W9-CKQ-948

PUBLICATIONS OF THE NEW CHAUCER SOCIETY

THE NEW CHAUCER SOCIETY

Studies in the Age of Chaucer, the yearbook of The New Chaucer Society, is published annually. Each issue contains substantial articles on all aspects of Chaucer and his age, book reviews, and an annotated Chaucer bibliography. Manuscripts should follow the *Chicago Manual of Style*, 16th edition. Unsolicited reviews are not accepted. Authors receive twenty free offprints of articles and ten of reviews. All correspondence regarding manuscript submissions should be directed to the Editor, Sarah Salih, Department of English, King's College London, Virginia Woolf Building, 22 Kingsway, London WC2B 6LE, United Kingdom; e-mail ageofchaucer@kcl.ac.uk. Subscriptions to The New Chaucer Society and information about the Society's activities should be directed to Ruth Evans, Department of English, Saint Louis University, Adorjan Hall 231, 3800 Lindell Blvd., St. Louis, MO 63108–3414. Back issues of the journal may be ordered from University of Notre Dame Press, Chicago Distribution Center, 11030 South Langley Avenue, Chicago, IL 60628; phone: 800-621-2736; fax: 800-621-8476; from outside the United States, phone: 773-702-7000; fax: 773-702-7212.

Studies in the Age of Chaucer

Studies in the Age of Chaucer

Volume 39
2017

EDITOR

SARAH SALIH

PUBLISHED ANNUALLY BY THE NEW CHAUCER SOCIETY
SAINT LOUIS UNIVERSITY IN ST. LOUIS

The frontispiece design, showing the Pilgrims at the Tabard Inn, is adapted from the woodcut in Caxton's second edition of the *Canterbury Tales*.

ISBN-10 0-933784-41-4
ISBN-13 978-0-933784-41-3
ISSN 0190-2407

CONTENTS

CONTENTS

REVIEWS

Studies in the Age of Chaucer

THE PRESIDENTIAL ADDRESS
The New Chaucer Society
Twentieth International Congress
July 11–14, 2016
Queen Mary University of London, Mile End

The Presidential Address

"The lytel erthe that here is": Environmental Thought in Chaucer's *Parliament of Fowls*

Susan Crane
Columbia University

Abstract

Chaucer's *Parliament of Fowls* traces his rejection of Neoplatonist and moral allegories, with their emphasis on transcendent truths and teachings. Instead, the *Parliament*'s dreamer observes and absorbs a richly sensual earthly environment, replacing mainstream allegory's guiding question "How shall I save myself?" with the more mundane question "What's happening here?" In exploring this latter question, the *Parliament* stages three contrasting ontologies—three models of how living things are interrelated—that continue to inform anthropological and environmental thought today. As dualism, animism, and totemism collide and intersect, Chaucer develops a productive uncertainty about the order of things. His ontological experiment offers a prehistory and a way forward for contemporary environmental theory.

Keywords

Chaucer, *The Parliament of Fowls*, environment, ontologies, nature, animism, totemism, animal studies, materiality, NASA Apollo missions

W HAT CONNECTION COULD CHAUCER possibly have with our own environmental moment? Many of us today feel that we are facing

I am grateful for the comments and suggestions of many colleagues who heard this lecture at the London Congress of the New Chaucer Society. Inspiration for the project came first of all from conversations with Pierre-Olivier Dittmar about his fascinating work in anthropologies of the Middle Ages. Draft versions improved substantially thanks to the expertise and generosity of Rita Copeland, Eleanor Johnson, and *primus inter pares* Paul Strohm.

Studies in the Age of Chaucer 39 (2017):3–29
© 2017 The New Chaucer Society

an unprecedented earthly crisis. Setting Chaucer's environmental thought and contemporary thought in dialogue looks wrong, on its face, because our "earth" has so radically changed. An earth that now appears depleted, fragile, and at risk, back then appeared dense and vast, stretching well beyond human reach. And our responses to the earth feel unprecedented to us: environmental theorists call for ruptures from past conceptions of life, seeking new theories of being—new ontologies—that will better integrate human and nonhuman interests. Yet I propose that Chaucer's *Parliament of Fowls* is pertinent to environmental posthumanism. Chaucer shares with our time a preoccupation with how beings, including human beings, are interrelated on earth; he shares our curiosity about what *human* being even is, and our dubiousness about species distinctions, and our eagerness for affective engagement with the material world. Despite the differences that separate Chaucer's fourteenth-century earth and perceptions of earth from ours, setting his *Parliament* in conversation with current environmentalism can illuminate our search for revised consciousness and practice.

My starting-point is how the earth looks from far away. *The Parliament of Fowls* opens with Chaucer's narrator reading a book, Macrobius's commentary on Cicero's *The Dream of Scipio*, in which Scipio's ancestor Africanus comes to him in a dream and lifts him up to "a sterry place"; "Thanne shewede he hym the lytel erthe that here is, / At regard of the hevenes quantite."[1] The geocentric universe of classical and medieval science, with its little earth surrounded by celestial spheres, is often visualized in manuscript illuminations (Fig. 1). Similarly, the photographs from NASA's Apollo missions between 1968 and 1972 gave our contemporaries their first look at a "little earth" afloat in vast space. (Fig. 2). The Apollo missions were designed to lead outward, to the moon and beyond, but the Apollo crews also turned their cameras back to look at earth from far away.

These two perspectives from above—from Scipio's eighth sphere and Apollo's moon orbit—gave rise to two contrasting ethical responses. In Scipio's dream, the radical change of physical perspective should prompt us to turn away from earthly things:

[1] Geoffrey Chaucer, *The Parliament of Fowls*, in *The Riverside Chaucer*, gen. ed. Larry D. Benson, 3rd ed. (Boston: Houghton Mifflin, 1987), lines 43, 57–58. All citations from works of Chaucer are from this edition.

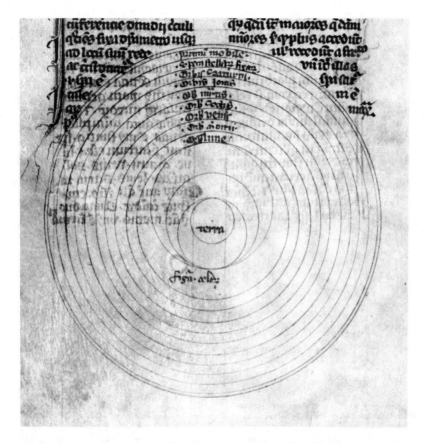

Fig. 1. Celestial spheres. John of Sacrobosco, *De sphaera*, Oxford, Bodleian Library, MS Ashmole 1522, fol. 25r (English, c. 1350). By permission of the Bodleian Library, University of Oxford.

> Than bad he hym, syn erthe was so lyte,
> And dissevable and ful of harde grace,
> That he ne shulde hym in the world delyte.
>
> (*PF*, 64–66)

Life on earth, says Africanus, is "but a maner deth"; life on earth should be directed toward winning a place in heaven (54). In contrast, NASA's Apollo missions, aimed up and away from earth, ironically launched a public movement of concern for earth's finite, fragile materiality. The

Fig. 2. Photo taken on NASA's Apollo 17 mission, December 7, 1972. Courtesy of the National Aeronautics and Space Administration. Photo no. AS17–148–22727.

Apollo photograph called "Earthrise," showing a partly shadowed earth rising above the moon's horizon, was an inspiration for the first international Earth Day in 1970; it has been called "the most influential environmental photograph ever taken."[2] The astronaut who shot "Earthrise" while orbiting the moon, William Anders, later commented on this turn of events: "We came all this way to explore the moon, and the most important thing is that we discovered the Earth."[3]

[2] "Apollo Astronaut Shares Story of NASA's Earthrise Photo," March 29, 2012, https://www.nasa.gov/centers/johnson/home/earthrise.html (accessed May 7, 2016).
[3] Bob Granath, "Astronaut Photography from Space Helped 'Discover the Earth,'" April 22, 2016, https://www.nasa.gov/feature/astronaut-photography-from-space-helped -discover-the-earth (accessed May 7, 2016).

Fascination with the little earth goes against Africanus's instruction to transcend earthly concerns. Chaucer's narrator, however, aligns himself with the earth rather than the heavens, by failing to join the celestial perspective of Africanus on "the lytel erthe *that here is*": this wording locates the narrator down on earth, here and now. He could easily have joined the lofty perspective of Africanus by ending this line with "the lytel erthe below" or "the lytel erthe adoun." Instead, Chaucer differentiates his narrator's perspective from that of Africanus, and emphasizes the differentiation by placing a verb at the line's eleventh syllable, producing a potential sixth stress in the line "Thanne shewede he him the lytel erthe that here *is*." The reference to *here* and *now* conjures a wider public around the narrator, shifting the perspective-point decisively back to earth. Africanus, like the Apollo missions, aimed outward and upward to ponder the heavens; Africanus, like the Apollo missions, turned to look back on earth in an instructional mode—philosophic, scientific—but in both cases an audience, Chaucer's narrator and the public of 1968, experienced a moment of cathexis, an investment of mental and affective energy in the earth. Indeed, *The Parliament of Fowls* persistently, systematically resists the belittling perspective of Africanus and his pedagogical certainty about turning our attention beyond earthly things. *The Dream of Scipio* teaches transcendence; Chaucer is more invested in pondering "the lytel erthe that here is."

I. Earthbound

Africanus steps off the page of "myn olde bok totorn" to reward his faithful reader with a new dream, but he does not lift the dreamer to the heavens (110). Rather, he leads him to a walled park, an earthly place of joys and pains. The truth status of the dream shifts as well, evoking the science concerning the possible causes of dreams: physical disturbances, mental preoccupations, and revelations from beyond.[4] "Can I not seyn," Chaucer's narrator avers, what kind of dream he had (106). Scipio's *somnium coeleste*, a dream vision from above, yields (apparently) to a *somnium animale*, a dream arising from mental preoccupation with Macrobius's book, as when "the juge dremeth how his plees

[4] On Chaucer's frequent deployment of a tripartite typology of dreams, see *The Riverside Chaucer*, 937, Explanatory Note to *NPT*, 2922–3157; 995, Explanatory Note to *PF*, 31; 1051, note to *TC*, V.358–85; A. C. Spearing, *Medieval Dream Poetry* (Cambridge: Cambridge University Press, 1976) 55–62, 91–92.

7

been sped" (101). Or, is this indeed a *somnium coeleste*, brought by Africanus—or by "Cytherea, thow blysful lady swete," Venus in her planetary form (113)? But no, if a planetary pull from "north-north-west" caused this dream, it's a *somnium naturale*, with physical causes, as when "the syke met he drynketh of the tonne" (117, 104). In obscuring the source of this dream, Chaucer diminishes its authority, retooling it from a vehicle for eternal truths to a vehicle pretty much earthbound, stuck at its literal level.

The dream's walled park declines analogously from ethereal perfection into subjection to time and violence. When Chaucer's dreamer first enters the park, he hears music so ravishing "That God, that makere is of al and lord, / Ne herde nevere beter" (199–200). This passage harks back to Scipio's dream, in which "the melodye herde he / That cometh of thilke speres thryes thre" (60–61). Likewise, the park at first recalls the classical *locus amoenus*: it appears to be a timeless place where plants grow but never wither, birds sing like angels, no one gets ill or old, night never falls, and joy is everlasting.[5] Soon, however, Chaucer unmakes these impressions of perfection, as a pantheon of lesser gods presides over mating, the sun sinks in the west, lovers suffer, birds squabble, and endless summer yields to the earthly cycle of seasons and years.[6]

The sinking effect intensifies as wise and preachy Africanus provides no guidance, disappearing or falling silent after bringing the dreamer through the park's gates. In place of lessons and interpretations, we experience the park through the dreamer's sensations—what he sees, hears, and feels. For example,

> Tho was I war of Plesaunce anon-ryght,
> And of Aray, and Lust, and Curteysie,
> And of the Craft that can and hath the myght
> To don by force a wyght to don folye—

[5] E.g., *PF*, 173, 185, 190–91, 204–10. Richard G. Newhauser, "The Multisensoriality of Place and the Chaucerian Multisensorial," in *The Five Senses in Medieval and Early Modern England*, ed. Annette Kern-Stähler, Beatrix Busse, and Wietse de Boer (Leiden: Brill, 2016), 212–14, most recently discusses *PF*'s park as a *locus amoenus*.

[6] E.g., *PF*, 214–17, 253–56, 265–66, 293–94, 321, 338–40, 357, 411, 489–90, 674. Stephen Knight, "Classicizing Christianity in Chaucer's Dream Poems: The *Book of the Duchess, Book of Fame*, and *Parliament of Fowls*," in *Chaucer and Religion*, ed. Helen Phillips and Helen Cooper (Woodbridge: D. S. Brewer, 2010), 143–55, focuses on *PF*'s turn backward from Scipio's transcendence to "revert to a troubled world"; the progression from Scipio to Venus to Nature "works in religious reverse" (154).

> Disfigurat was she, I nyl nat lye;
> And by hymself, under an ok, I gesse,
> Saw I Delyt, that stod with Gentilesse.
>
> (218–24)

These lines look conventionally allegorical: they feature personified abstractions around the Temple of Venus. Potentially, the scene could be parsing erotic love and revealing whether it should be rejected, or honored. Yet the mode of narration is neither diagnostic nor moralizing. The dreamer sees the personifications in their literal sense, and they are unproductive, oddly idle, just standing around as if on a break, waiting to be called back to work. The absence of interpretation stands out in the case of Craft, whose disfigured countenance could reveal that craftiness is morally flawed or a threat to lovers.[7] Yet the dreamer responds to Craft's appearance only. The challenge to courtship that she could potentially elucidate shrinks to whether or not to be honest about her appearance: "Disfigurat was she, *I nyl nat lye*" (222). The dreamer's focus on Craft's physical disfigurement dis-figures her rhetorically, stripping her of instructive allegorical potential. One could supply interpretations, drawing on Chaucer's intertexts or on historically informed perspectives, but Chaucer provides no Africanus, no philosophically minded narrator, and no telling two-leveled narration to help us out.

The *Parliament*'s resistance to abstracting meanings from its concrete representations has an important formal dimension. Chaucer's composition is turning against Neoplatonist and moral allegory. In these widely practiced forms, allegory presents visible figures and tangible events whose narrative action is designed to convey abstract ideas, principles, and teachings. This abstract register of significances generates a tangible narrative as a means toward manipulating and exploring abstract concepts such as Craft, Delyt, and Gentilesse.[8] In Alan of Lille's *Plaint of*

[7] Chaucer creates this interpretive impasse by citing just a fragment from Boccaccio's *Teseida delle nozze d'Emilia*. In Boccaccio's work, the surrounding context of Palamon's prayer and its fatal outcome supply Venus's temple with cautionary and predictive meanings. Gerald Morgan sets Chaucer's text alongside Boccaccio's, emphasizing the Chaucerian scene's disillusioning trajectory: "Chaucer's Adaptation of Boccaccio's Temple of Venus in the *Parliament of Fowls*," *RES* 56 (2005): 1–36.

[8] Mainstream medieval allegories (Realist, Neoplatonist, moral) aim above all to convey general truths, but they do admit a degree of feedback between concrete and abstract registers: Carolynn Van Dyke, *The Fiction of Truth: Structures of Meaning in Narrative and Dramatic Allegory* (Ithaca, N.Y.: Cornell University Press, 1985), 35–40; Barbara Newman, *God and the Goddesses: Vision, Poetry, and Belief in the Middle Ages* (Philadelphia: University of Pennsylvania Press, 2003), 30–37.

Nature, one of Chaucer's sources for the *Parliament*, the rips in the gorgeous garment of Nature make manifest that man "exempts himself by a nonconformist withdrawal" from Nature's "universal law."[9] In another source text, Jean de Meun's *The Romance of the Rose*, a priestly figure named Genius can be trusted to convey theological arguments. Alan's and Jean's kind of allegory "dematerializ[es] the material world," Angus Fletcher argues, since "only by wrenching his stories out of time can the allegorist start with an immaterial fact, such as a passion, and then invent *visibilia* to express such invisible facts."[10] In this traditional "allegory of ideas," Alan and Jean can certify that Nature and Genius are speakers of authoritative truths by declaring them to be transhistorical principles that do not originate in the living world's confusions. In contrast, Chaucer's *Parliament of Fowls* is closer to what Fletcher calls "allegory without ideas."[11] Fletcher traces this form to William of Ockham's nominalism, with its emphasis on human perceptions and worldly phenomena as the starting place for knowledge. Nominalism—and for Chaucer's times, Aristotelianism as well—begins the search for knowledge in observation and thought about the world, and then moves toward abstract ideas and concepts. But this merely mortal process, according to Ockham, may never attain perfect knowledge; the process is not visionary. Fletcher argues that nominalism gets poetic expression in an "allegory without ideas"—an apparently pedagogical narrative in which a level of tangible signs is activated, but higher levels of abstract meaning (the "ideas") are indistinct or compromised.[12] Whether or not

[9] Alan of Lille, *The Plaint of Nature*, ed. and trans. James J. Sheridan (Toronto: Pontifical Institute of Mediaeval Studies, 1980), 131. Peter T. Struck, "Allegory and Ascent in Neoplatonism," in *The Cambridge Companion to Allegory*, ed. Rita Copeland and Struck (Cambridge: Cambridge University Press, 2010), 57–70, provides background on classical allegory.

[10] Angus S. Fletcher, review of Gordon Teskey, *Allegory and Violence*, MLQ 59 (1998): 397–98; Fletcher also objects that C. S. Lewis and other scholars of mainstream allegory are overreaching when they accord the status of "fact" to the immaterial register as well as the material register of that allegory: "if something is a fact, in what sense—other than by radical figuration—can it even *be* immaterial?" (397, his italics). Fletcher prefers the term "idea" to "fact" in his later analysis of mainstream allegory's abstractions: Angus J. S. Fletcher, "Allegory without Ideas," in *Thinking Allegory Otherwise*, ed. Brenda Machosky (Stanford: Stanford University Press, 2010), 9–33.

[11] Fletcher, "Allegory without Ideas," 15.

[12] Ibid., 14–18. When Ockham's nominalism is translated into allegorical form, Fletcher concludes:

> we must then rethink our wall between the literal and the higher-order interpreted "meanings," the *significatio* of medieval exegesis. If nominalist, then there will be no ideas in a strict sense, no meanings segregated to a "higher" place on the interpretive

Chaucer knew something about Ockham's and Aristotle's methods, his *Parliament* accords with the nominalism of an "allegory without ideas" insofar as the narrator's dream abounds in sensual, visible scenes that dominate—and sometimes altogether obscure—a potential pedagogical register of abstract truths.

In these various thematic and formal ways, Chaucer diminishes his poem's metaphysical and didactic potential. But, in happy compensation, he offers a physical earth that brims over with sounds, sights, and creatures:

> For this was on Seynt Valentynes day,
> Whan every foul cometh there to chese his make,
> Of every kynde that men thynke may,
> And that so huge a noyse gan they make
> That erthe, and eyr, and tre, and every lake
> So ful was that unethe was there space
> For me to stonde, so ful was al the place.
>
> (309–15)

Here the earth is no longer "lytel." It is full, alive, vast, and various. Through an odd syntactic progression, the birdsong is so very noisy that

---

side of the wall. The so-called ideas of virtue and vice, good and evil, happiness and misery, fame and fortune will no longer be read as referring to universal notions. They will be mere functions of shared human speech and language, mere conventions, mere names and their grammar. The allegory without ideas could make no appeal to universals and hence could never legitimately establish belief in imagined higher values. (20)

Despite tracing its inspiration back to William of Ockham, Fletcher believes there are no exemplars of "allegory without ideas" in the medieval period; instead, non-transcendent allegory begins with "sophisticated later poets such as Andrew Marvell" (19). In contrast, Burt Kimmelman has pointed out Chaucer's gradually developing sense that "allegory was not a useful poetics" and, more specifically, the resonances between Ockham's philosophical writing and Chaucer's emphasis on "firsthand experience as a conduit for arriving at truth": "Ockham, Chaucer, and the Emergence of Modern Poetics," in *The Rhetorical Poetics of the Middle Ages: Reconstructive Polyphony; Essays in Honor of Robert O. Payne*, ed. John M. Hill and Deborah M. Sinnreich-Levi (Madison: Fairleigh Dickinson University Press, 2000), 177–205 (178, 183). Russell Peck, "Chaucer and the Nominalist Questions," *Speculum* 53 (1978): 745–60, emphasizes Chaucer's interest in nominalist questions over his interest in proving or disputing their truth: "Though he may not be interested in whether we can know with certitude only individual things, he is profoundly interested in how we know individual things" (745). See also Hugo Keiper, " 'I wot myself best how y stonde': Literary Nominalism, Open Textual Form and the Enfranchisement of Individual Perspective in Chaucer's Dream Visions," in *Literary Nominalism and the Theory of Rereading Late Medieval Texts: A New Research Paradigm*, ed. Richard J. Utz (Lewiston: Mellen, 1995), 205–34.

it takes up physical space: the "huge" sound "fills" earth, air, trees, and lakes, leaving almost nowhere to *stand*. This mind-boggling crush of sensations is a corrective to the dematerialization that conventional allegory works on the world. Here, and throughout the *Parliament*, the dreamer's senses, rather than his ideas, tend to convey the experience. At the park's gate, fear and boldness grip him until he catches comfort from Africanus holding his hand. The park's lush beauty gladdens him, he likes seeing Venus nearly naked, he walks to "solace" himself. "I saw," he reports, "I heard, I felt, I went, my ears ached, I found, I left, I noticed, I walked, I stood." This sensing, spongelike dreamer reinforces the textual orientation away from interpreting and teaching.[13]

Chaucer's somatically engaged dreamer anticipates posthumanist exhortations to draw less on intellect and more on senses when attempting to apprehend the living world. In his groundbreaking argument for knowing through the senses, Michel Serres looks beyond *logos* to intercorporeal connection as the definitional human trait. *Homo sapiens*, according to Serres, could best be translated *tasting man*.[14] Timothy Morton endorses a Romantic conviction that human consciousness "had the qualities of an Aeolean harp," a wind-harp thrumming to environmental sensations.[15] Branka Arsić recovers Henry David Thoreau's "literalization" of experience, his "desire to inhabit the perceived" at Walden Pond, "once his senses are entrusted to an unknown—conceptually unmediated—reality."[16] Moves such as these can supplement rational understanding with further perceptual resources; more ambitiously in posthumanism, these moves aim to discredit and revise humankind's definitional rationality.

In the several ways outlined above, the *Parliament* has avoided allegory's interpretive drive in favor of sinking into an earthly environment.

---

[13] In mainstream medieval allegorical works, a clueless or passive central figure such as the Boethian figure in *The Consolation of Philosophy*, the lover in *The Romance of the Rose*, and Dante in *Inferno* is thematically functional in that he stimulates instruction. In contrast, Chaucer's *PF* has no enlightening guide for the passive narrator, once Africanus disappears. This narrator must puzzle over an onslaught of sensations and conflicting views, rather than an onslaught of authoritative explanations.

[14] Michel Serres, *The Five Senses: A Philosophy of Mingled Bodies*, trans. Peter Cowley and Margaret Sankey (London: Continuum International Publishing, 2008), 235.

[15] Timothy Morton, *Ecology without Nature: Rethinking Environmental Aesthetics* (Cambridge, Mass.: Harvard University Press, 2007), 191.

[16] Branka Arsić, *Bird Relics: Grief and Vitalism in Thoreau* (Cambridge, Mass.: Harvard University Press, 2016), 8–10. A wide-ranging introduction to the "posthumanist" project that emphasizes its animal and environmental aspects is Cary Wolfe, *What Is Posthumanism?* (Minneapolis: University of Minnesota Press, 2010).

In contrast, the guiding question for mainstream medieval allegory, as Rosemond Tuve's monumental study of allegory recounts, is "How shall I save myself?"[17] Chaucer's dreamer, stranded on earth with no rocketship to raise him toward salvation, poses instead the question "What's happening here?"

II. Sinking into Nature

"What's happening here?" is a fundamental question for any society: how are beings on earth related to one another and how do they interact? This question is the focus today of an "ontological turn" across several disciplines.[18] Scholars of this turn note that a basic social preoccupation is making sense of the inconceivable complexity of living beings, by filtering that complexity through perhaps just three or four "cognitive schemata" or "framing devices" that reveal patterns of similarity and difference among worldly beings.[19] Each cognitive scheme of being (each "ontology," in the anthropological sense of this term) offers a clarified world of beings by emphasizing some of the data and ignoring some of them. Each scheme allows differently for maneuvering through specific situations, ranging from what to eat to what to believe.

I turn first to the ontology most familiar today and, in its medieval form, most familiar to Chaucer. From different perspectives including posthuman and environmental theory, science studies, and animal studies, scholars urge that the centuries-long domination of a "dualist" model of being, also called the "culture/nature dichotomy," can obscure other perceptions of how beings are interrelated in systematic accounts

[17] Rosemond Tuve, *Allegorical Imagery: Some Mediaeval Books and Their Posterity* (Princeton, N.J.: Princeton University Press, 1966): "the basic theme of allegory (salvation through holiness)" (49); "the basic allegorical theme . . . [is] the pilgrimage man takes through life to death and redemption" (145). Barbara Johnson, *The Wake of Deconstruction* (Oxford: Blackwell, 1994), 69–70 extends Tuve's thesis to John Bunyan's opening question in *Pilgrim's Progress*, "What shall I do to be saved?" And in Chaucer's *PF*, "Thanne preyede hym Scipion to telle hym al / The wey to come into that hevene blisse" (71–72).

[18] A debate on this developing area of work at the 2013 meeting of the American Anthropological Association, with contributions from John D. Kelly, Philippe Descola, Marshall Sahlins, Bruno Latour, Michael Fischer, and Kim Fortun, was published with subsequent responses to the session in *HAU: Journal of Ethnographic Theory* 4, no. 1 (2014): 259–360. A substantial introductory collection is Philippe Descola and Gísli Pálsson, eds., *Nature and Society: Anthropological Perspectives* (London: Routledge, 1996).

[19] Philippe Descola, "Modes of Being and Forms of Predication," *HAU: Journal of Ethnographic Theory* 4, no. 1 (2014): 271–80 (274).

of existence.[20] The dualist model of being is so ingrained in medieval and postmedieval western societies that it may be difficult to apprehend as just one possible model of being. Dualism conceives materiality—"creation," in medieval thought—to be structured by humankind's difference from, and superiority to, other forms of life. Despite our evident participation in physical life, certain traits—such as rational thought, language, original sin, an eternal soul, or the possession of culture—are thought to distinguish fundamentally humans from all other creatures; these others constitute an unchanging realm of "nature" that persists in stability until humans intervene to draw on its resources.[21] The dualist model of being is best known from its eighteenth-to-twentieth-century dominance in European science and philosophy, but its ancestry stretches back into classical and medieval philosophy. Of course, "western" and "European" thought is far from monolithic: even crucial biblical texts such as God's granting of dominion to Adam and God's covenant with Noah attracted a wide range of learned interpretations, and so did philosophical understandings of creation, language, and nature.[22] Across this range, however, dualism is persistently the dominant principle of medieval thought on how being is structured.

The Parliament of Fowls is hardly a systematic treatise on being, but it does interrogate dualism from two directions that anticipate contemporary environmental and anthropological critiques. First, Chaucer visibly revises his depiction of the goddess Nature over the course of the parliament, in ways that resist a dualist split between nature and humankind. In a second ontological shakeup, to which I will turn in the following sections of this essay, Chaucer intersects dualism with animism and totemism, two alternative models of being that are delineated and

[20] Foundational critiques of dualism are Jacques Derrida, *The Animal that Therefore I Am*, ed. Marie-Louise Mallet, trans. David Wills (New York: Fordham University Press, 2008); Philippe Descola, *Beyond Nature and Culture*, trans. Janet Lloyd (Chicago: University of Chicago Press, 2013); Bruno Latour, *We Have Never Been Modern*, trans. Catherine Porter (Cambridge, Mass.: Harvard University Press, 1993).

[21] Modern dualism spins off the supernatural into a third category of being, beyond the mechanistic laws governing "nature" and the human realm of "culture," whereas medieval versions of dualism accommodate an ongoing divine presence within all creatures, human and nonhuman.

[22] Admirably illustrating this range of interpretations are John M. Fyler, *Language and the Declining World in Chaucer, Dante, and Jean de Meun* (Cambridge: Cambridge University Press, 2007); Alastair Minnis, *From Eden to Eternity: Creations of Paradise in the Later Middle Ages* (Philadelphia: University of Pennsylvania Press, 2016); and Kellie Robertson, *Nature Speaks: Medieval Literature and Aristotelian Philosophy* (Philadelphia: University of Pennsylvania Press, 2017).

14

debated in philosophical anthropology. The *Parliament*'s alternative ontologies contribute depth and flexibility to Chaucer's environmental thought.

Medieval "nature" was both transcendent and earthly. In one sense, "nature" designated the idea that the regeneration of life forms accords with the timeless will of the Creator: in this sense, as Nature first appears in the *Parliament*, she is "the vicaire of the almyghtly Lord" (379). In another sense, *nature* designated traits that appear to be innate in life forms: mortal nature, gifts of nature, natural inclinations; for example, certain avian species eat worms "as hem Nature wolde enclyne" (325). This double *nature* offers Chaucer a final opportunity to shift his poem's focus from transcendent idealism to earthly engagement—from Scipio's "How shall I save myself?" to "What's happening here?" Well before the bird parliament opens, Chaucer has prepared for this final opportunity. As he brings the action back down from the eighth sphere, silences Africanus, generates an "allegory without ideas," and shoves us into a sensual creaturely realm, Chaucer positions us to read the bird parliament not vertically, from bird-signifier up to human-signified, but instead horizontally, across material creation, without presuming an exceptional status for the human.

Chaucer begins the bird parliament with the transcendent "noble goddesse Nature" who coordinates all creatures—all created things—that God "hath knyt by evene noumbres of acord" (303, 381). This cosmos-unifying Nature is not dichotomous with human culture. Nature rules all God's creatures alike; she oversees both the wormy diet of birds and the cultural conventions of courtly sublimation.[23] Soon I will turn to species questions; for the moment I assume it is uncontroversial that the *Parliament*'s birds refer to humans as well as to birds. Donna Haraway, writing against contemporary dualism, needs neologisms to recover this medieval inclusiveness: she rejects modernity's term "nature" as falsely dichotomized, in favor of the fused single word "naturecultures," and she rejects the isolation of the human in nature/

---

[23] This first version of Nature endows her with moral as well as generative authority: thus Melibee can assert that "Nature defendeth and forbedeth by right that no man make hym self riche un to the harm of another persone" (*Mel*, B.2774). Nature's moral authority does not require an overtly Christian framework: in Maying poetry of Chaucer's milieu, the realm of flower and leaf is both sensual and ethical, inviting expressions of courtly sublimation; Susan Crane, *The Performance of Self: Ritual, Clothing, and Identity during the Hundred Years War* (Philadelphia: University of Pennsylvania Press, 2002), Chapter 2.

culture dualism by using the cowboy slang "critters" for all living things—an earthy resurgence of the medieval term "creature" with its nondistinction between human beings and other beings.[24]

As Chaucer's poem unfolds, it not only evades depicting a dualist isolation of the human from everything else, it also challenges the dualist conception that nature (in contrast to culture) is a stable, transhistorical entity. Barbara Newman explains that the poets who personify Nature as a mediating "goddess" are shielding God from difficult theological questions, redirecting the questions to a nonbiblical, female figure.[25] ("Saint Valentine" similarly stands between God's love and sensual love, obscuring the problem of whether the sensual fully participates in the divine.) Chaucer's Nature soon betrays "deep-seated contradictions," as Newman shows, between the perfection of the music of the spheres and the various imperfections of physical life, and between Nature's universal "statute" that birds are to choose mates yearly and her suspension of the statute for the formel eagle.[26] As Kellie Robertson asks, are the divine and natural orders one, or are they two?[27] Chaucer's dream leans toward the latter option, as Nature slides from her first status as "vicaire of the almyghty Lord" toward mere equivalence with her squabbling creatures. In turning to ask the assembled species about the formel's suitors, Nature seems to forget her opening rule that the formel—not the others—must "agre to his eleccioun" (409). The realm of this "noble goddesse of kynde" includes "the cukkow ever unkynde" and the "stroyere of his owene kynde," the drake (672, 358, 360). In Marshall Leicester's summary of this development, "Chaucer's presentation shows the large-scale hypostasis *Natura* dissolving into the flux created by the drives, desires and interests of diverse individual *natures*."[28]

---

[24] Donna J. Haraway, *When Species Meet* (Minneapolis: University of Minnesota Press, 2008), see index under "critters" (403) and "naturecultures" (415).

[25] Newman, *God and the Goddesses*, 39–41.

[26] Ibid., 111–15 (113).

[27] Robertson, *Nature Speaks*, 243: Chaucer's *PF* "is a philosophical thought experiment that explores how humans conceptualize the divine and natural orders (are they one or are they two?)." Robertson reveals how deeply contested is the concept of nature in Chaucer's sources and intertexts: should nature be seen as a principle of generation set above living creatures, or as brute physical life itself, "a wild pig eating acorns in the woods" (184)? On medieval concepts of nature, see also Sarah Stanbury, "Ecochaucer: Green Ethics and Medieval Nature," *ChauR* 39, no. 1 (2004): 1–16.

[28] H. M. Leicester, Jr., "The Harmony of Chaucer's 'Parlement': A Dissonant Voice," *ChauR* 9, no. 1 (1974): 15–34 (27). Along similar lines, Carolynn Van Dyke, *Chaucer's Agents: Cause and Representation in Chaucerian Narrative* (Madison: Fairleigh Dickinson

Re-figuring the goddess Nature as "diverse individual natures" speaks to the second problem that contemporary theorists identify in modernity's culture/nature dualism: modern *nature* is falsely imagined as an entirely nonhuman realm, governed by unchanging laws, internally balanced in contrast to the turbulence within cultures. Translating back into medieval terms, Chaucer's first version of Dame Nature as "vicaire of the almyghty Lord" expresses a conviction that God's creative act continues to generate a realm of natural stability, from which humankind has been exiled since the original sin. As Chaucer's Nature comes instead to embody her contending creatures, as her "statut" and "ordenaunce" (387, 390) shift under pressure, and as human foibles intersect avian behavior, the *Parliament* anticipates contemporary environmental theory's resistance to modernity's conception of an unchanging natural world. More accurately, both human and nonhuman being unfold in "parallel and intersecting histories of experiments that continually succeed and fail."[29] Analogously, the *Parliament*'s park draws human and nonhuman alike into its contentious instability.

From two directions, then, Chaucer constructs an order of being that contrasts with the dualism of Scipio's cosmos. Human and nonhuman "critters" align and misalign in a single "natureculture" where eating worms and sublimating desire both have a place. As Nature herself expresses competing agendas and reverses her own rules of procedure, Chaucer credits living dissonance rather than cosmic harmonies. In these two ways, Chaucer is resisting the attraction of dualism, but not yet developing a counter-ontology.

University Press, 2005), 52–62, treats Nature's shifting status as one of the allegorical anomalies that characterize *PF*. Stephen Knight, *Rymyng Craftily: Meaning in Chaucer's Poetry* (Sydney: Angus and Robertson, 1973), 38 calls Chaucer's Nature "the abstracted essence of [the birds'] natures." Some instances of diversity in *PF* cut against heteronormativity: the "soleyn" cuckoo (607, 614); the goddess Venus "in a prive corner in disport" with her porter Richesse, a female personification (260); and the "weddid turtil, with hir herte trewe" (355), whose spouse is feminine ("though she deyede, I wolde non other make" [587]). A revelatory discussion of gender in *PF* is Kathleen Davis, "Hymeneal Alogic: Debating Political Community in *The Parliament of Fowls*," in *Imagining a Medieval English Nation*, ed. Kathy Lavezzo (Minneapolis: University of Minnesota Press, 2003), 161–87.

[29] Ursula K. Heise, "Lost Dogs, Last Birds, and Listed Species: Cultures of Extinction," *Configurations* 18, nos. 1–2 (2010): 49–72 (72). Cary Wolfe, "Each Time Unique: The Poetics of Extinction," in *Animalities: Literary and Cultural Studies beyond the Human*, ed. Michael Lundblad (Edinburgh: Edinburgh University Press, 2017), 22, similarly calls the radical change of species extinction "the most natural thing in the world."

III. Animism

Ontological thought often finds expression in models of the cosmos and in taxonomies of living beings.[30] The cosmos in *The Dream of Scipio* expresses a dualistic ontology as it shrinks "earth" to an undifferentiated lump of hardship, and shows humankind an escape route toward an eternal split with other earthly beings. This dualistic model of being has great cultural authority in Chaucer's time and our own, but the walled park of the *Parliament* also bears traces of two alternative ontologies. Most evidently, the tree catalogue and later the catalogue of birds offer pointed contrasts to the nine-sphere cosmos. Traditionally called rhetorical "catalogues," the term E. R. Curtius used for this classical device, Chaucer's tree and bird catalogues also meet the scientific definition of taxonomies: they classify living things according to their differentiating characteristics.[31] Medieval taxonomies tend to be in the form of lists, as in the encyclopedias, sometimes with internal sublists, as in the bestiaries' sublists of wild beasts, quadrupeds, birds, fish, and creeping things.

The *Parliament*'s taxonomic stanza on trees makes a deft transition from dualism to a second anthropological ontology: animism. In animist conceptions, all sorts of beings interact responsively with humans and share with them traits such as passions, abilities, and consciousness.[32] Chaucer's tree taxonomy looks familiarly dualist, but animism is pressing forward through its species figurations:

> The byldere ok, and ek the hardy asshe;
> The piler elm, the cofre unto carayne;
> The boxtre pipere, holm to whippes lashe;
> The saylynge fyr; the cipresse, deth to playne;

[30] Philippe Descola, "Societies of Nature and the Nature of Society," in *Conceptualizing Society*, ed. Adam Kuper (London: Routledge, 1992), 107–26.

[31] *The Riverside Chaucer*, 997, note to *PF*, 176–82: the "catalogue . . . is a fundamental poetic form that goes back to Homer and Hesiod." On scientific and folk taxonomies, see R. Bulmer, "Why the Cassowary Is Not a Bird," in *Rules and Meanings: The Anthropology of Everyday Knowledge*, ed. Mary Douglas (Harmondsworth: Penguin, 1973), 167–93; John Dupré, *The Disorder of Things: Metaphysical Foundations of the Disunity of Science* (Cambridge, Mass.: Harvard University Press, 1993); Susan Crane, *Animal Encounters: Contacts and Concepts in Medieval Britain* (Philadelphia: University of Pennsylvania Press, 2012), Chapter 3.

[32] Diverging views of animism that both fit the basic sense I invoke here are Descola, "Modes of Being and Forms of Predication," 275; and Marshall Sahlins, "On the Ontological Scheme of *Beyond Nature and Culture*," *HAU: Journal of Ethnographic Theory* 4, no. 1 (2014): 281–90.

> The shetere ew; the asp for shaftes pleyne;
> The olyve of pes, and eke the dronke vyne;
> The victor palm, the laurer to devyne.
>
> (176–82)

By means of the trope called metalepsis, the fate of each tree species is innate in its living form. A first meaning for *metalepsis* is the temporal transumption that is definitional for Isidore of Seville: "a trope designating what follows from what precedes it," or what precedes from what follows.[33] A familiar example is calling a living lamb "the sacrifice." In Chaucer's tree taxonomy, end use defines each species as coffin, beam, lash, pipe, mast, bow, arrow, and ceremonial artifact. Designating each species by its cultural use treats "nature" as an inert stock of resources, dualistically: the park's grove becomes a woodworking shop. But these tropes are more than just predictive. They are animate. To be sure, the "shetere ew" and the "saylynge fyr" can be understood to subsume the trees to human designs, but they can also evoke a weirdly animate present in which the yew tree is shooting its own bow, the fir tree is sailing its own ship, the oak tree is a builder, and so on, as if the trees were infused with human capacities. These animate trees fit a more complex understanding of metalepsis as "a process of transition, doubling, or ellipsis in figuration, of replacing a figure with another figure, and of missing out the figure in between in order to create a figure that stretches the sense or which fetches things from far off."[34] The yew, in a proleptic metaphor, is a bow, and the archer, metonymically, is that bow in action. The elided, missed-out bow pulls yew tree and archer into relationship "from far off," animating the tree with the archer's abilities.[35] Expanding the stanza's species alignments of men and trees,

---

[33] Isidore of Seville, *The "Etymologies" of Isidore of Seville*, trans. Stephen A. Barney, W. J. Lewis, J. A. Beach, and Oliver Berghof (Cambridge: Cambridge University Press, 2006), 61 (I.37.7).

[34] Brian Cummings, "Metalepsis: The Boundaries of Metaphor," in *Renaissance Figures of Speech*, ed. Sylvia Adamson, Gavin Alexander, and Katrin Ettenhuber (Cambridge: Cambridge University Press, 2007), 219. My thanks to Rita Copeland for this reference.

[35] Chaucer's stanza also illustrates the pleasure of metalepsis: "if a metalepsis comes off, part of the sheer thrill of success is precisely this sense of a sharing of something recondite or mysterious" (Cummings, "Metalepsis," 221). On the circulation of classical and medieval rhetorical concepts of metalepsis/transumption, see Rita Copeland, "Grammar, Rhetoric, and Figurative Language: Learned Innovations and Vernacular Receptions," in *Intellectual Culture in Medieval Scandinavia, c. 1100–1350*, ed. Stefka Georgieva Eriksen (Turnhout: Brepols, 2016), 226–32; on Chaucer's milieu specifically, see Martin Camargo, "Chaucer and the Oxford Renaissance of Anglo-Latin Rhetoric," *SAC* 34 (2012): 173–207.

a dove's act of choice and a god's gift of winemaking inhabit the "olyve of pes" and the "dronke vyne."

The form of Chaucer's tree taxonomy, the classical catalogue, joins metalepsis to evoke an animist Mediterranean mythology, whose inspirited trees and rivers, its randy gods pursuing pretty youths, its rocks coming to life, its metamorphosing Actaeon and Philomela, all retain a prominent place in medieval poetry.[36] Animism figures as well in medieval scientific and travel writing. The male and female diamonds of *The Book of John Mandeville* "beth noryshed with the dew of hevene, and they engendreth comunely and bryngeth forth other smale dyamaundes, that multeplieth and groweth all yeres."[37] Medieval herbals feature the mandrake, capable of taking vengeance on those who pull it screaming from the ground; Richard Kieckhefer finds animist principles informing further magical practices.[38] Posthumanist materialisms distribute animacy and agency more and less evenly across all existents.[39] The consonance between *The Parliament of Fowls* and these contemporary materialisms emerges as the shooter yew and the sailing fir reverse the deadly instrumentality of nature as use value. Mere use, which Jeff Dolven labels "the bogey of thing theory," becomes through troping a springboard into expanded life.[40]

Like the inspirited trees, the *Parliament*'s birds behave in self-determining, animate ways that cannot easily be reduced, as they were in earlier scholarship, simply to expressions of human self-determination. For earlier scholarship, the *Parliament*'s only subject was our species: "the comic, contradictory variety of men's attitudes toward love," or "a picture of how people discover civic charity through institutions for

---

[36] One medieval response, as illustrated by the *Ovide moralisé*, was to adjust animism to reflect Christian dualism, but other medieval poets do not baptize classical animism into Christian orthodoxy.

[37] Jeffrey Jerome Cohen, *Stone: An Ecology of the Inhuman* (Minneapolis: University of Minnesota Press, 2015), 246. Cohen's book abounds in further examples of medieval animist thought.

[38] Richard Kieckhefer, *Magic in the Middle Ages* (Cambridge: Cambridge University Press, 1989), 13–14.

[39] An interdisciplinary overview of contemporary materialisms, with contributions from more than thirty scholars and artists, appeared as "A Questionnaire on Materialisms," *october* 155 (Winter 2016): 3–110.

[40] Jeff Dolven, "A Questionnaire on Materialisms," 32 (his italics): "*Use* is the bogey of thing theory, or at least *mere use*. Its costs are practical (global warming: using up resources), existential (alienation from the thing-world), and intellectual (mistaking how the world works)."

speaking together."[41] Now scholars no longer dismiss the "royal egle" as a completely transparent signifier for "aristocrat" (330). Perhaps modern dualism generated that sharp distinction between bird-signifier and human-signified. In formal terms, dualism could require taking personification in its most conservative sense, as a rhetorical device that drops its tenor on the way up to signification, like a rocket dropping its first stage. But the *Parliament*'s several rejections of allegorical transcendence, outlined above, argue against dismissing the birds as mere signs, irrelevant as birds. To be sure, they shimmer with vital significance for humankind, but also with animate life of their own. The birds' coordination of avian specificity and human referentiality embodies a third ontological mode of perception, called totemism. Yet Chaucer soon abandons the birds' totemic role, freeing them to deliver a noisy challenge to all three ontologies that have shaped this little earth.

IV. Totemism and Beyond: From Bird Taxonomy to Species Uncertainty

To rephrase the inadequacy of "personification" for Chaucer's birds: indeed they persistently have to do with humans, but not by borrowing human traits through personification. Their mode of reference is not as rhetorical signs, but as totemic creatures, in a third ontological structure that supplements dualism and animism in Chaucer's *Parliament*. This third ontology imagines two hierarchies of being, one for humans and one for nonhumans, that mirror and explain one another. Whereas animism differs from medieval dualism in distributing mentality and agency broadly across living things, totemism organizes species differences so that they parallel status differences, justifying and strengthening our status differences by locating their templates beyond the human. In totemism, animal species are not evanescing signs for human status: animal and human both remain living entities.[42] Only a living world

---

[41] Charles Muscatine, *Chaucer and the French Tradition: A Study in Style and Meaning* (Berkeley: University of California Press, 1957), 292; Paul A. Olson, "*The Parlement of Foules*: Aristotle's *Politics* and the Foundations of Human Society," *SAC* 2 (1980): 56. As recently as 2005, Van Dyke, *Chaucer's Agents*, 73–75, noted widespread agreement among scholars that *PF*'s only subject is humankind.

[42] Totemism is among the oldest and most disputed anthropological categories. In a major turning-point for the concept, Claude Lévi-Strauss, *Totemism* (*Le totémisme aujourd'hui* [1962]), trans. Rodney Needham (Boston, Mass.: Beacon, 1973) argued that totemism is not about religion or taboo, but is instead a universal human strategy for explaining social segmentation; subsequent revisions to Lévi-Strauss emphasized that

of species can ground totemism's claim that our social hierarchies are inevitable—presocial—a fact of nature.

This claim that hierarchy is natural emerges in the bird taxonomy's "royal egle . . . and othere egles of a lowere kynde / Of whiche that clerkes wel devyse conne" (330, 332–33). Dame Nature similarly articulates her parliament's *social* hierarchy in terms of its *species* distinctions:

> The foul royal, above yow in *degre*, . . .
> He shal first chese and speken in his gyse.

> And after hym by order shul ye chese,
> After youre *kynde*
> (393–94, 400–401, my emphasis)

Rank ("degre") and species ("kynde") are coterminous, asserting that differences in rank are as innate as differences in species. Dame Nature's "rightful ordenaunce" gets broad cultural expression in the totemic heraldry and masking of medieval elites.[43] Species difference, when taken as a totemic validation for social difference, does not necessarily conflict with distributing animacy across species; Marshall Sahlins even proposes that "totemism is the animism of segmentary collectives."[44] Later in the parliament, the birds' comic infighting compromises their totemic authority, but this comic critique is itself an indication of totemism's imaginative power in Chaucer's milieu.

A stanza from the *Parliament*'s bird taxonomy illustrates both totemism and Chaucer's first steps beyond it:

---

totemism can both underpin social orders and establish cross-species relationships: Crane, *Performance of Self*, 107–25. Descola's totemism, in contrast, predominates in just certain cultures, in the way dualism, animism, and analogism predominate in certain other cultures; these ontologies are, in logical terms at least, not compatible with one another. In Descola's narrow sense, totemism allows only for a relationship of signifier to signified between an entire species and an entire social group, and does not allow for any relationship between specific members of the species or social group: Descola, "Modes of Being and Forms of Predication," 271–76. In *PF*, Chaucer deploys a sense of totemism that is closer to the views of Lévi-Strauss and of Sahlins, "On the Ontological Scheme of *Beyond Nature and Culture*."

[43] Crane, *The Performance of Self*, Chapter 4: totemism works its way into medieval lineages when families claim high status through descent from a powerful nonhuman creature, such as the serpent-woman Melusine and the swan-knight Elias. Melusine in her bathtub, where she turned into a serpent each Sunday, was the identifying crest for members of the Lusignan family.

[44] Sahlins, "On the Ontological Scheme of *Beyond Nature and Culture*," 283.

> The gentyl faucoun, that with his feet distrayneth
> The kynges hand; the hardy sperhauk eke,
> The quayles foo; the merlioun, that payneth
> Hymself ful ofte the larke for to seke;
> There was the douve with hire yën meke;
> The jelous swan, ayens his deth that syngeth;
> The oule ek, that of deth the bode bryngeth.
>
> (337–43)[45]

The stanza begins with a classic totemic relationship between falcon and king, as the raptor's dominating "kynde" mirrors the ruler's authority, and the ruler's "degre" confers gentility on the raptor. So far, so good for totemism's parallel between two distinct realms of being, avian and human, each realm stratified. Yet other species in the bird taxonomy are not aligned with human statuses, nor are the birds defined by their cultural usefulness (as were the trees in their taxonomy). Instead, the bird species are mostly engaged in mundane behaviors that define them in relation to one another. Totemism has provided a scaffolding for the parliament's social thought to come, but species thought is not thereby precluded. Indeed, the poem's interest in bird lore is exceptional—for example, in the length and detail of the full bird taxonomy, its focus on birds native to England plus a few exotics known there, and its addition of many birds of England that do not appear in Chaucer's source texts.[46] By densing up the details of species behavior, Chaucer urges that birds, as distinctive life forms, are being represented.

As the parliament unfolds, Chaucer moves decisively beyond both

---

[45] The bird taxonomy carries traces of philosophical anthropology's fourth ontology: analogism. These traces—the death-boding owl (343), the eel's foe (346), the predictive raven (363), and Venus's planetary influence (117)—are too sparse in *PF* to put immediate pressure on dualism, as do animism and totemism. Analogism weaves a web of connections between physical bodies. A familiar illustration of analogism is man as the microcosm of everything else. Analogism pervaded medieval and early modern science, as Michel Foucault traced in *The Order of Things: An Archaeology of the Human Sciences* (New York: Pantheon, 1971), Chapter 2.

[46] Melissa Ridley Elmes, "Species or Specious? Authorial Choices and *The Parliament of Fowls*," in *Rethinking Chaucerian Beasts*, ed. Carolynn Van Dyke (New York: Palgrave Macmillan, 2012), 233–47, determines that all the birds in Chaucer's stanzas are native to England or well-established exotics (such as the parrot), and that he adds "at least twenty-three birds whose descriptions are either absent in, or vastly different from, Chaucer's known sources" (238). Derek Brewer notes that the *PF*'s "list of birds . . . has a richness of meaning far beyond any comparable list in any other poet": Geoffrey Chaucer, *The Parlement of Foulys*, ed. D. S. Brewer (Manchester: Manchester University Press, 1972), 118 (note to line 364).

totemism and species specifics, to delight in cross-commingling the species instead of aligning them in patterns:

> "Now fy, cherl!" quod the gentil tercelet,
> "Out of the donghil cam that word ful right!
> Thow canst nat seen which thyng is wel beset!
> Thow farst by love as oules don by lyght:
> The day hem blent, ful wel they se by nyght.
> Thy kynde is of so low a wrechednesse
> That what love is, thow canst nouther seen ne gesse."
>
> (596–602)

Here bird species—tercelet, owl, implicitly goose—get human status descriptions—churl, gentil, wretched. This is classic totemism: species correspond to estates. But the two parallel realms also fuse, as further terms apply to both humans and birds: the goose's "kynde" could be her species or her sort; "low" might refer to social status or to living on the ground ("water-foul sat lowest in the dale" [327]); "see" is meant literally for owls, but figuratively for the cognitive goose and the human consciousness she also evokes. The "donghill" is the literal habitat of a bug-hunting goose, and simultaneously a rude synecdoche for a churl's agrarian habitat. A triple intersection identifies the goose as a churl behaving like an owl.

Throughout Nature's parliament, human–avian conflations multiply, as the formel and the turtledove blush, the second eagle asks to be hanged by the neck if the formel finds him false, and the duck swears by his hat. Terms for avian and human melt into one another, for example when Nature commands "of every folk men shul oon calle / To seyn the verdit for yow foules alle" (324–25). Terms for voice are especially fluid: the assembled birds make noise, sing, jangle, scorn, call, speak, answer, cry, say, murmur, tell, cackle, laugh, advise, jest, quack, and shout.[47] Fine recent work by Carolynn Van Dyke, Emma Gorst, and Aranye Fradenburg has illuminated such effects, which they have termed simultaneity, commonality, hybridity, and transmorphism.[48]

---

[47] E.g., PF, 312, 342, 345–46, 352, 415, 463, 465, 501, 520, 559, 562, 575, 579, 589, 594, 693. A suggestive discussion of the contiguity of animal sounds and speech in relation to language acquisition is Jonathan Hsy, "Between Species: Animal–Human Bilingualism and Medieval Texts," in *Booldly bot Meekly: Essays on the Theory and Practice of Translation in the Middle Ages in Honour of Roger Ellis*, ed. Catherine Batt and René Tixier, The Medieval Translator 14 (Turnhout: Brepols, 2017).

[48] Carolynn Van Dyke, "Touched by an Owl? An Essay in Vernacular Ethology," *postmedieval* 7, no. 2 (2016): 304–27; Emma Gorst, "Interspecies Mimicry: Birdsong in Chaucer's 'Manciple's Tale' and *The Parlement of Fowles*," NML 12 (2010): 147–54; Ara-

These effects, beyond their specific surprises, do away with ontologies' basic unit of comprehension—species or "kyndes" of being. I believe Chaucer's effort is underrepresented when characterized as blurring species boundaries or representing one species as another. When bodies are indeterminate (what's wearing that hat?) and when words fuse with calls ("in hire kakelynge / She seyde, 'Pes!'" [562–63]), we are invited to imagine a world of species uncertainty.

In this way, Chaucer transforms his *Parliament* into a forum for surpassing totemism, animism, and dualism together. Each of these ontological structures begins from a perceived contrast between human being and other beings.[49] Reviewing the *Parliament*'s specific models of being, Chaucer first evoked a dualist conception, as the ensouled Scipio was enjoined to reject a woefully material earth; next, he evoked an animist vision of archer, builder, and sailor in dynamic relationship with their artifacts of yew, oak, and fir; and next he evoked a totemism that justified the social estates by grounding them in a hierarchy of avian species. In these models of being, the nonhuman realm takes three distinctive shapes, while the human remains that realm's stable point of contrast. As species simultaneity and transmorphism emerge in the parliament's turbulent debate, Chaucer reaches beyond defining the human as the unique vantage-point from which creation's inconceivable complexity is reduced into patterns. Chaucer's species uncertainty expresses his ontological uncertainty.

The *Parliament*'s closing roundel, in the form reconstructed by Furnivall and Skeat, has been taken as the poem's return to ordered love and cosmic harmony.[50] I lack confidence that Saint Valentine can successfully invoke the Prime Mover in these sensuous lines whose every point of reference is earthly: summer and winter, day and night, blissful singing and mating, waking in soft sunshine. But in any case, the roundel's lines cannot bear much argumentative weight, since they are not

---

nye Fradenburg, "Among All Beasts: Affective Naturalism in Late Medieval England," in Van Dyke, *Rethinking Chaucerian Beasts*, 13–31.

[49] Philippe Descola, "Constructing Natures: Symbolic Ecology and Social Practice," in Descola and Pálsson, *Nature and Society*, 82–102 (85): "a common feature of all conceptions of non-humans is that they are always predicated by reference to the human domain."

[50] E.g., "What seemed a confusion of many voices during the parliament is resolved in a unified courtly roundel that glorifies love and community": Craig Bertolet, "'My wit is sharp; I love no taryinge': Urban Poetry and the *Parlement of Foules*," *SP* 93 (1996): 365–89 (389); "These rightly ordered birds imitate the [nine] spheres," especially if the roundel could be taken to have a three-line refrain to "end the poem's music with the same 'thryes thre' pattern with which that music begins": David Chamberlain, "The Music of the Spheres and *The Parlement of Foules*," *ChauR* 5, no. 1 (1970): 32–56 (51);

securely part of the *Parliament*.[51] More certain than the text and provenance of the roundel is its status as a sung performance, with a French
"note" and "wordes . . . swiche as ye may heer fynde, / The nexte vers,
as I now have in mynde" (677–79). Julia Boffey judges the *Parliament*'s
"nexte vers" to be "one of the most likely candidates [among Chaucer's
works] for performance of some kind."[52] Ardis Butterfield suggests that
the line "Qui bien aime a tard oublie," which appears in place of poetic
lines in several early copies, may be a vestigial or recreated "performance
cue."[53] As a sung performance embedded in its narrative, the *Parliament*'s roundel—whatever were its text and tune—would have continued the narrator's depiction of species conflation: the birds "chosen . . .
for to synge" (673) intersect with human singers in performing a French
"note" and its "wordes"; the "note" and "wordes" would look figurative
for birdsong until singers step forward, in live performance, to figure
singing birds. Tenor and vehicle simultaneously occupy both positions,
avian and human. This joyous confusion appropriately concludes the
narrator's avian performance all through the parliament, cackling and
kek-kekking and quacking bird calls along with bird opinions.[54]

---

the roundel is "surely one of the finest hymns to civic charity in existence": Paul A.
Olson, "The *Parlement of Foules*: Aristotle's *Politics* and the Foundations of Human Society," *SAC* 2 (1980): 53–69 (63).

[51] On the roundel's uncertain standing: Ralph Hanna, *London Literature, 1300–1380*
(Cambridge: Cambridge University Press, 2005), 185–90; Julia Boffey, "The Reputation and Circulation of Chaucer's Lyrics in the Fifteenth Century," *ChauR* 28, no. 1
(1993): 23–40. Between five and nine lines beginning "now welcome somer" appear,
after 1440, in just three MSS and Thynne's revised printing. Another three MSS, Caxton's edition, and Thynne's first printing have no roundel lines but instead represent a
tune, or its words, or both with a single line: "Qui bien aime a tard oublie" (Who
loves well does not soon forget). Four further MSS, including the important Cambridge
University Library, MS Gg.IV.27, either leave a blank space for the missing roundel or
silently close up the gap. From the MS evidence, Hanna argues in detail that "*Parliament*
680–92 is a mid-fifteenth-century intrusion, Chaucerian perhaps but not part of the
poem" (*London Literature*, 190). Boffey, "Reputation and Circulation of Chaucer's Lyrics," 34, notes "the air of solutions reached after the event."

[52] Boffey, "The Lyrics in Chaucer's Longer Poems," *Poetica* 37 (1993): 33. Boffey,
"Reputation and Circulation of Chaucer's Lyrics," 34, finds evidence that Chaucer
tended to keep lyrics separately from narrative MSS and to "tip in" lyrics later on in
composition or copying.

[53] Ardis Butterfield, *The Familiar Enemy: Chaucer, Language and Nation in the Hundred
Years War* (Oxford: Oxford University Press, 2009), 249, in the context of other occur-
rences of the phrase "Qui bien aime a tard oublie."

[54] Copyists intensify the avian sounds by revising " 'Ye queke,' seyde the goos" with
the first syllables "Kek kek," "Ee kekyl," and "Ye queke queke": *The Riverside Chaucer*,
1150, Textual Note to *PF*, 594. Michael J. Warren, " 'Kek kek': Translating Birds in
Chaucer's *Parliament of Fowls*," *SAC* 38 (2016): 109–32, observes that in such lines
"human and nonhuman utterances are bound up in ambiguous and interlocking

As the narrator and the roundel singers give sonorous form to the poem's emergent vision of species uncertainty, they anticipate a broadly posthumanist development over the last few decades: an "uncertainty about humans' status as a biological species."[55] Ursula Heise does not trace this contemporary development as far back as *The Parliament of Fowls*, but she does outline its fascinating recent history. Between the 1950s and the 1970s, the alien, the monster, and the postcolonial Other attacked the claim of the human to transhistorical and cross-cultural essence. The 1980s and 1990s turned attention to how technologies commingle with bodies and minds to generate cyborgian humans that grow and morph as their technologies advance. After the turn of the century, attention shifted to questioning the dichotomy between humans and other animals. To be sure, as Heise notes, it is tempting to "sketch worlds with a vast range of different forms of biological and technological consciousness, but in the end return to attributing a special status to authentic humanness."[56] Chaucer resists that special status for the human—in the form of Scipio's heavenward elevation—through his dream's compromised authority, his narrator's somatic engagement in the park's creaturely life, and especially through the uncertain species statuses of Nature's parliament. Environmental poshumanism is indebted to animal studies for a conception of being that intersects and commingles the human with other living creatures. Centuries earlier, Chaucer's *Parliament* also, on its own terms, recognized that images of species uncertainty can bump the human from its sovereign ontological perch.

V. To Dream

Chaucer's dreamer, in the final stanza, awakens to hope:

> I wok, and othere bokes tok me to,
> To reede upon, and yit I rede alwey.
> I hope, ywis, to rede so som day

---

exchange, and we are prompted to imagine, at least, that these calls carry meaning" (127). Warren also comments insightfully on the narrator as avian performer (121).

[55] Ursula K. Heise, "The Posthuman Turn: Rewriting Species in Recent American Literature," in *A Companion to American Literary Studies*, ed. Caroline F. Levander and Robert S. Levine (Malden, Mass.: John Wiley, 2011), 454–68 (454).

[56] Ibid., 465.

That I shal mete som thing for to fare
The bet, and thus to rede I nyl nat spare.
(695–99)

What is this hope? "That I shal mete som thing" is glossed in *The River-side Chaucer* and in D. S. Brewer's edition of the *Parliament* as "that I shall meet something" (*mēten*) rather than "that I shall dream something" (*mēten*).[57] Glossing "mete" as "meet" produces an expression of commitment to written authorities: the narrator reads in hope of meeting with something useful in his books. In contrast, glossing "mete" as "dream" produces a narrator who reads in order to move beyond reading into dreaming again. I would urge that hoping to "dream something" is more true to the *Parliament*'s ambitions than hoping to "meet something" in books. But any reader could agree that the double potential of the final stanza's "mete" neatly encapsulates the *Parliament*'s shift from reading to dreaming, and from seeking philosophical truths to envisioning a multisensory earthly scene.

The *Parliament*'s dream, with its destabilized truth value (by turns *somnium animale/naturale/coeleste/naturale*), revises Chaucer's sources in directions not so much respectful as interrogative and transformative. These revisionary directions become clearer when set in relation to environmental posthumanisms. Chaucer's poem and contemporary thought share an interest in validating diverse ontologies and mixing them up in order to think beyond the isolation of the human from everything else. Set alongside contemporary environmental thought, Chaucer's poem elucidates some unfamiliar contours of ontological speculation. And Chaucer, in turn, can illuminate posthumanism's task. Reading Chaucer's "olde bok" (110) can clarify the shadowed ontologies that structure cultural expression. Chaucer himself recognizes this as he mobilizes Africanus's dualism, classical mythology's animism, and medieval totemism, smashing them together to knock off rejected bits and rough out his

---

[57] *The Riverside Chaucer*, Glossary, 1269, "mete(n), meete v.2 meet"; *Parlement of Foulys*, ed. Brewer, Glossary, 158, "mete, v. meet, find." *The Middle English Dictionary* (Regents of the University of Michigan, 2001), http://quod.lib.umich.edu/m/med/ (accessed October 15, 2016) records a difference in pronunciation between the two long "e"s in the two verbs: open long "e" for "to dream" and closed long "e" for "to meet." The pronunciation difference was slight enough that Gower rhymes the two verbs in *Confessio Amantis*, IV.2091–92: "Otherwhile I dreme and mete / That I al one with hire mete"; *MED*, s.v. *mēten* (v.[3]), def. 1(a).

innovative model of species uncertainty. His *Parliament of Fowls* demonstrates that pondering ontologies is a cultural project with a long history, not a special distinction of our moment. And his creative mashup of dualism, animism, and totemism shows that such mixtures can have internal tensions and still make a kind of sense—poetic sense, dreamy sense, visionary sense.

In the *Dream of Scipio*, as Africanus answered the mainstream question of Neoplatonist and moral allegory, "How shall I save myself?," he dismissed earth's nonhuman realm, and urged Scipio to earn elevation beyond the earth. Chaucer's takedown of *The Dream of Scipio* reclaimed the little earth and juggled systems of being to investigate "What's happening here?" Now, in our time, what's happening here has changed so dramatically that a time-traveling Chaucer might well hope to dream again. Now, in our time, Scipio's question has shifted into compelling material terms: on this little earth that here is, how shall we save ourselves?

THE BIENNIAL CHAUCER LECTURE
The New Chaucer Society
Twentieth International Congress
July 11–14, 2016
Queen Mary University of London

The Biennial Chaucer Lecture

Chaucer's Silent Discourse

Stephanie Trigg
University of Melbourne

Abstract

This essay examines the trope of the "speaking face" in the poetry of Geoffrey
Chaucer. This trope draws on the familiar idea that we can read the "text" of
other people's faces, though that idea itself has a mixed and unwritten history.
Chaucer is the first writer in English to make his characters speak silently
through this facial discourse: his narrators and characters "read" the expression
on another character's face and translate that expression into words, such as
Criseyde's famous and silent rhetorical question, "What, may I nat stonden
here?" Chaucer borrows this trope from the French of Guillaume de Machaut
and the Italian of Giovanni Boccaccio, and develops a rhetorical repertoire
through which it can indicate character and personality, express emotion, or
enact interpersonal dynamics. To read the face in this way involves complex
cognitive acts, which do not simply represent human interactions; they guide
and direct them.

Keywords

Chaucer, faciality, speaking face, emotions, expressions, cognition, *The Book of
the Duchess*, *Canterbury Tales*, *Troilus and Criseyde*, *The Parliament of Fowls*

H OW DO WE KNOW what the face is saying? It has long been
regarded as one of the most expressive parts of the human body. We
look to the face to disclose identity and personality, as well as more
fleeting affects, emotions, and expressions. We read its shapes, colors,

My thanks to Helen Hickey and Anne McKendry for their assistance with this essay.
Research was supported by the Australian Research Council's Centre of Excellence for
the History of Emotions (project number CE110001011).

and aspects, and its conscious and unconscious movements and gestures. Normally, we expect these forms of recognition to be almost instantaneous, although factors such as cultural alterity, cognitive disability, and variable levels of empathy can affect our capacity to read other faces.

In western culture Cicero was one of the first to formulate the idea of the face as the index of the mind ("imago est animi voltus").[1] More evocatively, the eyes are sometimes described as "the windows to the soul," a phrase so resonant and apparently universal that it is frequently, though erroneously, attributed to William Shakespeare.[2] Equally familiar is the idea that the expression on the face can be read as a form of silent speech. For Saint Jerome (c. 347–420), "Speculum mentis est facies et taciti oculi cordis fatentur arcana" ("The face is the mirror of the mind, and eyes without speaking confess the secrets of the heart").[3] And sometimes, indeed, our facial expressions are as legible as writing. Shakespeare familiarizes this idea in English drama, helping his audience see something of what Lady Macbeth sees in her husband's face: "Your face, my thane, is as a book, where men / May read strange matters."[4]

For a more recent example, in *A Thousand Plateaus*, Gilles Deleuze and Félix Guattari explore the "abstract machine of faciality" (or "visagéité"), the process through which we apprehend what a face is, and how it works. They write about the way language is "embedded" in faces, and use an unusual metaphor to evoke the screaming expressivity of the face: "The face is a veritable megaphone."[5] Here, the face projects its meanings so forcefully, it is as if the noise were deafening up close.

[1] "Nam ut imago est animi voltus sic indices oculi" ("For as the face is the image of the soul, so are the eyes its interpreters"), in Marcus Tullius Cicero V, *Orator*, ed. Jeffrey Henderson, trans. H. M. Hubbell, Loeb Classical Library 342 (Cambridge, Mass.: Harvard University Press, 1962), XVIII.60.350–51.

[2] Pliny the Elder refers to the eyes as windows to the soul, but he is describing the cognitive processes through which the eyes help the mind comprehend the world. See *Naturalis historia*, Vol. 3, books VIII–XI, ed. Jeffrey Henderson, trans. H. Rackham, Loeb Classical Library 353 (Cambridge, Mass.: Harvard University Press, 1940), XI.146.522–23. "[A]utem uidimus, animo cernimus; oculi ceu uasa quaedam uisibilem eius partem accipiunt atque tramittunt" ("[I]in fact it is the mind which is the instrument of sight and of observation; the eyes act as vessels receiving and transmitting the seeing portion of the mind"); Mary Beagon, "The Curious Eye of the Elder Pliny," in *Pliny the Elder: Themes and Contexts*, ed. Roy Gibson and Ruth Morello (Leiden: Brill, 2011), 71–88 (77 n. 21).

[3] Saint Jerome, "To Furia, on the Duty of Remaining a Widow," in *Select Letters of St. Jerome*, ed. T. E. Page and E. Capps, trans. F. A. Wright, Loeb Classical Library 262 (London: William Heinemann, 1933), 250–53.

[4] William Shakespeare, *Macbeth*, ed. Kenneth Muir, Arden Shakespeare Second Series (London: Bloomsbury, 1997), I.v.62–63.

[5] Gilles Deleuze and Félix Guattari, *A Thousand Plateaus: Capitalism and Schizophrenia*, foreword and trans. Brian Massumi (1987; London: Continuum Press, 2008), 199.

If the idea of the face as a megaphone juxtaposes noise with silence, the more familiar trope of "reading the face" similarly jams visual and textual images up against each other. The acts of reading and looking produce very different kinds of information, which may or may not be reliable or consistent. And in fact, for all these metaphors of mirrors, windows, books, and megaphones that invoke the expressive power of the face, we actually prefer our facial knowledge to be a little opaque, a little clouded, a little resistant to easy reading. Why otherwise is the most beloved face in western art—Leonardo's *Mona Lisa*—such an enigmatic one, generating so many thousands of words to explain its mystery?

This cluster of ideas—silence, sound, discourse, and facial expression —sits at the heart of this essay, which considers the ways Chaucer both explores and exploits the ambiguous relationship between words and the appearance of the face. Literary discourse has long been fascinated by the problem of representing the visual appearance of the face, and Chaucer's works offer many intriguing examples. I will conclude with a more personal reflection on some of the ways facial recognition can go badly wrong.

Chaucer has Troilus ponder a secular aspect of facial mystery in Book III of *Troilus and Criseyde*. In one of the most intense and erotic encounters of medieval literature, the lovers are finally lying in bed together. Troilus kisses Criseyde's eyes and addresses them:

> O eyen clere,
> It weren ye that wroughte me swich wo,
> Ye humble nettes of my lady deere!
> Though ther be mercy writen in youre cheere,
> God woot, the text ful hard is, soth, to fynde!
> How koude ye withouten bond me bynde?[6]
> (III.1353–58)

At this moment of face-to-face mutuality, Troilus brings his mouth to Criseyde's face, to kiss her eyes and then to address them in an act of deep intimacy. But that intimacy is quickly displaced by distance and discourse. Troilus must close Criseyde's eyes in the act of kissing them, sealing off their expressive and seductive gaze in order to perform his

---

[6] All quotations from Chaucer are taken from *The Riverside Chaucer*, gen. ed. Larry D. Benson, 3rd ed. (Boston: Houghton Mifflin, 1987). Book and line numbers are given parenthetically in the text.

own erotic gesture. He then invokes the formalities of courtly discourse and the language of deferred desire by calling those eyes "nets," and referring to his lady in the distancing third person. While he correctly reads the "mercy" that is "written" in her face, he cannot say how he has come to that knowledge. He abstracts and mystifies that face by saying the text of his beloved's "chere"—her expression—is difficult to "fynde." To "fynde" in Middle English may mean to discover something, to come across a text by reading, but it may also mean to compose, translating Latin *invenire*.[7] Is Troilus a reader or a writer of this text? And how does he know how to read this mercy in her face? It is a "ful hard" erotic mystery, like Criseyde's power (or Criseyde's eyes' power) to bind Troilus without bonds. The mysteries of emotion and cognition are tightly entangled.

In *The Parliament of Fowls*, Africanus is a more confident reader, easily diagnosing the confusion written on the dreamer's face:

> And seyde, "It stondeth writen in thy face,
> Thyn errour, though thow telle it not to me;
> But dred the not to come into this place,
> For this writyng nys nothyng ment bi the,
> Ne by non but he Loves servaunt be."
>
> (155–59)

The narrator's mind is confused, but that unspoken confusion, his "errour," is clearly legible on his face. So legible, indeed, that Africanus uses the same word, "writen/writing," to refer equally to the expression on the dreamer's face and to the two material inscriptions in gold and black letters above the gateway into the park, before which the dreamer hesitates.

As Aranye Fradenburg put it so beautifully in her biennial lecture in Siena in 2010, "Living Chaucer," "human animals do love pondering what's going on in each other's minds. Chaucer distinctively invites us to accompany him in this highly psychological, yet highly social activity."[8] Fradenburg's key concept here is "intersubjectivity": the pleasurable work of understanding each other. She also shows how "Chaucer's words 'live on' because the patterns they create really do change our minds

---

[7] *MED*, s.v. *finden* (v.), def. 7(a), "To discover, find out, or learn by inspection, investigation, observation, or reflection."

[8] L. O. Aranye Fradenburg, "Living Chaucer," *SAC* 33 (2011): 41–64 (50).

and bodies."[9] These textual patterns have cognitive and empathetic implications for the relationships between texts and readers, as well as between characters in literary narratives.

Reading the text of facial expression—what the face says—is an ideal topic for the history of emotions, as it helps us locate gesture, affect, and emotion in precise literary and social contexts. In my first two examples, the ideology of courtly love conditions the way medieval characters read each other's faces. A woman's eyes are predatory or seductive nets; a man appears befuddled by *not* feeling interpellated by Love. Such examples help us tease out the relationship among gesture, emotion, and the social context in which emotions arise and are interpreted by others. Jerome's oft-quoted maxim, for example, is driven by a concern for the place of women in a patriarchal culture: he is warning the widow Furia against the company of handsome young men, lest her inevitable desires—"the secrets of the heart"—should appear on her face to her public shame.[10] My point here is simple: ideas about the face that seem to support the thesis of stable and universal expression often arise from very particular historical and social circumstances.

In what follows, I try to follow Fradenburg's lead, to consider some of the things Chaucer shows us about the emotional and cognitive acts of reading the expression on someone else's face.[11] Chaucer's poetry gives us some powerful examples, but I focus here on an even more precise rhetorical trope, one that he uses only a handful of times. This is the trope of the speaking face, when the expressive face or demeanor of another person is translated into conversational, though silent, speech. The most famous example will already be in your mind:

> To Troilus right wonder wel with alle
> Gan for to like hire mevynge and hire chere,
> Which somdel deignous was, for she let falle

---

[9] Ibid., 45.

[10] Elsewhere in the same letter, it is clear that the body that speaks in this way is the untempered female body: "Quid aliud pollicemur et aliud ostendimus? Lingua personat castitatem et totum corpus praefert inpudicitiam" ("Why do we profess one thing and display another? The tongue talks of chastity, but the whole body reveals incontinence"); Jerome, "To Furia," 240–41.

[11] For further discussion of the face in late medieval culture, see Ethan Knapp, "Faciality and Ekphrasis in Late Medieval England," in *The Art of Vision: Ekphrasis in Medieval Literature and Culture*, ed. Andrew James Johnson, Knapp, and Margitta Rouse (Columbus: Ohio State University Press, 2015), 209–23.

Hire look a lite aside in swich manere,
Ascaunces, "What, may I nat stonden here?"
(I.288–92)

What kinds of social, cognitive, and emotional acts are performed here, as Criseyde's moving body and demeanor produce a "look" that asks a silent question? What forms of intersubjectivity are at play, as our narrator shows us Criseyde's face through Troilus's eyes, in the midst of a crowded public gathering? What kind of volition can we attribute to Criseyde, who lets her look fall a little to the side in such a manner as if she were saying "What? Can't I stand here?" How do we all comprehend so clearly the narrative truth of this facial expression, and the translation of an unseen expression into words? Questions abound, and many Chaucer scholars have written illuminatingly on this passage.[12] Rather than lingering too long here, then, I would like to address some structural questions first, and then examine some less familiar examples.

This trope of the speaking face is a small but very powerful rhetorical machine, one that is intriguing to think with in the broader context of the history of emotions. In this arena, the face is a familiar object of study. Many modern scholars—especially in the fields of psychology and anthropology—argue that emotions can be captured and analyzed in their appearance on the human face. The long visual tradition of portraying emotions in this way became more analytic in the seventeenth century with Charles Le Brun, who produced a series of drawings, "The Expressions,"[13] and Charles Darwin similarly compared the faces of animals and humans in an attempt to isolate and identify the characteristic expressions and facial gestures associated with specific emotions.[14]

In the field of contemporary psychology, the use of single images of faces to signify or demonstrate emotional states is controversial. Paul

[12] See, for example, Jill Mann, "Shakespeare and Chaucer: 'What is Criseyde worth?,'" *Cambridge Quarterly* 18 (1989): 109–20; John Burrow, *Gesture and Looks in Medieval Narrative* (Cambridge: Cambridge University Press, 2002), 130; Mary Behrman, "Heroic Criseyde," *ChauR* 38 (2004): 314–36. See also Stephanie Trigg, "'Language in Her Eye': The Expressive Face of Criseyde/Cressida," in *Love, History and Emotion in Chaucer and Shakespeare: "Troilus and Criseyde" and "Troilus and Cressida,"* ed. Andrew James Johnston, Elisabeth Kempf, and Russell West-Pavlov (Manchester: Manchester University Press, 2016), 94–108.
[13] For a comprehensive study, see Jennifer Montagu, *The Expression of the Passions: The Origin and Influence of Charles Le Brun's "Conférence sur l'expression générale et particulière"* (New Haven: Yale University Press, 1994).
[14] Charles Darwin, *The Expression of the Emotions in Man and Animals* (1872; Chicago: University of Chicago Press, 1965).

Ekman is the most famous exponent of this practice. He suggests there is a limited number of "core" human emotions, though his method and his findings have been vigorously contested.[15] Arrays of faces linked to emotions also proliferate on social media platforms: for example, in the dizzying rows of emoji that compete for my attention when I simply want to send a text message. If you google images for "face and emotion" you can find many sequences of such facial arrays, where the infinite variations of the human face are abstracted into a kind of humanoid graphic language that, with only a few exceptions, has the effect of bypassing gender, age, and ethnicity. In the proliferation of such images, emotions are reduced to a series of choices, each of equal strength, each equally available to all.

In contrast, the speaking face trope is wordy and oblique. It resists repetition or formulaic iteration, as its words are always very specific to the occasion. It occurs in moments of thick description, often mediated by another character, and captures a somatic sense of the face in motion, using the full resources of spoken dialogue—the telling richness of interpersonal communication. In the literary text, the speaking face often constitutes a key moment of characterization or narrative development. The silent discourse of the face beautifully complicates the appealing simplicity of visual images as the key indices of emotions.

Furthermore, the speaking face trope insists on both the historicity and the sociability of emotional expression because it depends on both its textual and historical form (the words the face is said to say), and the presence of a second person (whether character or narrator) to witness and interpret it. The face "speaks," then, in a deeply social script, to borrow a phrase from Monique Scheer, because its expressivity and legibility depend on the habitus—in Pierre Bourdieu's sense—in which it acts.[16] Scheer views emotions as a form of cultural practice, embedded

---

[15] For a recent and comprehensive analysis of many of these arguments, see Jan Plamper, *The History of Emotions: An Introduction*, trans. Keith Tribe (Oxford: Oxford University Press, 2012), 147–63. Several essays in the recent special issue of *postmedieval*, *Facing up to the History of Emotions*, ed. Stephanie Downes and Stephanie Trigg, also consider Ekman's work and its implications for medieval studies. See Philippa Maddern, "Reading Faces: How Did Late Medieval Europeans Interpret Emotions in Faces?," *postmedieval* 8, no. 1 (2017): 12–34; and Kim M. Phillips, "The Grins of Others: Figuring Ethnic Difference in Medieval Facial Expressions," *postmedieval* 8, no. 1 (2017): 83–101.

[16] Monique Scheer, "Are Emotions a Kind of Practice? (and Is That What Makes Them Have a History?): A Bourdieuian Approach to Understanding Emotion," *History and Theory* 51 (2012): 193–220 (207).

in social settings, and involving somatic, cognitive, and other social factors. She might well be writing of the speaking face here: "Other people's bodies are implicated in practice because viewing them induces feelings."[17] A look or a glance between characters that is rendered into silent conversational speech can be a very powerful indicator of the role of emotions in social relationships, whether intimate or public. The long history of such discourse over several centuries and genres of writing might also register telling changes in the structures and conventions of such relationships, and the mediation between the private and public speech of lovers, family members, or between social classes, for example. This is a much more precisely textual and literary machine, then, than the Deleuzian "abstract machine of faciality," which is grounded in visual and conceptual phenomena, and the experience of looking at the face or an image of one.

In my thinking about how this trope works I take my chief inspiration from two writers whose work will be familiar to those working in the emotions. The first is William Reddy, who uses speech-act theory to develop his concept of "emotives": or "emotional utterances that take the form of first-person, present-tense emotion claims."[18] Emotives are neither simply descriptive nor performative, but in Reddy's words they still "do things to the world. Emotives are themselves instruments for directly changing, building, hiding, intensifying emotions, instruments that may be more or less successful."[19] His examples include expressions such as "I am angry," "I have always loved you." The silent discourse of the literary face often shares the same grammatical form. Similarly, it draws attention to the role of language in shaping and creating feeling, as well as simply expressing it. Reddy's insight encourages me to think about the speaking face, not just as the expression of feeling, but as an active emotional performance in the company of others.

Second, I follow the lead of Guillemette Bolens, who argues for the importance of "embodied cognition and kinesic intelligence" in our reading of literary texts.[20] The phrase "kinesic intelligence" comes from Ellen Spolsky, who refers to "our sense of the relationship of parts of the

[17] Ibid., 211.
[18] William M. Reddy, *The Navigation of Feeling: A Framework for the History of Emotions* (Cambridge: Cambridge University Press, 2011), 104.
[19] Ibid., 105.
[20] Guillemette Bolens, *The Style of Gestures: Embodiment and Cognition in Literary Narrative*, foreword by Alain Berthoz (Baltimore: Johns Hopkins University Press, 2012), 1.

human body to the whole."[21] We use kinesic intelligence to produce mental imagery, and for "recognizing the facial and bodily gestures of other people." Bolens's first example is the elaborate kinesic tracing of the memory of the smile of Françoise, in the early pages of *Du côté de chez Swann*. Proust's complex narrative easily lends itself to such analysis, but Bolens also works through the social concept of "face-work" and kinesic facial gestures in medieval narratives such as *Patience* and *Sir Gawain and the Green Knight*.[22]

Spolsky seeks to deflect attention *away* from language, and toward the nonverbal communication at work in the visual arts, or the kinesic intelligence at work when we look at pictures. In contrast, I am, like Bolens, more interested in what happens when we read: when we are told, for example, what Criseyde's face means through this act of verbalization, even though there is no visual description of its physical features in movement. We work backwards, as it were, from the silent discourse of her face to reconstruct, imagine, and perhaps even feel the facial movements and gestures that might give rise to this appearance. The speaking face depends on elaborate sequences that are cognitive, somatic, rhetorical, and emotional, in varying degrees.

The speaking face is used to great effect in the realist novel. One of its most accomplished exponents is Jane Austen, whose novels are often built around social scenes in which the characters who have most to say to each other cannot speak directly, so the speaking face often accomplishes intense, intimate, and emotional work in a crowded social context.[23] But fiction writers such as Chaucer and Austen sit in the middle of a wide range of cultural examples. In the field of philosophy and theology, we might cite Emmanuel Lévinas, for whom the human face is the primordial signifier, when it interpellates the other in the voice of God, as if it said, "Thou shalt not commit murder" ("tu ne commettras pas de meurtre"), or more simply, "Thou shalt not kill" ("tu ne tueras pas").[24] Lévinas returns to the trope of the speaking face many times in

---

[21] Ellen Spolsky, "Elaborated Knowledge: Reading Kinesis in Pictures," *Poetics Today* 17, no. 2 (1996): 157–80 (160).

[22] Bolens, *Style of Gestures*, 123–66.

[23] Stephanie Trigg, "Faces that Speak: A Little Emotion Machine in the Novels of Jane Austen," in *Spaces for Feeling: Emotions and Sociabilities in Britain, 1650–1850*, ed. Susan Broomhall (London: Routledge, 2015), 185–201.

[24] Emmanuel Lévinas, *Totality and Infinity: An Essay on Exteriority*, trans. Alphonso Lingus (The Hague: Martinus Nijhoff, 1979), 199; *Totalité et infini: Essais sur l'extériorité*, Phaenomenologica 8 (The Hague and Boston: Martinus Nijhoff, 1961), 217. Lévinas's use of this trope is irresistible to one commentator, Terry Veling, who glosses Lévinas's

his discussions of otherness: it becomes a kind of universal expression of humanity. In a similar fashion, he also describes the "I can" that is "spoken" by the body.[25] For Lévinas, the capacity of the face to speak in this way is a crucial aspect of its signifying function as the human other. By directly acknowledging the function of the speaking face trope in his work, we can further understand his simultaneous abstracting and literalizing of the face as the basis of human ethics.

The trope is also invoked in more mundane and popular contexts. On June 28, 2016, Jeremy Corbyn, the besieged leader of the UK Labour opposition, who was refusing to step down despite a massive vote of no confidence from his party's members of parliament, held a shadow cabinet meeting. He invited the Sky TV cameras to film it. In the *Guardian*, John Crace described a moment from the television footage: "On [Corbyn's] left was the deputy leader, Tom Watson, whose face was crumpled in abject misery. 'Get me out of here,' his eyes pleaded. 'I'm stuck in a room with the seriously unwell. Get me out of here in case it's contagious.' The eyes had it."[26] I like this example because even though television footage is available, Crace's attribution of Watson's silent discourse works as a Derridean "supplément," supplementing and supplanting the visual image for the readers of print or textual media. We don't need to have seen the footage, because Crace has given us the "real" meaning of Watson's face, inviting us to speculate with him about the unresolved layering of private feeling and public, or political, allegiance.

Elsewhere on the cultural and historical spectrum we might consider the banderoles used to indicate speech in medieval manuscripts; the sophisticated interplay between text and image in graphic fiction; our affectionate habit of ventriloquizing babies and animals to make them "speak" to us in the first person; or even the humorous textual caption, whereby we superimpose words and cultish dialogue onto photographs

---

speaking face over and over: "Every face says, 'I am other to you.' Every face says, 'I am not you.' Every face says: 'Don't kill me, don't absorb me into your world, don't obliterate me by making me the same as you. I am other. I am different. I am not you'"; Terry Veling, "Lévinas and the Other Side of Theology," *Jewish–Christian Relations, International Council of Christians and Jews* (August 1, 2002): 1–8 (4), http://www.jcrelations.net/Levinas + and + the + Other + Side + of + Theology.2234.0.html?L = 3 (accessed April 25, 2017).

[25] Lévinas, *Totality and Infinity*, 37; *Totalité et infini*, 26.

[26] John Crace, "Corbyn's Going Nowhere but Not in the Way He Means," *Guardian*, June 28, 2016, https://www.theguardian.com/politics/2016/jun/28/corbyns-going-nowhere-but-not-in-the-way-he-means (accessed April 25, 2017).

of cats and dogs. These can range from the sublime to the ridiculous. This internet meme even generated its own dialect, "lolcat": the systematic misuse of spelling and grammar modeled on the caption to an image of a cat apparently saying with joy "I can has cheezburger?"

Even the much maligned trivial speech acts associated with contemporary casual spoken discourse—for example, "I'm like, 'Oh my God'"—share some rhetorical features with the speaking face: the "like" here is comparable to the expression "as if to say" that underpins the rhetorical structure of silent facial discourse. Even without any specific content, we are invited to recognize some sense of shared feeling or anticipated response to a situation.

If literary examples sit in the middle of this spectrum from philosophy to cartoon captions, Chaucer uses the trope at the very beginning of its history in English literature. His earliest use of the speaking face trope comes in *The Book of the Duchess*, after the dreamer has suggested to the Knight who is dressed in black that he should tell his sorrows, to ease his heart:

> With that he loked on me asyde,
> As who sayth, "Nay, that wol not be."
> (558–59)

There is no description of any facial gesture here: no raised eyebrow; no twitch of the mouth or nostrils. Nor is the face an entity of any kind (in many medieval texts the nouns "chere" or "countenance" or "lokyng" are used to describe facial expression as a whole). Yet it is clear that the Knight's looking, the way he directs his gaze, is a facial effect, as well as a bodily gesture, and that its meaning is beyond doubt.

Prior to this point, the Knight has been speaking very politely with the dreamer, who is standing directly in front of him (515–56). When the dreamer first comes upon him, he is sitting with his head down, with his back against a tree, firmly embedded in the natural world (446–47). Now he looks at the dreamer (*he loked on me*), but apparently by turning his head or his eyes from another direction. This puts the reader in the position of the dreamer: seeking answers but being given only half a response, indirectly, from an angle. This looking aside is not incidental, but crucial: the face moves toward the dreamer at the same time as it moves into this expression.

The hermeneutic fulcrum here is the little phrase in the second line,

"As who sayth . . . ." This is usually glossed as meaning "like one who says . . ." or "in the manner of one who says . . . ."[27] These three words, from the larger family of the simile, or the "as if," inaugurate the cognitive processes of the emotional machine. They seem predicated on the idea that every face that expresses "Nay that wol not be" might move in a similar way. But at the same time, because the direct speech attributed to the face is so unequivocal, expressed with such narrative authority, it does not matter what the face looks like. This is one of the reasons this trope is so paradoxical. It seems to begin with the appearance of the face, but has the effect of displacing that appearance with words. Perhaps we may picture what that face might look like—but no more, really, than we picture a character whose spoken discourse is reported to us. Rather, I think this trope invites us to think and feel our way into imagining that facial movement as if it were our own; how would our own face move if those words were what we were thinking? This trope depends more on grammar, rhetoric, and bodily feeling than any visual impression. It is unashamedly textual; and its effect is immediate.

This example from *The Book of the Duchess* offers another layer of social meanings, as it implies that the dreamer's capacity to read the Knight's face and, by extension, his mind, is better than his ability to hear and understand what he actually says, later on, when he appears not to understand the Knight's complaint that his lady has died. This example shows us the expressivity of the aristocratic face, but also shows us how the dreamer is able to read that face for us. The distinctions of class are also apparent in the contrast between the Knight's expressive face, and the spoken words that come out of his mouth a moment later. His refusal—"Nay that wol not be"—would be blunt if spoken aloud, but it is displaced by the formal and polite speech that follows:

> "Graunt mercy, goode frend," quod he,
> "I thanke the that thow woldest soo,
> But hyt may never the rather be doo."
> (560–62)

Two polite expressions of gratitude, first in French ("Graunt mercy") and then in English ("I thanke the") soften his face's silent resistance to

---

[27] For a fuller analysis of a comparable trope, see Susan Yager, "'As she that': Syntactical Ambiguity in Chaucer's *Troilus and Criseyde*," *PQ* 2 (1994): 151–68.

the dreamer's suggestion that talking about his grief might provide any comfort.

The linguistic contrast here echoes an earlier contrast in discursive modes, when the dreamer first sees the Knight and overhears his lament. There, the dreamer observes his pale complexion and the rush of blood to his heart, as if he were nearly insane with sorrow. He bows and greets the Knight, who replies politely, excusing himself for not seeing him earlier. And the dreamer remarks:

> Loo, how goodly spak thys knyght,
> As it had be another wyght
>
> (529–30)

So the Knight is master of two levels of discourse: one that is more private and involuntary (the lyric and the silent discourse of the face); and one that is more well considered and formal (the spoken conversation with the narrator).[28]

It is worth noting that even though the face speaks in Chaucer only a few times, it always speaks in simple language of predominantly English vocabulary. My other examples do not draw this sharp contrast between unspoken English and spoken French words, but Chaucer's silent discourse always uses words that are English in origin. In the *Book of the Duchess*, Chaucer seems to imply a differential relationship between English and French vocabulary: instinctive body language is best rendered in English, but French is used to correct any apparent rudeness and replace it with courtly formality.

This is not to imply there is anything particularly "natural" about the speaking face trope, however. Chaucer seems to have found it first in his reading of French poetry, in the most direct source for this part of his poem, Machaut's *Jugement dou roy de Behaingne*.[29] In that poem, Machaut's dreamer/narrator observes an encounter between a courtly lady whose lover has died and a gentleman whose beloved has betrayed him. Lost in silent grief, the lady passes the man without noticing him.

---

[28] In *The Familiar Enemy: Chaucer, Language and Nation in the Hundred Years War* (Oxford: Oxford University Press, 2009), Ardis Butterfield makes a similar observation about *The Book of the Duchess* at this point, writing of the dream's "system of imperfect exchange, between a language honed for its specific courtly task and another that has up to now had an inferior and different position" (291).

[29] Guillaume de Machaut, *Le jugement dou roy de Behaingne*, ed. and trans. R. Barton Palmer, Garland Library of Medieval Literature 9, series A (New York: Garland, 1984).

She apologizes for her distraction, and as they begin to converse, the man suggests the woman should reveal her troubles. There is no silent facial discourse in their exchange. Chaucer adapts the emotional structure of this encounter for *The Book of the Duchess*, but adds the Knight's sideways look and silent expression, while putting himself in the middle of the scene, rather than as a hidden observer.

But Machaut does use the trope of the speaking face later in the *Jugement*, when the knight describes his first tentative approach to his beloved and begs for her mercy: this is the narrative that sits behind the Black Knight's later account of his love affair with White. In Machaut, the lady refuses the lover in a gentle speech that closes with a self-referential performative: "Adieu vous dit" ("I say goodbye to you").[30] His heart nearly breaks as she is leaving, but there is a more encouraging message in her face:

> Mais la douceur de son plaisant regart
> Par son dous art fist que j'en os regart;
> Qu'au departir de moy, se Diex me gart,
> Si doucement
> Me regarda qu'il m'iert vis proprement
> Que ses regars me disoit vraiement:
> "Amis, je t'aim trés amoureusement."[31]

In Barton Palmer's translation:

> But the sweetness of her pleasant look
> With its sweet craftiness made me dare look at her;
> So that as she left (may God protect me)
> So sweetly
> She did look my way that it truly seemed
> That her expression actually said:
> "Lover, I love you very much in Love's own way."[32]

[30] Ibid., 24–25.
[31] Ibid., 24, lines 553–59.
[32] Ibid., 25, lines 553–59. Helen Phillips paraphrases thus: "Although she says 'Adieu,' her look seems to say 'Friend, I love you very much,'" in Geoffrey Chaucer, *The Book of the Duchess*, ed. Helen Phillips, Durham and St. Andrews Medieval Texts 3 (Durham and St. Andrews: Department of English Language and Medieval Literature, Durham University; and Department of English, University of St Andrews, 1982), 175.

The contrast here between the lady's spoken refusal and her silent expression of love is built around the decorum of courtly behavior, but of course it also sets a dangerous precedent for the sexualized interpretation of a woman's word, where her spoken "no," or in this case her "Adieu," is apparently contradicted by her unspoken "I love you." As in Jerome's letter, the speaking face here is the face of female desire, as read by the male viewer.

Chaucer does not repeat Machaut's wish-fulfillment fantasy that the woman's face should speak something more promising than her spoken word. When the Black Knight first asks White for mercy, she says " 'Nay' / Al outerly" (that is, completely; 1243–44), but does not promise love with any silent expression. That is, she is not coy, or playful, or duplicitous; and nor does she express any yearning that would give the lie to her firm rejection of his suit. Her spoken "Nay" means "No"; and the Knight steals away and loves her in devoted service for another year before addressing her again. While Machaut uses the speaking face to dramatize a foundational myth of heterosexual seduction, Chaucer avoids this flirtatious usage and adapts the technique in the earlier narrative moment to dramatize the way that the Black Knight will overcome his own first instinctive facial "nay" with a spoken address to his interlocutor, saying the same thing, but in more polite discourse.

Later in the poem, Chaucer will use this trope to describe White's face, as part of a formal description:

> Hir eyen semed anoon she wolde
> Have mercy—fooles wenden soo—
> But hyt was never the rather doo.
> Hyt nas no countrefeted thyng;
> Hyt was hir owne pure lokyng
> That the goddesse, dame Nature,
> Had mad hem opene by mesure
> And close; for were she never so glad,
> Hyr lokynge was not foly sprad,
> Ne wildely, thogh that she pleyde;
> But ever, me thoght, hir eyen seyde,
> "Be God, my wrathe ys al foryive!"
> (866–77)

I have written about this description elsewhere so I will pause only to emphasize how the face—or in this case White's eyes—speaks in

English vocabulary.[33] This is more of a character description than a narrative encounter, but the expression on White's face shares many of the most stable features of this trope as an emotive in Reddy's sense (present tense, first-person expression involving an emotion word: *wrathe*), mediated by the emphatic presence of the observing, processing narrator, the Knight who describes her expression.

In dramatic contrast, Chaucer uses the same phrase, "as who saith," in the opening lines of his *Lenvoy de Chaucer a Bukton*, to introduce a speculation about the silent discourse of silence itself. This is by far the most complex example in Chaucer's writing:

> My maister Bukton, whan of Crist our kyng
> Was axed what is trouthe or sothfastnesse,
> He nat a word answerde to that axing,
> As who saith, "No man is al trewe," I gesse.
>
> (1–4)

This example is not technically a speaking face. Rather, it is the whole silent, unmoving demeanor of Christ—the *absence* of gesture—that seems to answer Pilate's question, "What is truth?," in this indirect way, by not saying a word.[34] With so little relational context, the same phrase of comparison, "as who saith," interpreting Christ's silence, depends strongly on its capacity to invoke a normative, familiar equivalence between negative gesture and silent discourse.

Like the discourse of the Knight's face, Christ's "No man is al trewe" is semantically simple, though there is a rare contextual ambiguity here. Chaucer manuscripts and early printed editions do not punctuate for direct speech, of course, but the end of this sentence is unusually uncertain. The Riverside editors put quotation marks around the "No man is al trewe," and leave the "I gesse" as if spoken by Chaucer—as if he were surmising what Christ's silence might signify. But one translator, Gerard NeCastro, includes the "I gesse" as part of Christ's response, when he translates the line, "as who should say, 'I believe no man is all

---

[33] Trigg, "'Language in Her Eye,'" 94–108.

[34] John 18:38. Chaucer's lyric conflates two different Gospel accounts. John is the only one to include Pilate's question, but it is clearly a rhetorical one, as Pilate immediately leaves Jesus. Matthew and Mark emphasize Jesus's silence but do not include Pilate's question about truth.

true.'"[35] It is a nice question: do we think Christ, or Christ's face, would use a concessive clause like "I gesse"? And if not, why not?

Because this instance is attributing words to *Christ's* silence it is particularly complex in its theology as well as its rhetoric. Lévinas and Deleuze and Guattari all privilege the face of God as the primordial or universal face, or the primordial example of facialization. If the face *is* Christ, as Deleuze and Guattari suggest, then perhaps it does not matter that there is no specific facial movement or gesture here to be interpreted. The implicit invocation of a speaking face, *any* face, is sufficient to suggest the face of Christ in his allegedly universal humanity. Yet the content of Christ's silent discourse—the idea that "no one is completely true"—complicates the sense that the silent discourse of the face is normatively truthful. If no one is completely truthful, then the discourse of their face, or the interpretation of that face, may not be completely true either.

This example recalls Saint Paul's doubts about the truthfulness and reliability of face-to-face interactions in the imperfect human world. He promises the Corinthians, "For now we see in a mirror dimly, but then face to face; now I know in part but then I will know fully just as I also have been fully known."[36] It is only in God's eternity that we will enjoy full and mutual knowledge with, and of, God, but Paul reminds us that all earthly knowledge is imperfect. And thus, when we look into a mirror, or into each other's faces now, all we can see are shadows, dim reflections, and difficulties. Paul's facial metaphor promises us perfect knowledge in eternity, but his "now" has the surprising effect of blurring our quotidian vision of each other's faces. Like Paul, we regularly use the face-to-face metaphor to suggest a form of unmediated knowledge, but facial expressions are often quite oblique. The impulse to render such expressions as (silent) direct speech is a way of forestalling those difficulties.

Of all Chaucer's works, the one most consistently concerned with facial expression is *The Clerk's Tale*. Comparison with Petrarch's Latin, Boccaccio's Italian, and the French *Livre Griseldis* analogues reveals that

---

[35] "My master Buckton, when it was demanded of Christ our Lord, what is truth or truthfulness, he answered not a word; as who should say, 'I believe no man is all true'"; Geoffrey Chaucer, "The Envoy of Chaucer to Buckton," trans. Gerard NeCastro, in *eChaucer: Chaucer in the Twenty-First Century* (University of Maine at Machias, 2007), http://ummutility.umm.maine.edu/necastro/chaucer/translation/short/short.html (accessed April 25, 2017).

[36] 1 Corinthians 13:12.

Chaucer consistently takes up the invitation to focus on the facial expressions throughout the *Tale* more than his sources do.[37] One of the most striking things in *The Clerk's Tale*—and Chaucer does carry this over from his sources—is that while many romances have an evil intent under a smiling face (the false steward, the false guardian, the false mother-in-law), Walter is often pleased with his wife but must pretend he is angry and sad.[38]

As a master manipulator of his own face, and of Griselda's emotions, it is Walter who expresses the greatest consciousness of its power, in a telling example of the speaking face that is hypothetical but forcefully contractual in nature. Here he is, setting out the terms of his marriage proposal to Griselda:

> "I seye this: be ye redy with good herte
> To al my lust, and that I frely may,
> As me best thynketh, do yow laughe or smerte,
> And nevere ye to grucche it, nyght ne day?
> And eek whan I sey 'ye,' ne sey nat 'nay,'
> Neither by word ne frownyng contenance?
> Swere this, and heere I swere oure alliance."
>
> (351–57)

Griselda's hypothetical "nay" can be spoken equally by word or by "frownyng contenance," in a passage that helpfully articulates the grammatical rules and conditions of the speaking face. Again, the discourse of that face is English, as the simple "ye" and "nay" (and "grucche" and "swere") give way to the French rhymes and the contractual vocabulary of the "alliance" that follows. We might compare the Merchant in the *Canterbury Tales* and his vision of marriage: "She seith nat ones 'nay,'

---

[37] Thomas H. Bestul, "True and False *Cheere* in Chaucer's *Clerk's Tale*," *JEGP* 82 (1983): 500–515 (501).

[38] "Letus ille responso, sed dissimulans visu mestus abscessit" ("He was happy with her response, but departed masked in melancholy"); Francis Petrarch, *Historia Griseldis: Petrarch's Epistolae seniles XVII.3*, in *Sources and Analogues of the "Canterbury Tales,"* ed. Robert M. Correale and Mary Hamel, Vol. 1 (Cambridge: D. S. Brewer, 2003), 119, lines 208–9. "Le marquis de ceste response fut moult liez en cuer, mais il dissimula et faingny qu'il feust courroucie et triste et se party d'elle" ("The marquis rejoiced at this response, but he dissembled his feelings and pretended that he was angry and sad, and took his leave of her"); *Le livre Griseldis*, in Correale and Hamel, *Sources and Analogues of the "Canterbury Tales,"* 151, lines 185–86. "Glad was this markys of hire answeryng, / But yet he feyned as he were nat so; / Al drery was his cheere and his lookyng, / Whan that he sholde out of the chambre go" (*ClT*, 512–15).

whan he seith 'ye' " (*MerT*, 1345). Walter clearly does not want the kind of nay-saying wife invoked by negative example in this passage, and seeks to forestall any resistance. These minimalist dialogues—the husband's "yes" and the wife's "no"—are important moments in the emotional history of marriage.

The earlier versions of the story vary in terms of the things that Walter asks Griselda to agree to, though they all emphasize the potential for her to differ from him in will and obedience. Petrarch alludes to the possibility of Griselda disagreeing through "resistance in your face or your words" ("sine ulla frontis aut verbi repugnancia te").[39] It is only Chaucer who adds the trope of the speaking face, and I suggest that it deepens the sense of emotional tyranny with which Walter will test his wife. Not only must Griselda not show resistance in her face; Walter anticipates the word her face *might* speak in order to inhibit that hypothetical silent discourse. A "nay" on Griselda's face would constitute a forceful act of resistance that would violate her marriage. She must not let her face move into such a gesture. Indeed, it might be safer not to let her face move into any gesture at all. It is one of the reasons so many readers find her character so unrealistic: conceiving of a face that does *not* respond to emotion has an inhibiting and distressing effect on our own kinesic imaginary. It is as if our own faces were equally stilled by Walter's prohibition.

The hypothetical nature of Griselda's imagined silent "nay" draws our attention to a further paradox of this trope. I have used the phrase "silent discourse," but if these poems were read aloud, these expressions would not be silent at all. How would Chaucer have performed this ventriloquized facial discourse? Would he have attempted to perform a female voice when describing the expression on the faces of White and Criseyde? Would he have attempted to perform Walter performing Griselda's voice? Or would his own face have performed the appropriate gestures? In the context of performance, the distinction between speech and silence would have become slightly blurred. It would also raise a different set of issues about inner feeling and the spoken word, for sometimes the face speaks silently to express emotion, at other times to communicate a message that may not readily be spoken aloud.

For my final examples, I return to *Troilus and Criseyde*. Chaucer prepares us for Criseyde's captivating speaking glance by first showing us

---

[39] Petrarch, *Historia Griseldis*, 117, line 156.

51

the silent discourse of Troilus's face as he mocks the young lovers in his company:

> And with that word he gan caste up the browe,
> Ascaunces, "Loo! is this naught wisely spoken?"
>
> (I.204–5)

Given that it follows his direct address to a member of his company about the folly of love, there is no great secret concealed in this silent discourse. In one sense, Troilus may as well have asked his rhetorical question out loud. But as a plot driver, his expression demonstrates the perceptive powers of the God of Love, who can interpret Troilus's raised eyebrow correctly, and, in his angry response, set the narrative wheels in motion. Chaucer also adds this silent discourse (there is no equivalent in the Italian text) to make a match with Criseyde's own rhetorical question:

> she let falle
> Hire look a lite aside in swich manere,
> Ascaunces, "What, may I nat stonden here?"
>
> (I.290–92)

Again, in both examples we find that the vocabulary of the speaking face is English, and in both cases the glance is associated with mobility, with a changing aspect. Just as the Black Knight looks *asyde* at the dreamer, Troilus *casts up* his eyebrows, and Criseyde *let falle hire look a lite aside*. These are all semi-conscious, deliberate acts of emotional expression that seem to involve the movement of the head as well as the silent discourse of the face.[40] Another pattern emerges, of Chaucer pairing the silent discourse of male and female faces: Troilus with Criseyde, the Man in Black with Lady White, and Walter's "ye" with Griselda's hypothetical "nay."

At this point in Boccaccio's *Il filostrato*, Criseyda holds her cloak out in front of her, and the narrator interprets this gesture less as a rhetorical question and more as a statement, "quasi dicesse:—E' non ci si puó

---

[40] The "ascaunces" is a composite word that joins English "as" with French "quanses," which itself can mean "as if to say," although it is difficult to disentangle from the later senses of "askance": that is, "askew or obliquely," or "with disapproval." *MED*, s.v. *ascaunce* (adv.), def. 2(a), "As if to say or indicate (sth.)."

stare" ("as if to say, 'No one may stand here' ").[41] Boccaccio's French translator, Beauvau, is even more taken with this trope. His heroine, Brisaida, like Boccaccio's, holds out her mourning cloak in front of her to make more room in the crowd:

et fist une façon de faire comme de dire: «Las! Je suis trop empressée.» Celle manière que elle fist, en soy tournant comme si elle fust ennoyée, pleut fort à Troylus, car il sembloit que elle vouloit dire: «Je ne peus plus durer.»

[and made a gesture as if to say: "Alas, I'm too crowded." The way she did this, turning as if she were annoyed, pleased Troilus very much, because it seemed as if she would say "I can bear it no longer."][42]

Beauvau's heroine's manner—not her face, as such—speaks twice. This passage is not discussed by those who have had most to say on the question of whether Chaucer worked from this French translation, but it is clear that Beauvau was struck by Boccaccio's "quasi dicesse," so much so that he deployed it twice within a few lines.[43]

Criseyde's "What, may I nat stonden here?" performs important emotional work. Even though her discourse does not use obviously emotional words, and is posed as a rhetorical question, it clearly has an emotional effect, as it eases her own feeling: "and after that hir loking gan she lighte" (I.293). Her expression also has a powerful effect on Troilus, the reader, and possibly the crowd around her in the temple. As the examples of Griselda and Troilus show, the silent discourse of the speaking face can also have a powerful effect on the world. For Griselda it has the potential to destroy her marriage; for Troilus it unleashes the wrath of Cupid; while for Criseyde it pulls Troilus into her orbit, with devastating results.

The speaking face, then, can be a powerful cognitive and emotional performance that ties characters, narrators, and readers together in shared acts of understanding and feeling. These examples, in their very literariness—in their sheer rhetorical bravado—insist that we do kinesic,

---

[41] Giovanni Boccaccio, *Il filostrato*, ed. Vincenzo Pernicone, intro. and trans. Robert P. apRoberts and Anna Bruni Seldis, Garland Library of Medieval Literature 53, series A (New York: Garland, 1986), 32, stanza 28.

[42] Pierre de Beauvau, "Le roman de Troïlus," in *Nouvelles françoises en prose du XIVe siècle, publ. d'après les manuscrits: Avec une introd. et des notes par L. Moland et C. D'Héricault* (Paris: P. Jannet, 1858), 117–303 (127). My translation.

[43] Ibid., 127.

and perhaps even somatic, work to comprehend the emotional performances being enacted before us. And that work has the capacity to bridge
distance, time, and cultures as well as bodies and minds.

This brings me to another dimension of the speaking face, and why I
have come to love it so much.

I am still a novice in thinking about cognitive processes, their successes, and their failures, but I have begun to consider some forms of
cognitive disability that affect facial interactions. People on the autism
spectrum, for example, sometimes struggle to read facial emotional
expressions, while other cognitive disabilities and traumatic memory loss
can result in the forms of visual agnosia—the failure to recognize
faces—made famous by Oliver Sacks.[44]

I am particularly interested in prosopagnosia, or face-blindness,
because I've read enough, and had enough awkward and embarrassing
experiences of not recognizing friends and colleagues, to realize I am
somewhere on that spectrum of impairment. For post-traumatic suffer-
ers with dramatic cognitive disability it is life-changingly devastating.
This is particularly the case if the faces of family members appear indis-
tinguishable from strangers, or if, like some of Oliver Sacks's patients, a
face becomes unrecognizable *as* a face. For me it's just sometimes
socially and emotionally awkward, or conceptually problematic if I am
watching a movie in which all the characters are white men in suits with
short hair. I cannot tell you whether a baby looks more like its mother
or father, and I don't always recognize my colleagues if they grow a
beard over summer, or their hair changes after chemotherapy. And as
my friends will delight in telling you, I once failed to recognize my ex-
husband.

Historical portraiture is problematic for me, as I found recently when
trying to compare the named portrait of John Gower with three other
portraits in the same manuscript that Sylvia Wright claims are images
of Chaucer. I find it very difficult to assess whether these images look
more like other Chaucer portraits, or like Gower, or are just a series of
old men with white beards.[45] Sometimes I think Bill Bailey looks like
Chaucer; sometimes I know that's only because of his parodic Chaucerian pub-joke and the way he has shaved his beard. And if Hoccleve

[44] See, for example, Oliver Sacks, *The Man who Mistook His Wife for a Hat* (London:
Picador, 1995), 5, 19–21.
[45] Sylvia Wright, "The Author Portraits in the Bedford Psalter-Hours: Gower, Chaucer and Hoccleve," *British Library Journal* 18 (1992): 190–201 (198, 200).

kindly arranges to have a portrait of Chaucer painted in a manuscript, I'll still depend more on his beard, clothes, and gestures to recognize him if I see other pictures of him.

Academic conferences are fraught with difficulty for prosopagnosiacs, because we cannot always make good judgments about how well we know you. So over the last few days, I may seem not to have remembered you as clearly as you might expect after our last sustained conversation on a previous occasion. Or I may have greeted you more enthusiastically and affectionately than you thought was warranted after having only shaken my hand once over the last six years. But one of the mysteries about prosopagnosia is that I will still be able to read the emotional expression on your face, and the dismay or confusion written there will help me realize if I have misjudged the degree of our acquaintance as a result of my failure to recognize you, and in my enthusiasm to over-compensate for that failure. That is, the emotional performance on your face will help my brain to recognize its own deficiencies. As psychologists show, the cognitive and neural systems we use for recognizing faces are different from those we use in interpreting facial expressions.[46]

But in the world of literature, I have no such problems. I never confuse one character with another. That's mostly because they come with their names and narrative histories firmly attached, of course. But nor do I have any trouble imagining a face whose expression seems always to be lightening in mood from anger to joy; or one that asks defensively whether it's all right to stand in a corner near the door. And most importantly, nor do I have any great difficulty in carrying that memory through five books and thousands of lines of rhyme royal.

The silent discourse of the face produces a strong sense of feeling and thinking that does not depend on the visual image. It is an argument in a nutshell for the study of literature as a changeable social, emotional, and historical practice. As we follow medieval narrators and characters interpreting and glossing the movements, gestures, and silences of others, we can build on the traditional claims about the capacity of literary texts to teach and show how human interaction works. For the trope of the speaking face teaches us proficiency in facial and emotional performance: how to read faces and, by implication, how to read each other. I

---

[46]See, for example, Alan Richardson, "Facial Expression Theory from Romanticism to the Present," in *Introduction to Cognitive Cultural Studies*, ed. Lisa Zunshine (Baltimore: Johns Hopkins University Press, 2010), 65–83 (65).

speculate that it is even possible that decades of reading literary texts have helped me grow a kind of cognitive prosthetic, helping me to compensate for my visual failures with another set of neural and emotional skills, for reading the emotions in faces and texts, medieval and modern.

As the first writer in English to make sustained use of this trope, Chaucer shows how we can make emotional and cognitive connections with each other: and by extension, with the past. Or, to put it another way, it's as if he were saying "Why use a picture when you can use a thousand words?"

Ripples on the Water? The Acoustics of Geoffrey Chaucer's *House of Fame* and the Influence of Robert Holcot

Neil Cartlidge
University of Durham

Abstract

Focusing on the Eagle's discussion of the principles of acoustics in lines 729–822 of *The House of Fame*, this essay offers a reconsideration of the nature of Chaucer's engagement with fourteenth-century physics. In particular, it offers a new interpretation of the sources for the Eagle's explanation of the mechanisms of sound in terms of an analogy with the ripples on the surface of a body of water. This passage is typically seen as an illustration of the extent to which Chaucer's thinking on natural science is highly traditional, wholly shaped by such venerable authorities as Aristotle, Macrobius, Boethius, and Vincent of Beauvais; but here it is argued that Chaucer was probably most directly influenced at this point in *The House of Fame* by a passage in the widely circulated Wisdom-commentary of the Dominican friar Robert Holcot (d. 1349). Even if Chaucer is unlikely to have been familiar with "cutting-edge" thinkers such as Robert Grosseteste (d. 1253), Walter Burley (d. 1344 or after), and the Oxford Calculators, Holcot himself certainly had direct access to the work of all of them. Perhaps more significantly, he may well have shown Chaucer how specifically "scientific" motifs could be turned to literary effect even in contexts that are otherwise predominantly moral and/or allegorical.

Keywords

Chaucer, *The House of Fame*, natural science, physics, sound, Robert Holcot, friars, dream visions

An earlier version of this paper was presented to the Manchester Medieval Society in October 2011 (as "Chaucer and Scientific Thinking in the Fourteenth Century"). I am grateful to the audience on that occasion for their comments. I would also like to thank the Leverhulme Trust, the Deutscher Akademischer Austauschdienst (DAAD) and Freiburg Institute of Advanced Studies (FRIAS) for their support during the time that I was revising this essay for publication. Finally, I am very grateful to Venetia Bridges, Mike Huxtable, and *SAC*'s two anonymous readers for their eagle-eyed comments.

Studies in the Age of Chaucer 39 (2017):57–97
© 2017 The New Chaucer Society

THE SECOND BOOK OF Chaucer's dream-vision poem *The House of Fame* begins with the arrival of a huge golden eagle, who swoops down, seizes the dreaming poet in his claws, and carries him off skyward.[1] The bird eventually introduces himself as the envoy of "the god of thonder / Which that men callen Jupiter" (lines 608–9); and he explains he has been sent by Jupiter to take Chaucer to a place called "the House of Fame," where the poet will be able to overhear a marvelous profusion of all the various things ever spoken by or about lovers (lines 661–98). The Eagle clearly expects the poet to be delighted by this prospect of so privileged an insight into the experiences of "Loves folke" (675). However, as it turns out, Chaucer's persona in the poem flatly refuses to believe even in the existence of the House of Fame, frankly doubting that so many sounds could ever be collected in one place: "For hyt / Were impossible," he insists, that Fame "shulde here al this" (701–2, 705). Apparently rather piqued by this disappointingly unenthusiastic (and indeed rather ungracious) response, the Eagle is moved to try to prove that the existence of such a place is an entirely logical deduction, not from any particular textual precedent (as the predominantly literary concerns of the poem up to this point might have led one to expect), but from the principles of acoustics. Rather than insisting on his authority as the ambassador of the gods, the Eagle apparently chooses to interpret Chaucer's skepticism about the possibility of so many sounds being gathered in one place as a challenge to his authority as a physicist. Accordingly, he seems to believe that if he can convince the poet (and perhaps implicitly the poet's readers) of his credibility as an expert on the laws of sound, then Chaucer's persona within the poem (and, by extension, we the readers of the poem) will also accept the reality of the House of Fame. Yet how convincing is the Eagle's lecture on acoustics meant to be? Are we really supposed to treat this lengthy disquisition within the context of a fantastic dream vision as an up-to-date and scientifically accurate account of the mechanics of the natural world? In

---

[1] Geoffrey Chaucer, *The House of Fame*, ed. John M. Fyler, in *The Riverside Chaucer*, gen ed. Larry D. Benson, 3rd ed. (Boston: Houghton Mifflin, 1987), 347–73; ed. Nick Havely in *Geoffrey Chaucer: The House of Fame*, 2nd ed., Durham Medieval and Renaissance Texts (Toronto: Pontifical Institute of Mediaeval Studies, 2013). All quotations here from *The House of Fame* are from Havely's 2013 edition. Other Chaucer quotations are from *The Riverside* unless otherwise stated.

any case, what would the science of physics have looked like to an educated layman (such as Chaucer) in the second half of the fourteenth
century? What models of the principles of sound were actually available
to him? And are any of the choices that the Eagle makes among them
significant for our understanding of the horizons of Chaucer's scientific
knowledge?

In the course of attempting to answer these broad questions, I am
going to propose a new source for one of the key moments in the Eagle's
lecture on acoustics, the analogy with ripples created by a stone thrown
into a body of water (in section III below). To be more precise, I will
argue for the primary importance to this portion of *The House of Fame* of
a source that is not exactly "new"—having long lurked at the fringes of
Chaucerian scholarship's consciousness—but that has never been seriously considered as a decisive influence on the Eagle's analysis of sound.
This source is the Wisdom-commentary of the Dominican friar Robert
Holcot (c. 1290–1349). It seems to me that the probable presence of
this text in Chaucer's mind at this point in *The House of Fame* invites
a fundamental reconsideration of the way in which the English poet
received—and used for literary effect—ideas about natural science. In
section IV, I provide an account of the central, and perhaps even pivotal,
position occupied by Holcot in the intellectual history of the fourteenth
century. However, before even attempting to define Holcot's influence
on the Eagle's acoustics, or to discuss the relevance of this to any assessment of Chaucer's indebtedness to fourteenth-century intellectual culture, it appears to me necessary to preface this with an account of what
seem to be the prevailing assumptions about the sources of Chaucer's
physics: in particular, the supposition that Chaucer's understanding of
natural science is, in essence, so profoundly and conventionally "Aristotelian" as to leave little room for the identification of any distinctively
fourteenth-century contributions in it (see section I). Such assumptions
have been challenged before, with Chaucer's physics being portrayed as
much more "cutting-edge" than is generally assumed, but only on the
basis of arguments that have not been subjected to sufficient scrutiny
(see section II). The possibility of Holcot's direct influence on the Eagle's
account of the principles of acoustics is perhaps most significant for what
it tells us about how Chaucer mediated between these alternatives—in
effect pretending to participate in the grand and venerable tradition of
scientific speculation about the natural world only by making use of

ideas that had already been given a distinct moral/rhetorical shape by a relatively near contemporary.

I. The "Aristotelian" Eagle?

It might be useful to begin with a summary of what the Eagle actually says: how, that is, he goes about attempting to justify his claim to authority as a natural scientist. Everything in the universe, the Eagle argues, is governed by a principle of attraction, such that every object has a natural tendency, a "kyndely enclynynge," to move toward a particular point: a "kyndely stede" (729–36). So, for example, anything made of a heavy substance such as stone or lead will always fall downward once it is released (737–41), and conversely, light things such as fire or sound or smoke naturally move upward, "seke upwarde on hight" (742–46). Similarly, every river is "enclyned" to run toward the sea; fish can only survive in water; and trees need to be rooted in the earth (747–52). What these instances illustrate, according to the Eagle, is the principle that every kind of thing has its own proper place in the universe: "every thinge, by thys reson, / Hath his propre mansyon / To which it seketh to repaire" (753–55); and he emphasizes that this is an opinion familiar in "every philosophres mouthe," not just Aristotle and Plato, but also "other clerkys, many oon" (757–60). Speech, moreover, is only a form of sound, and it is therefore governed by just the same rules that govern the behavior of sound in general. All sounds, the Eagle says, should be understood as disturbances in the air: as "eyre y-broken" (765). This includes speech (765–66), but the breaking of air can be effected "in many wise," so that the sounds made by pipes or harps, say, are very different (771–80). The movements of sound are analogous to the ripples on a body of water after a stone has been thrown into it (787–815). Just as ripples multiply in water, so too sound keeps on multiplying until, inevitably, it reaches the House of Fame (816–21). Since every thing is "enclyned" to move toward its proper place (its "kyndelych stede" [823–42]), and since the House of Fame is particularly capable of receiving sound (being "most conservatyf the soun" [843–47]), then the inevitable conclusion is that "every speche of every man" moves "kyndely to Fames place" (848–52). In other words, the eventual arrival of all tidings at the House of Fame is not at all so "impossible" as Chaucer's persona in the poem immediately assumes, but a necessary deduction from some of the most basic principles of medieval physics.

Admittedly, there is at least an amusing tension between the sheer earnestness and elaboration of this long discussion of the physical properties of sound, and the strangeness of the circumstances in which it is imagined to take place. If nothing else, it is at least ironic that the limits of what is physically "impossible" are discussed so thoroughly in the course of a conversation with an enormous talking bird. Indeed, one might have expected the poet to have been a little more willing to believe in the Eagle's account of the wonders of the House of Fame, given that the Eagle himself presents such an impressive contradiction of the ordinary rules of possibility. Certainly, Chaucer actually goes out of his way to emphasize the comedy of this encounter between the bird and his own persona within the poem.[2] When the Eagle first addresses "Chaucer" it is only to complain about how uncomfortable he is to carry (573–74), which should presumably be taken as a joke at the expense of the poet's waistline. The narrator-figure himself is preoccupied with the concern that he may be on the point of being "stellifye[d]" (586): transformed into a star, that is, like so many figures in classical mythology (and in Ovid's *Metamorphoses* in particular). But this only suggests a rather exaggerated view of his own significance, as well as a degree of pusillanimity. Throughout his journey in the Eagle's claws, in fact, "Chaucer" cuts an amusingly self-centered, testy figure—altogether more Arthur Dent than Dante[3]—and it is perhaps implicit that his terse rejection of the Eagle's description of the wonders of the House of Fame is not so much a serious challenge to his guide's scientific authority as a convenient way of giving vent to his irritation at finding himself in the undignified position of being in the Eagle's claws in the first place. Yet, despite the comedy implicit in the exchanges between the bird and its passenger, the description of the physics of sound to which they lead seems to be anything but frivolous. The Eagle's account of the movements of sound is painstakingly thorough and exact. There is nothing intrinsically comical about the substance of what he says, despite the ironies created by its context. Indeed, it could be argued that those ironies are only deepened by the fact that the Eagle's speech is so determinedly sober. By his own estimation at least, what he has to say about

[2] A. J. Minnis describes the Eagle with provocative concision as "Chaucer's funny fowl"; *Oxford Guides to Chaucer: The Shorter Poems* (Oxford: Clarendon, 1995), 201.

[3] For comparison of Chaucer's Eagle with Dante's, see ibid., 202.

the physics of sound seems to amount to a rational and philosophically coherent account of the mechanisms of the natural world.

Perhaps the best way of explaining the odd combination of weightiness and whimsy that characterizes the conversation between "Chaucer" and the Eagle is to see the Eagle's whole speech as an exercise in pastiche: that is, as a deliberately and playfully imitative use of an identifiably distinct mode of discourse for comical, but not necessarily satirical, effect. However, seeing the Eagle's speech in this way only intensifies the question of what particular discourses, cultural traditions, or "authorities" he might be said to be imitating. After all, pastiche is generally most effective when its mimicry is most accurate and well-informed. If the Eagle is, in effect, pretending to be an expert in the physics of sound, what kind of expert exactly is he pretending to be? The Eagle himself suggests an answer to this question when he cites Aristotle, Plato, and "other clerkys, many oon" (759–60). Aristotle is explicitly the first of the authorities cited by the bird, and even though it is emphasized that Aristotle's opinions were shared by Plato and many other philosophers, it is certainly true that nearly all of the Eagle's ideas can be found in Aristotle's works. For example, the suggestion that "every thinge . . . / Hath his propre mansyon" (753–54) is apparently a version of Aristotle's analysis of "the locomotions of the elementary natural bodies—namely, fire, earth, and the like," in terms of a certain kind of "influence," whereby "each [element] is carried to its own place, if unhindered, the one up the other down."[4] Similarly, the observation that it is natural for heavy things to fall and light things to rise, or, as Chaucer puts it, "Lyght thinge upwarde, and dounwarde charge" (746), seems to be at least a distant recollection of Aristotle's view that all bodies "have a natural tendency towards a certain position: and this is

---

[4] Aristotle, *Physics*, Book IV, cap. 4, 208b (according to the standard system of references to Bekker's 1831 edition of Aristotle's works), trans. R. P. Hardie and R. K. Gaye, in *The Complete Works of Aristotle: The Revised Oxford Translation*, ed. Jonathan Barnes, 2 vols. (1984; repr., Princeton: Princeton University Press, 1995), 1:315–446 (355); and for discussion of Aristotle's thinking on this point, see Edward Grant, *The Foundations of Modern Science in the Middle Ages: Their Religious, Institutional and Intellectual Contexts* (Cambridge: Cambridge University Press, 1996), 58–60. A version of this idea is also found in Plato's *Timaeus*, trans. Desmond Lee and Thomas Kjeller Johansen (London: Penguin, 2008); see for example 63d–e (according to the standard system of references to Stephanus's 1578 edition of Plato's works), trans. Lee and Johansen, 59: "the main aggregations of the basic kinds of matter occupy opposite regions to each other; and what is light or heavy or below or above in one region will be found to be or to become the direct opposite of, or to be at an angle to, or anyway different from, what has these characteristics in another region" (cf. also 56d–57c, trans. Lee and Johansen, 51–52).

what it is to be light or heavy, the former being determined by an upward, the latter by a downward, tendency."[5] Meanwhile, the notion that sound is essentially broken air ("eyre y-broken"), so that the substance of sound is air itself ("in his substaunce ys but aire" [768]), clearly resembles Aristotle's definition of sound specifically in terms of impact: "[air] must be struck with a sudden sharp blow if it is to sound."[6] The Eagle's emphasis on the way in which sound produces movements of air ("And of thys movynge, out of doute, / Another ayre anoon ys meved" [812–13]) apparently corresponds with Aristotle's assertion that "What has the power of producing sound is what has the power of setting in movement a single mass of air which is continuous up to the point of hearing."[7] And even the Eagle's passing reference to the different kinds of sound produced by harps and pipes (771–79), and his comparison between them and human voices (780), have a precedent in Aristotle's careful distinction between the real, animate voice of a living creature and the metaphorical "voice" of a musical instrument.[8]

To a large extent, then, the authority to which the Eagle lays claim

---

[5] Aristotle, *Physics*, VIII.4, 255b, trans. Hardie and Gaye, 427. In Plato's *Timaeus*, 52e–53a (trans. Lee and Johansen, 44), this tendency is explained in terms of a comparison with the process of winnowing:

> the things that were moved were constantly being separated and carried in different directions, rather like the contents of a winnowing basket or a similar implement for cleaning corn, in which the solid and heavy stuff is sifted out and settles on one side, the light and insubstantial on another. . . . It separated the kinds most unlike each other furthest away from each other and pushed those most like each other towards the same place, with the result that they came to occupy different regions of space even before they were arranged into an ordered universe.

In Calcidius's commentary, this winnowing is defined as the process by which "ea quae massa erunt secernuntur, grana quidem seorsum motu et agitatione, palaeae uero aliorsum ex iactatione; et leuia quidem uolitare, grauia uero residere" (*Timaeus, a Calcidio translatus commentarioque instructus*, ed. J. H. Waszink, in *Plato latinus* 4 [London: Warburg Institute, 1962], 344). In his study of the possible influence of Calcidius on Chaucer, Joseph E. Grennen picks out this last phrase ("leuia quidem uolitare, grauia uero residere"), and suggests that it is a "very apt translation of line 746" of *The House of Fame*; "Chaucer and Chalcidius: The Platonic Origins of the *House of Fame*," *Viator* 15 (1984): 237–62 (247). However, unlike Calcidius, Chaucer's application of this phrase is not specifically to the idea of winnowing.

[6] Aristotle, *On the Soul*, Book II, cap. 8, 419b, trans. J. A. Smith, in *The Complete Works*, ed. Barnes, 1:641–92 (668). What Aristotle seems to have particularly in mind is the sound created by the snapping of a whip. Cf. Plato, *Timaeus*, 67, trans. Lee and Johansen ("Sound may be generally defined as a stroke given by air" [page 63]).

[7] Aristotle, *On the Soul*, II.8, 420a, trans. Smith, 668.

[8] Ibid., II.8, 420b, trans. Smith, 669: "it [is] only by a metaphor that we speak of the voice of the flute or the lyre or generally of what (being without soul) possesses the power of producing a succession of notes which differ in length and pitch and timbre."

is clearly Aristotle's, and it is theoretically possible that Chaucer did have some direct knowledge of the relevant parts of Aristotle's corpus, via the commentaries of the twelfth-century Arabic philosopher Averroes (Ibn Rushd), Latin translations of which had been available in Europe since the first of half of the thirteenth century.[9] However, it has long been something of a consensus among Chaucerian scholars that the principal sources for the Eagle's acoustics are most likely to lie in the work of three eminent Latin authorities to whom Chaucer makes conspicuous reference elsewhere.[10] These are: first, the fifth-century philosopher Macrobius, who appears as a distinct figure within *The Parliament of Fowls* (lines 120–70) and whose commentary on Cicero's *Dream of Scipio* is mentioned on three other occasions in Chaucer's works;[11] second, the sixth-century philosopher Boethius, the author not just of *The Consolation of Philosophy*, but also, and more significantly in this context, a treatise on music, to which Chaucer clearly alludes in *The Nun's Priest's Tale* (VII.3293–94);[12] and third, the thirteenth-century encyclopedist Vincent of Beauvais, whom Chaucer names directly in the G-prologue to *The Legend of Good Women* (line 307).[13] Nearly all of the "Aristotelian"

[9] For a text of the Latin version of Averroes's "great" commentary on Aristotle's *De anima*, see *Averrois Cordubensis Commentarium magnum in Aristotelis De anima*, ed. F. Stuart Crawford (Cambridge, Mass.: Medieval Academy of America, 1953). On the influence of Averroes's interpretations of Aristotle's physics, see Ruth Glasner, *Averroes' Physics: A Turning Point in Medieval Natural Philosophy* (Oxford: Oxford University Press, 2009). On the reception of Aristotle in the Latin West more generally, see Bernard G. Dod, "Aristoteles latinus," in *The Cambridge History of Later Medieval Philosophy*, ed. Norman Kretzmann et al. (1982; repr., Cambridge: Cambridge University Press, 1996) (henceforth *CHLMP*), 45–79; C. H. Lohr, "The Medieval Interpretation of Aristotle," in *CHLMP*, 80–98. A set of useful resources in relation to Averroes can be found at the Digital Averroes Research Environment, http://dare.uni-koeln.de (accessed January 23, 2017).

[10] See, for example, Minnis, *Oxford Guides*, 203. This consensus seems to have been established at least since Wilbur Owen Sypherd's *Studies in Chaucer's "Hous of Fame,"* Chaucer Society 2nd Series 39 (London: Kegan Paul, 1904), where the three authors' influence on *The House of Fame* is tabulated at 97–100.

[11] Macrobius, *Commentarii in somnium Scipionis*, ed. James A. Willis (Leipzig: Teubner, 1970), trans. William Harris Stahl as *Commentary on the Dream of Scipio by Macrobius* (1952; repr., New York: Columbia University Press, 1990). Chaucer refers to Macrobius in *BD*, line 284; *NPT*, VII.3123; *Rom*, Fragment A, line 7.

[12] Boethius, *The Consolation of Philosophy*, ed. and trans. S. J. Tester, in *Boethius: The Theological Tractates; The Consolation of Philosophy*, ed. H. F. Stewart, E. K. Rand, and S. J. Tester (1918; repr., Cambridge, Mass.: Harvard University Press, 1990); Boethius, *De institutione musica*, ed. Gottfried Friedlein, in *Anicii Manlii Torquati Severini Boetii De institutione arithmetica libri duo, De institutione musica libri quinque . . .* (Leipzig: Teubner, 1867), trans. C. M. Bower as *Fundamentals of Music* (New Haven: Yale University Press, 1989).

[13] Vincent of Beauvais, *Speculum quadruplex*, Vol. 1, *Speculum naturale* (Strasbourg: Rusch, *ante* 1476). For a general set of resources in relation to Vincent, see *A Vincent of*

motifs that I have listed can also be found in the work of these three men.[14] Boethius and Vincent of Beauvais also provide analogues for the one distinctive feature of the Eagle's speech for which no clear precedent or inspiration is readily available in Aristotle, and which effectively provides the center-piece of the Eagle's whole argument: that is, the proof "by experience" (788) of throwing a stone into a body of water and watching the ripples spread.[15] Either one of these writers could be Chaucer's immediate source for this conceit: the parallels are, in each case,

---

Beauvais Website, http://www.vincentiusbelvacensis.eu/index.html (accessed January 23, 2017).

[14] For example, Aristotle's view that "each [element] is carried to its own place, if unhindered, the one up the other down" is reflected by Macrobius, *Commentary*, I.22, trans. Stahl, 181–82; and Boethius, *Consolation*, Book III, prosa 11, ed. and trans. Tester, 290–93. However, this idea was so widely known in the Middle Ages as to be something of a commonplace: it also appears, for example, in Saint Augustine of Hippo, *Concerning the City of God against the Pagans*, XI.28, trans. Henry Bettenson (London: Penguin, 1984), 463; Bernard Silvestris, *Cosmographia*, trans. Winthrop Wetherbee (1973; repr., New York: Columbia University Press,1990), 72; and William of Conches, *Dragmaticon philosophie*, II.6, trans. Italo Ronca and Matthew Curr as *A Dialogue on Natural Philosophy* (Notre Dame: University of Notre Dame Press, 1997), 33–34. Sound is defined in terms of impact or percussion in Macrobius, *Commentary*, II.1, trans. Stahl, 185–86; Boethius, *De institutione*, Book I, cap. 3, ed. Friedlein, 189 ("Idcirco definitur sonus percussio aëris indissoluta usque ad auditum"), trans. Bower, 11 ("Sound is defined as a percussion of air remaining undissolved all the way to the hearing"); and Vincent, *Speculum*, V.14 ("Sonus est aeris percussio indissoluta usque ad auditum"). Again, parallels for this idea seem to have been widely disseminated, particularly in the context of medieval grammar (see Martin Irvine, "Medieval Grammatical Theory and Chaucer's *House of Fame*," *Speculum* 60 [1985]: 850–76): for example, Donatus's definition of voice as "aer ictus sensibilis auditu" (Irvine, "Medieval Grammatical Theory," 854). Cf. also the allegorical description of the senses by Chaucer's near-contemporary Heinrich von Mügeln, who describes Hearing as one of the horses pulling the chariot of Reason: "sin futer was der lüfte slak, / das pfert nicht ander weide pflak" ("Its food was the striking of the air. The horse did not graze in any other way"), ed. and trans. Annette Volfing as *Heinrich von Mügeln: "Der meide kranz"; A Commentary* (Tübingen: Niemeyer, 1997), lines 1141–42 (211). In relation to the "movynge [of] ayre," cf. Boethius, *De institutione*, I.3, ed. Friedlein, 189 ("pulsus vero atque percussio nullo modo esse potest, nisi praecesserit motus"), trans. Bower, 11 ("pulsation and percussion cannot exist by any means unless motion precedes them"); Vincent, *Speculum*, V.14 ("Sonatum autem est motivum aeris"). For the distinction between wind and stringed instruments, see Boethius, *De institutione*, I.2, ed. Friedlein, 189, trans. Bower, 10; and Macrobius, *Commentary*, II.4, trans. Stahl, 197–98. See also J. A. W. Bennett's discussion of the sources of the Eagle's speech in *Chaucer's Book of Fame: An Exposition of "The House of Fame"* (Oxford: Clarendon Press, 1968), 76–80: he foregrounds Dante and Macrobius, and also suggests parallels with Vitruvius and Adelard of Bath, among others. More recently, Rebecca Davis's discussion of the Eagle's sources focuses on Dante and Boethius; "Fugitive Poetics in Chaucer's *House of Fame*," *SAC* 37 (2015): 106–11.

[15] Boethius, *De institutione*, I.14, ed. Friedlein, 200:

Tale enim quiddam fieri consuevit in vocibus, quale cum in paludibus vel quietis aquis iactum eminus mergitur saxum. Prius enim in parvissimum orbem undam colligit, deinde maioribus orbibus undarum globos spargit, atque eo usque dum

---

very strong, and there is no doubt that Chaucer might have known either or both of them directly. So it looks as though the case is already closed: the scientific tradition to which the Eagle lays claims is largely Aristotelian, and Chaucer could easily have sourced his Aristotelianism from the three venerable and widely cited authorities whose work he

---

defatigus motus ab eliciendis fluctibus conquiescat. Semperque posterior et maior undula pulsu debiliore diffunditur. Quod si quid sit, quod crescentes undas possit offendere, statim motus ille revertitur et quasi ad centrum, unde profectus fuerat, eisdem undulis rotundatur. Ita igitur cum aër pulsus fecerit sonum, pellit alium proximum et quodammodo rotundum fluctum aeris ciet, itaque diffunditur et omnium circum stantium simul ferit auditum.

[The same thing happens in sounds that happens when a stone, thrown from above, falls into a puddle or into quiet water. First it causes a wave in a very small circle; then it disperses clusters of waves into larger circles, and so on until the motion, exhausted by the spreading out of waves, dies away. The latter, wider wave is always diffused by a weaker impulse. Now if something should impede the spreading waves, the same motion rebounds immediately, and it makes new circles by the same undulations as at the center whence it originated. In the same way, then, when air that is struck creates sound, it affects other air nearby and in this way sets in motion a circular wave of air; and so it is diffused and reaches the hearing of all standing around at the same time.] (trans. Bower, 21)

Vincent of Beauvais, *Speculum*, V.17: "sonus efficitur secundum circulum maiorem et minorem; itaque minor circulus generat maiorem: et ille iterum maiorem. Cuius exemplum patet in lapillo in aqua proiecto in aquam, videlicet stantem. Ubi videlicet lapis cadens est centorum multorum circulorum successive generatorum [*read:* generator], eo quod una pars aque impulsata inundat super aliam circumquaque per circumferentiam." Cf. also Vincent, *Speculum*, XXVI.58: "Ad quod demonstrandum [i.e., how sounds are made] inducit idem Boecius tale exemplum: lapis proiectus in medio stagni facit breuissimum circulum, et ille alium, et hoc fit donec vel ad ripas pervenerit, vel impetus defecerit." In Calcidius's commentary on the *Timaeus*, this image is used to describe not sound, but the nature of primary matter: "Sed ut in stagnis, cum immobilis est aquae superficies, incidente aliqua grauiore mole primo nascitur initium motus, deinde agitatione facta totius elementi non solum agmen aquae mouetur, sed illud ipsum, quod incidit causamque motus praebuit, uicissim mouet, sic silua quoque ex initio corporum sumpto motu non solum ipsa omnifariam mouetur, uerum ipsa corpora, quae initium motus sunt, inuicem pellit" (ed. Waszink, 343; see also Grennen, "Chaucer and Chalcidius," 255–56). The same analogy is also used by Averroes, *Commentarium magnum*, 419b, ed. Crawford, 248:

Et debes scire quod sonus non fit in aere ita quod aer qui expellitur a percutiente movetur per se singulariter donec perveniat ad auditum, sed debes scire quod illud quod fit in aere de percussione corporum adinvicem est simile ei quod fit in aqua, quando lapis proiicitur in aquam, scilicet quia fit in aere apud percussionem figura sperica, aut prope spericam, cuius centrum est locus percussionis per expulsionem aeris ab illo loco equaliter, aut prope.

(Both of the references to the *Speculum naturale* in *The Riverside Chaucer*—"4.18 and 25.58"—are erroneous.)

claims himself to have known: that is, Macrobius, Boethius, and Vincent of Beauvais.

II. The "Cutting-Edge" Eagle?

The one thing that is troubling about this analysis is that it makes the Eagle's scientific horizons (and by extension, Chaucer's) seem so very old-fashioned. The implication is that Chaucer had no acquaintanceship with the remarkable scientific developments that had taken place in England since the middle of the thirteenth century, very often as a direct response to Aristotle's physics. This was a period that saw England (and Oxford in particular) develop a remarkable reputation for highly rigorous, innovative, and precise thinking about the workings of the universe. The possibility that Chaucer's thinking about the physics of sound could actually be more up to date than it might at first seem has been advocated most energetically by Joseph E. Grennen.[16] He defines the Eagle's speech as "a pastiche of terms and ideas drawn from contemporary scientific writing"; and he suggests, among other things, that it reflects the particular influence of Robert Grosseteste and Walter Burley. These claims are perhaps worth exploring more fully, in part because they imply that Chaucer's engagement with scientific thought was much deeper and more active than is usually assumed, and in part because they rely on correspondences of terminology and argument that are not easy to assess or interpret.

Grosseteste was not exactly a "contemporary" of Chaucer (he died in 1253), but he was a highly original thinker, in many ways at the cutting edge of scientific thinking in the thirteenth century, and he has at least a good claim to being the founding father of the English scientific tradition that I have just described.[17] Grosseteste wrote a set of Notes on Aristotle's *Physics* that seem to have been widely cited in Oxford well

---

[16] Joseph E. Grennen, "Science and Poetry in Chaucer's *House of Fame*," *Annuale mediaevale* 8 (1967): 38–45.

[17] On Grosseteste's science, and his mind in general, see A. C. Crombie, *Robert Grosseteste and the Origins of Experimental Science 1100–1700* (Oxford: Clarendon Press, 1953); R. W. Southern, *Robert Grosseteste: The Growth of an English Mind in Medieval Europe*, 2nd ed. (Oxford: Clarendon Press, 1992); James McEvoy, *Robert Grosseteste* (Oxford: Oxford University Press, 2000); Maura O'Carroll, ed., *Robert Grosseteste and the Beginnings of a British Theological Tradition* (Rome: Istituto Storico dei Cappuccini, 2003); Evelyn A. Mackie and Joseph Goering, eds., *Editing Robert Grosseteste* (Toronto: University of Toronto Press, 2003).

into the fourteenth century,[18] as well as a whole series of short, and in some cases brilliantly innovative, works on specific questions in physics, including one on the generation of sounds.[19] As lector to the Franciscans in Oxford and then bishop of Lincoln, Grosseteste exerted a powerful influence on the intellectual development of the university. A. C. Crombie even claims that "Grosseteste's theory of science determined the approach of the next generations of Oxford natural philosophers to the physical world" and that "their work was in many ways simply an elaboration in concrete detail of his general principles of investigation and explanation."[20] This formulation possibly overstates the case, but there is no question that Grosseteste is a very important figure in the history of English science, and certainly important enough for Grennen's suggestion of a connection between Grosseteste and Chaucer to invite further scrutiny.

As it turns out, Grennen's evidence for Chaucer's direct knowledge of Grosseteste's writing is not very convincing. He argues that "the eagle's definition of sound in terms as 'noght but eyr ybroken' [765] is probably Chaucer's deliberately garbled version of a current explanation not of sound *simpliciter* but of the echo—a reversal of sound caused by a *fractio radii* at the obstacle with which it collides, on the analogy with the reflection of light."[21] This seems like an unnecessarily complex explanation of what the Eagle actually says, given that the idea of sound as "broken air" was relatively commonplace in the Middle Ages, and readily available to Chaucer in the work of Boethius, Macrobius, and Vincent of Beauvais (and probably elsewhere as well). Grennen also suggests that *The House of Fame*'s reference to the air being "twyst with violence" (775) should be compared with a specific sentence from Grosseteste's commentary on Aristotle's *Posterior Analytics*, in which "the substance of sound" is defined as "light incorporated into the very finest air, [so that] when a sounding object is violently struck, parts of it

---

[18] *Roberti Grosseteste commentarius in VIII libros Physicorum Aristotelis*, ed. Richard C. Dales (Boulder: University of Colorado Press, 1963) . See also Neil Lewis, "Robert Grosseteste's *Notes on Physics*," in Mackie and Goering, *Editing Robert Grosseteste*, 103–34.

[19] Ludwig Baur, ed., *Die Philosophie des Robert Grosseteste Bischofs von Lincoln († 1253)* (Münster: Aschendorff, 1917); Cecilia Panti, ed., *Moti, virtù e motori celesti nella cosmologia di Roberto Grossatesta: Studio ed edizione dei trattati "De sphera," "De cometis," "De motu supercelestium"* (Florence: SISMEL/Galluzzo, 2001). Robert Grosseteste, *De generatione sonorum*, ed. Ludwig Baur, in *Die Philosophie*, 7–10, available online at the *Electronic Grosseteste*, http://www.grosseteste.org (accessed May 17, 2016).

[20] Crombie, *Robert Grosseteste*, 135.

[21] Grennen, "Science and Poetry," 42.

are necessarily scattered from the natural position that they occupy throughout the sounding body."[22] Grosseteste's commentary on the *Posterior Analytics* seems to have become a relatively well-known text in medieval universities, but there is no particular reason for thinking that Chaucer would have made direct use of it himself; and the sentence to which Grennen points actually has little in common with *The House of Fame* except for its shared heritage in Aristotle. That both the Eagle and Grosseteste refer to "violence" in the context of sound is not very telling in itself, since the violence in question is specifically that of impact, and the emphasis on impact goes back to Aristotle (the "sudden sharp blow" from which sound is created). There is certainly no parallel in the Eagle's speech for what is the most distinctive aspect of Grosseteste's acoustics: the suggestion that the substance of sound is ultimately light—"light incorporated into the very finest air."[23] There are several problems, finally, with Grennen's insistence that the Eagle's reference to both a "demonstracion / In myn ymagynacion" (727–28) and a proof "by experience" (787–88) reflects "the fourteenth-century physicist's distinction between problems conceived *secundum imaginationem* ('thought experiments') and those worked out *per experimentiam*." This, he suggests (following Crombie), was Grosseteste's peculiar "contribution" to the history of European science.[24] Here he makes too casual a conflation between the language of fourteenth-century scientific writing and the particular terms of Grosseteste's own thinking, as if it would have been impossible to draw any distinction between imagination and experience in the fourteenth century without specific deference to what Crombie sees as Grosseteste's uniting of "the two twelfth-century traditions of technology and logic." Grennen also insists too narrowly on the connection between these two moments in the Eagle's speech—that is, the "demonstracion / In myn ymagynacion" and the proof "by experience"—as if they were necessarily to be read as opposing terms in a single contrast, even though they are actually separated by some sixty lines.

[22] Robert Grosseteste, commentary on Aristotle's *Posterior Analytics*, II.4: "Substantia autem soni est lux incorporata in subtilissimo aere, et cum percutitur sonativum violenter necesse est partes eius disgredi a situ suo naturali quem habent in toto sonativo" (cited from Crombie, *Robert Grosseteste*, 115 n. 1).

[23] The Eagle argues at one point that sound is in "aire y-broke" in the same way as flames are "lyghted smoke" (769–70), but this is an analogy designed to explain only how sound is incorporated in air (just as flame is a kind of special form of smoke), not a suggestion to the effect that light provides any part of sound's substance.

[24] Grennen, "Science and Poetry," 42.

Grennen goes on to argue that "the most convincing proof . . . of Chaucer's familiarity with current speculation [in scientific thought]" is his apparent familiarity with Walter Burley's commentary on Aristotle's *Physics*.[25] Again, this would be a very significant connection—if it could be proved. Like Grosseteste, Burley is a very significant figure in the history of natural philosophy. He was a regular antagonist of William Ockham (who, like Burley, wrote on Aristotle's *Physics*);[26] and among the various issues on which Burley and Ockham disagreed was the way in which the quantity of motion inheres in any moving body.[27] It is perhaps worth emphasizing that Burley, like many thirteenth- and fourteenth-century English physicists, tended to subordinate questions on natural science to both theology and formal logic, in such a way as to make much of the "scientific thinking" in this period a dizzying mixture of the vastly philosophical and the narrowly terminological.[28] However, Burley's interest in physical questions, and in questions of motion in particular, is pronounced enough to mean that he is also sometimes seen as precursor to that group of extraordinarily brilliant English thinkers now known interchangeably as the Mertonians or the Oxford Calculators, whose particular contribution was the introduction, to this already heady mix of methodologies, of a large dose of mathematics.

[25] In fact, Burley seems to have engaged so continuously with Aristotle's *Physics* as to have produced several distinct versions of his commentary: see Rega Wood, "Walter Burley's *Physics* Commentaries," *Franciscan Studies* 44 (1984): 275–327. On Burley's career more generally, see Edith D. Sylla, "The Oxford Calculators and the Mathematics of Motion, 1320–1350: Physics and the Measurement by Latitudes," Ph.D diss. (Harvard University, 1970; published New York: Garland, 1991), 70–111; Jennifer Ottman and Rega Wood, "Walter Burley: His Life and Works," *Vivarium* 37 (1999): 1–23; M. C. Sommers, "Burley, Walter (b. 1274/5, d. in or after 1344)," *Oxford Dictionary of National Biography* (henceforth *ODNB*), article 4037.

[26] On Ockham generally, see Paul Vincent Spade, ed., *The Cambridge Companion to Ockham* (Cambridge: Cambridge University Press, 1999); and on Ockham's physics in particular, André Goddu, "Ockham's Philosophy of Nature," in Spade, *Cambridge Companion to Ockham*, 143–67.

[27] J. A. Weisheipl, "The Interpretation of Aristotle's Physics and the Science of Motion," in *CHLMP*, 521–36, esp. 530–32; see also Edith Dudley Sylla, "Walter Burley's *Physics* Commentaries and the Mathematics of Alteration," *Early Science and Medicine* 6 (2001): 149–184; Dirk-Jan Dekker, "Time and Motion in Walter Burley's Late *Expositio* on Aristotle's *Physics*," *Early Science and Medicine* 6 (2001): 185–203.

[28] For a concise and suggestive analysis of fourteenth-century intellectual culture generally, see John E. Murdoch, "The Development of a Critical Temper: New Approaches and Modes of Analysis in Fourteenth-Century Philosophy, Science and Theology," in *Medieval and Renaissance Studies: Proceedings of the Southeastern Institute of Medieval and Renaissance Studies; Summer 1975*, ed. Siegfried Wenzel (Chapel Hill: University of North Carolina Press, 1978), 51–79.

Burley is sometimes classed as a full member of this group, as he is, for example, by Edith Sylla, the author of what is still the most thorough and accessible study of the Calculators and their work,[29] even though much of Burley's own philosophical activity in this field predates what is probably the defining text in this intellectual movement, Thomas Bradwardine's treatise of 1328, *De proportionibus velocitatum in motibus*.[30] In this treatise, Bradwardine set out to remedy one of the most obvious defects in Aristotle's *Physics*, the lack of mathematical explanation of the principles governing acceleration and velocity, and it was this work (rather than Grosseteste's suite of short, speculative treatises on particular questions in physics) that seems to have set the dominant agenda for what was to develop into an extensive and distinctly Oxford-based tradition of work on the interrelationship among logic, physics, and mathematics, with a particular focus on problems in mechanics (i.e., on problems relating to forces and motions). This tradition includes work by such figures as William Heytesbury, John Dumbleton, Richard Kilvington, Richard Swineshead, and Roger Swineshead. Their achievements have been described as "a revolution in scientific thought,"[31] not just because of their treatment of the particular mechanical problems

[29] Sylla, "The Oxford Calculators and the Mathematics of Motion." See also Marshall Clagett, *The Science of Mechanics in the Middle Ages* (Madison: University of Wisconsin Press, 1959); Curtis Wilson, *William Heytesbury: Medieval Logic and the Rise of Mathematical Physics* (Madison: University of Wisconsin Press, 1956); J. A. Weisheipl, "The Place of John Dumbleton in the Merton School," *Isis* 50 (1959): 439–54; J. A. Weisheipl, "Ockham and Some Mertonians," *Mediaeval Studies* 30 (1968): 163–213; J. A. Weisheipl, "Repertorium Mertonense," *Mediaeval Studies* 31 (1969): 174–224; Sylla, "The Oxford Calculators," in *CHLMP*, 540–63; William J. Courtenay, *Schools and Scholars in Fourteenth-Century England* (Princeton: Princeton University Press, 1987), esp. the section on "The New Physics," 240–49; David C. Lindberg, *The Beginnings of Western Science: The European Scientific Tradition in Philosophical, Religious and Institutional Context, Prehistory to AD 1450* (1992; repr., Chicago: University of Chicago Press, 2007), 300–306; Keith Snedegar, "Merton Calculators (act. c. 1300–c. 1349)," in *ODNB*, theme 95034.

[30] H. Lamar Crosby, *Thomas of Bradwardine: His "Tractatus de proportionibus"; Its Significance for the Development of Mathematical Physics* (Madison: University of Wisconsin Press, 1955); Weisheipl, "The Interpretation of Aristotle's Physics," esp. 533–36; John E. Murdoch, "Thomas Bradwardine: Mathematics and Continuity in the Fourteenth Century," in *Mathematics and Its Applications to Science and Natural Philosophy in the Middle Ages: Essays in Honor of Marshall Clagett*, ed. Edward Grant and John E. Murdoch (Cambridge: Cambridge University Press, 1987), 103–37. For Bradwardine's logic, see *Thomas Bradwardine: Insolubilia*, ed. Stephen Read (Paris: Peeters, 2010). For his life, see Gordon Leff, "Bradwardine, Thomas (c. 1300–1349)," in *ODNB*, article 3213. Weisheipl sees Bradwardine as the "founder of the Merton School" ("Ockham and Some Mertonians," 189).

[31] Weisheipl, "The Place of John Dumbleton," 439.

they chose to solve, but also because of the precedent they set for the use of mathematics in natural science.[32] In popular histories of science,[33] the Oxford Calculators are now sometimes given particular credit for having anticipated Galileo in the formulation of the mean speed theorem (which describes the distance covered in a specified time by a uniformly accelerated or decelerated body);[34] but perhaps what is most striking is that, for them, the mean speed theorem was, as Sylla puts it, merely "a fairly routine lemma":[35] that is, only a relatively basic premise preliminary to addressing problems that were in themselves much more complex. The existence of this tradition in Oxford certainly demonstrates that scientific thinking in the fourteenth century extended well beyond the astrology, alchemy, and magic that student-guides to Chaucer tend to represent as the sum-total of medieval science,[36] but also

[32] Lindberg rightly comments that while "today the application of mathematics to motion needs no defense . . . it is only by hindsight and from a modern perspective that this conclusion is obvious; it would not have seemed plausible to many who worked within the Aristotelian tradition" (*Beginnings*, 299).

[33] See, e.g., James Hannam, *God's Philosophers: How the Medieval World Laid the Foundations of Modern Science* (London: Icon, 2009), 175 ("they [the Mertonians] almost certainly beat out the path later followed by Galileo and the other founders of modern science"), and 178–80 (where the mean speed theorem is described as "the most significant result of fourteenth-century physics"). However, as Lindberg observes, "medieval physics was not a primitive version of modern physics and cannot be legitimately judged by comparison with its modern namesake" (*Beginnings*, 286).

[34] In Heytesbury's formulation:

> For whether it [i.e., latitude or increment of velocity] commences from zero degree or from some [finite] degree, every latitude, as long as it is terminated at some finite degree, and as long as it is acquired or lost uniformly, will correspond to its mean degree of velocity. Thus the moving body, acquiring or losing this latitude uniformly during some assigned period of time, will traverse a distance exactly equal to what it would traverse in an equal period of time if it were moved uniformly at its mean degree [of velocity]. (William Heytesbury, *Reguli solvendi sophismata* [Venice: Locatellus, 1494], trans. Clagett, *Science of Mechanics*, 270)

See also Edward Grant, *Physical Science in the Middle Ages* (New York: Wiley, 1971), 55–59; Grant, *Foundations of Modern Science*, 100–104.

[35] Sylla, "The Oxford Calculators and the Mathematics of Motion," 174: "Aside from the fact that Swineshead gives four different proofs of the mean speed theorem, it would appear to be a fairly routine lemma. He does not give it any special importance, and does not even give it the honor of labelling it as a separate conclusion."

[36] See, e.g., Mahmoud Manzalaoui, "Chaucer and Science," in *Geoffrey Chaucer: The Writer and His Background*, ed. Derek Brewer (1974; repr., Cambridge: Brewer, 1990), 224–61; Irma Taavitsainen, "Science," in *A Companion to Chaucer*, ed. Peter Brown (2000; repr., Oxford: Blackwell, 2002), 378–96; J. A. Tasioulas, "Science," in *Chaucer: An Oxford Guide*, ed. Steve Ellis (Oxford: Oxford University Press, 2005), 174–89. Not one of these accounts of Chaucer's scientific horizons even mentions fourteenth-century English physics.

quite a long way beyond the relatively simple models and basic observations about the structure of things that characterize the Eagle's speech in *The House of Fame*.

It certainly seems hard to believe that Chaucer knew absolutely nothing at all about the Calculators' work in physics, even by reputation. After all, Thomas Bradwardine (the author of *De proportionibus*) is mentioned very prominently in *The Nun's Priest's Tale* (VII.3242); and it may well be that *The Nun's Priest's Tale* refers to him a second time (this time more codedly) in the plea for a benediction with which this tale concludes.[37] At the end of *Troilus and Criseyde* Chaucer submits the poem to the scrutiny of his learned friend Ralph Strode, who is probably to be identified with the logician who was a fellow of Merton College, like so many of the Calculators earlier in the century (including Walter Burley).[38] However, there is no indication that Strode himself had any particular interest in the kind of mechanical problems so characteristic of his predecessors at Merton; and the Nun's Priest invokes Bradwardine, not as the author of *De proportionibus*, but only as the author of the monumental philosophical treatise *De causa Dei*:[39] in other words, as a controversial theologian, rather than as a pioneer in the mathematization of physics. If it could be proved that Chaucer was directly acquainted with Burley's work on Aristotle's *Physics*, then it would be hard to deny that Chaucer would have been capable of appreciating this whole tradition of advanced scientific speculation.

Once again, however, Grennen's evidence for "Chaucer's familiarity with current speculation [in scientific thought]" turns out to be disappointingly thin; and the case he makes for Chaucer's knowledge of Burley's commentary on Aristotle's *Physics* is not, in itself, at all convincing. What Grennen argues, specifically, is that Chaucer's use of the word

[37] See David P. Baker, "A Bradwardinian Benediction: The Ending of the Nun's Priest's Tale Revisited," *MÆ* 82 (2013): 236–43; David P. Baker, "Literature, Logic and Mathematics in the Fourteenth Century," Ph.D. diss. (University of Durham, 2013), 104–7.

[38] See Rodney Delasanta, "Chaucer and Strode," *ChauR* 26, no. 2 (1991): 205–18; J. D. North, "Strode, Ralph (*d.* 1387)," *ODNB*, article 26673. On Strode's logic, see Wallace Knight Seaton, "An Edition and Translation of the 'Tractatus de consequentiis' by Ralph Strode, Fourteenth-Century Logician and Friend of Geoffrey Chaucer," Ph.D. diss. (University of California, Berkeley, 1973).

[39] Thomas Bradwardine, *De causa Dei contra Pelagium et de virtute causarum* (London: John Bill, 1618). There is no modern edition of this work; however, edited extracts with translations into modern German have recently been published by Edit Anna Lukács, in *Thomas Bradwardine: De causa Dei contra Pelagium et de virtute causarum; Auszüge Lateinisch–Deutsch* (Göttingen: V&R Unipress, 2013).

"conservatyf" (847) in the course of saying that the House of Fame is the place in the universe that best "conserves" sound was directly conditioned by Burley's use of the expression "virtutem conseruatiuam locati existentis" in the course of explicating Averroes's reading of Aristotle's fourth book of *Physics*. This phrase Grennen translates as "a power for conserving the placed thing." However, the passage in Burley's commentary from which Grennen cites this phrase is not nearly so relevant to the Eagle's concept of "kyndely place" (842) as Grennen suggests it is, since what is specifically at issue for Burley is how the "natural place" of each element ought to be defined in relation to the other elements, particularly in the light of Aristotle's proposition that "the place of a thing is the innermost motionless boundary of what contains it."[40] Burley is principally concerned here with Averroes's rejection of what might look like an obvious deduction from Aristotle's proposition: i.e., that if "the place of a thing is the innermost motionless boundary of what contains it," then the "natural place" of earth is therefore the "innermost motionless boundary" of the element that is naturally adjacent to it. But this deduction would be obviously wrong in a number of ways, as Averroes and Burley emphasize:

Certum est quod terra non moueretur ad superficiem aque ibi existentem, et propter hoc superficies aque non est locus naturalis per se ipsius terre, et hec est intentio Commentatoris commento .24. [*recte* .42.] huius capituli, ubi dicit quod "graue querit hunc finem [nisi] secundum quod est medium totius, et non secundum quod est finis aque. Et si non esset ita, tunc terra moueretur ad aquam ubicunque fuerit finis eius, sicut ferrum mouetur ad magnetem ubicunque fuerit. Sed hoc non sentit[ur] de aqua"[41]—hec Commentator. Dico igitur quod ultimum aque non est per se locus naturalis terre, nec eadem ratione est ultimum aeris locus naturalis aque.

[Certainly, earth is not attracted only so far as the surface of any water happening to be there, and therefore the surface of the water is not the "natural place" of earth in and of itself: this is what the Commentator means to say in his 24th {*recte* 42nd} comment on this chapter, where he says that "a heavy thing seeks this boundary {between earth and water}, not just to the extent that it seeks to reach the boundary of the water, but rather to the extent that it seeks to

---

[40] Aristotle, *Physics*, IV.4, 212b20, trans. Hardie and Gaye, 361.
[41] Averroes, commentary on Aristotle's *Physics*, 42 (Venice: Andreas Torresanus, 1483), fol. 54ra; (Venice: Lucas Antonius Iuncta, 1562), fol. 140v–b.

reach the middle of the whole. And if this were not the case, then earth would always be attracted to {the surface of} the water wherever it happened to be, just as iron is attracted to a magnet where it happens to be, but this is found not to be the case with water"—such {are the words of} the Commentator. I say, therefore, that the surface of water is not in itself the "natural place" of earth, nor by the same reason is the boundary with air the "natural place" of water.][42]

In effect, what Averroes and Burley argue is that, even if earth is always attracted downward such that it always passes through water until it reaches at least the boundary between earth and water, this does not mean that it is solely and particularly to this boundary that earth is attracted.

It is only in the course of trying to explicate this very technical point that Burley introduces what is, in effect, a distinction between two different ways of conceiving of the elements' attraction to their "natural place." It is not just that each element is drawn away from the other elements in such a way that it is always trying to reach at least the limits of the space occupied by any of the others. His point is that it is also drawn to its own proper sphere, in such a way that this elemental attraction always operates, regardless of the nature of each element's boundaries with the other elements:

Et si queratur quis igitur est locus naturalis terre per se, loquendo de loco locante et circumscribente, dico quod locus naturalis per se ipsius terre est ultimum aque secundum quod aqua est in tali situ, et in tali distantia ad orbem. Locus enim naturalis plus dic[o][43] quam ultimum corporis continentis, quia ultra ultimum corporis continentis, addit virtutem conseruatiuam locati existentis in corpore locante; et ideo si aer esset in loco totius aque, ultimum aeris esset locus naturalis terre, quia aer existens in tali situ, haberet virtutem conseruandi terram.

(fol. 106ra)

[And if it were asked what therefore is the "natural place" of earth in itself, I would say that the "natural place" in which earth is located and circumscribed, in and of itself, is the boundary with water {only} to the extent that water is in

[42] Walter Burley, commentary on Aristotle's *Physics* (Venice: Johannes Herbort, 1482), fol. 117v; (Venice: Simon de Luere, 1501; facsimile repr., Hildesheim: Olms, 1972), fol. 106ra.

[43] dico] dicit (in both the 1482 and 1501 editions)

that particular position and at some distance from the sphere {of earth itself}. I refer to "natural place"[44] rather than the boundary of a containing body {i.e., to the nature of attractive forces, rather than to Aristotle's conceptualization of extension in space}, since beyond the boundary of the containing body, this additionally confers the conserving power of an existing location {"virtutem conseruatiuam locati existentis"}. This means that, if the place of the water were wholly taken by air, the "natural place" of earth would then be the boundary of air, since air existing in that particular place would have the power to keep earth in position.]

It looks as if Burley may have been particularly indebted here to Saint Thomas Aquinas's commentary on Aristotle's *Physics*:

Videmus enim quod unumquodque horum fertur in suum proprium locum quando non impeditur, grave quidem deorsum, leve autem sursum. Ex quo patet quod locus habet quandam virtutem conservandi locatum: et propter hoc locatum tendit in suum locum desiderio suae conservationis. Non autem ex hoc ostenditur quod locus habeat virtutem attractivam, nisi sicut finis dicitur attrahere.

[For we observe that each of these bodies is carried to its proper place when it is not prevented, i.e., the heavy are carried down and the light upward. This shows that place has a certain power of conserving what is in place. For this reason, an object tends to its own place by the desire to conserve itself. This, however, does not prove that place has the power to attract, except in the sense in which the end is said to attract.][45]

Aquinas's "virtus conservandi locatum" (power of conserving what is placed) is simpler and more immediately comprehensible than Burley's "virtus conservativa locati existentis" ("conserving power of an existing location"), and it may well be that Burley's phrasing here should be interpreted merely as a version of Aquinas's formulation. Whether or not this is the case, it is clearly part of a relatively involved philosophical discussion, and the point it is designed to make is very specific to this discussion. It is difficult to see how Chaucer's Eagle's suggestion that

[44] Grennen translates: "non-natural place." He seems to have misexpanded the abbreviation for "enim," wrongly reading "non."

[45] Saint Thomas Aquinas, commentary on Aristotle's *Physics*, Book IV, Lectio 1, 412, ed. and trans. Pierre H. Conway (Columbus: College of St. Mary of the Springs, 1958–62), available online at http://dhspriory.org/thomas/Physics.htm (accessed May 17, 2016).

the House of Fame naturally conserves sound must necessarily reflect any of these complexities. There is simply no reason to think that this particular phrase would have captured Chaucer's attention, even if he had been reading Burley attentively and with profit.

III. Ripples on the Water

So far, then, my argument has been rather negative and inconclusive: I have simply observed that thirteenth- and fourteenth-century English physics seems to be conspicuous only by its absence from the Eagle's account of the mechanics of sound; and I have contested Grennen's suggestion that English physics is nevertheless visible in the Eagle's speech in the form of identifiable references to Grosseteste and Burley. However, I do not think that we are obliged to choose between assuming either that Chaucer's knowledge of physics was wholly old-fashioned—to the extent that he had no awareness of any writer on the subject more recent than Vincent of Beauvais—or that he must have had a direct and detailed acquaintance with the work of highly sophisticated thinkers such as Grosseteste and Burley. I will argue that Chaucer's approach to the themes of the Eagle's speech is decisively shaped by another writer who can be shown to have links with Grosseteste, Burley, and the Oxford Calculators—but who is hardly an innovative thinker on physics himself. I will also suggest that not only did this fourteenth-century writer provide Chaucer with several themes and metaphors of a broadly "scientific" kind: he also showed him how perspectives on physics could be used to effect even in contexts that are otherwise predominantly moral or allegorical. The writer I have in mind is Robert Holcot, the Dominican friar best known for his widely circulated commentary on the deutero-canonical book of Wisdom.[46] The

[46] There is no modern edition of the Wisdom-commentary. I have used the Hagenau 1494 edition (repr. in facsimile, Frankfurt: Minerva, 1974) (henceforth H); the Venice 1509 edition (V), available via the Bayerische Staatsbibliothek, http://reader.digitale -sammlungen.de/resolve/display/bsb10148926.html (accessed January 23, 2017); and the MS copy of the Wisdom-commentary in Oxford, Balliol College, MS 27 (O), using the photographs available at https://www.flickr.com/photos/balliolarchivist /sets/72157641118102464/ (accessed January 23, 2017). For a list of manuscripts and early printed editions of this work, see Friedrich Stegmüller, *Repertorium biblicum medii aevi*, 11 vols. (Madrid: Consejo Superior de Investigaciones Científicas, 1950–80), 5:143–47, no. 7416. On Holcot generally, see Beryl Smalley, *English Friars and Antiquity in the Early Fourteenth Century* (Oxford: Blackwell, 1960); and, more recently, Jenny Swanson, "Holcot, Robert (c. 1290–1349)," in *ODNB*, article 13485. On his theological *Quodlibeta*, see Richard E. Gillespie, "Robert Holcot's Quodlibeta," *Traditio* 27 (1971): 480–90; and Hester Goodenough Gelber, *Exploring the Boundaries of Reason: Three Ques-

strongest evidence for Holcot's influence on the Eagle's speech derives, perhaps surprisingly, from the one passage in *The House of Fame* that might seem least in need of any new suggestions about the nature of its sources: that is, the Eagle's description of the ripples produced when a stone is thrown into a body of water. As I have already pointed out, analogues for this passage can be found in both Boethius and Vincent of Beauvais. However, there is also a direct parallel for it in Holcot's Wisdom-commentary, a parallel that seems to have been noticed in Chaucerian scholarship only relatively recently.[47] Holcot's use of the ripples-on-the-water analogy in Lection 193 of this commentary is, in fact, remarkably close in phrasing to Chaucer's, much closer even than seems to have been realized, and in several respects noticeably closer to what the Eagle says than the corresponding passages in either Boethius or Vincent of Beauvais.

In Holcot's Wisdom-commentary Chaucer would have found a convenient summary, not just of Aristotle's thinking on the physics of sound, but also of the refinements on it offered by Aristotle's great "Commentator," Averroes:

Naturale autem generationem ipsius Echo declarat Aristoteles .ii. *De Anima*, textu[48] correspondente commento .viii. Est enim secundum Commentatorem "iteratio soni conseruando figuram suam":[49] et fit ab aere percusso et sonante cum reflexione ad aliquid obstaculum maxime concauum. Ponit autem ad hoc exemplum Aristoteles de lumine: Lumen multiplicatum in aere et reflexum ad aliquod politum[50] reflectitur versus illam partem in qua generatur, sicut manifestum est in corpore luminoso quod illuminatur, non solum per radios incidentes, sed per radios reflexos; aliter[51] esset vmbra[52] vbicumque non incidunt radii solis.

(Lection 193: V, fol. 164ra; O, fol. 286rb)[53]

---

tions on the Nature of God, by Robert Holcot, O.P. (Toronto: Pontifical Institute of Mediaeval Studies, 1983).

[47] John M. Fyler, *Language and the Declining World in Chaucer, Dante and Jean de Meun* (Cambridge: Cambridge University Press, 2007), 151, 250 n. 173. Fyler's observation is noted in *The House of Fame*, ed. Havely, note to lines 787–822, 184–85.

[48] textu] **O**; **HV** *om.*

[49] Averroes, *Commentarium magnum*, 419b25–419b33, ed. Crawford, 251.

[50] Ponit autem ad hoc exemplum Aristoteles de lumine: Lumen multiplicatum in aere et reflexum ad aliquod politum] **HV**; Ponit autem flexum ad aliquod corpus politum et tersum **O**

[51] aliter] **HV**; alias **O**

[52] vmbra] **HV**; tenebra **O**

[53] There are no page numbers in **H**.

[Aristotle explains the natural origins of this "Echo" in the second book of *On the Soul*: {see also} the corresponding commentary, distinction 8 {*recte* 80}, for according to the Commentator {i.e., Averroes} Echo is "the repetition of sound in such a way as to conserve its shape," and it is made out of air that has been struck and that resounds when it is reflected towards any obstacle that is as concave as possible. Indeed, in relation to this Aristotle suggests an analogy with light.[54] Light that is multiplied in air and thrown onto any polished surface is reflected back toward the point at which it is generated, just as is evident in the case of a luminous body that is illuminated not only by rays {of light} striking directly, but also by rays that are reflected: otherwise there would be shadow wherever the rays of the sun do not strike.]

It is at this point in his discussion of the physics of sound that Holcot introduces the analogy with the ripples created on the surface of a body of water by a falling object:

Aliud exemplum est in aqua. Si enim lapillus proiicatur in aquam, fiunt multe circulationes vbi cecidit[55] lapillus et minor circulus[56] pellendo causat maiorem et ille[57] alium, et sic deinceps[58] donec deficiat virtus primi pellentis.[59] Si autem circulationes ille occurrant alicui obstaculo priusquam virtus[60] primi pellentis deficiat, repercutiuntur:[61] et fiunt circulationes versus locum vbi prima percussio facta est per lapidem.

(Lection 193: V, fol. 164ra–b; O, fol. 286rb–ra)

[Another example of this is in water: for if a pebble is thrown into water, this creates many circles where the pebble fell; and each smaller circle causes the {next} larger one by impelling it outwards, and this then causes the next {larger one}, and so on successively, until the force of the initial impulsion is exhausted. If, however, these circles run into any obstacle before the force of the first

---

[54] Fyler seems to think that Holcot is misguidedly referring at this point to some Aristotelian work called "de Lumine" (*Language*, 250 n. 173), but this is not the case. Holcot's reference is to Aristotle, *On the Soul*, II.8, 419b, trans. Smith, 668: "What happens here must be analogous to what happens in the case of light: light is always reflected—otherwise it would not be diffused and outside what was directly illuminated by the sun there would be blank darkness."

[55] circulationes vbi cecidit] **HV**; circulationes quarum centrum est locus vbi cadit **O**

[56] circulus] **HV**; circulatio **O**

[57] ille] **HV**; illa **O**

[58] deinceps] **HV**; **O** *om.*

[59] pellentis] **HV**; inpellentis **O**

[60] virtus] **HV**; **O** *om.*

[61] repercutiuntur] **HV**; et repercutiuntur **O**

impulsion is exhausted, they are bounced back, and the circles return towards the point where the initial impact was made by the stone.]

Averroes makes use of this same analogy in the chapter immediately before the one that Holcot cites;[62] and it may well be that Holcot's own use of this analogy was most directly prompted by Averroes, rather than Boethius or Vincent of Beauvais,[63] neither of whom he mentions at this point.

In order to describe the effect of the stone falling into the water Holcot repeatedly uses the terms "circulationes" and "circulus," and *The House of Fame* could be taken to reflect this in its use of the word "sercle" at lines 791, 794, and 796. Vincent of Beauvais likewise makes repeated use of the word "circulus," but only in relation to sound in general, not when describing the spread of ripples as such. Even more striking, however, is the fact that Holcot specifically says that each of these circular ripples *causes* ("causat") the next one, since "cause" seems to have been a key-term in this context for Chaucer too. Neither Boethius, Vincent of Beauvais, nor Averroes refers specifically to "cause" in relation to the ripples created by a stone falling into water, whereas Chaucer's Eagle uses the term three times in quick succession (at lines 794, 796, and 800). Holcot also seems to have provided Chaucer with another term that is very prominent in the Eagle's speech: that is, "multiplication" (which appears at lines 784, 801, and 820).[64] Again, there is no precedent for this in Boethius, Vincent, or Averroes; however, Holcot says: "In the same way [as in the case of the ripples on the water], when sound is created in the air by the impact of something on something else, then that sound is *multiplied*, and it generates another sound, and this other sound generates another sound [and so on], radiating outwards, as long

---

[62] Averroes, *Commentarium magnum*, 419b, ed. Crawford, 248 (cited above, note 49).

[63] Boethius, *De institutione*, I.14, ed. Friedlein, 200, trans. Bower, 21; and Vincent, *Speculum*, V.17 (both cited above, note 15).

[64] Following Fyler (*Language*, 151), Havely notes that both Chaucer and Holcot refer to multiplication in this context (*HF*, note to lines 787–822 [pages 184–85]), but he also suggests that "There may be an allusion here to Robert Grosseteste" (note to line 784 [page 184]), on the grounds that " 'multiplication of species' or 'virtue' was part of his [Grosseteste's] optical theory." This comparison does not seem to me particularly compelling—or at least not so compelling as the comparison with Holcot's Wisdom-commentary. Nor am I persuaded by Havely's further suggestion (in his note to line 784) that Chaucer's "interest in the notion of multiplicity (versus unity) may well have been further stimulated by his reading about unity and diversity in Book 3 of Boethius's Cons[olation of Philosophy]" (cf. *Boece* 3, prosa II.16–73)."

as the strength of the initial impact lasts" ("Eodem modo, quando[65] ex percutiente et percusso[66] sit sonus in aere, ille sonus *multiplicatur* et sonus iste generat alium et ille alium[67] circulariter, quamdiu durat virtus primi percutientis") (Lection 193: **V**, fol. 164rb; **O**, fol. 286va; emphasis mine). Holcot's particular emphasis on both "cause" and "multiplication" in his account of the ripples on the water seems to be the immediate explanation for the Eagle's prominent repetition of these very terms in the course of his own use of this analogy (which I cite here with these key words in bold):

> Now, hennes-forth y wol the teche
> How every speche or noyse or soun,
> Thurgh hys **multiplicacioun**,
> Thogh hyt were piped of a mouse,
> Mote nede come to Fames house.
> I preve hyt thus (take hede now)
> By experience—for yf that thow
> Throwe on water now a stoon,
> Wel wost thou, hyt wol make anoon
> A litel roundell, as a sercle—
> Peraventure brode as a covercle—
> And ryght anoon thow shalt see wel,
> That sercle wol **cause** another whele
> And that the thridde, and so forth, brother,
> Every sercle **causynge** other,
> Wydder than hym self was.
> And thus, fro roundel to compas,
> Eche aboute other goynge,
> Causeth of othres sterynge,
> And **multiplyinge** ever moo,
> Til that hyt be so fer y-goo
> That hyt at bothe brynkes bee.
> [. . .]
> As I have of the watir preved—
> That every cercle **causeth** other—
> Ryght so of ayre, my leve brother:
> Everych ayre other stereth

---

[65] quando] **HV**; **O** *om.*
[66] percusso] **HV**; percussio **O**
[67] ille alium] **HV**; ille alius alium **O**

More and more, and speche upbereth,
Or voys or noyse or worde or soun,
Ay through **multiplicacioun**,
Til hyt be atte House of Fame . . .
(*HF*, 782–803, 814–21)

These parallels are suggestive in themselves, and they clearly indicate that, even if Chaucer were aware of the use of the ripples-on-the-water analogy by Boethius, Vincent of Beauvais, or Averroes, it is probably Holcot whose influence on Chaucer at this point was most direct. Yet it is perhaps the broader context in which Holcot discusses the physics of sound that is most suggestive about the nature of the relationship between the two English writers. Holcot's discussion of the nature of sound in the Wisdom-commentary comes as part of his analysis of "Echo," which, he emphasizes, is open to discussion from at least two distinct perspectives, the one "natural" ("naturale," or what might be called "scientific") and the other "fabulous" ("fabulosum," i.e., derived from classical mythology): "Circa generationem Echo notanda[68] sunt duo: vnum est naturale, aliud fabulosum" (Lection 193: **V**, fol. 164ra; **O**, fol. 286rb). Having offered us his account of the "natural" approach to the theme of echoes (by means of the analogy with the ripples on the water), Holcot then switches directly to the "fabulous":

Fabulose loquendo[69] Echo narrat Ouidius .iii. *Methamorphoses*.[70] Fuit enim virgo quedam mire eloquentie, que Junonem longa narratione[71] detinere solebat, dummodo Jupiter in montibus adulteria sua fecit cum puellis. Impediebatur igitur Juno per narrationes ipsius Echo ne deprehendere posset istas puellas, ipsis fugientibus Junone detenta per narrationes ipsius Echo. Tandem Juno hoc percepto, " 'Huius' ait, 'lingue que sum decepta[72] potestas./ Parua[73] tibi dabitur[74] vocisque breuissimus vsus.' "[75] Priuauit eam vsu loquendi, hoc solum sibi relinquens quod fines verborum ingeminat. Hec ergo Echo Narcissum iuuenem

---

[68] notanda] **HV**; videnda **O**
[69] fabulose loquendo] **HV**; fabulosum ortum ipsius **O**
[70] Ovid, *Metamorphoses*, III.359–510, ed. and trans. Frank Justus Miller, 2 vols. (Cambridge, Mass.: Loeb, 1984), 1:148–61.
[71] longa narratione] **HV**; longis narrationibus **O**
[72] decepta] **HVO**; delusa *Ovid*
[73] Parua] *Ovid*; Praua **HVO**
[74] dabitur] *Ovid* **O**; datur **HV**
[75] Ovid, *Metamorphoses*, III.366–67, ed. and trans. Miller, 1:150–51.

adamauit pulcherrimum, sed[76] ab eo repellitur. "Spreta latet siluis pudibun-
daque[77] frondibus ora/ Protegit et solus ex illo viuit in antris."[78] Fatigans[79] igitur eam amore, dolore et pudore cuius[80] corpus totum euanuit preter vocem et
ossa. Ossa vero conuersa sunt in saxa et tandem[81] sola vox remansit que vocatur
"Echo."

(Lection 193: V, fol. 164rb; O, fol. 286va)

[In mythological terms, Ovid tells the story of Echo in the third book of *Metamorphoses*. There was once a young woman of wonderful eloquence, who was
accustomed to detain Juno with long drawn-out storytelling all the time that
Jupiter was in the mountains committing adultery with his girlfriends. In this
way Juno was prevented by the stories of this Echo from being able to catch
any of these girls, for they fled from her while she was being detained by Echo's
stories. "That tongue of thine {she said}, by which I have been {deceived}
shall have its power curtailed and enjoy the briefest use of speech." Juno
deprived Echo of the power of speech leaving her only the power to repeat the
ends of words. So then this Echo fell in love with the beautiful Narcissus, but
was rejected by him. "Thus spurned, she lurks in the woods, hides her shamed
face among the foliage, and lives from that time on in lonely caves." In this
way exhausted by love, grief, and shame, her whole body vanished {into thin
air} apart from her voice and bones.[82] Her bones were changed into rocks, and
at length only her voice remained, which is what we call "Echo."]

In essence, what Holcot does here is to yoke together precisely the same
two modes of thinking that come together to such incongruous effect in
the Eagle's speech in *The House of Fame*: that is, the "naturale" and the
"fabulosum"—the "scientific" and the "mythological." Just as Holcot
chooses to read Echo both as a phenomenon in nature and as an invitation to analyze the moral dimensions of the classical legend of Echo, so
too Chaucer presents us with the Eagle, who is simultaneously both a
vehicle for what seems to be a determinedly scientific account of the
mechanics of sound and a figure straight out of classical mythology. In
other words, what Holcot offers Chaucer here is a precedent not just for

---

[76] sed} **HV**; **O** *om.*
[77] pudibundaque] **HV**; putibundaque **O**
[78] Ovid, *Metamorphoses*, III.393–94, ed. and trans. Miller, 1:152–53.
[79] Fatigans] *Ovid*; Fatigantibus **HVO**
[80] cuius] **HV**; **O** *om.*
[81] tandem] **HV**; sic tandem **O**
[82] Cf. *FranT*, V.951–52: "And dye he moste, he seyde, as dide Ekko / For Narcisus,
that dorste nat telle hir wo."

the particular analogy of the ripples on the water, but also for the explicit conjunction of "mythology" with "science."[83]

Such conjunctions are by no means unusual in the Wisdom-commentary. Another example can be found in Lection 187, where Holcot discusses Ovid's characterization of the House of Envy in the second book of the *Metamorphoses*. According to Holcot:

> Vult ergo dicere quod domus inuidie est situata in vallibus pro tanto quod[84] persone humiles inuident[85] superioribus, et omnis inuidus ideo inuidet, quia se inferiorem alio in aliquo quod appetit esse videt. Inferior planeta eclipsat superiorem, et non econtra, sicut patet de luna et sole, et ita regulariter illi qui minus valent et sunt gratiis et meritis inferiores obumbrare nituntur per inui-diam meliores.

> (Lection 187: **V**, fol. 159ra; **O**, fol. 277rb–va)

> [{Ovid} chooses to say that the House of Envy is situated in a valley {"in vallibus"}[86] because of the way that lesser folk envy their superiors; and every envious person is envious because he sees himself to be inferior to another in something that he desires. A lesser planet eclipses a greater, not vice versa, just as is clear with regard to the sun and the moon: and so it regularly happens that those who are worth less, and are inferior in their virtues and their merits, strive to overshadow their betters through envy.]

Here again we find that seemingly incongruous conjunction between the "fabulosum" and the "naturale": between the imaginative world of classical literature, that is, and the physical world of bodies moving in the cosmos. As it happens, Chaucer's description of the House of Fame's nearby annex, the House of Rumour, also includes the idea that it was situated in a valley ("Tho saugh I stond in a valeye, / Under the castel, fast by, / An house" [1918–20]), and it is possible that Chaucer was

---

[83] I should emphasize that this reading of Holcot's influence on Chaucer is not intended to be exclusive. There are other medieval authors who make use of something like this conjuncture of the "naturale" and the "fabulosum": see, for example, the *Roman de la rose*, lines 18013–91, ed. Daniel Poirion (Paris: Flammarion, 1974), 481–82, where references to scientific authorities such as Aristotle and Alhazen are pointedly juxtaposed with mythological figures such as Mars and Venus.

[84] quod] **HV**; quia **O**

[85] inuident] **HV**; semper inuident **O**

[86] Ovid, *Metamorphoses*, II.761–62, ed. and trans. Miller, 1:112–113: "domus est imis in vallibus huius / abdita" ("her home was hidden away in a deep valley").

particularly encouraged to include this detail by its prominence in Holcot's discussion of Ovid's allegorical architecture, as well as—or possibly even wholly instead of—Ovid's own text. Just as Holcot here uses the idea of movement of planets in eclipses in order to explain the architecture of a particular ethical/mythical construct (the House of Envy), so too, it could be argued, Chaucer uses the idea of the physical movements of sound-waves in order to explain the architecture of what is, in effect, a parallel and related concept (the House of Fame).

IV. The Place of Robert Holcot in Fourteenth-Century Intellectual Culture

What, however, is the wider significance of these correspondences? What is the nature of the relationship between Chaucer and Holcot—or, for that matter, between Holcot and Grosseteste, Burley, or the Oxford Calculators? Born around 1290, Robert Holcot was a contemporary of many of the Calculators: his career, like those of two of the most important Calculators, Bradwardine and Dumbleton, was cut short by the Black Death of 1348/49. In Oxford from at least 1326, he held the Dominican chair of theology there in 1334, followed by a second regency in Cambridge; and at some point after this he became part of the literary and book-collecting circle that gathered around the bishop of Durham, Richard Bury.[87] Bury is now best known to literary history as the putative author of a work called *Philobiblon* (or *The Love of Books*),[88] although in fact there is some evidence that Holcot was also involved in its authorship, to the extent that "we shall never know . . . how much of *Philobiblon* is Holcot's and how much de Bury's."[89] The group around Bury is described in the *Dictionary of National Biography* as "the single most notable circle or sequence of scholars under the patronage of one person in fourteenth-century England." Among its members were the Oxford Calculators Thomas Bradwardine and Richard Kilvington—and

[87] On Bury, see N. Denholm-Young, "Richard de Bury (1287–1345)," *Transactions of the Royal Historical Society*, 4th Series 20 (1937): 135–68; Christopher R. Cheney, "Richard de Bury, Borrower of Books," *Speculum* 48 (1973): 325–28; Courtenay, *Schools and Scholars*, 133–37; W. J. Courtenay, "Bury, Richard (1287–1345)," in *ODNB*, article 4153.

[88] '*Philobiblon*': *Richard de Bury; The Text and Translation of E. C. Thomas*, ed. Michael Maclagan (Oxford: Blackwell, 1970).

[89] Smalley, *English Friars*, 67. See, however, Bury, *Philobiblon*, xxxv–xxxvii.

also Walter Burley.[90] Some idea of this circle's activities might be deduced from the *Philobiblon*, where Bury says (or is imagined by Holcot to say):

ab aetate tenera magistrorum et scholarium ac diversarum artium professorum quos ingenii perspicacitas ac doctrinae celebritas clariores effecerant, relegato quolibet partiali favore, exquisitissima sollicitudine nostrae semper coniuncimus comitivae, quorum consolativis colloquiis confortati, nunc argumentorum ostensivis investigationibus, nunc physicorum processuum ac catholicorum doctorum tractatuum recitationibus, nunc moralitatum excitativis collationibus, velut alternatis et multiplicatis ingenii ferculis, dulcius fovebamur.

[From our early years we attached to our society with the most exquisite solicitude and discarding all partiality all such masters and scholars and professors in the several faculties as had become most distinguished by their subtlety of mind and the fame of their learning. Deriving consolation from their sympathetic conversation, we were delightfully entertained, now by demonstrative chains of reasoning, now by the recital of the physical processes and the treatises of the doctors of the Church, now by stimulating discourses on the allegorical meaning of things as by a rich and well-varied intellectual feast.][91]

The recital of the "physical processes" (*physicum processuum*) mentioned here might even be read as a direct reference to something very like the scientifically educational lecture that Chaucer's Eagle attempts to provide; while the *moralitatum excitative collationes* (literally, "stimulating assemblages of moral ideas") clearly imply a reference to some form of allegory, as E. C. Thomas's translation assumes ("stimulating discourses on the allegorical meaning of things").

While Holcot is very likely to have known Burley personally (as a fellow member of the Bury circle), the evidence is also very strong that he knew at least some of Grosseteste's work. Apart from anything else, he says that he did. He refers directly to Grosseteste as "Linconiensis"

---

[90] In addition to these three men (and of course Holcot), Bury's "household" between 1334 and 1345 seems to have included such figures as Richard Bentworth, Richard Fitzralph, Walter Segrave, John Maudith, and John Aton. On Fitzralph, see Katherine Walsh, *Richard Fitzralph in Oxford, Avignon and Armagh* (Oxford: Clarendon Press, 1981), and "Fitzralph, Richard (*b.* before 1300, *d.* 1360)," in *ODNB*, article 9267; on Maudith, J. D. North, "Maudith, John (*d.* in or after 1343)," in *ODNB*, article 18362; on Aton, F. Donald Logan, "Aton, John (*d.* 1349)," in *ODNB*, article 75.

[91] Bury, *Philobiblon*, 86–87.

(i.e., as bishop of Lincoln) in his commentary on Peter Lombard's *Sentences*;[92] and in Lection 83 of the Wisdom-commentary he copied an extensive passage almost verbatim from Grosseteste's *Dictum* 91, which he also ascribes to "Linconiensis."[93] In addition, Lection 100 includes a whole section borrowed word for word from Grosseteste's *Dictum* 60, although here Holcot seems to have thought that he was quoting from the work of Alexander Nequam.[94] From this perspective, Grennen's suggestion of Chaucer's indebtedness to Burley and Grosseteste is not so far off the mark after all. Whether or not Chaucer knew the work of either of these authors directly, it seems that he had access, in Holcot, to someone who largely shared their intellectual horizons.

These days, however, Holcot is probably best known, not for his membership of the Bury circle, or for his knowledge of Grosseteste, but

---

[92] Holcot, commentary on the *Sentences*, II, q. 2:

> Aliter aliqui dicunt ad istud argumentum quod vna multitudo infinita est maior alia: et concedunt quod plures fuerunt reuolutiones lune quam solis. Dicunt etiam quod sicut inter ternarium et binarium est sesquialtera proportio: ita inter ternarios infinitos et binarios infinitos est sesquialtera proportio: et infinito potest fieri additio. Et hec opinio est Linconiensis super librum physicorum. (Robertus Holkot, *In quatuor libros sententiarum questiones* [Lyon, 1518; facsimile repr., Frankfurt: Minerva, 1967], n.p.)

> [In response to this argument others say differently: {they say} that one multitude can be more than another; and they concede that there have been more revolutions of the moon than of the sun. They also say that just as the ratio between a cube and a square is three to two, so the ratio between an infinite cube and an infinite square is {still} three to two: and {therefore} there can be addition to an infinite. And this was the opinion of {the bishop} of Lincoln {in his commentary} on the books of *Physics*.]

According to Pierre Duhem: "The last assertion seems completely false: Robert Grosseteste says nothing not purely Aristotelian on the subject of the infinite in his Summa (which is so concise, so full of ideas), and nothing in particular that resembles what Holkot attributes to him"; Pierre Duhem, *Medieval Cosmology: Theories of Infinity, Place, Time, Void, and the Plurality of Words*, ed. and trans. Roger Ariew (Chicago: University of Chicago Press, 1985), 103. Duhem's view is contradicted by Neil Lewis ("Robert Grosseteste's *Notes on Physics*," 120), who interprets this passage as a direct reference to Grosseteste's *Notes on Physics*—although he mistakenly refers to Holcot as "John Holcot."

[93] The passage in question occupies most of the final third of Holcot's Lection 83. An edition of Grosseteste's *Dictum* 91 can be found at the *Electronic Grosseteste* website (cited above, note 19): the material borrowed by Holcot can be found at fols. 69vb–70ra in the base-text for this edition, Oxford, Bodleian Library, MS Bodley 798.

[94] The relevant passages are printed below, in the appendix. On *Dictum* 60, see also Servus Gieben, "Traces of God in Nature according to Robert Grosseteste," *Franciscan Studies* 24 (1964): 144–58.

for the leading part he plays in two other important fourteenth-century contexts.[95] First, he is generally regarded as one of the principal theological antagonists of Thomas Bradwardine: specifically, as one of the philosophers that Bradwardine chose to represent in *De causa Dei* as "Pelagians" (that is, philosophical skeptics in the tradition of Ockham), and against whom the *De causa Dei* was apparently directed.[96] For Bradwardine, whose views on the relationship between divine grace and human free will could certainly be said to veer toward theological determinism, Holcot seems to have been something of a *bête noire*, since, even by the standards of Ockham's followers, Holcot's skepticism was particularly strongly stated.[97] In his *Sentences*-commentary he even argued for the rather disconcerting proposition that God can lie and deceive, and that he can do so without impairing his perfection in any way.[98] Such antideterminism may well have appealed rather strongly to Chaucer, the poet who includes in Book IV of *Troilus and Criseyde* an

---

[95] From the point of view of the history of English literature, Holcot is also interesting as the only medieval writer who apparently shows a knowledge of the first long comic poem in the English language, the thirteenth-century poem known as *The Owl and the Nightingale* (ed. and trans. Neil Cartlidge [2001; repr., Exeter: University of Exeter Press, 2003]). This observation was made by Alan J. Fletcher in "The Genesis of *The Owl and the Nightingale*: A New Hypothesis," *ChauR* 34, no. 1 (1999): 1–17 (2–4).

[96] See Gordon Leff, *Bradwardine and the Pelagians: A Study of His "De causa Dei" and Its Opponents* (Cambridge: Cambridge University Press, 1957), esp. 221; Baker, "Literature, Logic and Mathematics," 49, 107–32; Courtenay, *Schools and Scholars*, 294–303; Calvin Normore, "Future Contingents," in *The Cambridge History of Later Medieval Philosophy*, ed. Norman Kretzmann et al. (Cambridge: Cambridge University Press, 1982), 358–81 (373–77); Bradwardine, *De causa Dei*, ed. Lukács, 33–36. On Holcot's relationship with Ockham, see E. A. Moody, "A Quodlibetal Question of Robert Holkot, O.P. on the Problem of the Objects of Knowledge and of Belief," *Speculum* 39 (1964): 53–74.

[97] Cf. Holcot's Wisdom-commentary, Lection 147 (**V**, fol. 128rb; **O** [here Lection 148], fol. 222vb):

> Multi confitentur iniquitatem suam, sed aduersus Deum. Quando enim inueniuntur in peccatis, [non (**O**; **HV** *om*.)] dicunt "Non feci hoc, aut non est hoc peccatum," sed "Deus voluit." Alii dicunt "fatum mihi fecit. Stelle mihi fecerunt et ita per circuitum nituntur venire ad accusandum Deum. Stellas enim ipse fecit et ordinauit." Et ita per eas voluit ostendere quod Deus fecit vt peccarent. Sed vere penitens dicit "Ego peccaui, non fatum, non fortuna, non Diabolus me coegit: sed ego persuadenti consensi." Hec Glosa: Vere igitur penitentes precogitant et deliberant quomodo possint semetipsos accusare: [sed (**O**; **HV** *om*.)] false penitentes deliberant quomodo possint Deum accusare [et excusare seipsos (**O**; **HV** *om*.)].

[98] Holcot, commentary on the *Sentences*: "Similiter nullum inconueniens videtur si dicatur Deum dicere falsum: vel permittere se facturum et non facere: sicut homo potest" (Likewise no contradiction seems to be entailed if it is said that God is able to say what is false, or to commit himself to doing something in the future and not do it—just as a human being can). *In quatuor libros sententiarum questiones*, II, q. 2 (n.p.); Baker, "Literature, Logic and Mathematics," 117–18.

extended illustration of the folly of narrow fatalism.[99] Second, Holcot is known for his membership of a group that Beryl Smalley long ago labeled as the "classicizing friars": a group of English writers characterized by a conspicuous penchant for incorporating classical material into what were essentially devotional and pastoral texts. Smalley considered Holcot the most "diversely gifted" of all these fraternal writers: and indeed, "no medieval moralist," she adds, "ever had a stronger sense of humour" than Holcot did.[100] The Wisdom-commentary is an undeniably engaging and accessible text, as well as an instructive one, which means that it is not hard to see why it eventually became, in Jenny Swanson's words, "one of the most popular commentaries of the late middle ages."[101] As Swanson explains, it "made [Holcot's] name famous throughout medieval Europe, and surviving catalogues show that every well-stocked library came to have a copy."[102] Nevertheless, the book's popularity waned in the sixteenth century; and the Wisdom-commentary is now (arguably) the most widely circulated and culturally significant medieval English text never to have appeared in a complete modern edition.

V. Holcot and Chaucer

The possibility that Chaucer was a reader of Holcot's Wisdom-commentary has, in fact, long been recognized. Some of the strongest evidence for it comes from the fact that Chaucer's discussion of dreams and their significance in *The Nun's Priest's Tale* seems to have been substantially influenced by several passages in the Wisdom-commentary. Both of the stories told by the cock Chauntecleer in support of the idea that dreams can be predictive of the future are found in the commentary (Lections 102 and 201);[103] and it was probably directly from Holcot that Chaucer

[99] On Troilus's fatalism in *Troilus and Criseyde*, see A. J. Minnis, *Chaucer and Pagan Antiquity* (Cambridge: Brewer, 1982), 93–99.

[100] Smalley, *English Friars*, 73. On Holcot's sense of humor, see also Katherine H. Tachau, "Looking Gravely at Dominican Puns: The 'Sermons' of Robert Holcot and Ralph Friseby," *Traditio* 46 (1991): 337–45.

[101] Jenny Swanson, "Holcot, Robert (c. 1290–1349)," in *ODNB*, article 13485.

[102] Ibid. Cf. J. C. Wey, "The *Sermo finalis* of Robert Holcot," *Mediaeval Studies* 11 (1949): 219–23 (219): "As the author of [the] . . . commentary on the *Book of Wisdom* Holcot became famous over night and his fame held throughout the next two centuries."

[103] Kate O. Petersen, *On the Sources of the "Nonnes Preestes Tale"* (Boston, Mass.: Radcliffe College, 1892); Robert A. Pratt, "Some Latin Sources of the Nonnes Preest on Dreams," *Speculum* 52 (1977): 538–70. Pratt refers to these Lections as 103 and 202 (rather than 102 and 201) because he based his reading of Holcot primarily on the

took them, rather than from Holcot's own principal source, Valerius Maximus. Indeed, Robert Pratt asserts that "In Holcot's fascinating Wisdom commentary [Chaucer would have] found opposing views on dreams and divination which he developed into stupendous mock-heroic discourses. He rifled Holcot—especially the sections on significative dreams—for Pertelote's discussion of humors and for most of Chauntecleer's argument."[104] Given the energy with which Pratt argues for Chaucer's dependence on the Wisdom-commentary for his material on dreams and divination, it seems rather surprising that Chaucerians have not sought more intensively for further examples of Chaucer's "rifling" of Holcot.[105] I have recently tried to lend support to Pratt's case for

---

manuscript copy of the Wisdom-commentary in O, where the numbering is slightly different.

[104] Pratt, "Some Latin Sources," 569.

[105] In the past A. J. Minnis has presented Chaucer's knowledge of the Wisdom-commentary as a certainty, stating bluntly that "[Robert Holcot's . . . popular commentary on the Book of Wisdom was known to Chaucer" (*Chaucer and Pagan Antiquity*, 3); cf. A. J. Minnis, *Medieval Theory of Authorship: Scholastic Literary Attitudes in the Later Middle Ages*, 2nd ed. (Aldershot: Wildwood House, 1988), 165: "Chaucer seems to have made use of Holcot's Wisdom-commentary when writing his *House of Fame* and the Nun's Priest's Tale." In support of these assertions he cites Petersen, *On the Sources*, and Pratt, "Some Latin Sources"; and (for *The House of Fame*) Sypherd, *Studies*, 74–76; but adds no specific evidence himself for Chaucer's use of Holcot. More recently, his views seem to have shifted a little: he expresses skepticism about Pratt's case for Chaucer's use of Holcot, but adds "let that pass for now: in principle I see no reason why Chaucer should or could not have read Holcot's Wisdom commentary" ("Looking for a Sign: The Quest for Nominalism in Ricardian poetry," in *Translations of Authority in Medieval English Literature: Valuing the Vernacular* [Cambridge: Cambridge University Press, 2009], 38–67 [40]). William H. Watts argues that:

the case for Holcot's influence on Chaucer is less clear-cut than the near-universal acceptance of the *Wisdom Commentary* as a source for *The Nun's Priest's Tale* would seem to suggest. While Petersen and Pratt are able to point to parallels between the *Commentary* and the *Tale*, there is little in Chaucer's work that must of necessity come from Holcot. The argument for Holcot's influence rests largely on similarities in verbal choices, in the structure of the argument, and in the narrative details Chauntecleer deploys in the exemplary tales that support his case for the prophetic value of dreams, but it would seem that these similarities can be accounted for without resorting to Holcot

and he suggests (unconvincingly in my view) that Chaucer is unlikely to have made use of the works of clerks such as Holcot if only because "we find in Chaucer's poetry a kind of anti-clericalism, focused not on the worldly abuses of the religious orders but on the hubris and misdirected studies of clerks"; "Chaucer's Clerks and the Value of Philosophy," in *Nominalism and Literary Discourse: New Perspectives*, ed. Hugo Keiper, Christoph Bode, and Richard J. Utz (Amsterdam: Rodopi, 1997), 145–55 (152–53). More recently, Peter Brown has argued that the influence of Holcot's Wisdom-commentary is visible in Chaucer's treatment of optics; *Chaucer and the Making of Optical Space* (Bern: Lang, 2007), esp. 107–8, 159–60, 311.

Chaucer's knowledge of Holcot by pointing out that the friar's influence is probably directly visible in the rather austere attitude that Chaucer takes in the *Canterbury Tales* toward parental, and particularly paternal, responsibility. So, for example, there is a close correspondence between Chaucer's Physician's warning that parents should be careful not to encourage immorality in their children either "by ensample of youre lyvynge / Or by youre necligence in chastisynge" (*PhyT*, 97–98) and Holcot's assertion in Lection 41 that when children turn out to be immoral it is either "Tum propter parentum imitationem, tum propter defectum castigationis" (either because of imitating their parents, or a lack of chastisement).[106] It is also the case that in *The Merchant's Tale* January's assertion that a man ought to "Take . . . a wyf with greet devocioun, / By cause of leveful procreacioun / Of children to th'onour of God above" (*MerT*, 1447–49) at least resembles the phrasing of Holcot's argument in Lection 37 that the generation of children should occur within the boundaries of marriage "in order to honour God" ("prolis propagatio ad laudem Dei").[107] A further close verbal correspondence can be found in the two writers' accounts of the story of Phaethon. Chaucer concludes his version by asking:

> Loo, ys it not a mochil myschaunce
> To lat a fool han governaunce
> Of thing that he can not demeyne?
> (*HF*, 957–59)

The particular phrasing of this rhetorical question seems to be a direct reflection of Holcot's observation in Lection 8 of the Wisdom-commentary that "This is what might happen to those fools and presumptuous people who complain about divine governance" ("Ita contingeret de istis *fatuis* et presumptuosis qui de diuina *gubernatione* murmurant"; my italics).[108] However, the case for Chaucer's dependence on Holcot rests not just on close verbal correspondences such as these, but also on the sheer accumulation of themes and motifs common to the two writers. So, for example, in Lection 191 of the Wisdom-commentary, Holcot tells the story of Ceyx and Alcyone, which Chaucer

---

[106] Neil Cartlidge, "Wayward Sons and Failing Fathers: Chaucer's Moralistic Paternalism—and a Possible Source for the *Cook's Tale*," *ChauR* 47, no. 2 (2012): 134–60 (146–47).

[107] Ibid., 147 n. 35.

[108] Lection 8: **V**, fol. 9vb. This sentence is in a passage omitted in **O**.

also uses in *The Book of the Duchess* (lines 62–230). In Lection 197, Holcot discusses the "Dulcarnoun," the Euclidian axiom to which Pandarus makes reference in *Troilus and Criseyde* (III.931).[109] And in Lection 16, he cites the case of the poet who is so moved by his feelings as to address his beloved's deserted house (the rhetorical device of *paraclausithyron*) much as Troilus does in *Troilus and Criseyde* (V.540–53).[110] In these cases, the verbal correspondences are not so close as to add much weight individually to the idea that Chaucer was making use of the Wisdom-commentary, but cumulatively they support the impression that, intellectually and imaginatively, the two writers inhabited very much the same world.

In the light of all this, the most efficient explanation for the parallels between Chaucer's use of the ripples-on-the-water analogy and Holcot's use of this same analogy is surely that Chaucer knew the Wisdom-commentary, and that he used it in the composition of the Eagle's speech. Indeed, many of the general principles of the Eagle's physics are at least implicit in Holcot's commentary;[111] and there is probably no need to assume that Chaucer's learning (either in classical literature or in fourteenth-century physics) necessarily extended very much beyond it. It may be that Chaucerian scholars have actually played into the poet's hands by attempting to identify his sources only in authorities much grander and more remote than the English friar. No doubt Chaucer would have been quite pleased to be credited with such deep erudition that he would have needed no guide to the thinking of such ancient intellectual eminences as Aristotle or Boethius.[112] However, in the Wisdom-commentary he would certainly have found just such a

[109] See Thomas Elwood Hart, "Medieval Structuralism: 'Dulcarnoun' and the Five-Book Design of Chaucer's 'Troilus,'" *ChauR* 16, no. 2 (1981): 129–70; and Baker, "Literature, Logic and Mathematics," 178–80.

[110] This particular parallel was noted by Smalley (*English Friars*, 169–70). See also Morton W. Bloomfield, "Troilus' Paraclausithyron and Its Setting," *Neuphilologische Mitteilungen* 73 (1972): 15–24. He discusses the possibility at 18–19 that Chaucer was at this point borrowing from Holcot, remarking: "It now seems very probable that Chaucer knew Holcot's *Commentary on Wisdom* which was one of the popular works of the later fourteenth century" (18).

[111] Cf., e.g., "Lyghte thinge upwarde, and dounwarde charge" (*HF*, 746); and Holcot's "Locus autem grauium est deorsum" (Holcot, Wisdom-commentary, Lection 188).

[112] On Chaucer's "emphasis on ancient authority and silence or obfuscation" in relation to his true sources, and the precedents for such a practice that he might have found in another writer whose own influence he signally fails to acknowledge (in this case Giovanni Boccaccio), see B. A. Windeatt, *Oxford Guides to Chaucer: "Troilus and Criseyde"* (1992; repr., Oxford: Oxford University Press, 1995), 39–40.

guide. It would have provided him with a convenient and engagingly presented digest of themes and motifs gathered from a wide range of different sources, which probably did much more to define his intellectual horizons than he would have liked to admit. At the same time, it could be argued that Chaucer's greatest debt to Holcot lies not so much in his adoption of any particular themes or motifs, as in what he learned from him about how to exploit them for literary effect: that is, in Holcot's demonstration of the very possibilities implicit in learned eclecticism as a kind of literary practice. What Holcot showed Chaucer, in particular, was how it might be possible to generate intellectual energy and a sense of abundance from the inventive juxtaposition of distinctly different kinds of authority. For Holcot, demonstrative eclecticism was a means of attracting and keeping the attention of his readers, and also of showing those readers (most of them, implicitly, clerks) how they too might attract and maintain the attention of their own congregations when they came to write sermons or lectures in their turn: but it also seems to be something of an end in itself, a challenge to his ingenuity and intellectual flamboyance at least as much as it was a means of exhibiting the breadth of his reading. It is perhaps in a very similar spirit that Chaucer incorporates his own displays of demonstrative, *compilator-ish* bookishness into his poetry—as, for example, here in the Eagle's speech in *The House of Fame*, but also recurrently throughout his work.[113] Thus, although it is possible, and indeed likely, that Chaucer quarried Holcot's Wisdom-commentary directly for some of the details of the Eagle's speech, what is perhaps most significant here is what he learned from Holcot in terms of literary technique. It may well have been Holcot in particular who encouraged Chaucer to imagine the Eagle precisely in the way he did: as a figure embodying in its very conception a clash between two very different types of authority, the classical/mythological

---

[113] Cf. Minnis, *Medieval Theory of Authorship*, 191:

Of Chaucer's debt to several of the great medieval compilations there can be no doubt. . . . My point is a different one, namely, that Chaucer was indebted to the compilers not only for their source-material and technical information but also for a literary role and a literary form. Chaucer seems to have exploited the compilers' typical justification of their characteristic role as writers, and to have shared, to some extent, the compilers' sense of *ordinatio partium*.

See also Ralph Hanna III, "*Compilatio* and the Wife of Bath: Latin Backgrounds, Ricardian Texts," in *Pursuing History: Middle English Manuscripts and Their Texts* (Stanford: Stanford University Press, 1996), 247–57.

and the scientific—the "fabulosum" and the "naturale." Holcot is not just a source for Chaucer's acoustics, in other words, but also, and perhaps more importantly, a model for the cultivated incongruity of making Jupiter's Eagle into an expert on physics in the first place. From this perspective, the Eagle's speech is an illustration not so much of Chaucer's Aristotelianism, as of his Holcotianism.

Appendix: Holcot's Use of Grosseteste[114]

1. Holcot, Lection 100[115]

Omnibus enim mobilibus mobilior est sapientia. Attingit autem ubique propter mundiciam suam. Vapor enim est virtutis dei, et emanatio quedam est claritatatis[116] *omnipotentis dei sincera, et ideo nihil inquinatum in illam incurrit.* [Sap 24:24–25] . . . Sicut[117] enim deducit magister Alexander cognomento[118] Nequam: In omni creatura corporea quantumcumque sit modica, potest[119] ratio humana videre infinitam Dei potentiam, infinitam sapientiam et bonitatem. Verbi gratia, ut de atomo fiat exemplum. Satis enim approbat humana ratio et acceptat quod mensura potentie agentis sumatur secundum proportionem facti ad illud de quo fit. Tanta enim videtur potentia facilitatis, quantum ipsum factum excedit illud de quo fit. Cum ergo ratio inuenerit atomum esse aliquid ex nihilo et sciat quod, si atomus excederet, nihil [ad][120] infinitum excederet, concludit quod potentia ducens atomum de nihilo ad esse est infinita. Secundo videbit ratio quod[121] cum atomus sit corpus, habet inter se tres lineas intersecantes se ad angulos rectos: in qua sectione posito circino conscribi potest sphera super[122] atomum et videt in sphera infinitos circulos posse describi; immo infinita corpora infra spheram esse imaginabilia, et vltra infra circulos omnes figuras fore inscriptibiles, que tamen sunt infinite,

---

[114] The translations here are mine.
[115] V, fol. 88rb; O, fols. 153vb–154ra.
[116] *claritatis*] *Vulgate*; *claritas* HVO
[117] Sicut] HV; Sed O
[118] cognomento] HV; O *om.*
[119] potest] HV; valoris potest O
[120] ad] HV *om.*; in O
[121] quod] VO; H *om.*
[122] super] HV; infra O

super quas infinite possunt erigi demonstrationes, tam de magnitudinibus, quam de numeris. Ergo videbit ratio humana in atomo vel in flore
infinitam scientiam objectiue descriptam. Infinitam vero scientiam non
potest descripsisse agens quodcumque nisi sapientie infinite. Ergo
humana ratio, si est bona, videbit et[123] inveniet in vno atomo infinitam
sapientiam Conditoris.

[*For wisdom is more active than all active things: and reacheth everywhere by
reason of her purity. For she is a vapor of the power of God, and a certain pure
emanation of the glory of the almighty God: and therefore no defiled thing cometh
into her.* . . . Indeed, this was the reasoning of Master Alexander
Nequam: that in every created body, no matter how small, human reason can perceive the infinite power of God, his infinite wisdom and
goodness. This is illustrated, for example, by the atom. Human reason
readily sees and accepts that the productive power of anything can be
measured as an amount equivalent to the proportion of {the value
of} what is produced to {the value of} what it is produced with. The
extent to which {the value of} the actual product exceeds {the value
of} what it is produced with is an index of the agent's effective power.
Therefore, since it is reasonable to assume that an atom is something
{produced} from nothing, and that, if the atom exceeds {what it is
produced with}, then it exceeds nothing to an infinite extent, so the
conclusion must be that the power required to call into being {even}
an atom out of nothing is infinite. Second, reason will see that since an
atom has a body, it must have within itself three intersecting lines at
right angles {i.e., it is three-dimensional}. With the compasses placed
at this point, a sphere can be drawn around this atom, and {reason}
sees that within the sphere an infinite number of circles can be drawn;
indeed an infinite number of bodies are imaginable within the sphere,
and moreover, within these circles every shape drawable can be placed
(but the number of these is infinite); and on this might be rested an
infinite number of proofs, in relation both to magnitudes and to numbers. Thus human reason will see even in a flower or an atom the infinity
of knowledge objectively depicted. Indeed, the infinity of knowledge
could not be described by any agent, except that of infinite wisdom.

---

[123] videbit et] **HV**; **O** *om.*

Therefore, human reason (as long as it is good) will see and discover in even a single atom the infinite wisdom of the Creator.]

2. Grosseteste, Dictum 60[124]

Videbit enim racio investigans, quod omnis potencia mensuratur per proporcionem facti ad illud ex quo fit. Tanta est enim facientis potencia, quanto factum excedit illud ex quo fit. Omne autem aliquid, quantumcumque vile et parvum, [in][125] infinitum excedit nichilum. Igitur, cum racio invenerit attomum esse aliquid ex nichilo, et decurrerit ab eo ad potenciam facientis, mensuraveritque eam per proporcionem facti ad illud ex quo fit, videbit attomum egressum in esse non a minori quam ab infinita potencia. Sic igitur egressus attomi in esse aliquid ex nichilo similacrum est infinite potencie efficientis.

Item, racio eadem considerans amplius inveniet attomum esse corpus, et in eo tres lineas intersecantes se ad angulos rectos, in qua sectione posito pede circino[126] describi[127] poterit sphera[128] intra attomum, et in sphera infinitos circulos et omnia corpora sphere inscriptibilia, et in circulis omnes figuras inscriptabiles circulis, que sunt infinite. Videbitque racio quod supra quamlibet illarum infinitarum figurarum potest erigi sciencia demonstrativa. Invenietque in attomo descripcionem infinite sciencie, non solum de magnitudinibus, sed eciam de numeris. Cum igitur invenerit racio attomum factum ex nichilo ab infinita potencia, videritque in attomo descripcionem infinite sciencie, perpendet eandem infinitam potenciam descripsisse in attomo a se facto infinitam scienciam. Sed non posset infinitam scienciam describere nisi per infinitam sapienciam. Videbit ergo infinitam potenciam fecisse attomum per infinitam sapienciam.

[Inquiring reason will see that power can be measured as a proportion of the {value of the work} done to the means by which it is done. For the power of any agent equals the extent to which what is done exceeds

---

[124] The text (henceforth **eG**) is taken from the *Electronic Grosseteste* (cited above, note 19), which is in turn based on Oxford, Bodleian Library, MS Bodley 798, fol. 47rb–vb.

[125] in] **eG** *om.* The Hagenau text of the Wisdom-commentary seems to share the same error at this point as the copy of the *Dictum* that **eG** uses as its base-witness.

[126] circino] circum **eG**. In this sentence, Holcot's version of this passage produces a better text than the one printed in **eG**.

[127] describi] describere **eG**

[128] sphera] spheram **eG**

that by which it is done. Every single thing, however, no matter how wretched and small, exceeds nothing to any infinite extent. Therefore when reason discovers an atom to be something {created} out of nothing, and it proceeds from this to the power of its producer, and, measuring it as a proportion of what is done to the means by which it is done, it will see that an atom could only emerge into being as a result of a power that is nothing less than infinite. Thus the emergence of an atom into being something out of nothing is a model of the infinite power of its producer.

Likewise, consideration by reason will discover that an atom is a body, and that within it there are three lines intersecting at right angles. With the foot of the compasses placed at this point, a sphere can be drawn within the atom, and inside the sphere an infinite number of circles and all the bodies of the sphere that can be drawn, and in the circles every shape that can be drawn in circles, and the number of these is infinite. Reason will see that any one of these innumerable shapes will support a demonstrable {understanding of} knowledge. And it will discover in the atom a description of infinite knowledge, as regards not just magnitudes, but also numbers. Since therefore reason will have found that {even} an atom made out of nothing requires infinite power, and sees in an atom a description of infinite knowledge, it might consider the very description of that same infinite knowledge by means of an atom as itself amounting to infinite knowledge. But infinite knowledge could not be described except by infinite wisdom. Reason will therefore see that the atom has been created by infinite power {only} by means of infinite wisdom.}

Loving Confession in the *Confessio Amantis*

Stephanie L. Batkie
Sewanee: The University of the South

Abstract

Gower's approach to the sin of forgetfulness as a form of Sloth in Book IV of the *Confessio Amantis* uses memory and desire to reveal a chiastic structure between the poem's discourses of love and confession. The subject in confession creates narratives that revise memories in order to enter into a confessional history that stretches from the past to the future; the subject in love creates exemplary narratives that remain in the present. For both, the problem of remembrance and representation becomes one of narrative agency—the ability to use one's will as a mechanism for subject-formation. As such, the narrative structures of both discourses echo one another, but they do not map onto a teleological or dialectical relationship (as much as we might like them to do so). In this, our desire as critics to reach a resolution between love and confession reflects Amans's own desire for success in love through confessional practice. The poem and the poet resist this desire and instead find in the crossing of the two discourses a source of narrative production and pleasure.

Keywords

Confessio Amantis, Gower, confession, amorous discourse, memory, forgetting, chiasmus, subjectivity, agency, narrative, history, Moses and Tharbis, Phyllis and Demophon

THERE ARE TWO THREADS running throughout the *Confessio Amantis*: there is confession, and there is love. Gower's Amans begins the poem as a passive (if not pacified) victim, struck with love's dart, and ends as an active producer of narratives in which he can no longer participate. At the same time he is, of course, also a confessant, responding to narratives in a penitential register and willfully transforming himself into a legible, confessional subject. The challenge for readers who approach the poem with an eye to taking its use of confessional discourse seriously is to determine the way in which one of these threads might speak to another. Inevitably, frustration emerges when we find that whatever relationship one might draw out of an exemplum, or one moment of conversation between Amans and Genius, or one moment of social critique from the Prologue, vanishes almost as quickly as it appears: by the next episode it will have shifted, if not have seemed to disappear entirely—as if it were never there.[1]

What I would like to propose in this argument is also twofold: first, I argue that we ought to see the relationship between the discourse of love and the discourse of confession not as that of one reflecting or commenting on the other, or one offering a training of the subject with an eye to the latter, or both speaking in meaningful ways to the political and ethical contexts of Gower's larger poetic project—although these arguments have certainly been made, and have been made well. Rather, I would like to offer an alternative perspective on the nature of how these discourses interact in the text, with the aim of proposing that our critical desire for harmonious complement (mirrored conveniently enough in Gower's own aspirations for his poem) has shaped our approach to the relationship among confession, desire, and the erotic in ways that inevitably cannot and should not hold across the span of the text. The productive space that opens between confession and love, however, offers perspective on how the subject of love is bounded by confessional discourse and amorous exemplum in Gower's text. Second, I would propose that much of our critical difficulty with the form of confession in the poem, particularly as it relates to erotic love, stems from our misreading of how confession structures subjectivity and

---

[1] On the whole, the dissatisfaction with Gower's choice of confessional discourse for the frame-narrative of the *Confessio Amantis* is well documented. For example, Katherine R. Chandler writes "the confession provides more the skeleton than the focus of *Confessio Amantis*; it does not constitute the majority of the poem," agreeing with James Murphy's reading of the tales as "loosely tied together through the device of a lover confessing to Genius, a priest of Venus." Karma Lochrie takes criticism of the frame device further, stating that "the very application of the penitential format to love renders the format itself absurd, even meaningless, as Genius warps it to fit everything from the petty infractions to the grand tragedies of love and in the process does violence to its stories." Katherine Chandler, "Memory and Unity in Gower's *Confessio Amantis*," *PQ* 71, no. 1 (1992): 15–30 (18); James Murphy, "John Gower's *Confessio Amantis* and the First Discussion of Rhetoric in the English Language," *PQ* 41 (1962): 401–11 (402); Karma Lochrie, *Covert Operations: The Medieval Uses of Secrecy* (Philadelphia: University of Pennsylvania Press, 1999), 221. See also C. S. Lewis, *The Allegory of Love: A Study in Medieval Tradition* (New York: Oxford University Press, 1936), 199–200.

desire. Rather than working through what Katherine Little calls the "violent and insistent" nature of hegemonic power over the narrative subject often associated with Foucault's imagining of medieval confessional practices, I argue that Gower's text hinges on how memory in narrative works to construct not confessional subjectivity, but confessional history.[2]

To begin with this second point, we cannot understand confession in the *Confessio* without understanding its relationship to memory and to forgetting. As a subspecies of Sloth, forgetfulness figures largely in medieval taxonomies of the sins and in discussions of confessional praxis. Indeed, forgetfulness and memory form the poles by which successful confession is measured, and explanations of confession in handbooks and sermons are often located in explanations of *accidia*. Contrition, confession, and penance, for example, make up the majority of the treatment of Sloth in the fourteenth-century preaching handbook the *Fasciculus morum*, and the text describes confession (at great length) as the primary spiritual defense against idleness.[3] Likewise, in *The Book of Vices and Virtues*, confession is both holy activity and contemplative labor, and it depends on the diligence of the will as pertains to memory: "After, he þat tarieþ to longe to schryue hyn forȝeteþ ofte his synnes. So vnneþes falleþ it þat he may be wel y-schryuve, for he forȝeteþ many of his synnes whiche he may neuere biþenke hym of, and so schal he neuere repente hym ne neuere be schryue þer-of, and þus it is wel gret perele."[4] Nearly every confessional manual emphasizes the necessity of full and complete confession in similar fashion, explicitly warning about the dangers of forgetfulness.[5] Gower, true to form, follows suit in his discussion

[2] Katherine C. Little, *Confession and Resistance: Defining the Self in Late Medieval England* (Notre Dame: University of Notre Dame, 2006), 11.

[3] *Fasciculus morum: A Fourteenth-Century Preacher's Handbook*, trans. Siegfried Wenzel (University Park: Pennsylvania State University Press, 1989), 429–555.

[4] *The Book of Vices and Virtues: A Fourteenth Century English Translation of the 'Somme le roi' of Lorens d'Orléans*, ed. W. Nelson Francis, EETS o.s. 217 (London: Oxford Unversity Press, 1942), 176.5.

[5] The stipulations for completeness and contrition as relates to confessional speech are, of course, well known. Consider the *Peniteas cito peccator* of William of Montibus: "Omnia peccata plangat contricio uera / Scrutans etates, sensus, loca, tempora, membra. / Vera sit, integra sit, et sit confessio uera, / Sit cita, firma, frequens, humilis, spontanea, nuda, / Propria, discreta, lacrimosa, morose, fidelis" (True contrition strikes at all sins, searching ages, feelings, places, times, and areas. It must be true, it must be whole, and it must be true confession; it must be quick, steady, full, humble, spontaneous, bare, individual, discreet, tearful, careful, and faithful). Greti Dinkova-Bruun, "Notes on Poetic Composition in the Theological Schools circa 1200 and the Latin Poetic Anthology from MS Harley 956: A Critical Edition," *Sacris erudiri* 43 (2004):

of forgetfulness in Book IV of the *Confessio*, and he does the same in his discussion of penance and confession in the *Mirour de l'omme*. Gower's treatise on confessional practice in his Anglo-Norman text comes as part of his discussion of knowledge—the virtue that serves as the counterpoint to the sin of negligence, a subspecies of Sloth.[6] Furthermore, in both the *Confessio* and the *Mirour* not only is confession tied to memory and Sloth in terms of Gower's explanation of the practice, but the formal positioning of the sin of Sloth within the larger arrangement of the text likewise argues for the critical relationship between this particular sin and the confessional structure. The *Mirour*, spanning approximately 30,000 lines, locates the discussion of negligence, knowledge, and confession in almost the very center of the poem (lines 14803ff.). Similarly, in the *Confessio* Sloth appears as the fourth of seven sins and as the fourth of nine books of the *Confessio* (taking the Prologue as its own entity), similarly situated, thereby, at the formal mid-point of the text. Forgetfulness in the *Confessio*, moreover, appears third out of the eight forms of Sloth, making it more or less centrally located in the discussion of this central sin.[7] In this way, if attention to memory and forgetting form the doctrinal center to the treatment of confession in a text such as the *Mirour*, bolstered as it is by contemporary sources, memory and forgetting likewise form the poetic center of the *Confessio*.

It is within this poetic mid-point that I propose to locate the absent center in the relationship between confession and love. Confessional narrative in the *Confessio* is, as we shall see, dependent upon a particular form of memory that looks not to expunge the past, but rather to revise its relationship with the present; absolution is not the same as erasure, and the confessing voice does not obliterate the past self through the process of narrating sin. If we are to consider the relationship between

---

299–391 (338–39). We see much the same in the confessional writings of Robert Grosseteste, Alain de Lille, Robert Mannyng of Brunne, Thomas Aquinas, etc., as well as in the *Confessio*.

⁶For this passage, see lines 14797–15096. All translated passages from the *Mirour* are taken from John Gower, *Mirour de l'omme (The Mirror for Mankind)*, trans. William Burton Wilson (East Lansing: Colleagues Press, 1992). Gower's original Anglo-Norman appears as in "The French Works," in *The Complete Works of John Gower*, ed. G. C. Macaulay, 4 vols. (Oxford: Clarendon Press, 1899–1902), Vol. 4.

⁷Gower distinguishes in the *Confessio* between forgetfulness and negligence, whereas in the *Mirour de l'omme* they appear together as forms of negligence. As in the *Confessio*, the order of sins in the *Mirour* appears as (1) Pride, (2) Envy, (3) Anger, (4) Sloth, (5) Avarice, (6) Gluttony, and (7) Lechery, once again situating negligence and forgetting at the center of the poetic arrangement as the final sub-sins of Sloth. For a helpful chart of the organization of the sins and their corresponding virtues in the *Mirour*, see Wilson's introduction to the *Mirour*, xx–xxi.

love and confession, then Gower's abundant interest in the relationship between confession and memory provides an opportunity to consider how narration, agency, and poetic making circulate in both discourses— not necessarily uniformly, but certainly productively. Peter Nicholson has described Gower's choice of joining the trials of a lover with the confessional discourse as a "genuine exploration" of the possibilities of the confessional frame, and the temptation to equate the one with the other, or to join them as two forms of ethical systems that speak to one another, or to read in amorous love a trace of divine love that will unify the world, is a strong one.[8] Understanding the dangers of a specific sin such as negligence or forgetfulness in terms of devotion certainly comments on the dangers of negligence in love, and we might also say that virtuous behavior in love plays into a habitus of attention that will shore up the lover against future sins, but to equate the one with the other is to flatten out the ways in which both discourses function in the poem and to diminish the narrative tension that Gower finds productive. The ambiguous space that opens between love and confession is not something to explain away but rather (borrowing Nicholson's term) something to explore as the poem unfolds.

We see a model of this ambiguous but proximate pairing in the headnote Gower offers for the sin of forgetfulness. In the passage, the verse is equally divided between the dangers of forgetfulness in each context, and the two discourses, moderated here by the sin to which they both are subject, share a formally chiastic relationship to one another:

> Mentibus oblitus alienis labitur ille,
> Quem probat accidia non meminisse sui.
> Sic amor incautus, qui non memoratur ad horas,
> Perdit et offendit, quod cuperare nequit.

[The forgetful one is lost from others' minds, whom sloth approves to have not been mindful of himself. Thus, incautious love, who is not mindful of the hours, loses and offends what cannot be seized.]

(*Confessio Amantis*, III.3)[9]

---

[8] Nicholson finds that Gower presents the subject of love as a force that binds the world together in God, as well as one that works on the lover as does Fortune's wheel: "blind, unpredictable, yet overpowering." Peter Nicholson, "The 'Confession' in Gower's *Confessio Amantis*," *Studia neophilologica* 58, no. 2 (1986): 193–204 (193).

[9] All passages from the *Confessio* are taken from John Gower, *Confessio Amantis*, ed. Russell A. Peck, 3 vols. (Kalamazoo: Medieval Institute Publications, 2003). I have made use of Andrew Galloway's translations of Gower's Latin from this edition elsewhere in this article, but in the instance of these four lines I offer my own translation to emphasize some of the poetic aspects of the quatrain.

Admittedly clumsy in translation, the Latin of the passage characterizes forgetfulness as a sin of passivity, of failing to be actively mindful, and the description is built around both isocolonic and chiastic modes. On the one hand, the verse creates an isocolon, or a parallel pattern, that moves from subject-verb to subject-verb in the "oblitus"–"labitur" and "amor"–"Perdit" pairing, but on the other, it includes an overlaid chiastic structure in the way the verbs of loss and memory are arranged; the verbs progress from loss to memory and from memory to loss: "labitur" to "meminisse" and "memoratur" to "Perdit." Building off this, Gower crosses a second set of poetic threads in the way in which allegorized concepts in the passage work on or through the sinner. Here, the text moves from act to personification, and from personification to act: first from "probat" to "accidia" and then from "amor" to "Perdit et offendit." We might also note that these chiastic patterns are further supported by the neatly divided structure of the verse, in which problems of forgetfulness as they relate to sin occupy the first two lines of the quatrain, and the problems of forgetfulness in love make up the subsequent pair. Following this poetic form, the comparison between love and confession "announces and projects a signifying difference" that "enables new meanings to emerge."[10]

In part, this is due to poetic arrangement, but it is also dependent upon the ambiguous nature of the ligature between confession and love, which comes in Gower's choice of "Sic" as the hinge for his chiastic structure. As the transition between the first two confessional lines and the second two amorous lines, "Sic" rather leaves something to be desired in terms of specificity. For example, we might take "Sic" to mean "thus," or "in this way," opening an analogous relationship between love and confession, or as a "yes—and," which allows for love to follow confession, but does not necessarily attribute any logical insistence to order per se, or we might read it as closer to "to such a degree," which offers the option of an analogy of urgency. Gower uses this structure to construct multiple openings and points of contact between the two discourses, allowing "Sic" to work as a hinge that invites qualities such as echo, balance, and contrast to cross over into one pair of lines from the other, but that also resists any sense of easy equivalence.

---

[10] William E. Engel, writing of chiasmus as a poetic form in *Chiastic Designs in English Literature from Sidney to Shakespeare* (Farnham: Ashgate, 2009), 4. Engel in this text also equates chiasmus with early modern mnemonic culture, albeit in a different way than I do here for the medieval.

Chiastic connections, be they poetic or more general figures of thought, depend upon arrangement to produce proximity between concepts, but as soon as they seem to promise what Robert Hariman terms "a stable array" between the terms they bring together, they defer the possibility of resolution as originating within their structure. Hariman notes that chiasmus

sets up and shows a pattern that can only be taken as a whole, which proves to be a process of continual movement secured only in the illusory permanence of the gaze. The chiasmus moves one towards a center that proves to be empty, a space only for crossing. As one thinks with chiasmus, the doubled modality of the term offers stability only to oscillate and then to spin off something beyond the binary, something asymmetrical.[11]

In Gower's poetics, chiasmus thus becomes a particularly valuable mode for seeking the *aporia* between the discourse of love and the discourse of confession, both of which move through these Latin lines. In defining their proximate relationship through poetics rather than exposition, Gower permits the two threads to circulate around and through one another but not to solidify or stabilize. As such, I argue that the quatrain holds a metonymic relationship to the larger circulation of love and confession throughout the poem, and that the chiastic pattern generates a sense of constant oscillation between the ways sin works in each context, drawing them together even as it maintains their distinct distance.

The promise and the frustration of the chiastic form is in its invitation to continually deferred comparison; we want to follow our desire to read through these structures in order to understand the similarities and the differences between the two threads running through them. This temptation is productive inasmuch as it allows brief moments of contact between two entities, but it cannot ever be completely satisfied by clear and static definitions of the relationship such moments form. It is in these chiastic moments of tension and contact that the work of the poem happens, and where Gower allows terms shared between the two discourses to circulate in productive ways. For example, in Gower's note on forgetfulness, the repetition of verbs of memory and the subject-verb,

---

[11] Robert Hariman, "What Is a Chiasmus? Or, Why the Abyss Stares Back," in *Chiasmus and Culture*, ed. Anthony Paul and Boris Wiseman (New York: Berghahn, 2014), 45–68 (51).

subject-verb isocolon open the comparison, with "meminisse" in the second line anticipating "memoratur" directly below it in the third. The shift here from past to present and from active to passive is an interesting one, but more telling is the shift in what these verb forms act on or through. In the first two lines, when the sinful person is forgetful, what he forgets is "sui," or himself. This is an essential claim for Gower's understanding of forgetfulness as a sin that eliminates the possibility of virtue by disrupting the habitus of prudence, which in turn depends upon reason and memory.[12] Whereas the fault of a sin such as cowardice, for example, lies in a problematic emotional state (that of fear rather than love), forgetfulness is the absence of reason rather than the absence of emotion; it is the failure to understand appropriate action in the world, and thereby it removes the forgetful person from the world. But if we cross over the "Sic" juncture to the second pair of lines, we find a very different problem: the forgetful lover forgets not himself but "the hours" or "the time" ("horas"). The danger of forgetting in love is not that the lover will fail to remember himself, but that he will fail to remember the beloved, and in so doing will lose her love through negligence and Sloth. Forgetting to act for the beloved is strikingly distinct from forgetting as an erasure of subjectivity; if the one depends upon the ability to understand virtue, the other depends upon the ability to behave virtuously.

In a similar way, the grammatical subject in both sets of lines is a forgetful one, but Gower syntactically differentiates the forgetful lover from the forgetful sinner, moving from the "oblitus" (the forgetful one) at the beginning of the first line to "amor incautus" (incautious love) at the beginning of the third. The adjectival form of *oblitus* is cleverly offered here as a substantive, allowing the description of being forgetful

[12] In the Latin marginal note to this section of the poem, Gower argues that forgetfulness of the past forecloses other virtues in the future: "Hic tractat Confessor de vicio Obliuionis, quam mater eius Accidia ad omnes virtutum memorias necnon et in amoris causa immemorem constituit" ["Here the Confessor treats about the vice of Forgetfulness, whose mother, Sloth, makes her forgetful of every memory of virtue even in the cause of love"] (IV.522ff. and note). For Aquinas's definition of habitus as the quality of will that guides the appetitive power, see *Summa theologiae*, I–II, q. 50 art. 5, ad. 1. For a much more complete argument about the power of habitus, see the first chapter of Katherine Breen, *Imagining an English Reading Public: 1150–1400* (Cambridge: Cambridge University Press, 2010). On prudence as it relates to memory, see Mary Carruthers, *The Book of Memory: A Study of Memory in Medieval Culture* (Cambridge: Cambridge University Press, 2008), 66. All references to the *Summa* are taken from Thomas Aquinas, *Summa theologica*, trans. Fathers of the English Dominican Province, 5 vols. (Westminster, Md.: Christian Classics, 1981).

literally to obliterate the absent nominative subject; the corresponding "incautious love" also creates distance between the lover and his description of forgetfulness, but in this case the line opts for allegorization and personified embodiment rather than grammatical erasure. Gower thus generates the promise of a relationship among forgetting, absence, and presence that echoes across the central "Sic," but the mechanics of any such relationship recalibrate as we move from one discourse to the other. In the same way, we find a similar distinction between absence and presence in the first and last lines. In the opening line, the "oblitus" slips from the "Mentibus . . . alienis," the "minds of others," and Gower warns that the danger of *accidia* is not just forgetting—it is being forgotten. However, Gower also syntactically encloses the forgetful one within the "Mentibus . . . alienis" in the line as "Mentibus oblitus alienis," ironically presenting what is supposedly being lost within the description of what is forgetting the forgotten. In addition to being a particularly deft bit of poetic arrangement, this sense of present absence echoes again across the "Sic"-hinge in the problematic verb "cuperare" in the last line of the verse. Translators have rendered this term as "seized" or "gained," taking it as a back-formation from *recuperare*, "to restore" or "to regain," both of which indicate that any potential conquest of the beloved has been lost through sin.[13] Seemingly unique to Gower, "cuperare" also cunningly echoes the more familiar *cupere*, "to desire": a more common and comfortable word choice for amorous discourse. (In fact, the echo of *cupere* is the only hint of emotion we are given in this passage.) In this way, just as the "oblitus" is present and then absent in the first two lines, so too are the grammatical and emotional traces of desire when love and forgetfulness become analogous to one another. Because imprudent love loses its sense of time through the loss of memory, the ability to desire and seize the beloved and to restore equilibrium to the self becomes impossible. As a piece of wordplay, "cuperare" thus gathers the idea of restoration, the seizing and possessing of an object, and the desire held for the object together, placing all of these in open conversation with knowledge and memory from the

---

[13] See Galloway's translation given in Peck's edition, and that in John Gower, *The Latin Verses in the "Confessio Amantis": An Annotated Translation*, trans. Siân Echard, Claire Fanger, and A. G. Rigg, Vol. 7, Medieval Texts and Studies 7 (East Lansing: Colleagues Press, 1991). The same definition of "seize" is given, with Gower's line as the only example, in the *Dictionary of Medieval Latin from British Sources*, ed. R. E. Latham and D. R. Howlett (London: Oxford University Press for The British Academy, 1975).

preceding pair of lines. In this way, the verse uses the chiastic relationship between love and confession, as enacted by poetic structure, to draw together confession and love through their divergent rehearsals of the sin. The one discourse is not defined by the other, but they both momentarily share terms across the space of the text.

Further attention to this quatrain reveals additional elements that chiastically trace the poetic and structural differences between love and sin, such as the way in which *accidia* as an external force is absent in the lines about forgetfulness in love, casting the neglectful lover as the sole cause of his own forgetfulness, whereas the sinner encounters a more concrete connection to the almost-allegorized vice. And there is the way in which we move from an easy, effortless erasure in "labitur" ("to slip," "to pass away") as the consequence of sin in the first line to the more destructive and direct "Perdit" ("to destroy," "to waste," "to lose") when it comes to forgetful love. All of these poetic elements, however, open rather than answer questions about the relationship between sin and sins of love, and all reflect back and forth across the "Sic"-hinge that connects them. In so doing they resolutely defer any easy mapping about agency or action that might stem from a result of an encounter with *accidia*. The terms in question are all in play, but they shift and resound along diffuse rather than schematic lines.

If we take this same view of the larger confessional and erotic structures of the *Confessio*, with an eye to finding the moments in which the two discourses speak to one another, much the same chiastic relationship develops. Within the sin of forgetfulness, fundamental as it is to Gower's understanding of confession as it relates to agency and the will, we are also invited to consider how agency, the will, and memory work for Amans's amorous history. Furthermore, we are asked to consider how the construction of narrated (and narrative memory) becomes integral to how Gower locates not just the desire for the beloved, but also the desire for agency in the text. To cast agency as part of Amans's desire shows us how our understanding of the amorous might play off of the confessional when it comes to exemplary narrative, but also the ways in which the two discourses, even as they cross one another, move off in formally and ethically different directions.

Memory and Confessional History

We have long been accustomed to reading confession as a process of subject-formation that, in critical approaches, is most often predicated on a Foucauldian system of discipline and power. If we follow Foucault's reading of confessional practice in his later work, the identity of the sinner enters back into the devotional community through the process of articulating past sin, in what Foucault memorably terms a "renunciation of the self." As such, it becomes impossible to disclose oneself in the hierarchical construct of confession without simultaneously destroying the autonomous will that caused the sin in the first place: "Here, obedience is complete control of behavior by the master, not a final autonomous state. It is a sacrifice of the self, of the subject's own will."[14] To seek absolution in medieval confession for Foucault, the speaker must submit to power and, in so doing, forget himself. Foucault's approach to subjectivity and confession is a remarkably durable one in critical contexts, especially inasmuch as it plays into the idea of absolution as a form of erasure. Indeed, the act of absolution, the act of forgiveness, would seem, as Paul Ricoeur reminds us, "to constitute the final stage in the process of forgetting," as it renders the act/s committed in the past no longer part of the confessing subject's present person.[15] Furthermore, as Paul Stegner argues, "spiritual transformation cannot occur without the appropriate remembering of sin, but the process can only be completed through the productive forgetting of the desire to sin."[16] In this model, the subject depends upon erasure and forgetting. Attention to the way in which memory, will, and narrative agency function in Gower provides, on the other hand, an alternative. Rather than the creation of the subject, I propose that in Gower we find that the exercise of narrative produces not the confessional subject, but confessional history. Gower's form of confession is both generative and historical; furthermore, it seeks not just to connect the confessant to his own past, but also demands that he look forward into the eschatological future.

[14] Michel Foucault, "Technologies of the Self," in *Ethics: Subjectivity and Truth*, ed. Paul Rabinow (New York: New Press, 1997), 223–52 (246). For more on the "will of the master" in confession, see Michel Foucault, *The History of Sexuality: An Introduction*, trans. Robert Hurley (New York: Vintage Books, 1978), 63–64.

[15] Paul Ricoeur, *Memory, History, Forgetting*, trans. Kathleen Blamey and David Pellauer (Chicago: University of Chicago Press, 2004), 412. Mary Flowers Braswell agrees, and argues that once absolution has been granted, any interest the penitential character might have offered is now gone: "The reformed penitent is never an individual, but a type. His confession has stripped him of those particular sins which have made him unique, and he has espoused the cardinal virtue of humility. His is a passive good; the goal of the confessional has been met, and we find him interesting not for his future activities but for his past." Mary Flowers Braswell, *The Medieval Sinner: Characterization and Confession in the Literature of the English Middle Ages* (East Brunswick: Associated University Presses, 1983), 13.

[16] Paul D. Stegner, " 'Foryet it thou, and so wol I': Absolving Memory in *Confessio Amantis*," *SP* 108, no. 4 (2011): 488–507 (489).

The mechanism creating this history is the temporal, emotional shift at the center of the confessional process: the movement from appetite, to guilt, to contrition. The causes of sin in Aquinas are the will (in completing the sinful act), the reason (in failing to exercise due rule), and the appetite (as inclining to sin).[17] Desire and appetite move the will through distraction or through the misunderstood good of the object, thereby leading to the sinful action the confessant recalls for the confessor.[18] For Aquinas, "it is impossible that God pardon a man for an offense, without his will being changed."[19] The movement from the appetite that disorders reason and leads to sin is, therefore, in confessional practice exchanged for the desire to be reunited with God through penance and absolution. This revision from desire-to-sin to desire-for-God stands at the heart of how medieval confession understands the effect of contrition in terms of the will, and how in confessional discourse the effects of contrition become encoded in the act of narration.[20]

The move to contrition in confession is thus grounded in the temporal, emotional revision of the recalled sin. No longer evidence of a disordered (and disordering) appetite, the actions remembered must now be narrated through the lens of an admission of guilt, through sorrow, and through a contrite heart.[21] Augustine famously "insists" on the flexibility of emotional recall when it comes to describing past events: memories in the *Confessions* become "modified images" that are necessarily changed through the act of remembering them.[22] Augustine describes

---

[17] See Aquinas, *Summa theologiae*, I–II, q. 75 art. 3, co.

[18] Ibid., I–II, q. 77 art. 1, co.

[19] Ibid., III, q. 86 art. 2, co.

[20] For Aquinas's definition of contrition as it relates to the will, and the use of the will in the destruction of sin, see ibid., III, q. 1 art. 2, co.

[21] NB this is what makes confessional recall different from the definitions of memory from Aristotle and other classical authors. Carruthers explains that accurate memories should access the contextual chains surrounding the recalled event, including the emotions experienced: "recollection was understood to be a re-enactment of experience, which involves cogitation and judgment, imagination, and emotion. Averroes and Aristotle both insist on this: 'the one who recollects will experience the same pleasure or pain in this situation which he would experience were the thing existing in actuality.'" Carruthers, *The Book of Memory*, 60. In the passage, she cites Averroes, *Epitome of "Parva naturalia,"* trans. Harry Blumberg (Cambridge, Mass.: Medieval Academy of America, 1961), II.i, page 30.

[22] "[I]n my mind alone I experienced being happy, and the knowledge of it stuck fast in my memory, so that I am able to remember it, sometimes with contempt and at other times with longing for the various things which I recall having enjoyed. I was formerly flooded with a kind of joy in depraved actions which I now recollect with

the ability to recall different aspects of a memory, expanding some and minimizing others, depending on the reason the memory is sought out. In the same way, emotions surrounding memory are likewise mutable inasmuch as one might remember with distaste a past joy, or take delight in events that previously caused grief. Emotions are part of memory, but in confession, they are distinct from the initial experience of the action.[23]

As such, the narrative revision that emerges through the medieval confessional process does not encourage forgetfulness, or any kind of "technical error" in the recall function. The remembered and subsequently recounted events are a deliberate re-formation of the past that reflect the discursive requirements of the confessional form: actions of the disordered will are historicized through sorrow and contrition rather than through an unruly appetite. Thus, the past in confession cannot be a static substance, dragged without alteration into the present through a perfect act of recollection. In order for memories to be useful, they must be read through the will of the present and, indeed, through the anticipation of the future. In this way, confession creates a history for the subject that returns him to the Christian timeline, suspending him between a revised past, and future, prudent action.

Gower's understanding of confessional memory follows this model with remarkable precision. As he explains in the *Mirour de l'omme*, the text in which he theorizes confession most completely, knowledge and

---

loathing and disgust." Augustine of Hippo, *The Confessions*, trans. Maria Boulding (New York: New City Press, 2001), 258.

[23] In much the same way, Ricoeur notes the importance in confession of separating the act from the actor; this is the only way in which forgiveness is possible: "Everything, finally, hangs on the possibility of separating the agent from the action. This unbinding would mark the inscription, in the field of the horizontal disparity between power and act, of the vertical disparity between the great height of forgiveness and the abyss of guilt"; *Memory, History, Forgetting*, 490. He uses here Derrida's earlier discussion of the *pardon conditionelle*: through the admission of guilt, which internalizes the sinful act in the person of the speaker, he who is forgiven is "no longer through and through the guilty party but already an other, *and better than* the guilty person. To this extent, and on this condition, it is no longer the guilty person as such whom one forgives"; Jacques Derrida, "Le siècle et le pardon," *Le monde des débats* (December 1999) (emphasis mine). In the same way, Larry Scanlon argues that any narrativized acts in confessional discourse "cease to exist as action, and they . . . become entirely superseded by the now sanctified language which describes them"; *Narrative, Authority, and Power: The Medieval Exemplum and the Chaucerian Tradition* (Cambridge: Cambridge University Press, 1994), 78. Carolyn Dinshaw reminds us of how central this idea of separating the act from the actor is in Foucault's notion of sexual identity in the Middle Ages in *Getting Medieval: Sexualities and Communities, Pre- and Postmodern* (Durham, N.C.: Duke University Press, 1999), 200–205.

the application of the will not only give the subject his own history, but also bring him into the historical frame.[24] *Scientia*, the appropriate answer to the sin of negligence in the *Mirour*, is closely connected with both memory and with prudence:

> Celle est de l'alme droit Priour,
> Q'el cloister de sa Conscience
> Le cuer du fine intelligence
> Et le voloir sanz nul errour
> Defent et guart par nuyt et jour.
> Du Reson est remembrançour,
> Que tout remeine en sa presence;
> Du temps passé et recordour,
> Et le present voit tout entour,
> Et le future pourvoit et pense.

[She is the right prior of the soul; day and night in the cloister of her conscience, she guards and defends the heart with complete intelligence and the will without any error. She is the remembrancer of Reason, in whose presence she brings back everything. She is the recorder of the past, the present she sees all around, and the future she foresees and thinks about.]

(*Mirour de l'omme*, 14595–604)

Knowledge's defense against sin rests on her ability, as Reason's memory, to act with multitemporal effect. This is more than memory intruding into the present as a goad to either action or inaction; rather, it is the ability of Knowledge to order responses to events according to a correct and prudent will. Whether she is acting as the "prior of the soul" or as the "remembrancer of reason," Knowledge assumes a supervisory position. Correct understanding leads to correct action, which is only possible through the application of knowledge across time, stretching

---

[24] Gower's French poem relies heavily on the penitential tradition for its organizing principle, and specifically, as R. F. Yeager notes, on Henry of Lancaster's *Le livre des seyntz medicines*. Both works arrange the major sins and their subsidiary vices in a fashion that seems designed to facilitate penitential study: sins of a kind are grouped together, their relationships discussed, and their corresponding virtues enumerated. Similarly, both texts end with extensive, personal prayers invoking the Virgin in "essentially the same voice—that of a sinner blackened beyond all other hope and deprived of all other appeal." R. F. Yeager, "Gower's French Audience: The *Mirour de l'omme*," *ChauR* 41, no. 2 (2006): 111–37 (115).

from the past (memory), to the present (action), and into the future (counsel).

Gower goes on to define the effect of having right knowledge through confessional praxis, and he outlines a progression from tale-telling, to memory, to desire, to the process of revision through self-narration that is familiar from other penitential sources:

> Molt est apris du bonne escole
> Cil q'a sa discipline tire;
> *Bien dist, bien pense et bien desire,*
> *Bien sciet, bien fait, bien se remire,*
> Du fine resoun se rigole,
> Fole ignorance fait despire,
> Bien sciet la meene voie eslire
> Parentre dure chose et mole.

[He who follows her teaching is taught in a very good school. *He speaks well, thinks well, desires well, knows well, does well, looks well about himself,* delights himself in good reason, despises foolish ignorance, and knows well how to choose the middle way between what is hard and what is soft.]

(*Mirour de l'omme*, 14609–16, emphasis mine)[25]

Here we find the "meene voie" that echoes the "middle way" of the Prologue in the *Confessio* alongside the speaking voice of the confessant.[26] Knowledge as pertains to memory and reason facilitates self-narration that, while it looks inward to desire, also turns its gaze outward: "Bien

[25] In the one surviving manuscript of the *Mirour* (Cambridge University Library, Add. MS 3035), part of this passage is underlined and highlighted in the margin with a pen drawing of a flower. The underlining runs from lines 14605 to 14613, and the flower appears at lines 14605–7. Additional underlining is found at lines 14625–28, with a manicule pointing to 14628. Two more marginal flowers appear at 14589–91 and 14749–51. It is worth noting that all of these appear to be later annotations, but are some of the very few that are present in the manuscript, indicating significant readerly interest in this particular section of the poem.

[26] NB whereas in his English work, Gower's poetic voice searches for the middle way between desire and knowledge, the Anglo-Norman subject of the *Mirour* looks for a *vita* partway between the "dure" and the "mole," the hard and the soft, pride and despair. In *Handlyng Synne*, we see the same concern over speech that is liberal but humble, or that treads the path between prideful declamation of sins and despairing silence before the gaze of the confessor: "Holde þe euene ham betwene, / Nat ouer-drede ne ouer-wene" (5163–64); Robert Mannyng, *Handlyng Synne*, ed. Idelle Sullens (Binghamton: Medieval and Renaissance Texts and Studies, 1983). For the fuller description of the relation between pride and humility in confessional speech, see lines 5131–202 of the same.

dist, bien pense et bien desire, / Bien sciet, bien fait, bien se remire."
The trios of speaking–thinking–desiring and knowing–doing–looking
in the passage outline the progression from the isolated subject who
speaks his desires in the moment to the prudent speaker who is able to
"remire" or "revise"/"review" his desires for his past, present, and future
actions. Or, in other words, this process should create a subject with
and within history. The process of speaking (*dire*) memories of sin, and
in altering one's emotional memory of desire (*desire*) through careful
thought (*penser*), leads to knowledge (*scire*), prudent action (*faire*), and a
new vision of one's place with respect to God and the world (*remire*).

In the *Mirour*, Gower's understanding of confession explicitly works
through a process of memory, the application of the will, and the production of narrative: events transpire and are subsequently accessed by
the memory; the remembering subject in turn narrates those events,
using the willful engagement of his agency to produce *historia*; these
narratives then become part of the larger history of salvation. We might
say that the purpose of this process of confession is to make the confessant legible to himself. Through the narration of past sins, a series of
exempla is formed out of memory, which not only permit absolution
but, more importantly for Gower, allow the will to exert prudent control over future action.[27] The confessing subject speaks, he thinks, he
knows, and in so doing becomes part of the larger salvific narrative.[28]

---

[27] In this, I follow J. Allan Mitchell's excellent discussion of the importance of confessional recollection in the *Confessio* as a continual, pragmatic requirement for ethical
action in the future: "the penitential activity of remembrance is based on the ongoing
possibility of imminent reconfigurations of the past, retroactive changes in self-image,
and thus never can it be said that confession is sufficiently completed in this life"; *Ethics
and Exemplary Narrative in Chaucer and Gower* (Cambridge: D. S. Brewer, 2004), 67.
Similarly, Ricoeur finds much the same connection among guilt, action, and temporality
in his description of forgiveness: "Under the sign of forgiveness, the guilty person is
considered capable of something other than his offenses and his faults. He is held to be
restored to his capacity for acting, and action restored to its capacity for continuing. . . .
And, finally, this restored capacity is enlisted by promising as it projects action toward
the future." *Memory, History, Forgetting*, 493.
[28] Hannah Arendt finds that it is both the history of sin and the history of forgiveness
that creates Christian community and Christian time:

Humanity's common descent is its common share in original sin. This sinfulness,
conferred with birth, necessarily attaches to everyone. There is no escape from it. It
is the same in all people. . . . Each individual already belongs to Adam (that is, to
the human race) by generation, not by imitation. The possibility of imitation, and
thereby of freely choosing the grace of God, did not exist until Christ revealed this
grace to all people through his historic sojourn on earth. (Hannah Arendt, *Love and
Saint Augustine*, ed. Joanna Vecchiarelli Scott and Judith Chelius Stark [Chicago:
University of Chicago Press, 1996], 102)

In this way, confessional narratives have two primary valences. First, any legibility gained through the generation of confessional narrative serves to create in the confessant the ability to render his own past as a (negative) exemplum, and to read his own narrative against the abstract definition (or definitions) of a given sin.[29] But second, in willfully creating exempla out of his own memories, and in joining his own understanding of his participation in the greater narrative of human salvation via grace to other, similar confessional narratives, the speaker becomes narratively part of eschatological time. As such, confessional narratives do not simply become a means by which the confessant enters into confessional history, they become the mechanism by which confessional history is created. Jean-Luc Nancy writes of the relationship between sin and history as a fundamentally generative one:

> The original condition is that man is a sinner, thus the sinner is more important than the sin itself; moreover, this is why that which is truly pardoned is the sinner. The sinner, once pardoned, is not, of course, wiped clean—one does not simply remove from her or him the stains of sin. The pardoned sinner is *regenerated* and reenters the history of salvation.[30]

Nancy describes here how, as the memories are recalled and recounted, they become the *catena* (or even the text) by which the sinner draws himself to God.[31] To remember a sin in confession is not to reexperience it, it is to reencounter it in time through confessional practice. As such, confession does not just revise the past, it more importantly creates a history for the confessing subject that, in turn, establishes the subject as suspended within and through Christian eschatology.[32]

[29] Mitchell describes this as casuistry, a process of judgment and a "diagnostic technique" that works through the interaction between the specific example under consideration and an abstract understanding generated from previous experience; Mitchell, *Ethics and Exemplary Narrative*, 24.

[30] Jean-Luc Nancy, *Dis-Enclosure: The Deconstruction of Christianity*, trans. Bettina Bergo, Gabriel Malenfant, and Michael B. Smith (New York: Fordham University Press, 2008), 155.

[31] I borrow this term from Carruthers's work on memory. She describes the act of recall as being closely linked to the textual: "A common image for items associatively grouped in memory is that of *catena*, or 'chain'; perhaps the very notion of *texta* itself, which literally means 'something woven,' derives from the same mental phenomenon." Carruthers, *The Book of Memory*, 62.

[32] As Nancy describes it, Christian history is continually suspended in eschatological time: "Christianity, stretched between the virtually infinite antecedence in which it never ceases deciphering the signs of its own anteriority and an infinite future into which it projects the final advent of its event in progress, is constitutively stretched between passage and presence." Nancy, *Dis-Enclosure*, 147.

Exemplarity and Amorous Memory

The terms Gower uses to establish confessional discourse as narratives of emotional revision also circulate through how Amans attempts to negotiate between his ability to act as a subject and his desire for his beloved. Memory, agency, narrative, and will are equally at stake in amorous exempla as they are in their confessional counterparts, but like the chiastic relationship between memory and agency in the Latin head-note, the ways in which exemplarity, legibility, and desire register in each context both inform and resist one another. If in confession, willful control over the way in which memory is reexperienced as narrative is essential for making the confessant legible to himself, then in love, the memory, the will, and narrative are equally (but not equivalently) essential for making the lover legible to the beloved. Confessional handbooks locate narrative on two levels: (1) in the exempla used to initiate the penitent's understanding and consideration of a given sin, and (2) in the speaker's contrite relation of past sins. Perhaps unsurprisingly, amorous exempla do much the same: tales of past lovers offer models for successes and failures in love, through which the would-be lover might analyze his own performance and the lover can tell of his love to his beloved, casting his emotional state and/or devotion in narrative form. Memory in both these forms of exemplarity works by creating legibility and negotiating desire. Amans, however, seems to lose the ability to represent himself to his beloved, even as he seems to gain the ability to do so to Genius. His problems in one discourse are chiastically related to his success in the other, as both pivot around narration, agency, and desire without offering any reconciliation among them.

For example (and to return to memory more directly), when Genius asks if Amans is guilty of forgetfulness in Book IV, Amans is quick to admit that he finds remembering himself impossible when it comes to articulating his desires. The violence of his longing, rather than facilitating his speech, has quite the opposite effect: it tends to overwhelm his ability to remember himself enough to speak of himself in even a perfunctory way. Amans complains to Genius that he is unable to convey the depth of his ardor to his beloved, and he locates his failure in his faulty memory. He recalls his repeated attempts to tell the lady of his passion but must confess that, whenever he sees her, he is rendered mute by the strength of his desire:

> And so recorde I mi lecoun
> And wryte in my memorial
> What I to hire telle schal,
> Riht al the matiere of mi tale.
> But al nys worth a note schale;
> For whanne I come ther sche is,
> I have it al forgete ywis
> (IV.562–68)

Amans's frustration here is poignant; he describes himself as a book whose letters have been erased (IV.580–81), and he cites the source of his difficulty as the overwhelming desire he feels—the same desire that should individuate him to his beloved. When the lady appears, he is "of hire adrad" (IV.572) as a man who has seen a ghost, and every thought he has ever had is struck from his heart (IV.593–94). The situation becomes so dire that he eventually reaches the point of complete incoherence: he cannot comprehend who he is, where he came from, or where he is going, so "overcome" (IV.592) he is by his disordered emotions: "So that for feere I can noght gete / Mi witt, bot I miself forgete" (IV.475–76).

At the point of contact, Amans is erased by his desire; he cannot remember himself enough to describe himself, making his choice of a book "in which is rased / The lettre" metaphor an apt one (IV.580–81). His personal narrative is no longer legible and, as a result, he cannot author a version to present to the lady—a lamentable situation for the lover looking to persuade his beloved to return his affections. Interestingly enough, however, at this moment Amans has no trouble describing to Genius the frustration he feels when he is confronted by the object of his desire, and his memory of paralyzing fear subsequently launches a spectacular tirade of unprompted yet extremely articulate self-chastisement (IV.598ff.). He is able effortlessly to translate his memory of frustrated embarrassment into an effective confessional narrative. This difference between Amans's ability to speak in confession and his inability to speak in love returns to the speaking–thinking–desiring triad from the *Mirour*; as a lover, Amans's fear overwhelms his ability to speak and think, and therefore his desire becomes frustrated, whereas in confession he appears to be able effectively to address the idea of how and what he desires, articulating his failure (in this case) with great success. Confessional discourse provides for Amans's *memoria* what Katherine Zieman describes as the "generalizability and stable contextualization that allows utterances to have meaning beyond their immediate moment."[33] The speech-act in confession is the result of interpretation inasmuch as it is produced as an effect and in recognition of a willful reevaluation of desire. But the speech-act in love, as we see here, is markedly different. There is no reevaluation of desire in Amans's attempt at speech when approaching his beloved—there are only absence and deferral. As a result, this failure can only become generative as a confessional exemplum, wherein Amans might read his inability to express his present desire in the amorous past through the expression of his remembered desire in the confessional present.

Like the "Sic"-verse, however, the relationship between tale-telling in confession and tale-telling in love is one that at this moment is neither perfectly analogous, nor perfectly contradictory. Rather, the two are made proximate through the relationship among memory, desire, narration, and agency in Amans's metaphor of the "letterless book." In the Latin headnote, forgetfulness is a problem here for both the confessant and the lover, but in Amans's complaint about his inability to speak to his beloved, his replete confessional narrative is not the inverse of his lack of success when it comes to expressing his desire to the lady. If anything, when he attempts to speak, his desire is too present, too overwhelming; he forgets not what he wants, but more specifically what he wants to say. Moreover, the agency that is lost in one context is gained in another, but through very different means: Amans is not looking to be absolved from his desire as a lover, he is looking to achieve it. Rather than divine forgiveness, he seeks amorous affirmation—confirmation of his identity as a lover. Even so, attention to the connection among memory, agency, and narrative in love stands, as it does in confessional discourse, at the heart of both what Amans desires and what he hopes to attain.

In his "letterless" despair, Amans abandons hope for amorous satisfaction and will settle for obliterating his desire to reclaim some form of agency over his will; this only becomes possible, he supposes, through the rejection of the self as a subject of desire. Moreover, he attempts to accomplish this renunciation by offering an exemplum of his own to

---

[33] Katherine Zieman, "Escaping the Whirling Wicker: Ricardian Poetics and Narrative Voice in the *Canterbury Tales*," in *Answerable Style: The Idea of the Literary in Medieval England*, ed. Frank Grady and Andrew Galloway (Columbus: The Ohio State University Press, 2013), 75–94 (80).

articulate his longing willfully to forget his desire. In a somewhat bitter response to Genius's question about his tendency to be forgetful in love, Amans recounts the tale of Moses and Tharbis.[34] The brief narrative describes Moses's military participation in the Egyptian war against the Ethiopians, and his marriage to Tharbis, an Ethiopian princess who betrays her city in exchange for his love. Extra-scriptural, it is most likely an attempt to explain the reference in Numbers to Moses's otherwise unexplained Ethiopian wife ("Locutaque est Maria et Aaron contra Moysen propter uxorem ejus Æthiopissam" [And Miriam and Aaron spoke against Moses, because of his Ethiopian wife]), and it becomes allegorized by Jerome as a description of the Church as deriving from the Gentiles rather than the Jews.[35] In the *Confessio*, Amans focuses not on the exegetical implications of Moses's marriage, but rather on how Moses manages to extricate himself from his new wife and return to Egypt by means of a magical ring of forgetfulness, crafted "thurgh his enchanting" (IV.648). Once placed on Tharbis's finger, her love for Moses is mysteriously obliterated beyond all reclaiming:

> Whan Tharbis hadde it on hire hond,
> No knowlechinge of him sche fond,
> Bot al was clene out of memorie,
> As men mai rede in his historie.
> And thus he wente quit away,
> That nevere after that ilke day
> She thought that ther was such on;
> Al was forget and overgon.
>
> (IV.677–84)[36]

---

[34] For an alternative reading of the tale focusing on the quality of *gentilesse*, see Rozalyn Levin, "The Passive Poet: Amans as Narrator in Book 4 of the *Confessio Amantis*," *EMSt* 3 (1986): 114–30.

[35] Num 12:1. "Moyses . . . id est lex Domini spiritualis, Aethiopissam de gentibus duxit uxorem. Et Maria [= Miriam], id est synagoga Iudaeorum; et Aaron, id est carnale sacerdotium, et non secundum ordinem Melchisedec, murmurant adversus legem, sed frustra" ["Moses . . . that is the spiritual law of God, took an Ethiopian wife from the Gentiles. And Maria, that is the synagogue of the Jews, and Aaron, that is the priesthood after the flesh and not after the order of Melchisedek, murmured against the law, but in vain"]. Jerome examines this passage in the *In Sophoniam*. Cited and translated in Mark Balfour, "Moses and the Princess: Josephus' *Antiquitates Judaicae* and the Chansons de Geste," *MÆ* 64, no. 1 (1995): 1–16.

[36] Versions of this story appear in Petrus Comestor's *Historia scholastica* (*Patrologia latina*, ed. J.-P. Migne, 221 vols. [1844–64; Alexandria, Va.: Chadwick-Healey, 1995], 198:1144); Godfrey of Viterbo's *Pantheon* (Basileae: Oporinus, 1559), cols. 134–37; Ranulf Higden's *Polychronicon* (London: Longmans, Green, 1869), II.322; and The Middle English *Genesis and Exodus*, ed. Olaf Arngart (Lund: C. W. K. Gleerup, 1968),

Tharbis's magical amnesia with regard to love is precisely what Amans desires; unfortunately (as the reader is well aware) it should rather be what he seeks to avoid. The telling of the tale is, after all, included in a conversation about the evils of forgetfulness—evils Genius is careful to lay out for his erstwhile charge at the beginning of the section. Thus, the failure of the exemplum is clear from the start: there is no way in which Amans can make his weakness and his longing to be released from the pains of love serve as an appropriate rejoinder to the problems of memory and desire.

In fact, it is difficult to imagine a worse response to Genius's query about Amans's tendency to forget himself than the Moses and Tharbis exemplum. It narrativizes, almost point by point, the problems with being forgetful and becomes a confession not of guilt, but of a desire to be guilty. Once the tale is completed, Amans complains that even with Moses's ring of forgetting he would still be in continual thrall to his beloved. He sees her, desires her, fears her, forgets himself, and sees her again in a continual and impotent progression. Supernatural intervention, however patristically authorized, is powerless when faced with the ravishment of love—desire will always return the lover to the same state, even with the aid of a magical talisman:

> For sche is evere faste by,
> So nyh that sche nym hearte toucheth,
> That for nothing that Slowthe coucheth
> I mai forget hire, life ne loth.
>
> (IV.666–69)

As with the initial impulse to sin, what Amans forgets here is the role of desire and the will in prudence. In a perverse rehearsal of confessional practice, his wish as expressed by the exemplum is to revise the remembered narrative of his desire: in the removal of desire, he will change his

---

I.2689–708. See also treatments in Gervase of Tilbury, *Otia imperialia*, III.3; Vincent of Beauvais, *Speculum historiale*, II.2; John Bromyard, *Summa praedicantium*, s.v. *Caro*, C, ii, 14; and the *Gesta Romanorum*, cap. 10. In the *Summa praedicantium* and the *Gesta Romanorum*, the story is of an Emperor Freundericus, who gives his wife a ring of hope and promise so he can leave her (Bromyard writes that the ring is of forgetting and "sicut Moyses"). Chaucer also mentions a similar magic ring in *The Squire's Tale*, and Larry D. Benson's notes in *The Riverside Chaucer* find that Chaucer gives Roger Bacon's *Opus maius* as a source; *The Riverside Chaucer*, gen. ed. Larry D. Benson, 3rd ed. (Boston: Houghton Mifflin, 1987), note to *SqT*, lines 250–51 (page 893). Further references to Chaucer are to this edition.

response to narrative events just as the penitential process revises memory of past sins by editing out the desire that accompanied them. Amans's desire for an *ars oblivionis* speaks to his desire to regain agency over his disruptive will, which, in turn, determines his response to the force exerting control over him—in this case, his ongoing lovesickness. He mistakenly looks to make forgetting into an event he can *will* into being. Forgetfulness is a *force*, a quality that affects, but it is not in itself an effect.[37] Amans's wish to be free of the constraints of his desire (his inability to turn his attention to anything save the object) is the desire to return agency to himself, free of the effects of controlling love. Like Moses, he looks for escape. But, unlike Moses, Amans cannot *will* this escape into being, magical ring or no.

Of course, what Amans should look to as a remedy for his loss of agency is not the destructive power of oblivion but rather, as the Latin verse opening the section reminds us, the power of reason accessed by careful attention to memory. If control over his subject-status is what Amans is after, he is looking in the wrong place. In response, Genius quickly rebuts Amans's longing for an erasure of desire with the tale of Phyllis and Demophon, cautioning Amans about the dangers of being unmindful in love. As a counter-narrative to Moses and Tharbis, the tale realigns both the problem of memory, desire, and love and also the way in which narrative works on the subject. In the tale, Demophon swears unending loyalty and devotion to his beloved, Phyllis, before leaving for the battlefield at Troy, whereupon he promptly forgets her. Upon his failure to return, she chastises him *in absentia* for his broken promise before hanging herself with a length of silk; the gods, in Ovidian fashion, respond by transforming her into a tree—a tree that subsequently becomes a public reminder of Demophon's guilt.[38]

In the tale, Genius very specifically casts Phyllis as a woman whose ardor has thrown her into insanity.[39] In her grief over her lover's

[37] Ricoeur notes that willful forgetting is an impossibility: "The arrival of memory is an event. Forgetting is not an event, something that happens or that someone causes to happen. To be sure, we can notice that we have forgotten, and we remark it at a given moment. But what we then recognize is the state of forgetfulness we had been in." Ricoeur, *Memory, History, Forgetting*, 502.

[38] For Gower's use of Ovid for this tale, see Conrad Mainzer, "John Gower's Use of the Mediaeval Ovid in *Confessio Amantis*," *MÆ* 41 (1972): 215–22. See also the notes to Peck's edition of the poem in Gower, *Confessio Amantis*, Vol. 2, 383.

[39] This is a departure from other versions of the tale: in the *Remedia*, Ovid uses Phyllis as a warning for lovers to avoid solitude, and in the *Heroides*, her plight is used as a critique against those who, like Demophon, fail to maintain loyalty as the appropriate response to generous hospitality. Chaucer's version of Phyllis in *The Legend of Good*

betrayal, her senses become deranged, keeping her from tending to even the basics of self-care:

> The days gon, the monthe passeth
> Hire love encresceth and his lasseth,
> For him sche lefte slep and mete.
> And he his time hath al forgete
>
> (IV.781–84)

As time wears on, Phyllis progresses beyond a failure to eat and sleep and becomes unable to determine the truth of the world around her, so overwhelming is her emotional distress. She cannot forget the time, as he does:

> Bot, she, which might noght do so,
> The tyde awayteth everemo,
> And caste hire yhe upon the see.
> Sometime nay, sometime yee,
> Sometime he cam, sometime noght,
> The sche desputeth in hire tought
> And wot not what she thenk mai.
>
> (IV.807–13)

As she loses her grasp on the physical reality of the world, Phyllis is losing herself through Gower's definition of Sloth in the headnote—in her grief she becomes forgetful of herself and falls into the position of the *oblitus*. Furthermore, this is a form of Sloth particularly pertinent to Amans. Like Amans's beloved, Phyllis's lover fails to respond at the appropriate time to her emotional attachment, and like Amans's, her grief escalates to the point of causing her bodily suffering. However, in Phyllis's story, even though Demophon is appropriately punished with public shame, she is the one who must serve as the negative model for Gower's earlier Latin warning against *accidia*. We might think of this as something of a "forked" exemplum: in Demophon we have "incautious love," who "forgets the time," but in Phyllis we have the woman who is becoming an *oblitus* through her lack of judgment and reason—she is forgetting herself even as she is forgotten. This is the danger Amans

---

Women rather focuses on Demophon as the "wikked fruit" of "a wikked tree" (2), perpetuating his father's caddishness when it comes to devotion in love.

faces: as he quite rightly points out, he is no Demophon. But Ger
reminds us that he is coming perilously close to becoming Phyllis,
whom even Venus takes no pity (IV.824).[40]

As an exemplum of Sloth, Phyllis works in concert with Demophon's
more obvious form of forgetfulness, wherein Phyllis's obliviation occurs
as her desire overpowers her reason and her will. She is not "mindful of
herself" as the Latin headnote advises; she is mindful only of the desire
that consumes her—desire that prevents her from exerting control over
her own body. As she gives over to her anxious vigil, she relinquishes
control over her mind to the point where even her faculties of perception
cease to function appropriately. The danger of her sin, therefore, is that
it masquerades as its opposite: Phyllis's busy mind, fixated as it is on
Demophon, appears to serve as the antidote for Sloth, particularly in
contexts of love. But the position of the tale in the confessional framework (and more pointedly in Book IV) shows that while her desire does
not cause her to forget love, it does drive her to forget everything else.
This is what makes her tale so pertinent for Amans. As an exemplum,
Phyllis embodies Amans's desire for oblivion even as her narrative
argues against it. She has relinquished her agency by forgetting herself
in love, and her sloth is in her willingness to give herself over to her
disordered reason.

Both Amans's and Genius's narratives about forgetfulness in love act
to some extent like confessional exempla: they offer models, and they
allow Amans to articulate and thereby examine his desire through the
application of his will. In this, the centrality of memory, narrative, and
desire in the two discourses finds their moments of proximate contact;
as in the headnote, terms move from one context to another, drawing
the two threads together. But also as in the headnote, the text resists
analogy as definition. The axiomatic claim that "Happy people have no
history," often associated with Denis de Rougemont's *Love in the Western
World* (1939), might also be said of lovers, but we must take the claim

---

[40] Venus's lack of compassion for Phyllis's pain is noteworthy here, and critics have
seen her indifference as an interpretive marker for the meaning of the tale. In contrast
to a character such as Pygmalion, for whom Venus intervenes even without a direct
petition, Phyllis's voiced despair leaves the goddess unmoved, and she shows her not
mercy, but rather how quickly time is slipping by without Demophon's return: "Bot al
for nough, sche was deceived, / For Venus hath hire hope weyved, / And schewed hire
upon the sky / How that the day was faste by, / So that withinne a litel throwe / The
daies lyht sche mihte knowe" (IV.823–28).

one step further: all lovers are without history.[41] If happy lovers are without history because, out of a lack of dramatic conflict they do not produce narratives, then unhappy lovers in Gower are without history because their narratives cannot extend past themselves, or past the present tense. Unlike confessional exempla, which move the confessant into the eschaton and into the world history of salvation, amorous exempla remain in the past, and speak only to the present. Lovers, successful or unsuccessful, might find themselves stretching into the future if their narrative is memorable enough, but only because they are always already part of the past. They may offer suggestions for future action, as Gower notes at the end of the *Traitié*: "Exemplo veteri poterunt ventura timeri" ("We may fear what is to come by the example of what is past") (3), or at the beginning of the *Vox clamantis*: "Scripture veteris capiunt exempla futuri" (The ancients' writings hold the future's examples).[42] However, even when amorous love becomes exemplary, it never moves past the present; it can have a past, but it can never have a future—love always looks backward in Gower. Even the hope of satisfaction or the prospect of present pleasure becomes an empty temporality. De Rougemont writes of romantic love as that which is "an impoverishment of one's being, an *askesis* without sequel, an inability to enjoy the present without imagining it as absent, a never-ending flight from possession."[43] This is an inversion of how Gower conceives of confessional practice, in which he finds a *techne* that anticipates its salvific end, a demand to revise the past by imagining it as present and productive, and a continual reach into grace and divine union.

Suspended Desire and the Production of Pleasure

In the *Confessio*, the difference between the lover and the confessant is in the relationship among their memory, their narratives, and their histories. Confession in Gower is a narrative praxis that uses the subject's willful revision of past desires to bring him into a shared, salvific future.

---

[41] Denis de Rougemont, *Love in the Western World* (1939; Princeton: Princeton University Press, 1983), 52.

[42] John Gower, *The French Balades*, ed. R. F. Yeager, TEAMS Middle English Texts Series (Kalamazoo: Medieval Institute Publications, 2011), Prol.1. The Latin from the *Vox* is taken from Gower, *Complete Works*, ed. Macaulay, Vol. 4. The translation is from a forthcoming edition and translation of the *Vox* by myself and Matthew Irvin.

[43] Rougemont, *Love in the Western World*, 285.

Amorous exempla, on the other hand, offer the lover an historical context through which to read and produce his present desire. But, of course, history, memory, and narrative are also precisely the same elements that draw the two discourses together in the poem; the chiastic nature of the relationship between love and confession is not merely unstable, it is also generative. To return to Hariman's definition, "The chiasmus moves one towards a center that proves to be empty, a space only for crossing."[44] For Gower, this absence (as in Amans's experience of love) is productive—it produces desire, and in Foucauldian terms, it produces an amorous subject. It does so, however, primarily through memory and narration. As a discursive nexus, confession and love in the *Confessio* thus offer us the possibility of a medieval intervention into Foucault's understanding of confession and sexuality. Whereas Foucault finds in confession that identity is generated out of the understanding of desire in terms of taxonomy, in terms of understanding categories of desire, in Gower we find that identity is produced from memory, and specifically from narrated memories. These memories are shaped by knowledge of sin, but more importantly it is the knowledge of the historical self that forms the subject.

This turn to memory as the grounds of the subject does two things for Foucault's structures of confession and desire. First, the construction of an historical subject in confession (while not precisely the same as an exemplary amorous subject) requires that the recalled sins of love presented to Amans are more than sexual events or acts that have transpired. Amans's recollection and narration of his desires, in fact, very rarely have to do with the flesh at all—he hasn't, after all, had much opportunity to pursue the more lascivious pursuits Foucault locates as the centerpiece of sexuality. What Amans is narrating is his desire, and (more often than not) the failure of his desire. As such, the history he produces bears little resemblance to the medieval confession Foucault describes, which, in order to be effective, must offer a "description of the respective positions of the partners, the postures assumed, gestures, places touched, caresses, the precise moment of pleasure—an entire painstaking review of the sexual act in its very unfolding."[45] Needless to say, this is not the confession Amans experiences or offers. Instead, his narrative of desire (or history of desire) creates for him the identity of a

---

[44] Hariman, "What Is a Chiasmus?," 51.
[45] Foucault, *The History of Sexuality*, 19.

lover, and in the terms of the articulation of his desire, his lack of satisfaction simply does not matter.[46] The lover is a creature of the present,
and even when Venus dashes Amans's hopes with her mirror his desire
is not erased—at best it merely moves into the past. Venus's revelation
in Book VIII is therefore neither a resolution nor a closing off of amorous pleasure; rather it is a moment that sends us (and Amans) back
into the *historiae* of the text. At the end of the poem we have the opportunity to see (aged) Amans as his own history—his story of himself as a
lover is certainly not erased, but neither is it resolved, and it certainly
does not move forward. If Venus were to send Amans/Gower off without
the command to write of what he knows of love, this would be a different matter. But she does urge him to write—she perpetuates the
unfolding, and returns us (and him) to history. Our (and his) desire is
not satisfied; it is summoned, named, and extended.

The second thing the move to memory and history does for the poem
is to serve as the hinge between the amorous and the confessional. Like
the "Sic" in the headnote, memory stands at the center of the two discourses, and, as the mechanism through which confession produces
meaningful narratives, it also finds purchase for Amans's amorous
reflections by refracting the way in which agency and desire produce
(or, in this case, trouble) the subject. Like the "Sic," however, memory
as a hinge between love and confession offers a shifting target, resisting
easy definition or analogy. Quite apart from evoking Amans's own
desire, bounded as it is on the one side by confession and on the other
by love, the chiastic relationship opened by memory invites our desire
as critics to engage in reading that moves dialectically, revealing our
own desire for transcendence and totality. We seek to resolve the perceived conflict between the discourses to understand better the structure
of the text as a component of our authoritative, critical voice. The desire
of the critic and the reader is an echo of Gower's own (Prol.1053–75),
and in many ways our search for discursive consummation also mirrors
the desire for absolution in confession—we are looking to move beyond
ourselves and, in so doing, establish and attest to our agency over text
and meaning, over memory and narrative. Gower, however, frustrates
this desire, just as Amans is so often frustrated in the poem. At this
point, the critic has two options: either to find in this frustration an

---

[46] In this, Amans looks much more like Foucault's understanding of the post-
seventeenth-century confessional subject than a medieval confessional subject. We
might say that Gower anticipates Foucault, and simply accelerates his chronology.

irresolvable structural problem, or to cast it, as James Simpson does, as an opportunity that shifts interpretive activity and textual resolution to the reader. Simpson argues that the purpose of the text is to work on, or *enform*, the reader, implying a dialectical hermeneutic that sublates both love and confession in order to reach an ethical subject. His argument about readership in the *Confessio* requires that we find a dialectical relationship between confession and love, and places the labor of ethical meaning in the hands of readers who move beyond the text as the poem becomes enacted in their interpretive process.[47] The problem with this approach is that the intersection of love and confession, especially as it relates to memory and agency, does not present a clear teleology (ethical or otherwise) that would permit transformational and transcendent reading. Confession alone might, but confession joined with love does not.

Our critical desire to reconcile confession with love, the two primary narrative engines of the poem, is both incited and denied as the text unfolds. In this, we might well feel our sympathies stirring for Amans, a character longing to exert agency over his own narrative. In a parallel way, critical readings of Gower's poem look to establish their own form of hermeneutic mastery by dialectically moving tension into transcendence. The end of confession is, after all, found in absolution, from *absolvo*, meaning "to finish" or "to complete," but also "to loosen" or "to free." The tension between loosening and completion is fruitful for Gower, and he maintains it throughout the poem, provoking and prolonging desire for closure but doing the same for delight in possibility. Our engagement with the poem places us neither as subjugated to a program of subject-formation, nor as exerting critical mastery over the

---

[47] It is important to note that Simpson does not discuss confession at length—his focus is on the formation of a political rather than a devotional subject. His notion of *enformation*, however, would call for readers to resolve the tension between the confessional and the amorous in order to experience the truth of the dialectical synthesis for themselves. For Simpson,

> [the] reader becomes the central locus of the poem, in which its strains are registered. Rather than being primarily referential, such poems are *enactive*—they draw readers into their action in such a way as to reproduce problems and/or experiences within the reader. It is through the reader's resolution of these problems and experiences— the reader's enformation—that the poems work most significantly . . . such works become the locus in which received ideas are experienced anew though the reader's resolution of, or struggle with, those ideas. (James Simpson, *Sciences and the Self in Medieval Poetry: Alan of Lille's "Anticlaudianus" and John Gower's "Confessio Amantis"* [Cambridge: Cambridge University Press, 1995], 120)

text, and this approach calls for a revision of our critical desire for a reading of the *Confessio* that either solves the problem of confession or ignores it in favor of other interpretive *desiderata*. Desire for the other, desire for God, desire for completion: these are central to any readerly experience with the poem. The trouble comes when desire becomes teleology and we demand a satisfaction that returns us, as critics, to ourselves.

To read the *Confessio* in this way is to read a poem about labor and longing—two qualities equally pertinent to love as they are to confession. But if we take this further and allow for a reading of the poem that works not to erase their presence but rather to produce it, and in so doing to create history for the subject, then not only do we have a different understanding of the working of confessional discourse for Gower, we have a different understanding of how the poem works as a whole. Our critical desire for the text is created in constraint, and our instinct is to work at the text in consummation of that desire. Gower, however, would rather produce and prolong desire, folding it back into itself, than bring it to textual satisfaction. Surprisingly, then, the presence of confession implicates desire as part of the text that is not denied, repressed, absolved, or erased. Rather, it is remembered and rehearsed over and again.

Seek, Suffer, and Trust: "Ese" and "Disese" in Julian of Norwich

Vincent Gillespie
University of Oxford

Abstract

Julian of Norwich's engagement with the passion meditation and *ars moriendi* traditions is more radically inventive than critics have noticed. Charting Julian's interactions with texts including Heinrich Suso's *Horologium sapientiae*, William Flete's *Remedies against Tribulation*, the *Stimulus amoris*, and the *Speculum Christiani*, this article proposes that Julian tactically synthesizes generic tropes to posit Christ as "the ultimate double signifier," at once physical and metaphysical, and the comfort proffered by his "destroying of death." Here, the *Revelations of Divine Love* is a literary artifact blending generic conventions, striving to elevate the deathbed repertoire beyond programmatic ethical schemes to a renewed understanding of Christ's redemptive suffering. Bodily sickness detaches the mind from regular consciousness, enabling fleeting, intuited access to God's ineffable compassion; Julian's abject body sees—and experiences—Christ's blood stream in the firmament. This radically deviates from the accepted generic shape of *ars moriendi*, refiguring Christ's sacrifice as both eternal salvation and temporal consolation. Julian redirects the genre from an affective focus on the dying process to the transcendent potential of *Christus moriens* as "a man dying and speaking to us." In the *Revelations of Divine Love* the abject liminality of "sekenes" brings the sufferer into a new affective relationship with Christ, beheld with "avisement" in the liminal space between time and immutability. Julian's newly holistic understanding of Christ's Passion affirms the potential of literature to inscribe the hypostatic sense-experience of dying revelation: her unfettered, syncretic creativity illuminates the ease offered to those who "seek, abide and trust" in God while passing beyond time.

Keywords

Julian of Norwich, abjection, liminality, disease, tribulation, *Revelations*, *ars moriendi*, *Christus moriens*, *Christus medicus*, kenosis, Passion, intertext, genre, linearity, temporality

Illness strips you back to an authentic self, but not one you need to meet. Too much is claimed for authenticity. Painfully we learn to live in the world, and to be false. Then all our defences are knocked down in one sweep. In sickness we can't avoid knowing about our body and what it does, its animal aspect, its demands.

Hilary Mantel[1]

Illness makes us disinclined for the long campaigns that prose exacts . . . In illness words seem to possess a mystic quality. We grasp what is beyond their surface meaning, gather instinctively this, that, and the other—a sound, a colour, here a stress, there a pause—which the poet, knowing words to be meagre in comparison with ideas, has strewn about his page to evoke, when collected, a state of mind which neither words can express nor the reason explain. Incomprehensibility has an enormous power over us in illness, more legitimately perhaps than the upright will allow. In health meaning has encroached upon sound. Our intelligence domineers over our senses. But in illness, with the police off duty, we creep beneath some obscure poem by Mallarmé or Donne, some phrase in Latin or Greek, and the words give out their scent and distil their flavour, and then, if at last we grasp the meaning, it is all the richer for having come to us sensually first, by way of the palate and the nostrils, like some queer odour.

Virginia Woolf[2]

I. The Poetics of Abject Liminality

And when I was thirty yers old and halfe God sent me a bodely sekeness in which I lay iii dayes and iii nights; and on the fourth night I tooke all my rites of holy church and wened not a levyd till day.[3]

---

[1] Hilary Mantel, in *London Review of Books Diary*, November 4, 2010: 41–42.

[2] Virginia Woolf, *On Being Ill* (London: Hogarth Press, 1930), xl. This is a revised version of the essay first published in *The New Criterion* 4, no. 1 (January 1926): 32–45.

[3] Julian of Norwich, *A Revelation of Love*, ed. Marion Glasscoe (Exeter: University of Exeter Press, 1993), cap. 3, 4. Unless otherwise noted, all quotation from Julian's Long Text (hereafter Long Text) will be taken from this edition, which uses the text in London, British Library, MS Sloane 2499, dating from the mid-seventeenth century. Other editions, such as *A Book of Showings to the Anchoress Julian of Norwich*, ed. Edmund Colledge and James Walsh, 2 vols., Pontifical Institute of Mediaeval Studies, Studies and Texts 35 (Toronto: Pontifical Institute of Mediaeval Studies, 1978); and *The Writings of Julian of Norwich*, ed. Nicholas Watson and Jacqueline Jenkins (University Park: Penn State University Press, 2006), prefer the Paris manuscript (Paris, Bibliothèque nationale de France, MS fonds anglais 40), written in an ornamental form of fere textura by an English hand in the third quarter of the sixteenth century. For an assessment of the textual problems and a good account of some aspects of Sloane's superiority, see Marion Glasscoe, "Visions and Revisions: A Further Look at the Manuscripts of Julian of Norwich," *Studies in Bibliography* 42 (1989): 103–20. See also the valuable but neglected discussion in Marion Glasscoe, "Means of Showing: An Approach to Reading Julian of

Julian of Norwich's description of the onset of her life-threatening illness in May 1373 is the point of departure for the most remarkable rumination on the process of dying in Middle English. Her text is transfused not only with extraordinary honesty about her responses to the process but also with her remarkable ability to use language to construct for her readers performative simulacra of those deathbed experiences and the dialogue and revelations from God that accompany them, and to track and transcribe her growing understanding and acceptance of the nature and meaning of her showings in all their existential tension and theological complexity.[4]

Julian's writing exists in a complex, polyphonic, and intertextual relationship with many other works of catechesis and penitential theology, devotion, Passion meditation, contemplation, and eschatology.[5] I have previously sketched out what seems to me to be a persistent strategy of parody, pastiche, and ventriloquism in the shifting and multilayered textures of Julian's text.[6] We are only just beginning to explore the

---

Norwich," *Analecta Cartusiana* 106, no. 1 (1983): 155–77. Colledge and Walsh give an account of their editorial method and the reasons for their preference for Paris at 1.1–28; Watson and Jenkins discuss their textual choices at 24–43.

[4] Cf. James T. McIlwain, "The 'Bodelye syeknes' of Julian of Norwich," *Journal of Medieval History* 10 (1984): 167–80; Marleen Cré, "The Literary Significance of Illness in Julian of Norwich's *A Vision Showed to a Devout Woman*," in *Convergence/Divergence: The Politics of Late Medieval English Devotional and Medical Discourses*, ed. Denis Renevey and Naoë Kukita Yoshikawa, *Poetica* 72 (special issue) (Tokyo: Yushodo Press, 2009), 43–57. Naoë Kukita Yoshikawa, ed., *Medicine, Religion and Gender in Medieval Culture*, Gender in the Middle Ages 11 (Cambridge: D. S. Brewer, 2015) contains several essays referring to Julian's illness. See also Caroline Walker Bynum, *Fragmentation and Redemption: Essays on Gender and the Human Body in Medieval Religion* (New York: Zone Books, 1991).

[5] For useful discussion of this important and contentious issue, see Anna Maria Reynolds, "Some Literary Influences in the *Revelations* of Julian of Norwich," *Leeds University Studies in Language and Literature* 7–8 (1952): 18–28; Lynn Staley Johnson, "The Trope of the Scribe and the Question of Literary Authority in the Works of Julian of Norwich and Margery Kempe," *Speculum* 66 (1991): 820–38; Denise Nowakowski Baker, "Julian of Norwich and Anchoritic Literature," *Mystics Quarterly* 19 (1993): 148–60; Denise Nowakowski Baker, *Julian of Norwich's Showings: From Vision to Book* (Princeton: Princeton University Press, 1994); Felicity Riddy, " 'Women Talking about the Things of God': A Late-Medieval Sub-Culture," in *Women and Literature in Britain 1150–1500*, ed. Carol M. Meale, 2nd ed. (Cambridge: Cambridge University Press, 1996), 104–27; Felicity Riddy, "Julian of Norwich and Self-Textualization," in *Editing Women*, ed. Ann M. Hutchison (Cardiff: University of Wales Press, 1998), 101–24; Christopher Abbott, *Julian of Norwich: Autobiography and Theology* (Cambridge: D. S. Brewer, 1999), 47–60; Felicity Riddy, "Text and Self in *The Book of Margery Kempe*," in *Voices in Dialogue: Reading Women in the Middle Ages*, ed. Linda Olson and Kathryn Kerby-Fulton (Notre Dame: University of Notre Dame Press, 2005), 435–53.

[6] See, for example, Vincent Gillespie, " '[S]he Do the Police in Different Voices': Pastiche, Ventriloquism and Parody in Julian of Norwich," in *A Companion to Julian of*

ways that Julian's showings interact with texts such as Heinrich Suso's *Horologium sapientiae* (composed 1334–37) and its vernacular translations, which contain a chillingly influential *ars moriendi*. These textual and subtextual interactions are even more extensive, I think, with the various incrementally developing versions of the *Remedies against Tribulation* of William Flete (d. after 1380), not to mention the late thirteenth-century Latin *Stimulus amoris* or its late fourteenth-century Middle English version, *The Prickynge of Love*.[7] With reference to Julian's deathbed experiences, Amy Appleford has recently explored the ways in which, especially in the Short Text, Julian's description of the stages of her illness and the attendance by clergy and members of her family closely echoes the admonitions in the *visitacio infirmorum* and *ars moriendi* tradition, and in the sacramental rituals associated with the ceremonies of the Last Rites.[8] But I want to argue that Julian goes much further

---

Norwich, ed. Liz Herbert McAvoy (Cambridge: D. S. Brewer, 2008), 192–207. This collection of essays offers a valuable starting-point for critical orientation on Julian's text.

[7] A recognition of this vernacular intertextuality is a particular strength of the annotations in *The Writings of Julian of Norwich: "A Vision Showed to a Devout Woman" and "A Revelation of Love,"* ed. Nicholas Watson and Jacqueline Jenkins, Brepols Medieval Women Series (University Park: Penn State University Press, 2006). The Latin *De remediis contra temptationes* was written by William Flete, probably between 1352 and 1358. The text had considerable circulation in Latin and English, undergoing at least three recensions and elaborations of the vernacular text along the way. On Flete, see M. B. Hackett, "William Flete and the *De remediis contra temptaciones*," in *Medieval Studies Presented to Aubrey Gwynn S.J.*, ed. J. A. Watt, J. B. Morrall, and F. X. Martin (Dublin: Three Candles, 1961), 330–48; Benedict Hackett, Eric Colledge, and Noel Chadwick, "William Flete's 'De remediis contra temptaciones' in Its Latin and English Recensions: The Growth of a Text," *Mediaeval Studies* 26 (1964): 210–30; and Edmund Colledge and Noel Chadwick, " 'Remedies against Temptations': The Third English Version of William Flete," *Archivio italiano per la storia della pietà* 5 (1968): 203–40. On the vernacular *Stimulus amoris*, see *The Prickynge of Love*, ed. Harold Kane, 2 vols., Salzburg Studies in English Literature (Salzburg: Institut für Anglistik und Amerikanistik, 1983).

[8] Carl Horstmann, ed., *Yorkshire Writers: Richard Rolle of Hampole, an English Father of the Church, and His Followers*, 2 vols. (London: S. Sonnenschein, 1895–96), 1:107–8. For the Latin *De visitatione infirmorum* attributed to Baudri de Bourgueil, which ascribes a curative function to looking at a crucifix, see *Patrologia latina*, ed. J.-P. Migne, 221 vols. (Paris: Migne, 1844–64), 40:1147–58. On the texts and their cultural impact and work, see the important recent work by Amy Appleford, "The 'Comene Course of Prayers': Julian of Norwich and Late Medieval Death Culture," *JEGP* 107 (2008): 190–214; Amy Appleford, "The Dance of Death in London: John Carpenter, John Lydgate, and the *Daunce of Poulys*," *JMEMSt* 38 (2008): 285–314; and the development of the argument in her *Learning to Die in London, 1380–1540* (Philadelphia: University of Pennsylvania Press, 2015), 24–25, 31–32, 36; and Amy Appleford, "The Sea Ground and the London Street: The Ascetic Self in Julian of Norwich and Thomas Hoccleve," *ChauR* 51, no. 1 (2016): 49–67. I have learned much from her work. For older accounts, see Mary Catharine O'Connor, *The Art of Dying Well: The Development of the "Ars Moriendi"*

than Appleford allows, and transforms the deathbed repertoire through her revelatory encounters with Christ. Julian's trajectory through the experience of learning how to die is revelatory as well as exemplary.

Not noticed by Appleford is that the age at which Julian's bodily sickness arrives has clear textual echoes of the age of the dying man in Heinrich Suso's *ars moriendi*, included as Chapter 5 in the early fifteenth-century Middle English *Seven Points of True Wisdom* and variously translated as a standalone guide by Thomas Hoccleve and others. The young man, who laments to the disciple that death has unexpectedly come upon him and found him unprepared, comments that "Loo alle my dayes ben passed, thritty ʒeere of myne age ben passed and loste and wrechedly perysched."[9] Suso's speaker hauntingly describes himself as "the liknesse of a man diynge and þerwith spekynge with the," a characterization rendered even more powerfully in Hoccleve as:

> Beholde now the liknesse and figure
> Of a man dyynge and talkyng with thee.[10]

Julian, and Suso's young man, are entering into the *selva oscura* of their death agonies at exactly the same point in the middle of their life journeys (and at the age when Christ was traditionally thought to have begun his public ministry). Appleford plausibly argues that Julian's

---

(New York: Columbia University Press, 1942); T. S. R. Boase, *Death in the Middle Ages: Mortality, Judgment and Remembrance* (London: Thames and Hudson, 1972); Nancy Lee Beaty, *The Craft of Dying: A Study in the Literary Tradition of the "Ars Moriendi" in England* (New Haven: Yale University Press, 1970); Paul Binski, *Medieval Death: Ritual and Representation* (London: British Museum Press, 1996); Caroline Walker Bynum and Paul H. Freedman, *Last Things: Death and the Apocalypse in the Middle Ages* (Philadelphia: University of Pennsylvania Press, 2000).

[9] Carl Horstmann, "*Orologium sapientiae; or, The Seven Poyntes of Trewe Wisdom*, Aus Ms Douce 114," *Anglia* 10 (1888): 323–89 (360). For the Latin text of the *Horologium sapientiae*, see *Heinrich Seuses "Horologium sapientiae,"* ed. Pius Künzle (Fribourg: Universitätsverlag, 1977). On the vernacular English reception, see Roger Lovatt, "Henry Suso and Medieval Mystical Tradition in England," in *The Medieval Mystical Tradition in England II: Dartington, 1982*, ed. Marion Glasscoe (Exeter: University of Exeter Press, 1982), 47–62; Stephen Rozenski, "Authority and Exemplarity in Henry Suso and Richard Rolle," in *The Medieval Mystical Tradition in England: Exeter Symposium VIII*, ed. E. A. Jones (Cambridge: D. S. Brewer, 2013), 93–108; Sarah James, "Rereading Henry Suso and Eucharistic Theology in Fifteenth-Century England," *RES* 63 (2012): 732–42.

[10] *Orologium sapientiae*, ed. Horstmann, 358; "Ars vtillissima sciendi mori," in Thomas Hoccleve, *"My Compleinte" and Other Poems*, ed. Roger Ellis (Exeter: University of Exeter Press, 2001), lines 85–86. For recent discussion of this version, see Stephen Rozenski, "'Your Ensaumple and Your Mirour': Hoccleve's Amplification of the Imagery and Intimacy of Henry Suso's *Ars Moriendi*," *Parergon* 25 (2008): 1–16.

recurrent concern that her experiences and her showings should be of spiritual benefit to those at her bedside and, later, in the Long Text, to all her *euen-cristen*, suggests that Julian has configured her teaching persona in the *Showings* quite deliberately as a version of Suso's "man dyynge and talkyng with thee."

By evoking the conventional texts of deathbed preparation, as well as the more sophisticated and spiritually ambitious agenda of Suso's exploration of the *mors improvisa*, or unforeseen and unprepared-for death, Julian constructs a protagonist who shares with Suso's dying man the same liminality, poised on the threshold of leaving life and approaching death. Hoccleve's Suso captures this powerless liminality in his chiastic line: "Thyn eende is comen: comen is thyn eende."[11] The dying man who speaks is a profoundly paradoxical double signifier: a synapse of meaning forged from the hyperactive stasis of the critical moment before life is extinguished. He represents what the Middle English Suso, the *Seven Points of True Wisdom*, calls a "felable ensaumple."[12] He functions like the atemporal Passion image of the Man of Sorrows, who speaks from a non-linear and non-chronological "nowhere."[13] Similarly Julian's comment to those around her bed that "it is today doomsday with me" dresses her in a little brief authority, endowing her with the same sense of liminality.[14] There is something Beckettian about these deathbed voices, speaking from the lip of the grave, living but in some sense already dead; already dead but in some sense still living.[15]

Julian blends elements of the *ars moriendi* tradition (well described by Appleford) with aspects of the narrative velocity offered by other literary

[11] Hoccleve, "Ars vtillissima sciendi mori," line 134.

[12] *Orologium sapientiae*, ed. Horstmann, 358.

[13] On the static image Man of Sorrows, see now Catherine R. Puglisi and William L. Barcham, eds., *New Perspectives on the Man of Sorrows*, Vol. 1, *Studies in Iconography* (Kalamazoo: Medieval Institute Publications, 2013).

[14] Long Text, cap. 8, 13. It also stresses her sense of being an exemplar to her *euen-cristen*, and her engagement with a wider emotional community: see, for example, Barbara H. Rosenwein, *Emotional Communities in the Early Middle Ages* (Ithaca, N.Y.: Cornell University Press, 2006), Chap. 2, "Confronting Death"; Jill Sirko, "Making 'Penance Profitable': Julian of Norwich and the Sacrament of Penance," *Journal of Medieval Religious Cultures* 41 (2015): 163–86.

[15] For more on this liminality in Middle English literature, see Vincent Gillespie, "Dead Still/Still Dead," *The Mediaeval Journal* 1 (2011): 53–78; Jane Gilbert, *Living Death in Medieval French and English Literature* (Cambridge: Cambridge University Press, 2011); Robert Mills, *Suspended Animation: Pain, Pleasure and Punishment in Medieval Culture* (London: Reaktion, 2005).

genres, such as Visions of the Otherworld.[16] She restlessly looks to move beyond the bland and passive submissiveness of the Uses of Tribulation tradition. In particular, she makes one important change to tradition: she largely avoids the extensive narrative scripts of purgatory and hell commonly found in such texts (or rather uses them only in a highly tactical and local manner in describing her temptation by demons), because the focus for her is always already on the transformative powers of the transfigured bleeding head of Christ.

The curtains of blood that close off the face of Christ in the second revelation mark her desire to move her showings away from conventional Passion meditations and the affective and cognitive scripts of devotional aspirations, to feel compassion with the suffering Christ. These conventional scripts are initially embodied and exemplified in the three spiritual gifts and wounds that she requests at the start of her Long Text (cap. 2). She asks for mindfulness of the Passion (including a "bodily sight" of the Crucifixion); bodily sickness at the age of thirty; and three inner wounds of contrition, compassion, and willful longing for God. But she finds them and her being transfigured onto a different plain of perception and understanding by the force of her showings and the affective crucible of her responses to them:

And one time I saw how halfe the face, begyning at the ere, overrede with drie blode til it beclosid to the mid face, and after that, tuther halfe beclosyd on the same wise, and therewhiles in this party even as it came. This saw I bodily, swemely and derkely, and I desired more bodily sight to have sene mor clerely. And I was answered in my reason: "If God wil shew thee more, he shal be thy

[16] On this class of texts, see Robert Easting, *Visions of the Other World in Middle English* (Woodbridge: D. S. Brewer, 1997); Mary Erler, "'A Revelation of Purgatory' (1422): Reform and the Politics of Female Visions," *Viator* 38 (2007): 321–47. Takami Matsuda, *Death and Purgatory in Middle English Didactic Poetry* (Woodbridge: D. S. Brewer, 1997) is a useful compendium of vernacular motifs and imagery in death narratives. The popular account of the visionary Monk of Eynsham on his deathbed, with visions linked to the *triduum* of Easter (Holy Thursday to Easter Saturday), bears interesting comparison with the nature and duration of Julian's visions: *The Revelation of the Monk of Eynsham*, ed. Robert Easting, EETS o.s. 318 (Oxford: Oxford University Press, 2002), 22–23, 29ff. The text closely observes the changing colors of the face of the dying monk, and a bleeding crucifix and bright lights beside the cross also feature. Appleford, "Comene Course," 209, notes that the "Sermon of Dead Men," roughly contemporary with Julian, also ruminates on the changing appearance of the dying man: *Lollard Sermons*, ed. Gloria Cigman, EETS o.s. 294 (Oxford: Oxford University Press, 1989), 207–40 (207).

light. Thee nedith none but him." For I saw him [and sought hym]; for we arn now so blynd and so unwise that we never sekyn God til he of his godenes shewith him to us; and we ought se of him graciously, than arn we sterid by the same grace to sekyn with gret desire to se him more blisfully; and thus I saw him and sowte him, and I had him and I wantid hym. And this is, and should be, our comon werkeyng in this, as to my sight.[17]

The apophatic curtains of blood veil the scene of human suffering, denying bodily sight, and shifting the focus onto the light of divine revelation to reveal instead the kenotic drama of the soteriological act.[18] This is emphatically not what Julian thought she was signing up for when she made her initial requests:

Methought I would have beene that time with Mary Magdalen and with other that were Crists lovers, and therefore I desired a bodily sight wherein I might have more knowledge of the bodily peynes of our saviour, and of the compassion [of] our lady and of all his trew lovers that seene that time his peynes, for I would be one of them and suffer with him.[19]

Indeed, her request in Chapter 10 for more bodily sight is entirely consistent with her initial desire to "see" the "bodily peynes" and to have compassion comparable to that enjoyed by Mary Magdalen and those at the foot of the cross.[20] In her opening requests in the Short Text, she

[17] Long Text, cap. 10, 14–15.
[18] See further Vincent Gillespie and Maggie Ross, "The Apophatic Image: The Poetics of Effacement in Julian of Norwich," in *The Medieval Mystical Tradition in England: 5th Symposium Papers*, ed. Marion Glasscoe (Cambridge: D. S. Brewer, 1992), 53–77; Vincent Gillespie, "Postcards from the Edge: Interpreting the Ineffable in the Middle English Mystics," in *Interpretation Medieval and Modern: The J. A. W. Bennett Memorial Lectures; Perugia 1992*, ed. Piero Boitani and Anna Torti (Cambridge: D. S. Brewer, 1993), 137–65. Both are reprinted, with other essays, in Vincent Gillespie, *Looking in Holy Books: Essays on Late Medieval Religious Writing in England* (Turnhout: Brepols, 2011).
[19] Long Text, cap. 2, 3.
[20] For discussion of Julian's perceptual triad of bodily sight, ghostly sight, and "word formed in the understanding," see Nicholas Watson, "The Trinitarian Hermeneutic in Julian of Norwich's *Revelation of Love*," in Glasscoe, *Medieval Mystical Tradition in England*, 79–100; Barbara Newman, "What Did It Mean to Say 'I Saw'? The Clash between Theory and Practice in Medieval Visionary Culture," *Speculum* 80 (2005): 1–43, provides a helpful overview of the reception and development of the Augustinian theories. Glasscoe, "Means of Showing," is still a wise reflection on this subject. It is striking that the borrowings in *The Chastising of God's Children* from Alphonse of Pecia's *Epistola solitarii ad reges*, a key text in the development and popularization of techniques *discretio spirituum*, use Augustine and Gregory the Great's *Moralia in Job* to explore similar modalities of visionary reception: *The Chastising of God's Children and the Treatise of Perfec-*

asks for all the experiences that she would have "if I shulde die": it is never more than an "as if," a hypothetical scenario, a theatrical engagement.[21] What she gets is very different. The apparent imminence of her own death transposes her engagement with the death of Christ onto a different plane. The interpretative and imaginative matrix that these changed circumstances generates is far more radical, profound, and non-linear than the usual Passion meditation scenarios.[22] Her desire to see the bodily pains of Christ is not the same as the vivid reality of her sharing in death's agony. The actual position of fear and abjection she finds herself in is a very different experience for her and for us from looking at the Passion of Christ from the psycho-affectively generated and directed compassionate responses taught by the devotional tradition.[23]

---

tion of the Sons of God, ed. Joyce Bazire and Eric Colledge (Oxford: Blackwell, 1957), to which should be added the newly purchased copy in Oxford, Bodleian Library, MS Don. c. 287, previously unprovenanced. For recent discussions, see Annie Sutherland, *"The Chastising of God's Children*: A Neglected Text," in *Text and Controversy from Wyclif to Bale: Essays in Honour of Anne Hudson*, ed. Helen Barr and Ann M. Hutchison (Turnhout: Brepols, 2005), 353–73; Kathryn Kerby-Fulton, *Books under Suspicion: Censorship and Tolerance of Revelatory Writing in Late Medieval England* (Notre Dame: University of Notre Dame Press, 2006), 247–323; Marleen Cré, "Contexts and Comments: The *Chastising of God's Children* and Marguerite Porète's *Mirour of Simple Souls* in Oxford, MS Bodley 505," in *Medieval Texts in Context*, ed. Graham Caie and Denis Renevey (London: Routledge, 2008), 122–35. On *discretio spirituum* generally in the context of Julian of Norwich, see Rosalynn Voaden, *God's Words, Women's Voices: The Discernment of Spirits in the Writing of Late-Medieval Women Visionaries* (Woodbridge: D. S. Brewer, 1999).

[21] Short Text, section 1, 63.

[22] On this break with the linearity of Passion meditation, see James H. Marrow, *Passion Iconography in Northern European Art of the Late Middle Ages and Early Renaissance: A Study of the Transformation of Sacred Metaphor into Descriptive Narrative* (Kortrijk: Ghemmert, 1979); Henk W. van Os, *The Art of Devotion in the Late Middle Ages in Europe, 1300–1500* (Princeton: Princeton University Press, 1994); Jeffrey F. Hamburger and Anne-Marie Bouche, eds., *The Mind's Eye: Art and Theological Argument in the Middle Ages* (Princeton: Princeton University Press, 2006). Aspects of this are discussed in Vincent Gillespie, " 'Lukynge in Haly Bukes': *Lectio* in Some Late Medieval Spiritual Miscellanies," in *Spätmittelalterliche geistliche Literatur in der Nationalsprache*, ed. James Hogg (Salzburg: Institut für Anglistik und Amerikanistik, 1984), 1–27; Vincent Gillespie, "Strange Images of Death: The Passion in Later Medieval English Devotional and Mystical Writing," in *Zeit, Tod und Ewigkeit in der Renaissance Literatur* (Salzburg: Insitut für Anglistik und Amerikanistik, 1987), 111–59. Both are reprinted in Gillespie, *Looking in Holy Books*. For recent work on that other static icon—the vernicle—referred to by Julian, see Lisa H. Cooper and Andrea Denny-Brown, eds., *The Arma Christi in Medieval and Early Modern Material Culture: With a Critical Edition of "O Vernicle"* (Farnham: Ashgate, 2014).

[23] On which see, for example, the recent studies by Jennifer Bryan, *Looking Inward: Devotional Reading and the Private Self in Late Medieval England* (Philadelphia: University of Pennsylvania Press, 2007); Sarah McNamer, *Affective Meditation and the Invention of Medieval Compassion* (Philadelphia: University of Pennsylvania Press, 2010); Michelle

Real, serious, life-threatening illness entails a radical simplification of the self, focusing inward, perhaps making the barriers between the conscious and unconscious mind a little more permeable. The abject man or woman, reduced to their bare humanity, can achieve a focused attentiveness to matters of life and death, and potentially to matters of spiritual significance.[24] Yet Suso's young man dying laments that his fear of death has removed from him the power to think and prepare spiritually for his end. He is mesmerized by his own mortality and by an unavoidable awareness of his pain and imminent death: nothing can get through or past that fear. This is one of the great risks of dying unprepared. Illness can turn you inward, can create self-fueling and solipsistic loops of fear and paralyzing anxiety. Julian describes this as being "turnyd and left to myselfe in hevynes and werines of my life and irkenes of myselfe that onethis I coude have patience to leve," and she spends a lot of her text performing and counseling a move away from the futility of what she calls this "beholding of selfe" toward a beholding of God: "for in the beholding of God we fall not, in the beholding of selfe we stond not."[25] But Julian dramatizes that these states do not exist in clean and clear opposition to each other: instead the abject liminality of serious illness precipitates a restless and troubling oscillation between them:

And than the peyne shewid ageyn to my feling, and than the ioy and the lekyng, and now that one, and now that other, dyvers times—I suppose aboute xx tymes. And in the same tyme of ioy I migte have seid with Seynt Paul:

Karnes, *Imagination, Meditation, and Cognition in the Middle Ages* (Chicago: University of Chicago Press, 2011).

[24] Mikhail Bakhtin comments that "events of the grotesque sphere are always developed on the boundary of dividing one body from the other and, as it were, at their points of intersection"; *Rabelais and His World*, trans. Hélène Iswolsky (Bloomington: Indiana University Press, 1984), 322, quoted by Frederick Christian Bauerschmidt, *Julian of Norwich and the Mystical Body Politic of Christ* (Notre Dame: University of Notre Dame Press, 1999), 73, whose Chapter 3, 63–123, contains many helpful insights. Elaine Scarry, *The Body in Pain: The Making and Unmaking of the World* (Oxford: Oxford University Press, 1985), 147, notes that pain is resistant to language and indeed requires a "shattering of language." Jeffrey Butcher, "*Absolute Essence* of the Suffering Mystic: The Visions of Elisabeth of Schönau," *Journal of Medieval Religious Cultures* 40 (2014): 173–91. See also Paul Ricoeur, *Oneself as Another*, trans. Kathleen Blamey (Chicago: University of Chicago Press, 1992); and *Living up to Death*, trans. David Pellauer (Chicago: University of Chicago Press, 2009), which have powerful reflections on suffering and wisdom.

[25] Long Text, cap. 15, 23; cap. 82, 131.

"Nothing shal depart me fro the charite of Criste." And in the peyne I migte have seid with Peter: "Lord, save me, I perish."[26]

Julian is keen to teach that the "comon werkyng" of mankind ought to be to seek out God in the hope that he will show himself to us. Julian becomes abject through her illness, but in her abjection she realizes that she has always been the object of the unwavering beholding of Christ and enfolded in his transformative love.[27] This is one of her key remedies or mitigations for pain and suffering: seeking the loving beholding of Christ leads her understanding into wider metaphysical perspectives, and raises the mind and soul up from the grinding pain and solipsistic terror of mortal illness:

And this vision was a lernyng to myn vnderstondyng that the continual sekyng of the soul plesith God ful mekyl; for it may do no more than *sekyn, suffrin and trosten*, and this [is] wrought in the soule that hath it be the Holy Ghost; and the clernes of fyndyng is of his special grace whan it is his will. The sekyng with feith, hope and charite plesyth our lord, and the finding plesyth the soule and fulfillith it with ioy. And thus was I lernyd to myn vnderstondyng that *sekyng is as good as beholdyng for the tyme that he will suffer the soule to be in travel. It is God wille that we seke him to the beholdyng of him*, for be that he shall shew us himselfe of his special grace whan he wil. And how a soule shall have him in his beholdyng he shal teche himselfe; and that is most worshipp to him and profitt to thyself, and most receivith of mekenes and vertues with the grace and ledyng of the Holy Goste; for a soule that only festinith on to God with very troste, either be sekyng or in beholdyng, it is the most worshipp that he may don to him, as to my sight.[28]

Julian tells us that it is the lot of mankind to "sekyn, suffrin and trosten," which she immediately glosses as seek, abide, and trust. Initially

[26] Ibid., cap. 15, 23.

[27] Cf. ibid., cap. 48: "And grace werkyth oure sorowfull dyeng in to holy, blyssyd life." I am indebted to Annie Sutherland for this cross-reference. For recent reflections on Julian's poetics of enclosure, see Laura Saetveit Miles, "Space and Enclosure in Julian of Norwich's *A Revelation of Love*," in McAvoy, *A Companion to Julian of Norwich*, 154–65. This is linked to her use of images of spiritual and physical pregnancy: see note 52.

[28] Long Text, cap. 10, 16–17; emphasis my own. The Paris text reads here: "It is gods will that *we seke into the beholdyng* of hym," but this turns the process away from kenotic traveling hopefully into one of theological examination and interrogation, and probably reflects a Counter-Reformation ideology at work on this copy.

at least this is pretty much a standard deployment of tribulation material for local, tactical purposes: you have to put up with your lot and
hope for better in the next life.[29] William Flete says that one of the uses
of tribulation is that we should learn to "suffren mekely and abyden
pacyently," while the hugely popular *XII Profits of Tribulation* asserts in
a very Julianish way that "more mede is in desirande and sekande god
þen likande in hym."[30] The Middle English Suso exhorts "be perseuerant
askynge, knokkynge & sechynge tille þou haue þi askynge."[31]

But Julian's development of these stock ideas is endlessly synthetic
and inventive, balancing the aspiration of the human soul against the
sole agency of the Trinity in bringing about such changes. Through the
course of her Long Text, she deepens and widens her understanding of
the therapeutic utility of this perichoretic Trinity of "sekyn, suffrin and
trosten." By this means she takes her audience on a journey away from
programmatic and conventional responses toward something more radical and complex. Unlike Suso's dying young man, who has misspent his
thirty years in revelry and the pleasures of the world, Julian's years of
service to God (for which Christ thanks her explicitly in Revelation 6
[cap. 14] in a way that also alludes to Flete and Suso), her own willed
and sustained liminality in a paradoxical state of "wilful abiding," and
her patient ruminations on her showings have all allowed to her to
develop a modality for blending these archetypal teachings on preparation for death with a profound theology of love and salvation:

And how a soule shall have him in his beholdyng he shal teche himselfe; and
that is most worshipp to him and profitt to thyselfe, and most receivith of
mekenes and vertues with the grace and ledyng of the Holy Goste; for a soule
that only festinith on to God with very troste, either be sekyng or in beholdyng, it is the most worshipp that he may don to him, as to my sight. These

---

[29] Julian, *Writings*, ed. Watson and Jenkins, 212; and *Book of Showings*, ed. Colledge
and Walsh, 37, argue for *The Chastising of God's Children* as an analogue to much of this
tribulation language. But similar sentiments are common in anchoritic texts such as
Ancrene Wisse, and develop incrementally in vernacular versions from the early thirteenth
century onward.

[30] Colledge and Chadwick, "Remedies against Temptations," 221. *The XII Profits of
Tribulation* is often pseudonymously associated with Peter of Blois or Gerard of Liège;
this version printed in Horstmann, *Yorkshire Writers*, 2.57–60; another version at 2.391–
406. The same sentiment is expressed in *The Book of Tribulation*, ed. Alexandra Barratt,
Middle English Texts 8 (Heidelberg: Carl Winter, 1983), 108: "it is a gretter merit to
seche the delityng in God and to abide it, than it is to delite in him."

[31] *Orologium sapientiae*, ed. Horstmann, 341.

arn two werkyng that mown be seene in this vision: that on is sekyng, the other is beholdyng. The sekyng is common; that, every soule may have with his grace, and owith to have that discretion and techyng of the holy church. It is God wil that we have thre things in our sekyng: the first is that we *sekyn wilfully and bisily*, withouten slauth, as it may be throw his grace, gladly and merili withoute onskilful hevynes and veyne sorow; the second is that we *abide him stedfastly* for his love, withoute gruching and striveing ageyns him, in our lives end, for it shall lesten but awhile; the thred that we *trosten in him mightily of fulsekird feith*, for it is his wil. We knowen he shall appere sodenly and blisfully to al his lovers; for his werkyng is privy, and he wil be perceivid, and his appering shal be swith sodeyn, and he wil be trowid, for he is full hend and homley— blissid mot he ben![32]

Julian's exposition of the "seek, suffer, and trust" triad is noteworthy. Seeking and trusting are theologically pretty straightforward, but suffering is, in every respect, harder. The literature on the uses of tribulation always stresses the importance of patience, typified by William Flete's exhoration to "suffren mekely and abyden pacyently."[33] As Flete says, "a man þat stondeþ in disese, he is holden to seken alle þe wyes he may comforte hym self."[34] Julian wants to engage with common experience and common teachings, but aspires to drive them into deeper taxonomies and syntheses of understanding. "Suffer" is glossed by Julian as meaning to "abide him stedfastly . . . withoute gruching and striveing ageyns him, in our lives end, for it shall lesten but awhile."[35] Julian is characteristically and forcefully impacting several lexical layers into each other with this formulation. "Suffer" means to wait for or abide, of course, but, in the context of her own illness and of the bleeding head of Christ, it also by this date already carries unmistakeable lexical overtones of pain and tribulation.[36] And the gloss reads equally well as referring to the patience of those with a serious or terminal illness, who wait

[32] Long Text, cap. 10, 16–17; emphasis my own.
[33] There are also underlying references to the two kenotic Beatitudes: "Blessed are the pure in heart for they shall see God" and "Blessed are the poor in spirit for the kingdom of heaven is theirs." Julian not only inhabits the theological parameters of the Beatitudes but also creates a multidimensional environment within which its meanings can be explored and, somatically at least, experienced by the imaginative force of her presentation of the showings. The patient will conquer (*pacientes vincunt*): the potential application of this to radical illness and tribulation is obvious; see, for example, G. J. Schiffhorst, ed., *The Triumph of Patience: Medieval and Renaissance Studies* (Orlando: University Presses of Florida, 1978).
[34] Colledge and Chadwick, "Remedies against Temptations," 226.
[35] Long Text, cap. 10, 17.
[36] MED, s.v. *sufferen*.

without complaint for the passing pain to cease, as it does to the more abstract theological patience of those waiting for the grace of God to manifest itself at the end of time or at the end of human life.[37]

This kind of performative twinning of ideas is typical of the ways in which Julian uses language and syntax to complicate and collocate theological ideas: Julian's punning and playful linguistic explorations of the ways in which *sickness* can give way to *sekirnes* (or security) by way of *seeking*; or the ways that *disease* can lead to discovery of where true *ease* can be found; or the ways in which being able to *trow* can lead to *troste* and then to *Truth*. Such word-knots are all examples of her exploration of a holistic view of life and death. Indeed, her ideas of wholeness play tirelessly with notions of physical wellness and wholesomeness (*hole* and *hele*), and are underpinned by her sense that the whole of her showings are a teaching about spiritual health and wholeness, which will eventually allow the crutch of referential and metaphorical language to fall away, for "the godenes of God is ever hole, and more nere to us withoute any likenes."[38] But her linguistic journey to such ideas of health and wholeness will take her through a renegotiation of the core terms and images of the Passion tradition, represented through the filter of the *ars moriendi*. By the end of it her own role as a version of Suso's "man dyying and speking to us" will stand not as the main focal point of the text but as a *myse en abyme* of a much more radical teaching modality. Julian's text traces the trajectory "fro the peyne that we felen into the bliss that we trosten" but it does so in no glib or superficial fashion.[39]

II. "In this sodenly": Transfiguring *Sekenes* into *Sekirnes*

When a ryghtful man laboreʒ in the laste seknes to dye, the gud aungel, [his] kepar, comeʒ wyth multitude of angeles and takeʒ vp hys soule fro the preson

[37] On the eschatological subversion of human time in suffering and transfiguration, see Long Text, cap. 64: "And in thys worde, Sodeynly thou shalte be taken, I saw that God rewardyd man of the pacience that he hath in abydyng Goddys wylle and of hys tyme."

[38] Long Text, cap. 6, 9, in an explicit denial of similitude or analogy. On Julian's word-knots, see further Gillespie and Ross, "The Apophatic Image"; and Gillespie, "Postcards from the Edge." Annie Sutherland points out to me that the oscillation between dying/drying in Long Text, cap. 16 represents another word-knot.

[39] Long Text, cap. 81, 130. On therapeutic uses of vernacular literature in this period, see, for example, Daniel McCann, "Heaven and Health: Middle English Devotion to Christ in Its Therapeutic Contexts," in *Devotional Culture in Late Medieval England and Europe: Diverse Imaginations of Christ's Life*, ed. Stephen Kelly and Ryan Perry (Turnhout: Brepols, 2014), 335–62; Daniel McCann, "Medicine of Words: Purgative Reading in Richard Rolle's *Meditation on the Passion A*," *The Mediaeval Journal* 5 (2015): 53–83.

of body and lede3 hym to the heuenly paleyse in-to gostly paradyse wyth song of gretteste and swetest melodye, wyth gret lyght and sottest sauour and odour.[40]

According to the popular pastoral handbook the *Speculum Christiani*, composed on the cusp of the fifteenth century, but using vernacular and Latin materials from the fourteenth century, the death of a good man will be marked by an apotheosis of his senses, and he will pass over enfolded in light, harmony, and sweet smells. His passing is not to be lamented because, according to Jerome, "deth es the gate be whych the frendes of god fle fro the handys of enmyes vnto mercy and glorie."[41] His good deeds will follow him and will speak in his defence at his particular judgment. Freed from the miseries of human existence, at the Last Judgment, the resurrected bodies of the saved will be perfected and transfigured, shining as if they were sunbeams, with golden hair, noble bearing, and perfect proportions and stature. Compared to their last days and hours in their death agonies, all shall quickly be sweetness and light for them: "Al men dyen feble, freel, ful of passions; bot aftyr this lyfe the chosen creaturs schal a-rise and be stronge, stable, 3onge, fayre, and immortalle. Such es the chaunge of the gudnes and power of god."[42] Once across the threshold of death, their stability or impassibility will mark them out as freed from the turbulent passions of human existence, and the relentless changes and challenges that life and death on earth require. Their resurrected attributes will make them immune to fear,

---

[40] *Speculum Christiani: A Middle English Religious Treatise of the 14th Century*, ed. Gustaf Holmstedt, EETS o.s. 182 (London: Oxford University Press, 1933), 48.

[41] Ibid., 50. For the date (at least twenty-five years later than that posited by Holmstedt), see Vincent Gillespie, "The Evolution of the *Speculum Christiani*," in *Latin and Vernacular: Studies in Late-Medieval Texts and Manuscripts*, ed. Alastair J. Minnis (Cambridge: D. S. Brewer, 1989), 39–62; Vincent Gillespie, "Chapter and Worse: An Episode in the Regional Transmission of the *Speculum Christiani*," *English Manuscript Studies 1100–1700* 14 (2008): 86–111. This popular pastoral manual, surviving in over fifty copies, also contains pertinent sections on the nature of prayer, tribulation, temptation, and penance, and was designed to assist parochial clergy in their pastoral, catechetic, and homiletic duties. For the suggestion that Julian's advice to Margery Kempe on the subject of tears uses patristic quotations found in *Speculum Christiani*, see *Book of Showings*, ed. Colledge and Walsh, 38, reporting Hope Emily Allen. On the medieval sensorium, see now Richard Newhauser, ed., *A Cultural History of the Senses in the Middle Ages, 500–1450* (London: Bloomsbury, 2014); and Stephen G. Nichols, Andreas Kablitz, and Alison Calhoun, eds., *Rethinking the Medieval Senses: Heritage, Fascinations, Frames* (Baltimore: Johns Hopkins University Press, 2008).

[42] *Speculum Christiani*, 50. The translation of the Latin sections of the text into the vernacular was produced c. 1450 and survives in a single copy.

decay, loss, and disease. Indeed, as the Maiden in *Pearl* shows, the resurrected body will manifest physical perfection, traditionally at the age of Christ's adult mission, which is also, tellingly, the age of Suso's dying man, and of Julian when she suffers her life-threatening illness. The perfected body will also display an impassible ease of mind and heart that will be a counterpart to the *claritas* and *agilitas* of its new being with God.[43] None of this is something it can achieve for itself, because, as the *Speculum Christiani* stresses, "such es the chaunge of the gudnes and power of god." The transformation from disease to ease will be at the will and subject to the power of God's benevolence. This is the idea behind Saint Paul's teaching in his First Letter to the Corinthians:

Ecce mysterium vobis dico: Omnes quidem resurgemus, sed non omnes immutabimur. In momento, in ictu oculi, in novissima tuba: canet enim tuba, et mortui resurgent incorrupti: et nos immutabimur.

[Behold, I tell you a mystery. We shall all indeed rise again: but we shall not all be changed. In a moment, in the twinkling of an eye, at the last trumpet: for the trumpet shall sound, and the dead shall rise again incorruptible: and we shall be changed.][44]

The sudden transformation promised by Paul is always part of the divine covenant in Scripture: Paul's comments echo Isaiah's "Præcipitabit mortem in sempiternum: et auferet Dominus Deus lacrymam ab omni facie" ("He shall cast death down headlong for ever: and the Lord God shall wipe away tears from every face"), and both are later echoed in the Book of Revelation: "et absterget Deus omnem lacrymam ab oculis eorum: et mors ultra non erit, neque luctus, neque clamor, neque dolor erit ultra, quia prima abierunt" ("And God shall wipe away all tears from their eyes: and death shall be no more, nor mourning, nor crying, nor sorrow shall be any more, for the former things are passed away").[45]

[43] Cf., for example, Kevin Marti, "Traditional Characteristics of the Resurrected Body in *Pearl*," *Viator* 24 (1993): 311–35.

[44] 1 Cor 15:51–52. All Bible quotations come from *Biblia Sacra iuxta Vulgatam Clementinam*, ed. Albertus Colunga and Laurentius Turrado (Madrid: Biblioteca de Autores Cristianos, 1965). Translations are from *The Holy Bible: Douay-Rheims Version* (Baltimore: John Murphy, 1899). Annie Sutherland, "'Our feyth is groundyd in goddes worde': Julian of Norwich and the Bible," in *The Medieval Mystical Tradition in England: Exeter Symposium VII*, ed. E. A. Jones (Cambridge: D. S. Brewer, 2004), 1–20; Annie Sutherland, "Julian of Norwich and the Liturgy," in McAvoy, *A Companion to Julian of Norwich*, 88–98.

[45] Is 25:8, 21:4.

These resonant clichés of the literature of Christian consolation lie at the heart of Julian of Norwich's great meditation on death in her eighth and ninth revelations. Julian's text is a profoundly, indeed restlessly complex and subtle, working-through of the ontology and teleology of human suffering and death. Sudden change is central to the eddying whirlpool of images, laconic and enigmatic spoken and unspoken words uttered by Christ, and flashingly intuited or carefully articulated ideas that constitute her revelations and their unfolding exposition. But Paul's promised sudden change from disease to ease, from darkness and pain to light and joy, from *Tod* to *Verklärung*, has a problematic glibness that provides little comfort and only thin justification for the existential dread and pain of the end of a human life.[46] It is hardly surprising that *timor mortis conturbat nos*. Everyone facing their own illness and likely death has to steer a perilous psychological route avoiding despair and presumption, servile fear, and debilitating dread. For this final escape from time and causality, from change and decay, cannot be assumed to be securely available for all. Of the two thieves only one was saved: to be on the wrong side of the division into sheep and goats is a literally dreadful fate, as the *Speculum Christiani* also makes clear:

When the wycked man lyth in hys laste ende to dye, deueles cluster togyders, comen wyth greteste noyse, horrible of syght, ferdful of apperynge and doynge, that casten out a-noon the synful soule fro the body wyth grete turmentes and cruelly drawen it to the cloystre of helle . . . The soule es departede fro the body with gret drede, wyth gret dolours; for the horrible places shal appere than sodenly of peynes, the cloude gret and derke, the blac shadow of derknes, the gastfulnes of wrechednes and of confusion, the tremlynge of anguysch, the drede of tribulacion, the sorwe of ferde-ful vysion, the feer of quauerynge dwellynge, wheyr that schal be weylynge of wepynge creaturs, grystynge of teeth, fretynge of wormys venemose, clamour of sorwynge, wepynge of sor-wynge men, and voyce of creatures clamerynge and criynge: Wo, wo, wo to vs, moste wreches, chyldren of Eue! Then al hys werkes, as it were spekynge, schal sey to hym: Thou hast wroght vs; we ben thi werkes; we schal go wyth the to the doom.[47]

---

[46] Cf. Scarry, *The Body in Pain*; Esther Cohen, *The Modulated Scream: Pain in Late Medieval Culture* (Chicago: University of Chicago Press, 2009).

[47] *Speculum Christiani*, 50, 52. Cf. Long Text, cap. 76, 123, where Julian redeploys this self-castigating penitential register, and puts it in the mouth of the devil as part of his temptation to the soul to wallow in self-hatred and despair. Colledge and Walsh's suggested analogue from Walter Hilton's *Scale of Perfection*, II.12 (*Book of Showings*, ed. Colledge and Walsh, 687) is unpersuasive. Similar play of voices is found in the Middle English version of the pseudo-Augustine (Paulinus of Aquilea), *Epistola ad Julianum vel*

Whereas the good man's death is transfigured by the power and goodness of God, the death of the wicked man triggers diabolic actions and
an assault on the senses, enacted by iterative and obsessive variations of
terms for fear and dread, and a performative stridency in description of
the torments of the damned. This is well represented in the Middle
English translator's lexical choices and variations on a small repertoire
of terms from noun to adjective via recurrent present participles, but is
perhaps even more mordantly iterative and relentless in the original
Latin:

Tunc enim subito apparebunt horribilia loca penarum, chaos & caligo tene-
brarum, horror miserie & confusionis, tremor angustie, timor tribulacionis,
dolor horrende visionis, terror tremende mansionis, ubi luctus flencium, stridor
dencium, morsus vermium, clamor dolencium, fletus gemencium & vox cla-
mancium.[48]

The process of separation between soul and body is painful and traumatic (one popular account describes the process as like a tree with its
roots deep in a man's lungs being violently and protractedly dragged
out of the mouth and entrails).[49] The unfortunate soul is delivered to a
place of darkness, noise, and torment, with a stress on multiple voices
crying out: the voices of the man's evil deeds, of the demons, and of the
suffering and damned. The noisiness of these conventional accounts of
the process of dying, with its cacophony of clashing and conflicting
voices, is an important basis for comparison with Julian's own visionary
experiences, where darkness, disembodied voices, and clamor form an
important part of the sensory world into which she finds herself thrust

---

Henricum comitem (Liber exhortationis), ed. S. L. Fristedt, in The Wycliffe Bible, Vol. 2, The
Origin of the First Revision as Presented in "De salutaribus documentis," Stockholm Studies in
English 21 (Stockholm: Almqvist & Wiksells boktr., 1969). The use of the Penitential
Psalms in times of tribulation, suffering, and hardship will also have been in the textual
mix of Julian's reflections on such moments. See Lynn Staley, "The Penitential Psalms:
Conversion and the Limits of Lordship," JMEMSt 37 (2007): 221–69 (237–44); Clare
Costley King'oo, Miserere mei: The Penitential Psalms in Late Medieval and Early Modern
England (Notre Dame: University of Notre Dame Press, 2012).
   [48] Speculum Christiani, 51.
   [49] See, for example, the "Sermon of Dead Men," in Lollard Sermons, ed. Cigman, 215;
discussed in Appleford, "Comene Course," 208–9. The image also occurs somewhat
earlier, in the hugely popular Prick of Conscience, as part of a lengthy rumination on death
and dying that deploys most of the standard topoi of the ars moriendi tradition: Ralph
Hanna and Sarah Wood, eds., Richard Morris's "Prick of Conscience," EETS o.s. 342
(Oxford: Oxford University Press, 2013), lines 1900–25; see lines 1665–2689 for the
full meditation on death.

in the course of the revelations. The *Speculum Christiani*'s account of the demonic torments of the dying man is reflected not only in the rhetorical patterning that Julian deploys in her accounts of her own demonic temptations, but also in her highly ornate and patterned account of the dying moments of Christ on the cross.

As *ex post facto* readers of her revelations, we accept her assurance, hard won over many years of reflection, that "I conceived treuly and mightily that it was himselfe shewed it me without ony mene" (Long Text, cap. 4), but on the face of it her early experiences are poised as uncertainly on the threshold between the divine and the diabolic as she is poised on the threshold between life and death.[50] Indeed, her first experience of the sort of sudden change often referred to in homiletic and pastoral descriptions of the process of dying leaves her literally uneasy at the sudden change from disease to ease:

All that was beside the cross was uggely to me as if it had be mekil occupied with the fends. After this the other party of my body began to dyen so ferforth that onethys I had ony feleing, with shortness of onde. And than I went sothly to have passid. And, *in this sodenly* all my peyne was taken fro me and I was as hele, and namely in the other party of my body, as ever I was aforn. I mervalid at *this soden change* for methought it was a privy workeing of God and not of kinde. And yet by the feleing of this ease I trusted never the more to levyn; ne the feleing of this ease was no full ease to me, for methought I had lever a be deliveryd of this world.[51]

The liminality of Julian's state of mind mirrors the abject liminality of her physical health, breathlessly poised on the point of dissolution. She expects and longs for delivery from the world, but, like the pregnancy metaphors that see her conceiving Christ without any *mene* or intermediary, she needs to understand deliverance in a new way.[52] This delivery

[50] Long Text, cap. 4, 5.
[51] Long Text, cap. 3, 5; emphasis my own.
[52] On pregnancy imagery in Julian, see Tarjei Park, "Reflecting Christ: The Role of the Flesh in Walter Hilton and Julian of Norwich," in *The Medieval Mystical Tradition in England: 5th Symposium Papers*, ed. Marion Glasscoe (Cambridge: D. S. Brewer, 1992), 17–37 (33–34); Maud Burnett McInerney, "'In the meydens womb': Julian of Norwich and the Poetics of Enclosure," in *Medieval Mothering*, ed. Bonnie Wheeler and John Carmi Parsons (New York: Garland, 1996), 157–82; Tarjei Park, *Selfhood and "Gostly Menyng" in Some Middle English Mystics: Semiotic Approaches to Contemplative Theology* (Lewiston: Edwin Mellen Press, 2003); Claire Sisco King, "The Poetics and Praxis of Enclosure: Julian of Norwich, Motherhood, and Rituals of Childbirth," *Comitatus* 35 (2004): 71–82. See also note 27, above, on enclosure imagery.

will, like most pregnancies, be the result of much labor, pain, anxiety, and uncertainty, and sorrow suddenly gives way to joy. Julian's text shows that the sudden change is not just a magical transformation, as it can sometimes appear to be in Scripture. Rather, it is about radically transfiguring sickness into *sekirnes* and about learning how to transform the clichés of tribulation literature, or at least to inhabit them with new force.[53]

III. *Christus medicus* and *Christus moriens*

In Chapter 66, on the verge of the final showing, this force is brutally demonstrated. Julian's ease and relief from physical pain and suffering, which have lasted for the duration of her first fifteen showings, are suddenly removed, and she is thrown back into the maelstrom of illness and spiritual desolation:

I have seid in the begynnyng "And in this al my peine was sodenly taken from me"; of which ipeyne I had no grefe, no disese, as long as the xv shewings lestid folowand; and at the end al was close and I saw no more. And sone I felt that I shuld liven and langiren; and anon my sekenes cam agen: first in my hede, with a sound and a dynne; and sodenly all my body was fu[l]fillid with sekenes like as it was aforn, and I was as baren and drye as I never had comfort but litil. And as a wretch I moned and hevyed for felyng of my bodily pey[n]es and for fayling of comfort, gostly and bodily.[54]

Sekirnes has given way once more to sickness. Her loss of ghostly comfort is linked to her dryness, a spiritual as well as physiological desiccation.[55] But rather than making the physical pain a metaphor for spiritual desiccation and disease, Julian has been steadily working since the early revelations to separate the two and to avoid facile linkage. This stage in her

---

[53] Pertinent here is Allan F. Westphall, "Walter Hilton's *The Prickynge of Love* and the Construction of Vernacular 'Sikernesse,'" in *The Pseudo-Bonaventuran Lives of Christ: Exploring the Middle English Tradition*, ed. Ian Johnson and Westphall (Turnhout: Brepols, 2013), 457–502.

[54] Long Text, cap. 66, 107–8. On creative aspects of loss, absence, and dread in late medieval theological contexts, see the recent discussion by Simon D. Podmore, "*Mysterium horrendum*: Mystical Theology and the Negative Numinous," in *Contemporary Theological Explorations in Christian Mysticism: Opening to the Mystical*, ed. Louise Nelstrop and Simon D. Podmore (Farnham: Ashgate, 2013), 93–116.

[55] Cf. the cognate account of Christ's agonizing and protracted 'dry dying' in Long Text, caps. 16–17.

developing understanding is typically enacted in long chains of reflection and observation that need to be quoted at length to give the full flavor of her unfolding wisdom. In Chapter 15, for example, despite having had her pain and paralysis lifted, she experiences a fluctuating sense of the presence of God and his comfort. This feeling is linked to her understanding of the theology of fear: throughout her text she oscillates between "peynful drede" (*timor servilis*, a self-regarding and self-serving existential dread and fear of punishment) and "reverent drede" (a state of awe and respect for the power and grace of God that yields the initiative to him).[56] She seeks, and suffers, but fails to be able to trust:

I was fulfillid of the everlesting sekirnes migtily susteinid withoute any peynful drede. This felyng was so gladd and so gostly that I was in al peace and in reste that there was nothing in erth that should a grevid me. This lestinid but a while and I was turnyd and left to myselfe in hevynes and werines of my life and irkenes of myselfe that onethis I coude have patience to leve. There was no comfort nor none ease to me but feith, hope and charite, and these I had in truthe, but litil in feling. And anone, after this, our blissid lord gave me ageyne the comfort and the rest in soule, in likyng and sekirnes so blisful and so mycti that no drede, no sorow, ne peyne bodily that might be suffrid should have desesid me. And than the peyne shewid ageyn to my feling, and than the ioy and the lekyng, and now that one, and now that other, dyvers times—I suppose aboute xx tymes. And in the same tyme of ioy I migte have seid with Seynt Paul: "Nothing shal depart me fro the charite of Criste." And in the peyne I migte have seid with Peter: "Lord, save me, I perish." This vision was shewid me, after myn vndestondyng, that it is spedeful to some soulis to fele on this wise, somtime to be in comfort, and somtyme to faile and to be left to hemselfe . . . But frely our lord gevyth when he wille, and suffrith us in wo sumtyme. And both is one love; for it is Godds wil we hold us in comfort with al our migte, for blisse is lestinge withoute ende, and peyne is passand and shal be browte to nougte to hem that shall be savyd. And therefore it is not Godds wil that we folow the felyng of peyne in sorow and mornyng for hem, but sodenly passing over and holden us in endless likyng.[57]

[56] The theology of fear, with its divisions into *timor initialis*, *timor servilis*, and *timor filialis*, is a patristic commonplace discussed in Peter Lombard, Bonaventure, and Thomas Aquinas. More often in pastoral contexts there is a distinction drawn between obedience to God driven by *timor* and that driven by *amor*. For vernacular uses, see Rosemary Woolf, *The English Religious Lyric in the Middle Ages* (Oxford: Clarendon Press, 1968), 72–73.

[57] Long Text, cap. 15, 23–24.

Yet it soon emerges that it is indeed trust that is the key to deliverance from pain and illness. Julian's mature response to the age-old moral problem of evil and suffering is to see pain not as a state to be escaped from but as a condition of our humanity, deeply equated in her thinking with the corrosive and corrupting force of sin in the world.[58] Pain is transient; bliss is eternal. After death, man will be eternally removed from the region of pain, and this is a sounder solution than the transient relief achieved by pain being taken from man in this life. By this stage of her progress, Julian shows that one fruit of her "wilful abiding" is that simple answers reveal that one is asking the wrong questions.

It is ful blisfull, man to be taken fro peyne, mor than peyne to be taken fro man; for if peyn be taken fro us it may commen agen. Therfore it is a severen comfort and blissfull beholdyng in a lovand soule [that] we shal be taken fro peyne; for in this behest I saw a mervelous compassion that our lord hath in us for our wo, and a curtes behoting of clene deliverance; for he will that we be comforted in the overpassing; and that he shewid in these words: "And thou shalt come up aboven; and thou shal have me to thi mede; and thou shall be fulfillid of ioye and bliss." It is God will that we setten the poynte of our thowte in this blisfull beholdyng as often as we may, and as long tyme kepen us therin with his grace; for this is a blissid contemplation to the soule that is led of God, and ful mekil to his worship for the time that it lestith. And we falyn ageyn to our hevynes and gostly blyndhede and felyng of peyens gostly and bodily be our frelte, it is God will that we knowen that he hath not forgetten us. And so menith he in thes words and seith for comfort: "And thou shall never more have peyne, no manner sekenes, no manner mislekyng, non wanting of his will, but over ioy and bliss withouten ende."[59]

The echoes of Isaiah and Revelation in Christ's words at the end of this passage are surely not accidental. This is the true consolation that Christ offers Julian: not an earth-bound escape from pain and suffering, from disease and sickness, but rather a guarantee of overpassing bliss and an assurance that passing pain in our sensuality or humanity will not quell or suppress the true life of the substance of man, which is united to God in its essence and nature. And it is achieved primarily by her education

---

[58] On this, see especially Grace Jantzen, *Julian of Norwich: Mystic and Theologian*, new ed. (London: SPCK, 2000), esp. Part 4, "Wounds into Honours."

[59] Long Text, cap. 64, 105. See the usefully schematic account in Anna Minore, "Julian of Norwich and Catherine of Siena: Pain and the Way of Salvation," *Journal of Medieval Religious Cultures* 40 (2014): 44–74.

in the true meaning of the Passion of Christ, a meaning that transcends the affective banalities of most meditations and narrative accounts. Suso's Wisdom advises the disciple: "My passioun putte eek twixt my doom and thee, / Lest, more than neede is, adrad thow be."[60]

If the role of the *moriens* in the *ars moriendi* tradition is to serve as a *memento mori* for those present at the deathbed or reading such texts for personal devotion, Appleford's important argument that Julian fulfills the same function in her own text ultimately gives an incomplete account of what she is doing in the showings. After all, Julian recovers her health and lives to write another day. The only person who actually dies in her book is Christ. This is the true genius of her showings: in the core revelations, Julian goes well beyond her own role as the liminal *moriens*, the double signifier poised on the brink and instructing her *euencristen* how to die. For, in a stroke of powerful imaginative synergy, she presents to us Christ the Man of Sorrows as the ultimate "felable ensaumple" of "a man dying and speaking to us." Christ, God and man, is of course already the ultimate double signifier, a theological synapse of powerful liminality, who is simultaneously the way, the truth, and the life. But, crucially, whereas Suso's dying man was trapped in the stasis of his own inactivity and his previous dissolute life and spiritual sloth, Julian's man dying and speaking to us—the *Christus moriens*— offers to Julian the symbolic and spiritual answer to the existential fear of pain and death.

Nearly all the Passion showings take place within the first "sodeynly" of her earliest revelation ("In this sodenly I saw . . ." [cap. 4]): in that respect they participate in the sudden changing that scriptural tradition had asserted. But while the powerful and protracted account of Christ's lingering death in the eighth revelation (especially caps. 16–17), with its dry dying and languorous teetering on the edge of dissolution, fulfills her earlier request to see the sufferings of Christ and to have compassion with him, it goes well beyond it in the intensity of its staging. Verbally marked by the traditional signs of death from lyric and medical literature (and also found in Suso's man dying and speaking), it takes place in a dystopian non-landscape of muted dark colors, like the non-representational backgrounds of Man of Sorrows iconography, an eschatological setting swept by an unnaturally cold and drying wind.[61] This

---

[60] Hoccleve, "Ars vtillissima sciendi mori," lines 832–33.

[61] On Julian's subtle and dynamic use of light and color, see Vincent Gillespie, "The Colours of Contemplation: Less Light on Julian of Norwich," in Jones, *Medieval Mystical Tradition: Exeter Symposium VIII*, 7–28; Elizabeth Robertson, "Julian of Norwich's

is a place out of time where the changes wrought by Christ's death are both feared and desired by the observer: feared because they mark the apparent death of God, and desired because they mark the end of suffering:

After this Criste shewid a partie of his passion nere his deyeng. I saw his swete face as it was drye and blodeles with pale deyeng; and sithen more pale, dede, langoring, and than turnid more dede into blew, and sithen more brown blew, as the flesh turnyd more depe dede . . . This was a swemful chonge to sene this depe deyeng, and also the nose clange and dryed, to my sigte, and the swete body was brown and blak, al turnyd oute of faire lifely colowr of hymselfe onto drye deyeng; for that eche tyme that our lord and blissid savior deyid upon the rode it was a dry, harre wynde and wond colde, as to my sigte; and what tyme the pretious blode was blede oute of the swete body that migte pass therfro, yet there dwellid a moysture in the swete flesh of Criste, as it was shewyd. Blodeleshede and peyne dryden within and blowyng of wynde and cold commyng fro withouten metten togeder in the swete body of Criste. . . . And thow this peyne was bitter and sharpe, it was full long lestyng, as to my sighte, and peynfully dreyden up all the lively spirits of Crists fleshe. Thus I saw the swete fleshe dey, in semyng be party after party, dryande with mervelous peynys. And as longe as any spirit had life in Crists fleshe, so longe sufferid he peyne. This longe pynyng semyd to me as if he had bene seven night ded, deyand, at the poynt of out passing away, sufferand the last peyne.[62]

The "swemful chonge" creates a looping existential dread, where Julian's language enacts a self-perpetuating and self-fueling combination of acute anxiety and chronic ennui that is painfully familiar to anyone who has watched at a deathbed or has experienced life-threatening illness themselves.

But because it is Christ himself who is the *moriens*, a man dying slowly, interminably, and horribly, and speaking to Julian, his words do not teach the conventional perils of unexpected death. Despite the fact that the language she uses borrows rhetorical velocity from the sorts of transit narratives found in the *Speculum Christiani*, Christ's death is willed and planned and wholeheartedly embraced: he embodies and personifies the wonderful but hidden "great deed" that God has done and will do.

Unmediated Vision," in *Medieval and Early Modern Devotional Objects in Global Perspective: Translations of the Sacred*, ed. Robertson and Jennifer Jahner (London: Palgrave Macmillan, 2010), 97–114.

[62] Long Text, cap. 16, 24–25.

He is a different kind of exemplar, a model of *kenosis* and love that gives an answer to the stasis and debilitating fear expressed by the traditional *moriens* (and indeed initially by Julian herself).[63] His sudden change of cheer will unexpectedly and transformatively disrupt this seemingly ineluctable linear trajectory to dissolution and despair (the repeated "ands" in this passage convey something of the radical anaphoric causality of her suddenly changing perspective):

And I loked after the departing with al my myght and {wende} have seen the body al ded, but I saw hym not so. And ryth in the same tyme that methowte, be semyng, the life myght ne lenger lesten and the shewyng of the end behovyd nedis to be, sodenly, I beholdyng in the same crosse, he chongyd his blissfull chere. The chongyng of his blisful chere chongyd myn, and I was as glad and mery as it was possible. Than browte our lord merily to my mynde: "Where is now ony poynte of the peyne or of thin agreefe?" And I was full merry. I understode that we be now, in our lords menyng, in his crosse with hym in our peynys and our passion, deyng; and we wilfully abydyng in the same cross with his helpe and his grace into the last poynte, sodenly he shal chonge his chere to us, and we shal be with hym in hevyn.[64]

Julian's Christ refuses to play by the script: tearing up the rules of illness and suffering, refusing the logic of lingering death, and frustrating the narrative and medical expectations that "the shewyng of the end behovyd nedis to be." Julian's compassion with the suffering Christ is transformed instead into a celebration of Christ's compassion with our

[63] See further Gillespie and Ross, "The Apophatic Image." In recent years, *kenosis*, *apophasis*, and issues surrounding the ineffability of God have become much more central to and familiar in discussions of English contemplative writing. See, for example, Nicholas Watson, "Conceptions of the Word: The Mother Tongue and the Incarnation of God," *NML* 1 (1997): 85–124; Cynthia Masson, "The Point of Coincidence: Rhetoric and the Apophatic in Julian of Norwich's *Showings*," in *Julian of Norwich: A Book of Essays*, ed. Sandra J. McEntire (New York: Garland, 1998), 153–81. For useful recent accounts of the broader theological and philosophical background, see Onno Zijstra, ed., *Letting Go: Rethinking Kenosis* (Bern: Peter Lang, 2002); C. Stephen Evans, ed., *Exploring Kenotic Christology: The Self-Emptying of God* (Oxford: Oxford University Press, 2006); William Franke, *On What Cannot Be Said: Apophatic Discourses in Philosophy, Religion, Literature, and the Arts*, 2 vols. (Notre Dame: University of Notre Dame Press, 2007); Michael Kessler and Christian Sheppard, eds., *Mystics: Presence and Aporia* (Chicago: University of Chicago Press, 2003); Michael A. Sells, *Mystical Languages of Unsaying* (Chicago: University of Chicago Press, 1994).

[64] Long Text, cap. 21, 30–31. On the text of this showing, see Marion Glasscoe, "Changing Chere and Changing Text in the Eighth Revelation of Julian of Norwich," *MÆ* 66 (1997): 115–21.

sufferings. Julian comes to realize that it is not a matter of us being in pain because he is in pain: the traditional sense of compassion. Rather, she stresses that "when we were in pain he was in pain." He has love and compassion with us: he is the supreme exemplar of affective compassion. It is a transactional and profoundly therapeutic reversal of expectation and of normal devotional strategy. It brings about sudden changes of perspective and expectation.[65]

In the endless present participles of these chapters on the dying Christ, Julian dramatizes waves of fear, grief, anxiety, despair, and creates a paradoxical and powerful hybridity between physical and spiritual states. She creates disease, suffering, and discomfort in the ways that she refashions the Christ of the Passion meditation tradition as the speaking dead man of the Suso *ars moriendi*. But whereas Suso's dying man had no hope and no answers and was beyond consolation or reprieve, Christ shows that he holds the answers for her. He has been there, done that and got, if not the tee-shirt, then at least the vernicle. The Word made Flesh is the lexical synapse that can turn sickness into *sekirnes*. Suso talks about the work of the Passion as: "for to make þe feyre & semely þorhe his abieccione and vnsemelynessse . . . Wherfore hit foloweþ opunlye þat þe abieccione and vnsemelynesses of the vttere manne, þat he toke of þe bitternese of passione, is raþer chewynge and profe of loue þanne mater of reprefe."[66] This is the transformational paradox of Philippians 2:5–9, one of the strikingly few Scripture passages explicitly cited by Julian at precisely this point in the Short Text:

Swilke paines I sawe that alle es to litelle that I can telle or saye, for it maye nought be tolde. Botte ilke saule, after the sayinge of Sainte Paule, shulde "feele in him that in Criste Jhesu."

[65] I am grateful to Dr. James Hanvey S.J. for his helpful comments on this section of the article:

> Is it too much to think that here in this experience of joy Julian is also expressing an eschatology, but one that is lived now, in this present, a sort of magnificat? Much more then than your usual mystical experience but something that is for every Christian life in the circumstances of its real existence. The fear of death is removed not only because of future hope but because of a present reality of knowing (understanding and experiencing) now in this life something of the reality and promise of heaven. At the deepest level, this is because the dynamic *ekstasis/kenosis* in and through the cross and death of Christ is a genuine eucharistic moment; not out of the world but in it. (personal communication, March 17, 2016)

[66] *Orologium sapientiae*, ed. Horstmann, 338.

Hoc enim sentite in vobis, quod et in Christo Jesu: qui cum in forma Dei esset, non rapinam arbitratus est esse se aequalem Deo: sed semetipsum exinanivit, formam servi accipiens, in similitudinem hominum factus, et habitu inventus ut homo. Humiliavit semetipsum factus obediens usque ad mortem, mortem autem crucis. Propter quod et Deus exaltavit illum, et donavit illi nomen, quod est super omne nomen.

[For let this mind be in you, which was also in Christ Jesus: Who being in the form of God, thought it not robbery to be equal with God: But emptied himself, taking the form of a servant, being made in the likeness of men, and in habit found as a man. He humbled himself, becoming obedient unto death, even to the death of the cross. For which cause God also hath exalted him, and hath given him a name which is above all names.][67]

Exaltation follows abjection; obedience leads to freedom, humility to eternal reward, suffering and pain to joy and bliss. The logic of the world is torn up.

The exhortation to "Seek, suffer, and trust" is reworked in Julian's later chapters into polyphonic variations on a theme, with Christ speaking directly to her soul: "But take it, leve it, and kepe the therin and comfort the therwith and trost thou therto; and thou shalt not be overcome."[68] This allows her to summarize that "therfore in what manner he techith us, he will we perceivyn him wisely, receivyn him swetely, and kepin us in hym feithfully."[69] As the therapeutic triads overlay each other semantically and lexically, so her ability to "wilfully abide" the sufferings and tribulations of life and of death appear to be enhanced by her confidence that they will quickly and permanently pass over. She has learned that the abjection of human sickness can be suddenly

---

[67] Short Text, section 10, as edited in "A Vision Showed to a Devout Woman," in *The Writings of Julian of Norwich*, ed. Nicholas Watson and Jacqueline Jenkins, Medieval Women: Texts and Contexts 5 (Turnhout: Brepols, 2006), 83; Phil 2:5–9. Both Brant Pelphrey, *Love Was His Meaning: The Theology and Mysticism of Julian of Norwich*, Salzburg Studies in English Literature 92, no. 4 (Salzburg: Institut für Anglistik und Amerikanistik, 1982), 261; and *Book of Showings*, ed. Colledge and Walsh, 97, discuss the influence of this passage on Julian. Neither sees it as fundamental to her overall textual strategy. Colledge and Walsh argue, for example, that the whole eighth revelation, on Christ's lingering death and double dryness, is an extended meditation on Philippians 2 (97).

[68] Long Text, cap. 68, 111.

[69] Ibid., cap. 70, 113.

changed into a willed *kenosis* of love.[70] In this way, Julian's vividly performative account of the Passion of Christ provides a transferable model for her own behavior in the face of sickness and death, which in turn becomes a model for all her *euen-cristen*. Just as her friends and family watched round her own deathbed at the start of the showings, so she watches for the death of Christ. Her text is a repetitious *mise en abyme* of Suso's man dying and speaking to us, a spiritual fractal endlessly reflecting and conforming to a paradigm of goodness that originates in Christ's Passion.

If love was indeed Christ's meaning, then Julian performs in her text not only the injunction of Paul in Philippians 2, but also the linked injunctions in the First Epistle of Saint John:

Timor non est in caritate: sed perfecta caritas foras mittit timorem, quoniam timor poenam habet: qui autem timet, non est perfectus in caritate. Nos ergo diligamus Deum, quoniam Deus prior dilexit nos.

[Fear is not in love: but perfect love casteth out fear, because fear hath pain. And he that feareth, is not perfected in love. Let us therefore love God, because God first hath loved us.][71]

Julian develops this in her own way: "And therefore he will that we redily entenden to his gracious touching, more enioying in his hole love than sorowand in our often fallings . . . And therefore he will that we

---

[70] This is in keeping with the kenotic thrust of Julian's thought: noughting of self leads to oneing with God in the mathematical paradox beloved of contemplative theologians. Hilton comments that:

> he may not lyven to God fulli, until he die first unto the world. This dyynge to the world is this myrkenesse, and it is the gate of contemplacioun and to reformynge in feelynge, and noon othir than this . . . But he that can brynge himsilf firste to nought thorugh grace of mekenesse and dien on this maner, he is in the gate, for he is deed to the world and he lyveth to God. (Walter Hilton, *The Scale of Perfection*, II.27, as printed in *The Scale of Perfection*, ed. Thomas H. Bestul [Kalamazoo: Medieval Institute Publications, 2000]).

This recalls Jerome's aphorism "Nudis Christum nudum sequi," a popular Patristic theme. For discussion of this theme, see Karl Heinz Steinmetz, "'Thiself a cros to thiself': Christ as *Signum Impressum* in the *Cloud*-Texts against the Background of Expressionistic Christology in Late Medieval Devotional Theology," in *The Medieval Mystical Tradition in England: Exeter Symposium VII*, ed. E. A. Jones (Cambridge: D. S. Brewer, 2004), 132–48.

[71] 1 Jn 4:18–21.

setten our herts in the overpassing: that is to sey, fro the peyne that we felen into the bliss that we trosten."[72] Touching leads to wholeness: this is *Christus medicus* at work in the guise of *Christus moriens*.[73] The phrase "redily attenden" implies a focused attentiveness (a powerful combination of attention and intention) that allows our hearts to aspire to an overpassing of pain and grief.

In one of the most powerful formulations of her entire book, Julian explains pain and suffering from the divine perspective, but she is only able to do so because she has learned how to "behold with avisement": a special kind of agendaless and non-analytical attention that allows her to see things in a metaphysical context and allows God to take the spiritual and indeed the semantic initiative.[74] A proper "beholding" of the loving face of Christ triggers a transformation in outlook, a response to his gracious touching, and a performative passover from dread to love, distracting from fear and pain by radically remodeling the parameters of human attentiveness from the linear and physical (illness leads to pain and then death) to the *sodeynly* atemporal and metaphysical. Suso's man dying warns of the paralysis of pain and fear; Julian's *Christus moriens* liberates from it. Julian does nothing to minimize pain, illness, disease. But by placing them in a wider and deeper perspectival setting she perhaps breaks the spiritual stasis and frozen, existential dread that *timor mortis* can assert over the frailty of our living:

And ryte as in the first worde that our good lord shewid, menyng his blissfull passion—"Herwith is the devill overcome"—ryte so he seid in the last word with full trew sekirness, menand us all: "Thou shalt not ben overcommen." And all this leryng in this trew comfort, it is generall to all my even cristen as it is afornseid, and so is Gods will. And these words: "Thou shalt not ben

---

[72] Long Text, cap. 81, 130.

[73] The image of *Christus medicus* derives ultimately from Matthew 9:12, and is widely used by Augustine in his *Ennarationes in psalmos*; Rudolph Arbesmann, "The Concept of *Christus medicus* in St. Augustine," *Traditio* 10 (1954): 1–28; Reinhard von Bendemann, *Christus medicus* (Neukirchener: Neukirchen-Vluyn, 2009).

[74] On the particular importance of *beholding* as a key concept in Julian's theology, see now Martha Reeves, "Behold Not the Cloud of Experience," in *The Medieval Mystical Tradition in England: Exeter Symposium VIII*, ed. E. A. Jones (Cambridge: D. S. Brewer, 2013), 29–50; Vincent Gillespie and Maggie Ross, " 'With mekenes aske perseverantly': On Reading Julian of Norwich," *Mystics Quarterly* 30 (2004): 125–40. For a more cautious interpretation, see Pelphrey, *Love Was His Meaning*, 229–47; Roland Maisonneuve, *L'univers visionnaire de Julian of Norwich* (Paris: OEIL, 1987), 125–53.

overcome," was seid full sharply and full mightily for sekirness and comfort agens all tribulations that may comen. He seid not "Thou shalt not be tempesteid, thou shalt not be travelled, thou shalt not be disesid," but he seid: "Thou shalt not be overcome."[75]

Tribulations will come, but they will also be overcome. Despite tempest, travail, and disease, she asserts that her *euen-cristen* will not be overcome, provided they learn how to seek, suffer, and trust. For Julian, a central understanding of her showings seems to be that the radical liminality of sickness places the *euen-cristen* into the synapse of potential spiritual efflorescence from the shackles of fear, pain, and existential terror:

God will that we taken heede at these words, and that we be ever myty in sekir troste, in wele and wo; for he lovith and lekyth us, and so will he that we love him and lekin him and mytily trosten in him; and al shal be wele. And sone after al was close and I sow no more.[76]

The tight verbal patterning here enacts the enfolding and enclosing love of God that Julian feels to be at the heart of her showings: strength, security, might, delight, wele, and woe lead to love and liking, or likening. The result of this for Julian is a "sekir troste" in the existential guarantee offered by *Christus medicus et moriens*, whose painfully realistic death has surrealistically destroyed death and the fear of death. T. S. Eliot, a profoundly perceptive reader of Julian's text, captures the point perfectly:

> The wounded surgeon plies the steel
> That questions the distempered part;
> Beneath the bleeding hands we feel
> The sharp compassion of the healer's art
> Resolving the enigma of the fever chart.
>
> Our only health is the disease
> If we obey the dying nurse.[77]

If Christ is indeed the word uttered by God, then, for Julian, when properly attended to, he is also truly the medicine of words: a man dying and speaking to you.

[75] Long Text, cap. 68, 111.
[76] Ibid.
[77] T. S. Eliot, "East Coker," in *Four Quartets* (London: Faber and Faber, 1959), 29: cf. ". . . to be restored, our sickness must grow worse."

"O sweete and wel biloved spouse deere": A Pastoral Reading of Cecilia's Post-Nuptial Persuasion in *The Second Nun's Tale*

Mary Beth Long
University of Arkansas

Abstract

This essay reconciles the sweet wife Cecilia who appears at the beginning of Chaucer's *Second Nun's Tale* with the public preacher she has become by the end by attending to what pastoral books, such as confessional manuals and hagiographical narratives, said and assumed about wives, women saints, and preachers. Reading the tale from this perspective offers a way to understand Cecilia's speaking behaviors and, by extension, how her *passio* is wholly congruent with the Second Nun as teller. Here, Cecilia is an orthodox wife whose persuasive skills are as evident in her initial nuptial conversation with her husband Valerian as in her conventional hagiographical debate with the pagan Almachius. Contextualized by pastoral expectations of wives and late medieval assessments of women's speech, this interpretation of Cecilia suggests her potential as a rhetorical model to late medieval readers who wanted to emulate her persuasive talent and commitment to orthodoxy regardless of marital or clerical status.

Keywords

Chaucer, Saint Cecilia, hagiography, pastoral, Benedictine, speech, sweetness, persuasion, wives, preaching, *Canterbury Tales*, orthodox, medieval, England

CHAUCER'S SPLICING TOGETHER of Dominican and Franciscan source texts in *The Second Nun's Tale* gives us Cecilia's authoritative voice in what seem like two very different registers: as a sweetly persuasive wife to Valerian, and as a fierce, insulting preacher in her confrontation

Studies in the Age of Chaucer 39 (2017):159–189
© 2017 The New Chaucer Society

with Almachius.[1] Previous readings leave unexplained this shift in Cecilia's social and rhetorical roles from wife to widowed martyr within the text, as well as the seemingly jarring juxtaposition of the Second Nun as teller with the married, defiant Cecilia as subject. Cecilia's combative speech with Almachius attracts disproportionate attention from scholars, as does her preaching, largely because both have been read as such a contrast to the Second Nun herself.[2] Modern readers have been, if not quite scandalized by Cecilia's speech, eager to describe it as subversive or to label her as feistier than her situation calls for, despite its conformity to similar speeches in other virgin martyrs' *passiones*.[3] But the less sexy truth is that Cecilia is a rule-follower, not -breaker: in Chaucer's

[1] Chaucer's version of Cecilia's *vita* is derived from two mendicant sources, the Dominican *Golden Legend* and a Franciscan breviary. See Sherry Reames, "A Recent Discovery Concerning the Sources of Chaucer's 'Second Nun's Tale,'" *MP* 87, no. 4 (1990): 337–61; and her "The Second Nun's Prologue and Tale," in *Sources and Analogues of the "Canterbury Tales,"* ed. Robert M. Correale and Mary Hamel, 2 vols. (Cambridge: D. S. Brewer, 2002), 1:491–527. Mary-Virginia Rosenfeld suggested as early as 1940 that Chaucer may have consulted a breviary for this tale and others; "Chaucer and the Liturgy," *MLN* 55 (1940): 357–60 (358). Sherry Reames has pointed out that Chaucer's manipulation of his sources highlights Cecilia's speech; "The Office for Saint Cecilia," in *The Liturgy of the Medieval Church*, ed. Thomas J. Heffernan and E. Ann Matter (Kalamazoo: Western Michigan Press, 2001), 219–42. Here and henceforth, like every other modern scholar of this tale, I am heavily indebted to Reames's groundbreaking archival work, although I do not always agree with her conclusions. I am equally indebted to the anonymous readers of previous versions of this essay who offered incisive suggestions for its improvement.

[2] Readers have long speculated about or tried to reconcile the mismatch of the Second Nun with the other pilgrims and of her *Prologue* with the *Tale(s)*. V. A. Kolve notes that the Nun's voice is not "significantly individuated in the tale she tells" (139), so that the *passio* is "uncolored by the idiosyncrasies of a personal narrative voice"; "Chaucer's *Second Nun's Tale* and the Iconography of Saint Cecilia," in *New Perspectives in Chaucer Criticism*, ed. Donald M. Rose (Norman: University of Oklahoma Press, 1981), 137–74 (157). Karen Arthur attempts to reconcile the quiet piety of the Second Nun with Cecilia's outspokenness by highlighting the relationship between virginity and vocality for teller and subject; "Equivocal Subjectivity in Chaucer's *Second Nun's Prologue* and *Tale*," *ChauR* 32, no. 3 (1998): 217–31. The scholarly consensus seems to be that Chaucer's having written this tale long before compiling the rest of the *Canterbury Tales* is explanation enough, as though he simply needed filler for the collection and was unconcerned with matching tale to teller: this explanation is given in numerous editions of the *Tales*.

[3] Karen Winstead, for example, includes Cecilia in a group of virgin martyrs she calls "shrewish," and describes her "aggressiveness" in *Virgin Martyrs: Legends of Sainthood in Late Medieval England* (Ithaca, N.Y.: Cornell University Press, 1997), 64, 83. Carolyn Collette calls her "defiant" but contextualizes her claim that "the central action of the tale revolves around Cecile's public confrontation with Almachius" with reference to the Virgin Mary's presence and influence in the tale; *Performing Polity: Women and Agency in the Anglo-French Tradition, 1385–1620* (Turnhout: Brepols, 2006), 97. The prologue's invocation of Mary is outside the scope of this essay, but as Collette has pointed out, the model of Mary as speaker hovers over the prologue and tale. I discuss Mary's connection to Cecilia in a forthcoming project.

hybrid translation of her *vita*, her consistent falling into line is highly rewarded. To grasp this, we must consider the biases of the tale's initial culture of reception, which would have read both the Second Nun and Cecilia as vocal points along the same short spectrum of orthodoxy, and which would have absorbed Cecilia's preaching along with her private speaking by shoehorning both into the speech categories available to pious women.

The past few decades of scholarship on Chaucer and on devotional reading point to the logic of reading this text not only as one example from the *Canterbury Tales*, but as a hagiographical narrative modified to suit an audience with Benedictine, or at least pastoral, sympathies.[4] Like Chaucer's Prioress, the Second Nun is usually identified as Benedictine, as was a monastery that Mary Giffin once posited was the original beneficiary of Chaucer's translation.[5] Giffin's suggestion that this tale was composed as a gift to the Benedictines at Norwich Cathedral Priory in honor of their former monk Cardinal Adam Easton[6] is plausible enough that it is often cited without question or comment.[7] Widely acknowledged as it is, Giffin's theory has not, to my knowledge, been incorporated into any serious

---

[4] The mocking of friars throughout the *Tales* may be an obvious pattern to mention here, as is the potential for an inside joke on Chaucer's using mendicant sources to tell a story by and to Benedictines. Nancy Bradley Warren has done important archival work on Chaucer's texts in other religious houses, tracing Syon and Amesbury nuns' use of Chaucer for political and rhetorical purposes; "Chaucer, the Chaucer Tradition, and Female Monastic Readers," *ChauR* 51, no. 1 (2016): 88–106. For approaches to Chaucer's connections to theology and the Church, see Helen Phillips, ed., *Chaucer and Religion* (Woodbridge: D. S. Brewer, 2010).

[5] The Prioress has traditionally been affiliated with the Saint Leonard's Benedictine convent. On nuns' literary culture see Mary Erler, *Women, Reading, and Piety in Late Medieval England* (Cambridge: Cambridge University Press, 2002) for discussion of networks of women's reading materials passed across enclosure and generational lines slightly later than the period considered here; and Virginia Blanton, Veronica O'Mara, and Patricia Stoop, eds., *Nuns' Literacies in Medieval Europe: The Hull Dialogue* (Turnhout: Brepols, 2013), and *Nuns' Literacies in Medieval Europe: The Kansas City Dialogue* (Turnhout: Brepols, 2015).

[6] There has been some debate about the exact nature of Easton's role as cardinal and as inspiration for Chaucer's Cecilia. In brief: he was made cardinal of the Church of Saint Cecilia at Trastevere in Rome in 1381; there was already a holder of the Cecilia title, but Easton was referred to as cardinal of Saint Cecilia starting in 1382; he lost the title after a fair amount of trouble with Pope Urban VI and was deprived of benefices in 1385, but resumed it in 1389; intriguingly, Richard II called Easton "the cardinal of Norwich" in a letter to Pope Urban but "the cardinal of Saint Cecilia" to Boniface IX. See Margaret Harvey, *The English in Rome 1362–1420: Portrait of an Expatriate Community* (Cambridge: Cambridge University Press, 1999), 206.

[7] See Mary Giffin, "Hir hous the Chirche of Seinte Cecilie highte," in *Studies on Chaucer and His Audience* (Quebec: Les Editions l'Eclair, 1956), 29–48. The many editions of the *Canterbury Tales* that cite Giffin's theory include those most widely used in class-

literary analysis of the tale.[8] This seems an obvious gap in scholarship, as reading the tale from the perspective of the proposed original Benedictine audience offers a way to understand Cecilia's speaking behaviors and, by extension, how her *passio* is wholly congruent with the Second Nun as teller. If Giffin is right, then the prologue serves to remind Chaucer's later readers to interpret Cecilia as the Norwich Benedictines and users of their library would have, with an awareness of what their books, such as mendicant-authored confessional manuals and hagiographical narratives, said and assumed about wives, women saints, and preachers.

The Benedictines of Norwich certainly had both space and time to do serious reading. Barbara Dodwell asserts that by 1382–83 the Norwich Benedictines seem to have had the workings of a common library, and by 1386–87 had a designated room for communally held books. By 1574 the library was demolished, so piecing together what was in the collection has been a decades-long unfinished task.[9] Further, the Norwich Benedictines' reading community may have involved readers outside its cloister. Richard Copsey has described the monasteries' functioning as a kind of community college for the 90 percent of clergy who didn't make it to university, and as a first stage of higher education for those who did: any book owned by the monastery would thus potentially be accessible to a wide readership of other preachers.[10] In addition, while the nearby Carrow Abbey apparently had its own library, it is not outside the realm of possibility that its nuns also had access to texts

---

rooms, such as *The Riverside Chaucer*, gen. ed. Larry D. Benson, 3rd ed. (Boston, Mass.: Houghton Mifflin, 1987); and *The Canterbury Tales*, ed. Jill Mann (London: Penguin, 2005).

[8] Although for an interpretation of the tale based on its possible connection to the papal schism and contemporary debates about the Church, see Lynn Staley Johnson, "Chaucer's Tale of the Second Nun and the Strategies of Dissent," *SP* 89, no. 3 (1992): 314–33.

[9] See Barbara Dodwell, "The Muniments and the Library," in *Norwich Cathedral: Church, City, and Diocese, 1096–1996*, ed. Ian Atherton, Eric Fernie, Christopher Harper-Bill, and Hassell Smith (London: Hambledon, 1996), 325–38 (337). In the same volume, see also Norman Tanner, "The Cathedral and the City," 255–80, esp. 270–72. Roberta Gilchrist notes that the archeological "identification of at least twenty book cupboards confirms that the cloister at Norwich was used for reading and study," and speculates that it may have been fitted with carrels; *Norwich Cathedral Close: The Evolution of the English Cathedral Landscape* (Woodbridge: Boydell, 2005), 92.

[10] See Richard Copsey, "The Formation of the Medieval English Friar: From Dominican Model to Carmelite Practice," in *Omnia disce: Medieval Studies in Memory of Leonard Boyle, O.P.*, ed. Anne J. Duggan, Joan Greatrex, and Brenda Bolton (Ashgate: Aldershot, 2004), 245–62.

from the larger monastery's collection.[11] In either case, Chaucer's Second Nun herself might easily be imagined as a reader and as part of this original audience. We might also remember here Julian of Norwich's claim to have heard the story of Cecilia in church: the influence of Benedictine-owned texts should not be underestimated. The potential audience for this text would have been a group of readers thinking in pastoral as well as readerly terms, and with an eye toward other texts accessible and useful to the Benedictine community. In the setting that Giffin imagines, then, Chaucer's *vita* of Cecilia could have been experienced by individual study or by the communal reading of saints' lives that would have likely taken place at mealtimes or other communal gatherings; it would have been accessible to a relatively wide range of readers and reading experiences. Reading Cecilia with the eyes of this diverse pastoral audience gives us new tools with which to consider both Cecilia's behavior and the Nun as her narrator: it turns out that, by the standards of texts commonly found in Benedictine libraries, both are speaking absolutely according to form. Shifting our critical attention with these readers to the conventionality of Cecilia's first speech as a married woman helps us see that it, like her dialogue with Almachius, attempts to demonstrate women's potential agency within orthodoxy.

The prologue's criticism of idle speech and Cecilia's purposeful (rather than idle) speeches in the tale make clear that this is a narrative interested in the outcomes of orthodox (rather than gossipy) women's speech that is obedient to confessional demands and geared toward proselytical productivity. Spoken by a Benedictine nun, the prologue reminds us that our reading of the married Cecilia's words should be with an eye toward clerical expectations of wifely behaviors: amidst the many texts criticizing women's illicit speech, this tale explores what will happen if a woman's speech is *always* orthodox.[12] Specifically, the descriptions of women's speech and marital conversation in confessional manuals and

[11] See Marilyn Oliva, *The Convent and the Community in Late Medieval England: Female Monasteries in the Diocese of Norwich, 1350–1540* (Woodbridge: Boydell, 1998), 67. See also Walter Rye, *Carrow Abbey* (Norwich: Agas H. Goose, 1889).

[12] For recent work on the topic of women's speech, see Sandy Bardsley, *Venomous Tongues: Speech and Gender in Late Medieval England* (Philadelphia: University of Pennsylvania Press, 2006); and Susan E. Phillips, *Transforming Talk: The Problem with Gossip in Late Medieval England* (University Park: Penn State University Press, 2007). See also Edwin D. Craun, *Lies, Slander and Obscenity in Medieval English Literature: Pastoral Rhetoric and the Deviant Speaker* (Cambridge: Cambridge University Press, 1997).

hagiographical texts would prompt a Benedictine or pastoral reader's interpretation of the married virgin martyr Cecilia to consider her speech first as a wife, and only later as a preacher. By the standards of those genres, she is highly successful, achieving all her goals. Because we are not reading like Benedictines, we are less likely to notice the means of persuasion she uses on her wedding night to convince her husband Valerian to remain chaste and ultimately convert to Christianity,[13] although apart from a prayer, this address is her first, and is the linchpin of the whole narrative:

> O sweete and wel biloved spouse deere,
> Ther is a conseil, and ye wolde it heere
> Which that right fain I wolde unto yow seye,
> So that ye swere ye shul it nat biwreye.
>
> (SNT, 144–47)[14]

With this bedroom speech and the ones that follow, Cecilia demonstrates what a good and orthodox wife she is and intends to remain. In a pastoral reading of the tale, it is Cecilia's persuasion of Valerian on their wedding night that drives all the action that follows, from Valerian's agreement to keep the marriage chaste to Cecilia's own trial, when the widowed Cecilia abandons wifely persuasion in favor of a more conventional-hagiographical combative interaction with Almachius— that is, when she moves from acting like a good wife to acting like a good preacher. As I will argue, even as she demonstrates her persuasive skills as a wife, Cecilia is also training Valerian in how to speak as a proselytizing Christian.[15] Cecilia herself becomes a public figure—that

---

[13] In fact, speaking in a slightly different context, Reames has argued that "the persuasive gifts of Cecilia are ultimately irrelevant. God does not use persuasion"; Sherry L. Reames, "The Cecilia Legend as Chaucer Inherited It and Retold It: The Disappearance of an Augustinian Ideal," *Speculum* 51, no. 1 (1980): 38–57.

[14] Quotations are from *The Riverside Chaucer*. The phrasing is consistent with that of Chaucer's sources, the *Golden Legend* and the Franciscan abridgment: i.e., "O dulcissime atque amantissime iuvenis, est misterium quod tibi confitear si modo tu iuratus asseras tota te illud observantia custodire" (Reames, "The Second Nun's Prologue and Tale," 505); "O sweetest and most loving young man, I have a secret to confess to you, on condition that you swear to keep this secret entirely to yourself" (*The Golden Legend: Readings on the Saints*, ed. and trans. William Granger Ryan [Princeton: Princeton University Press, 2012], 704–5); and from the abridgment, "O dulcissime atque amantissime juvenis, est secretum quod tibi confitear, si modo tu juratus asseras tota te illud observantia custodire" (Reames, "A Recent Discovery," 357).

[15] Elizabeth Robertson considers the first of Valerian's imitations of Cecilia, rather than Cecilia's speech that provokes it, as the crux of the narrative: "From *his* ultimatum springs the drama of the tale" (emphasis), in "Apprehending the Divine and Choosing

is, a speaker in the public sphere—only after her role and speech are legitimized by men. She thus reinforces wives' submissive roles as outlined by confessional manuals and other pastoral texts.

Most importantly for Chaucerian, hagiographical, and pastoral contexts, Cecilia's initial address to Valerian is spoken as his legal wife. That first line, "O sweete and wel biloved spouse deere," suggests she is not interested in changing the status of their new relationship. Cecilia's identity as a Chaucerian wife has long been discussed; Donald Howard famously proposed that hers is the ideal Chaucerian marriage in part because it is chaste and ends in martyrdom, but he does not mention Cecilia's persuasive skills, and glosses over her navigation of the late medieval Christian role of wife.[16] As a saint, too, Cecilia's marital status is noteworthy because the *vitae* of female saints more often featured unmarried virgin martyrs.[17] Frequent admiring references to Cecilia in the biographies of would-be chaste women, such as the betrothed Christina of Markyate; the married Margery Kempe and Marie d'Oignies; and, as Sharon Farmer discovered, the eleventh-century German noble wife Ermengard, make clear that female readers of Cecilia's *vita* saw her primarily as a wife whose orthodox inflection justified their citing her

---

to Believe: Voluntarist Free Will in Chaucer's *Second Nun's Tale*," *ChauR* 46, nos. 1–2 (2011): 111–30 (111).

[16] The first modern scholar to raise the subject may have been Henry Hinckley, who mentions in passing that Cecilia's "unconsummated marriage" should qualify the tale as part of the Marriage Group in "The Debate on Marriage in the *Canterbury Tales*," *PMLA* 32, no. 2 (1917): 292–305 (303). Sherry Reames reads the relationship as "an alternative model of marriage" (as opposed to "monastic asceticism") in "Mary, Sanctity and Prayers to Saints: Chaucer and Late-Medieval Piety," in *Chaucer and Religion*, ed. Helen Phillips (Woodbridge: D. S. Brewer, 2010), 81–96 (94). Howard explains that Cecilia's marriage "involves something more than the subjugation of the woman to the man's will. There is a kind of mutuality in their relationship, a lack of any noticeable element of 'maistrye'" (229)—though I suspect most modern readers would agree that Cecilia is very much in charge. See Donald R. Howard, "The Conclusion of the Marriage Group: Chaucer and the Human Condition," *MP* 57, no. 4 (1960): 223–32.

[17] See Marc Glasser, "Marriage in Medieval Hagiography," *Studies in Medieval and Renaissance History* n.s. 4 (1981): 3–34; and Dyan Elliott, *Spiritual Marriage: Sexual Abstinence in Medieval Wedlock* (Princeton: Princeton University Press, 1993). Saints' lives were often used as anecdotes to spice up medieval sermons, and thus are regularly found in preachers' books, and certainly in monastic libraries. They offer a particular, if formulaic, model for human behavior, most popularly that of the virgin martyr, a type who is almost invariably abrasively vocal and confrontational with a pagan, male oppressor. See Donald Weinstein and Rudolph M. Bell, *Saints and Society: The Two Worlds of Western Christendom, 1000–1700* (Chicago: University of Chicago Press, 1982); Sarah Salih, ed., *A Companion to Middle English Hagiography* (Woodbridge: D. S. Brewer, 2006); and Jocelyn Wogan-Browne, *Saints' Lives and Women's Literary Culture c. 1150–1300: Virginity and Its Authorizations* (Oxford: Oxford University Press, 2001).

example.[18] Cecilia is mentioned more often as a model for wives than for unmarried virgins: it is her conduct within marriage that makes her admirable, as she manages to conform to parameters for wifely behavior without violating those of sanctity.[19] That Cecilia is married at all suggests her powers of negotiation were not available to her as a daughter: shouldn't someone so bent on chastity have been able to persuade her parents against contracting this marriage?[20] This implicit failure of persuasion coupled with the absence of discussion of parental consent foregrounds Cecilia's role as wife, rather than daughter.

In hindsight, Cecilia's marital status seems inevitable: the text opens with her desire to remain chaste, not to remain unmarried; her first words are a prayer uttered at her wedding; and as she speaks directly to Valerian for the first time, she instantly assumes a wifely persona. (Cecilia begins their conversation not with Christianity but with a tantalizing "conseil" that carries the implication of sexuality: an "angel," suspected by Valerian to be "another man" in line 167, protects her. She knows what is on Valerian's mind on this wedding night.) In addition, Cecilia does not abandon the domestic setting of their first conversation until line 379, more than halfway through the tale. For the majority of the narrative, she remains in the nuptial bedroom, reminding us that however universal her faith and authority may be, her body is ensconced in domestic space for the duration of her marriage. Yet for pastoral readers, the validity of that marriage depends on her abilities to convert

[18] Sharon Farmer, "Persuasive Voices: Clerical Images of Medieval Wives," *Speculum* 6, no. 3 (1986): 517–43 (536). Wives are not the only admirers of Cecilia, of course; Catherine Sanok opens *Her Life Historical: Exemplarity and Females Saints' Lives in Late Medieval England* (Philadelphia: University of Pennsylvania Press, 2007) with Cecilia as prime example of a saint whose imitable behaviors might vary depending on readers' historical and social context. Much would depend on modes of access. Cate Gunn pieces together how Julian of Norwich may have heard the Cecilia story—as a nun at Carrow Priory, as a parishioner in the Dominican church that was destroyed in 1413, or from the Benedictine priory—in "'A recluse atte Norwyche': Images of Medieval Norwich and Julian's Revelations," in *A Companion to Julian of Norwich*, ed. Liz Herbert McAvoy (Woodbridge: D. S. Brewer, 2008), 32–41 (33).

[19] Among models of good wives are also "bad" ones, such as Medea: her complaint throughout Seneca's play is that in her total submission to Jason she has lost herself; medieval readers likely noted that even apart from infanticide she was unwilling to subjugate herself wholly to her husband, as wives were supposed to do.

[20] In fairness, James Brundage points out that couples were not always informed about their betrothal until after it was arranged. Once contracted, the betrothal was not easy to dissolve, sometimes requiring evidence of a clandestine marriage to undo the agreement. See James A. Brundage, *Law, Sex, and Christian Society in Medieval Europe* (Chicago: University of Chicago Press, 1987).

Valerian. According to Raymond of Penyafort, author of a thirteenth-century penitential manual and a *Summa de matrimonio*, Christians were not held to a marriage contract with nonbelievers unless the latter converted: "[Si] fidelis contrahit cum infideli . . . nullum est matrimonium. Sponsalia tamen potest fidelis cum infideli contrahere sub conditione ut infidelis convertatur ad fidem" ("[If] a believer contracts marriage with an unbeliever . . . there is no marriage. However, a believer can contract an engagement with an unbeliever with the condition that the unbeliever be converted to the faith").[21] It is not physical consummation of the marriage that matters to Raymond, who argues that a chaste marriage is consummated with holiness.[22] Rather, in a neat twist, the legality of Cecilia's marriage depends on Valerian's conversion, and as we will see, the strength and orthodoxy of her persuasive words depend on her being and staying married. Much hinges on Valerian's response to Cecilia: if he ignores or disbelieves her claims, the marriage can be invalidated; if he consequently attempts rape, her chastity will be threatened, and the angel will physically attack him. The integrity of Cecilia's legal and spiritual status, then, as well as Valerian's physical safety, all depend on Cecilia's powers of persuasion in this first speech and within this domestic space. The speech marks her acceptance of her role as Valerian's spouse and acknowledges that his validation of her words is crucial to his own conversion and, ultimately, her sanctity.

Further, the non-Chaucerian manuscript evidence points to the importance of this textual passage: nearly every version of Cecilia's life, with the exception only of a very few liturgical texts, includes the opening speech in its entirety, while the preaching and combative speech later in the text is more often minimized or omitted.[23] Sherry Reames has argued that

[21] See Raymond of Penyafort, *Summa de matrimonio*, ed. Xaverio Ochoa and Aloisio Díez, Universa Bibliotheca Iuris, Vol. 1, tomus C (Rome: Commentarium pro religiosis, 1978), 951; and Raymond of Penyafort, *Summa on Marriage*, trans. and ed. Pierre Payer (Toronto: Pontifical Institute of Mediaeval Studies, 2005), Title X, "Dissimilar Religion," 51ff.

[22] "Quod perfectum et consummatum dicitur coniugium sanctitate, etiam ante carnalem copulam"; Raymond, *Summa*, ed. Ochoa and Díez, 923 ("a marriage is called completed or consummated through holiness, even before carnal copulation"; Raymond, *Summa*, trans. Payer, 27).

[23] Even in the liturgy, the wedding night dominates: Reames's work on the late medieval breviaries shows that what was most often heard at Matins as lessons from the saint's life was the nuptial scene:

The easiest and most old-fashioned way of shortening a set of lessons was just to copy some excerpts from the parent text, dividing them into the desired number of

secular English breviaries—i.e., those written primarily for clergy who were expected to work with the laity—seem more concerned than the monastic ones to provide models that conform with late medieval ideas of how laymen and -women should behave. In the case of Cecilia . . . they tend to omit or rewrite extensively those parts of the legend which portray her as transgressing the usual norms of womanly behavior: two scenes in which she is shown as a powerful and authoritative teacher of the faith, preaching first to Tiburce and then publicly to the officers sent to arrest her; and the dramatic trial scene in which she stands up to the prosecutor, Almachius, defying his commands and scoffing at the power he claims to have.[24]

Reames suggests that this editing is an attempt to deemphasize or even ignore Cecilia's confrontation with Almachius. However, Cecilia's behavior in that exchange is consistent with that of other virgin martyrs in late medieval hagiography. I suggest that it is because pastoral readers privileged and endorsed Cecilia's nuptial persuasion, and not because her confrontation with Almachius is considered out of line, that the later speech is often omitted.

It is, then, the nuptial speech to Valerian rather than that to Almachius to which we should be paying attention. In that address, Cecilia is a near-perfect example of the clerical ideal of wifely persuasion that appears in confessional manuals. Sharon Farmer first described this ideal in 1986, and Mary Carruthers has discussed it more recently in her work on the rhetoric of "sweetness."[25] Cecilia becomes "sweeter" as a speaker,

---

lessons. In the case of Cecilia, the breviaries that use this method tend overwhelmingly to take their excerpts from the opening scenes of the legend . . . it is probably no accident that the breviaries with verbatim excerpts from the Cecilia legend tend to reproduce the same portions of the legend that were emphasized in the chants for her Office: the initial description of her piety, her hair shirt and fasts and fervent prayers before her wedding, *her wedding-night conversation with Valerian*, his baptism, and his return to find the angel made visible. (Reames, "Office for Saint Cecilia," 233–34 [emphasis mine])

[24] Ibid., 239.
[25] Farmer, "Persuasive Voices"; Mary Carruthers, "Sweetness," *Speculum* 81, no. 4 (2006): 999–1013. Farmer's arguments are invoked, though not cited, in Silvana Vecchio, "The Good Wife," in *A History of Women in the West*, Vol. 2, *Silences of the Middle Ages*, ed. Christiane Klapisch-Zuber (Cambridge, Mass.: Harvard University Press, 1992), 105–35, which summarizes the intellectual development of this issue from the thirteenth to the fifteenth century. Cecilia is not the only Chaucerian wife to utilize persuasion; Jane Chance notes that the Wife of Bath, in her way, follows the model of a woman whose role it is to influence her husband, "to show that vicious *husbands* need to be taught by their wives," in *The Mythographic Chaucer: The Fabulation of Sexual Politics*

wife, and saint if we examine her opening speech through the lens of confessional manuals that often called attention to the danger of women's speech, but also to its power to encourage positive change in a man's behavior. She could potentially function not only as a model of how medieval preachers and confessors were advising laywomen to influence their husbands, but also as a model for how members of the clergy could influence those in positions of power.

The genre of confessional manuals developed from the Fourth Lateran Council's requirement of yearly individual confession beginning in 1215.[26] Raymond of Penyafort wrote his *summa* between 1220 and 1245; William Peyraut wrote his *Summa de vitiis* in the 1230s; Thomas of Chobham began *Summa cum miserationes* well before the Fourth Lateran Council, edited it just after the end of 1215, and completed and circulated it in 1216.[27] These differed from earlier penitential manuals not only in their emphasis on private over public remission of sins, but also in their provision of detailed analyses of types of sins and sinners and in their training for confessors on how to hear, understand, and

---

(Minneapolis: University of Minnesota Press, 1995), 216, with reference to Farmer in note 11; see also Charles Koban, "Hearing Chaucer Out: The Art of Persuasion in the 'Wife of Bath's Tale,'" *ChauR* 5, no. 3 (1971): 225–39.

[26] Thomas Tentler counts one- or two-dozen *summae*, depending on the definition: there were no *summae* until 1215; the last one appeared in 1520. See Thomas Tentler, "The Summa for Confessors as an Instrument of Social Control," in *The Pursuit of Holiness in Late Medieval and Renaissance Religion*, ed. Charles Trinkaus and Heiko A. Oberman (Leiden: Brill, 1974), 103–26 (103). Around 1303, Robert Mannyng of Brunne composed the first English version of the genre: *Handlyng Synne*, a Middle English verse translation of *Manuel des péchés*. Scholarship relevant to confession manuals and sexuality is relatively scant but impressive: besides Pierre J. Payer's splendid scholarly trilogy of medieval theological approaches to sexual sin (*Sex and the Penitentials: The Development of a Sexual Code 550–1150* [Toronto: University of Toronto Press, 1984]; *Sex and the New Medieval Literature of Confession, 1150–1300* [Toronto: Pontifical Institute of Mediaeval Studies, 2009]; and *The Bridling of Desire: Views of Sex in the Later Middle Ages* [Toronto: University of Toronto Press, 1993]), see Karma Lochrie, *Covert Operations: The Medieval Uses of Secrecy* (Philadelphia: University of Pennsylvania Press, 1999); and more broadly, Michel Foucault, *The History of Sexuality* (London: Allen Lane, 1979).

[27] See *Thomae de Chobham Summa confessorum*, ed. F. Broomfield (Louvain: Editions Nauwelaerts, 1968), lxii. Peyraut's *summa* will appear as William Peraldus, *Summa de vitiis*, ed. and trans. Siegfried Wenzel, Richard Newhauser, Bridget Balint, and Edwin Craun, 3 vols., forthcoming from Oxford University Press. For penitential manuals— conflated, for most purposes, with confessional manuals—see Robert of Flamborough, *Liber poenitentialis*, ed. J. J. Francis Firth (Toronto: Pontifical Institute of Mediaeval Studies, 1971); Joseph Goering, "The *Summa de penitentia* of Magister Serlo," *Mediaeval Studies* 38, no. 1 (1976): 1–53; and Joseph Goering, "The *Summa de penitentia* of John of Kent," *Bulletin of Medieval Canon Law* 18 (1988): 13–31. Goering has made a transcription of Wetheringsett's *Qui bene present*, but it has not yet been published.

handle each type.[28] Mendicant authors' rush to produce these manuals and their popularity with both clerical and lay readers suggest that the ideas therein found a wide audience.[29] As Farmer and Pierre Payer have pointed out, we can learn how that audience interpreted human behavior by considering how the confessional manuals advise doing so.[30]

What has not been considered is how the manuals affected their readers' interpretations of other *texts*, such as the narratives about saints' lives with which they were often bound in manuscript. For literary scholars, this lack of attention seems an oversight, especially because the close physical proximity of these texts within the same manuscript occurs often enough to merit notice.[31] While texts needn't be bound together to suggest intertextuality, the frequency with which such binding occurs raises the question of whether the relatively new genre of confession manuals had the power to change how medieval readers

[28] In language that intriguingly echoes that of the prologue, Phillips, *Transforming Talk*, notes that confession works in line with, rather than in opposition to, penitential rules (17), although it is "continually besieged by idle talk, vulnerable to gossip at almost every stage of its process" (42).

[29] For this reason, they are also useful to historians: as Jacqueline Murray has said, these texts "provide us with a window onto the moral universe of the Middle Ages and present the values and behaviours that the Church was trying to promote . . . at the very point at which they were being disseminated to the laity through the mediation of the confessor"; "Gendered Souls in Sexed Bodies: The Male Construction of Female Sexuality in Some Medieval Confessors' Manuals," in *Handling Sin: Confession in the Middle Ages*, ed. Peter Biller and Alistair Minnis (York: York Medieval Press, 1998), 79–93 (81).

[30] See Farmer, "Persuasive Voices," and Payer, *Sex and the New*. Brundage notes that while the form of the *summa* was somewhat outdated by the end of the fourteenth century, attitudes about (marital) sex stayed consistent from before until after the Black Death, and laypersons would not normally be reading the legal commentaries and treatises that replaced the *summa*; Brundage, *Law, Sex*, 487–90.

[31] I provide here only a small sampling of British Library manuscripts that contain selections from both saints' lives and confessional manuals: MS Royal 8 C.VII (13–15th cent.; includes a lectionary and confessional tract with a formula for priest's confession); MS Royal 8 E.XVII (includes Bozon's lives, Raymond's *Summa*, and three lives from the *Golden Legend*); MS Royal 9 A.XIV (late 13th cent.; includes Richard Wetheringsett's *summa* "Qui bene presunt"; John of Kent's *Summa de penitentia*; and several saints' lives, some from the *Golden Legend*, some from older sources; as well as Grosseteste's tract on confession); MS Royal 13 A.XIV (Ireland, 13th–early 14th cent.; includes Wetheringsett's *summa*, the martyrdom of Thomas of Becket, and "notes on Apostles, Holy Women, & the Assumption"); Add. MS 6716 (mid–late 15th cent.; includes Grosseteste's work on confession and saints' lives); Add. MS 41069 (a legendary that includes questions to be asked at confession); MS Arundel 201 (13th cent.; includes a *Liber poenitentialis* and verses on Cecilia); and MS Arundel 330 (14th cent. Carthusian legendary that includes the life of Cecilia and a penitential tract). The pattern holds across multiple preachers' books in the various archives where I have examined them, including the Vatican Library, Biblioteca Casanatense, and Biblioteca Angelica in Rome.

approached the ancient one of hagiography. Saints' lives are ubiquitous in archives: they get bound with all kinds of texts, not just religious ones, and it might seem presumptuous to claim that confessional manuals necessarily have some magical power to influence a medieval reader's interpretation of hagiography more than do romances, nautical sketches, recipes, or medical treatises. However, the confessional manual offers something we don't see in any previous genre: a key to what is considered normative behavior. They reveal a new way of thinking about other people as individuals with psyches, not simply as holders of phlegmatic or choleric tendencies.

Confessional manuals were widely distributed among monastic libraries, and it is fair to assume that the mendicant authors of both Chaucer's sources were familiar with them: aside from their sharing the common educational experience of religious elites across Europe, both were members of preaching orders that would have found a confessional manual especially useful. The depiction of Cecilia's persuasion of and submission to Valerian even in Chaucer's sources, then, was likely informed by these manuals' values. Preaching manuals are certainly a relevant genre for Chaucer: his *Parson's Tale* has sources in Raymond of Penyafort's *Summa de poenitentia* and William Peyraut's *Summa de vitiis*,[32] and Cecilia herself does a fair amount of preaching, so pastoral readers might be remiss *not* to consider how preaching manuals might assess her behavior.[33] Certainly the Wife of Bath's direct engagement with Jerome and other

[32] According to Payer, a high proportion of space in the confessional manuals was devoted to avarice—the subject of *The Pardoner's Tale*, and thus one Chaucer had familiarity with—as well as to marital relations; e.g., avarice ranks third, after homicide and sex, among the most discussed sins in Robert of Flamborough's *summa* (Payer, *Sex and the New*, Appendix A, 197). Payer notes that Chaucer's use of the term *luxuria* in *The Parson's Tale* to indicate lechery indicates his familiarity with confession manuals' vocabulary for cataloguing and tabling sins; *Sex and the New*, 200. See also Richard Newhauser, "The Parson's Tale," in Correale and Hamel, *Sources and Analogues*, 1:529–613. Emma Lipton links the clerical interest in sacramental marriage to the rise of lay piety; *Affections of the Mind: The Politics of Sacramental Marriage in Late Medieval English Literature* (South Bend: University of Notre Dame Press, 2007).

[33] While we do not tend to think of the Benedictines primarily as preachers, there is some evidence that they were preaching to the laity in late medieval England. See Siegfried Wenzel, *Monastic Preaching in the Age of Chaucer*, The Morton W. Bloomfield Lectures on Medieval English Literature 3 (Kalamazoo: Medieval Institute Publications, 1993); see also Patrick Horner, "Benedictines and Preaching in Fifteenth-Century England: The Evidence of Two Bodleian Library Manuscripts," *Revue bénédictine* 99 (1989): 313–32. In particular, as Joan Greatrex notes, Adam Easton himself had been valued enough for his preaching that the prior recalled him to Norwich at least twice during his studies at Oxford for preaching duties; Joan Greatrex, "Benedictine Sermons: Preparation and Practice in the English Monastic Cathedral Cloisters," in *Medieval*

Church fathers suggests Chaucer was thinking of his female narrators in conjunction with the prevailing clerical arguments of the day. At the very least, Chaucer could assume his readers would be familiar enough with those arguments to note when the wives in his *Tales* strayed from or adhered to their precepts.

Pastoral values would necessarily be colored by confessional manuals, or at least their principles as passed down by [other] priests, which had to be taken seriously by those committed to pastoral care.[34] Hearing confession, in particular, was recognized as a subjective practice, so readers were expected to learn to "read" and analyze individuals as well as texts.[35] Leonard Boyle points out that these manuals were also used as lower-level resources for basic knowledge about all aspects of pastoral care for candidates for the parochial priesthood in fourteenth-century England.[36] These readers, then, might "read" Cecilia as a woman and penitent, as the manuals trained readers to do, but could equally "read" her as an eloquent preacher or pastor, as the manuals trained readers to be.

Whether or not we accept Giffin's theory that Chaucer's translation was intended to honor an English priest in Rome (where Cecilia was considered a model of how women should treat their husbands), *The*

Monastic Preaching, ed. Carolyn Muessig (Leiden: Brill, 1998), 257–78 (261). Dodwell reminds us that university education was considered training for preaching, and observes that Benedictines owned several sermon collections and preaching manuals; "Muniments and the Library," 336.

[34] Leonard Boyle summarizes Grosseteste's approach to pastoral care as "governed" by precepts such as "A bishop is directly responsible to God for every soul in his diocese"; "Robert Grosseteste and the Pastoral Care," *Medieval and Renaissance Studies* 8 (1979): 3–51.

[35] Jacqueline Murray reminds us that "confession developed originally in a masculine monastic environment . . . the sacrament of confession and the literature associated with it ultimately reflected male concerns and values"; Jacqueline Murray, "The Absent Penitent: The Cure of Women's Souls and Confessors' Manuals in Thirteenth-Century England," in *Women, the Book, and the Godly: Selected Proceedings of the St. Hilda's Conference, 1993*, ed. Lesley Smith and Jane H. M. Taylor (Cambridge: D. S. Brewer, 1995), 13–26 (15).

[36] See Leonard E. Boyle, "Aspects of Clerical Education in Fourteenth-Century England," in *The Fourteenth Century*, ed. Paul E. Szarmach and Bernard S. Levy (Binghampton: State University of New York Press, 1977), 19–32 (20). For more discussion of other texts in this genre, which Boyle credits with "popularization" of "the theological and legal advances of the twelfth century" (245), see Leonard Boyle, "The *Summa confessorum* of John of Freiburg and the Popularization of the Moral Teaching of St. Thomas and of Some of His Contemporaries," in *St. Thomas Aquinas, 1274–1974: Commemorative Studies*, ed. Armand Maurer and Etienne Gilson, 2 vols. (Toronto: Pontifical Institute of Mediaeval Studies, 1974), 2.245–68.

Second Nun's Tale's potential appeal to pastoral readers becomes clearer when we accept Farmer's nudge to consider proscriptive descriptions of wifely behavior in confessional manuals such as the one by Thomas of Chobham, an English subdean of Salisbury Cathedral, which survives in over 160 manuscripts. According to Neil Ker, a fourteenth-century copy of Thomas's *Summa* (Cambridge University Library, MS Ii.i.22) was at the Priory of Holy Trinity in Norwich, so these Benedictine readers would have been familiar with its arguments as they read the life of Cecilia; one inventory of the priory's books lists a *Summa confessorum* along with a *Legenda aurea*.[37] Thomas's *Summa* assigns the responsibility for a man's sins to his wife and argues that women's seductive powers of persuasion can be positively exploited for spiritual edification:

Mulieribus tamen semper in penitentia iniungendum est quod sint *predicatrices* virorum suorum. Nullus enim sacerdos ita potest cor viri emollire sicut potest uxor. Unde peccatum viri sepe mulieri imputatur si per eius negligentiam vir eius non emmendator. Debet enim in cubiculo et inter medios amplexus virum suum blande alloqui, et si durus est et immisericors et oppressor pauperum, debet eum invitare ad misericordiam; si raptor est, debet detestari rapinam; si avarus est, suscitet in eo largitatem . . . Prima ergo sacerdotis et precipua providentia ista debet esse ut mulierem hoc modo instruat.

[In imposing penance, it should always be enjoined upon women to be *preachers* to their husbands, because no priest is able to soften the heart of a man the way his wife can. For this reason, the sin of a man is often imputed to his wife if, through her negligence, he is not corrected. Even in the bedroom, in the midst of their embraces, a wife should speak alluringly to her husband, and if he is hard and unmerciful, and an oppressor of the poor, she should invite him

---

[37] See Neil Ker, "Medieval Manuscripts from Norwich Cathedral Priory," *Transactions of the Cambridge Bibliographical Society* 1, no. 1 (1949): 1–28. See also Neil Ker, *Medieval Libraries of Great Britain: A List of Surviving Books*, 2nd ed. (London: Royal Historical Society, 1964), 284–86, for Norwich Cathedral library. Broomfield argues that *Summa* was written in England, with English readers as Thomas's target audience, based partly on geographical circumstance and partly on some English terminology and textual examples. Another inventory lists 228 books belonging to Adam Easton, whose library was eventually sent back to Norwich. The inventories, by W. T. Bensly (chapter clerk for the dean of Norwich Cathedral) and M. R. James, are cited in H. C. Beeching, "The Library of the Cathedral Church of Norwich," *Norfolk Archaeology; or, Miscellaneous Tracts Relating to the Antiquities of the County of Norfolk*, 19, no. 1 (1915–17): 67–116. Harvey discusses some texts that Easton owned, as well as the circumstances of the delivery of Easton's library—six barrels of books—to the monastery, in *English in Rome*, 222–23. They arrived seventeen years after he'd shipped them, ten years after his death; two barrels are thought to have gone missing.

to be merciful; if he is a plunderer, she should denounce plundering; if he is avaricious, she should arouse generosity in him . . . Therefore, this ought to be the first and foremost concern of the priest, that he instruct the wife in this way.][38]

Thomas's term "preachers" ("predicatrices") suggests that he would consider Cecilia a "preacher" from the very beginning of the *Tale*; the distinction between her private and public speeches is thus only a function of social context. While other writers do not employ Thomas's semantics, his attitude toward wives' responsibility and ability to modify their husbands' behaviors appears in several clerical texts to which Chaucer, Easton, and the Norwich Benedictines would have had ready access. Thomas's contemporary Robert of Courson similarly expects a wife to exert influence "emoliendo cor viri sui" (by softening [her husband's] heart) and, if he is still "impoenitens et incorrigibile" (unrepentant and incorrigible), to refuse to accept financial support from him—though he clarifies "sed numquam thori" (that she should "never [refuse to share] his bed").[39] In both cases cited here, the wives exercise persuasive power in the bedroom, with its access to private speech and potential for sexual activity. Robert's stipulation that the wife continue to share her husband's bed acknowledges the implication of sexual bargaining, with its insistence that the persuasion must occur verbally, not physically. That preference (and assumption) is maintained across different contexts: in a pro-Crusades treatise in 1306, Peter Dubois reiterates and expands these clerics' ideas, proposing that Christian women should be trained to seek out and convert non-Christian husbands:

[38] Thomas of Chobham, *Summa confessorum*, 375; translated in Farmer, "Persuasive Voices," 517 (emphasis mine).

[39] Both Thomas of Chobham and Robert of Courson are concerned with wives of men who commit usury, a major thirteenth-century theological issue. The full passage from Robert:

Cum uxor feneratoris agit causam spoliaterum, vivat parce de iis quae ministrat ei vir suus de spoliis usurae, non quia ipse possit ei dare, cum non sint suae, sed quia ipsa advocatrix est spoliatorum pro melioranda corum causa, emoliendo cor viri sui, & inducendo virum suum ad faciendam condignam restitutionem sic ablatorum. Si autem invenerit cor viri sui impoenitens & incorrigibile, & se nihil erga ipsum perficere posse pro facienda debita restitutione; tunc tenetur modis omnibus quaerere separationem mensae ejus & convivii; sed numquam thori, ut prius mendicet ab amicis vel aliis quo veseatur & vestiatur, quam hujusmodi tam morticino & quasi idoloto foedae usurae contra Deum pascatur. ("Consilium parisiensis, 1212," Part 5, chap. 10, in *Sacrorum conciliorum nova et amplissima collectio*, ed. J. D. Mansi, 31 vols. [Florence, 1759–98], 22.852)

Forte majoribus Saracenis quibus alii injuriantur, guerras movent, auferunt terras suas, alia bona rapiunt, poterunt dari uxores perite provisionis istius, salva fide earum, ut non communicent cum eorum ydolatria; per quas cum auxilio Dei et discipulorum predicantium, et ut subsidium habeant a catholicis, quia de Saracenis non possunt confidere, poterunt ad fidem catholicam *induci* et perduci.

[While others are pursuing a policy of inflicting injury on the Saracens, making war upon them, seizing their lands, and plundering their other property, perhaps girls trained in the proposed schools may be given as wives to the Saracen chiefs, although preserving their faith lest they participate in their husbands' idolatry. By their efforts, with the help of God and the preaching disciples so they may have assistance from Catholics—for they cannot rely on the Saracens—their husbands might be *persuaded* and led to the Catholic faith.][40]

Dubois argues that these trained wives "per quas sic litteratas, articulos et sacramenta more romano credentes, liberos suos et maritos ad sic tenendum, credendum, et sacrificandum contingeret informari longe forcioribus rationibus et occasionibus illis, que per consilium mulierum induxerunt Salomonem, summum sapientem, ad ydolatrandum" ["with such education, who held the articles of faith and the sacraments according to Roman usage, would teach their children and husbands to adhere to the Roman faith and to believe and sacrifice in accordance with it. They would employ *arguments* and opportunities far more effective than those which by the wiles of his wives led Solomon, the wisest of men, into idolatry"]; again, the power of rhetoric is preferred to the use of physical seduction, although clearly the sexual appeal of the women sweetens the authority of their words.[41]

[40] Emphasis mine; he adds "quod plurimum appeterent eorum uxores, eo quod quilibet ipsorum multas habet" ("Their wives would strive the more zealously for this because each one of [the men] has many wives"). See Pierre Dubois, *De recuperatione terre sancte*, ed. Charles-Victor Langlois (Paris: A. Picard, 1891), 57; English translation in Pierre Dubois, *The Recovery of the Holy Land*, trans. and ed. Walther I. Brandt (New York: Columbia University Press, 1956), 124. Dubois also outlined a formal education program, with courses in theology as well as practical medical knowledge, for the girls who would be sent to do this work; this training would be above and beyond his expectation that all girls learn grammar, logic, and a foreign language (Dubois, *De recuperatione*, 50–52 and 71; Dubois, *Recovery*, 119 and 139).

[41] Dubois, *De recuperatione*, 51–52; Dubois, *Recovery*, 119 (emphasis mine). In related discussions, Paul Strohm's chapter "Queens as Intercessors" expresses skepticism about how much actual power this role granted queens; *Hochon's Arrow: The Social Imagination of Fourteenth-Century Texts* (Princeton: Princeton University Press, 1992), 95–120. Collette emphasizes the power as well as the danger of Cecilia's private-to-public speech as

Given Cecilia's status later in the poem as preacher, it makes sense that during the brief nuptial moment to which we are privy she adheres to the description of wifely behavior found in preachers' manuals. Cecilia's first words to Valerian convince him (1) not to consummate the marriage, (2) to convert to Christianity, and (3) to risk his life by seeking out an outlaw (here, a pope) to confirm her claims. Thanks largely to Cecilia's quick mastery of wifely rhetoric—she has, after all, only been a wife for a few hours—Valerian shows himself pliable to all her directions, confirming monastic assessments of wives' persuasive potential. Chaucer's portraying Cecilia as such a smooth talker required delicate dancing along the cultural party line on women's speech, which was legally and religiously suspect.[42] As Sandy Bardsley has explained, "wives were encouraged to speak gently, privately, and on appropriate topics, [but] speech outside these very circumscribed bounds was open to suspicion."[43] Bardsley's work has shown that women's public speech was highly regulated in the post-plague fourteenth century.[44] Women could be prosecuted for being "scolds," for disturbing the status quo, and for slander; their public words could interfere with their husbands' social and spiritual standing.[45] Pastors' books contained plenty of examples of women's "bad" speech, as well: Edwin Craun cites an anecdote from *Handlyng Synne* that renders a mother's curse on her child literal, and an exemplum of a man who pushes his talkative wife overboard.[46] Craun observes that pastoral tracts advise habitual silence to combat "sins of the tongue," noting that the Benedictine rule of silence was an attempt at "breaking the tongue's habit of sinning"; readers of those

---

sanctioned and authorized by Mary; "The Power of the Virgin," in *Performing Polity*, 79–98 (79).

[42] Chaucer's other *Tales* are clearly aware of the discourse and restrictions on speech: the Pardoner's, Cook's, and Parson's tales all concern speech and slander, and *The Wife of Bath's Prologue* can be read as an experiment in all the permitted and prohibited possibilities of women's speech. See Craun, *Lies*, 225–57 for a discussion of the Cook's and Parson's tales—the last of which is a mini-treatise on penitence. Lee Patterson traces Alisoun's connections to antifeminist literature in "For the Wyves love of Bathe: Feminine Rhetoric and Poetic Resolution in the *Roman de la rose* and the *Canterbury Tales*," *Speculum* 58 (1983): 656–95.

[43] Bardsley, *Venomous Tongues*, 68.

[44] For examinations of *men's* speech, see Sandy Bardsley, "Men's Voices in Late Medieval England," in *The Hands of the Tongue: Essays on Deviant Speech*, ed. Edwin D. Craun (Kalamazoo: Medieval Institute Publications, 2007), 163–83; and Derek Neal, "Husbands and Priests: Masculinity, Sexuality, and Defamation in Late Medieval England," in Craun, *Hands of the Tongue*, 185–208.

[45] See Bardsley, *Venomous Tongues*, 6, 47, 48, 51.

[46] Craun, *Lies*, 1, 51.

tracts doubtless would have assessed speech (particularly women's speech) quite differently than we do.[47] Too much talking was associated with lechery; idle speech risked attribution to minstrels; and Christians' words were expected to be salvific.[48]

Within that context, wives had a pastoral dispensation to speak at home, and their words are ascribed weight precisely because of their fleshly status.[49] Claire Waters clarifies that women's speech is "suspect . . . not . . . because of its unimportance but because of its perceived power."[50] For thirteenth- and fourteenth-century religious readers, persuasion as a technique had feminine and sexual overtones. Thomas of Chobham attributes to wives a special power of speech in persuasion because he views women largely as sexual rather than intellectual beings.[51] Farmer notes that monastics considered "speech as a sensuous and physical phenomenon, and they therefore associated speech with the physical realm and with women . . . in part because they associated both women and oral persuasion with seduction and magic."[52] The power and potential danger of wives' speech were perceived as merely a less potent form of witchcraft: Jacqueline Murray provides Serlo's and Robert of Flamborough's citations of women's nonverbal influence over

[47] Ibid., 53. Gilchrist notes that silence was the default in the monastery; *Norwich Cathedral Close*, 13.

[48] Craun, *Lies*, 26–47, 172 n. 47, 173.

[49] Bardsley's chapter "The Sins of Women's Tongues in Literature and Art," in *Venomous Tongues*, 58–62, discusses several examples of women whose husbands should beware their wives' speech, including Eve, Noah's wife, and the Wife of Bath.

[50] Claire M. Waters, *Angels and Earthly Creatures: Preaching, Performance, and Gender in the Later Middle Ages* (Philadelphia: University of Pennsylvania Press, 2004), 97.

[51] Among other things, he argues that women should be churched early so their husbands won't go looking elsewhere for sex, and allows the husband's sins and preferences to overshadow those of the wife's even in her confession and penitence. See Murray, "Absent Penitent," 23. Further, he permits women to read religious texts publicly—because he doesn't think they'd be intellectually capable of adding anything to the meaning or distorting the interpretation of a text. See Waters, *Angels and Earthly Creatures*, 20. In Murray's words: "the very structure of confessors' manuals reinforced the notion of women as primarily, even exclusively, sexual. In the process, therefore, the salvation of women's souls was linked to their sexuality and to their sexuality alone"; "Gendered Souls," 83.

[52] Sharon Farmer, "Softening the Hearts of Men: Women, Embodiment, and Persuasion in the Thirteenth Century," in *Embodied Love: Sensuality and Relationship as Feminist Values*, ed. Paula Cooey, Farmer, and Mary Ellen Ross (San Francisco: Harper & Row, 1987), 115–34 (116). Farmer further explains: "Christian theologians associated false rhetoric—that in which men and women were persuaded of something that was contrary to Christian doctrine—with magic or seduction, while they associated true rhetoric—that which persuaded men and women to believe and obey Christian doctrine—with divine inspiration or assistance" (117).

men through potions and other physical means.[53] These assumptions imbue Cecilia's private speech to Valerian on their wedding night with significant authority. Waters observes that "beauty, intimacy and rhetoric" were considered particularly useful for persuasion—and of course, Cecilia achieves her first persuasive victory as Valerian's wife in their nuptial bedroom.[54]

Chaucer's translation frames the wedding-night conversation with some sensitivity to its provocative implications. As Joseph Grossi and Lynn Staley have noted in other contexts,[55] he reworks its uses of terms such as "secret" and "hidden," removing the *Golden Legend*'s description of Cecilia's faith as "nutrita absconditum" from lines 122–23 and from the bedroom itself ("cubiculi secreta silencia").[56] Absent these terms, Chaucer must locate the couple not merely in their chamber but "to bedde . . . as ofte is the manere" (141–42), and specify that Cecilia speak "pryvely" (143) to her husband in that bed (promising intriguingly to reveal a "conseil"). In this seemingly redundant phrasing, the "intimacy" Waters mentions as useful to persuasion is clarified as close proximity, with implied sexual tension—but it is not hidden ("secreta"). This seems appropriate, since others are privy to Cecilia's faith as well as to her bedroom: apart from the tale's readers, both Urban (by his inference) and Tiburce (by his presence) will have access to what transpires there. Given this dynamic, Cecilia's powerful bedroom talk always has potential to be public: while she may appear conventional, she will not be an ordinary wife, even as she borrows the persuasive speech of one. Throughout the scene, Chaucer's language reflects Cecilia's double role as Valerian's wife and pastor. For example, her greeting him as "wel biloved" (144) rather than "amantissime" does not just shift agency from him to herself: the "biloved" she bestows can be interpreted as either spousal or pastoral. Yet while Chaucer's translation subtly reminds readers that Cecilia's speech serves multiple functions, the success of this scene depends on her taking on the guise of a wife, and on Valerian's

---

[53] Murray, "Absent Penitent," 21.

[54] Waters, *Angels and Earthly Creatures*, 96.

[55] See Joseph Grossi, "The Unhidden Piety of Chaucer's 'Seint Cecilie,'" *ChauR* 36, no. 3 (2002): 298–309 (300); and Lynn Staley, "Chaucer and the Postures of Sanctity," in *The Powers of the Holy: Religion, Politics, and Gender in Late Medieval English Culture*, ed. David Aers and Staley (University Park: Penn State University Press, 1996), 179–259 (206).

[56] Reames, "The Second Nun's Prologue and Tale," 505.

belief that she fully inhabits that role. She becomes a model of persuasion not by transcending her spousal role as a purely sexual being but by exploiting it in this conversation with her husband.

Mary Carruthers reminds us of the specific Latin terms for "sweetness" that appear in theological discussions of wives' potential influence on their husbands: chiefly *suavitas*, meaning sweetness, pleasantness, agreeableness; and *persuadeo*, meaning to persuade. As she points out, *persuadeo* therefore means literally to sweeten, or as we still say in English, to sweet-talk.[57] This term comes to have a morally ambivalent sense for clerical writers, for it is most often women who employ sweetness to cajole their husbands; even seduction can be described as "sweet."[58] (We might note that the related "suave" now has the connotation of slickness in English.) For medieval thinkers, eloquence or beauty can be suspect, for it distracts from the main message: the thirteenth-century Dominican Thomas Aquinas argued that while a woman's physical form and beauty do provoke lust, "the *sweetness* of her voice and the pleasure of her words do so still more."[59] For all these reasons monks were suspicious of women's speech, but as Farmer points out, persuasion was also (perhaps grudgingly) acknowledged as useful for both preachers and monks to influence others' behavior: men of God needed therefore to employ the rhetorical tools of a wife. Clerical writers' approval of wives' persuasive methods (particularly Thomas of Chobham's equating them with preachers) explains why Cecilia's ability to convert influential men with "sweet persuasion" could be instructive, even for Benedictines who considered women tainted and their presence a defilement of their own sacred spaces.[60]

The opening line of Cecilia's first speech to Valerian, "O sweete and wel biloved spouse deere" (144) is the only time Cecilia herself uses the word "sweet."[61] In this scene, Cecilia is clearly employing sweet talk but cleverly attributing "sweetness" to Valerian (who is, after all, learning on his wedding night that his wife wants to remain a virgin). I have yet to find "sweetness" or its various Latin forms in any version of the *vita* referring to Cecilia herself; Cecilia is stunningly persuasive but is never

---

[57] Carruthers, "Sweetness," 1008.

[58] Ibid., 1003.

[59] Waters, *Angels and Earthly Creatures*, 100 (emphasis mine).

[60] See Gilchrist, *Norwich Cathedral Close*, 16, who mentions "the medieval understanding of sacred space, which regarded seculars, and women in particular, as potential polluters and prohibited their access to parts of the church and cloister."

[61] See note 14, above.

called such directly in the tale or in either of Chaucer's sources for the *vita*. Perhaps Chaucer's sources purposefully distanced Cecilia and her rhetoric from the concept of sweetness as persuasive technique because it might be perceived as overly slick or as undermining the seriousness of her message. However, it is more likely that Cecilia's persuasive talent is self-evident and need not be explicitly mentioned: we are seeing sweetness in action. When terms for sweetness do appear in the tale, in either Latin source or in Chaucer's translation, they refer to her reputation ("soote savour" in *SNP*, 91); Valerian (*SNT*, 144, as shown above); Valerian's affection for his brother Tiburce (in his source, but not in Chaucer); or the scent of the lilies and roses that Cecilia's guardian angel gives them ("soote savour" or "sweete smell"; *SNT*, 229, 247, 251). Assuming Chaucer's sources were aware of the nuanced connotations of sweetness, we can read these other uses of the term as pointing to the effects of Cecilia's influence: the flowers symbolize her own purity and upcoming martyrdom, after all, and their sweet scent renders Tiburce more susceptible to conversion.[62] Given the positive effects, from a clerical perspective, of Cecilia's persuasion, we can read these references to sweetness as an authorial vote in favor of her methods.

Cecilia's commitment to orthodoxy, revealed early by her desire for chastity, both affirms and justifies her sweetness. When Cecilia does as Thomas suggests, addressing Valerian "in the bedroom, in the midst of their embraces . . . [speaking] alluringly to her husband," her first goal is to convince him to be celibate. Her skill in doing so is a testament to Cecilia's ultimate powers of persuasion as a wife: using her proximity and potential sexuality to convince Valerian to abstain from taking advantage of these temptations. As is typical of virgin martyrs, Cecilia's virginity has been her chief concern up to this point. Preserving it assures her sanctity. But paradoxically, she must lay her virginity on the line in order to demonstrate her power as a sweet-talker.[63] Her first words to Valerian—on their marriage bed—concern her desire (coupled with a threat) that he leave her untouched:

---

[62] They also recall the Virgin's popular association with those flowers—reminders to readers of her presence behind the tale. See Miri Rubin, *Mother of God: A History of the Virgin Mary* (New Haven: Yale University Press, 2010), 310–11.

[63] She is certainly doing her part to "make sex less sexy," to borrow a phrase from Sarah Salih, "Unpleasures of the Flesh: Medieval Marriage, Masochism and the History of Heterosexuality," *SAC* 33 (2011): 125–47 (131).

> O sweete and wel biloved spouse deere,
> Ther is a conseil, and ye wolde it heere
>
> . . .
>
> I have an aungel which that loveth me,
> That with greet love, wher so I wake or sleepe,
> Is redy ay my body for to kepe.
> And if that he may feelen, out of drede,
> That ye me touche, or love in vileynye,
> He right anon wol sle yow with the dede.
>
> (*SNT*, 144–45, 152–57)[64]

Here Cecilia prefaces what amounts to a death threat with words of tenderness that would never be heard from another virgin martyr. The sweet talk (and, importantly, her status as wife) takes immediate effect: Valerian swears not to betray Cecilia in lines 148–50, *before* she mentions the angel or his potential violence. We see Cecilia employing a wife's method of sweet persuasion—one that conforms with Thomas's ideal—to achieve the promise of her virginity, and by extension her sanctity. Her success in this rhetorical gamble validates her as a wife (because she is so good at persuasion) and as a saint (because she keeps her virginity). Further, it will point the way to her success as a preacher later on, as Valerian will mimic and validate her words here as well as the message she wants preached. Cecilia's warning to Valerian not to "touche" her here reminds us of Payer's observation that "touch" in the confessional manuals is usually treated as a feature of illicit sexual situations. Pastoral readers would thus be primed to associate this warning with confessional manuals' treatment of sin and inappropriate behavior, contrasting Cecilia's holiness with Valerian's still-pagan status, a prompting that handily sets up Valerian's conversion and the couple's consequent teamwork as further evidence for clerical promotion of wifely persuasion.

---

[64] Again, from the *Golden Legend*: "O dulcissime atque amantissime juvenis, est misterium quod tibi confitear si modo tu juratus asseras tota te illud observancia custodire . . . Angelum Dei habeo amatorem, qui nimio zelo custodit corpus meum. Hic si vel leviter senserit quod tu me polluto amore contingas, statim feriet te, et amittes florem tue gratissime juventutis"; Reames, "The Second Nun's Prologue and Tale," 505 ("O sweetest and most loving young man, I have a secret to confess to you, on condition that you swear to keep this secret entirely to yourself . . . I have a lover, an angel of God, who watches over my body with exceeding zeal. If my angel senses that you are touching me with lust in your heart, he will strike you and you will lose the flower of your gracious youth"; *Golden Legend*, ed. Ryan, 704–5).

After their initial bedroom conversation, in which Cecilia achieves Valerian's chastity and conversion, Cecilia and Valerian develop an unusual level of trust and encouragement. The focus of the tale moves quickly from Cecilia's virginity to the way she carries out her persuasive role as wife. In fact, most of the narrative is missing the usual male–female face-off of the virgin martyr genre. This is at least partially because Valerian—and nearly every other man in the story—acquiesces completely to Cecilia; except for a brief expression of doubt about the specifics of her guardian angel, Valerian follows all of her instructions without question. Cecilia is as successful at persuading men to give her what she wants as any Chaucerian wife: she convinces almost every man she encounters to convert, and they basically do so simply because she asks them to. (Converting his brother Tiburce is Valerian's idea, but Tiburce listens to the reasoning of Cecilia, not his brother.) Their susceptibility to feminine persuasion reveals a male aural vulnerability to women's words that is only implicit in the confessional manuals' emphasis on wifely persuasion.[65] The clerical assumption that a wife can compel a husband's ears to hear her requires his willingness to be manipulated. It is only Cecilia's orthodoxy—and Valerian's adoption of it—that keeps him from looking foolish and weak.

Cecilia does not appear to possess magnetic charm; the initial sweet talk with which she indulges Valerian apparently carries her through the rest of the tale. Her only secret, in personal persuasion as well as preaching, is in the detailed explanation she offers of what to do or what to believe: her (orthodox) knowledge gives her authority. When she tells Valerian how to get baptized by Pope Urban, she explains exactly what to do and say: "Sey hem right thus, as that I shal yow telle. / Telle hem that I, Cecile, yow to hem sente" (175–76).[66] The message is clear: her

---

[65] Bardsley offers several warnings culled from advice manuals of the failure of men to listen critically and of wives as dangerous or inaccurate speakers; *Venomous Tongues*, 48ff. Patterson has similarly mentioned the "foolish incapacity as a listener" of Alisoun's Midas; "For the Wyves love of Bathe," 657. He later discusses the titillation of the feminine voice and the stereotype of women revealing masculine secrets (in *Roman de la rose* and elsewhere); 662. Cecilia might *seem* to be doing this in mentioning the angel who protects her, but she is in fact accurate and orthodox.

[66] In the late fourteenth-century *Northern Homily Cycle* version of the *vita*, Cecilia explicitly requires Valerian to go to Urban for confession before he can be baptized: "And tell him all thi life till end, / No so that he may thi mis amend" (109–10). *The Life of St. Cecilia: From MS Ashmole 43 and MS Cotton Tiberius E. VIII. With Introduction, Variants and Glossary*, ed. Bertha Ellen Lovewell, Yale Studies in English 3 (Boston, Mass.: Lamson, 1898), 93.

connections are what matter, not his. Valerian does not even pause to ask questions about his newly espoused doctrine before going to be baptized. Likewise, it is only *after* declaring his belief in Christianity that Tiburce learns the implications of his decision or even major Christian doctrines. In their domestic setting, Cecilia preaches to Tiburce about subjects he should have known before converting, introducing some of Christianity's most basic mysteries. His questions express astonishment at the possibility of death ("Algate ybrend in this world shul we be!" [318]) and confusion about the Trinity ("Ne seydestow right now in this manere, / Ther nys but o god, lord in soothfastnesse? / And now of thre how maystow bere witnesse?" [334–36]). Such basic questions reveal that he was not fully aware of conversion's meaning. He was too swept up in her sweet talk, too easily persuaded to something he doesn't understand—and this despite the fact that he should be less susceptible to her words, since she is not his wife. It is Tiburce whose questions make explicit the risks he and Valerian are taking on. Given the perceived dangers of women's speech, he is lucky that Cecilia's is beyond reproach.

Importantly, Cecilia's words are not only believed by Valerian, but are also confirmed by Urban. He acknowledges her success as a sweet-talker by expressing praise:

> For thilke spouse that she took but now,
> Ful lik a fiers leoun, she sendeth here
> As meke as evere was any lamb.
>
> (197–99)

Readers have not actually seen evidence of Valerian's fierceness, but apparently what has rendered him as "meek as a lamb" is Cecilia's speech: after all, at this point in the narrative, she hasn't actually done anything but talk. However, a few lines earlier, Urban has given thanks in prayer for "The fruit of thilke seed of chastitee / That thow hast sowe in Cecile" (193–94). The "fruit" here is, apparently, Valerian himself: an interesting, if jarring, analogue to the fruit of the chastity sown in the Virgin Mary that was Jesus. Urban's lack of clarity about whether it is Cecilia's chastity or her speech that produces the "fruit" of Valerian underscores a sticking-point for medieval theologians. The same clerical and biblical sources that affirm that women should try to convert their husbands tend to privilege holy deeds and behavior, such as chastity or altruism, rather than speech.[67] Outside the bedroom context, of course, moral probity mattered as much as sweet talk; men like Urban and the pastoral readers of this tale had to demonstrate virtue as well as rhetorical skill to be persuasive. And certainly the orthodoxy of Cecilia's speech, supported by the virtue of her behavior, matters: speaking God's rhetoric gets women permission and justification to speak publicly, even if they, like the Second Nun who is telling this story, are not wives.[68] To hear Urban tell it here, Cecilia has converted Valerian through both her chastity and her speech—a quiet reminder of theologians' belief that Christ got his humanity from Mary, and the implication that in Urban's mind Cecilia functions more like a mother than a wife. But he is not privy to her pillow talk as we are: we know that she is able to preserve her virginity *because* of that pretty speech she gave Valerian, a speech whose effectiveness is dependent at least in part on her role as his wife. Further, Valerian himself values her rhetorical moves enough to imitate them when trying to convert his brother:

> I have an aungel which that loveth me,
> That with greet love, wher so I wake or sleepe,
> Is redy ay my body for to kepe
>
> . . .

---

[67] Farmer synthesizes the argument; Augustine of Hippo based his argument about how one might convert one's spouse on 1 Peter 3:

> And with regard to unbelievers, the rule is that by a *good mode of life and conduct (bona sua conversatione moribus)* a believing husband is to try to gain his wife to the faith, and the believing wife is to try to gain her husband. So, they ought not to hide their *good works (bona opera sua)* from each other, for by those good works one is attracted to the other in such measure that one may be able to attract the other to the communion of the Christian faith.

The author of 1 Peter "emphasizes the wife's submission to the husband, and he specifically avoids any discussion of the woman's use of spoken language": "Likewise let wives be subjected to their husbands, so that some, though they do not believe in the word, may be won *without a word (sine verbo)* by the *behavior (conversationes)* of their wives, when they see your reverent and chaste behavior." Finally, Farmer points out that "Medieval authors often asserted that by itself speech could not bring about conversion, the desired effect of evangelism." "Persuasive Voices," 528, 532, 540.

[68] For a fuller discussion of women's "good" speech, see Bardsley, *Venomous Tongues*. Aside from the ubiquity of women speaking orthodoxy publicly in saints' lives, the *Pearl*-poet's *Cleanness* offers a contemporary analogue of wives being able to speak in the public sphere; Adam's, Noah's, and Lot's wives may smirk at Godly ideas, but their laughter and complaints are always private; Balthaser's wife can speak publicly because she expresses God's truth. See also Craun, *Lies*, 97ff.; and note 52, above.

And if that ye in clene love me gye,
He wol yow love as me, for youre cleneness,
And shewen yow his joye and his brightnesse.
(152–54; 159–61)

Valerian seyde, "Two corones han we,
Snow white and rose reed, that shynen cleere,
Whiche that thyne eyen han no myght to se;
And as thou smellest hem thurgh my preyere,
So shaltow seen hem, leeve brother deere,
If it so be thou wolt, withouten slouthe,
Bileve aright, and knowen verray trouthe."
(253–59)

Valerian's copying of the structure of Cecilia's speech—making sure even to address Tiburce as "leve brother deere," not too far from "wel biloved spouse deere"—suggests he sees power in the rhetoric of her sweet talk. He seems to have learned tools of persuasion as well as chastity from Cecilia's rendering his "fiers leoun" into a "meke lamb." Significantly, despite his relative ignorance and lack of Christian experience, Valerian's imitation sweet talk works: Tiburce converts, and while it is Cecilia who then explains Christian doctrine to him, it is the same rhetoric of her initial appeal to Valerian that engages Tiburce. In this text, then, sweet talk is not just for wives, but a useful all-purpose method of persuasion.

Chaucer changes source texts just after this scene, moving from the *Golden Legend*, which downplays Cecilia's role in the second half of the story, to the Franciscan abridgment, which highlights Cecilia's speech. That Chaucer gives so much attention to Cecilia's eloquence—even switching to a source that cuts major events in the narrative to give proportionally more space to her words—suggests that he, like Thomas of Chobham, believes in the power of sweet talk and sees her preaching to and persuasion of Valerian as of a piece with her vocal interactions with Almachius. Moreover, Cecilia's persistent chastity confirms to a monastic readership that her sweet talk is not tainted by the dangerous temptation of female sexuality, and the effects of her speech are always those the monastic audience should be hoping for anyway. Unlike the virgin martyrs who achieve mass conversions mostly by public performance (by undergoing bodily pain and enacting miracles), Cecilia persuades people one conversation at a time, as Adam Easton could, as perhaps individual monastic or conventual readers could, via promises, rewards, and sometimes threats. This text, then, serves to validate Thomas's approval of the rhetoric of sweetness: Cecilia achieves and maintains authority throughout the tale largely as a function of having first persuaded her husband to accept her point of view.

Ironically, the success of Cecilia's methods requires her adherence to proscribed wifely behavior. That her speech must first be validated by a pope and imitated by a husband before her message enters the public sphere (mediated through the preaching and ultimate martyrdom of her husband and brother-in-law) suggests that her words cannot stand apart from male sanctioning: their effectiveness depends on her working within the gendered hierarchy that the confessional manuals reinforce. As a wife, Cecilia is not a threat to the status quo, as Winstead has suggested.[69] She consistently demonstrates that she respects male authority: in submitting to her father's arrangement of the marriage to Valerian, in making her husband's conversion central to the first episode in her own *vita*, in staying home while Tiburce and Valerian legitimate her words with their brief public ministry, and in waiting for the legal and economic status of widowhood before confronting Almachius and ultimately donating her legally inherited house to the Church.[70] Her acting like a submissive wife allows her to be taken seriously by the men she encounters and by pastoral readers.

This is most obvious in Cecilia's attention to Valerian's conversion. Her persuasive speech allows him to take center-stage, preaching her message, ultimately to be martyred, in *her vita*. In effecting Valerian's conversion, Cecilia fulfills the expectations of confessional manuals that see Christian wives as not only capable of persuasion but responsible for their husbands' souls.[71] Jacqueline Murray's work on manuals by

---

[69] See Winstead's chapter "Unruly Virgins and the Laity," in *Virgin Martyrs*, 64–111.

[70] Here, Cecilia uses her secular, economic power as a widow for spiritual benefit. That is, having had her speech authorized by Valerian and Tiburce, she is only now legally authorized to donate her property to the Church. See Sue Sheridan Walker, ed., *Wife and Widow in Medieval England* (Ann Arbor: University of Michigan Press, 1994); and Michael Sheehan, "The Influence of Canon Law on the Property Rights of Married Women in England," *Medieval Studies* 25 (1963): 109–24. Sanok reads this as confirmation of Cecilia's authority as preacher: "When Cecilia turns her house into a church, it gives her a forum for the pastoral work reserved in late medieval England to male clerics. She now 'preaches' to those she had once 'fostered' . . . the Second Nun refuses to circumscribe Cecilia's authority"; Sanok, *Her Life Historical*, 169.

[71] A few years later, Christine de Pizan would also advocate that women should take some responsibility for their husbands' spiritual well-being in her 1405 *Livres de trois virtues*.

Thomas of Chobham, Serlo, and Wetheringsett has shown that women's agency is consistently compromised as ancillary to men's spiritual status.[72] Payer agrees, describing the confessional manuals as "radically androcentric," noting that, with few exceptions, the manuals are not addressed to women, nor do they offer much discussion of women's spiritual states.[73] Cecilia's job as wife, according to the manuals, is to ensure her husband behaves like a Christian, not to focus on her own spiritual development. She demonstrates her understanding and acceptance of doctrine by keeping Valerian in line: to "submit" by temporarily biding her time as he takes the spotlight is to act in her own self-interest.

In other words, Cecilia earns her freedom to speak publicly—like a traditional virgin martyr or preacher—by first acting like a good wife. She chooses to focus on Valerian's spiritual state, first as a convert and then as a preacher and martyr, rather than on her own status as a potential saint and public speaker. Because of this adherence to form, Valerian and Tiburce are fully convinced by her speech, so much so that they proclaim her message publicly, anticipating and promoting her ideas so she can't later be confused with a gossip, scold, or rabble-rouser.[74] The result is that Cecilia's preferences take center-stage in the narrative even as she steps briefly out of the limelight. Cecilia easily avoids the "idle speech" the prologue warns about: she speaks with reason and orthodoxy, privately, and maintains her domestic identity until Valerian and Tiburce, as men preaching her message in the public arena, make her words more palatable.

Until this point, Cecilia's success has largely been confirmed by men's responses to and assessments of her. Once she has proven herself as a Christian wife, Urban has affirmed her orthodoxy, and Valerian and

[72] Murray, "Absent Penitent," 20–24. For example, consensual adultery is a violation of another man's bed, with penance ascertained according to the status of the woman whom a man has violated, rather than a sin equally committed by men and women. See Murray, "Absent Penitent," 20 n. 28. Thomas of Chobham expresses concern that a victim of *stuprum* is deprived of the hundredfold reward of chastity, and that being knocked out of the marriage market might give her occasion to sin (*Summa confessorum*, 355–56). Payer suggests that the manuals' treatment of *stuprum* (the sexual violation of a virgin) actually offers some equity in this discussion; he lists various confessional manuals' required penance, usually related to paying [her father] for the woman's loss but also making the offender responsible for sexual sin the victim might commit afterward (*Sex and the New*, 122–23).

[73] Payer, *Sex and the New*, 8, 9 n. 15.

[74] See Phillips, *Transforming Talk*; and Bardsley, *Venomous Tongues*.

Tiburce have validated her speech, she is finally able to confront Almachius without attention to (Christian) male judgment. In this hagiographical public setting, his being pagan matters more than his sex, just as her position as preacher, honed throughout the narrative, outweighs hers. The authority that Cecilia has built with her orthodox persuasion and proselytizing (mostly by proxy) can now be cashed in: because her speech and behavior are unquestionably orthodox, her manner of speaking to Almachius and his opinions of her are irrelevant for pastoral readers. Cecilia's insults, defiance, and jeers are not surprising in this genre; virgin martyrs such as Katherine of Alexandria and Margaret of Antioch invoke similar language in their *passiones*. Cecilia may call Almachius ugly names, but because she is and has consistently been speaking doctrine, she is no less or more a preacher than she was back in the bedroom with Valerian. Her rhetorical techniques are no longer those of a wife, in part because conversion of Almachius is not her goal: getting doctrinal truths uttered in public is, and she has already achieved that through the process of persuading her husband to say them.

Part of what marks Almachius as pagan, and thus for pastoral readers is wrongheaded in his reaction to Cecilia, is his misreading of her role in this scene and in previous events of the narrative. He assumes that removing Cecilia's voice from the public sphere will end her influence. Almachius condemns Cecilia to be boiled in a bathtub "in hire hous" (514), where he also orders the executioner to behead her (523–34). Yet the importance and complexity of Cecilia's voice are only underscored by her forced return "home til her hous" (514) for her martyrdom, rather than the confinement in a government prison or execution at a public site that is more typical for virgin martyrs. In the context of this tale, Almachius does not realize the power of a Christian wife's words, of what she can achieve at home—in short, that a wife can be a preacher. As we have seen, until her confrontation with Almachius, most of Cecilia's speech has been uttered in domestic spaces, either her own or the convert Maxime's (368–90). That she preaches in her own home for three days before dying (537–39) makes explicit the connection between her roles as wife and as preacher. Almachius's misreading of what a wife can do ultimately allows the circumstances for the famous donation of Cecilia's house to the early Christian Church, a contribution that for medieval readers derives directly from her role as a recent wife, now a widow and head of household.

The suggestion that wives' orthodox submission leads to autonomy becomes heavy-handed by the end of the tale, when the very site at which a noblewoman has employed wifely persuasion becomes a holy place of worship. The types of sermons that Cecilia preached in her nuptial bedroom and from her bloody bathtub are presumably given now by men, as "Men doon to Crist and to his seint servyse" (553). The *vita* thus allows us to track Cecilia's words from her domestic space to the public arena, showing that her speech and message are transferable, as worthy to be stated by men as by a young wife. She may appear to be a deviant speaker if we focus only on her public voice late in the tale or on Almachius's response to her, but in her deference to Christian male authority throughout the text and willingness to allow Valerian and Tiburce to "go first" (and to speak her words for her), she upholds and reinforces the gendered expectations of the confessional manuals—and ultimately regains the central focus of the tale, along with, of course, sanctity.

Chaucer's choice of Cecilia as subject is not simply coincident with the name of the patron saint of Adam Easton's new church. It provides confirmation of the feminine behavior depicted in confessional manuals and other pastoral texts, and offers a model for those thinking in terms of how to speak persuasively. There is much in this text to appeal to a pastoral readership: a good wife, whose piety is such that the pope knows her personally, uses her persuasiveness to achieve her husband's conversion (and proselytizing), which leads indirectly to her own validation (and further proselytizing). Her ability to speak depends on her husband's affirmation and her own respect of social boundaries; his spiritual state depends on her orthodoxy. Chaucer, his target readers, and the Second Nun herself—who is, after all, also telling a story publicly, to be assessed by a man, and protected by the orthodoxy of her narrative—would recognize both registers of Cecilia's voices as congruent with their pastoral values.

Sleep and the Transformation of Sense in Late Medieval Literature

Michael Raby
McGill University

Abstract

The poets and philosophers of the late Middle Ages were fascinated by the phenomenon of dreaming. The Scholastics provided detailed accounts of how dreams are generated by the misperception of sense impressions. Similarly, the dream-vision genre often included narrative frames that allowed readers to see how the external circumstances of the dreamer condition the content of their dreams. This essay examines how three of the most important writers in the medieval dream-vision tradition—Dante, Machaut, and Chaucer—explored the sensory origins of dreaming. The scenes examined here raise the possibility that not all of the senses close completely during sleep and, in so doing, call into question the boundary between waking and sleeping. Drawing on readers of Aristotle from Albert the Great to Freud, the essay argues that an Aristotelian framework can help us better to understand how literary dreams provoke questions about the workings of perception and the relation between art and life.

Keywords

sleep, dream vision, history of the senses, Dante, Machaut, Chaucer

NEAR THE END OF THE *Purgatorio*, the Dante pilgrim falls asleep while listening to a hymn of unbearable beauty. He struggles to depict the moment of his nodding off:

> S'io potessi ritrar come assonnaro
> li occhi spietati udendo di Siringa—

An earlier version of this paper was delivered at the Nineteenth Biennial Congress of the New Chaucer Society, Reykjavik, Iceland, July 2014. I would like to thank the anonymous reviewers for *SAC* as well as the following people for their comments on various drafts: Ian Drummond, Madeleine Elson, Alexandra Gillespie, Bill MacLehose, Richard G. Newhauser, Maura Nolan, Will Robins, and Michael Van Dussen.

li occhi a cui pur vegghiar costò sì caro—
come pintor che con essempro pinga
disegnerei com' io m'addormentai,
ma qual vuol sia che l'assonnar ben finga.
 Però trascorro a quando mi svegliai,
e dico ch'un splendor mi squarciò 'l velo
del sonno, e un chiamar: "Surgi: che fai?"[1]

[If I could portray how the cruel eyes fell asleep when they heard of Syrinx—those eyes whose wakefulness cost so dear—like a painter painting from a model, I would depict how I fell asleep; but he must be one who imitates sleepiness well. Therefore I pass on to when I awoke, and I say that a brightness rent the veil of sleep for me, and a call: "Arise: what are you doing?"]

It is not easy to observe oneself falling asleep. After all, the descent into sleep seems to extinguish the very capacity for observation. We can more easily observe others as they fall asleep—the external signs at least. If Dante were able to depict someone else falling asleep, he muses, he could then apply that description to his own experience. He invokes one of the most famous depictions of nodding off in classical literature: Ovid's account of how Argus, the hundred-eyed watchman, was lulled to sleep by Mercury's tale of the nymph Syrinx and then beheaded.[2] But if we turn to the *Metamorphoses*, we discover that Ovid himself has failed to represent Argus's nodding off. Part way through his story Mercury notices that all of Argus's eyes have already closed in sleep. The precise moment of their closing goes unobserved and unnarrated. We are left doubting whether there is anyone who can "imitat[e] sleepiness well." Part of the difficulty lies in determining when exactly sleepiness tips over into sleep proper. As Augustine notes, "falling asleep is not being asleep, nor is waking up being awake; there is a passage from one state into the other."[3] The problem is that being asleep is not a stable, self-

---

[1] Dante Alighieri, *The Divine Comedy: Purgatorio*, ed. and trans. Robert M. Durling, intro. and notes Ronald L. Martinez and Durling (Oxford: Oxford University Press, 2003), XXXII.64–72. Subsequent references are cited parenthetically. See discussion of this passage in Teodolinda Barolini, *The Undivine "Comedy": Detheologizing Dante* (Princeton: Princeton University Press, 1992), 160–61.

[2] Ovid, *Metamorphoses: Books 1–8*, trans. Frank Justus Miller, rev. G. P. Goold, 3rd ed., Loeb Classical Library (Cambridge, Mass.: Harvard University Press, 1977), I.622–721.

[3] Augustine of Hippo, *De libero arbitrio*, ed. W. M. Green (Turnhout: Brepols, 1970), 193.24.73.254: "Velut in somno et uigiliis neque id est dormire quod obdormiscere neque id est uigilare quod expergisci, sed transitus quidam ex altero in alterum." The English translation is from Augustine of Hippo, *"On the Free Choice of the Will," "On Grace*

identical state; it consists of substates, variations in depth and cadence.[4] Even Argus, whose wakefulness is emblematized and telegraphed by his hundred open eyes, sleeps in phases: after the watchman's eyes have closed, Mercury uses his magic wand to deepen his sleep. And yet as deep as Argus's sleep may be, it retains some element of wakefulness; otherwise, Mercury would not need to cut off his head, for he would already be dead. In the words of Merleau-Ponty, "the sleeper is never completely isolated within himself, never totally a sleeper"; he remains in the world "through the anonymous alertness of the senses," the "last link [that] makes waking up a possibility: through these half-open doors things will return or the sleeper will come back into the world."[5] It is through the partly open doors of the senses that Dante is summoned back into the world by the bright light and the command to arise. This essay examines how Dante and other late medieval thinkers represented sleep as a state constituted by varying degrees of wakefulness. The kernel of wakefulness in the sleeper is not simply the capacity to be awakened, but a potential for perceiving things through the half-open doors of sense that would not otherwise be perceptible.

"Sleep," writes Jonathan Crary, "has a dense history, as does anything presumed to be natural. It has never been something monolithic or identical, and over centuries and millennia it has assumed many variegated forms and patterns."[6] In recent years, historians and literary critics have started to document the forms and patterns that make up the premodern history of sleep.[7] According to A. Roger Ekirch's important study

---

and Free Choice," and Other Writings, ed. and trans. Peter King (Cambridge: Cambridge University Press, 2010). Cited in Thomas D. Hill, " 'Half-waking, half-sleeping': A Tropological Motif in a Middle English Lyric and Its European Context," *RES* n.s. 29 (1978): 50–56 (54–55).

[4] As Jean-Luc Nancy observes, "rocking movements put us to sleep because sleep in its essence is itself a rocking, not a stable, motionless state"; *The Fall of Sleep*, trans. Charlotte Mandell (New York: Fordham University Press, 2009), 30.

[5] Maurice Merleau-Ponty, *Phenomenology of Perception*, trans. Colin Smith (London: Routledge, 1962), 190. See the discussion of this passage in Peter Schwenger, *At the Borders of Sleep: On Liminal Literature* (Minneapolis: University of Minnesota Press, 2012), 1–2.

[6] Jonathan Crary, *24/7: Late Capitalism and the Ends of Sleep* (London: Verso, 2013), 11. This observation qualifies the bolder claim that "sleep is a ubiquitous but unseen reminder of a premodernity that has never been fully exceeded, of the agricultural universe which began vanishing 400 years ago" (11).

[7] See, for instance, A. Roger Ekirch, *At Day's Close: Night in Times Past* (New York: Norton, 2005); William MacLehose, "Sleepwalking, Violence and Desire in the Middle Ages," *Culture, Medicine and Psychiatry* 37 (2013): 601–24; William F. MacLehose, "Fear, Fantasy and Sleep in Medieval Medicine," in *Emotions and Health, 1200–1700*,

At Day's Close, up until the industrial age, sleep was segmented into two discrete periods separated by a waking interval. After waking from the "first sleep," sleepers could fill the interval with reading, prayer, meditation, or sex.[8] Or they might find themselves drifting between sleep and wakefulness. In Old French, this liminal state was called *la dorveille*. Michel Stanesco and Michel Zink argue that horse riders traversing long distances would have spent much of their time in a *dorveille*-like state in which "the mind maintains only a distant relationship with reality or even loses contact with it, but without actually giving way to sleep."[9] They locate traces of this "technique of the body" in the troubadour tradition, particularly the well-known poem about "nothing" that Duke William IX of Aquitaine (1071–1126) claimed to have composed while dozing on a horse.[10] Later poets turned to the dream vision to explore the boundary between waking and sleeping, as well as the analogy between composing poetry and dreaming.[11] Dream visions often include

---

ed. Elena Carrera (Leiden: Brill, 2013), 67–94; and Jean Verdon, "Dormir au Moyen Age," *Revue belge de philologie et d'histoire* 72 (1994): 749–59.

[8] Ekirch, *At Day's Close*, 301–23. Ekirch notes Chaucer's reference to "first sleep" in *SqT*, 367: Canacee wakes up after sleeping her "firste sleep" and sets out on a pre-dawn walk. *The Riverside Chaucer*, gen. ed. Larry D. Benson, 3rd ed. (Boston: Houghton Mifflin, 1987); subsequent references to Chaucer's works are to this edition. Another reference to "first sleep" appears in *Visio Anglie*, the first book of Gower's *Vox clamantis*. After spending the day wandering through a paradisal wooded area, the speaker beds down for the night, but, after the passing of "first rest" ("prima quies aberat"), his eyes remain untouched by sleep, his anxious wakefulness spilling into and out of the allotted interval. John Gower, *Visio Anglie*, in *Poems on Contemporary Events: The "Visio Anglie" (1381) and "Cronica tripertita" (1400)*, ed. David R. Carlson, trans. A. G. Rigg (Toronto: PIMS, 2011), line 143. Cf. Ovid, *Metamorphoses*, VIII.83–84: "prima quies aderat, qua curis fessa diurnis pectora somnus habet" ("the first rest had come, when sleep holds the heart weary with the cares of day").

[9] Michel Zink, "The Allegorical Poem as Interior Memoir," trans. Margaret Miner and Kevin Brownlee, *Yale French Studies* 70 (1986): 100–126 (109); Michel Stanesco, *Jeux d'errance du chevalier médiéval* (Leiden: Brill, 1988), 148–72, esp. 169. Both Zink and Stanesco draw on the work of Marcel Mauss, "Techniques of the Body," trans. Ben Brewster, *Economy and Society* 2 (1973): 70–88 (81). On the tropological significance of the *dorveille*, see Hill, "Half-waking, half-sleeping."

[10] Guilhem IX, duke of Aquitaine, "Farai un vers de dreit nïen," in *Songs of the Troubadours and Trouvères: An Anthology of Poems and Melodies*, ed. Samuel N. Rosenberg, Margaret Switten, and Gérard Le Vot (New York: Routledge, 1998), 38–39. Zink, "Allegorical Poem," 109; Stanesco, *Jeux d'errance*, 149–50.

[11] The secondary literature on the medieval dream vision is extensive. Important works include Steven F. Kruger, *Dreaming in the Middle Ages* (Cambridge: Cambridge University Press, 1992); A. C. Spearing, *Medieval Dream-Poetry* (Cambridge: Cambridge University Press, 1976); and Kathryn L. Lynch, *The High Medieval Dream Vision: Poetry, Philosophy, and Literary Form* (Stanford: Stanford University Press, 1988). For a useful recent survey of Middle English dream visions that takes as its thematic focus the boundary between waking and sleeping, see Peter Brown, "On the Borders of Middle English Dream Visions," in *Reading Dreams: The Interpretation of Dreams from Chaucer to Shakespeare*, ed. Brown (Oxford: Oxford University Press, 1999), 22–50. On the parallels

sequences that provide a glimpse into the dreamer's surroundings or waking state of mind; such glimpses allow the reader to observe parallels between the content of the dream and the external circumstances that undergird it. The idea that bodily sensations or residual emotions could affect dreaming was commonly accepted by premodern dream theorists. The late antique philosopher Macrobius identified a type of dream that "arise[s] from some condition or circumstance that irritates a man during the day and consequently disturbs him when he falls asleep."[12] As a variety of "false dream," the *insomnium* does not warrant much in the way of exegesis or explanation. Other highly influential thinkers such as Augustine and Gregory the Great maintained that certain dreams could be attributed to somatic processes.[13] As Steven Kruger has demonstrated, interest in the physiology of dreams picked up in the twelfth century as philosophical and medical treatises written in Greek and Arabic became increasingly available to western Europe.[14] By the early thirteenth century, Aristotle's treatises on sleep and dreams had been translated into Latin and were providing stimulus to Scholastics such as Albert the Great, who expended much energy and ingenuity trying to account for the physiological processes behind sleep and dreaming; instances of parasomnia were of particular interest, including cases of those who, like William, managed to ride horses and even conduct conversation while asleep. To be sure, the Aristotelian models did not replace established late antique and patristic theories; as Kruger notes, late medieval thinkers, even the most Aristotelian among them, tended to synthesize the "newer" learning with "older" theories that were better able to explain divinely inspired dreams. Yet, owing partly to the outsize role that Macrobius's typology continues to play in medieval literary criticism, scholars have been slow to read dream visions in the light of Aristotelian theory.[15]

---

between poetic creation and dreaming, see Kruger, *Dreaming in the Middle Ages*, 123–49.

[12] Macrobius, *Commentarii in somnium Scipionis*, ed. Jacob Willis (Leipzig: Teubner, 1970), 1.3.5. The English translation is from Macrobius, *Commentary on the Dream of Scipio*, trans. William Harris Stahl (New York: Columbia University Press, 1952).

[13] See, for example, Augustine of Hippo, *De Genesi ad litteram*, ed. J. Zycha (Vienna: F. Tempsky, 1894), 12.19.41; Gregory the Great, *Dialogi*, ed. Adalbert de Vogüé, Vol. 3, Sources Chrétiennes 265 (Paris: Cerf, 1980), 4.50.2.

[14] Kruger, *Dreaming in the Middle Ages*, 70–82.

[15] C. H. L. Bodenham argues that, despite name-checking Macrobius in its opening lines, the *Roman de la rose* can more productively be read against the background of Aristotelian dream theory; "The Nature of the Dream in Late Mediaeval French Literature," *MÆ* 54 (1985): 74–86. On the tendency of literary critics to overvalue the influence of Macrobius, see also Alison M. Peden, "Macrobius and Mediaeval Dream Literature," *MÆ* 54 (1985): 59–73.

One of the goals of this essay is to demonstrate that medieval poets were more interested in so-called "false dreams" than a Macrobian hermeneutic would have us believe,[16] and that an Aristotelian framework can better illuminate how these dreams provoke questions about the nature of perception and art. The increasing attention that medievalists are paying to the history of the senses makes an investigation into the perceptual processes underlying dreams especially timely.[17] After an opening discussion of two commentaries by Albert the Great, I turn to a series of literary scenes; my major examples are drawn from the works of three of the most influential authors in the dream-vision tradition—Dante's *Purgatorio*, Chaucer's *Troilus and Criseyde*, and Machaut's *Fontaine amoureuse*. Surfacing in these scenes are questions that vexed Albert and his colleagues: can the senses remain open in sleep? If so, which ones and to what extent? The Scholastics attempted to answer these questions while preserving a conceptual division between sleep and wakefulness. The poets examined here are fascinated by moments in which it is difficult to tell if one is fully asleep or awake, if one is dreaming or perceiving. These scenes are characterized by the interweaving of dream imagery and bodily sensations; they do not simply reduce the phantasmatic to its physiological inputs, but rather create a split vantage that allows for reflection on the nature of image-making, on the process of transforming sensation into dream, experience into art.

Sleepwalkers and Dreams of Honey: The Aristotelian Tradition

Three of the treatises that make up Aristotle's *Parva naturalia* (*Short Treatises on Nature*) focus on sleep and dreams—*De somno et vigilia* (*On Sleep and Waking*); *De insomniis* (*On Dreams*); and *De divinatione per somnum* (*On Divination through Sleep*). Included within these texts are some

---

[16] For critics who have made this point in different ways, see Zink, "Allegorical Poem"; Michel Zink, "Séduire, endormir: Note sur les premiers vers d'un poème du XVe siècle," *Littérature* 23 (1976): 117–21; Barolini, *Undivine "Comedy"*; and Yasmina Foehr-Janssens, "Songes creux et insomnies dans les récits médiévaux (Fabliaux, dits, *exempla*)," in *Le rêve médiéval*, ed. Alain Corbellari and Jean-Yves Tilliette (Geneva: Droz, 2007), 111–36.

[17] For a useful recent overview of sensory studies in the Middle Ages, see Richard G. Newhauser, "The Senses, the Medieval Sensorium, and Sensing (in) the Middle Ages," in *Handbook of Medieval Culture: Fundamental Aspects and Conditions of the European Middle Ages*, ed. Albrecht Classen, Vol. 3 (Berlin: De Gruyter, 2015), 1559–75. There are a few brief references to sleep in C. M. Woolgar, *The Senses in Late Medieval England* (New Haven: Yale University Press, 2006), e.g. 9, 29.

of the most important discussions of key Aristotelian concepts such as the *sensus communis* (Gr. *koinē aisthēsis*), the imagination, and the phantasm. Aristotle begins his inquiry by positing sleep as the privation of waking.[18] Given that perceiving is the defining feature of waking life ("we take every waking person to be perceiving either something external or some movement within himself"), it then follows that sleep entails the cessation of perception.[19] Aristotle supports this claim by adducing the closed eyes of the sleeper. Taking sight to be the paradigmatic sense, he claims that the other senses are equally incapacitated during sleep.[20] As his inquiry proceeds, Aristotle modifies his opening position by allowing that there is a qualified form of perception at work in sleep. In an obscure formulation, he states that dreaming is the work of the perceptual part of the soul in its imaginative capacity.[21] By imagination (*phantasia*), Aristotle refers to the faculty that, among other capabilities, retains traces of sense objects and from these traces generates new images.[22] The dreaming person "perceives" impressions of now-absent sense objects that persist in both the superficial and deeper structures of perception. Once again the paradigmatic sense is sight. Aristotle demonstrates his claim by pointing to the phenomenon of after-images, such as traces of sunshine that remain in the field of vision even when the eyes are now closed. While awake, we encounter a variety of sensory stimuli, many of which we disregard because we are focused on the most salient. In sleep these unnoticed residual impressions receive, as Philip J. van der Eijk puts it, "a second chance to 'present themselves.'"[23] They

---

[18] Aristotle, *De somno et vigilia*, in *Aristotle on Sleep and Dreams*, ed. and trans. David Gallop (Warminster: Aris and Phillips, 1996), 453b24–31. English translations are from this edition. On Aristotle's theories of sleep and dreaming, see, among others, Philip J. van der Eijk, *Medicine and Philosophy in Classical Antiquity: Doctors and Philosophers on Nature, Soul, Health and Disease* (Cambridge: Cambridge University Press, 2005), 169–205; Mark A. Holowchak, "Aristotle on Dreaming: What Goes on in Sleep when the 'Big Fire' Goes Out," *Ancient Philosophy* 16 (1996): 405–23; and Marcia Sá Cavalcante Schuback, "The Hermeneutic Slumber: Aristotle's Reflections on Sleep," trans. David Payne, in *The Bloomsbury Companion to Aristotle*, ed. Claudia Baracchi (London: Bloomsbury, 2014), 128–43.

[19] Aristotle, *De somno*, 454a4–5.

[20] Aristotle, *De insomniis*, in *Aristotle on Sleep and Dreams*, 458b3–9.

[21] Ibid., 459a14–22.

[22] On the faculty of the imagination in Aristotle and his medieval commentators, see Murray W. Bundy, *The Theory of Imagination in Classical and Mediaeval Thought* (Champaign: University of Illinois Press, 1927); Gerard Watson, *Phantasia in Classical Thought* (Galway: Galway University Press, 1988); and Michelle Karnes, *Imagination, Meditation, and Cognition in the Middle Ages* (Chicago: University of Chicago Press, 2011).

[23] Van der Eijk, *Medicine and Philosophy*, 183.

are carried inward toward the controlling sense located in the area of the heart, where they are perceived, albeit in distorted forms. Dreams, ultimately, are born out of acts of misprision. Dreamers mistake the jumbled images for objects that they resemble, and it is only upon waking that they can reconstruct the circumstances behind their generative errors.

By the early thirteenth century, Aristotle's three treatises, along with Arabic commentaries, had been translated into Latin.[24] Albert the Great wrote two extensive paraphrases on the treatises: one that appears in *De homine*, the second part of what was long known as his *Summa de creaturis* (c. 1242); and a second, *De somno et vigilia*, which formed part of his *Parva naturalia* (c. 1255–60).[25] At times, we can see Albert attempting to square away inconsistencies or unpack enigmatic passages in his source texts. He expands Aristotle's allusive reference to sleepers who "move and perform many actions akin to waking ones" by explaining the mechanics of sleepwalking.[26] According to Albert, sleep occurs when the process of digestion produces a coldness that binds the external senses and the *sensus communis*. The *sensus communis* is the inner sense that collates, compares, and synthesizes the various sensations that arrive

---

[24] On the medieval reception of Aristotle's sleep and dream treatises, see Kruger, *Dreaming in the Middle Ages*, 83–122; and Christophe Grellard, "La réception médiévale du *De somno et vigilia*: Approche anthropologique et épistémologique du rêve, d'Albert le Grand à Jean Buridan," in *Les "Parva naturalia" d'Aristote: Fortune antique et médiévale*, ed. Grellard and Pierre-Marie Morel (Paris: Publications de la Sorbonne, 2010), 221–37.

[25] Albert the Great, *De homine*, ed. Henryk Anzulewicz and Joachim R. Söder, in *Opera omnia*, Vol. 27, Part 2 (Münster: Aschendorff, 2008); Albert the Great, *De somno et vigilia*, ed. A. Borgnet, in *Opera omnia*, Vol. 9 (Paris: Vives, 1890). On the dating of these works, see James A. Weisheipl, "Albert's Works on Natural Science (*libri naturales*) in Probable Chronological Order," in *Albertus Magnus and the Sciences: Commemorative Essays 1980*, ed. Weisheipl (Toronto: Pontifical Institute of Medieval Studies, 1980), 565–77. Albert also discusses sleep in *Quaestiones super De animalibus* (*Questions Concerning Aristotle's "On Animals"*), IV.9–12. Albert's writings on sleep have yet to be studied in detail. See Christina Thomsen Thörnqvist, "Sleepwalking through the Thirteenth Century: Some Medieval Latin Commentaries on Aristotle's *De somno et vigilia* 2.456a24–27," *Vivarium* 54 (2016): 286–310; MacLehose, "Sleepwalking, Violence and Desire"; and Roberto Lo Presti, "'For sleep, in some way, is an epileptic seizure' (*somn. vig.* 3, 457a9–10)," in *The Frontiers of Ancient Science: Essays in Honor of Heinrich von Staden*, ed. Brooke Holmes and Klaus-Dietrich Fischer (Berlin: De Gruyter, 2015), 339–96.

[26] Aristotle, *De somno*, 456a24–28. In *De generatione animalium*, Aristotle makes a brief reference to sleepwalking: "There are those who get up while asleep and walk about and can see as well as anyone awake. The reason is that they are aware through their senses of what is going on, and though they are not awake, still this awareness is different from that of a dream." The nature of this awareness is tantalizingly unspecified. *Generation of Animals*, ed. and trans. A. L. Peck (Cambridge: Harvard University Press, 1943), 5.1, 779a16–19.

through the external senses.[27] Normally when the *sensus communis* is immobilized so are all of the particular senses. However, it can sometimes happen that the *sensus communis* remains immobilized in sleep, while one or more of the particular senses become unfettered.[28] Interestingly, Albert's two paraphrases differ on precisely which senses are loosened. According to the account in *De homine*, the distal senses (namely, sight and hearing) are released by a certain kind of bodily heat, which also releases the motive power (*virtus motiva*), thus enabling movement.[29] Sleepwalkers can perceive their surroundings to some degree, although the present sensations are impressed more weakly than dream images, which is why it is easier to remember dreams than "waking actions" performed while asleep. This explanation comes at the cost of pathologizing somnambulism, though, as the heat that releases the senses and the motive power is produced by choleric blood rising to the head, the kind of circulation found in those who are predisposed to madness (*phrenesis*). In the account in *De somno*, on the other hand, it is the sense of touch that becomes unbound while the other senses remain immobilized. And, unlike in *De homine*, the bodily heat that releases touch can be generated by more quotidian factors—anger at an enemy, desire, hot food. With the organ of touch unbound, the limbs are free to move. The movements of sleepwalkers are not guided by sensation—they do not see or hear their surroundings—but rather by interacting with dream images; thus, dreaming that they will find their enemies at a certain place, they "go in darkness as in the light, and sometimes it happens that their enemy is there and that they beat him; but sometimes it happens that they attack a column or some wood or something

[27] Following Avicenna, Albert identifies five inner senses: the *sensus communis*, the imagination, the estimative power, fantasy (*phantasia*), and memory. On the inner senses in Albert's writings, see Nicholas H. Steneck, "Albert the Great on the Classification and Localization of the Internal Senses," *Isis* 65 (1974): 193–211. For a broader history of the concept of the *sensus communis*, see Daniel Heller-Roazen, *The Inner Touch: Archaeology of a Sensation* (New York: Zone, 2007).

[28] Jean de Meun's continuation of the *Roman de la rose* includes a passage that echoes Albert's explanation for sleepwalking. According to Jean, sleepwalkers move about while "their common senses sleep and their individual senses are all awake" ("si con li san conmun someillent / et tuit li particulier veillent"); Guillaume de Lorris and Jean de Meun, *Le roman de la rose*, ed. Félix Lecoy, 3 vols. (Paris: Champion, 1965–70), lines 18279–80. The English translation is from Guillaume de Lorris and Jean de Meun, *The Romance of the Rose*, 3rd ed., trans. Charles Dahlberg (Princeton: Princeton University Press, 1995).

[29] Albert the Great, *De homine*, 1.5.3.

else in place of their enemy."[30] If these sleepfighters were guided by sensation, they would be less likely to fall accidentally and die as they sometimes do, but they perceive in a limited, confused manner through the sense of touch alone. While the two accounts differ on which senses are released in cases of somnambulism, both insist that the center of perception, the *sensus communis*, remains incapacitated, and, by doing so, are able to preserve the coherence of the Aristotelian axiom that sleep and perception proper are mutually exclusive.

Medieval readers of Aristotle's sleep treatises would have encountered another passage that complicated the distinction between perceiving and dreaming, waking and sleeping. While Aristotle was generally skeptical of the prophetic potential of dreams, he acknowledged their diagnostic value. Physicians pay attention to dreams because they magnify minor and incipient sense impressions that can indicate potential illness. In *De divinatione per somnum*, for instance, he writes: "People think it is lightning and thundering, when faint echoes are sounding in their ears; or that they are enjoying honey and sweet flavours, when a tiny drop of phlegm is running down; or that they are walking through fire and feeling extremely hot, when a slight warmth is affecting certain parts."[31] Whereas in *De insomniis* Aristotle had claimed that dreams were composed of residual sense impressions left over from waking life, here he uses examples of sensory stimuli that are occurring in the present moment as the dreamer is sleeping. These present impressions are misconstrued as other objects according to the process of misprision that generates dream activity.[32] Significantly, none of Aristotle's examples is visual. Earlier he had invoked the closed eyes of the sleeper as evidence of the supposed cessation of perceptual activity in sleep; now he seems to admit that the other senses do not close as tightly. Albert adapts the passage in his discussion of the bodily causes of dreams, but, as with his analysis of somnambulism, he provides two contrasting accounts of which particular senses might be open. In *De homine*, he omits the thunder example, drawing instead exclusively from the domain of touch: we

[30] Albert the Great, *De somno*, 1.2.5: "Et ideo vadunt in tenebris sicut in lumine, et aliquando contingit quod est ibi, et tunc percutiunt eum: aliquando autem contingit, quod columnam vel lignum vel aliud quod impugnant pro inimico."

[31] Aristotle, *De divinatione per somnum*, in *Aristotle on Sleep and Dreams*, 463a12–16.

[32] In an attempt to reconcile Aristotle's examples with his previous definitions of dreams as the product of residual, not present, sense impressions, Philip J. van der Eijk writes: "We might consider the possibility that the experiences mentioned here are not examples of dreams, but effects of a more general mechanism which is operative in sleep, and of which dreams are a different species"; *Medicine and Philosophy*, 200.

dream we are in a fire when a warmth affects the body, or that we are eating honey when phlegm touches the palate and tongue, or that we are submerged in snow or water or ice when we are cold.[33] Earlier in this text Albert had insisted that the organ of touch remains asleep even in sleepwalkers, but his version of the passage from De divinatione per somnum suggests that touch is operating in some capacity, providing the sense impressions that will be transformed into dream imagery. We are given a different list in De somno. Not only does Albert reinstate the thunder example, he adds the sense that was conspicuously absent from Aristotle's catalogue: when little sounds strike our ears and small lights twinkle ("parva micant lumina"), we believe we are in a thunderstorm.[34] Albert goes on to include Aristotle's two other examples—phlegm as honey and bodily warmth as fire—appending to the latter the claim that such a misconstrual is especially possible if the affected bodily part is internal (e.g., the stomach). The clarification draws attention to the fact—more obvious in De somno than in De homine—that the sleeper's body is not insulated from external or internal sense impressions in sleep. On the contrary, these impressions, which would not be noticeable during waking hours, can become in modified forms the central focus of the sleeper's attention. In other words, the closing of sense that occurs in sleep is also an opening.

The Eagle and the Swallow

The Commedia famously begins with its sleep-filled ("pien di sonno") protagonist taking a wrong turn and finding himself in a dark wood.[35] Sleep is commonly read symbolically here, as a figure for sin, but, as my opening discussion has already indicated, Dante was interested in the

[33] Albert the Great, De homine, 2.5.1: "Ex parte corporis quidem, sicut quando aliquis videt se esse in igne vel in parte, vel in toto, ex eo quod in toto vel in parte in naturali calore calefactus est; et aliquis somniat se comedere mel, eo quod flegma dulce tangit palatum et linguam. Aliquis etiam somniat se esse in nive vel aqua vel glacie, eo quod in parte vel in toto nimis infrigidatus est."

[34] Albert the Great, De somno, 3.2.1: "Arbitramur enim fulgura cadendo micare, et tonitrua fieri, quando parvi soni in auribus nostris fiunt, et parva micant lumina, et melle et dulcibus saporibus perfrui videmur nobis, quando tenue et dulce phlegma a capite fluit ad linguam, et somniamus nos ambulare per ignem et calefieri vehementer parvo calore facto circa partes aliquas corporis: et praecipue si in interioribus corporis fit."

[35] Dante Alighieri, The Divine Comedy: Inferno, ed. and trans. Robert M. Durling, intro. and notes Ronald L. Martinez and Durling (Oxford: Oxford University Press, 1996), I.11.

non-figurative aspect of sleep as well.[36] Given the centrality of Albert the Great and his pupil Thomas Aquinas to the philosophical background of the *Commedia*, it is likely that Dante would have been familiar with at least the rudiments of Aristotelian sleep theory.[37] In the *Purgatorio*, Dante repeatedly explores the structural parallels between sleep and *ecstasis*. As the pilgrim emerges out of "an ecstatic vision" ("una visïone / estatica") and his soul returns its focus to external things, Virgil chides him for shuffling along, eyes veiled and legs stumbling like someone who has just woken up (XV.85–86). Sleepiness has a much different valence here than at the beginning of the *Inferno*; Dante inserts himself within a lineage of somnolent visionaries that includes Saint John, the author of Revelation, who, later in the *Purgatorio*, walks by "asleep, with his face alert" ("dormendo, con la faccia arguta") (XXIX.144). In Canto XVII, the pilgrim is granted another ecstatic vision, one in which images rain into his "deep fantasy" ("l'alta fantasia") from above (XVII.25):

> De l'empiezza di lei che mutò forma
> ne l'uccel ch'a cantar più si diletta
> ne l'imagine mia apparve l'orma,
>   e qui fu la mia mente sì ristretta
> dentro da sé che di fuor non venìa
> cosa che fosse allor da lei ricetta.
>
> (XVII.19–24)

[The wickedness of her who changed her form into the bird that most delights to sing, appeared as a trace in my imagination, and here my mind was so bound up within itself that it would receive nothing then that came from outside.]

[36] Teodolinda Barolini makes this point convincingly in *Undivine "Comedy."* I am indebted to her analysis in this paragraph and the next. See also Robert Hollander, who notes: "Dante's fascination with the state between dream and waking is a notable part of his program of investigating the mental state of humans." Dante Alighieri, *Purgatorio*, trans. Jean Hollander and Robert Hollander, intro. and notes Robert Hollander (New York: Anchor Books, 2003), 382. See also William Anderson, *Dante the Maker* (London: Routledge, 1980).

[37] On Dante's engagement with Aristotelian philosophy, particularly regarding sleep and dream theory, see Natale Busetto, "Saggi di varia psicologia dantesca: Contributo allo studio delle relazioni di Dante con Alberto Magno e con san Tommaso," *Giornale dantesco* 13 (1905): 113–55, esp. 143–55; and Patrick Boyde, *Perception and Passion in Dante's "Comedy"* (Cambridge: Cambridge University Press, 1993). Bruno Nardi identifies parallels between Dante's *Convivio* and Aristotle's *De somno*; "Raffronti fra alcuni luoghi di Alberto Magno e di Dante," in *Saggi di filosofia dantesca* (Florence: La Nuova Italia, 1967), 63–72.

The brief allusion is to Procne, the sister of Philomela. According to the Ovidian version of the myth, Philomela is raped by Procne's husband Tereus, who then cuts out her tongue to prevent her from telling anyone. Philomela weaves a representation of the rape into a tapestry that is eventually deciphered by her sister. In an act of revenge, Procne murders her infant son and feeds the body to his unwitting father. When Tereus discovers the secret ingredient in his meal, he chases the sisters, who are transformed into birds. In the Latin tradition, Procne becomes a swallow and Philomela a nightingale, but Dante seems to have it the other way around.[38] The image of Procne's wickedness is produced in the pilgrim's mind without any sensory input; his imagination has instead been moved by a heavenly light (XVII.17). In an instructive passage from his discussion of prophetic dreams, Albert describes a similar process in which the mind, detached from the senses, is able to receive heavenly forms that are ordinarily overlooked because of external distractions.[39] As in sleep, though, the pilgrim's detachment from his senses is not complete:

> Come si frange il sonno ove di butto
> nova luce percuote il viso chiuso,
> che fratto guizza pria che muoia tutto:
> così l'imaginar mio cadde giuso
> tosto che lume il volto mi percosse,
> maggior assai che quel ch'è in nostro uso.

[38] It is possible that the sister intended here is Philomela, but Ovid's association of Procne with anger and impiety makes Procne more likely. See Jessica Levenstein, "Philomela, Procne, and the Song of the Penitent in Dante's *Purgatorio*," in *Writers Reading Writers: Intertextual Studies in Medieval and Early Modern Literature in Honor of Robert Hollander*, ed. Janet Levarie Smarr (Newark: University of Delaware Press, 2007), 40–57.

[39] Albert the Great, *De somno*, 3.1.9:

Similiter igitur per omnia videtur dicendum, quod formae coelitus evectae ad nos, corpora nostra tangentes fortissime movent, et suas imprimunt virtutes, licet non sentiantur propter exteriorem tumultum: et ideo quando alienatio fit a sensibus, quocumque modo illud fiat, tunc percipiuntur motus sicut patiens percipit motum passionis, licet non moveat ut passio, sed potius ut signum, et quaedam causa futurorum: anima autem imaginativa ad quam pervenit motus hujusmodi formae, recipit motum secundum modum possibilem sibi, et hoc est ad formas imaginationis.

Cited in Dante, *Purgatorio*, ed. Durling and Martinez, 284. For a discussion of Albert's theory of prophetic dreams, see Tullio Gregory, *Mundana sapientia: Forme di conoscenza nella cultura medievale* (Rome: Edizioni di storia e letteratura, 1992), 347–87.

(XVII.40–45)

[As sleep is shattered when suddenly new light strikes our closed eyes, but wriggles as it breaks, before it dies completely: so my imagining fell down as soon as the light struck my face, much greater than we are accustomed to.]

It is an external stimulus, albeit a supernaturally bright one, that breaks up the vision.

Earlier in the *Purgatorio*, Dante portrays a sleeping vision that is less disconnected from the sensory world. On his way to the gates of purgatory, the pilgrim falls asleep and dreams:

> Ne l'ora che comincia i tristi lai
> la rondinella presso a la mattina,
> forse a memoria de' suo' primi guai,
>   e che la mente nostra, peregrina
> più da la carne e men da' pensier presa,
> a le sue visïon quasi è divina,
>   in sogno mi parea veder sospesa
> un'aguglia nel ciel con penne d'oro,
> con l'ali aperte e a calare intesa.
> [. . .]
>   Poi mi parea che, poi rotata un poco,
> terribil come fólgor discendesse
> e me rapisse suso infino al foco.
>   Ivi parea che ella e io ardesse,
> e sì lo 'ncendio imaginato cosse
> che convenne che 'l sonno si rompesse.
>   (IX.13–21, 28–33)

[In the hour near morning when the swallow begins her sad lays, perhaps in memory of her first woes, and when our mind, journeying further from the flesh and less taken by its cares, is almost a diviner in its visions, in dream I seemed to see an eagle hovering in the sky, with golden feathers and open wings, intent to swoop [. . .] Then it seemed to me that, having wheeled a little, it descended terrible as lightning, and carried me off, up as far as the fire. There it seemed that it and I burned, and the imagined fire was so hot that my sleep had to break.][40]

---

[40] Translation modified.

Augustine points out that when we narrate our dreams, we usually elide the fact that we are seeing representations of objects instead of actual objects, saying, for instance, "I saw a mountain," rather than the more precise "I saw an image of a mountain."[41] Dante is something of an exception: he often marks his dream images as images by using, as he does here, the verb *parere* (to seem) and modifiers such as *imaginato* (imagined).[42] The dream begins against the background of the morning song of the swallow, another oblique reference to Procne/Philomela. That early morning dreams tended to be more prophetic in nature was a well-established tenet of medieval dream theory.[43] The passage thus sets us up to expect a divinely inspired oracular dream, but once the pilgrim awakes, the dream is recast in a different light. The pilgrim wakes up in an unfamiliar place, sun shining overhead. Virgil explains to him that a woman named Lucia ("light") appeared while he slept, carried his sleeping body some distance, and then deposited him at the entrance to purgatory. Virgil's account of the external events that coincided with the dream encourages us to read the dream in accordance with Aristotelian logic, as a phantasmatic misconstrual of the sensations experienced by the sleeping pilgrim—the heat and brightness of the sun on his body, the feeling of being lifted and carried by Lucia.[44] Virgil appears to confirm such a reading when he tells the pilgrim that his soul did not journey from his body, as we were initially invited to believe, but remained inside him while he slept (IX.53). Whereas the ecstatic vision of Procne appears when the pilgrim is largely if not completely separated from his senses, the golden eagle emerges in a sleep that retains contact with the surrounding world.

Chaucer was evidently quite struck by the dream of the golden eagle. He parodies the scene in *The House of Fame*, recasting the eagle as a verbose pedant who complains about the weight of the dreamer as they wheel through the heavens.[45] A less obvious reworking of the passage

---

[41] Augustine, *De Genesi ad litteram*, 12.4.10.

[42] On Dante's use of *parere* to signal visionary or counterfactual content more generally, see Barolini, *Undivine "Comedy,"* 150–51.

[43] On the veracity of early morning dreams, see Charles Speroni, "Dante's Prophetic Morning-Dreams," *SP* 45 (1948): 50–59; and Kruger, *Dreaming in the Middle Ages*, 72.

[44] Natale Busetto glosses the golden eagle dream with Albert's observation that dreams of walking through fire can arise from a slight feeling of warmth in the body (see *De somno*, 3.2.1; Aristotle, *De divinatione per somnum*, 463a12–16); "Saggi di varia psicologia dantesca," 146–47. See also Boyde, *Perception and Passion*, 127.

[45] On the eagle in *The House of Fame*, see John Leyerle, "Chaucer's Windy Eagle," *UTQ* 40 (1970): 247–65.

occurs in *Troilus and Criseyde*. At the beginning of Book II, we are given a brief glimpse into the private life of the character who is so adept at invading the private spaces of others. Pandarus has just agreed to help his lovesick friend Troilus win the good graces of the woman he covets, Criseyde, who happens to be Pandarus's niece. Here, though, we see Pandarus as a physician unable to heal himself. Pierced by "loves shotes keene," he spends the night tossing and turning.[46] It is a conventional pose. In the *Roman de la rose*, the God of Love details the nocturnal suffering experienced by his servants: as the Middle English *Romaunt of the Rose* puts it, lovers can expect to "turne full ofte on every side" and spread their arms like soldiers defeated in war; they will delight in an image of their beloved's "shap," believing that they hold her naked body in their grasp, only to wake and realize that the vision was nothing more than a "fable."[47] The restless Pandarus is visited by a different kind of "shap":

> The swalowe Proigne, with a sorowful lay,
> Whan morwen com, gan make hire waymentynge
> Whi she forshapen was; and evere lay
> Pandare abedde, half in a slomberynge,
> Til she so neigh hym made hire cheterynge
> How Tereus gan forth hire suster take,
> That with the noyse of hire he gan awake,
>
> And gan to calle, and dresse hym up to ryse,
> Remembryng hym his erand was to doone
> From Troilus, and ek his grete emprise.
>
> (*TC*, II.64–73)

Like the Dante pilgrim, Pandarus's early morning slumber is accompanied by the song of a swallow—in this case, Procne. While the allusion to *Purgatorio*, IX has been noted by Winthrop Wetherbee and others, Chaucer reads the Dantean intertext, and its implied theory of dreaming, more closely than has previously been recognized.[48] The background noise is amplified into two overlapping kinds of sound:

---

[46] *TC*, II.58.

[47] *Rom*, Fragment B, 2560, 2566, 2578.

[48] Winthrop Wetherbee, *Chaucer and the Poets: An Essay on "Troilus and Criseyde"* (Ithaca, N.Y.: Cornell University Press, 1984), 154–58. Wetherbee argues that Pandarus does not actually dream: "it is a symptom of his lack of an inner dimension that, lying half asleep, he should hear only the 'cheterynge' of Procne about Tereus's rape of her sister Philomela and be aroused by it to set in motion the seduction of his own niece"

"cheterynge," an onomatopoeic word for the twittering of birds, and "waymentynge" (wailing, or lamenting).[49] The two registers of sound— one associated with the nonhuman, the other with the human—evoke an oscillation between perception (bird chattering) and dream (Procne's lament), waking and sleep. Pandarus's half-slumber, I suggest, is an attempt to translate the translation that structures the dream of the golden eagle, that is, the translation of sensation into dream imagery. With one major difference: by transforming the chatter into lament and then back again, it reverses the tropic trajectory of Dante's dream (and of the Ovidian metamorphosis as well), in which a woman is trans- formed into a bird. The impetus for Chaucer's rewriting of the scene can be found within the *Purgatorio* passage itself. Note the careful use of "perhaps" ("forse") in Dante's description of the swallow: "when the swallow begins her sad lays, perhaps [forse] in memory of her first woes." Like *parere* and *imaginato, forse* is an important indicator for Dante of the counterfactual.[50] Perhaps the swallow is the mournful Procne or perhaps she is just a swallow. Chaucer highlights the indeterminacy by transposing the sound into a moment of waking sleep, the region of the "perhaps."

It might be helpful at this juncture to turn momentarily to a more modern theorist of dreaming—Freud. In *The Interpretation of Dreams*, Freud addresses the Aristotelian legacy of dreaming as a fundamentally somatic process.[51] He acknowledges that sensory impressions play a role in the formation of dreams, whether they are left-over day residue or occurring while the dreamer is asleep. For Freud, tracing dream imagery back to sensory impressions has a limited interpretative value; for the most part, the impressions simply comprise the "ready to hand" material

---

(158). Jane Chance contrasts the eventual seduction of Criseyde with the spiritual rav- ishment of the Dante pilgrim; *The Mythographic Chaucer: The Fabulation of Sexual Politics* (Minneapolis: University of Minnesota Press, 1995), 123–25.

[49] *MED*, s.vv. *chiteringe, waimenting.*

[50] Barolini, *Undivine "Comedy,"* 163–64.

[51] Freud writes: "Aristotle was aware of some of the characteristics of dream-life. He knew, for instance, that dreams give a magnified construction to small stimuli arising during sleep." Freud goes on to cite Aristotle's example of dreamers who imagine they are walking through fire when they feel a slight warmth in certain body parts. Sigmund Freud, *The Interpretation of Dreams*, in *The Standard Edition of the Complete Psychological Works of Sigmund Freud*, ed. and trans. James Strachey, vols. 4–5 (London: Hogarth Press, 1953), 3. Subsequent references are cited parenthetically. On Freud's knowledge, or non-knowledge, of premodern dream theory and dream-vision literature, see Aranye Fradenburg, "(Dis)continuity: A History of Dreaming," in *The Post-Historical Middle Ages*, ed. Elizabeth Scala and Sylvia Federico (New York: Palgrave, 2009), 87–115.

that is shaped into a dream by psychic forces (237). If the sleeper is bombarded by a particularly intense stimulus, a dream may function to prolong sleep by weaving the intrusive stimulus into a dreamscape, thus suppressing the reminder of the outside world. So, for instance, a sleeper is able to snatch a few extra moments of sleep by transforming the sound of his alarm clock into church bells that peal above him as he walks through a churchyard in his dream (26–27). Freud invokes the tenet that dreams are the guardians of sleep to explain the most well-known dream analyzed in *The Interpretation of Dreams*—the dream of the burning child. After the death of the sick child he has been watching over, a father goes into an adjoining room and falls asleep. He dreams that "his child was standing beside his bed, caught him by the arm and whispered to him reproachfully, 'Father, don't you see I'm burning?'" (509). Upon waking, the father notices a bright glare in the next room and discovers that the arm of his dead child has been burned by a tipped-over candle. Why, Freud asks, does the father construct a dream in response to the glare that filters through his closed eyes instead of waking up immediately to deal with the fire? According to Freud, the dream fulfills the father's wish to see his child as once more alive, but, more prosaically, it also serves to prolong his sleep by momentarily deferring the pressing demands of the external world. Freud's insistence on this latter function of the dream has been questioned by various readers, including Lacan, who proposes that it is the dream itself, particularly the son's "fire-brand" of a question, that awakens the father, not the encroaching external stimulus.[52] The point of contention here—does

[52] Jacques Lacan, *The Seminar of Jacques Lacan, Book XI: The Four Fundamental Concepts of Psychoanalysis*, ed. Jacques-Alain Miller, trans. Alan Sheridan (New York: Norton, 1998), 59. Slavoj Žižek provides a useful gloss of Lacan's position. In the Lacanian reading:

the subject does not awake himself when the external irritation becomes too strong; the logic of his awakening is quite different. First he constructs a dream, a story which enables him to prolong his sleep, to avoid awakening into reality. But the thing that he encounters in the dream, the reality of his desire, the Lacanian Real—in our case, the reality of the child's reproach to his father, "Can't you see that I am burning?," implying the father's fundamental guilt—is more terrifying than so-called external reality itself, and that is why he awakens: to escape the Real of his desire, which announces itself in the terrifying dream. (*The Sublime Object of Ideology* [London: Verso, 1989], 45)

For an important reading of Lacan's reading of the dream, see Cathy Caruth, *Unclaimed Experience: Trauma, Narrative, and History* (Baltimore: Johns Hopkins University Press, 1996).

the catalyst for awakening come from inside or outside the dream?—is a central ambiguity in a number of literary dream visions.

One of the most interesting examples I have encountered occurs in William Neville's *Castell of Pleasure* (1518), an early Tudor dream vision that owes much to the Chaucerian tradition. Having fallen asleep after reading Ovid's *Metamorphoses*, the dreamer is met by Morpheus, son of Hypnos (Sleep), who leads him through the countryside to the Castle of Pleasure, where they witness a debate among a number of allegorical figures. The debate climaxes with a joyful sounding of musical instruments. The "penytrable noyse" causes the agoraphobic and noise-sensitive Morpheus to vanish, and, as he disappears, the dreamer awakes.[53] Taking Morpheus as an obvious figure for the dreamer's sleep, we are led to believe that the dreamer is awoken by the commotion within the dream. Upon waking, however, the dreamer offers another explanation from a perspective outside his dream, a reconstructed, *post facto* perspective:

> The daye was comyn and kest a dymme lyght
> The sonne under clowdes by weder tempestyouse
> Oryble thonder & lyghtnynge sore troubled my syght
> And therwith a betynge shour a storme rygorouse
> Waked me out of slepe it was so Ieoperdouse
> And where as I wened I had be waked with mynstrelsy
> It was contrary whiche made my mynde so troublouse.
>
> (855–61)

He concludes that it was the storm that woke him up, not the music within the dream. In retrospect, we can note how the narrator adumbrates this corrected interpretation of the circumstances of his awakening with the *parere*-like qualifier "me thought" in "me thought I herde the sownynge of many an instrument," as well as with the adjective "penytrable" in "penytrable noyse" (848–49). He thought he heard musical instruments, but what he actually heard was the noise of the storm that had penetrated into his dreamscape from outside. Yet, even after tracing the content of his dream back to his physical surroundings, the narrator imagines that the penetration could work the other way as

[53] William Neville, *The Castell of Pleasure*, ed. Roberta D. Cornelius, EETS o.s. 179 (London: Oxford University Press, 1930), line 849. Subsequent references are cited parenthetically.

well: rising from his bed, he looks out of the window in the hope of catching a glimpse of the Castle of Pleasure, as if somehow the dream-world could infiltrate the natural landscape.

Might we read Pandarus's half-slumber along similar lines, taking Procne to be the guardian of his sleep? Such a reading would see Panda-rus prolong his fitful sleep by weaving the annoying "noyse" of the swal-low into a dream narrative in the same way that Freud's sleeper transforms his ringing alarm clock into church bells or the narrator of *The Castell of Pleasure* misconstrues thunder as music. And then when the stimulus becomes too loud—Procne comes "so neigh"—Pandarus awakes. But Pandarus does not awake simply because the "cheterynge" gets too loud; the line continues: it is her "cheterynge / *how* Tereus gan forth hire suster take." It is at the most critical moment in Procne's narrative—just as she is beginning to relate the rape of her sister—that Pandarus awakes. The abrupt termination reenacts the traumatic silenc-ing at the heart of the Procne–Philomela myth.[54] Once again, Philo-mela's voice is cut off, prevented from retelling (via Procne) the circumstances of the sexual violence inflicted on her. Whereas *The Castell of Pleasure* definitively locates the catalyst for waking outside the dream, Pandarus's dream shares with the Dante pilgrim's dream of the golden eagle a certain indeterminacy regarding the cause of its termination. We are left wondering whether the catalyst comes from inside the dream-space, from the phantasmatic correlate rather than the impinging sense impression; we are left wondering, in other words, whether it is the intensity of Procne's message rather than the intensity of the swallow's chattering that proves unbearable.

Readers have proposed a number of plausible interpretations of how the dream of the golden eagle reflects or prefigures the Dante pilgrim's experience.[55] It is more difficult to say what Pandarus's truncated encounter with Procne means, how it condenses or anticipates the move-ments of his waking life.[56] Pandarus himself has little patience for the

---

[54] Chaucer's telling of the Procne–Philomela narrative in *The Legend of Good Women* ends prematurely as well, but after Procne has deciphered Philomela's message. Corinne J. Saunders comments: "By ending with Philomela's depiction of her rape, rather than with her metamorphosis, Chaucer leaves his audience with the sense of the woman's need for a voice within a patriarchal world that threatens silence and death"; *Rape and Ravishment in the Literature of Medieval England* (Cambridge: D. S. Brewer, 2001), 277.

[55] For an overview of some of these theories, see Dante, *Purgatorio*, ed. Durling and Martinez, 152; and Dino S. Cervigni, *Dante's Poetry of Dreams* (Florence: Olschki, 1986), 95–116.

[56] C. David Benson cautions against answering this question with too much certi-tude; *Chaucer's "Troilus and Criseyde"* (London: Unwin Hyman, 1990), 66–67. According to Aranye Fradenburg, "the allusion simply joins a chain of stories of violence and

interpretation of dreams. He will later chalk up Troilus's nightmares to his "malencolie," and exclaim "Ther woot no man aright what dremes mene" (V.360, 364). But, despite his dim view of the portentous potential of dreams, Pandarus's waking actions do appear to be influenced by Procne's song. At the end of Book I, he had promised Troilus that he would visit Criseyde and tactfully press his suit. But, unlike in Boccaccio's *Filostrato*, wherein Pandaro heads to Criseida's house directly, Pandarus puts off the visit, waiting for an appropriate time and place. Now, upon waking, he remembers his "erand" and sets off to Criseyde's. Instead of hearing a note of warning or recrimination in the bird song, he apparently hears a spur to action, to desire. Pandarus's response to Procne's lament recapitulates a habit of mishearing the Philomela narrative that plays out in medieval poetry at large. Tom Shippey points out how the medieval reception of the Ovidian story is shaped by a literary tradition that makes Philomela "stand for the impulse to sexual love . . . , a tradition which overpowers completely the plainest statements of her reluctance."[57] For instance, even after depicting the sexual violence inflicted upon Philomela, the author of the *Ovide moralisé* represents her as a figure of deceptive, fleshly desire.[58] Another of Shippey's examples—John Gower's *Confessio Amantis*—presents a more complex case. According to Genius, the metamorphosed Philomela hides out of shame during the winter, but reappears in spring to sing:

> Wher as sche singeth day and nyht,
> And in hir song al openly
> Sche makth hir pleignte and seith, "O why,
> O why ne were I yit a maide?"
> For so these olde wise saide,
> Which understoden what sche mente,

---

rape [in *Troilus and Criseyde*] whose import is rendered ambiguous"; *Sacrifice Your Love: Psychoanalysis, Historicism, Chaucer* (Minneapolis: University of Minnesota Press, 2002), 224. Drawing on a psychoanalytic framework, Marvin Mudrick argues that the Procne dream helps Pandarus to endure the "lonely recognition of his own failure and of his looming treachery to Criseyde"; "Chaucer's Nightingales", repr. in *Chaucer's "Troilus": Essays in Criticism*, ed. Stephen A. Barney (Hamden: Archon, 1980), 91–99 (95). A more compelling reading that links Pandarus's suffering with Philomela's wounding is offered by Patricia Clare Ingham, "Chaucer's Haunted Aesthetics: Mimesis and Trauma in *Troilus and Criseyde*," *College English* 72 (2010): 226–47.

[57] Thomas Alan Shippey, "Listening to the Nightingale," *CL* 22 (1970): 46–60 (48). See also R. J. Dingley, "The Misfortunes of Philomel," *Parergon* 4 (1986): 73–86.

[58] *Ovide moralisé*, ed. Cornelius de Boer, Vol. 2 (Amsterdam: Johannes Müller, 1920), VI.3755–56.

Hire notes ben of such entente.[59]

Philomela "openly" laments the loss of her virginity without specifying that it was violently seized from her. Nor, in Gower's version, does the transformed Procne mention the fact that her sister was raped; she simply castigates "false Tereus" for being one "spousebreche" (adulterer) among many (6029, 6014). Chaucer's Procne is unusual in her explicitness that Tereus's crime was not just adultery, but the commission of rape and incest. But the passage from the *Confessio* is interesting because it foregrounds the interpretative filters that have been layered over Philomela's voice. It seems aware of its complicity in the re-silencing of Philomela.[60] We only hear her song through the ears of "these olde wise" who know what her "notes" mean. She goes on to recite a string of clichés about love's "wofull blisse," but here too the meaning of her song has been interpreted for us in advance by "hem whiche understonde hir tale" (5993–97). The repeated emphasis on the mediation of her song opens up the possibility that her notes might be heard differently by someone else. The quickness with which Pandarus resumes waking life and its amorous errands similarly draws attention to the distortion and suppression of Philomela's voice by the tradition represented by "old wise" like Pandarus himself. For Aristotle, dreams give sounds that were lost, or would be lost, in the clamor of the day another chance to present themselves, albeit in modified forms. Pandarus's half-slumber reconfigures the Aristotelian formulation by imagining how a bird's "cheterynge" might fleetingly become the "waymentynge" of a voice that continues to be marginalized through more pernicious acts of exclusion.

Consolation Prize: Shared Sleep in Machaut's *Fontaine amoureuse*

Guillaume de Machaut's *Fontaine amoureuse* (c. 1360) offers a more expansive investigation of the sensations underlying dreams than the

---

[59] John Gower, *Confessio Amantis*, ed. Russell A. Peck, Vol. 3 (Kalamazoo: Medieval Institute, 2004), V.5976–82. Subsequent references are cited parenthetically.

[60] Clare Regan Kinney argues that "Gower/Genius speaks *for* Philomela; a second forcible silencing has taken place, as, implicitly including himself among 'hem which understonde hire tale,' he occludes her voice"; " 'Who made this song?': The Engendering of Lyric Counterplots in *Troilus and Criseyde*," *SP* 89 (1992): 272–92 (284). Carolyn Dinshaw similarly observes: "The conventional discourse of love here converts the experience of forcible rape into desirable, idealized, elite love; those must be only a select few who 'understonde hir tale' when Philomela sings it"; "Rivalry, Rape and Manhood: Gower and Chaucer," in *Chaucer and Gower: Difference, Mutuality, Exchange*, ed. R. F. Yeager (Victoria: English Literary Studies, 1991), 130–52 (140).

highly compressed twin passages from the *Purgatorio* and *Troilus*. The narrative opens with the narrator, a poet-clerk, lying, like Pandarus, in a state of *dorveille* caused partly by an excess of melancholic thoughts.[61] (Indeed, given that Chaucer knew the *Fontaine* well—he borrowed from it heavily in *The Book of the Duchess*—it is possible that the *Fontaine*-narrator's *dorveille* provided something of a model for Pandarus's melancholic half-slumber).[62] On the verge of finally succumbing to the natural rhythm of sleep, the *Fontaine*-narrator is disturbed by a sound:

> Mais quant repos en moy nature
> Voloit prendre, une creature
> Oÿ, qui trop fort se plaignoit.
>
> (69–71)

[But just as nature intended me to fall asleep, I heard a creature that complained very loudly.]

He is terrified that the voice belongs to a malevolent spirit:

> Mais einsi com je l'escoutoie,
> Dedens mon cuer ymaginoie
> Que c'estoit aucuns esperis
> Dont je peüsse estre peris.
>
> (85–88)

[But just as I heard it, in my mind I imagined it was a ghost that could kill me.]

[61] Guillaume de Machaut, *Le livre de la fontaine amoureuse*, ed. Jacqueline Cerquiglini-Toulet (Paris: Stock, 1993), line 63. Subsequent references are cited parenthetically. English translations are from Guillaume de Machaut, *"The Fountain of Love" ("La fonteinne amoureuse") and Two Other Love Vision Poems*, ed. and trans. R. Barton Palmer (New York: Garland, 1993). Occasionally I have modified the translation in accordance with the original.

[62] On Chaucer's use of the *Fontaine* in *The Book of the Duchess*, see James I. Wimsatt, *Chaucer and the French Love Poets: The Literary Background of "The Book of the Duchess"* (Chapel Hill: University of North Carolina Press, 1968); William Calin, *The French Tradition and the Literature of Medieval England* (Toronto: University of Toronto Press, 1994), 273–370; and Ardis Butterfield, *The Familiar Enemy: Chaucer, Language, and Nation in the Hundred Years War* (Oxford: Oxford University Press, 2009), 276–91. According to Andrew Galloway, "Machaut made this ambiguous state of mind [i.e., *la dorveille*] fashionable for all following French and English dream-vision writers"; "Visions and Visionaries," in *The Oxford Handbook of Medieval Literature in English*, ed. Elaine Treharne, Greg Walker, and William Green (Oxford: Oxford University Press, 2010), 256–75 (266).

It was commonly thought that sleepers on the edge of sleep were susceptible to demonic attacks. Macrobius notes that during the transitional period between waking and sleeping people sometimes imagine that they see a host of weird things, including specters (*incubi*) that press down on their bodies.[63] The Scholastics would devote more attention to the underlying mechanism of these hallucinations, developing intricate physiological explanations that trace the subjective experience of being attacked by a demon back to the misconstrual of sensations generated through the processes of respiration and digestion.[64] In the *Fontaine*, it eventually becomes clear that the narrator has indeed misconstrued the aural sensations that have jarred him out of his *dorveille*. Listening carefully, he hears the familiar sound of a male lover addressing his absent beloved: "Farewell my lady, I'm going away" ("Adieu, ma dame, je m'en vois") (200). The voice belongs to a human, not a phantom. The scene thus represents an inversion of Pandarus's half-slumber: if Procne's metamorphosed voice reverts back into the swallow's chattering as Pandarus awakes, here the waking of the narrator—and the concomitant sharpening of his perceptual acumen—clarifies the noise of the "creature" into recognizable, human speech. In his discussion of how dreams are generated by mistaking residual sense impressions for other objects, Aristotle points out that strong emotion can induce similar misjudgments in waking life: so, for example, the fearful person believes based on some slight resemblance that he sees his enemies.[65] Recognizing his error, the *Fontaine*-narrator is gladdened by the voice and drawn out of his melancholic mood. He assembles his writing tools and begins to transcribe the complaint. The entangling and disentangling of the real and the phantasmatic will be repeated throughout the *Fontaine*.

Machaut likely wrote the *Fontaine amoureuse* for his patron Jean de Berry, who, like the nobleman overheard by the narrator, undertook a reluctant journey—in Jean's case, to England to stand as a hostage in

---

[63] Macrobius, *Commentarii in somnium Scipionis*, 1.3.7.

[64] MacLehose, "Fear, Fantasy and Sleep in Medieval Medicine," 84. See also Maaike van der Lugt, "The *Incubus* in Scholastic Debate: Medicine, Theology and Popular Belief," in *Religion and Medicine in the Middle Ages*, ed. Peter Biller and Joseph Ziegler (Woodbridge: York Medieval Press, 2001), 175–200. At the same time, Albert and other Scholastics preserved the patristic idea that actual spirits—whether good or evil—could inspire dreams. See Kruger, *Dreaming in the Middle Ages*, 107–15.

[65] Aristotle, *De insomniis*, 460b3–11. Cf. Albert the Great, *De somno*, 2.1.7.

place of his imprisoned father.[66] A few years earlier Machaut had composed *Le confort d'ami* (1357) for another aristocrat facing difficult times, the imprisoned Charles II of Navarre. The *Confort* blends together various strains of advice, ranging from biblical exempla to Boethian bromides to the kind of political strategizing found in the genre of the mirror for princes. One section is devoted to allaying the prisoner's erotic despair. The speaker advises him to construct and worship in his heart an image of his lady, who, if pleased with his devotion, will grant him consolation:

> Se tu gis a la terre dure
> Sans tapis et sans couverture,
> Seur fainc, seur estrain, ou seur paille,
> Ou sus lit dur, s'on le te baille,
> Elle t'ara si anobli
> Que tu mettras tout en oubli
> Et tous tes maus et ta grevence
> Penras en bonne pacience.[67]

[If you're sleeping on the hard ground, having no rug or coverlet, on the dirt, on leaves or straw, or on a crude bed, supposing one's provided you, she'll ennoble you so much, you'll forget everything, bearing with good patience all your misery and hurt.]

The mental image of the lady functions as phantasmatic insulation against uncomfortable sensations. For many readers of Machaut, the *Confort*-narrator's recourse to the remedial power of the image encapsulates the main thrust of his "poetics of consolation." Sylvia Huot has argued that Machaut repurposes the Boethian mode to construct a model of consolation that encourages the suffering lover to transition from a state of unproductive desire to one of hope by focusing on an idealized mental image of the love object; the lover thus gains access to the absolute through a form of love whose "true import lies not in bodily

---

[66] For Machaut's biography, including his relationship with Jean de Berry, see Lawrence Earp, *Guillaume de Machaut: A Guide to Research* (New York: Garland, 1995), 3–51.

[67] Guillaume de Machaut, *Le confort d'ami (Comfort for a Friend)*, ed. and trans. R. Barton Palmer (New York: Garland, 1992), lines 2201–8. The English translations are from this edition.

contact but in private contemplation; not in communication with a particular individual but in communion with a sovereign perfection."[68] It is worth noting, though, that the *Confort* ends with a brief coda that casts some doubt on the effectiveness of the narrator's consolatory regimen.[69] These enigmatic lines purport to allow the addressee of the poem to respond in his own voice; he does so by requesting further consolation from his friend and making clear that he is still deeply affected by the suffering inflicted upon him by his enemies. With the *Fontaine*, I argue, Machaut models a form of consolation that is quite different from the textually mediated, largely monologic dynamic that structures the *Confort*. He explores what the editors of an important recent collection call "the erotics of consolation." In her contribution to that volume, Sarah Kay locates Machaut within a community of late medieval poets, who, influenced in part by Aristotelian readings of Boethius, envisioned "a consolation that was more consoling, more physical, which made more concessions to the here and now of the embodied individual, allowed him his particular circumstances and his perspective."[70] As the editors add in their introduction, this consolation might come about through "an embodied touch, ethical or otherwise."[71] The *Fontaine* makes the case for the consoling potential of mental imagery, but it also shows how these images are grounded in sensation, especially touch. Put another way, Machaut's dream vision redraws the sleeping scene from

[68] Sylvia Huot, "Guillaume de Machaut and the Consolation of Poetry," *MP* 100 (2002): 169–95 (195). Huot's argument is expanded upon by Elizabeth Elliott, *Remembering Boethius: Writing Aristocratic Identity in Late Medieval French and English Literatures* (New York: Routledge, 2012). An important discussion of the consolatory role of the imagination is found in Douglas Kelly, *Medieval Imagination: Rhetoric and the Poetry of Courtly Love* (Madison: University of Wisconsin Press, 1978). See also R. Barton Palmer's argument about the Boethian drive to transcend the individual and the contingent in the *Fontaine*: "Vision and Experience in Machaut's *Fonteinne amoureuse*," *Journal of the Rocky Mountain Medieval and Renaissance Association* 2 (1981): 79–86.

[69] On the problematic ending of the *Confort*, see R. Barton Palmer, "Guillaume de Machaut and the Classical Tradition: Individual Talent and (Un)Communal Tradition," in *A Companion to Guillaume de Machaut*, ed. Deborah McGrady and Jennifer Bain (Leiden: Brill, 2012), 241–60 (251–52).

[70] Sarah Kay, "Touching Singularity: Consolation, Philosophy, and Poetry in the French *dit*," in *The Erotics of Consolation: Desire and Distance in the Late Middle Ages*, ed. Catherine E. Léglu and Stephen J. Milner (New York: Palgrave, 2008), 21–38 (36). See also Sarah Kay, *The Place of Thought: The Complexity of One in Late Medieval French Didactic Poetry* (Philadelphia: University of Pennsylvania Press, 2007); and Jessica Rosenfeld, *Ethics and Enjoyment in Late Medieval Poetry: Love after Aristotle* (Cambridge: Cambridge University Press, 2011).

[71] Catherine E. Léglu and Stephen J. Milner, "Introduction: Encountering Consolation," in Léglu and Milner, *Erotics of Consolation*, 1–18 (14).

the *Confort* by adding a layer of skin between the sleeper and the hard ground.

The narrator listens as the lover next door conjures up the specter of his beloved. The lover confesses to his phantasmatic addressee his overwhelming desire for her physical presence. The problem is that the real beloved has no idea how he feels. He cannot bring himself to let her know, either in person or via epistolary proxy. Over the course of his complaint, he comes up with a more outlandish method of disclosure. He prays to the God of Sleep, not for rest—as the sleepless narrator of Chaucer's *Book of the Duchess* will do—but for a different kind of benediction. The lover recounts the Ovidian tale of Alcyone: after praying for knowledge about the fate of her husband who is missing at sea, Alcyone was granted a dream in which Morpheus assumed the shape of Ceyx and informed her of his death. Similarly, the insomniac lover in the *Fontaine* requests that Morpheus adopt his half-dead form, visit his beloved over the course of several nights, and induce her into thinking obsessively about him, whether she is asleep or awake, in bed or at the table. If Morpheus were to grant this improbable beneficence, the lover would consider himself more fortunate than Pygmalion, another famous Ovidian supplicant. As it stands now, the lover resembles Pygmalion prior to Venus's intervention, complaining to the image of his beloved, the "earthly god" ("mon dieu terrien") he assiduously worships (1012).[72] However, we know that even though his lady cannot hear him, his complaint is not falling on deaf ears. In fact, his words provoke in the eavesdropping narrator much the same response that he hoped Morpheus's intercession would inspire in his lady. It is the narrator whose sleep is disturbed by an apparition with a sad story to tell, the narrator who attends carefully to every word of that story, who acknowledges that the emotion behind the words is genuine, and who is motivated by the complaint to seek out the lover in person.

In the morning, the narrator introduces himself to the owner of the lamenting voice, a handsome prince lodging next door. The two men hit it off. The meeting is marked by contingency. They have been brought together, the prince later notes, by "aventure" (1440). But their meeting is contingent in the root sense of the word as well (*con* + *tangere*, to

---

[72] As Katherine Heinrichs notes, the lover's comparison of his beloved to Pygmalion's image was highly conventional in medieval lyrics and *dits*; *The Myths of Love: Classical Lovers in Medieval Literature* (University Park: Pennsylvania State University Press, 1990), 135 n. 32. Machaut plays with the convention extensively in his *Voir dit*.

touch). The narrator pledges his heart and body to the prince, and the prince takes him up on the offer (1266). For much of the *dit*, the two figures remain physically inseparable. After the prince lifts the kneeling narrator up, they enter a beautiful garden hand in hand ("main a main") (1291). At the center of this *locus amoenus* is a marble fountain inscribed with images of the Trojan War that was constructed (the prince points out) by Pygmalion at the behest of Venus. Eventually the prince leans on his companion and falls asleep in his lap. The narrator nods off as well, tired from his sleepless night. Sleep, and the "veritable" dream it brings, arise out of bodily exhaustion (1567). Bodies in the *Fontaine* need to sleep and eat. Two beautiful ladies appear, Venus and the prince's beloved. Venus states her intention to comfort the prince, whose heart, she notes, remains tormented while asleep and awake. Before doing so, she explains the backstory of the golden apple she carries, how it was bestowed upon her by Paris, who in return was granted the heart and body of Helen. Venus complains that unlike Paris the prince has failed to acknowledge the extent of her powers. While awake, the narrator and prince had carefully examined the fountain's depiction of Paris courting Helen; now, in the dream, these perceptions resurface.[73] Michel Zink has demonstrated how Machaut's near-contemporary Watriquet de Couvin composed *dits* that transpose "day residue" into the allegorical dreamscape; for instance, in the *Dit de l'araignée et du crapaud* (*Poem of the Spider and the Frog*), the poet falls asleep in an orchard while listening to birdsong and then dreams he meets Reason under a walnut tree at a castle named Bec Oisel (Bird's Beak). According to Zink, Watriquet's juxtaposition of the dream itself and the circumstances behind its origination "function to present the universal teaching of the allegory as the result of chance circumstances and subjective impressions."[74] The *Fontaine* is similarly invested in laying bare the "chance circumstances and subjective impressions" that produce the prince's consoling dream. It is

[73] William Calin notes how "manifest dream content mirrors day residue" in the *Fontaine*: "both the Narrator and the Knight had thought endlessly of ladies and love, the Knight told and the Narrator overheard the myth of Ceyx and Alcyone, and both of them spoke of Venus, among the other gods who built the *fonteinne amoureuse*, on which are represented Paris's abduction of Helen and the subsequent history of Troy." *French Tradition*, 279.

[74] Zink, "Allegorical Poem," 114. According to Sylvia Huot, "Watriquet's works enjoyed a considerable popularity and prestige during the fourteenth century; it is likely that Machaut was aware of them"; *From Song to Book: The Poetics of Writing in Old French Lyric and Lyrical Narrative Poetry* (Ithaca, N.Y.: Cornell University Press, 1987), 299 n. 15.

not only visual and aural impressions that filter into the dreamscape. Despite feeling slighted by the prince, Venus takes pity on him and, reprising her role as animatrix, she vivifies the image of his beloved. The Pygmalion–Galatea roles are now reversed: the animated image of the lady addresses the mute, immobile form of the sleeping prince. She takes him "by the bare hand" ("par la main nue"), and, after exhorting him to keep her close in thought if not in body, she embraces him with her right arm and orders him to get up (2197, 2500). The lady's palpable ministrations echo the earlier, pre-dream interactions between the prince and narrator, when the prince raised the kneeling narrator by seizing his right hand and shortly afterward led him "par la main nue" into the garden (1219, 1291).[75] In the illustrated version of the *Fontaine* that appears in Manuscript A—possibly produced under the supervision of Machaut himself—there is a miniature that reminds us of the continuing physical touch that undergirds the lady's phantasmatic embraces (Fig. 1).[76] Her introduction and subsequent holding of the prince's hand are illustrated not by an image of the lady, as we might expect, but by an image of the prince and narrator asleep in front of the fountain. The miniature cuts away from the dream vision and momentarily refocuses our gaze on the circumstances of its production. The image highlights an irony present in the lady's disavowal of presence—the fact that her insistence that the prince accept the phantasmatic image of her as a "substitute for communion in the flesh" (as Huot puts it) arises in a sleep founded on fleshly communion.[77]

The narrator and prince awake at the same moment. Their intertwined bodies have generated an intertwining of dreams: "both of us dreamt one dream" ("tous deus un songe songames") (2520). It is the kind of shared private dream that Augustine assumed was impossible in his influential discussion of dreams and visions in Book XII of *De Genesi*

---

[75] In the introduction to her edition, Jacqueline Cerquiglini-Toulet notes the doubling of the phrase "par la main nue" in her argument that the text occasionally conflates the characters of the narrator and prince and their respective functions as poet and lover; *Fontaine amoureuse*, 20.

[76] Paris, Bibliothèque nationale de France (BnF), Fr. 1584, fol. 169r. A digital facsimile is available online at Gallica: http://gallica.bnf.fr (accessed May 27, 2017). On Manuscript A, see Lawrence Earp, "Machaut's Role in the Production of Manuscripts of His Works," *Journal of the American Musicological Society* 42 (1989): 461–503. On the *Fontaine* miniatures in Manuscript A, see Deborah McGrady, "Machaut and His Material Legacy," in McGrady and Bain, *Companion to Machaut*, 361–85.

[77] Sylvia Huot, "Reading the Lies of Poets: The Literal and the Allegorical in Machaut's *Fonteinne amoureuse*," *PQ* 85 (2006): 25–48 (36).

Fig. 1. Bibliothèque nationale de France, fr. 1584, fol. 169r (detail). Reproduced by permission of Bibliothèque nationale de France.

ad litteram.[78] Readers of the *Fontaine* have tended to overlook the fact that the dream does not initially console the prince. On the contrary— upon seeing his lady vanish, he suffers "toutes peinnes" and rejects the very possibility of consolation: "For if he couldn't see her soon, then nothing else would ever please him" ("Car s'adés vëoir la peüst, / Jamais riens ne li despleüst") (2629–30). Even when fully awake, he continues to wonder how he lost his lady (2699–702). In this sense, he is not unlike the lover in the *Roman de la rose* who wakes from his erotic fantasy to find his bed empty; or, for that matter, Alcyone, who wakes in order to embrace the figmentary Ceyx.[79] For these dreamers, phantasmatic bodies prove inadequate substitutes, highlighting, rather than redressing, loss. It is only after the narrator, seeing the prince's bemusement, reminds him of what transpired in the dream—the lady's gracious looks, her kisses, the ring that she placed on his finger—that he is comforted. Once again, the narrator proves an invaluable mediator of the prince's psychic life. After attending mass and eating dinner together, the prince requests that the narrator see him off on his journey, declaring his reluctance to separate from his companion. Indeed, the final miniature in Manuscript A imagines how difficult this separation will be: as his ship departs, the prince clutches the narrator's hand, pulling him forward on his horse as if to bring him along (Fig. 2).[80] The miniature is less optimistic than the text that the prince will be able to maintain his equanimity in the absence of the narrator's consoling touch. The *Fontaine* ends with a provocation: "Tell me, was this well dreamed?" ("Dites moy, fu ce bien songié?") (2848). What does "this" refer to? The shared dream within the poem? Or the events preceding and following the dream as well? Was it all just a dream? The line is disorienting because it deprives us of the scene of nodding off, the kind of waking context that the poem and its illustrations repeatedly draw our attention to. One way to read

[78] In his explanation of a "lucid dream" involving a conversation with a friend, Augustine dismisses the possibility that both he and his friend could have access to the same phenomenal dreamspace; *De Genesi ad litteram*, 12.2.3.

[79] As Helen J. Swift observes, after waking up, Alcyone finds herself "in a state of prolonged grief that is exacerbated by the degree to which her beloved appears so vividly." Swift contrasts Alcyone's vision and her subsequent mourning of Ceyx's actual death with the prince's "autoerotic fantasy," which consoles a perceived erotic loss, but I would add that at least initially the dreams provoke similar responses in the two dreamers. Helen J. Swift, *"Tamainte consolation / me fist lymagination*: A Poetics of Mourning and Imagination in Late Medieval *dits*," in Léglu and Milner, *Erotics of Consolation*, 141–64 (150). See also Huot, "Reading the Lies of Poets," 37.

[80] Paris, BnF, Fr. 1584, fol. 173r.

Q̇ vous me veilhes cõgier
aj ins quil ne vous doie annuier
C̣ ar ianm tant voſtre conpaignie
Q̇ ne dire mient la departie
j e li dis que ie le feroie
m̊ oult volentiers et que grãt ioie
Ⱥ noie de ceſte requeſte
C̣ ar ferme anoie en ma teſte
Q̇ compaingnie li feiſſe
Ꝑ t qua li le congie preiſſe

Fig. 2. Bibliothèque nationale de France, fr. 1584, fol. 173r (detail). Reproduced by permission of Bibliothèque nationale de France.

the closing line is as Machaut's playful acknowledgment that he has constructed the *Fontaine* as a wish-fulfillment dream of his own, the culmination of which is the prince's decision to thank the narrator by giving him all of his land. What court poet wouldn't want a patron like that? Or, conversely, what patron wouldn't want a poet so attuned to his every movement?[81] The idealized poet–patron relationship in the *Fontaine* is modeled on the reciprocity of touch. And it is moments when bodies touch—while walking; conversing; and, most importantly, sleeping—that give rise to a form of collaborative, consoling image-making.

Perhaps the closest Dante comes to narrating the fall of sleep is in *Purgatorio*, XVIII. After growing sleepy listening to Virgil expound the psychology of desire, the pilgrim is roused by a crowd of penitents who run by him performing their penance for sloth. As they fade into the distance, the pilgrim starts to nod off again:

> Poi quando fuor da noi tanto divise
> quell' ombre che veder più non potiersi,
> novo pensiero dentro a me si mise,
> del qual più altri nacquero e diversi;
> e tanto d'uno in altro vaneggiai
> che li occhi per vaghezza ricopersi,
> e 'l pensamento in sogno trasmutai.
> (XVIII.139–45)

[Then when those shades had gone so far from us as to be seen no more, a new thought came into me, from which a number of other, different ones were born; and from one to the other I so wandered on, that I closed my eyes in drowsiness and transmuted thinking into dream.]

---

[81] Commenting on Machaut's depiction of patronage in his work, Douglas Kelly writes: "Machaut's prince, as patron, is represented as generous donor; as source, planner, and architect of artistic productions; as pupil sitting at the feet of his sagacious mentor; and as *patron* or model and pattern for conduct. Whatever the actual organization of the prince's court may have been, Machaut represents its majesty as the expression of princely genius, to which the poet gives praise and expression." Douglas Kelly, "The Genius of the Patron: The Prince, the Poet, and Fourteenth-Century Invention," *Studies in the Literary Imagination* 20 (1987): 77–97 (79–80). For a different view of the power dynamic structuring the poet–patron relationship, see Deborah McGrady, " 'Tout son païs m'abandonna': Reinventing Patronage in Machaut's *Fonteinne amoureuse*," *Yale French Studies* 110 (2006): 19–31.

The dream that follows incorporates textual echoes of the lesson he has just received from Virgil and thus seems to bear out the claim that the pilgrim "transmuted thinking into dream."[82] As Durling and Martinez note, the line acts as something of a précis for the *Commedia* as a whole. We have seen how the transmutation of waking life into dream is thematized in the dream of the golden eagle. The subject is taken up by Dante's literary successors Chaucer and Machaut, who together explore how the respective senses of hearing and touch remain partly open in sleep. Machaut's *Fontaine* draws attention to the sensations that are transformed into phantasmatic representations, while Procne's lament, on the other hand, resists reduction back into its base elements. They populate these moments of waking sleep with figures drawn from the ur-text of transformation—Ovid's *Metamorphoses*—mapping the transformations of characters such as Procne and Galatea onto the transition from waking to sleeping. There is something a bit odd, however, about Dante's use of the verb "trasmutai" (I transmuted). As any insomniac knows well, the transition from thinking to dreaming cannot be effected by an act of will. The phrase suggests the presence of an "I" superintending the transmutation, a form of wakefulness persisting into sleep. We can hear in this phrase, I think, the voice of the poet acknowledging the parallel between the scene of sleep and the scene of writing as sites that facilitate the transformation of old images into new configurations. For poets concerned with the nature of their ability to form and reform images, the allure of waking sleep is the promise of observing a corollary process of image-making.

---

[82] On the dream of the siren as "a mosaic put together from elements related to his guide's earlier account of the functioning of love in human beings," see Zygmunt G. Barański, "Dante's Three Reflective Dreams," *Quaderni d'italianistica* 10 (1989): 214–36 (216).

Sir Thopas: A Story for Young Children

David Raybin
Eastern Illinois University

Abstract

This article proposes that Chaucer's *Tale of Sir Thopas* is a children's story—that is, to borrow F. J. Harvey Darton's succinct definition, a work designed "to give children spontaneous pleasure, and not primarily to teach them." Previously, no English children's books have been identified prior to the sixteenth century: *Sir Thopas* is by some 100 years the oldest extant children's story in England. The article further proposes that *Sir Thopas* is part of an extended experiment in writing for and about children. The tale's placement in Fragment VII of the *Canterbury Tales* between *The Prioress's Tale* and *The Tale of Melibee* signals Chaucer's interest in writing for and about children, and encourages us to appreciate his pioneering artistry in an important new way. Looking out for a fresh device, Chaucer recognized that children like to see themselves in a story; that they can enjoy a story without understanding everything in it; that they can read or listen without having things explained to them; and that it is acceptable if, like young Thopas, they are simply laughing and playing.

Keywords

Chaucer, children's literature, *Canterbury Tales* Fragment VII, play, *Tale of Sir Thopas*

"THERE WERE," wrote F. J. Harvey Darton in his classic 1932 study, *Children's Books in England: Five Centuries of Social Life*, "no children's books in England before the seventeenth century, and very few even then." By "children's books," Darton explained, he meant "works produced ostensibly to give children spontaneous pleasure, and

I am grateful to Susanna Fein, Sarah Salih, and *SAC*'s anonymous readers for their tough critiques of earlier versions of the essay. Astute responses to my presentations at the 2016 MLA Convention and Canada Chaucer Seminar encouraged me to pursue the project.

not primarily to teach them, nor solely to make them good, nor to keep them *profitably* quiet." To be sure, there were "plenty of schoolbooks and guides to conduct, but none which would openly allow a child to enjoy himself with no thought of duty nor fear of wrong."[1] The earliest English works containing "elements of later children's books" mentioned in Darton's volume are a translation of the *Gesta Romanorum* story compilation in an early fifteenth-century manuscript, Caxton's 1484 translation of Aesop's Fables, and a few works mentioned in the bookseller John Dorne's 1520 sales ledger for which printed editions were later published as children's books: the *Geste of Robyn Hode* (in Wynkyn de Worde's c. 1510 edition), the ballad *The Squire of Low Degree*, the romance *Bevis of Hampton*, and the comic tale *The Friar and the Boy*.[2]

Twenty-first-century scholarship has brought forth two principal challenges to Darton's narrow definition of what constitute "children's books." Nicholas Orme's *Medieval Children* argues that "Medieval story literature might be primarily meant for adults, but it contained much that would appeal to children or adolescents."[3] Orme acknowledges that "All of the works recommended to the young before 1500, like Chaucer and Gower, are ones which we normally think of as adult"; that "fiction for children . . . is lacking from the recommended reading lists"; and that fiction written "especially for young people . . . whose central characters are children or teenagers . . . is harder to identify before 1500."[4] Indeed, he identifies only one such work, hedging that comic tales such as *The Friar and the Boy*, whose earliest surviving instances are in late fifteenth-century manuscripts and Caxton's eight-leaf printed edition of 1510–13 ("the earliest illustrated children's story, just as it is the first printed story centered on a child"), might reflect a pre-print popular genre.[5] While Orme's single instance may push Darton's dating back to the turn of the sixteenth century, his thinking about "story literature" is in line with the scholarly consensus that medieval adolescents and

---

[1] F. J. Harvey Darton, *Children's Books in England: Five Centuries of Social Life*, 3rd ed., rev. Brian Alderson (1932; Cambridge: Cambridge University Press, 1982), 1. Darton further explains that he has excluded "all schoolbooks, all purely moral or didactic treatises, all reflective or adult-minded descriptions of child-life, and almost all alphabets, primers and spelling-books."

[2] Ibid., 35; discussion of "The Legacy of the Middle Ages" at 9–50.

[3] Nicholas Orme, *Medieval Children* (New Haven: Yale University Press, 2002), 273–304 (286).

[4] Ibid., 285, 285, 289.

[5] Ibid., 298; see page 294 for Caxton's single illustration, a woodcut showing the boy and friar.

children would have appreciated the many romances purchased and read by their parents.[6] He leaves us searching for a medieval story intended primarily for children.

In his introduction to the collection *Medieval Literature for Children*, Daniel T. Kline goes at Darton's definition from a different angle, speaking not of "children's books" but of "children's literature," and advocating for the inclusion of didactic literature in this broader category. Kline argues that "the line between purpose and pleasure is neither static nor simply determined"; that even now, as in the Middle Ages, "we look to children's literature to teach social norms and positive values"; and, turning polemical, that "denying medieval didactic texts the status of literature ignores contemporary literary theory's insistence upon recognizing the ideological dimensions of any textual product and the cultural currents it negotiates."[7] It is notable that none of these challenges—each supported by the essays in Kline's collection—questions the non-existence of medieval children's books as measured by Darton's definition: works designed for nothing other than to "give children spontaneous pleasure."

My purpose here is to establish, first, that Geoffrey Chaucer's late fourteenth-century *Tale of Sir Thopas* is just such a work, a story about a child calibrated to amuse young children, and, second, that the tale's placement in Fragment VII of the *Canterbury Tales* between *The Prioress's Tale* and *The Tale of Melibee* signals Chaucer's interest in writing for and about children, and encourages us to appreciate his pioneering artistry

---

[6] On children as making up a significant part of the target audience for medieval popular romance, along with a survey of criticism on the subject, see Phillipa Hardman, "Popular Romances and Young Readers," in *A Companion to Medieval Popular Romance*, ed. Raluca Radulescu and Cory James Rushton (Cambridge: D. S. Brewer, 2009), 150–64. Mary E. Shaner proposes that the versions of three late fifteenth-century Middle English romances in Edinburgh, National Library of Scotland, Advocates MS 19.3.1—*Sir Amadace*, *Sir Ysumbras*, and *Sir Gowther*—were "edited for the entertainment and instruction of the young," and argues that "these revised romances have implications both for the history of children's literature and for our understanding of the medieval conceptions of the child and of education"; Mary E. Shaner, "Instruction and Delight: Medieval Romances as Children's Literature," *Poetics Today* 13 (1992): 5–14 (14). Cindy L. Vitto, "*Sir Gawain and the Green Knight* as Adolescent Literature: Essential Lessons," *Children's Literature Association Quarterly* 23 (1998): 22–28, similarly contends that *Sir Gawain and the Green Knight* is "not just a romance for an adult audience but . . . a work quite possibly written with older children—in particular, male adolescents of noble birth—in mind" (22).

[7] Daniel T. Kline, "Medieval Children's Literature: Problems, Possibilities, Parameters," in *Medieval Literature for Children*, ed. Kline (London: Routledge, 2003), 1–11 (3, 3, 4).

in an important new way. When we recognize that *Sir Thopas* is a children's story, its complex integration of traditional romance elements, absurd and incongruous details, and a minimal plot acquires novel purpose. The tale's many trumpeted flaws—amalgamated in the critique, assigned by Chaucer to the opinionated but not always wise Harry Bailly, of the tale's "drasty speche" (VII.923), "rym dogerel" (VII.925), and "drasty rymyng . . . nat worth a toord" (VII.930)—fall by the wayside.[8]

The Genre of *Sir Thopas*

Until John Burrow pointed out that the poem has three distinct parts, or *fits*, each half the length of the one before (eighteen stanzas, nine stanzas, four-and-a-half stanzas), critics tended to assume that Chaucer left the tale unfinished simply to highlight Harry's critique that it was too bad to continue, or they sought to uncover a hidden serious meaning that might explain Chaucer's assigning bad poetry to his pilgrimage persona.[9] We now recognize that the poem is complete as intended, and the tale's precise structure—to get his self-consuming stanza count right, Chaucer placed Harry's interruption not just in the middle of a stanza, but in the middle of a line—argues for Chaucer's care in composition. Burrow's intervention was pivotal for critical response to the poem because it opened up the possibility that Chaucer had artistic intention beyond the double measure of parody of tail-rhyme romance and ideational contrast with *The Tale of Melibee*—*Sir Thopas* displaying *solaas* without *sentence*, *Melibee* illustrating *sentence* without *solaas*—that had been the prevalent scholarly evaluation.[10] It is in this vein that scholarship on *Sir Thopas* has largely focused on the tale's echoes of tail-rhyme romance, as literary historians debate whether Chaucer knew the early fourteenth-century Auchinleck manuscript, in which many of the romances named in the tale's closing stanzas are housed, and whether

---

[8] Citations of Chaucer's works, by line number, are taken from Larry D. Benson, gen. ed., *The Riverside Chaucer*, 3rd ed. (Boston, Mass.: Houghton Mifflin, 1987).

[9] J. A. Burrow, " 'Sir Thopas': An Agony in Three Fits," *RES* n.s. 22 (1971): 54–58. For a list of many mid-twentieth-century attempts to find *sentence* in *Thopas*, see C. David Benson, "Their Telling Difference: Chaucer the Pilgrim and His Two Contrasting Tales," *ChauR* 18, no. 1 (1983): 61–76 (75 n. 14).

[10] See Alan T. Gaylord, "*Sentence* and *Solaas* in Fragment VII of the *Canterbury Tales*: Harry Bailly as Horseback Editor," *PMLA* 82 (1967): 226–35.

he was mocking the tail-rhyme romances of northern and western England or paying them tribute.[11]

I agree that recognition of the tale's generic play is crucial if we are to appreciate the full extent of Chaucer's accomplishment, but contend that a persistent representation of *Sir Thopas*'s sole genre as parody or burlesque has led readers to miss another, no less significant generic innovation. The evidence that the tale offers a sustained parody of tail-rhyme romance is massive and indisputable, with critics locating numerous linguistic parallels in the romances that survive in Auchinleck and other early manuscripts that Chaucer might conceivably have known.[12] I credit Derek Pearsall's appreciation of the "glee" with which Chaucer appropriates the matter of romance, which the poet treats with "affectionate contempt": "the tale is funny because it is so ineffably, exquisitely bad . . . it would be worth reading all the popular Middle English romances for no other reason than to savour the more its delicious absurdity."[13] So, too, Alan Gaylord is surely correct when he argues for the artistry in Chaucer's mastery of "a form, the tail-rhyme, which epitomizes the mingling and confusing of royal romance with the popular idiom."[14] Yet one can hardly deny that *Thopas*'s independent interest as a romance is limited by the tale's short length, and Harry's intervention reflects that what he has heard, even were it extended, does not give signs of leading to an especially engaging chivalric romance. *King Horn*, *Bevis of Hampton*, *Guy of Warwick*, *Lybeaux Desconus*, and *Percival*—the tail-rhyme romances Chaucer names in *Sir Thopas*'s closing fit—all get

---

[11] Chaucer's knowledge of the Auchinleck manuscript was proposed by Laura H. Loomis, "Chaucer and the Auchinleck MS: 'Thopas' and 'Guy of Warwick,'" in *Essays and Studies in Honor of Carleton Brown* (New York: New York University Press, 1940), 111–28. It has been contested most recently by Christopher Cannon, "Chaucer and the Auchinleck Manuscript Revisited," *ChauR* 46, nos. 1–2 (2011): 131–46. The question is treated as secondary by Helen Phillips, "Auchinleck and Chaucer," in *The Auchinleck Manuscript: New Perspectives*, ed. Susanna Fein (Woodbridge: York Medieval Press, 2016), 139–55.

[12] For discussion of Chaucer's sources for *Thopas* and extracts from the romances he parodies, see Joanne A. Charbonneau, "Sir Thopas," in *Sources and Analogues of the "Canterbury Tales*," ed. Robert M. Correale and Mary Hamel, 2 vols. (Cambridge: D. S. Brewer, 2002–5), 2:669–714. On *Thopas* as self-parody and an indication of Chaucer's stylistic indebtedness to English romance, see Nancy Mason Bradbury, "Chaucerian Minstrelsy: *Sir Thopas*, *Troilus and Criseyde*, and English metrical romance," in *Tradition and Transformation in Medieval Romance*, ed. Rosalind Field (Cambridge: D. S. Brewer, 1999), 115–24.

[13] Derek Pearsall, *The Canterbury Tales* (London: Allen & Unwin, 1985), 161–62.

[14] Alan T. Gaylord, "Chaucer's Dainty 'Dogerel': The 'Elvyssh' Prosody of *Sir Thopas*," *SAC* 1 (1979): 83–104 (102).

the narrative action under way more quickly and recount more thrilling stories. A response that limits the interest of *Thopas* to its success as burlesque thus obscures a key part of Chaucer's effort. For beyond composing a playfully appreciative acknowledgment of the youth-oriented pleasures in so many tail-rhyme romances, Chaucer fashioned a poem in a genre for which we know of no English literary precedents: a story designed as an entertainment for *young* children. The romances that Chaucer directly parodies all recount the exploits of boys whose serious adventures lead them out of their childhood, usually to avenge a slain father or replace an absent one. *Sir Thopas* is unique in focusing on a child who does nothing but play pretend games in which he enacts his own made-up stories. His father is alive and well, and by "Goddes grace" the "lord . . . of that contree"—that is, of the town of "Poperyng" in the far-off country of "Flaundres" (VII.719–23). There are no moral lessons to be uncovered, none of the growing up that one finds in a *Bildungsroman*, just the story of a boy at play, with a good measure of silliness mixed in.[15] Already close to a century old when it was first printed by Caxton in 1476—a good three decades before his printing of *The Friar and the Boy*—Chaucer's *Tale of Sir Thopas* is, by the terms of Darton's definition, a classic children's book, the first known example in English.

The Children's *Tale of Sir Thopas*

The tale's story line is slight. Bearing a light lance in his hand and long sword by his side, valiant Sir Thopas spurs forth through a forest, enjoying sweet odors and bird song until the call of the wood-thrush draws him into love-longing, stirring him to spur more fiercely. Grown weary, he lies on the grass and prays to Mary, pledging that he will love no woman but an elf-queen. He then remounts and spurs his way to wild fairy country, where he comes upon the giant Olifaunt, who threatens to kill him unless he leaves the fairy queen's land. As the brave knight retreats, promising to return in armor on the morrow, the giant slings stones at him, but through God's grace and his own good bearing he escapes. Returned home, Thopas orders his servants to ready him to fight the giant and commands his minstrels to recite romances. After

[15] Benson, "Their Telling Difference," describes *Thopas* as "pure fun without the slightest desire to edify or improve" (66) and "pleasant nothingness" (67).

the servants bring food and wine, he arms himself richly and sets forth once more. The tale is interrupted as Thopas drinks water from a well.

As many a reader has noticed, the tale's interest doesn't lie in this minimal plot, which lacks the essential elements of conflict, complication, and character development.[16] In place of these narrative features, Chaucer offers descriptive detail, lively rhythm, and the imagined adventures of a young boy at play—what Lee Patterson calls "a boy dressing up as a knight"[17]—and directs this to a similarly juvenile audience. To demonstrate what I have up to now been asserting, I offer here an annotated reading of *Sir Thopas* as a story about a very young boy.

The Prioress's Tale, of a seven-year-old boy's miraculous singing after his throat has been slit, has just ended, and "every man / As sobre was that wonder was to se" (VII.691–92) when Harry Bailly turns to Chaucer and mockingly asks him for "a tale of myrthe, and that anon" (VII.706). Chaucer's response, "a rym I lerned longe agoon" (VII.709), purported to be the only tale he knows, is an apt counterpart to *The Prioress's Tale*: a lively story about an equally young child.[18] The opposition between the two tales' protagonists is, on its most basic level, quite simple. Where the "litel clergeon" of *The Prioress's Tale* (VII.503) is murdered as he sings loudly of the gracious mother of the Redeemer, "child

---

[16] See Susan Crane, *Gender and Romance in Chaucer's "Canterbury Tales"* (Princeton: Princeton University Press, 1994): "Thopas has a father, but filial duty, patrimony, and family honor receive no challenge; Thopas is in love, but his devotion to an elf-queen is neither in conflict with his dynastic and feudal obligations nor an occasion for self-transformation" (29).

[17] Lee Patterson, "'What man artow?': Authorial Self-Definition in *The Tale of Melibee* and *The Tale of Sir Thopas*," *SAC* 11 (1989): 117–75 (130). Patterson's thinking on the subject was confined to one paragraph, and, as far as I can tell from the criticism, few Chaucerians have noticed what is to my mind a defining moment in Chaucer's writing for young audiences. J. Allan Mitchell, *Becoming Human: The Matter of the Medieval Child* (Minneapolis: University of Minnesota Press, 2014), figures Thopas as a "petite, doll-like creature," an "artifactual and mechanical" device with a "painted-on appearance and meager frame," "a toylike contrivance," "an imitation knight" (109–11). Mitchell draws briefly on Patterson and more heavily on Ann S. Haskell, "Sir Thopas: The Puppet's Puppet," *ChauR* 9, no. 3 (1975): 253–61, which sees Thopas as a puppet, "a manufactured figure" manipulated by the pilgrim Chaucer, "himself a diminutive, manufactured figure for whom thought and action are supplied by a controlling figure" (253). Yvonne J. Truscott, "Chaucer's Children and the Medieval Idea of Childhood," *Children's Literature Association Quarterly* 23 (1998): 29–34 (31), seconds Patterson in an insightful essay.

[18] For a discussion of language linking *Thopas* to *The Prioress's Tale* and the Prioress's *General Prologue* portrait, see Adrienne Williams Boyarin, *Miracles of the Virgin in Medieval England: Law and Jewishness in Marian Legends* (Woodbridge: D. S. Brewer, 2010), 156–58.

Thopas" (VII.830) is entirely secure, even as he imagines himself threatened by a giant, and he asks that songs be sung in *his* praise.

Chaucer announces his light intention in the tale's opening lines:

> Listeth, lordes in good entent,
> And I wol telle verrayment
> Of myrthe and of solas.
> (VII.712–14)

A listening audience is asked to receive with good will a story of mirth
and pleasure, with the *sentence* that has governed *The Prioress's Tale* not
even hinted at. As we quickly learn, the tale's protagonist is "sire Thopas," a knight "fair and gent / In bataille and in tourneyment"
(VII.715–17) and born "in fer contree, / In Flaundres, al biyonde the
see" (VII.718–19)—that is, across the Channel from England in the
Flemish town of Poperinge, where the boy's father rules; the misrepre-
sentation of what is in actuality a rather short distance reflects a child's
limited understanding of geographic distance.[19] Were he a proper
knight, the face of this "doghty swayn" (VII.724) would be incongruous, as it possesses the red-and-white coloring characteristic of either a
woman in a romance or of a child ("Whit was his face as payndemayn, /
His lippes rede as rose; / His rode is lyk scarlet in grayn" [VII.725–
27]).[20] Surprising emphasis is placed on Thopas's stanza-closing "semely
nose" (VII.729), a facial feature that seems calibrated to elicit a child's
giggle.

The phrase that follows is the first strong indicator of Thopas's age:
"His heer, his berd was lyk saffroun, / That to his girdel raughte adoun"
(VII.730–31). The peculiar detail cannot but signify a young boy's fake
beard. Let us try to imagine a real beard extending down to a twenty-
or thirty-something man's waist. It is possible—terminal length for a
beard seems to be a maximum of two to three feet, and an electronic
search for "long beards" images does show a handful of waist-length
beards among a vast collection of mid- to upper-chest examples—but

---

[19] Thus David Wallace figures premodern Flanders "as a territory (like Scotland or
Wales) immediately adjoining—or blending into—England . . . 'In Flaundres' sounds a
retreat from the epic register: 'al biyonde the see'/'In Flaundres'—40 miles from
Dover"; *Premodern Places: Calais to Surinam, Chaucer to Aphra Behn* (Oxford: Blackwell,
2004), 92, 99.

[20] See J. A. Burrow's Explanatory Notes to *Sir Thopas*, 725–27, in *The Riverside Chaucer*, 917–23 (918).

most men's beards cannot grow longer than a foot.[21] In any case, there is no evidence that waist-length "saffroun" (that is, bright yellow or red) beards were fashionable in fourteenth-century England or Flanders, and I have not been able to find medieval images that depict beards of this length of any color. As a point of comparison, the titular Green Knight's remarkable beard "ouer his brest henges . . . abof his elbowes"—that is, extends to the middle of his chest—and at Bertilak's castle the host's beard is described without reference to its length: "Brode, bryȝt watz his berde, and al beuer-hwed."[22] Thopas's beard is a prop, such as a boy playing at being a knight might attach, and the boy must be quite young: adolescent boys do not commonly dress up in imitation beards as they engage in solitary make-believe.

As the tale progresses, the range of young Thopas's age is further narrowed by his behavior and imagination. Though Thopas is a knowledgeable hunter and hawker, and a good bowman, his greatest talent lies in a sport more associated with the marketplace than with the manor: "Of wrastlyng was ther noon his peer, / Ther any ram shal stonde" (VII.740–41).[23] As with Shakespeare's Orlando, his athletic skills render him attractive to girls, but with a twist that suggests the childishness in his sportive wrestling and occasions another smile:

> Ful many a mayde, bright in bour,
> They moorne for hym paramour,
> Whan hem were bet to slepe.
>
> (VII.742–44)

[21] For a comprehensive study of beards across the ages, see Christopher Oldstone-Moore, *Of Beards and Men: The Revealing History of Facial Hair* (Chicago: University of Chicago Press, 2015). For an historical study with a focus on beards in gay culture, see Kevin Clarke, *Beards: An Unshaved History* (Berlin: Bruno Gmünder, 2013). Images of various beards may be found in Allan D. Peterkin, *One Thousand Beards: A Cultural History of Facial Hair* (Vancouver: Arsenal Pulp Press, 2001).

[22] *Sir Gawain and the Green Knight: A New Critical Edition* (Chicago: University of Chicago Press, 1984), ed. Theodore Silverstein, lines 182, 845. The length of the Green Knight's beard is more fully described as: "A much berd as a busk ouer his brest henges, / Þat wyth his hiþlich here þat of his hed reches / Watz euesed al vmbetorne abof his elbowes / Þat half his armes þerunder were halched in þe wyse / Of a kyngez capados þat closes his swyre" (lines 182–86).

[23] William Askins urges that the "inherently ludicrous" idea of Thopas wrestling for the prize of a ram in Flanders, where the absence of sheep required that wool be imported from England, is an in-joke reflecting Chaucer's position as controller of the Wool Custom, Wool Subsidy, and Petty Custom; "All that Glisters: The Historical Setting of the *Tale of Sir Thopas*," in *Reading Medieval Culture Essays in Honor of Robert W. Hanning*, ed. Robert M. Stein and Sandra Pierson Prior (Notre Dame: University of Notre Dame Press, 2005), 271–89 (271–72).

The mourning maidens "bright in bour" reflect conventional romance imagery, but the tongue-in-cheek line "Whan hem were bet to slepe" is evocative of parental admonition. The innocence of youth is signaled in the boy's lack of interest in insomniac ladies and also in mock-romance language that likens the sweetness of his character to the dog-rose, the prickly wild shrub that bears the rose-hip:

> But he was chaast and no lechour,
> And sweete as is the brembul flour
> That bereth the rede hepe.
> (VII.745–47)

The diction has the veneer of romance, but lines such as these are "all wrong," as Gaylord puts it, "because too pretty."[24] At the same time, the unwitting parodic effect is exactly right for a boy's imaginative integration into his fantasy of the language of popular romance that he and the tale's juvenile readers have enjoyed.

Toy spear ("launcegay") in hand and "long swerd by his side" (VII.752–53), Thopas mounts "his steede gray" (VII.751)—what I take to be a stick horse such as that which Chaucer's contemporary Jean Froissart says he played upon as a child or that which appears in manuscript illustrations such as Paris, Bibliothèque nationale de France, Fr. 218, fol. 95 (Fig. 1, from Barthélémy l'Anglais, *Livre des propriétés des choses*)[25]—and rides among the trees by his house where may be found "many a wilde best" (VII.755)—a ferocious-sounding phrase promptly

---

[24] Gaylord, "Chaucer's Dainty 'Dogerel,'" 90.

[25] Jean Froissart, "L'espinette amoureuse," in *Jean Froissart: An Anthology of Narrative and Lyric Poetry*, ed. and trans. Kristen M. Figg, with R. Barton Palmer (New York: Routledge, 2001), 110–11: "Et sai souvent dun bastonciel / Fait un cheval nomme grisiel" ["And, as well, I often made from a stick / A horse that I called Grisel"] (lines 213–14). Orme discusses this and other references to stick horses, including a citation from King Alfred noting how "children ride their sticks and play many games in which they imitate their elders," and includes an image of a stick horse in a 1495 London printing of *De proprietatibus rerum*; *Medieval Children*, 174–75, 7 (Fig. 3). Additional fifteenth- and sixteenth-century images of children at play on stick horses appear in Paris, BnF, Fr. 995, fol. 7 (*La danse macabre*, available at http://gallica.bnf.fr/ark:/12148 /btv1b9059983v/f8.image [accessed February 15, 2017]); Oxford, Bodleian Library, MS Douce 276, fol. 124v (available at http://bodley30.bodley.ox.ac.uk:8180/luna/servlet /view/all/what/MS.%20Douce%20276 [accessed February 15, 2017]); Oxford, Bodleian Library, MS Douce 12, fol. 16; Vienna, Österreichische Nationalbibliothek, MS 12820, fol. 182r; and London, British Library, Add. MS 24098, fol. 23v (The Golf Book, available at http://www.bl.uk/onlinegallery/ttp/golf/accessible/images/page11full.jpg [accessed February 8, 2017]).

Fig. 1.

diminished as referencing deer and hares ("Ye, bothe bukke and hare" [VII.756])—and an assortment of sweet, exotic southern Asian herbs (none of them native to Flanders except in a child's imagination) such as a boy might relish: "lycorys," "cetewale" (a kind of ginger), "clowe-gylofre" (clove), and "notemuge" (VII.761–63). Indeed, in the tale's restful second section we will find young Thopas enjoying a snack consisting of the "roial spicerye" of gingerbread, licorice, cumin, and sugar (VII.853–56).

As he spurs his mount to the cheerful song of melodic birds (VII.766–71), Thopas falls into the state of "love-longynge" (VII.772) one might anticipate in a romance hero, but the boy's enthusiastic activity evinces unrestrained juvenile energy: though he is given no obvious reason for haste, he "pryked as he were wood" (VII.774), to the point that his

handsome steed "So swatte that men myghte him wrynge" (VII.776)—
one may imagine the stick horse bathed in the exuberant boy's perspiration.[26] Excessive spurring is not uncommon in romance, where
overtaxed horses sometimes break down beneath their riders' demands,
but such effusive equine sweat is not a literary norm, and the consequence of Thopas's exhausting "prikyng" is not knightly:

> Sire Thopas eek so wery was
> For prikyng on the softe gras,
> So fiers was his corage,
> That doun he leyde him in that plas.
>   (VII.778–81)

The intermediary line, "So fiers was his corage," is especially telling.
One might hear ironic humor in the idea that Thopas was "so fiers"
that he "leyde" himself "doun" on "softe gras," but I catch the child's
perspective, his justification for experiencing a weariness that only a
superbly "fiers" knight would feel: "My spurring is just too powerful!"
The instinctive self-justification also explains the subsequent transfer-
ence of the boy's own exhaustion to his horse: heavy-eyed Thopas may
have laid himself down, but it was "To make his steede some solas"
(VII.782). Affirmation that it is the child's thoughts we are observing
comes shortly afterwards in the deflection of responsibility for the boy's
make-up game that marks his first-person account of a vision apparently
witnessed not in Thopas's present slumber but the previous night:

> Me dremed al this nyght, pardee,
> An elf-queene shal my lemman be
> And slepe under my goore.
>   (VII.787–89)

No "In towne" (VII.793) maiden may be worthy of the boy's imaginative fantasy, but the pursuit of an elf-queen surely justifies an exciting
adventure undertaken "By dale and eek by downe!" (VII.796).

Revived by his nap—for surely that is what we have witnessed—
Thopas proceeds to the savage "contree of Fairye" (VII.802), where no

---

[26] Chaucer pictures hardy "prikyng" and an even sweatier horse to great effect in *The
Canon's Yeoman's Prologue*, VIII.559–86, where the horse's abundant foam is linked to its
rider's no less profuse perspiration: "His forheed dropped as a stillatorie" (VIII.580).

women or children dare approach him. In this make-believe land, Thopas's tender age takes linguistic center stage: "a greet geaunt"—further hyped as a "perilous man of dede" (VII.807, 809)—mockingly calls him "Child," the "child" responds, and then "child Thopas" escapes (VII.810, 817, 830). In a harmless reversal of the David and Goliath story, when Thopas flees, it is the giant Olifaunt who casts stones with a sling-shot, the inversion drawing attention to the citation of the most famous account of juvenile bravery in the Bible, a story every English boy would know. It is proper to both the parody and a child's imagination that Thopas answer the giant's Saracen exclamatory "by Termagaunt" (VII.810)—a common oath among the pagans of romance and chanson de geste—with a Christian-inflected *par ma fay* (VII.820); proper too that Thopas escape "thurgh Goddes gras" (VII.831); but amusingly boastful and further indicative of the heroic protagonist's extreme youth that the prudent retreat also be attributed to "his fair berynge" (VII.832).

All this busy adventure occurs in the tale's first "fit," of which one may note in passing how throughout these eighteen stanzas Chaucer plays with discreet sexual innuendo, a recurrent element in stories that adults read to children. Young children are able to enjoy adult stories without understanding or even noticing their erotic implications. In a children's tale such as *Sir Thopas*, it is not surprising that the prepubescent hero imagines maidens pining for him in their bowers, a fairy queen sleeping under his cloak, and himself "prikyng" wildly, his fancy (like that of the tale's juvenile audience) picking up on motifs common to tail-rhyme romances and love lyrics without being distracted by sexual connotations at which adults may smile but that are irrelevant to the childish excitement of the silly narrative.

The nine-stanza second fit has almost no action, as Thopas rests at home after his tiring escapade. First, the boy announces to his attendants that "nedes moste he fighte / With a geaunt with hevedes three" (VII.841–42), the three heads an impressively imaginative addition to his adventure, and another strong indicator of the boy's age. Make-believe is common play behavior for children from around age two-and-one-half through age six or seven, and is considered by specialists in child development to be a key indicator of cognitive and social growth.[27]

---

[27] See Scott Barry Kaufman, Jerome Singer, and Dorothy G. Singer, "The Need for Pretend Play in Child Development," http://www.psychologytoday.com/blog/beautiful-minds/201203/the-need-to-pretend-play-in-child-development (accessed February 15, 2017); and Doris Bergen, "The Role of Pretend Play in Children's Cognitive Develop-

He now calls for his minstrels and tale-tellers to amuse him and enter-
tain him with tales ("To make hym bothe game and glee" and "to tellen
tales" [VII.840, 846]); refreshes himself with a cloying snack of "sweete
wyn," "mede," "roial spicerye / Of gyngebreed," more "lycorys,"
"comyn," and excellent "sugre" (VII.851–56); and goes through a
lengthy ceremony of boyish dress-up that begins, indelicately were he
not a child, with his underpants:

> He dide next his white leere
> Of cloth of lake fyn and cleere,
> A breech and eek a sherte.
>   (VII.857–59)[28]

The scene continues with Thopas being armed in many layers of equipment, each introduced by the phrases "And next" or "And over that"
(VII.860, 861, 863, 866), the repetition hinting at the boy's delight in
how many layers there are. His other accoutrements are notable for their
luster: a shield "al of gold so reed" and embossed with a "bore's heed" and
a "charbocle" (VII.869–71); a helmet of "latoun bright"; an ivory sheath
and saddle; and a bridle that "as the sonne shoon, / Or as the moone
light" (VII.876–80), the "as . . . Or as" option suggesting that the boy
couldn't quite decide which was the more pleasing comparison. In the
midst of this arming, Thopas has another snack, swearing boastfully over
"ale and breed / How that the geaunt shal be deed" (VII.872–73), with
the catalogue proceeding as though uninterrupted. As Mark DiCicco has
noted, the extended scene of epic arming is somewhat bizarre: the
described armor is more suitable for display than for martial use.[29]

The four-and-one-half-stanza third fit also lacks exploit, as Thopas is
likened to the child heroes of romance, from "Horn child," "Ypotys,"
"Beves and sir Gy," and "sir Lybeux and Pleyndamour" (VII.898–90)
to Percival, whose example provides the boy with a model for temperate
drinking: "Hymself drank water of the well, / As dide the knyght sire

---

ment," *Early Childhood Research & Practice* 4, no. 1 (2002): 2–15, http://ecrp.uiuc.edu
/v4n1/bergen.html (accessed February 15, 2017).

[28] On the atypicality of Thopas's underpants, see Helen Cooper, "Chaucerian Representation," in *New Readings of Chaucer's Poetry*, ed. Robert G. Benson and Susan J. Rid-
yard (Cambridge: D. S. Brewer, 2003), 7–29 (23).

[29] On the absence of plate armor as indicative of the burlesque quality of the arming
scene, see Mark DiCicco, "The Arming of Sir Thopas Reconsidered," *N&Q* 244 (1999):
14–16.

Percyvell" (VII.915–16).[30] Thopas, like many a child playing at pretend, is of course the finest of them all:

> But sir Thopas, he bereth the flour
> Of roial chivalry!
>
> (VII.901–2)

Thopas begins this second sortie with the curious motion of gliding ("he glood" [VII.904]) even as his horse's imagined hooves stir up sparks ("As sparcle out of the bronde" [VII.905]), an inconsistency that passes unnoticed in a children's story where the interest of each individual element is more important than the various elements' compatibility. The narrative is interrupted without any event taking place beyond Thopas using his helmet as a pillow (another nap!) while his horse nibbles on the grass (VII.912–14). The overall sense of the tale's substance is that the first fit describes an engaging outing, the second fit adds an epic set-piece, and the third fit fades away, in content as well as in length.

The Playful Manuscript Layout of *Sir Thopas*

Phillipa Hardman opens her study of "evidence for the provision of small books for young child readers of English in the late fifteenth century" by referencing an earlier allusion to such reading, "Chaucer's description of the seven-year-old schoolboy in *The Prioress's Tale* learning his little book."[31] It is likely that younger children would have looked on as parents, nurses, or tutors read to them, and one can imagine six- and seven-year-olds reading *Sir Thopas* on their own.[32] The leaves on

---

[30] The list of child heroes in medieval popular romance is long. As Hardman writes, "So marked is the presence of children in Middle English popular romances that it might even be thought of as a defining feature" ("Popular Romances," 153). Ypotis is not a hero of romance but the principal speaker in a dialogue in which the young boy instructs the Roman emperor Hadrian on Christian belief; see Judith Deitch, "Ypotis: A Middle English Dialogue," in Kline, *Medieval Literature for Children*, 227–48. Pleyndamour has not been satisfactorily identified.

[31] Phillipa Hardman, "'This litel child, his litel book': Narratives for Children in Late-Fifteenth-Century England," *JEBS* 7 (2004): 51–66 (51). *Thopas*'s brevity suits this analysis.

[32] Nicholas Orme, *Medieval Schools: From Roman Britain to Renaissance England* (New Haven: Yale University Press, 2006), postulates that "The home must have been a common place for learning to read, perhaps more common than schools," and notes a few examples of parental reading instruction (60–61, quotation on page 61). See also Orme, *Medieval Children*, 242–46, who includes an image of Anne teaching Mary to

which the tale appears would have caught the observer's eye immediately, since a distinctive feature of the presentation of *Sir Thopas* in many *Canterbury Tales* manuscripts, including Ellesmere and Hengwrt—the earliest witnesses and those linked most closely to Chaucer—is a "peculiar diagrammatic layout": a system of "graphic tail-rhyme" in which "tail-lines are set off to the right in their own column, linked to their relevant couplets by brackets."[33] Rhiannon Purdie calls this layout, suppressed in almost all print editions, including all modern editions apart from facsimiles, "an important element of the humour of *Sir Thopas*."[34] Its appearance in authoritative manuscripts derived from different exemplars suggests that the graphic tail-rhyme in *Sir Thopas* manuscripts is likely to have been authorial.

The use of graphic tail-rhyme is not in itself remarkable: though uncommon, the feature appears in French, English, and Latin manuscripts from the late twelfth through the early sixteenth centuries as a marker of tail-rhyme in poems of many genres.[35] Unique to *Sir Thopas* manuscripts, however, is a complication whereby a second set of brackets links matching tail-rhymed lines, and a haphazard third set of brackets for bob-lines occasionally extends the text to the far-right edge of the page; Helen Cooper has famously likened the layout to "a pattern that is reminiscent of a schedule for a tennis tournament with an inconvenient number of players."[36] As most of the tail-rhyme romances Chaucer cites have exemplars that include bracketing, the common scholarly

---

read found in Oxford, Bodleian Library, MS Rawlinson Liturg.d.1: a late fourteenth-century missal for the use of Whitby Abbey, Yorkshire (245, Fig. 88). Images depicting this apocryphal scene were "popular in England, where it is found in manuscripts, wall paintings, and stained-glass windows" (244).

[33] Rhiannon Purdie, "The Implications of Manuscript Layout in Chaucer's *Tale of Sir Thopas*," *Forum for Modern Language Studies* 41 (2005): 263–74 (263). Purdie and other subsequent critics build upon the work of Judith Tschann, "The Layout of *Sir Thopas* in the Ellesmere, Hengwrt, Cambridge Dd.4.24, and Cambridge Gg.4.27 Manuscripts," *ChauR* 20, no. 1 (1985): 1–13, who reported that among the fifty-three *Thopas* manuscripts, "twenty-nine use brackets to join rhymes," "twenty also write the tail-rhyme lines to the right, making a separate column of tail lines," and "fifteen also mark the bob," with eleven carrying out the layout "consistently and intelligibly" (2). Wynkyn de Worde prints tail-rhymes to the right of the page (without brackets) in his 1498 edition, *The Boke of Chaucer Named Caunterbury Tales* (Westminster, 1498).

[34] Purdie, "The Implications," 263.

[35] Jessica Brantley, "Reading the Forms of *Sir Thopas*," *ChauR* 47, no. 4 (2013): 416–38, locates graphic tail-rhyme in numerous "medieval manuscripts apart from romance: Latin, French, Anglo-Norman, and Middle English" (422), and in genres as diverse as medieval Latin verse, liturgical song, "devotional vernacular lyrics apart from hymns" (425), historical lyric, courtly complaint, and fifteenth-century dramatic manuscripts, where its use is "strikingly consistent" (427).

[36] Helen Cooper, *Oxford Guides to Chaucer: The "Canterbury Tales"* (Oxford: Clarendon Press, 1989), 300.

explanation for Chaucer's use of the complex textual arrangement is that his expansion is an element in his parody of such romances. This is surely true, but I propose that Chaucer's playful complication of the layout is also calculated to appeal to a youthful audience. The confused design would have amused young children as they looked at the text being read to them, whether sitting in a lap or peeking over a shoulder, and the more curious among them might have tried to decipher the complicated lines on their own. Chaucer was, in effect, illustrating the text of *Sir Thopas* for the delight of his readers and listeners.

Fragment VII: The Children's Group

To recognize that *Sir Thopas* is a children's tale illuminates its placement in the *Canterbury Tales*. Fragment VII comprises the longest and most varied continuous sequence of the *Canterbury Tales*, with six distinct genres and five metric forms. The fragment has been dubbed "the Literature Group" (Alan Gaylord); an interrogation into "the status of language" (Helen Cooper); "a sustained reflection on the nature and devices of art" (Robert Edwards); a "thorough-going investigation of the problem of writing" (Ann Astell); and, most recently, "a metapoetic quest for a fully realized supreme fiction" (Peter Travis).[37] To this insightful list I would like to add the label "Children's Group."[38]

The fabliau *Shipman's Tale* is surely not a children's story—its subject is the intersection of sex and commerce in an amoral French household—but one of its oddest elements is a "mayde child" (VII.95) who appears only briefly when she accompanies the fiscally and sexually adroit wife as she dallies with Daun John in her garden while her merchant husband balances his books in his counting house. It is unclear whether this child, labeled as "yet under the yerde" (VII.97) and perhaps the merchant and wife's daughter, understands what she witnesses. The interplay between wife and priest might offer tutelage in amorous discourse and behavior—as would be appropriate in a tale originally

---

[37] Gaylord, "*Sentence* and *Solaas*," 227; Helen Cooper, *The Structure of the "Canterbury Tales"* (Athens: University of Georgia Press, 1984), 162; Robert R. Edwards, *The Dream of Chaucer: Representation and Reflection in the Early Narratives* (Durham, N.C.: Duke University Press, 1989), xvi; Ann W. Astell, "Chaucer's 'Literature Group' and the Medieval Causes of Books," *ELH* 59 (1992): 269–87 (282); and Peter W. Travis, *Disseminal Chaucer: Rereading "The Nun's Priest's Tale"* (Notre Dame: University of Notre Dame Press, 2010), 30.

[38] If one accepts the Ellesmere order, the group would be introduced by *The Physician's Tale* and *The Pardoner's Tale* of Fragment VI, the former focusing on a child, the latter featuring a scary story of a kind children like.

assigned to the Wife of Bath (as per Peter Beidler)—but as the girl's age is unclear it is also possible that she be deemed too young to appreciate the significance of the pair's negotiation of their fiscal and sexual desires (as argued by Karla Taylor).[39] The import of this easily passed-over crux thus involves whether the child receives behavioral instruction in the manner of impetuous Melibee or is as innocent in the ways of love as playful Thopas. Each of Fragment VII's ensuing tales explores in its own particular way the question of how an author—an adult—might choose to speak to children.

The Prioress's Tale, a pathos-laden Marian miracle about a victimized holy child, begins a series of five tales directed to audiences including children and usually featuring children. The Prioress's Prologue sets the juvenile tone as the narrator likens herself to "a child of twelf month oold, or lesse" (VII.484). The tale's martyred protagonist, a widow's seven-year-old son, is repeatedly called "litel" and "yong[e]," as the tale's ostensibly artless language is fashioned to elicit pity for a tender-aged "innocent" (VII.566) too young to give thought to the effect his loud singing has on the auditors to his passage through the Jewish quarter. As a religious folktale, The Prioress's Tale offers, among other things, a cautionary story for children: be careful where you go; watch what you say; and, most importantly, pray lovingly to Mary.

In contrast, The Tale of Sir Thopas tenders a lilting poetic account of the imagined and thoroughly secular adventures of a child certainly no older than The Prioress's Tale's "litel clergeon." Here the child's innocence is not placed in question—it is what one would expect in a little boy amusing himself in his garden—and there is no didactic purpose. Though they are directed to audiences of similarly juvenile listeners, the two tales' opposed tones (piteous vs. bubbly), subject matters (child's martyrdom vs. child's play), purposes (to caution vs. to amuse), and genres (miracle of the Virgin vs. silly adventure) could hardly be more extreme.

The titular protagonist of The Tale of Melibee is a "yong man" (VII.967), and the dominant genre of this moral treatise is the "Mirror for Princes," that is, a text intended to instruct young men in proper

---

[39] See Peter G. Beidler, "Medieval Children Witness Their Mothers' Indiscretions: The Maid Child in Chaucer's Shipman's Tale," ChauR 44, no. 2 (2009): 186–204; and Karla Taylor, "Social Aesthetics and the Emergence of Civic Discourse from the Shipman's Tale to Melibee," ChauR 39, no. 3 (2005): 298–322 (304–5, 308–9).

morality and behavior.[40] *Melibee* is thus precisely the kind of didactic text recent scholarship has asked us to treat as medieval children's literature. Chaucer inscribes his English translation into the *Canterbury Tales* by contriving a scenario in which Harry Bailly condemns *Thopas* as vapid, to which Chaucer responds with a tale that has been universally received as presenting *sentence* without *solaas*, thereby juxtaposing the two extremes of literature for children.

The Monk's Tale is a collection of short exemplary stories of a type common in collections designed for family recitation. The brief tragedies respond to Melibee's tutored response by presenting archetypal instances in the *Fall of Princes* tradition. The various accounts—some amusing, others stark, many involving children[41]—offer abbreviated accounts of the rises and falls of well-known biblical and historical figures, with a few modern instances thrown in. Notwithstanding the Knight's and Host's subsequent complaints about the stories' heaviness, they are suitable for youths with undeveloped attention spans—twenty-first-century university students often like them. The brief stories contrast, of course, with the brilliance of Fragment VII's final element, *The Nun's Priest's Tale*, which also incorporates a collection of tragic stories but integrates them into a lively and imaginative frame. The fragment, and with it this Children's Group, therein closes with a tale in another genre traditionally directed to children as well as adults: the beast fable, here expanded to incorporate all of the fragment's many strategies for speaking to an audience that includes children of various ages, interests, and understanding: humorously coded sexual negotiation and disputation; sage advice; miraculous escape; meditation (here comic) on free will and moral choice; collection of exemplary stories; and, in its overall character, non-didactic children's story.[42]

[40] Patterson has pointed out that Chaucer's source for *Melibee*, Renaud de Louen's 1336 French translation of Albertano de Brescia's Latin, was addressed to a noblewoman for the teaching and profit of her son, along with any other princes who might wish to listen and attend to it, and that Albertano's original 1246 text was intended for the instruction of his own youngest son ("What man artow?," 139, citing Renaud: "a l'enseignement et au profit de mon tres cher seigneur, vostre filz, et de tous autres princes et barons qui le vouldront entendre et garder").

[41] The tales featuring children are *Nabugodonosor* (Daniel, "the wiseste child of everychon" [VII.2155]), *Cenobia* ("Two sones . . . hadde she, / The whiche she kepte in vertu and lettrure" [VII.2295–96]), *Hugelino* ("his litel children thre; / The eldest scarsly fyf yeer was of age" [VII.2411–12]), *Nero* ("in youthe" taught by Seneca [VII.2512]), and *Cresus* (who knew his "doghter" to "in heigh sentence habounde" [VII.2747–48]).

[42] That Chaucer would compose a Children's Group is consonant with his history of writing about children. Children are omnipresent in the *Canterbury Tales*, where young or adolescent children appear in every tale save the Friar's and Canon's Yeoman's. See

Chaucer as a Writer for Children, Then and Now

Chaucer says very little about his immediate audience. He addresses lyrics to "My maister [Peter or Robert] Bukton" (*Buk* 1), Henry "Scogan, that knelest at the stremes hed / Of grace" (*Sco* 43–44), Philip la "Vache" (*Truth* 22), and "Adam scriveyn" (*Adam* 1), and he directs *Troilus and Criseyde* to "moral [John] Gower" and "philosophical [Ralph] Strode" (*TC*, V.1856–57).[43] These adults are not, however, the only audience that Chaucer names. Most notably, the *Treatise on the Astrolabe* is explicitly directed to "Lyte Lowys my sone," in whom Chaucer recognizes an "abilite to lerne sciences touching nombres and proporciouns" and a desire for instruction evidenced in the ten-year-old Lewis's "besy praier in special to lerne the tretys of the Astrelabie" (1–5). Chaucer deliberately composes the *Astrolabe* not in the Latin of "eny commune tretys of the Astrelabie" (54–55) but "in my lighte Englissh" (50–51), confident that he can show "as many and as subtile conclusiouns" in the vernacular "as ben shewid in Latyn" (53–54). "I . . . have it translatid in myn Englissh oonly for thy doctrine" (61–64), he writes, specifying that he will show Lewis the workings of an astrolabe "under full light reules and naked wordes in Englissh, for Latyn canst thou yit but small, my litel sone" (26–28). Indeed, as Sigmund Eisner has documented, the prose of Chaucer's "*Treatise* brings a delightful youth-oriented approach to fourteenth-century technical instruction," using a style that employs

---

D. S. Brewer, "Children in Chaucer," *Review of English Literature* 5, no. 3 (1964): 52–60; and Jill Mann, "Parents and Children in the *Canterbury Tales*," in *Literature in Fourteenth-Century England*, ed. Piero Boitani and Anna Torti (Cambridge: D. S. Brewer, 1983), 165–83. Eve Salisbury, *Chaucer and the Child* (New York: Palgrave Macmillan, 2017), appeared while this essay was under review; in a brief discussion of *Sir Thopas*, Salisbury calls the tale "innovative and experimental, an imaginative foray into an enchanted world weirdly attached to a material environment. The landscapes and the creatures inhabiting them are as elemental as they are magical" (54).

[43] During Chaucer's lifetime, a few fellow poets reference his writing. Eustache Deschamps names the *Roman de la rose* and Lewis Clifford in a poem with the refrain "Grant translateur, noble Geoffrey Chaucier"; Thomas Usk has Philosophy praise "myne owne trewe servaunt the noble philosophical poete in Englissh . . . in a treatise that he made of my servant Troylus" (*Testament of Love*, III.559–60, 563) and alludes to *Troilus* frequently; Gower has Venus send greetings to Chaucer in the *Confessio Amantis* (first recension) ("And gret wel Chaucer whan ye mete, / As mi disciple and mi poete" [*8.2941–42]); and Thomas Hoccleve claims to have known Chaucer and, if Simon Horobin is correct, was the editor of the Ellesmere manuscript ("Thomas Hoccleve: Chaucer's First Editor?," *ChauR* 50, nos. 3–4 [2015]: 228–50).

simple words and sentences; clarifying analogies; helpful repetition; and, frequently, the first- and second-person discourse children appreciate.[44]

As an instructional manual addressed to a child, Chaucer's *Astrolabe* is remarkable. Aside from school books, most overtly pedagogical medieval texts were aimed not at children but at their parents and instructors, especially tutors of princes and mothers who might use the lessons to teach their sons and daughters proper behavior. *The Tale of Melibee*, which Chaucer may initially have translated with the young Richard II in mind, is just such a text.[45] Chaucer himself names *Melibee* "a moral tale vertuous" (VII.940), points to his use of "somwhat moore / Of proverbes than ye han herd bifoore" (VII.955–56), and emphasizes that Melibee is an emotionally charged and hasty "yong man" (VII.967) in much need of a prudent woman's patient instruction. When one considers *Melibee* as a text that a parent might have read to a child, it makes a curious kind of sense when, at the treatise's end, Harry Bailly wishes that "Goodelief, my wyf, hadde herd this tale" (VII.1894).[46]

Beyond these authorial indicators of a child audience, scholars have judged the inclusion of works by Chaucer in books containing conduct manuals or romances with child heroes as an indication that fifteenth- and sixteenth-century parents saw his tales as offering beneficial models of courtly or domestic behavior.[47] As with the romances that seem to have been read aloud in family groups including children, Chaucer's designation of the *Canterbury Tales* as a collection that valorizes "Tales of best sentence and moost solaas" (I.798) would seem to have appealed to those compiling books for a mixed audience of juveniles, adolescents, and adults.[48]

[44] Sigmund Eisner, "Chaucer as a Teacher," *Children's Literature Association Quarterly* 23 (1998), 35–39 (46). See also Sigmund Eisner and Marijane Osborn, "Chaucer as Teacher: Chaucer's *Treatise on the Astrolabe*," in Kline, *Medieval Literature for Children*, 155–87, which includes Osborn's translation of the *Astrolabe*.

[45] See Patterson, "What man artow?," 139–40, following Albert H. Hartung, "A Study of the Textual Affiliations of Chaucer's Melibeus Considered in Its Relation to the French Source," Ph.D. diss. (Lehigh University, 1957); and Dolores Palomo, "What Chaucer Really Did to *Le livre de Melibee*," *PQ* 53 (1974): 304–20 (313–15).

[46] On mothers as teachers, see Orme, *Medieval Children*, 243–45. The question has been treated most recently by Michael Clancy, "Did Mothers Teach Their Children to Read?," in *Motherhood, Religion, and Society in Medieval Europe, 400–100: Essays Presented to Henrietta Leyser*, ed. Conrad Leyser and Lesley Smith (Farnham: Ashgate, 2001), 129–53.

[47] See Hardman. "Popular Romances," 154; Shaner, "Instruction and Delight."

[48] Scholars have speculated on the general nature of those for whom Chaucer was writing. Thus Paul Strohm sees those named by Chaucer and a few others (including

That many of the *Canterbury Tales* offer good reading for children is further evidenced by the numerous nineteenth- and twentieth-century adaptations of selected tales in illustrated books.[49] Charles Cowden Clarke's 1833 *Tales from Chaucer in Prose, Designed Chiefly for the Use of Young Persons* stands out as the first edition of Chaucer identifying children as its primary audience.[50] As the century advanced, the 1870 second edition of this book was joined by Francis Storr and Hawes Turner's 1878 *Canterbury Chimes; or, Chaucer Tales Retold for Children*, and two volumes by the scholar-artist Mary Eliza Haweis (1852–98): *Chaucer for Children* in 1877 and *Chaucer for Schools* in 1881.[51] For the dual-language *Chaucer for Children*, Haweis used Richard Morris's text as the base for her translations and illustrations of abridged versions of *The General Prologue* and the Knight's, Friar's, Clerk's, Franklin's, and Pardoner's tales, working on the assumption that children enjoy good storytelling when the mature subjects are appropriately edited.[52] Her commentary sometimes speaks to children directly ("Do you like hearing stories? I am

John Clanvowe, William Beauchamp, Richard Stury, and William Nevill) as constituting "Chaucer's most intimate circle . . . a constantly shifting group" of literary-minded members of "the king's affinity" (*Social Chaucer* [Cambridge, Mass.: Harvard University Press, 1989], esp. 41–46 [45]), and Derek Pearsall locates Chaucer in "a clubbable coterie of men" ("The *Canterbury Tales* and London Club Culture," in *Chaucer and the City*, ed. Ardis Butterfield [Woodbridge: D. S. Brewer, 2006], 95–108 [103]). I do not question these conjectures, but hope to expand our understanding of Chaucer's audience beyond groups of learned readers. Helen Cooper has proposed that in undertaking the *Canterbury Tales* project, Chaucer was reacting against an audience of merchant-founded "London and Southwark Poetic Companies": "When the pilgrim Chaucer rode out of the city to join Harry Bailey and the company of pilgrims in the inn at Southwark, he was turning his back on a certain kind of civic performance as well as on the poetry of princely courts"; "London and Southwark Poetic Companies: 'Si tost c'amis' and the *Canterbury Tales*," in Butterfield, *Chaucer and the City*, 109–25 (117). I suggest that the poetry *toward* which he was turning is distinguishable as a literature suitable for children.

[49] See Charlotte Morse, "Popularizing Chaucer in the Nineteenth Century," *ChauR* 38, no. 2 (2003): 99–125.

[50] Charles Cowden Clarke, *Tales from Chaucer in Prose, Designed Chiefly for the Use of Young Persons* (London: Effingham Wilson, 1833).

[51] Francis Storr and Hawes Turner, *Canterbury Chimes; or, Chaucer Tales Retold for Children* (London: C. Kegan Paul, 1878); Mary Eliza Haweis, *Chaucer for Children: A Golden Key* (London: Chatto & Windus, 1877), and *Chaucer for Schools* (London: Chatto & Windus, 1881). Margaret Connolly, "'Dr Furnival and Mother like the same old books': Mary Haweis and the Experience of Reading Chaucer in the Nineteenth Century," in *Eminent Chaucerians? Early Women Scholars and the History of Reading Chaucer*, ed. Richard Utz and Peter Schneck, *Philologie im Netz* (Supplement 4, 2009), 5–20, treats Haweis as scholar and author, with particular attention to her ideas about the value of mothers reading Chaucer to children in his original verse (6–8).

[52] See David Matthews, "Infantilizing the Father: Chaucer Translations and Moral Regulation," *SAC* 22 (2000): 93–114 (94–96). Velma Bourgeois Richmond, *Chaucer as*

going to tell you of some one . . . who told more wonderful stories than I shall be able to tell *you* in this little book") and elsewhere instructs parents that children will appreciate the sounds of Chaucer's English: "The mother should read to the child a fragment of Chaucer with the correct pronunciation of his day."[53]

In the past century, the efforts of these nineteenth-century proponents of juvenile engagement with Chaucer's tales have been supplemented by dozens of children's editions of Chaucer's poetry: Candace Barrington gives a count of "at least twenty-seven" editions.[54] Most of these juvenile adaptations perceive the *Canterbury Tales* as excessively challenging for children, who require versions of the tales that are cleansed, simplified, and modernized to articulate contemporary values often quite foreign to Chaucer.[55] In contrast, the reading of *Sir Thopas* that I have offered here locates a story authorially directed to a child audience without need of cleansing or simplification, a story that "openly allow[s] a child to enjoy himself with no thought of duty nor fear of wrong."

My point is not to say that Chaucer wrote *Sir Thopas* to amuse a particular child—how could we possibly know? Neither am I suggesting that Chaucer imagined parents hiring scribes to copy out the tale for their children—we have no evidence of any such activity. What I do

---

Children's Literature: Retellings from the Victorian and Edwardian Eras (Jefferson: McFarland, 2004) treats adaptations of the *Canterbury Tales* for children from Charles Cowden Clarke to World War I.

[53] Quoted in Mary Flowers Braswell, "The Chaucer Scholarship of Mary Eliza Haweis (1852–1898)," *ChauR* 39, no. 4 (2005): 402–19 (406). Haweis was unusual in seeing children as capable of understanding and enjoying something close to the original Chaucer. In her 1887 *Tales from Chaucer*, directed to lower-class readers, Haweis includes *The Miller's Tale*, and while she disguises the sexuality a bit, she follows Cowden Clarke in providing facing-page Middle English that allows an observant reader to tell what is lurking beneath the surface. Haweis's retelling of *The Miller's Tale* is discussed in Mary Flowers Braswell, " 'A completely funny story': Mary Eliza Haweis and the *Miller's Tale*," *ChauR* 42, no. 3 (2008): 244–68.

[54] Candace Barrington, "Retelling Chaucer's Wife of Bath for Modern Children: Picture Books and Evolving Feminism," in *Sex and Sexuality in a Feminist World*, ed. Karen A. Ritzenhoff and Katherine A. Hermes (Newcastle upon Tyne: Cambridge Scholars Press, 2009), 26–51 (28). Barrington's focus is on how child-oriented twentieth-century retellings of *The Wife of Bath's Prologue and Tale* mirror (or, sometimes, react against) evolving feminist conceptions of women's roles. Siân Echard, "Bedtime Chaucer: Juvenile Adaptations and the Medieval Canon," in her *Printing the Middle Ages: Material Texts* (Philadelphia: University of Pennsylvania Press, 2008), 126–61, explores how Victorian and modernist juvenile adaptations of the *Canterbury Tales* reflect declining appreciation for sentimentality.

[55] Barrington, "Retelling Chaucer's Wife," 27.

propose depends on a simpler assumption that is in line with Chaucer's practice in exploring a multiplicity of literary forms. I ask us to envisage a Chaucer who, as he contemplated writing a burlesque of the youth-oriented Matter-of-England romances that were so large a part of his literary culture, shaped in his mind an idea for which we have no literary precedents: a frivolous tale designed to amuse young children. Looking out for a fresh device, Chaucer recognized that children like to see themselves in a story; that they can enjoy a story without understanding everything in it; that they can read or listen without having things explained to them; and that it is acceptable if, like young Thopas, they are simply laughing and playing.

"A suffisant Astrolabie": Childish Desire, Fatherly Affection, and English Devotion in *The Treatise on the Astrolabe*

Jamie K. Taylor
Bryn Mawr College

Abstract

This essay examines the affective motivations in Chaucer's prologue to his *Treatise on the Astrolabe*, dedicated to his young son, Lewis. It argues that Chaucer conceptualizes Lewis as a metonym for vernacular readers, projecting an imagined ideal of "Englishness" that coalesces around paternal love and technological learning. More broadly, this essay explores the ways Chaucerian children, including Lewis, embody the aspirational possibilities of vernacular community.

Keywords

child, toy, astrolabe, envy, sufficiency, astral science, vernacularity

CHAUCER DEDICATES HIS *Treatise on the Astrolabe* to his ten-year-old son Lewis, giving him an astrolabe and an instruction manual so he can learn the complexities of astral sciences. He gives these gifts to Lewis as much to express fatherly love and friendship as to ensure his son can calculate planetary movements. "That for as moche as a philoso-fre said, 'he wrappith him in his frend, that condescendith to the right-fulle praiers of his frend,'" Chaucer explains, "'therfore have I yeven the a suffisant Astrolabie as for oure orizonte, compowned after the latitude of Oxenforde" (*Astr*, 5–10).[1] As "suffisant" as Lewis's astrolabe is to support complex scientific calculations, its manual will meet Lewis at

I would like to thank Elly Truitt, Darin Hayton, Colby Gordon, Jane Hedley, Alice Dailey, Lisa H. Cooper, Karma Lochrie, Patricia Ingham, Shannon Gayk, and Bethany Schneider for their sharp, generous engagement with this essay as it developed.
[1] All citations of *The Treatise on the Astrolabe* and other Chaucerian texts are from *The Riverside Chaucer*, gen. ed. Larry D. Benson, 3rd ed. (Boston: Houghton Mifflin, 1987). Line numbers are given parenthetically in the text.

his inchoate abilities, providing thorough instruction using "naked wordes in Englissh," since Lewis's Latin is "yit but small" (26–27). Chaucer ends by assuring Lewis that this "swerd"—that is, the *Astrolabe* prologue, Lewis's astrolabe, or perhaps even astral knowledge itself—will "sleen envye" (64).

Chaucer thus bookends his vernacular translation of a scientific treatise with affective reassurances, framing it as an act of paternal devotion and protection. In doing so, Chaucer theorizes the relationship between astrolabic understanding, desire, and parental love. Specifically, I argue here, the prologue to *The Treatise on the Astrolabe* depicts the three working together in the service of a vernacular imaginary in which technological instruction can formulate "Englishness" as a sign of and call for communal devotion. Lewis is both audience and strategy, the rhetorical and ideological center of an argument in which the child represents the aims and desires of a communal body. This strategy is one Chaucer turns to again and again throughout his works, especially the *Canterbury Tales*, and reading little Lewis as one of Chaucer's children contextualizes the *Astrolabe* prologue within an ongoing program of portraying children and childishness in the service of theorizing "Englishness."

Jill Mann argues that "the parent–child relationship is one of the central motifs of the *Canterbury Tales*," and investigations of Chaucer's portrayal of children over the last few decades have demonstrated that children and childishness are critical to Chaucer's self-depictions as a sophisticated poet or as an immature vernacular writer.[2] In fact, Chaucer

---

[2] Jill Mann, "Parents and Children in the *Canterbury Tales*," in *Literature in Fourteenth-Century England*, ed. Piero Boitani and Anna Torti (Cambridge: D. S. Brewer, 1993), 163–83 (165). See also Sigmund Eisner and Marijane Osborn, "Chaucer as Teacher: Chaucer's *Treatise on the Astrolabe*," in *Medieval Literature for Children*, ed. Daniel T. Kline (New York: Routledge, 2003), 157–87; and Thomas J. Jambeck and Karen K. Jambeck, "Chaucer's *Treatise on the Astrolabe*: A Handbook for the Medieval Child," *Children's Literature* 3 (1974): 117–22. For broader discussions of children's literature and childhood in the Middle Ages, see C. H. Talbot, "Children in the Middle Ages," *Children's Literature* 6 (1977): 17–33; Susan S. Morrison, "Medieval Children's Literature," *Children's Literature Association Quarterly* 23, no. 1 (1998): 2–6; Yvonne J. Truscott, "Chaucer's Children and the Medieval Idea of Childhood," *Children's Literature Association Quarterly* 23, no. 1 (1998): 29–34; Nicholas Orme, *Medieval Children* (New Haven: Yale University Press, 2001); Barbara A. Hanawalt, *Growing Up in Medieval London: The Experience of Childhood in History* (Oxford: Oxford University Press, 2003); Seth Lerer, *Children's Literature: A Reader's History, from Aesop to Harry Potter* (Chicago: University of Chicago Press, 2009), 57–80; Nicholas Orme, "Children and Literature in Medieval England," *MÆ* 68, no. 2 (2010): 218–46; and Rachel E. Moss, *Fatherhood and Its Representations in Middle English Texts* (Cambridge: D. S. Brewer, 2013). These studies counteract Philippe Ariès's longstanding argument that the Middle Ages did not much value

repeatedly explores communication and literacy, playfulness and sobriety, power and subordination through depictions of children.[3] As an overtly instructional text, *The Treatise on the Astrolabe* perhaps comes closest to Chaucerian "children's literature," and indeed, several fifteenth-century manuscripts title it "Brede and milke for children," taking literally Chaucer's claim that it is written in simplified language appropriate for young, science-minded adolescents.[4] But we might consider the *Astrolabe* an example of children's literature from a different angle: that is, as a text that deploys the figure of the child and its affective attachments. Little Lewis is but an introductory figure through which Chaucer can address "every discret persone" (41). He is, in other words, a child-reader that stands in for all English readers.[5] The *Astrolabe* thus constructs Lewis as the nodal point of vernacular community, in which Lewis can use his Oxford-oriented astrolabe to anchor himself at home even as the text radiates outward to include anyone who speaks or reads "lighte English." Accordingly, the *Astrolabe*'s prologue can be understood as a kind of "sovereign fantasy," to use Patricia Ingham's phrase, drawing upon little Lewis's desires, ambitions, and hopes as a means to project an imagined sense of "Englishness" that can coalesce around paternal love, childish stargazing, and technological learning.[6]

The idea that astral learning might serve political interests is certainly not unique or peculiar to Chaucer. Astrology was understood to be an important area of expertise for rulers, at least on the Continent,

---

or even demarcate childhood: *Centuries of Childhood: A Social History of Family Life*, trans. Robert Baldick (New York: Cape, 1962).

[3] See Eve Salisbury's *Chaucer and the Child* (New York: Palgrave, forthcoming). I am grateful to have been given access to this book before publication.

[4] Seth Lerer, "Chaucer's Sons," *UTQ* 73, no. 3 (2004): 906–15 (908). For a discussion of the *Astrolabe* as an example of grammar-school style, see Christopher Cannon, *From Literacy to Literature: England, 1300–1400* (Oxford: Oxford University Press, 2016), 85–124.

[5] Derek Pearsall claims that there is "no steadily growing sense of national feeling" in the fourteenth century, and Ardis Butterfield argues that Chaucer reflects a volatile political climate. Derek Pearsall, "Chaucer and Englishness," in *Proceedings of the British Academy 101* (Oxford: Oxford University Press, 1999), 77–99; Ardis Butterfield, "Nationhood," in *Chaucer: An Oxford Guide*, ed. Steve Ellis (Oxford: Oxford University Press, 2005), 50–65. For a crucial discussion of what "national identity" might mean in the Middle Ages in England, see Thorlac Turville-Petre, *England the Nation: Language, Literature, and National Identity, 1290–1340* (Oxford: Clarendon Press, 1996); and for an excellent summary of the various discussions of Chaucer and English nationhood, see Kathy Lavezzo, "England," in *Chaucer: Contemporary Approaches*, ed. Susanna Fein and David Raybin (University Park: Penn State University Press, 2009), 47–64.

[6] Patricia Ingham, *Sovereign Fantasies: Arthurian Romance and the Making of Britain* (Philadelphia: University of Pennsylvania Press, 2001).

although English rulers were less eager to incorporate astrological knowledge and prediction into their political affairs.[7] Edward III, for example, heeded Thomas Bradwardine's skepticism about the utility and veracity of astrological predictions, even as mathematicians at Merton College focused more and more attention on astral sciences.[8] Richard II was perhaps more amenable than Edward to including astrology in political decision-making; he commissioned a large, illustrated compilation of texts (in Latin) about governance and rulership, which included a lengthy geomancy and elaborate astrological tables (Oxford, Bodleian Library, MS Bodley 581).[9] Notably in the context of Lewis's astrolabe treatise, the compiler of MS Bodley 581 explains that he deliberately produced a text young Richard could understand:

Since the science of astronomy is both of great difficulty and time-consuming to learn, for which the present life is scarcely adequate, I have compiled this present little book of geomancy, not from my own views, but from the rules and precepts of established authorities in this art, up to the year of our lord 1391, in the month of March.[10]

Both little Lewis and young Richard inspire the production of simplified scientific manuals, and both Lewis's and Richard's child-appropriate science manuals assume broader influence than their immediate audiences.

In tracking how Chaucer's vernacular technological treatise authorizes itself via parental love and guidance, I turn to a wide range of texts, both within Chaucer's oeuvre and outside it, including pastoral manuals, craft instructions, and vernacular exempla. I thus stretch *The Treatise on the Astrolabe* well beyond its immediate or obvious contexts. I do so not to argue that the *Astrolabe* draws explicitly or directly from these texts, but rather to offer a kind of constellation of adjacent vocabularies and conceptual structures through which we might understand the relationships Chaucer develops here among vernacular translation, communal devotion, and fatherly affection. Indeed, as I hope to show

---

[7] Darin Hayton, "Astrology as Political Propaganda: Humanist Responses to the Turkish Threat in Early Sixteenth-Century Vienna," *Austrian History Yearbook* 38 (2007): 61–91. See also Tamsyn Barton, *Ancient Astrology* (New York: Routledge, 1994).

[8] Hilary M. Carey, *Courting Disaster: Astrology at the English Court and University in the Later Middle Ages* (New York: St. Martin's Press, 1992), 79–116.

[9] Katharine Breen, "A Different Kind of Book for Richard's Sake: MS Bodley 581 as Ethical Handbook," *ChauR* 45, no. 2 (2010): 119–68.

[10] Oxford, Bodleian Library, MS Bodley 581, fol. 9a. Cited and translated in Carey, *Courting Disaster*, 103.

here, Chaucer's *Astrolabe* prologue must be aligned with texts that seem very far from its immediate avatars to make sense of the ideological work it wants to accomplish.

Vernacular Citizenship and the Sovereign Child

The *Astrolabe* prologue's investments in parental devotion and vernacular instruction coalesce around ten-year-old Lewis, and Chaucer's introductory citation about responding to the prayers of one's friends makes an immediate link between feeling (both paternal and friendly), astrolabic knowledge, and Englishness. But it is not clear precisely to whom "a philosofre" might refer.[11] Walter Skeat suggests that the general ideal of friendly obligation is Ciceronian, but Chaucer's address to Lewis here looks more like Aristotle's description of parental friendship in the *Nicomachean Ethics*, insofar as it conceptualizes the possibility of friendship within families and places family love and friendly devotion along the same continuum. Aristotle explains that parents and children, like friends, love one another because they see reflections of themselves, but he adds "Parents know their offspring with more certainty than children know their parentage; and progenitor is more attached to progeny than progeny to progenitor, since that which springs from a thing belongs to the thing from which it springs."[12] Later, he builds on that claim to produce an analogy between parental and artisanal affection: "The same thing happens with the artist," he says. "Every artist loves his own handiwork more than that handiwork if it were to come to life would love him. This is perhaps especially true of poets, who have an exaggerated affection for their own poems and love them as parents love their children."[13] This Aristotelian framework provides a series of connotative associations, ones that subtend Chaucer's *Astrolabe* prologue in its layering of parental love and vernacular translation.

The Aristotelian analogy between child and poem takes on a specifically Chaucerian bent in his repeated associations between childishness and vernacularity, in which he persistently registers his own English writings as immature or as-yet unformed. In the prologue to *Sir Thopas*,

---

[11] For a discussion of friends as readers of the *Astrolabe*, see Edgar Laird, "Chaucer and Friends: The Audience for the *Treatise on the Astrolabe*," *ChauR* 41, no. 4 (2007): 439–44.

[12] Aristotle, *Nicomachean Ethics*, ed. and trans. H. Rackham (Cambridge, Mass.: Loeb, 1926), VIII.xii.2.

[13] Ibid., IX.vii.3–4.

for example, the Host describes Chaucer as a "popet" with an "elvyssh" face who will tell a Middle English tail-rhyme romance, a "deyntee thyng" of little consequence (*Th*, VII.711). In that tale, Chaucer cites several insular romances, including those "of Horn child," as well as *Ypotis*, *Bevis of Hampton* and *Guy of Warwick*, all of which feature children as central characters (VII.898–900). (For example, *Ypotis* is a dialogue between a three-year-old Ypotis and Emperor Hadrian about moral governance; as it turns out, Ypotis is the Christ-child, who has been instructing the emperor all along.[14]) *Sir Thopas* thus "suggests that Chaucer intends for the English reader, the reader who knows many of these romances, to identify their central connecting feature: they all feature heroes who are children, even if they eventually, and in the cases of the very long romances Beves of Hampton and Guy of Warwick, grow up."[15]

Whereas the gestures toward childishness in *Sir Thopas* assert a playful denunciation of English *auctoritas*—Chaucer, the puppetish pilgrim, tells a failed romance abruptly cut off by the Host—Chaucer turns to his own child in the *Astrolabe* to authorize English *auctoritas* and to conceptualize a community unified around love, desire, and friendship. For Chaucer, using "lighte" English here is both a way to speak directly to his young son and an ideological claim on behalf of the vernacular in the service of learning and community alike. Thus, in the *Astrolabe* prologue he establishes himself specifically as an English writer, rather than a writer whose work is quasi-continental, international, or "foreign."[16] Andrew Cole has persuasively shown that the *Astrolabe* prologue uses Wycliffite vocabularies ("naked wordes") to argue on behalf of a vernacular that draws its authority directly from insular models of translation circulating among English theologians.[17] In many of his other works, Chaucer "effaces much of the nexus of English vernacular literature," but here he clearly and deliberately deploys English terminology to

---

[14] See "Ypotis," in *Codex Ashmole 61: A Compilation of Popular Middle English Verse*, ed. George Shuffelton (Kalamazoo: TEAMS, 2008), item 27.

[15] D. Vance Smith, "Chaucer as an English Writer," in *The Yale Companion to Chaucer*, ed. Seth Lerer (New Haven: Yale University Press, 2006), 87–121 (103).

[16] Elizabeth Salter, "Chaucer and Internationalism," in *English and International: Studies in the Literature, Art and Patronage of Medieval England*, ed. Derek Pearsall and Nicolette Zeeman (Cambridge: Cambridge University Press, 1988), 239–44; on the vernacularity of the *Astrolabe*, see Glending Olson, "Chaucer," in *The Cambridge History of Medieval English Literature*, ed. David Wallace (Cambridge: Cambridge University Press, 1999), 580–84.

[17] Andrew Cole, "Chaucer's English Lesson," *Speculum* 77, no. 4 (2002): 1128–67.

write a "vernacular cosmology."[18] Moreover, as Seth Lerer claims, the *Astrolabe* sees its technical education as secondary to and supportive of its assertion of English, rather than French, as the language of the realm and of the king.[19] This is why, once Chaucer establishes a childish vernacular as his instructional mode, he writes "And preie God save the king, that is lord of this langage, and alle that him feith berith and obeieth, everich in his degre, the more and the lasse" (56–59).

Chaucer's move from expressing love for his son to calling for devotion to the king positions Lewis as the inaugural point for a more general emotional connection among English subjects. Drawing upon Lauren Berlant's vocabulary, we might think of Lewis as a kind of "infantile citizen": that is, an idealized political subject who relates to the nation affectively, through love, faith, and trust.[20] The infantile citizen is a passive canvas onto which the fantasies that structure aspirational political cohesion can be mapped, whose childlike acquiescence and obedience to communal ideologies are rewarded with rights and citizenship. The figural child—silent, passive, innocent—is a powerful allegory to imagine national or cultural coherence. In this sense, Lewis works for the *Astrolabe* as Sophie does for the *Melibee*, as a child who propels a large-scale prose translation in the service of political fantasy. The *Melibee* begins with the lifeless, brutalized body of Melibeus's daughter, beaten by his enemies, who "wounded his doghter with five mortal woundes in five sondry places—/ this is to seyn, in hir feet, in hire hands, in hir erys, in hir nose, and in hire mouth—and leften hire for deed, and wenten away" (*Mel*, VII.971–72). The tale explicitly catalogues Sophie's injuries to generate empathy for Melibeus's ferocious response. Moreover, the tale, like her perpetrators, leaves her for dead. We do not know whether she lives or dies; we do not know how she might narrate her experience of the incident, given the chance.

Voiceless and passive, Sophie functions less as Melibeus's daughter or

[18] Smith, "Chaucer as an English Writer," 100. The Parson's claim that he "kan nat geeste 'rum, ram, ruf'" (*ParsP*, 43) is perhaps the clearest example of such effacement. For a discussion of the *Astrolabe* as "vernacular cosmology," see Jenna Mead, "Geoffrey Chaucer's *Treatise on the Astrolabe*," *Literature Compass* 3, no. 5 (2006): 973–91.

[19] Seth Lerer, *Inventing English: A Portable History of the Language* (New York: Columbia University Press, 2007), 70–84. For a fascinating discussion of astrology, cartography, and vernacularity, see Daniel Birkholz, "The Vernacular Map: Re-Charting English Literary History," *NML* 6 (2003): 11–77.

[20] Lauren Berlant, *The Queen of America Goes to Washington City* (Durham, N.C.: Duke University Press, 1997), 27–28.

a character in a tale than as a narrative opportunity through which Meli-beus and Prudence can, at length, meditate on the delicate balance between revenge and justice.[21] As such, Sophie embodies the economy of sacrifice and desire that reaches toward what we might call, perhaps anachronistically, "patriotic" feeling, insofar as the term "patriotism" captures the devotional affect sutured to *patria*, or "fatherland." As L. O. Aranye Fradenburg explains with respect to chivalric devotion, dying on behalf of country animates a critical dialectic between specific and universal that shapes the desire that is necessary for community-formation.[22] In sacrificing himself on behalf of *patria*, the soldier is swallowed up by the imaginary or fantastical nation, becoming a structural figure of national love and fidelity rather than a dead individual. But in turn, by sacrificing himself to a communal imaginary, the solider reasserts his exemplary singularity. In other words, the dead solider is both individual and representative, specific and universal. This dialectic structures the profound feelings of loss, righteousness, and glory necessary to inspire the kind of devotion around which the state can develop.

The Chaucerian child, also simultaneously individual and representative, functions the same way. When Melibeus comes home to find his daughter almost dead, he "lyk a mad man rentynge his clothes, gan to wepe and crie" (VII.973). His robust reaction exemplifies the immediate response required by a child, and the rest of *The Tale of Melibee* channels those feelings into a philosophical debate in which Melibeus's rage and madness are tempered by Prudence's counsel for measured action. The *Melibee* sacrifices Sophie in the name of governmental prudence, rendering her an allegorical opportunity to imagine wisdom (*sophia*) as the foundation of justice. Lee Edelman has argued that the child emerges as a powerful political allegory particularly because he or she poses the fantasy of "unmediated access to Imaginary wholeness."[23] The Child (which Edelman capitalizes to indicate its ideological function, distinguished from any individual child) allegorizes the impossible desire for the coherence of the Symbolic. In other words, the Child animates a political vision in which the fragmentary Symbolic might be

[21] On this balance, see Conrad Van Dijk, *John Gower and the Limits of the Law* (Woodbridge: D. S. Brewer, 2013), 139–88.

[22] L. O. Aranye Fradenburg, "Pro patria mori," in *Imagining the Medieval English Nation*, ed. Kathy Lavezzo (Minneapolis: University of Minnesota Press, 2003), 3–38 (9).

[23] Lee Edelman, *No Future: Queer Theory and the Death Drive* (Durham, N.C.: Duke University Press, 2004), 10.

transformed into a communal and ideological whole. Such Imaginary wholeness, both Berlant and Edelman claim, relies on the emotional charge the Child sparks, in that pity and protectiveness ignite a desire for a political future in which the nation unites around its concern for the Child's welfare and, consequently, in which citizens' pity and protectiveness toward the Child expand to produce affection toward and recognition of one another.

To contextualize Lewis as a Chaucerian Child recognizes the ideological, even aspirational, work Lewis is pressed to perform. Yet there are significant differences between Melibeus's Sophie and Chaucer's Lewis. For one, Chaucer (probably) did have a son named Lewis, whereas Sophie is an obvious allegory for *sophia*.[24] More critically, Lewis does not suffer bodily harm, as Sophie and many other Chaucerian children do, and thus Lewis relies on, but does not fully reflect, the sacrificial model of Child ideology Chaucer elsewhere depicts.[25] We need only think of the Prioress's little clergeon or the Physician's Virginia to recognize that Chaucerian children are usually dead, subjects of violence, or, at best, mere background for conflict between adults. For the little clergeon and Virginia, as for Sophie, the description of bodily harm stimulates a pathetic response designed to unite an audience's sympathies around a common ideology or set of beliefs. *The Prioress' Tale*, for example, animates a "vision of an ideal theocracy" purged of cultural and religious impurities in the image of a beatific child, reminiscent of the Christ-child.[26] Similarly, *The Physician's Tale* presents a sacrificial economy upon the body of a fourteen-year-old girl, in which her intact virginity stands in for intact Christian patriarchy.[27] Many Chaucerian children are sacrificed, like soldiers, in the name of communal sanctity, insofar as their

[24] It is not entirely clear who "Lewis" is—whether the son of John of Gaunt and Chaucer's wife Philippa, Chaucer and Philippa, Chaucer and Cecily Champaigne, or perhaps an imagined construct. See Paul Strohm, who suggests Chaucer was separated from his wife when Lewis may have been conceived: *Chaucer's Tale: 1386 and the Road to Canterbury* (New York: Viking, 2014), 42–43.

[25] Daniel T. Kline, "Textuality, Subjectivity, and Violence: Theorizing the Figure of the Child in Middle English Literature," *EMSt* 12 (1995): 23–38. See also "'That child may doon to fadres reverence': Children and Childhood in Middle English Literature," in *The Child in British Literature: Literary Constructions of Childhood, Medieval to Contemporary*, ed. Adrienne E. Gavin (New York: Palgrave, 2012), 21–37.

[26] Denise L. Despres, "Cultic Anti-Judaism and Chaucer's Litel Clergeon," *MP* 91, no. 4 (1994): 413–27 (423).

[27] Daniel T. Kline argues that Virginia resists the hagiographic and legal discourses espoused in the tale, which are designed to preserve the patriarchal authority that subtends Christian community; "Jephtha's Daughter and Chaucer's Virginia: The Critique of Sacrifice in *The Physician's Tale*," *JEGP* 107, no. 1 (2008): 77–103.

violent deaths produce the pitiable feelings around which community devotion and future-oriented state ideologies can be forged.

But not all children are so violently sacrificed, and in the *Astrolabe* prologue, we get a different affective picture. There, parental love, rather than an imperiled child, formulates patriotic aspirations. As both the inspiration for and authorization of a translation of a dense scientific manual into "lighte English," Lewis encapsulates the fantasy of a vernacular *patria*, a fatherland tied conceptually to the love of a father for his son and enacted in an English treatise that both attends to Lewis's particular childish skill-set and imagines his skill-set as a metonym for a wider vernacular community. We can turn to *The Man of Law's Tale* for a similar formulation. There, a beloved child takes on the aspirational possibilities of English community. *The Man of Law's Tale* deploys Custance, and then her son Maurice, as child-objects in the service of *translatio imperii*. In the beginning of the tale, Custance's father, the Roman emperor, sends his daughter to Syria to marry the sultan once he promises to convert his court to Christianity. Custance models the kind of emotional resignation we likewise feel about this transfer, as she responds like a good daughter should, with both dismay and obedience:

> "Fader," she seyde, "thy wrecched child Custance,
> Thy yonge doghter fostred up so softe,
> And ye, my mooder, my soverayn plesance
> Over alle thyng, out-taken Crist on-lofte,
> Custance youre child hire recomandeth ofte
> Unto youre grace, for I shal to Surrye,
> Ne shal I nevere seen yow moore with ye."
>
> (*MLT*, II.274–80)

Custance's multiple self-references as the emperor's child emphasize the pitiable tragedy of the situation: she must go to the "Barbre nacioun" out of daughterly obligation and love, which her father exploits for imperial power. Of course, the transfer is disastrous, as the sultaness of Syria ships Custance away in a rudderless boat after murdering everyone who has converted, including the sultaness's own son. When Constance lands on the Northumberland shore and her obvious piety converts the community, including King Alla (her eventual husband), she finds herself again shipped off in a rudderless boat by an angry queen, this time with her infant son, Maurice.

When Custance and Maurice wash ashore in another "heathen" land, a traveling Roman senator discovers them and escorts the two back to Rome. The reunion of Custance, her father, Maurice, and Alla (who has traveled to Rome on pilgrimage) is both emotional and expedient. Alla's "sobbyng and bitter peyne" when he sees his thought-dead wife and son, and the emperor's "piteous joye" when reunited with his daughter signal the emotional recognition of familial and communal ties between Roman and Northumberland leaders. Their reunion leads to the papal appointment of Maurice as rightful Roman emperor. The end of the tale thus affectively reframes the beginning: whereas Custance operated as the tragic child-object of *translatio imperii* in her pitiable transfer from Rome to Syria, Maurice successfully links Rome to England via the happy affirmation of an intact family. Significantly, only once Maurice is made emperor does the tale use the word "Engelond" rather than "Northumberland," claiming that Alla and Custance returned there "the righte way" (II.1130). As in the *Astrolabe* prologue, then, *The Man of Law's Tale* imagines English *patria* through affective response to a Child. Moreover, it envisions Rome as a sign for imagined national wholeness, in which "Engelond" can subsume "Northumberland" and in which an Englishman can sit at the helm of the Roman empire.[28] As I explore in the final section, the *Astrolabe* prologue likewise takes Rome as a universalizing term, by which "Englishness" can be produced and preserved.

Chaucerian children such as Sophie, Virginia, Maurice, and Lewis thus perform ideological work in the service of future- and fantasy-oriented communal sanctity, invoking crucial emotions that can formulate a sense of communal devotion. Lewis specifically operates as both a recipient of and nodal point for the vernacular community that might coagulate around "lighte English," generating and passing on Chaucer's translation-as-fatherly-affection. In other words, Lewis provides an emotional center for a text that ultimately seeks to conceptualize the stakes of writing in English. A vernacular astrolabe treatise in particular provides the opportunity to consider the ways technological expertise and "lighte English" might work in tandem to bring together an imagined community of English-speakers and -readers. Indeed, as I examine in the next section, the *Astrolabe* prologue navigates between high-level

[28] Kathy Lavezzo, *Angels on the Edge of the World: Geography, Literature, and English Community, 1000–1534* (Ithaca, N.Y.: Cornell University Press, 2006), 112.

scientific knowledge and childish desire and abilities, to authorize vernacular translation as a kind of love.

Craft, Community, and Expertise

When Chaucer begins his *Treatise on the Astrolabe* by citing fatherly love and friendship as inspiration for his vernacular translation, he formulates an analogy between his personal, familial devotion to his child and devotion to a vernacular community. At the same time, the citation gestures to how technical knowledge in particular can support and be supported by such communal devotion. By turning again to Aristotle as a possible background, we can retrieve conceptual connections between parental affection and affection for handiwork or craft (*techne*), through which Chaucer composes a link between a vernacular translation of a scientific manual and sovereign fantasies. The father–son friendship works, according to Aristotle, like the artisan–craft relationship, insofar as the artisan loves his handiwork more than the handiwork could ever love its artisan. Such is particularly the case with poets, he says, whose works assume the status of children. Aristotle thus imagines a circle of love that loops around from parent to craftsman to poet and back again. Chaucer's prologue relies on this affective loop to yoke his own craft to the Child. He does so by conceptualizing the astrolabe itself as an artisanal product for his son: that is, as a toy.

For Chaucer, *techne* is the implicit fulcrum among his positions as Lewis's father, his role as *Astrolabe* translator, and his status as an English subject.[29] Yet Chaucer overtly disavows his own craftsmanship: "But considre wel that I ne usurpe not to have founden this werk of my labour or of myn engyn. I n'am but a lewd compilator of the labour of olde astrologiens, and have it translatid in myn Englissh oonly for thy doctrine" (59–64). In doing so, he follows idiomatic models of authorial self-effacement, in which compilers asserted that they added "nothing of their own" to a work that brings together the ideas of older *auctores*.[30]

---

[29] See Lisa H. Cooper, *Artisans and Narrative Craft in Late Medieval England* (Cambridge: Cambridge University Press, 2011).

[30] A. J. Minnis, *Medieval Theory of Authorship: Scholastic Literary Attitudes in the Later Middle Ages* (Philadelphia: University of Pennsylvania Press, 1988), 191–204. For a discussion of compilation in the *Astrolabe* specifically and in astrolabe treatises more generally, see Edgar Laird, "Geoffrey Chaucer and Other Contributors to the *Treatise on the Astrolabe*," in *Rewriting Chaucer: Culture, Authority, and the Idea of the Authentic Text*, ed. Thomas A. Prendergast and Barbara Kline (Columbus: Ohio State University Press, 1999), 145–65.

Chaucer's version of that self-effacement draws explicitly on artisanal language, focusing on his "werk" and his "labour," which in turn build on the "labour" of the astral scientists he translates. Such mechanical vocabulary would become common in the late fifteenth and early sixteenth centuries in the macaronic compilations produced by and circulated among London merchants; here in the *Astrolabe*, Chaucer looks both back to Scholastic models of compilation and forward to mercantile ones.[31] The prologue thus conceptualizes the manual as a text both intellectual and "practical," offering understanding of high-level astral science and the mechanical operations of astrolabes alike.

The most critical and telling term Chaucer uses here is "engyn," a word that derives from *ingenium* and, in the later Middle Ages, was "increasingly linked to mechanical contrivances and other idiosyncratic things."[32] Gesturing to both the excitements and the suspicions of human ingenuity, late medieval *ingenium* rinses itself of the anxieties of (dis)ingenuous machinations by turning to childish enchantment and whimsical creativity. Whereas the term "engyn" can register ambivalence or anxiety about the deceitfulness possible in human creations, "in the hands of children, and deployed in the service of young love, these counterfeit machinations gleam untarnished, their makers above reproach."[33] In the *Astrolabe* prologue, Chaucer uses the term to assert the overlaps between mechanical and linguistic operations particularly by drawing upon its possible childlike connotations to suggest his translation might offer the opportunity for fantasy, that its vernacular "trewe conclusions" might reach toward an imagined ideal of Englishness. Although he explicitly tries to assert that he offers unaltered "trewe conclusions," nothing especially playful or "ingenious," he also opens the possibility that "engyn," if attached to Lewis, might more positively connote ingenuity and childlike play. Chaucer's most sustained exploration of such childish "engyn" occurs in *The Squire's Tale*, in which the exuberant Squire tells a meandering romance that features three magical

[31] Jonathan Hsy, *Trading Tongues: Merchants, Multilingualism, and Medieval Literature* (Columbus: Ohio State University Press, 2013), 157–93.

[32] Patricia Ingham, *The Medieval New: Ambivalence in an Age of Innovation* (Philadelphia: University of Pennsylvania Press, 2015), 80. See also Scott Lightsey, *Manmade Marvels in Medieval Literature* (New York: Palgrave, 2007), 8–12; and E. R. Truitt, *Medieval Robots: Mechanism, Magic, Nature, and Art* (Philadelphia: University of Pennsylvania Press, 2015), 49–50.

[33] Ingham, *Medieval New*, 81.

devices gifted to Cambysukan and his daughter, Canacee. The "ingenious construction" of the Squire's horse enables us to press upon Chaucer's "engyn" in his *Astrolabe* prologue to think about the mechanics of both a toy and vernacular text given to a child as a gesture of affection. The young, eager Squire (described in *The General Prologue* as "fressh as is the month of May" (*GP*, 92) begins his tale with an authorial disavowal. He cannot describe Canacee's beauty because it exceeds his immature rhetorical skills: "I dar nat undertake so heigh a thyng," he says, "Myn Englissh eek is insufficient" (*SqT*, V.36–37). He then goes on to tell a romance of wonders, in which a knight enters Cambysukan's court bearing objects from his lord, the "the kyng of Arabe and of Inde" (V.110).

The Squire devotes most of his attention to the magical brass horse that can take the rider anywhere in the world. As he explains,

> This steed of bras, that esily and weel
> Kan in the space of o day natureel—
> This is to seyn, in foure and twenty houres—
> Wher-so yow lyst, in droght or elles shoures,
> Beren youre body into every place
> To which youre herte wilneth for to pace,
> Withouten wem of yow, thurgh foul or fair.
>
> (V.115–21)

The horse permits movement without regard to terrestrial space—that is, one might go "wher-so yow lyst"—but it must adhere to the conditions of natural time. Indeed, the Squire is careful to affirm that this horse is not magical, exactly; it works according to "gyn," in which the user turns a pin that dangles from the horse's ear. Marijane Osborn argues that this pin registers this horse as "astrolabic," in that it echoes the operations of an astrolabe.[34] As Chaucer describes in his *Treatise*, "Than is there a large pyn in manere of an extre, that goth thorugh the hole that halt the tables of the clymates and the riet in the wombe of the moder; thorugh which pyn ther goth a litel wegge, which that is clepid the hors, that streynith all these parties to-hepe" (I.14.1–6). We should note here that Chaucer turns to maternal language ("the wombe of the moder," a likely translation of the Arabic *al-umm* or Latin *mater*)

---

[34] Marijane Osborn, *Time and the Astrolabe in the "Canterbury Tales"* (Norman: University of Oklahoma Press, 1982), 34–54.

to describe the hollowed-out plate into which all the other astrolabe plates fit. In the *Astrolabe* treatise proper, then, the material form of the tool emerges as a metaphor for child-nurture and -development. *The Squire's Tale* makes a similar gesture (that is, describing an object's child-like properties) but from the opposite direction: it materializes an astrolabe in whimsical, but childishly literal, terms. The young Squire translates an astrolabic "horse" and "pin" into an actual toy horse with an ear-pin. He thus carefully positions the horse between the wondrous and the technical, providing clues to how it works but asserting that no one in the court could move it. "It stant as it were to the ground yglewed," he says, "Ther may no man out of the place it dryve / For noon engyn of wyndas or polyve; / And cause why? For they kan nat the craft" (V.182–85). Here, as in the *Astrolabe*, "craft" is the linchpin between childish wonder and technical expertise. Chaucer positions Lewis as the fulcrum between "engyn" and "trewe conclusions" offered by his translation, and as such, Lewis authorizes the veracity of the *Astrolabe* treatise as well as the calculations it enables.

Moreover, Lewis's Oxford-compounded astrolabe is both locally anchored and imaginatively expansive: that is, it can only be used properly in Oxford and thereabouts, but from there it can make available the entire cosmos. Such a dialectic between real place and imagined space supports the prologue's efforts to frame the astrolabe and its treatise as gifts from father to son as well as tools to envision a community lovingly devoted to an English sovereign. In contrast, "Englishness" seems barely at stake in *The Squire's Tale*. The tale begins "At Sarray, in the land of Tartarye," an exotic site of inexplicable wonders and magic. Only when the Squire momentarily likens the knight from Araby and India to Gawain does an English text surface as background (V.95–97). But the Squire betrays some investment in insular civic identity when he describes the brass steed as perfectly proportioned, exceeding both nature and art in its construction:

> For it so heigh was, and so brood and long,
> So wel proporcioned for to been strong,
> Right as it were a steede of Lumbardye;
> Therwith so horsly, and so quyk of ye,
> As it a gentil Poilleys courser were.
> For certes, fro his tayl unto his ere

> Nature ne art ne koude hym nat amende
> In no degree, as al the people wende.
> (V.191–98)

Lifelike ("quyk of ye") and "so horsly" that it seems like a noble Lombard horse, the Squire asks us to think about how this gift, which transcends spatial boundaries with the turn of a pin, might nonetheless register the geopolitics of poetic craft.[35] It is both local and expansive, mobile across any and all space yet yoked conceptually to specific places.[36] In addition, the Squire's citation of the noble horses native to Apulia and Lombardy also, significantly, gestures back to Fragment IV (*The Clerk's Tale* and *The Merchant's Tale*, which *The Squire's Tale* immediately follows), entirely set in Lombardy. Indeed, the beginning of *The Clerk's Tale* offers another example of such tension between mobility and locality, in which the Clerk says that Petrarch, his tale's source-author, wrote a prologue in which he describes Piedmont; Saluzzo; the Apennine mountains; the hills of West Lombardy including Mount Vesuvius; and the mouth of the River Po as it flows toward Emilia, Ferrara, and Venice. "And trewely, as to my juggement," the Clerk says, "Me thynketh it a thyng impertinent / Save that he wole conveyen his mateere; / But this his tale, which that ye may heere" (IV.53–56). Listing Petrarch's places only to claim that geographical specificity is a "thing impertinent" is how the Clerk asserts his own expertise as translator and author. He's done his reading, to be sure, but he believes proper "mateere" transcends the specific conditions of its production.[37]

We get a similar gesture in the *Astrolabe* prologue: that is, the gesture toward its sources accompanied by an assertion that the "mateere"—in the *Astrolabe*, "conclusions"—is profitably dislocated from the particularities of language or geography. But if we read the use of "engyn" here through *The Squire's Tale*, we can consider another angle: that Lewis's childishness, like the Squire's, reframes the relationship between ingenuity and translation. For the Squire, his "astrolabic" horse animates a childish, wondrous imagination that is unmarred by the knowledge of

---

[35] John M. Fyler, "Domesticating the Exotic in the *Squire's Tale*," in *Chaucer's Cultural Geography*, ed. Kathryn L. Lynch (New York: Routledge, 2002), 32–55.

[36] Apulian and Lombard horses were long considered the best and most beautiful in Europe. See Sir William Ridgway, *The Origin and Influence of the Thoroughbred Horse* (Cambridge: Cambridge University Press, 1905), 318.

[37] David Wallace, *Chaucerian Polity: Absolutist Lineages and Associational Forms in England and Italy* (Stanford: Stanford University Press, 1999), 287.

"craft." The Squire's horse, akin to a real Lombard horse but an ingenious contraption that can travel anywhere, animates the operations both of an astrolabe and of translation. In other words, the horse alerts us to the ways astrolabic mechanics and scientific translation are rooted geographically and linguistically even as they enable wide-ranging observations of the entire cosmos and transcend the particularities of specific languages and vocabularies.

Lewis's astrolabe and its manual expose their double investments in the universality of the conclusions they offer and the translational work that go into their use. By thinking through *The Squire's Tale* and its childish excitement for its wondrous objects and gadgets, we can conceptualize Lewis's astrolabe as a toy as much as a tool, and in doing so, we can expose its underground geopolitical operations.[38] Allan Mitchell has argued that toys expose the complicated and powerful relationship between play-objects and forms of identity, belonging, and self.[39] Such "toy ontology" is particularly clear in medieval playthings, which both orient and disorient by depicting an intended use without requiring it. A miniature knight atop a horse, for example, may encourage militaristic play and teach chivalric habits, but it cannot demand that kind of play nor directly instruct. "Toys are more or less oblique to systems of reference and everyday utility," Mitchell states. When children play with toys they both create and destroy little worlds.[40] To think of the astrolabe as a toy, then, is to think of it as an imaginative device that can dismantle and reconstruct space and time according to the whims and desires of the user. Still, we cannot simply think of an astrolabe as a toy, or as only a toy; it is, of course, also a scientific device. Mitchell explains: "That is partly why we may think of *mappae mundi* and astrolabes as *allied* to toy ontology, distracting from rational, routine procedures, without denying that those same technologies could have abetted mature ideological programs (e.g., drawing borders, marginalizing races, choreographing imperial expansion)."[41] Those mature ideological programs structure a child's understanding of the world, as Walter Benjamin reminds us: "A child is no Robinson Crusoe; children do not constitute a community cut off from everything else. They belong to the

---

[38] Salisbury, *Chaucer and the Child*, 44.
[39] Allan Mitchell, *Becoming Human: The Matter of the Medieval Child* (Minneapolis: University of Minnesota Press, 2014), 65–115.
[40] Ibid., 91.
[41] Ibid.; my emphasis.

nation and class they come from. This means that their toys cannot bear witness to any autonomous separate existence, but rather are a silent signifying dialogue between them and their nation."[42] Chaucer's astrolabe gift is Lewis's toy and a scientific device equally, and it is thus an object that can press childish play—even "engyn"—into communal ideology and vernacular subjectivity.

Envy, Sufficiency, and Diversity in Rome

Chaucer ends his *Astrolabe* prologue by promising that "this swerd" will "sleen envie" (64). Although this promise is perhaps surprising, it returns us to his initial dedication to Lewis by continuing to argue for an analogy between parent–child devotion and subject–community devotion. The *Astrolabe* prologue's ending recalls the beginning's ties between fatherly affection and the production of community, promising to mitigate the envy that might snag the affective bonds between neighbors. We can contextualize the promise that Lewis's "suffisant Astrolabie" can slay envy across an astonishingly wide range of texts that depict envy as a worry for children and communities alike, as well as those that insist sufficiency is envy's remedy. These texts—from practical artisans' manuals to pastoral instructions to vernacular exempla—help us recognize that Chaucer's promise to "sleen envie" reaffirms parental devotion as an impetus for larger patriotic fantasies and aspirations.

Augustine attributes envy to babies and children, claiming that infants cry to express jealousy when a mother pays attention to someone else and that young children must negotiate envy as they manage their multiple interests in school and in games. In the *Confessions*, for example, he recalls when he slacked off a bit and ignited the (understandable, he says) disciplinary attention of his teachers:

Non enim aut minus ea metuebamus aut minus te de his evadedis deprecabamur, et peccabamus tamen minus scribendo aut legendo aut cogitando de litteris, quam exigebatur a nobis. Non enim deerat, domine, memoria vel ingenium, quae nos habere voluisti pro illa aetate satis, sed delectabat ludere, et vindicabatur in nos ab eis qui talia utique agebant. Sed maiorum nugae negotia vocantabur, puerorum autem talia cum sint, puniuntur a maioribus.

[42] Walter Benjamin, "The Cultural History of Toys," in *Walter Benjamin: Selected Writings, 1927–1934*, Vol. 2, trans. Rodney Livingstone et al. (Cambridge, Mass.: Harvard University Press, 1999), 113–21 (116).

[And yet for all our fears, we too often played the truants; either in writing, or reading, or thinking upon our lessons, less than was required of us. For we wanted not, O Lord, either memory or capacity (for which, considering our age, thou pleasedst to bestow enough upon us) but our mind was all upon playing; for which we were beaten, even by those masters who were doing as much themselves. But elder folks' idleness, must, forsooth, be called business, and when children do the like, the same men must punish them.][43]

Here, Augustine offers a binary—childish play is antithetical to adult study or "business"—which Chaucer's *Astrolabe* prologue reconceptualizes as a continuum. But Augustine then suggests that the schoolmaster who had beaten him for ignoring his books had emotional motivations of his own:

idem ipse, a quo vapulabam, qui si in aliqua quaestiuncula a condoctore suo victus esset, magis bile atque invidia torqueretur quam ego cum in certamine pilae a conlusore meo superabar.

[my master, who, if foiled in any trifling question by another schoolmaster, was presently more racked with choler and envy at him than I was when, at a tennis match, I lost the game to my play-fellow.][44]

Augustine's descriptions map unexpected overlaps between knowledge-acquisition, authority, and envy, in which the child's choice to play offers the excuse for a teacher to take out his envy on the body of the child. In contrast, Chaucer's promise to "sleen envy" protects Lewis against such assaults, arming him with an astrolabe (or toy), astrolabic knowledge, and the kind of fatherly love that can sufficiently defend his child (and, potentially, a Child). And Chaucer's affective framework stretches to include vernacular subjects from similar attacks, thinking of this instructional manual as useful for all readers of "lighte English."

Although envy goes unmentioned in Chaucer's immediate astrolabic sources, such a turn toward envy is not entirely unprecedented in instructional manuals more broadly conceived, and those manuals argue that making knowledge available to all is key to mitigating the kind of

[43] Augustine of Hippo, *Confessions*, ed. and trans. Carolyn J. B. Hammond (Cambridge, Mass.: Loeb, 1912), I.ix.15.
[44] Ibid.

envy that might destroy communal good feeling.[45] Theophilus's twelfth-century *De diversis artibus*, for example, explains that accessible instructions obviate the envy that surfaces when knowledge is kept secret for those "in the know."[46] Chaucer's suggestion that his treatise can "slay envy" thus links it generically with craft instructions to claim his instructional manual can helpfully disaggregate envy and expertise. Similarly, Robert Mannyng asserts knowledge-hoarding as immorally envious and insists that "maystrye" requires sharing one's craft:

> ʒyf þou euer on any manere
> Lettydyst any man for to lere
> Crafte, or ouþer queyntyse,
> But fordeddyst hys apryse
> For þou shuldest furþeryd be,
> And more ynprys preysed þan he;
> Beþenke þe weyl, ʒyf þou do þus,
> Þat þyn herte ys ful enuyus.[47]

Handlyng Synne demonstrates the moral imperatives of sharing craft-knowledge, yoking artisanal manuals such as Theophilus's to pastoral instruction. Mannyng follows with an exemplum attributed to Saint Gregory, which describes God's punishment of envious sinners with measles and demonstrates just how universal envy is: "þat enuye is a cursed synne, / Any man to falle þer-ynne."[48] Yet he sums up his discussion of envy by outlining cultural proclivities toward certain sins. The French, he says, are especially prone to lechery, whereas the English are prone to envy.[49] So what he insists is a universal moral failing for "any man" turns out to be culturally inscribed. Chaucer amplifies Mannyng's momentary turn to cultural morality, bringing up the peculiarly English

---

[45] See R. T. Gunther, *Chaucer and Messahalla on the Astrolabe* (Oxford: Oxford University Press, 1929), 195–231. See also Paul Kunitzsch, "On the Authenticity of the Treatise on the Composition and Use of the Astrolabe Ascribed to Messahalla," *Archives internationales d'histoire des sciences* 31 (1981): 42–62; and Carol Lipson, "'I n'am but a lewd compilator': Chaucer's *Treatise on the Astrolabe* as Translation," *Neuphilologische Mitteilungen* 84 (1983): 192–200.

[46] Theophilus, *De diversis artibus*, ed. and trans. C. R. Dodwell (Oxford: Oxford University Press, 1961), 4.

[47] Robert Mannyng of Brunne, *Handlyng Synne*, ed. Frederick James Furnivall, EETS o.s. 119, 123 (London: EETS, 1901), 1:3945–52.

[48] Ibid., 1:4231–32.

[49] Ibid., 1:4151–52.

proclivity toward envy only to "slay" it with accessible astrolabic instruction. Thus, whereas Mannyng identifies the English as especially envious, Chaucer offers Englishness itself (via vernacular translation) as a bulwark against envy.

Elsewhere, discussions about envy—particularly the worrisome possibility that fortunes, whether as tangible goods or intangible successes, can be all-too-easily exchanged—turn on how cultural difference might invite it. This sub-mode of envy—supplantation—animates particular anxieties about what Jessica Rosenfeld calls "imitative treachery," in which the social and mechanical processes of likeness, imitation, and identification (we might add translation to this list) can be pursued with malevolent intent.[50] For example, in Book II of the *Confessio Amantis*, Gower worries at length about the treacherous possibilities of envious supplantation, which Genius explains to the Lover by way of a metaphorical compass: "Thus goth he with his sleyhte about / To hindre and schowve another oute / And stonden with his slyh compas / In stede there another was."[51] The "sly compass," a tool of orientation, works here in the service of social disorientation when the user translates its readings to support his nefarious intentions. In other words, Gower worries that disinterested data can be manipulated to support rather than suppress envy. He tries to solve the problem of imitative treachery in a series of exempla that collectively assert the imperial sovereignty of Rome. For him, Rome's putative universality can mitigate envy by smoothing perceived differences in fortune.

Specifically, in the "Tale of the False Bachelor," the threat of such imitative treachery is resolved only when Rome emerges to mitigate the insufficient legal policies of foreign places. The exemplum tells the story of the Roman emperor's son, who is bored with the peace at Rome and goes abroad ("in strange marches") in search of war, accompanied by his good friend. The two join an ongoing war between the sultan of Persia and the caliph of Egypt, on behalf of the sultan. The sultan is happy to have help, particularly "whan that he wiste he was Romein" (II.2565). In fact, he is so happy with the knight's performance that he promises his daughter to the Roman emperor's son, giving him a gold ring; whoever holds the ring will marry his daughter. Once the knight shows his

---

[50] Jessica Rosenfeld, "Compassionate Conversions: Gower's *Confessio Amantis* and the Problem of Envy," *JMEMSt* 42, no. 1 (2012): 83–105 (91).

[51] John Gower, *Confessio Amantis*, vol. 2, ed. Russell A. Peck (Kalamazoo: TEAMS, 2013), II.2339–42. Hereafter cited parenthetically by book and line number.

friend the ring, however, his friend grows envious and steals it, replacing it with a fake.

Despite the knight's discovery of his friend's treachery, the "tokne was so sufficant" that the promise it symbolizes must be followed, no matter the changed circumstances (II.2700). The envious friend thus marries the sultan's daughter and becomes the new sultan of Persia. The despondent knight writes his father to describe his sorrow, whereupon the Roman emperor steps in to right the wrongs suffered by his son. But there is a legal complication. Although in Rome the envious friend would be killed for his treachery, according to Persian law, a crowned sultan cannot be put to death. "And thus," Genius tells us, "the skiles ben diverse" (II.2770). This troublesome "diversity" is overcome only once the Persian people grant that the friend be taken to Rome, where justice can be meted out: "And thus acorded ful and plein, / The qwike body with the dede / With leve take forth thei lede, / Wher that Supplant hath his juise" (II.2778–81).

Rome functions in the *Confessio* as a sovereign place through which "ful and plein" accord might be achieved. Indeed, such accord caulks the fissures between the "diverse" laws of Persia and those of Rome by covering them over with Roman imperial authority. Gower's "ful and plein" accord, which reveals the sanctity of Roman authority, sounds a lot like Chaucer's "naked words in Englissh," which can adequately express the same technological mechanics articulated in other languages.[52] As Chaucer reassures Lewis,

But natheles suffise to the these trewe conclusions in Englissh as wel as sufficith to these noble clerkes Grekes these same conclusions in Grek; and to Arabiens in Arabik, and to Jewes in Ebrew, and to Latyn folk in Latyn; whiche Latyn folk had hem first out of othere dyverse langages, and writen hem in her owne tunge, that is to seyn, in Latyn. And God woot that in alle these langages and in many moo han these conclusions ben suffisantly lerned and taught, and yit by diverse reules; right as diverse pathes leden diverse folk the righte way to Rome.

(*Astr*, 28–40)

---

[52] For a discussion of the "horizontal multilingualism" of this list of scientific languages, see Gila Aloni and Shirley Sharon-Zisser, "Geoffrey Chaucer's 'Lyne Oriental': Mediterranean and Oriental Languages in the *Treatise on the Astrolabe*," *Mediterranean Historical Review* 16 (2001): 69–77; see also Jenna Mead, "Reading by Said's Lantern: Orientalism and Chaucer's *Treatise on the Astrolabe*," *Medieval Encounters* 5, no. 3 (1999): 350–57.

Chaucer affirms (and persistently reaffirms) the sufficiency of English here, by tying the diverse rules, diverse paths, and diverse folk to Rome. In doing so, he makes Rome the unifying signifier around which "trewe conclusions" can withstand multiple modes of expression. He also links Oxford with Rome, insofar as Lewis's Oxford-based astrolabe enables him (and every other "discret persone") to perform the same calculations; collect the same data; and, ideally, come to the same conclusions. "Rome" becomes a kind of logos around which meaning can take shape, and accordingly, it both authorizes and flattens linguistic and cultural diversity. We might note here that Oxford was peculiarly insular at the end of the fourteenth century, since it did not have the financial resources to support foreign students and, during the Schism and Hundred Years War, was isolated from other, more cosmopolitan university sites, such as Paris.[53] Linking Oxford and Rome is thus prescriptive rather than descriptive, in which Oxford emerges from its provincial isolation onto a global stage via the mobility of technology and translation both.

Indeed, like Gower, Chaucer's investment in diversity in the *Astrolabe* focuses on linguistic and cultural differences, which can and must come together under the condition of "trewe conclusions" and communal unity, for which "Rome" stands in. This dedication to linguistic diversity departs from other astrolabe treatises' discussions of diversity, which focus on the variety and plenitude in the spheres and earth. Take, for example, the opening justification of Rudolf of Bruges's twelfth-century astrolabe treatise:

Cum celestium sperarum diversam positionem stellarum diversos ortus diversosque occasus mundo inferiori ministrare manifestum sit huiusque varietatis descriptio ut in plano representetur sit possibile . . .

[Since it is clear that the diverse position of the celestial spheres, the diverse risings and settings of the stars, governs the lower world, and since it is possible for the description of this variation to be represented on a plane . . .][54]

[53] Kathy Kerby-Fulton, "Oxford," in *Europe: A Literary History, 1348–1418*, 2 vols., ed. David Wallace (Oxford: Oxford University Press, 2016), 1.223.
[54] Richard Lorch, "The Treatise on the Astrolabe by Rudolf of Bruges," in *Between Demonstration and Imagination: Essays in the History of Science and Philosophy Presented to John D. North*, ed. Lodi Nauta and Arjo Vanderjagt (Leiden: Brill, 1999), 60. I am grateful to Kersti Francis for her astute translation.

Rudolf uses the term "diversas" repeatedly to emphasize the range of cosmological and planetary origins, positions, and movements that can be described. In contrast, Chaucer emphasizes the diversity of the modes of description, gathering them together with the term "Rome."

Chaucer also "solves" the problem of linguistic diversity by asserting the "sufficiency" of English to express technological data, akin to any other language. In the *Astrolabe*, "sufficiency" is repeatedly summoned: Lewis's "suffisant Astrolabie" permits Lewis "suffisantly" to learn astronomy in English, itself a "sufficient" language in which to learn. The sufficiency of the vernacular here represents a bit of a sea-change from Chaucer's earlier worries about English's "litel suffisaunce," as in the Squire's conceit of immaturity (voiced as "insufficient English"). Likewise, in *The Complaint of Venus* Chaucer adopts a passive stance when performing a translator's role in order to reconcile his own textual production with his reliance on sources (75).[55] Here in the *Astrolabe*, however, he undercuts the professed passivity of being a mere "lewd compilator" with his insistence on the sufficiency of English as a technological language. In doing so, he offers a kind of *translatio scientiae* that reconceptualizes the relationship between source and translation, in which the stability of an observed, calculated conclusion mitigates the possibility of mistakes or misinterpretation on the part of the translator. Strikingly, Gower offers the same vocabulary in the "Tale of the False Bachelor": the gold ring's "sufficiency" enables the envious friend to supplant the knight's good fortune and thus put in motion the series of events that elevate Roman legal, ethical, and moral authority.

Elsewhere, sufficiency can mitigate envious feelings and thus obviate imitative treachery. In *The House of Fame*, for example, the narrator, Geffrey, argues that his own self-sufficiency obviates the gossipy envy that attends fame. "Sufficeth me, as I were ded," he says, "That no wight have my name in honde. / I wot myself best how y stonde" (*HF*, 1876–78).[56] Criseyde makes a similar argument about self-sufficiency, vowing to ignore the envious gossips who will deride her decision to flee Diomede's camp and find Troilus:

[55] See Jocelyn Wogan-Browne, Nicholas Watson, Andrew Taylor, and Ruth Evans, eds., *The Idea of the Vernacular: An Anthology of Middle English Literary Theory* (University Park: Penn State University Press, 1999), 9.

[56] Alcuin Blamires, " 'I nolde sette at al that noys a grote': Repudiating Infamy in *Troilus and Criseyde* and *The House of Fame*," in *Chaucer and Fame: Reputation and Reception*, ed. Isabel Davis and Catherine Nall (Cambridge: D. S. Brewer, 2015), 75–86.

> For whoso wol of every word take hede,
> Or reulen hym by every wightes wit,
> Ne shal he nevere thryven, out of drede;
> For that that som men blamen evere yit,
> Lo, other manere folk comenden it.
> And as for me, for al swich variaunce,
> Felicite clepe I my suffissaunce.
>
> (*TC*, V.757–63)

Not only does Criseyde claim that her own happiness is sufficient to block the nasty words of those who condemn her, she conceptualizes her self-sufficiency as the mitigating factor for diversity, or "swich variaunce." In other words, "suffissaunce" soothes both the perception of Criseyde's variable desires and the various rumors envious gossips will spew.

Likewise, the Parson tells us that sufficiency is the proper antidote to envy, and notably, he registers sufficiency in regnal and even national terms:

> Of thilke bodily marchandise that is leveful and honest is this: that, there as God hath ordeyned that a regne or a contree is suffisaunt to hymself, thanne is it honest and leveful that of habundaunce of this contree, that men helpe another contree that is moore needy. And therfore ther moote been marchantz to bryngen fro that o contree to that oother hire marchandises. That oother marchandise, that men haunten with fraude and trecherie and deceite, with lesynges and false othes, is cursed and dampnable.
>
> (*ParsT*, X.777–79)

The Parson explains envy with a series of analogies that move from exchange of goods to international or imperial magnanimity. A "regne or a contree" that is self-sufficient ought to support needier countries materially, with honest merchants transferring goods from one to the other. The kind of personal self-sufficiency elevated by Geffrey and Criseyde here functions at the regnal level, too, in which financial and material stability can be the source of support rather than envy between countries.

It also returns us to Chaucer's fatherly affection for Lewis at the beginning of his *Astrolabe* prologue. That sufficiency works as a palliative against envy constructs Lewis's "suffisant Astrolabie," that "swerd," as a defensive tool on behalf of his son and on behalf of an imagined vernacular community. The treatise thus works in multiple directions, for multiple audiences: as an instructional manual for a curious son, a justification for vernacular translation, an aspirational gesture to community built around an English sovereign. Its "lighte English" serves all of these purposes and audiences, and in doing so, it both participates in and builds on the depictions of Chaucerian children scholars are now beginning to trace. More broadly, as I hope to have shown here, the *Astrolabe* prologue operates as a kind of constellation or cosmology in its own right: a celestial assemblage of terms, tropes, illusions, and references that demand imaginative, even wondrous, observation and navigation.

Materials of Wonder: Miraculous Objects and Poetic Form in *Saint Erkenwald*

Anne Schuurman
University of Western Ontario

Abstract

This essay contends that *Saint Erkenwald*, a poem about a speaking object and the problem of signification, offers a strikingly apt contribution to new materialist discourse. It considers the miraculous objects in the poem—the corpse and the tear—as nonhuman agents rather than as vehicles of meaning; it also considers the poem itself as an object, as something finally opaque, a thing that invites contemplation but resists interpretation. This object-oriented reading illuminates the central mystery of the poem, the sacrament of baptism, at the same time as it suggests the limits of the new materialism. Object-oriented criticism tends to equate materialism with physicalism, insofar as it equates consciousness with vitality or energy, and does not restrict it to human being. The poem, however, insists on the transcendence of human consciousness, even as it enjoins us to heed the call of irreducible objects. The poet thus reminds us that to meditate on objecthood is not only to wonder at a world full of surprising transformations; it is also to meditate on all that decays and passes away—on history, but also, ultimately, on death itself.

Keywords

Middle English, miracles, objects, materialism, object-oriented ontology, poetics, baptism

AT THE CLIMAX OF THE Middle English poem *Saint Erkenwald*, a talking corpse reports the miraculous transport of his soul from limbo to heaven. There was a bright flash of light in the darkness of hell, announces the body, followed by his arrival in the celestial dining hall, where his hunger will be satisfied at last (336).[1] At this, the perfectly preserved body dissolves into a heap of black dust (344), and the

---

[1] Unless otherwise indicated, quotations from the poem are from *Saint Erkenwald*, ed. Clifford Peterson (Philadelphia: University of Pennsylvania Press, 1977).

Studies in the Age of Chaucer 39 (2017):275–296
© 2017 The New Chaucer Society

poem concludes with the joyful sound of bells ringing throughout the city in celebration (350–52). These remarkable sights and sounds form an appropriate ending to a poem rich in description of material and sensory objects, a poem that is very much concerned with the relation of material to spiritual reality, but also with the ways in which that relation is conditioned by the unfathomable depths of matter—objects that can be touched, seen, and heard, but not known.

In this essay, I suggest that the mystery of material objects in *Saint Erkenwald* offers fertile ground for object-oriented reflection. The "new" materialism in philosophy and literary studies attempts to "articulate the elusive ideas of a materiality that is itself heterogeneous, itself a differential of intensities, itself a life."[2] The term "new materialism" covers a wide and diverse area, and there are important differences among scholars who identify with speculative realism, new vitalism, object-oriented ontology (OOO), thing theory, or actor-network theory.[3] Nonetheless, this cluster of movements shares a refusal to reduce objects to their relations with subjects, concomitant with an insistence on the ethical imperative of humility and wonder before a material world of objects that are not static, but rather are always becoming, and are "withdrawn" or "hidden," inaccessible to the human knower, and resistant to epistemological categorization.[4] They also seek to challenge the modern narrative of disenchanted rational subjects with counter-narratives about objects that are surprising, wonderful, elusive, and agential.[5]

[2] Jane Bennett, *Vibrant Matter: A Political Ecology of Things* (Durham, N.C.: Duke University Press, 2010), 57. She continues, "In this strange, *vital* materialism, there is no point of pure stillness, no indivisible atom that is not itself aquiver with virtual force" (57).

[3] In his most recent work, Graham Harman, who is widely considered to be the founder of OOO, sharply distinguishes it from new materialism. He associates the latter with the political materialism of the New Left, and designates his concern with objects (not necessarily matter) as "immaterialism." See Graham Harman, *Immaterialism: Objects and Social Theory* (Cambridge: Polity Press, 2016), 13–20. Despite this insistence, OOO is widely considered to be one of the new materialisms, and as leading the critical turn, after post-structuralism, away from subjectivity, epistemology, and discourse, to objectivity, ontology, and material things. See below.

[4] The idea that objects are, in their essence, "withdrawn" from all relation is Graham Harman's: see *Guerilla Metaphysics: Phenomenology and the Carpentry of Things* (Chicago: Open Court Press, 2005), 73–124. He elaborates: "If there are objects, then they must exist in some sort of vacuum-like state, since no relation fully deploys them. . . . An object may drift into events and unleash its forces there, but no such event is capable of putting the object fully into play. Its neighbouring objects will always react to some of its features while remaining blind to the rest. The objects in an event are somehow always elsewhere, in a site divorced from all relations" (81).

[5] For a good overview of the field, see Diana Coole and Samantha Frost, *New Materialisms: Ontology, Agency, Politics* (Durham, N.C.: Duke University Press, 2010). A 2001 special volume of *Critical Inquiry*, edited by Bill Brown and titled *Things*, is often cited

Object-oriented ontology in particular insists on the autonomy of objects and rejects the reduction of objects to their relations.[6] The consequence of subject-oriented thinking is that it renders "all other entities in the world . . . *vehicles* for human contents, meanings, signs, or projections."[7] Object-oriented philosophy, by contrast, insists that "ontology precedes epistemology."[8] Rather than silencing objects by instrumentalizing them—making them vehicles for human meanings—object-oriented ontologies seek to "make [objects] talk."[9]

A text that is fundamentally about a speaking object and the problem of signification, *Saint Erkenwald* offers a strikingly apt contribution to new materialist discourse. As I will show here, an object-oriented reading of *Saint Erkenwald* illuminates the central mystery of the poem, the sacrament of baptism, by considering the miraculous objects in the poem—the corpse and the tear—as nonhuman agents rather than as vehicles, but also by considering the poem itself as an object, as something finally opaque, a thing that invites contemplation but resists interpretation. This reading emphasizes some continuities between modern and medieval materialisms, but does not attempt to elide the differences between them. Object-oriented ontologies seek to think "a *subjectless* object . . . an object-for-itself that isn't an object for the gaze of a subject, representation, or a cultural discourse."[10] The corpse, on the other

as marking a shift in the dominant mode in theory from New Historicism to new materialism. See also Bill Brown's essay, "Thing Theory," *Critical Inquiry* 28 (2008): 1–22. A series of articles in a 2012 issue of *New Literary History* marked the incursion of speculative realism and related theories into the domain of literary studies specifically: in that issue, see especially Graham Harman's "A Well-Wrought Broken Hammer: Object-Oriented Literary Criticism," *NLH* 43, no. 2 (2012): 183–203. Jeffrey Jerome Cohen offers a medievalist application of OOO in his recent book *Stone: An Ecology of the Inhuman* (Minneapolis: University of Minnesota Press, 2015).

[6] Harman has coined the terms "undermining" and "overmining" to denote such reduction. Undermining is the downward reduction of objects to their constituent parts, and overmining is their upward reduction to their properties, appearances, or effects. See Graham Harman, *The Quadruple Object* (Winchester: Zero Books, 2011), 7–19.

[7] Levi Bryant, *The Democracy of Objects* (Ann Arbor: Open Humanities Press, 2011), 22.

[8] Ibid.

[9] Bruno Latour, *Pandora's Hope: Essays on the Reality of Science Studies* (Cambridge, Mass.: Harvard University Press, 1999), 79. Bennett similarly stresses the need to listen to objects, to "give a voice to a thing-power" (*Vibrant Matter*, 2).

[10] Bryant, *Democracy of Objects*, 19. Object-oriented ontology and speculative realism have emerged as a response to Kantian finitude and what Quentin Meillassoux terms "correlationism." In Meillassoux's critique, philosophy since Kant has been stuck in an epistemological loop of subjectivity, such that it seems impossible to think of human subjecthood without defining it against the world of objects, and to think of objects without thinking of human subjects, but possible to think only of an ineradicable correlation between subjects and objects, the human and the world. This loop, in turn, has

hand, talks to us as a *soulless* object, but only because its soul has departed and continued to exist elsewhere after death. If humans are objects among objects, as new materialists argue, the poem suggests that, nonetheless, the human object alone suffers consciousness of its own finitude; the human object alone can anticipate its own death, and is also inescapably aware of the limits of its own mind. New materialisms tend to equate materialism with physicalism, insofar as they equate consciousness with vitality or energy, and do not restrict it to human being. The poem, however, insists on the transcendence of human consciousness, even as it enjoins us to heed the call of objects in all of their irreducibility. *Saint Erkenwald*'s inspirited matter thus evinces a mystical, rather than a physicalist, materialism.[11]

This mystical materialism has much to say to contemporary theories about objects, for to read *Saint Erkenwald* in the context of the miracle genre is to be reminded that the vital, objective materiality sought by Bennett, Harman, et al., and the very fact of its elusiveness, have a medieval history. As Kellie Robertson, Andrew Cole, and D. Vance Smith have pointed out, this history has been forgotten in contemporary discussions about objects and materiality, in which "ideas of matter retrospectively labeled 'modern' [displace] their medieval antecedents while nevertheless silently absorbing continuities with these earlier concepts."[12] *Saint Erkenwald* challenges such displacement and disavowal by linking materiality to temporality in ways that are both complex and

---

made the question of ontology—does a real world exist outside human consciousness?—impossible; see Quentin Meillassoux, *After Finitude: An Essay on the Necessity of Contingency*, trans. Ray Brassier (London: Continuum, 2008), esp. 5–16. In his articulation of OOO, Graham Harman affirms the impossibility of absolute knowledge—that is, he affirms Kantian finitude—but extends it "beyond the human realm to include all relations in the cosmos—including inanimate ones" (Harman, "Well-Wrought Broken Hammer," 185).

[11] Cf. Harman's recent work *Immaterialism*, in which he designates "immaterialism" as the more appropriate label for OOO, insofar as it designates an approach to a reality that "exists as a surplus even beyond the causal interactions of dust and raindrops, never fully expressed in the world of inanimate relations any more than in the human sphere" (18).

[12] Kellie Robertson, "Medieval Materialism: A Manifesto," *Exemplaria* 22, no. 2 (2010): 99–118 (101–2). Andrew Cole and D. Vance Smith are among the medievalists who have pointed out the unavowed medievalism of the "new" vitalism: in 2013, a special section in the *Minnesota Review* was dedicated to "The Medieval Turn in Theory" and featured a series of articles discussing and critiquing the key ideas of speculative realism and object-oriented ontologies. See Andrew Cole, "The Call of Things: A Critique of Object-Oriented Ontologies," *Minnesota Review* 80 (2013): 106–18; Bruce Holsinger, "Object-Oriented Mythology," *Minnesota Review* 80 (2013): 119–30; D. Vance Smith, "Death and Texts: Finitude before Form," *Minnesota Review* 80 (2013): 131–44.

explicit.[13] If the new materialisms have tended toward a kind of amnesia—as Jonathan Gil Harris puts it, "freezing not just the object in time but also the time in the object"—*Saint Erkenwald*, *qua* medieval materialism, offers a much-needed corrective, since, for the *Erkenwald*-poet, material objects are defined above all by their changeability over time.[14] The poet thus reminds us that to meditate on objecthood is not only to wonder at a world full of surprising transformations; it is also to meditate on all that decays and passes away—on history, but also, ultimately, on death itself.

I. Corpse

The newness of new materialism is sometimes conceived as a response to a world that faces unprecedented catastrophe. A sense of the uniqueness of the present moment pervades the writing of Timothy Morton, for example, who asserts that "all humans . . . are *now* aware that they have entered a *new* phase of history in which nonhumans are *no longer* excluded or merely decorative features of their social, psychic, and philosophical space. . . . This phase is characterized by a traumatic loss of coordinates, 'the end of the world.'"[15] Morton has coined the term "hyperobject" to designate those nonhuman things that have precipitated this apocalypse. Hyperobjects, such as black holes and global warming, are "massively distributed in time and space," so as to "end the possibility of transcendental leaps 'outside' physical reality."[16] A similar presentism characterizes Graham Harman's distinction between speculative

[13] Cf. Ruth Nissé, "'A Coroun Ful Riche': The Rule of History in *St. Erkenwald*," *ELH* 65, no. 2 (1998): 277–95, who sees the poem's concern with temporality as a response to Richard II's absolutist policies in the 1390s. Specifically, she argues the poem invokes historical memory as a means of critiquing the poet's political present. While my reading also sees the poem's concern with history and historiography as central, I do not find the same level of anxiety about history that Nissé does; she considers the poem "a strikingly anxious work" (277). Likewise, Jennifer Sisk, in "The Uneasy Orthodoxy of *St. Erkenwald*," *ELH* 74 (2007): 89–115, contends that the poem is "underwritten—surprisingly—by deep insecurity about the stability of the conversion it describes" (89). As I argue below, the poem's depiction of sacramental and magic-like language can be understood as part of its depiction of material objects as unfathomable and agential; as such, this language provokes much wonder but not much anxiety, at least not in the world of the poem.

[14] Jonathan Gil Harris, *Untimely Matter in the Time of Shakespeare* (Philadelphia: University of Pennsylvania Press, 2009), 16.

[15] Emphasis added. Timothy Morton, *Hyperobjects: Philosophy and Ecology after the End of the World* (Minneapolis: University of Minnesota Press, 2013), 22.

[16] Ibid., 2.

realism and the "naïve realism" of earlier centuries.[17] This new ontology, far from that espoused by "oppressive and benighted patriarchs," inscribes "a *weird* realism in which real individual objects resist all forms of causal or cognitive mastery."[18]

But just as this is not the first epoch to experience an apocalyptic, "traumatic loss of coordinates"—the Black Death comes to mind—so too is "weird realism" an apt descriptor for *Saint Erkenwald*'s depiction of material reality. The corpse is the poem's central resistant object, and it functions like a hyperobject insofar as it confounds all subjective attempts to grasp its true nature and origin and the full scope of its effects. But the corpse also confronts the subjects in the poem, and the reader of the poem, with the inevitability of historical change and the inescapability of historical recurrence.

Morton writes that the timescale of hyperobjects is characterized by "temporal undulation," a term that might also describe the temporality of the corpse. Because "we can't see to the end of them," hyperobjects are necessarily "uncanny"; they provoke an unsettling sense of "strange familiarity and familiar strangeness" in part because of our own belated awareness of them.[19] Hyperobjects "are [always] already here" and might go on being here long after humans are extinct.[20]

Coincidentally, one of the examples Morton uses to illustrate the temporal strangeness of hyperobjects is the city of London:

The appearance of things . . . is the *past* of a hyperobject. . . . The streets beneath the streets, the Roman wall, the boarded-up houses, the unexploded bombs, are records of everything that happened to London. London's history is its form. Form is memory. . . . There is no difference between causality and aesthetic experience.[21]

Insofar as it also collapses causality into aesthetic experience, the discovery of the tomb in *Saint Erkenwald* serves as a dramatic illustration of history-as-form. The descriptions of the workmen excavating the site of

[17] Harman, "Well-Wrought Broken Hammer," 196. On the other hand, Harman's most recent publication is titled *Dante's Broken Hammer* and applies OOO in a critical interpretation of *The Divine Comedy*. Perhaps this work signals a shift in Harman's approach, but the volume has come out too recently to be included in the present study (Winchester: Repeater Books, 2016).

[18] Harman, "Well-Wrought Broken Hammer," 188.

[19] Morton, *Hyperobjects*, 55.

[20] Ibid., 29.

[21] Ibid., 90–91.

Saint Paul's, the gleaming marble of the tomb and its carved symbols, and the "bryȝt" body inside it, construe the physical form of the tomb wonder as a record of England's pagan past.[22] The poem's temporal but also its physical setting are thus characterized by strange familiarity and familiar strangeness. The discovery of the tomb is uncanny because of the temporal rupture it signals: the workmen have been descending through layers of time, like archaeologists moving down through soil layers, but instead of finding fossils or decay, they find something apparently brand new that has somehow been existing in its own secret space, unknown to the bustling community above, outside of taken-for-granted reality. The tomb and the preserved body inside it are objects that cannot be defined solely in terms of their relations with subjects; they are also, like hyperobjects, both ancient and new. The body's clothes, for instance, are described as "als bryȝt of hor blee in blysnande hewes / As þai hade ȝepely in þat ȝorde bene ȝisturday shapen" (87–88).When the corpse explains that his soul has been languishing in limbo because he, though a just and righteous judge, lived long before the time of Christ and the sacrament of baptism, the implications of this temporal anomaly become chillingly clear: the body, neither alive nor entirely dead, has been inhabiting this hidden space for countless years, in freakish, solitary, suspended animation.

The narration in the opening lines telescopes the conversion history just as the tomb transgresses the bounds of time:

> At London in Englond noȝt full long sythen
> Sythen Crist suffrid on crosse and Christendome stablyd,
> Ther was a byschop in þat burgh, blessyd and sacryd;
> Saynt Erkenwolde as I hope þat holy man hatte.
>
> (1–4)

The slightly confused syntax ("sythen"/"Sythen") registers a confusion of the actual historical span—Erkenwald became the bishop of London in 675 CE—and the poet's characterization of those six centuries as

---

[22] Cynthia Turner Camp, "Spatial Memory, Historiographic Fantasy, and the Touch of the Past in *St. Erkenwald*," *NLH* 44, no. 3 (2013): 471–91, similarly links the geography of the poem with the history it depicts when she writes about "the spatial memory of the past" in *Saint Erkenwald*: "urban locales are 'lived spaces that shape collective imaginaries'"; therefore, the urban space of medieval London in the poem "becomes a contested site for creating a multidimensional civic identity from remembered and unremembered—visible and hidden—fragments of the past" (473).

"noȝt full long." From Christ and Erkenwald we move immediately to "Hengyst dawes" and Augustine of Canterbury's mission to convert the Anglo-Saxons, and finally to an ambiguous present tense, in which the adverb "Now" refers not to the poet's present but back to the past London of Erkenwald: "Now þat London is nevenyd hatte þe New Troie" (25). In this way, the process of conversion that is the subject of these lines becomes, like the tomb itself, ever ancient *and* new. The tomb and the history it embodies correspond, not to eternity, but to a timescale so great it defies precise numbering and human imagining.

This evocation of history-as-form is similarly at work in the poet's adaptation of the familiar motifs of *inventio*, motifs associated with the discovery of a saint or his remains.[23] The body of a saint or martyr is typically discovered by means of a vision or the voice of the saint, and is either miraculously incorrupt, or decayed but emitting a heavenly perfume. Once the body or remains have been moved to their final, appropriately sanctified, resting place (the *translatio*), healing miracles are thereafter reported at the site of the new shrine. By placing his version of these motifs in the context of the re-Christianization of pagan Britain, the poet depicts the discovery as a kind of public works construction project, in which the pagan temple sitting on the future site of Saint Paul's Cathedral is razed to the ground for the "new" structure to be erected in its place. The detailed, poetic descriptions of human activity here create a degree of literary realism typically lacking in the miracle genre: spiritual conversion is made possible by the labour of "merry masons" and by the sweat of diggers who proceed stone by stone, shovel by shovel (36–45).[24] This realism in an otherwise conventional miracle story functions like magic realism *avant la lettre*, precluding sharp distinctions between the natural and the supernatural, the mundane and the magical. As T. McAlindon puts it, through such realism, "the marvelous character of the story is at once thrown into relief and endowed with complete verisimilitude."[25] The poet's masterful juxtaposition of quotidian London busy-ness with stone crypt silence underscores the eerie disjunction between the ordinary limits of human perception and knowledge on the one hand, and, on the other, the hidden depths of

[23] See Monika Otter, *Inventiones: Fiction and Referentiality in Twelfth-Century English Historical Writing* (Chapel Hill: University of North Carolina Press, 1996).
[24] On the realism of *Saint Erkenwald*, see T. McAlindon, "Hagiography into Art: A Study of *St. Erkenwald*," *SP* 67 (1970): 472–94.
[25] Ibid., 480.

material reality: the body had been sitting there, enrobed and bejeweled, defying the laws of "kynde," for generation after generation, but no one knew about it (157). Since we are not in a vaguely realized world of conventional tropes but in the everyday "real" world of London, the miracles, too, seem part of the normal course of things.[26] Or, conversely, normal, sensory objects seem liable to act of their own accord: when miracles are made common, the common can be seen as miraculous.

The distinction between ordinary and miraculous matter is blurred to an even greater extent in the poet's adaptation of another familiar trope of hagiography: the miracle of incorruptibility, in which saints' remains or relics are miraculously preserved long past the time of natural decay.[27] Gaston Paris, for instance, tells a version of this miracle in which the incorrupt tongue of Emperor Trajan is discovered during an excavation in Rome.[28] When Gregory the Great commands it to speak, the tongue explains that Trajan's soul is languishing in hell even though he lived a life of exemplary virtue. Saint Gregory is filled with pity and asks God to restore the body to life long enough to receive the sacrament of baptism; God does, and the baptism administered by Saint Gregory has the effect of transporting Trajan's soul to heaven.

In this way, strange familiarity is produced through creative repetition, as the poet borrows well-known elements of plot, character, and symbol, and combines them in surprising ways.[29] Not only London's Trojan history, the motifs of *inventio* and incorruptibility, and Augustine of Canterbury's mission as told by Bede, but also the miracle stories associated with Erkenwald and collected in the *Miracula sancti Erkenwaldi* and the *Vita sancti Erkenwaldi* are here echoed with variation.[30] In these collections, Erkenwald is a hero of ecclesiastical orthodoxy; he is

---

[26] As McAlindon puts it, the miracle of the preserved corpse "acquires much of its authenticity and intensity by being set in an environment which is both concrete and invested with an air of workaday reality" (ibid., 480).

[27] See, for example, Rachel Koopmans, *Wonderful to Relate: Miracle Stories and Miracle Collecting in High Medieval England* (Philadelphia: University of Pennsylvania Press, 2011), 28–46.

[28] Gaston Paris, *La légende de Trajan*, Bibliothèque de l'École des hautes Études, Fasc. XXXV, 1878.

[29] McAlindon observes that the poem is "an intentional hybrid" composed "by a poet who was expert in the specifically narrative art of exciting expectations which are fulfilled in a wholly unexpected manner" ("Hagiography into Art," 475).

[30] Both collections have been published in *The Saint of London: The Life and Miracles of St. Erkenwald*, ed. and trans. E. Gordon Whatley (Binghamton: Medieval & Renaissance Texts & Studies, 1989).

also closely associated with the city of London and with the building of churches.[31]

The poet's method of repetition and recombination embodies the repetition characteristic of the miracle genre as a whole. Rachel Koopmans has explained the "clustering of similar stories" as the natural result of the oral creation and transmission of reports that were written down at various degrees of temporal and spatial distance from the original source.[32] Consequently, modern scholars have tended to find miracle collections "extraordinarily repetitive"; "stereotyped"; "highly conventionalized"; "schematized and topoi-ridden."[33] Miracles associated with the cult of Saint Erkenwald are a case in point. In the *Miracula sancti Erkenwaldi*, a collection composed around 1140 by a canon of Saint Paul's named Arcoid, ten out of the eighteen miracles recorded are healing miracles: a blind, crippled, deaf, or ill person invokes the saint or comes into contact with a relic or the tomb of the saint, and is healed. Five are "punitive miracles," in which the saint personally punishes a profaner of his tomb or neglecter of his feast.[34] Two are what we might call preservation miracles, in which the saint intervenes to protect his own relics or remains; and two are what we might call wish-fulfillment miracles, one in which a prisoner is set free and the other in which a schoolboy who has failed to study calls on the saint and is spared the teacher's rod. The basic narrative structure of problem–invocation–solution is repeated in all of the healing and wish-fulfillment stories (the saint need not be invoked when he is acting on his own behalf), and each of the types represented in this particular collection is represented

[31] E. Gordon Whatley, "Heathens and Saints: *St. Erkenwald* in Its Legendary Context," *Speculum* 61, no. 2 (1986): 330–63, esp. 353–59.

[32] Koopmans, *Wonderful to Relate*, 30–33. See also Koopmans's nuanced analysis of the cultural processes of miracle reporting and collecting, 34–46.

[33] Jonathan Sumption, quoted in ibid., 151; Michael Goodich, *Miracles and Wonders: The Development of the Concept of Miracle, 1150–1350* (Aldershot: Ashgate, 2007), 305; Kathleen M. Ashley and Pamela Sheingorn, *Writing Faith: Text, Sign, and History in the Miracles of Sainte Foy* (Chicago: University of Chicago Press, 1999), 24; Simon Yarrow, *Saints and Their Communities: Miracle Stories in Twelfth-Century England* (Oxford: Oxford University Press, 2005), 16. Gordon Whatley agrees, contending that the Erkenwald collections themselves consist of "mainly implausible, stereotyped, repetitive episodes largely devoid of interesting factual or contextual material"; Gordon Whatley, "*Opus Dei, Opus Mundi*: Patterns of Conflict," in *De cella in seculum: Religious and Secular Life in Late Medieval England*, ed. Michael Sargent (Cambridge: D. S. Brewer, 1989), 82. See also Barbara Abou-El-Haj, *The Medieval Cult of Saints: Formations and Transformations* (Cambridge: Cambridge University Press, 1994), 33.

[34] The punitive miracle is one of the "core scenes" identified by Abou-El-Haj in her survey of illustrated narrative cycles of saints' lives (*Medieval Cult of Saints*, 45–46).

with little variation in countless other collections, including the plethora devoted to that other famous English miracle-worker, Thomas Becket.[35] It seems, then, that miracle stories do not aim for surprise or newness, but precisely the opposite: a repetition of motifs and plots concerning material transformations. The paradox of flux through sameness that is embodied in the corpse is, at the same time, embodied in the poem as repetition with variation, and the poem, in turn, embodies a genre defined by the creation of wonder through repetition.

In *Saint Erkenwald*, the preserved body is a relic in the sense of being a vestige of a life that retains some kind of miraculous agency, but it is not the relic of a Christian saint whose efficacy can be understood as the result of some holy provenance. Thus, when the corpse begins to speak, we are told not that it has been resurrected but that it is imbued with "sum lant goste lyfe" – some kind of ghost-like life, though what kind of life that is exactly remains unclear (192). Indeed, the exact text and meaning of this line, which reads "through some lent ghost life [loaned] by Him who rules all," seems deliberately ambiguous. Peterson emends the manuscript to "þurghe sum Goste lant lyfe," capitalizing "Goste" to support his interpretation that the "ghost" here is "clearly the Holy Ghost which at Pentecost gave the gift of 'speaking in tongues' to the apostles."[36] But William Quinn argues that "the apparently deliberate mysteriousness of the 'ghost' in question should be maintained as such."[37] Miracles are inherently baffling; thus it seems likely that "the poet did intend to create such bafflement by his refusal to identify the agent *goste lyfe* as other than 'some.'"[38] Levi Bryant contends that "questions of ontology must precede questions of epistemology"; the thirteenth-century author of *De rerum principio* writes that even rocks and stones "live with an imperfect sort of life, although our dull sense does not comprehend that life."[39] The corpse, too, has a life of its very own, a kind of existence that can be neither categorized nor explained.

[35] On the cult of Becket, see, for example, the classic study by Edwin A. Abbott, *St. Thomas of Canterbury: His Death and Miracles* (London: A. and C. Black, 1898); and, more recently, Frank Barlow, *Thomas Becket* (Berkeley: University of California Press, 1986).
[36] *St. Erkenwald*, ed. Peterson, 104.
[37] William Quinn, "The Psychology of *St. Erkenwald*," *MÆ* 53 (1984): 180–93 (180).
[38] Ibid., 180.
[39] Bryant, *Democracy of Objects*, 18; *De rerum principio*, quoted in Lynn Thorndike, *A History of Magic and Experimental Science*, Vol. 2 (New York: Columbia University Press, 1964), 7.

The strangeness of the situation simultaneously demands and refuses explanation: we find out that the corpse was a pagan judge in life, centuries ago, but what is the nature of the thing that speaks at the behest of the bishop? If the corpse's soul is in purgatory, how are its earthly remains able to recount the soul's memories and deeds to the citizens of London? Such questions are never answered in the poem, but they are figured in the clerks and their fruitless searching in library and archives for answers to the mystery of the corpse's identity. The dean of the cathedral voices their bafflement when he complains

> . . . we have oure librarie laitid þes long seven dayes,
> Bot one cronicle of þis kyng con we never fynde.
> He has non layne here so long, to loke hit by kynde,
> To malte so out of memorie bot mervayle it were.
>
> (155–58)

The mystery of the corpse is here a failure of historiography (we cannot find a chronicle that mentions this king) and a failure of memory (we have forgotten someone who seems to have been alive only moments ago). When Erkenwald addresses the corpse and asks it to explain the mystery, therefore, the miracle of the corpse's reply is a particularly literal instantiation of the idea of history-as-form. The object speaks to the baffled subjects, and what it utters is an account and a reminder of their cultural and religious past. For the poet's immediate audience, this is a historical account that would resonate with familiar strangeness, for the corpse lived during the time of Geoffrey of Monmouth's New Troy, when "bold Britons" such as Belinus and Brennius ruled (208–16), when the law of the land was both the same (noble dukes and sceptered kings) and different ("þe lagh þat þen þis londe usit" [200]). This reference to popular legendary history reminds the corpse's and the poem's audience of the pagan otherness of their past and, simultaneously, of their current common knowledge. The corpse-as-hyperobject paradoxically embodies historical change, even as it has miraculously stayed the same.

II. Tear

After hearing the dead pagan's story of righteousness in life and suffering in hell, Erkenwald is moved to tears, and conveys his sympathy by saying out loud the baptismal formula he wishes he could perform, but thinks he cannot, while one of his tears happens to fall on the corpse's face at the very moment he is speaking:

> "Our Lord lene," quod þat lede, "þat þou lyfe hades,
> By Goddes leve, as long as I myȝt lacche water,
> And cast upon þi faire cors and carpe þes wordes,
> 'I folwe þe in þe Fader nome and his fre Childes
> And of þe gracious Holy Goste,' and not one grue lenger."
>
> (315–19)

Despite the conditional mode of the utterance, which means that the bishop cannot be said to intend to perform the sacrament in this moment, the baptism works and the soul is instantly transported to heaven.

This inadvertent baptism, like the miracle of incorruptibility, recalls earlier accounts of Saint Gregory's intercession on behalf of Emperor Trajan's soul in which the saint's prayers lead to the emperor's posthumous salvation.[40] This hagiographical context has led many critics to see the theological problem of the salvation of a just pagan as the poem's central concern. But critical opinion has been split between two opposing interpretations of the nature of this concern: some have seen the miraculous baptism as evidence of the poet's semi-Pelagianism while others have seen it as evidence of his conservative orthodoxy.[41] The problem is that, while the poem insists on the necessity of baptism for salvation, it also divorces the intent behind Erkenwald's words from their

---

[40] For examples of these accounts, see Cindy L. Vitto, *The Virtuous Pagan in Middle English Literature* (Philadelphia: American Philosophical Society, 1989); and Gordon Whatley, "Heathens and Saints: *St. Erkenwald* in Its Legendary Context," *Speculum* 61, no. 2 (1986): 330–63; Frank Grady, *Representing Righteous Heathens in Late Medieval England*, The New Middle Ages Series (New York: Palgrave Macmillan, 2005).

[41] Ruth Morse, in her introduction to *St. Erkenwald* (Cambridge: D. S. Brewer, 1975) makes a case for the poem's "Pelagianism" (19–31); McAlindon implies a similar position when he writes that, in the world of the poem, God's justice would be "found wanting" if he were not to save the righteous judge on grounds of merit (McAlindon, "Hagiography into Art," 28–29). Gordon Whatley, however, argues that the judge's righteousness only makes the case for orthodoxy stronger, for the "poet reveals that even such a flawless exponent of rational justice and civic probity cannot be saved outside the sacramental church" ("Heathens and Saints," 360). Likewise, William Kamowski, in "*St. Erkenwald* and the Inadvertent Baptism: An Orthodox Response to Heterodox Ecclesiology," *Religion and Literature* 27, no. 3 (1995): 5–27; and Christine Chism, in *Alliterative Revivals* (Philadelphia: University of Pennsylvania Press, 2002), 41–65, argue that the poem is not only firmly orthodox but specifically anti-Wycliffite. Most

effect. The lack of intent to baptize renders the bishop's role in the sacrament incidental rather than essential. The poet's depiction of the workings of baptism thus conflicts with most orthodox and Scholastic accounts of how baptism works, even as it affirms the orthodox view, perhaps against the Lollards, that the sacrament is indeed necessary for salvation.

Caroline Walker Bynum has traced the increasingly prominent role of "holy matter" in religious practice from 1100 to 1500; in this period, she argues, not only the Eucharistic wafer and other sacramental materials but also devotional images and relics increasingly "speak or act their physicality in particularly intense ways that call attention to their per se 'stuffness' or 'thingness.'"[42] By contrast, medieval theologians taught that sacred objects were merely signs and symbols. Peter Lombard and Thomas Aquinas, for example, do not even include the corporeal element in their definition of a sacrament (although Lombard considers the sacraments "visible forms of invisible grace"), and they emphasize the signifying and institutional purpose of the ritual and the inner orientations of all participants, insisting on the faith of the catechumen and on the intention of the priest to baptize as conditions for efficacy.[43] But the experience of many medieval people seems to have contradicted these teachings: "Formulae for blessing objects such as water and bread suggest that power lies *in* them. People behaved as if relics were the saints. The Eucharist itself *was* Christ."[44] Indeed, although preachers decried the abuse of Eucharistic elements, laypeople frequently took away consecrated wafers by keeping them under their tongues so they could use

---

recently, David Coley, in "Baptism as Eucharist: Orthodoxy, Wycliffism, and the Sacramental Utterance in *St. Erkenwald*," *JEGP* 107, no. 3 (2008): 327–47, demonstrates the poem's orthodoxy once again by showing that its representation of sacramental speech affirms a "forceful" repudiation of Wycliffism in the cause of orthodoxy (330).

[42] Caroline Walker Bynum, *Christian Materiality: An Essay on Religion in Late Medieval England* (Cambridge, Mass.: MIT Press, 2011), 28–29. Bynum continues: "[Medieval cult objects] were not like life; they (at least sometimes) lived. And they were not more apt to come alive or animate—bleed, weep, move, glow with life—the more they approached resemblance to human beings. Pieces of wood or bone, bread, wine, bits of wall or paint animated. It seems that their life or agency lay not in their naturalism or similitude but in their materiality" (282).

[43] Peter Lombard, *Sententiae in IV libris distinctae*, 2 vols. (Grottaferrata: Collegii S. Bonaventurae ad Claras Aquas, 1981), IV.i.2. Thomas Aquinas, *Summa theologiae*, ed. David Bourke (London: Blackfriars and Eyre and Spottiswoode, 1975), 3a q. 60, art. 1. See also Marilyn McCord Adams, *Some Later Medieval Theories of the Eucharist: Thomas Aquinas, Giles of Rome, Duns Scotus, and William Ockham* (Oxford: Oxford University Press, 2010), esp. 33–34, 57–60, 279–80.

[44] Bynum, *Christian Materiality*, 34.

them later to heal diseases or help the fertility of their livestock.[45] Such acts express belief in the power and agency of the material object itself, even when it is taken out of its sacramental context and evacuated of divine intentionality.

Like Lombard's and Aquinas's discussions of the sacraments, Augustine's writings on signs and signification explicitly reject the "thingness of objects" and insist instead on a hermeneutical imperative: all objects must be read as signs. Augustine's theory also inaugurates the widespread medieval association between materialism and spiritual death, in which the elevation of the material sign over its spiritual meaning is a confusion of created objects with the divine subject who created them. Augustine mistrusted both the affective nature of wonder and the sensory means by which miracle stories induce it, for fear the sign might be confused with the spiritual reality it signified. Writing around 390, he argues that an established Church has no need of miracles, and that God ceased to perform them, "lest the soul should always seek visible things and lest the human race should become indifferent [to them] through the customary occurrence [of events] whose novelty had once set them aglow."[46] As Giselle de Nie comments, "Refusing to allow the affective surprise of a miracle to paralyse or deform cognitive activity, Augustine, then, regarded miracles, like Scripture, as divine words or texts to be 'read.'"[47] All miraculous phenomena, indeed all sensory objects, were to be *seen through*, insofar as they were to be read as signs in the book of creation.

In this way, Augustine's hermeneutical imperative prefigures the reduction of objects that Graham Harman calls "overmining," insofar as Augustine reduces miraculous events to their effects as symbols.[48]

---

[45] Ibid., 139.

[46] Quoted in and translated by Giselle de Nie, *Poetics of Wonder: Testimonies of the New Christian Miracles in the Late Antique World* (Turnhout: Brepols, 2011), 226. Original text: Saint Augustine of Hippo, *De vera religione*, XXV.47, lines 25–31, CCSL 32, 216–17.

[47] De Nie, *Poetics of Wonder*, 365.

[48] Augustine's reluctance cuts two ways. By definition, miracles cannot happen with the regularity attested by the frequency of popular reports; but miracles do happen all the time, because the whole of the natural world is miraculous, in the sense that all being comes from the unknowable divine, but we do not recognize it as such because we are accustomed to it. Writing later in his career, Augustine modified his position somewhat, allowing that God also created miracles that surprise by *appearing* to contradict nature, specifically to counteract the danger of familiarity that kills wonder, thus defying human categories of thought and expectation—including theological categories. These "seminal causes" are made manifest in history in the form of miracles, which serve as reminders that the natural world is permeated by the divine (*De Trinitate*, III.7). For

Following an Augustinian logic, Wyclif and his followers reject sacramental materialism as idolatry. While Wyclif focuses most of his polemical attention on the sacraments of the Eucharist and penance, he does doubt the efficacy of baptism to remove the taint of original sin; he also censures clerics who baptize instead of preach—clerics who perform rites rather than educate the laity.[49] Above all, Wyclif insists that the "miracle of the Eucharist conform to the demands of the sense and reason. If the consecrated host looks like bread, it really must be bread."[50] Wyclif's rationalism extended, unsurprisingly, to the question of miracles in general, and was joined in his Latin and English writings to his attacks on clerical greed and hypocrisy. In *De potestate pape*, he targets ecclesiastical claims to miracle-producing sanctity in particular. But he also precludes the metaphysical possibility of post-apostolic miracles:

As for miracles, it is evident that they have ceased today in our bishops, since it is sufficient, in an age after faith in the gospel has been published, to strengthen the impression of that faith through pious encouragements. Therefore, since God does not give anything superfluously, it follows that God does not grant our prefects, as He once did the disciples, the power to work miracles, and consequently they do not have that power.[51]

While Augustine warned against confusing the allegory for its meaning, therefore, the Lollards, following Wyclif, warned against confusing the holy object for the divine agency it channeled. Indeed, the eighth conclusion of the Lollards mocks, not the abuse of relics for monetary

---

Augustine, the main purpose of recording and telling saints' lives and miracle stories is to issue such reminders, to evoke an appropriate sense of the majesty and mystery of creation. See also Thomas Heffernan, *Sacred Biography: Saints and Their Biographers in the Middle Ages* (New York: Oxford University Press, 1988), 94–95.

[49] See John Wyclif, *De ecclesia*, ed. Johann Loserth (London: Trübner, 1886), 467–68; and "Speculum de Antichristo," in *The English Works of John Wyclif*, ed. F. D. Matthew, EETS o.s. 74 (London: Kegan Paul, Trench, Trübner, 1902), 112. See also Anne Hudson, *The Premature Reformation* (Oxford: Clarendon Press, 1988), 290–92; and Coley's discussion in "Baptism as Eucharist," 330.

[50] Dallas G. Denery, "From Sacred Mystery to Divine Deception: Robert Holkot, John Wyclif and the Transformation of Fourteenth-Century Eucharistic Discourse," *Journal of Religious History* 29, no. 2 (2005): 129–44 (134).

[51] John Wyclif, *Tractatus de potestate pape*, ed. Johan Loserth (London: Trübner for The Wyclif Society, 1907). Wyclif writes, "Quantum ad miracula, patet quod cessant hodie in nostris episcopis, cum satis est post fidem in evangelio divulgatam ipsam impressam sanctis exhortacionibus confirmare. Cum igitur Deus non dat quicquam superflue, sequitur quod Deus non dat nostris prepositis, ut olim dedit discipulis, potestatem faciendi miracula, et per consequens nunc non habent" (106).

gain, but the very idea of causality implied in the veneration of material objects as such:

Þe correlari is þat þe seruise of þe rode, don twyes euery ӡer in oure chirche, is fulfullid of ydolatrie, for if þe rode tre, naylis, and þe spere and þe coroune of God shulde ben so holiche worchipd, þanne were Iudas lippis, qwoso mythte hem gete, a wondir gret relyk. But we preye þe, pilgrym, us to telle qwan þu offrist to seyntis bonis enschrinid in ony place, qweþur releuis þu þe seynt þat is in blisse, or þe pore almes hous þat is so wel enduwid?[52]

In other words, by insisting that wood, water, bread, and wine are not agents but signs, the Lollards reject an object-oriented ontology and follow Augustine's subject-oriented hermeneutics.

In these theological and ecclesiastical contexts, the accidental baptism in *Saint Erkenwald* serves as a testament to the power of material objects (tears, bodies) to act on each other, regardless of institutional setting and human intention. The poet's representation of the sacrament seems deliberately to court the Lollard accusation of idolatry: the baptism functions more like a "chemical reaction" than a divinely authored trans-formation.[53] In this way, *Saint Erkenwald* is a materialist rejoinder to the Augustinian imperative to treat miraculous objects strictly as vehicles of meaning. In this, the poet shares some ground with the mystical theolo-gies of Bernard of Clairvaux and Hugh of Saint Victor. Hugh, for instance, writes that the sacraments are effective not only because they are signs of grace, but because they are the material means by which that grace is conferred. In Hugh's definition, "a sacrament is a corporeal or material element set before the senses without, representing by simili-tude and signifying from institution and containing by sanctification

---

[52] *Twelve Conclusions of the Lollards*, in *Selections from English Wycliffite Writings*, ed. Anne Hudson (1978; Toronto: University of Toronto Press and Medieval Academy of America, 1997), 27. The logic of the Lollards' position, however, far from marking them as heterodox, puts them squarely in line not only with Augustine's reluctance to endorse reports of miracles but also with Thomas Aquinas's definition of relics. Aquinas had argued that the veneration of relics is not the same as *latria*, or divine worship, but is a form of *adoratio*. He describes the relics as means to the end of adoring the saints, but is careful to distinguish the material object from the spiritual agency of God: "God fittingly does honour to such relics by performing miracles in their presence [*in earum praesentia*]" but the relics themselves do not possess such power (Aquinas, *Summa theolog-iae*, 3a q. 25, art. 6).

[53] I borrow this phrase from J. A. Burrow and Thorlac Turville-Petre's introduction to the poem in *A Book of Middle English*, 3rd ed. (Malden: Blackwell, 2005), 222.

some invisible and spiritual grace."[54] Accordingly, Hugh places special weight on the material elements and does not require human intentionality. In baptism, there is something essential about water that makes this kind of material, and no other, necessary for the washing away of original sin; as he writes, water alone "has perfect cleanness. All other liquids indeed are purified by water. . . . Therefore in water alone is the sacrament of cleanness established."[55] According to Hugh, sacramental matter must contain spiritual grace because of the total physical and spiritual corruption of fallen man: "And so sacraments had to be sanctified in things that the matter of man might be sanctified, as works in deeds, as words in speech; in that way the whole indeed may be holy, both what is man and what is of man."[56] Likewise, in the poem, objects, including the materials of the sacraments, are signs that mean *and* things that act, just as a poem written in ink on parchment is an artifact that both means and does things in the world.

III. Poem

The baptism is also prefigured in the "roynysche" letters carved into the tomb and the other "Saynt Austyn's" incantatory renaming of the temples, and both seem deliberately to challenge the Lollards' contempt for popular belief in an enchanted causality:

> He hurlyd owt hor ydols and hade hym in sayntes,
> And chaungit chevely hor noms and chargit him better;
> That ere was Appolyn is now of Seynt Petre,
> Mahoun to Saynt Margrete oþir to Maudelayne,
> Þe Synagoge of þe Sonne was sett to oure Lady,
> Jubiter and Jono to Jesu oþir to James.

> (17–22)

---

[54] Hugh of Saint Victor, *On the Sacraments of the Christian Faith*, trans. Roy J. Deferrari (Cambridge, Mass.: The Medieval Academy of America, 1951), 155.

[55] Ibid., 301.

[56] Ibid., 164. Hugh also differs from later Scholastics in the inclusiveness of his definition, which makes room for "myriads of rites and ceremonies"; Bryan D. Spinks, *Early and Medieval Rituals and Theologies of Baptism: From the New Testament to the Council of Trent* (Aldershot: Ashgate, 2006), 140. Hugh specifies only baptism and the Eucharist as sacraments necessary for salvation, but includes "others which, although they are not necessary for salvation, since without them salvation can be possessed, are yet of benefit to sanctification . . . for example the water of aspersion and the reception of ashes and others like these" (164). Notably absent from the "necessary" sacraments is penance, which is also, arguably, precluded by Hugh's insistence on the corporeal element.

The carved lettering is clearly visible ("full verray" [53]) just as the verbal formula with which Augustine performs the rededication is efficacious, but the meaning of the words is obscure or arcane in both cases; both are instances of language that *performs* rather than *means*. Indeed, in the renaming scene, we are not even told what the words are (the dedication of a church?), simply that they have the power to change "chevely hor noms." The runes perform the tomb's exotic antiquity, instilling awe and wonder in all who see them, and as such they resist the Augustinian injunction to interpret the materials of wonder. The poet dramatizes this resistance: "Bot all muset hit to mouth and quat hit mene shuld; / Mony clerke in þat clos with crownes ful brode / Þer besiet hom aboute noȝt bryng hom in wordes" (54–56).

The spell-like baptism and the runish language are also embodied in the form of the poem itself. The poem's structure mirrors its content in that it, too, is "roynysche": it tells a story but it is also an objet d'art, a text that *is* what is *says*, a kind of pattern poem. Though the precise numerical organization of the poem is typically lost in modern editions, the Harley 2250 scribe clearly marks the poem's external structure of an introduction of eight alliterative quatrains followed by eighty stanzas. The main plot of the poem unfolds over eight days, with clerks scouring history books "þes longe seven dayes" (155), and the exact center of the poem (176) falling on the dawn of the eighth day when Erkenwald discovers the body's identity and baptizes it. Human activity, busy-ness, and movement dominate the first half of the narrative, from the rapid-fire renamings of the opening lines (15–24), to the offstage travels of the saint (107–8), to the studious but fruitless labors undertaken in library and archive (155–58). As Russell Peck observes, the poem's "symmetrical structure, then, is not 32 + 144 + 176 lines as modern editions suggest, but rather 8 stanzas (32 lines) + 144 lines, then 144 lines + 8 stanzas (32 lines)." In medieval numerology, eight symbolizes baptism and related themes of newness, rebirth, Pentecost, and Resurrection. It also symbolizes a return to oneness after diversity and multiplicity—the union with God constituted by salvation.[57]

This numerical mid-point of the narrative is marked in the manuscript by a space and a red capital letter at the beginning of line 176.[58]

[57] See Russell Peck, "Number Structure in *St. Erkenwald*," *Annuale mediaevale* 14 (1973): 11–12. See also Augustine's discussion of the seven ages of man, after which the eighth "age" constitutes the return to eternity and the transcendence of time (*De Trinitate*, IV.iv.7).

[58] London, British Library, MS Harley 2250, fols. 72v–75v.

These textual features signal the shift in the narrative from the above-ground concerns of the first half to the crypt-centered action of the second half. Narrative time slows when the body is discovered and urban busy-ness comes to a sudden stop as London citizens, both lay and religious, "of all kynnes so kenely mony," rush to the cathedral to see the marvel (63). We are given an image of the entire population of London crowded into the hidden crypt, and the poet remarks that it was as if "alle þe worlde were þider walon wythin a honde-quile" (64). As the varied citizens gaze upon the brilliance of body, crown, and scepter, we gaze upon the spectacle conjured by alliterating description. Insofar as it distills complexity ("of all kynnes so kenely mony") into an aesthetic and miraculous singularity ("þe mysterie is meruaile þat men opon wondres"), this is an image of the poem itself, possibly of all poems—an image "of a confined space overflowing with life and significance."[59]

Because the poem has a perfectly bifurcated structure that is mirrored in both its content and its alliterative lines, marked by caesurae, its structure hinges open on every level, ostensibly to reveal the answers not found by the clerks with their learning. This opening is figured in the action of the poem both in the diggers' opening of the earth with their "eggit toles" (40) and in the prying open of the coffin by the "wyȝt werke-men" (69). But the self-referential relation of form and content means that the discursive, doctrinal answers offered by the poem are unstable, at best. The mystery that the clerks sought to fathom was the mystery of the body's identity, and this is solved only in part. The precise historical and chronological details of the judge's life the poet leaves unclear ("þe lengthe of my lyinge here, þat is a lewid date, / Hit is to meche to any mon to make of a nommbre" [205–6]). Christ's neglect to save the pagan's soul during the Harrowing of Hell is left dramatically unexplained, as is the fact that the pagan's body is preserved in a miracle of incorruptibility even though he is neither saint nor martyr.[60] The

[59] McAlindon, "Hagiography into Art," 481.

[60] Although scriptural evidence for the Harrowing is apocryphal and ambiguous, and has therefore generated much debate, many orthodox medieval theologians held that Christ rescued the Old Testament patriarchs, unbaptized infants, and exemplary pagans. Aquinas writes, "it cannot be concluded that all who were in Purgatory were delivered from it, but that such a benefit was bestowed upon some persons, that is to say, upon such as were already cleansed sufficiently, or who in life, by their faith and devotion towards Christ's death, so merited, that when He descended, they were delivered from the temporal punishment of Purgatory" (*Summa*, 3a, q. 52, art. 8).

pagan's story cannot be interpreted as a model for imitation, as its report of its soul's salvation is, as Frank Grady explains, "exceptional."[61] In truth, the poem merely answers mystery with mystery, as one unfathomable object leads to another. Where the hermeneutics of allegory and reformist theology alike would hope to find spiritual truth housed in, but distinct from, its earthly, material shroud, the poem reveals only its own aesthetic, material being—the self-referential relation of form and content imagined as a beautiful, dead body inside a perfect stone tomb.

Read through the lenses of OOO, the accidental baptism is not a theological problem to be explained away but a mystery to be contemplated, and the kind of contemplation demanded by the baptism is analogous to the wonder of the tomb and the form of the poem itself. But these wonders of material sacrament and of aesthetic form are fearful wonders, for together they change the corpse from a state of vocal animation to a silent pile of dust. Hope for eternal life is offered in the corpse's report of the soul's offstage transport, but the concrete image with which we are left is an image of death and its remains: the citizens of London "now" clustered together, startled and blinking at the black "mold."

The poem's conclusion, then, points to the ultimate end of mystical contemplation, when "We shall perceive with our mind, and in a manner of speaking we shall perceive with our bodies too; for, when our bodily senses are themselves converted into reason, and reason into understanding, then understanding will pass over into God, to whom we shall be united."[62] The end for which the mystic longs and practices is death, and it is a death imagined specifically as the death of signification, the dissolution of the division between body and mind, matter and spirit, *res* and *ratio*—between object and subject. The confusion of sign and signified that Augustine warns against is, paradoxically, also anticipated ecstatically as union with the divine. To read *Saint Erkenwald* is therefore to look at the "menskefully" carved tomb, to gaze upon an icon that pulls its viewer into perceptual union in order to point beyond itself, to prepare the viewer for mystical union in death.

In its patterned, numerical structure, the poem is an object as the relic is an object, an opaque thing that can be read but whose meaning

---

[61] Frank Grady, "*Piers Plowman*, *St. Erkenwald*, and the Rule of Exceptional Salvations," *YLS* 6 (1992): 61–88.

[62] Hugh of Saint Victor, "De arche Noe," in *Selected Spiritual Writings*, ed. Aelred Spire (New York: Harper & Row, 1962), 67.

can never be exhausted. It is also a thing that performs, in its theme and structure of repetition and reiteration, a kind of ritual of sacramental transformation. In this, the poem anticipates Graham Harman's image of a "universe made up of objects wrapped in objects wrapped in objects."[63] Insofar as the poem's form is figured in the form of the corpse, *Saint Erkenwald* reminds us that death is also an object that can be seen and heard—it can be concretized in symbol and allegory—but not known, for to know death is to be dead. In the poem, this knowledge that we cannot know is an absence marked by linguistic sign and poetic form, a paradox that is dramatized in the material sight and sound of the corpse, whose being *is* death.

[63] Harman, *Guerilla Metaphysics*, 76.

REVIEWS

Jenny Adams and Nancy Mason Bradbury, eds. *Medieval Women and Their Objects*. Ann Arbor: University of Michigan Press, 2017. Pp. x, 294. $70.00.

Material Women and Their Objects, edited by Jenny Adams and Nancy Mason Bradbury, is a rich volume of essays dedicated to Carolyn P. Collette, who has contributed enormously to medieval literary scholarship. The essays in this collection investigate the complicated relationships between gender and materiality in the culture of later medieval England and France. The contributions are varied and multifaceted, using the tools of literary, historical, art-historical, and legal scholarship. While some of the authors reexamine the objectification of historical or fictional women, others consider how medieval women used objects to negotiate or even to subvert gender roles. Still others view the idea of the "object" more loosely, focusing on intangibles such as words or songs, or on women's objects of desire.

The collection is divided into three equally compelling sections. Part 1, entitled "Objects and Gender in a Material World," focuses on fictional women who use material objects to challenge gender roles and the structure of patriarchal power. The essays in Part 2, "Buildings, Books, and Women's (Self-) Fashioning," examine objects possessed by historical figures, using them as sources for insight into the women who owned them. Part 3, "Bodies, Objects, and Objects in the Shape of Bodies," inquires into complicated relationships between women's bodies and material objects, in which the border between the categories of agent and object often overlap or blur.

Part 1: "Objects and Gender in a Material World"

Each of the three essays in Part 1 focuses on one of the *Canterbury Tales*, providing fresh perspectives into these well-read texts. In "The 'Thyng Wommen Loven Moost': The Wife of Bath's Fabliau Answer," Susanna Fein rereads Alisoun's Arthurian romance as a fabliau. Using two lesser-known French tales as models of romance–fabliau hybrids, Fein cogently argues that the Wife uses fabliau elements to subvert the message of her tale; the real object of desire, the "thing wommen loven moost," is, in fact, not sovereignty but the male phallus.

Nancy Mason Bradbury's essay, "Zenobia's Objects," argues that in *The Monk's Tale*, the conquered queen's exchange of objects—her warrior's helmet for *vitremyte*—represents more than a misogynistic punishment for female transgression. Although scholars have traditionally viewed Cenobia's new headgear as humiliating, Bradbury instead sees this new object more neutrally as a "soft, feminine headdress." She argues that while Cenobia has indeed fallen victim to Fortune, the occupation with which she lives out her days demonstrates not her abject humiliation but rather her engagement in the laudable industry of a virtuous woman.

In "The Object of Miraculous Song in 'The Prioress's Tale,'" Howell Chickering analyzes the narrative's three central objects: the corpse of the "litel clergeon"; his song, the "Alma redemptoris mater"; and the grain the Virgin places under the boy's tongue. In doing so, he reexamines the tale's traditional dual critical status as both a satire on the character of the Prioress's worldliness and an expression of her devotion to the Virgin, and offers a new reading of the "greyn" as analogous to Chaucer's use of the Prioress as agent of the tale.

Part 2: "Buildings, Books, and Women's (Self-) Fashioning"

In contrast to the first section, Part 2 focuses on historical women and investigates the relationship between these women's identities and objects they possessed or created. Michael T. Davis, in "A Gift from the Queen: The Architecture of the Collège de Navarre in Paris," looks into Jeanne de Navarre's influence in establishing the first academic campus in Europe, the "Maison des Escholiers," in which she sought to combine moral and scholastic instruction. Through an examination of contemporary writings and later, nineteenth-century plans for reconstruction, Davis attempts to piece together the original architectural plan for the school. He concludes that in conceiving of this architectural "object," the French queen outlined a deliberate geometrical scheme for the school, a logical structure for a space dedicated to study, and sheltered from the city and the outside world. Lynn Staley's piece, "Anne of Bohemia and the Objects of Ricardian Kingship," looks to contemporary poets—Richard Maidstone, Geoffrey Chaucer, and John Clanvowe—as alternative sources for learning about Anne of Bohemia. Contemporary chroniclers provide us with a dark and shady picture of the queen, in which she is used primarily as a sign for Richard II's failings. However, representations in the chronicles conflict with poets' depictions of Anne of Bohemia. Staley argues that reading poetic descriptions of Richard's queen reveals a more nuanced picture of Anne as a person in her own right: this method offers insight into the queen's role as mediator between the English public and the king, as well as one of Richard's ethical advisers. Her essay raises some salient issues about the role of literary production in shaping as well as representing history.

The next essay of Part 2, "Royal Biography as Reliquary: Christine de Pizan's *Livre des fais et bonnes meurs du sage roy Charles V*" by Nadia Margolis, investigates Christine's approach to royal biography. Margolis argues that Christine used a variety of sources—chronicles, ethical manuals, and guides as well as myths and legends—to produce a work that not only memorializes Charles himself but also presents his virtuousness as inevitable, fore-ordained by ancient history and foretelling the future greatness of France. Jill C. Havens's essay, "A Gift, a Mirror, a Memorial: The Psalter-Hours of Mary de Bohun," examines an elegant and richly illustrated book of hours dating from the end of the fourteenth century. Havens argues that the manuscript, most likely commissioned by Joan Fitzalan as a gift to her daughter Mary, came to embody the relationship between mother and daughter, carrying a separate meaning for each woman. Jocelyn Wogan-Browne's contribution, " 'Parchment and Pure Flesh': Elizabeth de Vere, Countess of the Twelfth Earl of Oxford, and Her Book," calls attention to the understudied francophone spirituality of fifteenth-century East Anglia. The "chaste matron" Elizabeth de Vere's manuscript, which was donated to Barking Abbey in 1474, forms a "portable spiritual library" of French religious treatises. The varied collection of devotional materials attests to the multilingual nature of East Anglian devotion and reflects seemingly contradictory values of aristocratic *courtoisie* and religious abjection embraced in fifteenth-century devotional culture.

Part 3: "Bodies, Objects, and Objects in the Shape of Bodies"

The essays in Part 3 move to the realm of blurred boundaries and indistinct categories; in these studies, material objects sometimes merge with women's bodies and selves; here, the lack of defined borders can render women vulnerable to objectification but can also, in some cases, challenge male efforts to define and contain women's roles and identities. In "Objects of the Law: The Cases of Dorigen and Virginia," Eleanor Johnson investigates the issue of a woman's access to legal agency. Johnson focuses on *The Franklin's Tale* and *The Physician's Tale*, placing them in opposition to that of the Man of Law, whose protagonist, Custance, shifts from a powerless victim of earthly law to an agent of God's justice. Johnson contends that both the Franklin and the Physician represent the law as dangerous, particularly to women, since legal contracts have the potential to transform agents of the law into objects, subject to sexual exchange. Robert R. Edwards, in "Galatea's Pulse: Objects, Ethics, and Jean de Meun's Conclusion," argues that de Meun's conclusion to the *Roman de la rose* traces a movement from the long-lasting, repetitive nature of romantic, erotic desire to the material, carnal craving for sexual fulfillment. The Lover, in undergoing this transformation from idealized desire to carnal appetite, misses the moral message and fails to understand that material objects have meaning not in themselves but rather in what they signify.

Jenny Adams's essay, "Transgender and the Chess Queen in Chaucer's *Book of the Duchess*," moves to a different challenge to classification—gender crossing—to argue that Chaucer uses the game of chess to represent permeability between masculine and feminine, animate and inanimate, life and death. In reconsidering the much-studied chess metaphor as a moment of transgendering, of transgressing seemingly fixed boundaries, Adams both provides insight into Chaucer's preoccupation with gender crossing and creates new possibilities for reading other chess scenes in medieval literature. The final essay in the volume, "Statues, Bodies, and Souls: St. Cecilia and Some Medieval Attitudes toward Ancient Rome," was inspired by Collette's earlier study in which she notes the stark contrast the *The Second Nun's Tale* makes between the material and the spiritual. C. David Benson contrasts Cecilia's desire to depart the world of Rome for the realm of the spiritual, and the tale's lack of interest in Cecilia's physical remains, with the *Stacions of Rome*, in which the remains of Saint Cecilia's body represent not the materiality of the world but rather the hope of spiritual renewal.

Medieval Women and Their Objects, in its multifaceted, pluralistic approach to gender and to the relationship between women's bodies and material objects, underlines the importance of late medieval material culture and contributes much to its study.

MAIJA BIRENBAUM
University of Wisconsin—Whitewater

AMY APPLEFORD. *Learning to Die in London, 1380–1540*. Philadelphia: University of Pennsylvania Press, 2015. Pp. ix, 320. $65.00.

This assessment of a group of texts that surprisingly have received relatively little scholastic attention is a valuable contribution to the growing interest in the long fifteenth century. Interdisciplinary studies are especially important because literature scholars are generally particularly adept at "reading" texts, while the development of ideas surrounding reception, in addition to authorship, has done considerable service to our understanding of late medieval and early modern culture. One of the consequences of such approaches has been the realization of the significance of regional and local differences, but also paradoxically the importance of networks that crossed and recrossed these boundaries, spreading shared ideas in a wide variety of ways.

For many scholars London is seen as the hub, or at the very least a part of such networks, which means Amy Appleford's analysis of several *ars moriendi* texts in the context of fifteenth-century London is sensible, particularly because she can demonstrate their circulation among the city's elite. Moreover, as she rightly says (4), her study builds on the excellent work of London historians, especially Caroline Barron, thereby contributing to our greater understanding of England's only urban society comparable to the great cities on the European mainland. By bringing together her texts and their London context, Appleford is able to explore communal and individual attitudes toward dying that highlight continuity as much as change over time. This more nuanced perspective, which rejects Huizinga's ideas of the period's morbidity, could be extended fruitfully in the future using as a model the textual 'Geographies of Orthodoxy' project (Queen's University Belfast) to examine issues of networking, regionalism, and cultural specificity.

As Appleford notes in her introduction, her first three chapters consider several Middle English texts, at times focusing on specific versions that she believes indicate contemporary attitudes toward governance of the self, household, and city (6). At the heart of Chapter 1 is her comparison between the A version and slightly later E version of *The Visitation of the Sick*, which she sees as indicative of the change toward a more active role for the laity gathered around the deathbed. She develops her hypothesis by first examining the history and form of the liturgical *Ordo ad visitandum infirmum*. This and similar texts almost invariably accompany *Visitation* A in the extant clerically owned manuscripts. In contrast, the longer *Visitation* E includes passages she considers could have been employed "as a practical script [by laymen] for a deathbed performance" (39), but was equally appropriate for readers who, by working through the text, could prepare themselves for death at some point in the future. As well as demonstrating the greater versatility of the second text through her close reading, in the final section of the chapter Appleford discusses the texts found in several manuscripts containing *Visitation* E. These often didactic pieces, for example *How Lordis and Housbondemen Schulden Tecte Goddis Commaundementis*, regarding good governance at the level of the individual or household/family, can, she believes, offer an understanding of the likely fifteenth-century lay audience, and how householders might have employed these texts collectively to fulfill their pastoral responsibility to those under their authority. Such development she envisages as illustrative of the increasing laicization of late medieval English society, one of the themes that run throughout the book.

Keeping with this idea of the laity's role of social responsibility and pastoral care, in Chapter 2 Appleford deploys the example of Richard Whittington and the various projects undertaken in his name by his executors, especially the city's common clerk John Carpenter. The book's cover, depicting Whittington's deathbed, as illustrated in the vernacular translation of the ordinances for his almshouse founded from his vast fortune, is used by Appleford to highlight the hierarchical composition of those gathered there. This arrangement she sees as reinforcing the greater importance of and active roles undertaken by the laity, as patrons and governors of the almshouse and as its beadsmen whose regime, she believes, was less prescriptive than that seen in earlier hospitals and almshouses (69). Such an idea is interesting but probably not as innovative as Appleford implies because certain earlier hospitals in Kent, for example, exhibited these same characteristics.

Her examination of Carpenter's activities regarding London's Guild-hall, especially the library and his own work the *Liber albus* (which has some interesting parallels to the work of an early fourteenth-century common clerk from Sandwich, Kent), as well as another of his civic projects, the *Daunce of Poulys*, offers further evidence of this intertwining of spiritual care and civic responsibility as vested in London's elite. Regarding the latter, with its images of Death's dance with representative figures from society, Appleford explores in detail both its setting at the Pardon Churchyard at Saint Paul's and the extant manuscript versions of Lydgate's *Dance of Death* poem to consider ideas about authorship and reception.

Chapters 3 and 4 move from the ideas of London's elite respecting communal aspects of dying well to focus on the individual, where she discusses texts favored by the Carthusians that draw on the eremitical tradition. Asceticism through tribulation and mortification are key factors that Appleford assesses in terms of the readers she posits for a number of texts, especially of those manuscripts that contain several, where the reader was expected to experience a range of feelings and emotions as he meditated on the practice of death. Her principal subject is William Baron, who moved in the same circles as Carpenter, but Appleford believes his pious inclinations differed from Whittington's generation. Concentrating on some of the texts, including *Pety Job*, in the book he eventually gave to his granddaughter at the Dominican priory of Dartford (Oxford, Bodleian Library, MS Douce 322), she believes Baron was part of a group of leading laymen who were drawn to ideas of 'self-separation from the world through spiritual suffering' (111).

This sense of the separation of the individual in the process of dying, and the fallacy of looking to communal pious measures, forms the core of Appleford's assessment of Hoccleve's *Series*, thereby leading into Chapter 4, where she investigates in detail *The Book of the Craft of Dying*. Initially she discusses the importance of printing, as well as the role of European influences on later fifteenth-century London in the form of ideas mediated through a growing body of texts that were brought, translated, and copied in the capital. However, in addition to the availability of these favored texts among London's leading citizens, she seeks to stress further shifts in attitudes toward dying and death, considering that her chosen text highlights the notion that "although death *rehearsal* remains an individual practice, death *performance* demands the reconstitution of a renewed version of the communitarian religiosity long practiced by the generality of Londoners' (143).

Yet Appleford seeks to demonstrate that not all owners of *The Craft of Dying* were able to follow and so benefit from its directives, and in Chapter 5 she examines a new set of death texts, including Martin Luther's *Sermon von der Bereitung zum Sterben*. These were influenced by and part of the religious questioning that was taking place in mainland Europe, in addition to the new humanistic ideas that are probably most well known in the works of Desiderius Erasmus and Thomas More for early sixteenth-century England. By interweaving their writings on preparation for death with those of others, such as Richard Whitford and Thomas Lupset, she assesses the relationship of new and traditional ideas from England and abroad with particular reference to the different understanding and role of fear at the deathbed. Appleford believes this interplay of ideas is especially pertinent during the increasingly dangerous times of the 1520s and 1530s that, in particular, engulfed members of London's elite, in part because of their proximity to Westminster.

Drawing together these many and disparate texts (and threads) on dying and death from across the long fifteenth century is a challenging task. In her conclusion Appleford argues that these texts collectively offer a bridge between what she believes are unhelpful dichotomies of "public and private," "religious and secular," and "medieval and early modern," which are still to be found in current scholarship. In this she is not a lone voice and it is good to see another set of nails in this particular coffin. Thus, this book on the *ars moriendi* in a particular geographical setting is a fascinating and important contribution to our understanding of cultural changes and continuities in the two centuries after the Black Death, and will appeal to literary scholars and historians alike.

SHEILA SWEETINBURGH
Canterbury Christ Church University

HEATHER BLURTON AND HANNAH JOHNSON. *The Critics and the Prioress: Antisemitism, Criticism, and Chaucer's "Prioress's Tale."* Ann Arbor: University of Michigan Press, 2017. Pp. 228. $70.00.

There are few books that place the literary critic, rather than the text, beneath the analytical lens as cogently and delightfully as Heather Blurton and Hannah Johnson's excellent new account of the scholarship on

Chaucer's *Prioress's Tale*. Following in the footsteps of Florence Ridley's *The Prioress and the Critics* (1965), Blurton and Johnson document how a range of debates about the tale's anti-Semitic content, highly gendered narrator, and investment in Marian theology have revealed almost as much about the historical and theoretical affinities of the critic as they have about the text itself. Moreover, as they argue, the discipline of medieval literary studies has itself been shaped by the controversies at play with regard to Chaucer's Prioress; through the prism of that "greet cite" in "Asye," Blurton and Johnson identify the sometimes irreconcilable conflicts that have come to light between the demands of the aesthetic and the ethical. In *The Prioress's Tale*, four or five generations of critics have found a ready space to explore the limits of literary pleasure and moral responsibility.

Blurton and Johnson begin the book with a chapter that previews and encapsulates much of the material that is to follow. It is here in this chapter, titled "The Critics and the Prioress: A Retrospective," that the two authors directly engage the dominant theme of critical discussions of Chaucer's poem: the rampant anti-Semitism of the story it tells. The facts of the tale—the child-like Prioress, the little clergeon murdered by Jews, the Jews murdered in turn by vengeful Christian justice, the Virgin Mary's intervention on behalf of the little clergeon—form a façade of stability around which the sharp changes in critical interpretation have thronged. This chapter is a masterpiece of literary and critical cohesion, and its potential as a reference tool for future scholars of Chaucer is limitless. I thought I had read almost all the extant criticism on *The Prioress's Tale*, but found almost immediately that I had not. The chapter is particularly strong on the postwar critics of the tale, and its commentary on the way in which satirical reading became the tool to exculpate Chaucer from identification with the anti-Semitism of his own text is fully persuasive. Blurton and Johnson draw a clear line between postwar satirical readings that focus on the character of the Prioress (almost always to that lady's disadvantage) and those non-satirical postwar readings that emphasize the literary, aesthetic, and devotional.

Not only is this opposition well argued, but it masterfully sets the stage for the next critical opposition to be discussed by Blurton and Johnson, namely that between "ethics and historicism." If the previous section divided critical opinion according to the critic's comfort or discomfort with an anti-Semitic Chaucer, then here Blurton and Johnson establish a critical conflict according to whether the critic treats the tale as an object of cruelty or beauty in their analysis. Those critics who wished to find beauty within the story followed earlier scholars in shunting the brutality of the narrative onto its narrator, whereas those critics who considered the tale a direct ethical challenge to the contemporary reader focused not on the aesthetic, but on Chaucer (and the critic's) culpability in perpetuating such a violent literary artifact. And yet, while Blurton and Johnson tend to emphasize the disagreements among critics in this section, they increasingly acknowledge the overlaps among critical methodologies. For example, while they take Louise Fradenburg's significant 1989 essay "Criticism, Anti-Semitism, and the Prioress's Tale" as the pioneering text for the ethical move, they also note that the dichotomy Fradenburg drew between herself and "historicists" such as Lee Patterson and Lawrence Besserman became quite blurred over time, with both Patterson and Besserman producing work that merged a historicist perspective with an ethical concern.

In this sense, it is worth mentioning the limits of Blurton and Johnson's orderly but rigid organizational scheme, which divides scholars into what they call "critical camps." While this approach pays proper heed to the difference between a satirical or an ethical reading, for example, it risks losing the necessary perspective that recognizes how distant both are from a reading that subsumes the anti-Semitism of the story to its devotional, sentimental, or aesthetic qualities. Moreover, they cite many scholars who appear in multiple "camps" of their account at different times, so that the historical development of these theories becomes a bit muddled. Blurton and Johnson's choice of method sometimes can operate at the expense of a more historical or genealogical perspective that both traces intergenerational continuities and embeds each scholar within a particular social and institutional milieu. It would have been useful, for instance, when citing H. K. Root's early sentimental reading of *The Prioress's Tale* to reflect upon his entrenchment in Woodrow Wilson's Princeton, with its quota of 200 Jews a year; it would have been equally valuable to point out that when Greg Wilsbacher, in his 2005 essay, speaks of the *Shoah* rather than the Holocaust, his choice of language appears to testify deliberately to a Jewish presence now visible on both sides of the text.

The "critical camps" methodology of organization effaces what might otherwise be a more critical account of Chaucer studies itself; it privileges the textual experience of racism and discrimination over its institutional deployments at the very time that much of this criticism was being written. This is a *tactful* retrospective—albeit an erudite, thoughtful, and valuable one. And with that tact comes a certain confusion of origin and development, both in how these ideas came to take precedence within the field (or at least as major controversies within the field) and in how specific scholars came to espouse them.

There is no such confusion in the later chapters of this book. Blurton and Johnson perform a brilliant intellectual feat in Chapter 2, as they examine the source analogues and text networks of the tale in order to establish why, precisely, this story is considered a "masterpiece" of its anti-Semitic genre. They make a strong argument here as well that the modern desire to delineate carefully among stories of blood libels, ritual murders, and general Jewish violence may be a modern imposition upon a medieval text; the medieval audience was fully capable of recognizing the links between the story Chaucer sets before them and that of the ritual murder of Hugh of Lincoln, particularly since the Prioress prays to that infant saint directly. In particular, they make a convincing case that a network-based model of texts allows one to look past the author (Chaucer) of this text and instead focus upon his audience and their textual expectations. What modern critics have seen as the pinnacle of an admittedly horrid genre, medieval audiences would have seen as an interwoven textual product, capable of reaffirming other similar stories. If I complained of the lack of a historicist genealogy in the previous chapter, here Blurton and Johnson's upending of such a narrative with regard to source-texts is brilliant, sure, and endlessly enlightening.

In the third chapter, Blurton and Johnson note how profoundly gendered readings of the Prioress have become, particularly among those scholars who wish to place the onus of the tale's anti-Semitism upon the Prioress herself rather than upon its author. Blurton and Johnson argue that such readings depend far more upon *The General Prologue*'s portrait of the Prioress than upon the substance of her tale; these critics blend together the potential anticlericalism and misogyny of *The General Prologue*'s Prioress with the childishness and primitivism of *The Prioress's Prologue*, in order to argue for a narrator hopelessly (and deliberately) undermined by her own feminine inadequacies. Blurton and Johnson include some particularly unsettling assessments of the Prioress from critics in the 1960s and 1970s that tie her sentiment and "foolishness" to contemporary, generalized female behavior; yet even after the decades of important feminist readings of the tale, they argue, treatments of the

Prioress still tend to comment on her anti-Semitism through prejudicial characterizations of her femininity.

It is this play between the feminine and the anti-Semitic that Blurton and Johnson's final chapter explores, through a consideration of the fifteenth-century reception of the tale. They note that this tale was one of Chaucer's most popular in the century after his death, and one of the most commonly anthologized. And yet, its circulation in the fifteenth century was tied to its strong Marian themes rather than its attribution to Geoffrey Chaucer; Blurton and Johnson document numerous occasions upon which the tale appears without any reference to its author. In fact, they have discovered that it appears frequently paired with the Marian works of Thomas Hoccleve and John Lydgate; moreover, they argue that because of the tale's absorption into an established devotional culture, Hoccleve and Lydgate responded directly to its Marian identification in creating their own religious works. This is a significant argument for our understanding of how Chaucer's fifteenth-century successors understood his poetic authority, and Blurton and Johnson's naming of Chaucer as a "Marian poet" in this period is a profoundly provocative revision of the traditional narrative.

In summation, Blurton and Johnson have produced a work of criticism that has a great deal to offer Chaucerian scholars, particularly those who work on issues of anti-Semitism, gender, and devotion. In addition, they have also produced a work with deep insights into the interplay between text and critic, and the way in which centuries-old texts are reborn anew, in every generation, to meet the needs of those who read them. This is a book about Chaucer and his Prioress, but it is also a book about what it means to read. The ethical responsibilities of the critic never appear far from the consciousness of either author, and if I have critiqued them for looking backwards with too much tact, I have no quibble with the vision they shape of a future criticism enriched by its own self-knowledge and self-reflection.

SAMANTHA KATZ SEAL
University of New Hampshire

MICHAEL CALABRESE. *Introduction to "Piers Plowman."* Gainesville: University Press of Florida, 2016. Pp. xxx, 355. $79.95 cloth; $29.95 paper.

Michael Calabrese's *Introduction to "Piers Plowman"* stands as a welcome addition to the previously available handbooks, guidebooks, and companions. The volume provides what no aid to *Piers* has offered before: a "navigational summary" (xiii) of the A-, B-, and C-texts that proceeds not from A to B to C but simultaneously across the three main versions of Langland's poem, "one parallel set of passūs at a time" (xv). Scholars braving their first adventures with A. V. C. Schmidt's parallel-text edition now have a handy road map that introduces the varying movements of these three versions. Even seasoned readers of Langland's poem know how challenging it can be to hold a view of multiple versions of the text in the mind at one time. This effort can be overwhelming for college students and other new readers unless they have significant help. For such readers, that help is exactly what this volume provides. However, many (probably most) new readers encounter the poem in a student-friendly edition of only one of these versions (usually B; sometimes C; occasionally A), an initial approach that is practical but nonetheless limited in the vision it provides of Langland's evolving life work. Calabrese understands that problem and addresses those readers too: with his volume as a companion, that limitation is significantly mitigated, and first-time readers with only one version of the poem to hand can, with the help of his volume, now comprehend a reasonable view of all three.

The main body of Calabrese's *Introduction* is the "Narrative Reading Guide," each chapter of which offers discussion of parallel passus across the three versions (or across B and C for later parts of the poem that do not have analogous sections in A). Each chapter begins with a conspectus outlining the basic content of that section of the poem and briefly highlighting significant differences among the versions; more sustained discussion follows. This is not an overview of scholarship or a commentary on the state of the field: as Calabrese describes it, "its voice and approach to *Piers*, intentionally critically independent, often draws on classroom experience and keeps the new reader in mind by focusing mainly on an internal experience of the poem" (xv). His philosophy governing what to include and to emphasize can be found in his preface, where he articulates as his goal "to generate excitement and accessibility, while only minimally entangling the reader in the infinite webs of knowledges and discourses that the poem employs" (xiii). Knowing full well that Langland's work can be alienating, Calabrese chooses not to overwhelm and instead to nurture those passions and enthusiasms that the poem rightly stimulates in readers even today. Attention is duly paid to those matters without an understanding of which any sense of the text's coherence (such as it is) would be lost; more important for Calabrese's purpose, the Narrative Reading Guide also draws on the author's considerable experience in the college classroom to focus generously on the many ways in which teachers today can "show" the poem's relevance—"not 'make' it relevant"—for a twenty-first-century audience (xvi). In a testimony that resonates with my own experience teaching the poem to undergraduates, Calabrese writes "I am frankly amazed at how vitally the poem works in class and how students embrace it as both prescient and applicable to a range of current social issues" (xvi). At many junctures, for example, he draws attention to Langland's interest in social justice (a discourse just as vital today as in the fourteenth century), and he peppers the text with intentionally provocative statements such as this: "The poem exposes humans as curious, contentious, carnal, addictive, appetitive, and yet in constant search of love and the divine rewards of a salvation that they can barely convince themselves they deserve. Readers must determine just how 'medieval' and how 'modern' such conditions are" (xvi). This is excellent food for thought for students and teachers alike, and the exhortation ("Readers must determine . . .") is emblematic of the interpretative calls this volume offers.

While the Narrative Reading Guide is the heart of the volume, Calabrese supplements it with other materials that will be particularly useful to students of the poem. The Guide is preceded by a chronology of events relevant to *Piers* and its publication history and a section entitled "Life of the Poet," which introduces the matter of the author's identity (what little is known of it) and the rather different matter of the authorial presence suggested by the poem, which Calabrese cites George Kane as calling "elusive but inescapable" (9). In my own experience, one of the great difficulties of introducing *Piers* to students accustomed to novels by authors whose biographies are well known is preparing them for the experience of meeting Langland's dreamer-narrator, who appears, as Calabrese notes, "in many guises, with no guarantee of a single coherent *vita* nor any assurance that that *vita* faithfully reflects the real life of the poet" (9). The placement of this section prior to the Guide does much of this work.

The Narrative Reading Guide is followed by additional supplementary aids. The first is a section called "Langland and His Contemporaries" that provides further context for the poem through a discussion of medieval dream-vision literature and brief accounts of works of continental and English authors with which Langland's poem can be brought into "dynamic dialogue" (271). Two appendices follow. The first is an alphabetically arranged glossary of "Persons, Personifications, and Allegorizings in *Piers Plowman*," which provides brief sketches or definitions while also encouraging readers to supplement the glossary by pursuing its terms further in the *MED*. The second is an overview of Langland's phonology and meter that is subtitled "Reading *Piers Plowman* Aloud." Noteworthy here is Calabrese's insistence that reading the poem aloud "dramatically helps readers to comprehend and appreciate" it, that "reading Langland means 'hearing' Langland, which means 'vocalizing' Langland, which means 'feeling' the reverberations in the mouth and through the entire body" (309). Scholars, teachers, and students will all do well to remember that *Piers* is above all poetry—and, as poetry, it is sonic experience.

Calabrese's *Introduction to "Piers Plowman"* has as its stated purpose "to make the poem fundamentally accessible and comprehensible for new readers" (xi). In closing, I want to dwell on this volume's admirable commitment to access. We can only ensure the future of *Piers Plowman* studies if we continue to equip new readers with the tools they need to get over the prodigious hurdle that the poem initially poses. Calabrese disarms initial resistance to the reading experience by saying what is absolutely true and worth repeating to students: it is a normal response to the poem—possibly even a success and not a failure of reading—when, turning from it, we find ourselves "like Will the dreamer, puzzled, resentful, frustrated, or sleepy" (xiii). Experiencing resistance in the face of this poem is part of the work of understanding it. But that resistance can either provoke bitterness and apathy or a more affectionate bewilderment productive of further interest, depending on whether readers know to expect this response and whether they bring to it some recognition that it is a natural byproduct of Langland's own grappling with issues that have no easy answers: issues, Calabrese contends, that "all peoples and societies must struggle with" in one way or another (xvi). The great ethic of *caritas* that the poem supports asks that we read and teach with this in mind, and in my view Calabrese is a great leader in this effort. I admire both his honesty about what he has learned from his own students about *Piers* and the music of Langland's poetry and also what this volume reveals that he has generously given back to them. His receptivity to his students has tuned him in to the new reader's experience of Langland, which is something that becomes harder and harder for most of us to access as increased familiarity with *Piers* normalizes its mysteries, rendering less and less accessible the confusion, wonder, and frustration that it rightly invokes. Thus, even as Calabrese's *Introduction* speaks to new readers, it also reminds the rest of us of the initial pain this poem can—perhaps even should—cause. That is something that teachers, in particular, would do well not to forget. Langland does not ask his readers to do something easy, and that is part of his point. If we obey the injunction *redde quod debes*, then we will repay Langland's passionate effort to speak truth in the texts we have inherited with our own dedicated efforts to understand what he wrote. If our students join us, then perhaps we will see realized the final entry forecast in Calabrese's chronology, dated "20??," when *"Piers Plowman* joins Chaucer's *Canterbury Tales* as the most read and most beloved works of Middle English literature" (xxx).

JENNIFER SISK
University of Vermont

MICHAEL CALABRESE AND STEPHEN H. A. SHEPHERD, eds. *"Yee? Baw for Bokes": Essays on Medieval Manuscripts and Poetics in Honor of Hoyt N. Duggan*. Los Angeles: Marymount Institute Press, 2013. Pp. x, 296. $64.95.

It is a real accomplishment for a festschrift to achieve an impressive methodological range while retaining an equally impressive thematic unity. Hoyt Duggan's friends, colleagues, and students speak to the full range of this scholar's influence on Langland studies, the digital humanities, metrical analysis, manuscript studies, and medieval literary scholarship more generally. The contributors' exemplary essays simultaneously express the interrelationships among these subjects as they examine, for example, the value of digital editions for understanding the history of meter, or the importance of codicological study for recon-structing Langland's early reception—questions of immediate relevance to twenty-first-century scholarship. The volume itself is divided into two sections: one with six essays on "Composition and Authorship," and another with seven essays on "Reception and Use." Together, these two halves on textual production and postproduction create an illuminating collection of essays that offer new perspectives on some of the most vexing, long-standing questions in the study of Langland and the work of his contemporaries.

Of the first six essays on "Composition and Authorship," the first four deal with questions of meter. Thorlac Turville-Petre's opening piece promotes the *Piers Plowman Electronic Archives*' edition of a Bx archetype for its ability to improve future attempts at metrical analysis. Ralph Hanna identifies Richard Formande's *The Bridges of Abingdon*, a publicly displayed poem surviving on a single vellum broadsheet, as an example of "alliterative chronicle poetry" that documents and celebrates the building of bridges to make Abingdon commercially accessible. Written in an alliterative style that may have been influenced by interregional literary exchange, this fifteenth-century poem's local "liberation narra-tive" records how this community project frees the town from the abbot of Abingdon's oppression (35). The next two essays reexamine the lin-guistic status of final -*e* in fifteenth-century Middle English metrical practices. Problematizing the accepted history of final -*e*, John Burrow studies Hoccleve's holograph manuscripts in order to reveal how the poet's consistent use of final -*e* as an unstressed syllable most likely aligns with his own spoken pronunciation and with an audience able to understand the role this -*e* plays in his meter. Judith Jefferson's study of the final -*e* in *On Husbondrie*, a Middle English translation of Palladius's *Opus agricultura*, reveals a "more restricted" use of final -*e* for syllable count than Hoccleve used a few decades earlier.

The last two essays in this section address problems associated with non-Langlandian composition in *Piers*'s manuscript tradition. Because these pieces deal with the work of Langland's scribe-redactors, who also act as interpreters and readers, these two could easily fit into either section of the book, justifying their somewhat liminal position between the sections. Thomas A. Pendergast's excellent contribution argues that the famous John But ending merges the author-figure and reader-figure in a way that reflects the redactor's understanding of *Piers*'s "inherently complex authorial quality" and of "Langland's invitation to blur the distinctions between the reception and the making of the poem" (68). This author-continuator's "poetics of reception" voices the audience's presence while also setting up Will's writing of the B- and C-versions. Turning to the substantial gaps in an A-text manuscript, Míċeál F. Vaughan suggests that, despite its missing quire at the end, Dublin, Trinity College, MS 213 (sigil E) might be a fourth witness to A manuscripts containing Passus XII. He bases his argument on the average line count in the extant folios as well as on E's genetic relationship with other copies of the A-text that share a displacement of lines from Passus VII into Passus I, which may have larger implications for editing the A-text. Thus, while these two essays may intimate the limitations of artificially imposed organizing principles in edited collections, they also usefully bridge the content between the book's two sections.

The next seven essays on "Reception and Use" showcase a range of approaches to manuscript studies, with the first five examples focusing on a single manuscript each, four of which feature *Piers*. Examining the dramatic Jew in the Wakefield manuscript, and especially the metaphors of scribal activity used in the Crucifixion play, Regula Meyer Evitt argues that instead of the "traditional construction of the Jew as passive, embodied textual witness to the truth of Christianity," some of the Jews in the Wakefield plays become somatic and constitute a "viscerally aggressive threat to Christ as enfleshed text of the Christian Word" (113). Michael Calabrese provides a useful model for analyzing manuscript anthologies in his exploration of Huntington Library, MS HM 128 as a "pedagogical and pastoral" anthology, focusing on the connections between the volume's most unlikely companions, *Piers* and the *Expositio aequentiarum* (128). The *Expositio*'s combining of grammar and doctrine exemplifies Langland's conception of Study, offering "a window into the actual world of Latin learning in Langland's culture" (140). In the next essay, Stephen Shepherd reads the images in MS Douce 104 as intertextual interpretations that draw on sources the illustrator read alongside *Piers*, perhaps coming from a well-stocked library that belonged to the manuscript's patron. Even though his speculations tend to rely on circumstantial evidence, he balances them with thought-provoking insights about text–image relationships and the more specific text–image–text articulations he believes are present in the Langland tradition's only extant illustration cycle. Revisiting the Ilchester manuscript to study *Piers* as an "anticodicological" text full of disruptions and rebeginnings, D. Vance Smith suggests that Ilchester represents a scribal attempt at archival revision using loose sheets with C material meant for updating their older copies (204). Patricia Bart's exceptional piece on Huntington Library, MS HM 114 demonstrates just how heavy-handed and involved the Ht scribe was when revising the manuscript's unique A, B, and C composite version of *Piers*. The scribe's Latinity and reliance on French forms alongside the ink color variances from multiple rounds of emendation indicate the scribe's leading role in shaping this copy from multiple exemplars.

Bringing the volume to a close are two essays that consider the textual afterlives of Langland and Lydgate. Robert Adams addresses early Protestant interpretations of Langland as a proto-Protestant, not because Langland necessarily thought of himself that way, but because he shares "a troubled ambivalence about the Church" with many of these readers (252). *Piers*'s reformist stances on the pope, sacramentalism, and apocalypticism stand out as major touchstones for understanding their mutual, though diachronic, interests. Drawing upon the evidence for provenance in two large-format, fifteenth-century Lydgate manuscripts (Manchester, John Rylands Library, MSS English 1 and English 2), A. S. G. Edwards identifies two distinct types of textual reception among these manuscripts' noble audiences. English 1, a wealthy bibliophile's copy of the *Troy Book*, belonged to readers who would be uninterested in sharing their luxury book with a wide audience, while English 2, a copy-text for the first printed edition of the *Fall of Princes*, belonged to an audience more interested in its commercial value within a newly forming print culture.

Many of these essays challenge scholars to rethink some deeply held, long-standing assumptions in the field of Middle English. Whether these assumptions deal with the status of individual manuscripts and their texts, or the value of digital tools more generally for literary study, it is perhaps in this constant questioning and reevaluating that the real value of this volume lies. The great organizational care taken by the editors and the quality of the scholarship throughout make this tome in honor of Duggan a truly valuable resource for Middle English scholars.

KARRIE FULLER
University of Notre Dame

CHRISTOPHER CANNON. *From Literacy to Literature: England, 1300–1400.*
Oxford: Oxford University Press, 2016. Pp. xv, 297. $55.00.

In this handsome volume from Oxford, Christopher Cannon works into book form material from six of his previous publications in such journals as *The Yearbook of Langland Studies, Publications of the Modern Language Association of America, New Medieval Literature,* and *ELH: English Literary History,* now molded together with new material and a new rhetorical framework appropriate to a monograph, convenient for those wanting a "greatest hits" compilation of Cannon's engaging work (with bonus tracks) in the field of grammar and learning. Unifying the current volume, Cannon shows throughout how the various exercises learned at school equipped the major Ricardian poets for poetic creation in English. The book will mainly appeal to scholars and advanced graduate students, but the chapters that offer concrete examples from the major poets (Chaucer, Langland, and Gower) may be useful for classroom teaching, as they illustrate how poets cleverly transformed school exercises into some of the most famous, beloved, and intriguing moments of Middle English literature in texts such as the Wife of Bath's and Pardoner's prologues, *The Tale of Melibee,* the Monk's portrait, the *Troilus,* endless episodes in *Piers Plowman,* and many other examples that Cannon marshals in detailed comparisons of the school texts and the poets' verses. For the schoolboys, we learn, were inherently poets in training; as Cannon writes, "if poetry is usually the culmination of literacy training, it is almost always that training's first step" (2). In reading all these chapters collectively, one certainly does get a sense of what it was like to be a medieval schoolboy, and the monograph as it now stands makes a major contribution to our understanding of medieval grammar schools and their role in educating some of the major canonical poets in English medieval literature.

Chapter 1's section "Fiant Latina!" (Let there be Latin!), argues that students were (despite what medieval chroniclers have said) trained in "a fundamentally Latin pedagogy" (37). And the poets later wrote major works in English because of their growing awareness that English too has a grammar that can be understood and put to use creatively. Cannon's coinage "grammaticalization" may not be elegant, but it encapsulates the processes of learning and creativity at work in the schoolboys turned poets, as Cannon takes us beyond the traditional understanding of education as training in ethics to reveal it also as "a primer in literary possibility" (14). "There is a remarkably straight line," Cannon argues, from the schoolbooks that survive . . . through the agile understandings of Chaucer, Gower, and Langland, to the techniques that made the literature these three writers produced distinctive" (15).

Chapter 2, "The Ad Hoc School," reconsiders the texts and even the physical structures of the schools, arguing that the notion of a standardized curriculum and mode of instruction have been overstated, for education was much more improvisatory than previously thought, as a collection called "Cato" might not even include Cato. Cannon continues: "Whenever a medieval person had occasion to write about how he learned to read and write, in fact, he almost always described a local tutelary relationship rather than an institution" (59). In "Schoolboy Improvisation" Cannon argues that certain classic texts about writing that we usually associate with Chaucer such as the *Poetria nova* are works Chaucer would have studied later in life, for he would have already acquired instruction in the making of poetry in grammar school. Cannon then follows with a series of examples of school verses made in English where it's hard to tell the difference between an exercise and a poem, displaying the birth of poetic invention arising out of exercises in learning Latin. In fact many of the free-standing poems we "now value as literature" were produced in the mode of a schoolroom translation exercise, so learning Latin and creating verses in English were taught and practiced simultaneously. For this reason "the idea that he might write English verse of his own was almost impossible for such a schoolboy *not* to have" (83).

Chapter 3, "The Basic Grammar and the Grammar-School Style," traces what Cannon calls a "feedback loop as the learning of Latin worked backward to the schoolboy's understanding of his own English" (85). In grammatical pedagogy a "certain vivacity" and dramatic narrative style emerges, with the school texts "creating subjects and putting them into action" (88). Cannon traces ultimately "how the 'grammar school' style became a literary style" (89) because the realism wrought in the pedagogy will be translated into a certain realism in writing; as Cannon asserts, in literary history, "a certain vivacity in language and narrative was," for many readers, "Chaucer's signature achievement" (90). A section called "Bread and Milk for Children" focuses on Chaucer's *Treatise on the Astrolabe*, in which a major poet actually writes an elementary text that "shared a pedagogical task with the basic grammars and addressed a student at exactly the same age" (105). Instructive evidence is then marshaled from various "scenes of instruction" in Chaucer's *Troilus* (111)

"Grammaticalization and Literary Form" features a section on the recalcitrant grammatical analogy about Lady Mede in the C-text of *Piers Plowman*, with Cannon making a telling contrast between Chaucer and Langland: "whereas a genealogy is required to see the connections between the technique of the grammars and Chaucer's style, Langland's grammaticalizations hewed much more closely to the forms of grammar-school teaching that he often simply repurposed wholesale" (128–29). In the section "Grammar-School Poetry" Cannon asserts, in perhaps the most affecting moment in the book, that "Middle English poetry was born" not in the work of the great poets per se but when "the schoolboy, etching his translations dutifully with his stylus on his wax tablet . . . decided to move beyond the lines of Latin verse set him for translation to write a line or two of his own invention" (139). In a related discussion, Cannon ponders Langland's bilingualism, noting that he often treated Latin lines "of a piece with his English" (155), something that those of us who teach in bilingual communities have long recognized—all the more true, since, as Cannon asserts importantly, 1,200 lines of *Piers Plowman* are in Latin (11).

In Chapter 5, on the concept of "form," Cannon analyzes closely some school texts that are "extraordinarily unimaginative" (169), but he then cleverly observes that these texts ultimately "seem to be *about* nothing so much as the grammar-school boy, piecing out the pattern of the his [*sic*] life as if they were a single text whose defining formal principal [*sic*] was the treatment of this one subject from a variety of angles," including such issues as marriage and adolescent sexuality (173). The section concludes somewhat murkily concerning what a schoolboy was supposed to be reproducing from his curriculum: "what that form finally taught best was not how to reproduce each of the similar forms that constituted it, but, rather, how to reproduce the *canon* by piecing together a form out of variegated parts" (174). A reader's understanding may be suspended for a moment here, but the next sections, "The Poetry of Patchwork" and "The Middle English Poet as a Schoolboy," substantiate the argument with literary examples, including verses from *The Second Nun's Tale*, of how "texts signify by means of a patchwork, making meaning by the manner in which precept and narrative are combined" (177). A series of fascinating instances follow, where Cannon traces what he calls "the complete absorption" (194) of a patchwork of schoolroom quotations that appear seamlessly in medieval poems (including the Wife of Bath's famous question about who painted the lion), as if to make the original sources completely invisible. The chapter ends by noting the exceptionalism of the *Gawain*-poet, who "must have had a very different sort of education from the other major Middle English poets" (197), and so he simply does not display the paradigm that Cannon traces in this book.

Chapter 6, "Equipment for Living," makes the provocative and compelling argument that the content of all the works discussed from the grammar schools actually did not have any ethical effect on its readers' behavior "because it was fundamentally useless" (199). Rather, students were taught "how to use a wisdom that provided happiness to the extent that its possessor could be sure that it was always *there*" (201). This raises some compelling questions about the very nature of learning. Does studying make us wise or just make us feel wise? And does learning prepare us to act properly or does it allow us to "come to terms with an event once it has occurred," serving "not [as] a guide to the future but [as] an *interpretation of the past*" (209)? A welcome study of Chaucer's underappreciated *Tale of Melibee* proves the point, because in this tale, "the comfort provided by such wisdom finally swamps its propositional content" (211).

The final chapter, "The Experience of Learning," continues to display how proverbs and wisdom only become meaningful in retrospect, as illustrated by the dramatic scene of conversion in Augustine's *Confessions*. The final sequence of the book focuses again on how Langland, in revision, was constantly being drawn back to school texts, tugging at a web of references, proverbs, quotations, and allusions, revealing that his poetic revision was so often bound to his reengagement with school texts, concerning such evolving questions, for example, as which beggars are worthy of charity. The book ends anecdotally with a discussion of Austen, Woolf, and Henry James, concerning how people often return to books for well-worn wisdom.

Several glitches in copy-editing may distract, and Cannon's prose can at times be tortuous, as he works through some complex materials and complex psychological effects along the continuum from literacy to literature. But his voice can also be strong and teacher-like at the right moments. In all fields of aesthetics there is an unknown component, the intoxication of creativity, rooted in natural talent and ambition, which have not much to do with the specifics of grammar-school training. Not all schoolboys became great poets. But only the Apollonian leaves behind evidence, and Cannon, with deep learning, vast research, and acute critical insight has painstakingly mastered and documented that Apollonian record, which so clearly, we now can see, provided matter for so many moments in the great poetry of the Ricardian authors. Cannon's book significantly develops our understanding of medieval education, experienced, remembered, and reimagined by our poets. And modern-day readers, teachers, and students will gain access here to many important texts and documents in the history of education (so many otherwise inaccessible) that are tremendously informative and engaging. A robust bibliography and finely detailed index round out this penetrating and serious piece of scholarship.

MICHAEL CALABRESE
California State University, Los Angeles

LOUISE D'ARCENS. *Comic Medievalism: Laughing at the Middle Ages*. Cambridge: D. S. Brewer, 2014. Pp. x, 209. £19.99.

It is a truism that nothing kills a joke faster than explanation. This situation becomes dire when the joke crosses national boundaries, languages, generations, occasions, speakers, all of those things that target jokes to their intended and knowing audience. We've all had this experience and yet, somehow, in the decade since its uploading to YouTube, the Norwegian skit *Øystein og jeg* (*Medieval Help-Desk*), with English subtitles alone, has had 5,124,763 (and counting) views. How? Why? *Comic Medievalism: Laughing at the Middle Ages* gamely rides into this anarchy and sets about bringing some analytic rigor to its examination.

Comic Medievalism has four main parts, each with two chapters. The introduction provides a crisp "set-up" by sharpening the focus from simply laughing to laughing *at*, *with*, and *in* the Middle Ages; noting the ubiquity of "comic representations of the medieval past"; clarifying such representations as "based on a cluster of practices, rituals, beliefs, people and events that have come to be constituted as quintessentially 'medieval'"; and nominating such representations as "a vehicle for commentary on the present as well as the past" (6). D'Arcens calls on Umberto

Eco's (non-comic) *The Name of the Rose* to model three categories of comic medievalism: representations of the Middle Ages that are patently "risible" and provoke "a kind of modern-centric Schadenfreude" that laughs, with relief, *at* the past age (Mark Twain's *A Connecticut Yankee in King Arthur's Court*); representations that collapse temporal distinctions, allowing us to laugh, via comic identification, *in* the Middle Ages (Bill Bailey's "Pubbe Gagge"); and representations where "resilient folk comedy" allows us to laugh *with* the Middle Ages as a form of comic resistance (Andrei Tarkovsky's *Andrei Rublev*) (10, 11). Comic medievalism, as it whizzes through generic forms, engages periodicity through its reflections on modernity, inflects historicism by revealing the affect in our relations to past temporalities, and offers an ethico-political agenda in its grounding in social commentary.

In Chapter 1, Miguel Cervantes's *The Ingenious Gentleman Don Quixote of La Mancha* makes an entrance as "seminal comic forebear," and D'Arcens recognizes Cervantes's novel as having shaped "modernity's view of the Middle Ages" (25): not only through plot and character, rhetoric, and comic wattage from bathos to slapstick as the novel satirizes chivalric romance, but also through its exposé of the social effects of exactly the fanatical devotion that drives medievalism in the first place. It's this double-layered, ethical, and narrative conception that changed the form of the novel and gives *Don Quixote* its status as meta-medievalism. Since D'Arcens's book is developing a "genealogical account" (25), the discussion offers only a brief plot summary in order to make connections to other instances of comic medievalism—*The Tale of Sir Thopas*, *The Knight of the Burning Pestle* (1607), *The Cable Guy* (1996)—and identify some persistent features, including anachronism; verbal parody; historical mismatch; "premodern farcical and buffonic modes" (32); and a maneuver described as a "performative collapse of the dichotomy between laughing subject and comic object" (32), or ambiguity, as when Don Quixote entirely fails to distinguish between fictions and hacks Master Pedro's Moorish puppets to pieces. D'Arcens is keen to analyze what kind of humor is at work in comic medievalism, and so the discussion exposes a range of critical views that mimics the forms of comic medievalism itself. Some fix on an "epochal divide" between sophisticated "modern" forms (satire, parody, wit, irony) and premodern, "pre-novelistic," popular forms devoid of "ideological, social or existential reflection," thus laughing *at* the Middle Ages; others rely on Mikhail

Bakhtin to elevate *Don Quixote*'s "popular-festive matrix" to a "carnivalesque logic of grotesquery and social inversion," thereby laughing *in* the Middle Ages; Erich Auerbach's *Mimesis* allows us to laugh *with* the Middle Ages because the social satire is (formally and necessarily) weak, since Cervantes's grand project is "Spanish life in its colour and fullness," a.k.a. realism (39).[1]

Part 2 begins with "Scraping the Rust from the Joking Bard," and examines "Chaucer" in the literary imaginary of the long (English) eighteenth century, in which the transformative power of modernization rescued Joseph Addison's "merry *Bard*," to be lauded by Thomas Warton as "the first who gave the English nation, in its own language, an idea of HUMOUR," and dubbed by George Sewell as "Our Bard [who] Had Strength, and Vigour, and an English Face": one of James Thomson's "indigenous 'forebears,'" with all the ethnographic complexity those words suggest. D'Arcens gives a deft account of the push–pull factors— "antique" language; embarrassing bawdiness; "obscur'd" wit; sheer medievalness; Gothic, as against powerful linguistic, metrical, temporal primacy—to be managed before Chaucer could be admitted to the sublimity of the Augustans' republic. Rather than tracking this recasting of Chaucer through comic medievalism's social critique,[2] D'Arcens turns to formal analyses of taste, a version of aesthetics, which find their apogee in whatever it was that Alexander Pope did to *The Miller's Tale* to give us couplets such as the immortal "And Absolon, before he smoak'd the jest, / Ev'n on her bum a luscious kiss imprest" (61).

"Medievalist Farce as Anti-Totalitarian Weapon: Dario Fo as Modern *Giullare*" returns us to one of the compelling strengths of this book, namely the specific social and political situatedness of comic medievalism. In Dario Fo, D'Arcens finds an artist who cares about the (Italian) Middle Ages: cares enough to research the period; to be emotionally committed to one of its social pivots (the *giullare*); to risk a "dialectical" relation between modern and medieval; and, above all, to dramatize the *giullare* as a fearless and courageous body in the vicious world of popular

---

[1] This is a traditional reading of Erich Auerbach's most influential work; cf. Emily Apter's brilliant rereading of Erich Auerbach and his legacy, beginning with "Global *Translatio*: The 'Invention' of Comparative Literature, Istanbul, 1933," *Critical Inquiry* 29, no. 2 (2003): 253–81.

[2] Cf. Stephen Knight, 'Medieval Comic Relief: Cannibal Cow, Duck's Neck and Carry On Joan of Arc,' *Comic Medievalisms*, ed. Louise D'Arcens, special issue of *postmedieval*, 5, no. 2 (2014): 154–68.

antifascist satire. Fo's *Mistero buffo*, for instance, operates in a dense historical context where Antonio Gramsci's philosophical heft drives social-justice satire through the postmedieval reworking of the "socially dangerous farce of the *giullare*" (74), ramping up scatology, grotesquery, and cacophony into resistant subversion on behalf of a disempowered *popolo*. D'Arcens suggests links among Fo's praxis and that of Russian Futurist Vladimir Mayakovsky's *Mystery-Bouffe* (1918–21) and Mikhail Bakhtin's *Rabelais and His World* (1965), producing a dense textual, politically mandated, as well as transcultural, network for Fo's *giullare* as a leftist strand of comic medievalism. His secular *giullare* opens onto the figure of the holy fool—a shift into film: Roberto Rossellini's *Francesco, giullare di Dio* (1950) and Fo's notorious dark twin, Pier Paolo Pasolini, especially *La trilogia della vita* (1971–74) with its excoriating attacks on the apparatus of Church and state. D'Arcens has too little space for the rich complexity of materials here that careers between subtle and lurid, but we understand that this is a volatile version of (Italian) comic medievalism.

Part 3's "Pre-Modern Camp and Faerie Legshows: Travestying the Middle Ages on the Nineteenth-Century Stage" looks at burlesque's two targets of choice: Shakespearean plays and the Middle Ages. This material is mainly English with a handful of colonial references: a reminder that the civilizing mission of colonialism reached from the sublime to the "gor blimey." D'Arcens notes burlesque's "pedantry and irreverence" (92), its lampooning of medieval history, its working the slipstream of Victorian England's obsession with historical-realist theater (Charles Kean's *Sardanapalus*) and imperial nationalism, its topicality, its self-awareness: "Don't on this nonsense waste a witticism, / When all burlesque's one great anachronism" (108). The use of Susan Sontag's "Notes on 'Camp'" (*Partisan Review* [Fall 1964], 515–30) is a reminder that theory too has specific histories: despite Sontag's note 2 ("It goes without saying that the camp sensibility is disengaged, depoliticized —or at least apolitical"), here camp provides a transition to queer; though it leaves the dynamic of class, fundamental to British comedy, largely unremarked.

The companion piece in Part 3 on performing and parodying medievalism surveys cinematic medievalism in "Up the Middle Ages: Performing Tradition in Comic Medievalist Cinema." Here, a generosity of material that is illuminating and hilarious, including many film citations and identifying a diversity of cinematic tropes, restricts D'Arcens from developing three moments of critical acuity. First, "archaeological comedy" (114) surfaces as a mode (potentially) useful for analyzing both the performance history of individual films *and* anachronistic portrayals of the Middle Ages together with the films' enclosing temporalities. Second, D'Arcens shifts into the more responsive auteur mode to examine the films of Mario Monicelli, thus leveraging the theatrical and literary texts, the pervasive social realist mode of Italian cinema, and interview material, as well as Monicelli's cinematic narrative technique, to unpack his "counter-historical strategy": "I wanted to show this was the real Middle Ages in Italy—barbaric and uncivilized, savage, grotesque" (121). Third, the insight that cinematic medievalism—especially in comic form—"lampoons not so much the Middle Ages as the preposterous and contradictory ways in which modern perceptions of the past have been formed through popular entertainment" (117)—is right at the core of this book. All three moments suggest something of what laughing at the Middle Ages, aside from a good time, can give us.

Part 4's first chapter—" 'The Past Is a Different and Fairly Disgusting Country': The Middle Ages in Recent British 'Jocumentary' "—changes gear in terms of content and methodology. This is a quite formal discursive account of comic representations of medieval British history on syndicated UK television by three presenters (Tony Robinson, Terry Jones, and Terry Deary), whose impeccable credentials are as comedians first and "autodidactic" historians second. The material format is the franchise; the economic template is commodification. D'Arcens's coinage, "jocumentary," is useful in tracing the traditional association between pedagogy and humor, here in the public teaching of history, and pinpoints the ethical question of whether the past is "dignified, diminished or otherwise distorted" (159) by comic methodologies. It's a version of contempt that gives the comic its edge. Jocumentary's partner in market share, edutainment, is the focus of the final chapter, "Smelling the Past," offering a synoptic discussion of comic medieval heritage tourism and the popularity of olfactory display to outline a "phenomenology of comic nostalgia" (170). Meditating on the smells of selected British heritage sites allows D'Arcens to speculate on the tacit agreement between promoters and visitors to treat inauthenticity as an ironic substitute for realism that shows up the sanitized and deodorized "bodily régimes of postmodern Western society" (179) as laughable.

This book is not so much a monograph—"a detailed written study of a single specialized subject or an aspect of it"—as a report from a new field of inquiry still in process, and thus, for the most part, combines survey with brief analytic interventions rather than offering a sustained exposition of a hypothesis or sequenced argument. After more than forty years of scholarly inquiry; the publication of reference works—such as *Medievalism Key Critical Terms*, to which D'Arcens is a contributor—and journals in various formats, including special issues of which D'Arcens herself has been an editor; numerous conference events; and institutional recognition including the establishment of professorial positions, medievalism is a recognized academic formation in which comic medievalism now appears as a subset. The effects of this new subset include energy, spaciousness, a sense of adventure, and a glimpse of further disciplinary possibilities. And the afterword, coming after and looking forward, suggests three more nuanced questions that have ghosted these notes from the field. Comic medievalism depends, from its Cervantean paradigm onward, upon versions of humanism: how to rethink that humanism now, in a time of rancorous political appropriations of medievalism and the seismic shifts of the anthropocene, notwithstanding the foreclosure of the posthuman? D'Arcens typically investigates her case studies through agile forays into (diachronic) literary history and (synchronic) close reading. If close reading, as Barbara Herrnstein Smith argues,[3] remains the go-to methodology for textual studies as a disciplinary formation, does it risk simply normalizing comic medievalism, given the dynamic and proliferating array of its formats, versions, sources, temporalities, acculturations? Then too, for D'Arcens, comic medievalism is a way of "understanding"; in other words, in the midst of the laughter, there's a nascent epistemology and yet, time and again, comic medievalism depends upon tacitly agreed un-knowing, ignorance, fabrications: so how might this knowing be curated? *Comic Medievalism* will be an excellent pedagogical resource as well as shaping future developments in the field, and these are significant achievements.

JENNA MEAD
University of Western Australia

[3] Barbara Herrnstein Smith, "What Was Close Reading? A Century of Method in Literary Studies," *Minnesota Review* n.s. 87 (2016): 57–75.

REBECCA DAVIS. *"Piers Plowman" and the Books of Nature*. Oxford: Oxford University Press, 2016. Pp. xv, 272. $90.00.

"Piers Plowman" and the Books of Nature offers a rare thing: an "optimistic" reading of *Piers Plowman*. Rebecca Davis presents her monograph, which argues that Langland finds divine presence in the created world, as an answer to the more common "pessimistic" sense of Langland as a poet of failure and privation. That optimism is hedged and complicated over the course of the book, and the advocates of more pessimistic readings—notably, Nicolette Zeeman—prove productive interlocutors throughout. But Davis's argument is a convincing challenge to read *Piers Plowman* anew, alongside discourses that call forward the poem's reparative and generative qualities rather than its negations and discontinuities.

Specifically, the first three chapters of *"Piers Plowman" and the Books of Nature* trace the connections between Langland's *kynde* and multiple traditions of medieval thought on nature. *Kynde* is a multivalent word in *Piers Plowman*, not only a name for nature but also a component of knotty Langlandian terms such as *kynde knowynge*, and Davis's introduction ably covers those multiple meanings in their contexts and the critical debates they have spawned. But two points in the B-text of the poem, the book's primary focus, prove particularly crucial for what follows. The first is the explication of the Trinity offered by Langland's Samaritan: comparing the Trinity first to a hand and then to a candle, the Samaritan offers the crucial depiction of God as the "formour and shappere" whose power rests "in makynge of þynges" (B XVII.170–71).[4] *Kynde* is nowhere in the Samaritan's speech, but his images of creating God and incarnate Christ suggest that created nature provides access to God, according to the bravura close reading with which Davis concludes her introduction. The second point is the personification Wit's definition of *Kynde*. *Kynde* "is creatour of alle kynnes þynges," he says—not just nature, but "þe grete god þat gynnyng had neuere" (B IX.26–28). As Davis notes, Wit's speech is the only place in Middle English where *kynde* names God. Together, these two moments suggest a ligature in Langland's thought between *natura naturans*, creating nature (or nature's creator), and *natura naturata*, created nature. God is

---

[4] I cite from *Will's Visions of Piers Plowman and Do-Well: Piers Plowman; The B Version*, rev. ed., ed. George Kane and E. Talbot Donaldson (London: Athlone, 1988).

manifest in the world twice, as creator and created, and the whole of creation reveals his presence. Davis returns repeatedly to this intermingling of creator and created in her discussion of the place of nature in *Piers Plowman* and the discourses from which it draws.

The book's first chapter traces the career of the allegorical figure Nature from late antiquity through Bernard Silvestris to Alan of Lille and, from him, to Jean de Meun and Guillaume de Deguileville. Though the *Natura* tradition will be familiar to many medievalists, Davis's treatment of it is thorough and careful, and her approach is distinguished by its narrative of decline, what she calls "the secularization of Natura" (77). In Davis's telling, twelfth-century Neoplatonic humanism valorized the study of the created world as a way to understand its creator, while later Aristotelianism divided creator from creation, assigning Nature a diminished earthly role. In the book's only extended discussion of a Middle English poem other than *Piers Plowman*, *The Parliament of Fowls* is treated as a terminus of this decline: Chaucer's Nature echoes her Neoplatonic antecedents, but is ultimately circumscribed in the earthly realm.

Kynde in *Piers Plowman*, on the other hand, restores "the moral and spiritual value attached to nature" in earlier thought (84). Chapter 2 returns to the concerns and textual field of the introduction to argue this point, suggesting that Langland aligns *kynde* with both God the creator and the incarnate Christ, whom Langland repeatedly describes as a mediator between humanity and God. This chapter is particularly valuable in connecting *Piers Plowman* to relatively neglected predecessors and analogues, the plural "books of nature" that complement the *Natura* tradition described in the first chapter. Davis traces Langland's incarnational theology, for instance, back to Robert Grosseteste's depiction of the Incarnation as the meeting of *natura naturans* and *natura naturata* in his *Château d'amour*. Chapter 3 turns to *other* "books of nature," bestiaries and medieval encyclopedias, to explicate the seemingly failed engagement with nature in Will's "vision of *kynde*" in Passus XI. In a powerful explication of Will's vision and what follows, Davis argues that Langland's Imaginatif draws on encyclopedic and exemplary modes in order to teach "how natural facts can be translated into spiritual facts" (168).

Shorter fourth and fifth chapters turn inward from these wide-ranging discussions of *kynde*. Rather than taking in the fullness of nature, these chapters address more narrowly human ethical concerns, and their fourteenth-century contexts and concerns will be comparatively familiar to most Langlandians. The fourth chapter turns to the fourteenth century's emergent equity law, which Davis sees reflected in *Piers Plowman*'s "lawe of kynde." The fifth examines the poem's rhetoric of conversion, finally finding grounds for pessimism in Langland's soteriology: *kynde* alone is, ultimately, insufficient grounds for salvation. A short epilogue, which turns from *kynde* to *cortesie* and thus from nature to grace, returns to optimism.

The challenge of an optimistic approach to *Piers Plowman* is how often the poem undercuts its own tenuous moments of optimism. A skeptical reader might be suspicious of Wit's equation of *kynde* with God, for instance: why should we take his word, when the poem routinely impeaches such authoritative claims to knowledge? This book is at its strongest when Davis buries such skepticism under wide-ranging readings of the poem and its surrounding "books of nature," as in the second and third chapters, which set local oddities such as Wit's speech into broader currents of late medieval thought. But if Davis's optimism about *Piers Plowman* is convincing, I sometimes found myself wishing that she allowed herself to look beyond the poem: the book is admirably clear about how Langland draws on multiple medieval traditions of thought about nature, but there is no consideration of how those traditions look different with *Piers Plowman* in them. The book likewise makes few concessions to a non-specialist audience. Key terms such as "fullness" and "natural capacity" are introduced unglossed, and readers are expected to keep up.

Despite these caveats, the force of Davis's claim is easy enough to grasp and its stakes are clear. Langland finds divine presence, and the potential access to spiritual knowledge, in the things, animals, people, and words of the created world. In its approach to Langland's poetics, *"Piers Plowman" and the Books of Nature* thus offers a particularly learned contribution to a long-standing tendency in formalist thought on the poem. More than fifty years ago, for instance, Nevill Coghill suggested that Langland's poetics offered a "mixture of a homely naturalism with mystery."[5] (Davis's introduction gestures to Erich Auerbach's "Figura," but the more relevant essay might be his *"Sermo humilis,"* which argues

---

[5] Nevill Coghill, "God's Wenches and the Light that Spoke (Some Notes on Langland's Kind of Poetry)," in *English and Medieval Studies Presented to J. R. R. Tolkien on the Occasion of His Seventieth Birthday*, ed. Norman Davis and C. L. Wrenn (London: George Allen & Unwin, 1962), 200–18 (214).

that the Incarnation licenses the Christian sanctification of everyday language.)[6] More recently, Jill Mann's major essays on the poem, clearly an important influence, anticipate some of Davis's arguments in their broad strokes. But in presenting *Piers Plowman* as a coherent statement, a work whose local failures serve a unified creative purpose, the book also speaks to a new crop of more theologically inclined studies of the poem, such as David Aers's *Beyond Reformation?* and Ryan McDermott's *Tropologies*. Davis's method and archive are unique, however. By disclosing the origins of Langland's creative purpose and poetics in multiple traditions of thought about nature, she has made a major contribution to *Piers Plowman* studies. Davis indeed offers an optimistic Langland—but pessimists would also benefit from considering the *Piers Plowman* that emerges from her book: a poem of plenitude rather than privation.

SPENCER STRUB
University of California, Berkeley

MARY DZON. *The Quest for the Christ Child in the Later Middle Ages*. Philadelphia: University of Pennsylvania Press, 2017. Pp. 424, $65.00.

What happened between Christ's Nativity and his first documented public appearance in Jerusalem at age twelve, in which he went missing and was eventually found—to his parents' relief and astonishment—in the temple arguing with Jewish doctors? Of the gospel writers, only Luke recounts this episode; chronologically, the next canonical incident from Jesus's life appears to be his baptism by John, which occurred when both were already grown men.

In this fascinating and thought-provoking study, Mary Dzon tackles the "hidden years," as she terms them, of Jesus' childhood—particularly the time between his birth and the episode with the temple doctors in Jerusalem.

The book focuses on the later Middle Ages and places particular emphasis on textual and iconographic sources from England, though it by no means focuses narrowly on English materials. Dzon takes her

[6] Erich Auerbach, "*Sermo humilis,*" in *Literary Language and Its Public in Late Latin Antiquity and in the Middle Ages*, trans. Ralph Manheim (1965; Princeton: Princeton University Press, 1993), 25–66.

readers from the apocryphal Infancy Gospels to English vernacular lyrics to Thomas Aquinas; from Francis of Assisi to Brigitta of Sweden and back to England and Margery Kempe. To trace the complex routes and intersections of the material and its transmission across Europe is a challenging task, which Dzon has mastered with great skill, and with a verve that makes the book a joy to read.

Dzon places medieval people's desire to know more about the young Jesus in the context of Christocentric affective piety and the emerging interest in the humanity of Christ, propagated by the Cistercians and Franciscans. Popular curiosity gave rise to the Infancy Gospels, widely influential apocryphal texts that closed the biographical void left open by the canonical Gospels. Drawing on topoi from romance and other popular genres, these apocryphal legends of Jesus' early life piqued the interest of medieval readers and aroused the suspicion of members of the clergy, as Thomas Aquinas's extensive engagement with the topic demonstrates. At the same time, the Franciscans played an important role in resuscitating the Christ Child, and their founder, in particular, seems to have actively promoted this devotional trend. A strong Franciscan influence, in turn, can be detected in Brigitta of Sweden's *Revelations*, a text that brings together the affective devotion to the Christ Child and to his humanity with a decidedly maternal perspective.

Dzon's introduction not only provides a succinct overview of the chapters that follow, but also surveys previous scholarship on the topic. Though this overview comes rather abruptly (in the form of a standalone section), it ultimately proves highly useful because it contains a nuanced discussion of the different interests that have tended to underlie previous scholars' works (i.e., feminist approaches; Eucharistic devotion; the social history of childhood; the advent of affective piety, particularly as it relates to the Passion). Because many previous scholars studied legends of the Christ Child as a means to understanding some broader topic, their treatment of the material covered by Dzon has seemed sketch-like and at times one-sided. Given this context, it is obvious why a book devoted to the apocryphal Infancy Gospels and their medieval reception is an important contribution to existing knowledge.

The first chapter ("The Christ Child in Two Treatises of Aelred of Rievaulx and in Early Franciscan Sources") analyzes the Cistercian and early Franciscan role in establishing the Christ Child as an object of affective devotion, focusing in particular on Aelred's treatises *De Jesu puero duodenni* (c. 1153–57) and *De institutione inclusarum* (1160s). In both texts, Aelred champions an experiential approach and invites his readers—respectively, his friend Ivo, and his sister, a recluse—to achieve closer proximity to Jesus through meditation and by contemplating his humanity. The Christ Child proves central to both texts. Dzon argues that Francis of Assisi's treatment of the childhood of Christ is even more forceful, thanks to its emphasis on the poverty of the innocent baby. Francis aligned himself explicitly with the lowly conditions of the Christ Child, reflected alike in Franciscan iconography and writing (including the *Meditationes vitae Christi*, which Dzon analyzes meticulously). If hagiography is to be believed, Francis's identification with the Christ Child apparently culminated in the famous episode at Greccio on Christmas Eve in 1123, in which Francis staged a live tableau of the Nativity for devotional purposes. In this chapter, Dzon eloquently weaves together textual, iconographic, and performative evidence, never losing sight of the overall argument: the Christ Child as the focal point of people's fascination and devotion.

Chapter 3 ("Aquinas and the Apocryphal Christ Child in the Later Middle Ages") is the one I enjoyed the most. Here, Dzon provides a detailed interpretation of Thomas Aquinas's views of the apocryphal stories about Christ's childhood. In the *Summa theologiae*, and in a number of other writings, Aquinas rejects the non-canonical narratives because he claims that a miracle-working Christ Child would have made people doubt the humanity of the baby. Instead of strengthening the believers' faith in the miracle of God becoming human, the child would have been regarded as a demon or magician rather, thereby countering the divine purpose of the Incarnation. Dzon carefully takes apart Aquinas's arguments and places them within the wider context of the hugely popular apocryphical accounts. She provides a succinct overview of the texts in question: the *Protoevangelium Jacobi* and the *Infancy Gospel of Thomas*, both of which influenced the later *Gospel of Pseudo-Matthew*. Against the backdrop provided by this overview, Aquinas's objections are thrown into sharp relief, and his concerns about the possibly detrimental effect of popular fascination with the Christ Child become vivid and tangible. What makes Dzon's argument particularly enjoyable is that she, whenever possible, adds evidence from vernacular texts that correspond either to Aquinas's critique and/or to the apocryphal Latin narratives that preoccupied him. Aquinas's use of terms related to "fantasy" (*phantasma, phantasia, phantasticus*) leads Dzon to a very suggestive discussion of changelings and the potential links between the baby Jesus and Merlin, arguably one of the most famous medieval figures engendered by an incubus. The "quest" in the title of Dzon's book is thus more than a catchy selling-point; as Dzon argues, the stories of the Christ Child bear uncanny resemblance to Merlin's conception and early years. The synergies that seem to have existed between popular romance and the infancy narratives, Dzon suggests, in turn may have been influenced by the Scholastic arguments against overly fanciful depictions of the Christ Child, and in particular the suggestion that Jesus would likely have been crucified prematurely if he had exhibited the supernatural powers attributed to him in popular accounts of his infancy.

The fourth and final chapter ("A Maternal View of Christ's Childhood in the Writings of Brigitta of Sweden") concentrates on Brigitta of Sweden's *Revelations*, particularly the depiction of the Christ Child found in the Virgin Mary's account of her experiences as she tells them to Brigitta. Especially striking is the way in which Brigitta's devotion is connected to certain material objects that are indicative of a specific female perspective on the Christ Child. A major theme in Brigitta's writings is the Proleptic Passion, i.e., the conception that Christ's whole life was an act of suffering. Dzon offers a compelling reading of Brigitta's texts against the backdrop of the wider traditions that informed her thinking, such as the legend of the seamless tunic that Mary made for Jesus. Here, iconographic evidence is considered as well. Among other aspects, Brigitta stresses the humanity of the Christ Child and the need to swaddle him. The swaddling clothes become the prop for an associative chain that links the Nativity to the Passion and to Christ's burial shroud. The female perspective promoted by this focus on the material realities of women's work seems to have appealed to Margery Kempe, who at one point in her *Book* imagines herself tending to the newborn baby. Dzon's argument comes full circle when she closes the chapter with a brief discussion of the extent to which Franciscan thought may have influenced Brigitta's writings, especially her focus on the Christ Child's poverty and lowliness.

Even though each of the chapters is devoted to a detailed examination of one author's writings and the contexts that illuminate them, Dzon keeps a number of threads running throughout the whole book. The overlaps and intersections among the multifarious traditions Dzon traces (biblical, apocryphal, Scholastic, Cistercian, Franciscan, mystic) leave us with the impression of a dense intertextual web that demonstrates how permeable the various parts of medieval society and culture were. I feel that I cannot do full justice to how brilliantly Dzon manages the richness of the material; there are a plethora of observations she makes in passing that are worth reflecting upon and perhaps following up on in further studies. I am thinking, in particular, of the Jews' role in both the Scholastic arguments against the Infancy Gospels and in vernacular narratives, but also of Dzon's mentions of the Christ Child as an object of Passion devotion in art and literature, as well as her discussions of the narrative strategies that allowed for an experiential engagement with the humanity of Christ in devotional contexts. This is truly a thought-provoking study, not only for anyone interested in the Christ Child, but also for readers who wish to deepen their understanding of the intricacies of medieval devotional culture.

EVA VON CONTZEN
University of Freiburg, Germany

THELMA FENSTER and CAROLYN P. COLLETTE. *The French of Medieval England: Essays in Honour of Jocelyn Wogan-Browne.* Cambridge: D. S. Brewer, 2017. Pp. xvii, 340. $99.00.

The theme of this festschrift in honor of Jocelyn Wogan-Browne must have picked itself. *The French of Medieval England* is the subtitle of the influential collection *Language and Culture in Medieval England*, which she edited, and is also firmly embedded in the French of England Translation Series, which she founded. As the editors write in their introduction (and Felicity Riddy in her foreword), Jocelyn's work has been trailblazing, and this collection shows the richness of the vistas that she has opened up.

The first essay deals with the *Comput* by Philippe de Thaon, the earliest named vernacular French author. Thomas O'Donnell examines the Latin glosses to the Anglo-Norman text in one of the manuscripts (Cambridge University Library, MS Add. 4166, Fragment 9), and reflects on the historical circumstances following the Norman Conquest in which it made sense to gloss Anglo-Norman into Latin rather than vice versa. An edition of the glosses is provided in an appendix to the essay. After a more theoretical discussion of translation by Emma Campbell, we come to some close readings of Anglo-Norman poems. Monika

Otter compares the French and English versions of the Prisoner's Lament with the Latin song that provided the melody, the Latin *Planctus ante nescia*. The Latin text is given in an appendix, followed by French and English verses with syllable counts (my counts for some of the English verses are different). Fiona Somerset achieves the same satisfying balance of textual analysis and contextualization in her discussion of two thirteenth-century political songs, both extant in interestingly different versions, all of them printed, with translation, at the end of the essay. Andrew Taylor contributes an essay on the *Chanson d'Aspremont*, addressing the intriguing question of why the Benedictine Abbey of Saint Augustine's in Canterbury may have wanted to acquire, and perhaps produce, a chanson de geste. Robert Grosseteste's *Chasteau d'amour* is the topic of Nicholas Watson's essay, which shows exactly what Langland's *Piers Plowman* owes to Grosseteste and where these two allegorical poets diverge from each other.

The term "The French of England" has certain advantages over Anglo-Norman and Anglo-French, but a drawback of the term is that this French was spoken and written not just in England, but also in Wales, Scotland, and Ireland. It is good to see this recognized in Serge Lusignan's analysis of a set of surviving documents (many of them by Scottish writers) relating to the Anglo-Scottish Wars. An illuminating table shows the correlations between text type and language choice: some genres of documents are predominantly in Latin (e.g., debentures and warrants) while others (letters and petitions) are typically in French.

Two essays focus on text collections that Jocelyn Wogan-Browne has helped us to rediscover. Richard Ingham looks at French borrowings in the *South English Legendary*. The received wisdom is that it was the social prestige of the "upper classes" that encouraged lexical borrowing from French, but, as Ingham clearly shows, the semantic domains of French-derived items in the *South English Legendary* go well beyond "posh" words: there are, for instance, "action verbs" (e.g., exchange, pass, cry), verbs for abstract relations (accord, betray) and for emotional states (e.g., annoy, suffer). The community most likely to be responsible for this lexical diffusion is the clergy. The case is convincing, though the separation of the clergy from the secular "upper classes" is perhaps over-schematic (they often came from the same families). Christopher Baswell's essay analyzes the saints' lives in the Campsey manuscript. He focuses on disability, and the focus is amply justified by his exposition of the narrative possibilities generated by disabled bodies in these texts.

The chapters by Mark Ormrod and Maryanne Kowaleski are concerned not with the French of English people, but with French speakers who migrated to England. Amongst the "EU migrants" who feature in Ormrod's essay is the remarkable John Gournay, who, according to a local jury, had come to England not for business purposes but to improve his English. Kowaleski uncovers a surprisingly large community of French-speaking immigrants in Devon, many of them associated with Devon's maritime economy.

There are two essays that take us beyond the Middle Ages. Paul Cohen discusses what sixteenth- and seventeenth-century French intellectuals made of the "French of medieval England," while Delbert Russell celebrates the achievements of that great discoverer in the field of Anglo-Norman, Paul Meyer.

The penultimate essay is by R. F. Yeager, who argues there is much more to Gower's French balades in his *Traitié* than first meets the eye and successfully demonstrates this in a detailed close-reading of Balade 2. Some of the French quotations needed checking, and I would venture a different translation of lines 8–9, "A l'espirit qui fait la providence / Ne poet failir de reguerdon suiant," than that offered by Yeager ("From the spirit which does this, Providence cannot withhold a subsequent reward"). I think this means "The spirit that enacts God's providence will not go without the subsequent reward." The final essay, by the late Robert Stein, notes how often "England" and "English" royalty feature in the songs of the troubadours, and claims that "the songs of the troubadours are . . . an entirely uninterrogated witness for the place of England during the high Middle Ages." Readers interested in the topic should consult Jean Audiau, *Les troubadours et l'Angleterre* (1927).

The collection concludes with an "Afterword" by Robert W. Hanning that sums up both the value of the contributions in this collection and the immense value of Jocelyn Wogan-Browne's scholarship over four decades.

AD PUTTER
University of Bristol

JAMIE C. FUMO. *Making Chaucer's "Book of the Duchess": Textuality and Reception*. Cardiff: University of Wales Press, 2015. Pp. 272. $125.00.

This is the first comprehensive study of Chaucer's first major work, *The Book of the Duchess*. Until now, the poem has been the subject of only one major scholarly study, James Wimsatt's 1968 *Chaucer and the French Love Poets: The Literary Background of the "Book of the Duchess,"* which focuses on its literary sources. *The Book of the Duchess* may be the least examined of Chaucer's dream visions because of its roots in submission and service, both personal and literary. Not only is this narrative dream vision heavily invested in its French sources, it is also rooted in historical events and figures, with the Man in Black, whom the melancholy dreamer encounters after falling asleep over a volume of Ovid, identified as John of Gaunt, and the young wife that he mourns Blanche of Lancaster, who died of the plague in 1368. The poem illustrates Chaucer and his wife, Philippa's, deep personal investment in and service to this branch of the royal family.

Jamie C. Fumo's project here is to take into account not only the literary sources of *The Book of the Duchess* but also its reception and dissemination, including its place in current Chaucer studies. *Making Chaucer's "Book of the Duchess"* includes chapters on critical trends in the interpretation of the poem, especially in relation to the production of the text as a book (putting the "book" back into *The Book of the Duchess*). The "Making" in the title thus refers to Chaucer's own, active and self-conscious "making" of the book, as well as its ongoing construction as a literary artifact. Fumo makes *The Book of the Duchess* relevant to twenty-first-century studies by highlighting its investments in active processes of reading and rereading, interpretation and reinterpretation, multilingual and polyglot cultures, and the fluidity of the self and of constructions of identity and reality.

Chapter 1 provides a valuable overview of scholarly discussions of the work, illustrating how scholars "made" *The Book of the Duchess*. It ranges from the dismissive responses by early Chaucerians such as J. M. Manly, who scoffed at its "thin prettiness," reflecting the prevailing Victorian opinion of the text as marginal and derivative, to George Lyman Kittredge's acknowledgment of the poem's elegiac power, and twentieth-century scholars' emphasis on its originary status, in terms of its expression of authorial identity and English literature coming into its own as a literary language. This chapter includes discussions of dating and the poem's historical occasion, the process of composition and evidence of authorial revision, and the poem's generic investments in elegy, the French *dit amoreux*, and the dream vision.

Chapter 2 pursues the subject of scholarly discussion of the poem by looking closely at the key interpretative issues of concern in contemporary critical discussion of the poem: miscommunication, consolation and Boethianism, gender and grief, illness narratives, and interlingualism. These interpretative issues all resonate with broader critical issues in the field of literary studies. The miscommunication between the Dreamer and the Man in Black, for example, represents a drama of thwarted communication and misinterpretation that speaks to the broader theoretical issues raised by deconstruction. The discourses of insomnia, fainting, and melancholy, not to mention the devastation wrought by the Black Death, speak similarly to current critical interests in the body, illness, and medicine. The question of the poem's relationship to its French sources is especially pertinent to theoretical topics of intertextuality, translation, and cultural hybridity.

While the previous two chapters are admirable in their ability to synthesize broad critical trends and histories, Chapter 3 provides, instead, an original and exciting thesis about the text's inscription of its own textuality through Chaucer's vocabulary of "making" and the "book," and self-consciousness about reading and writing. Chaucer's representation of acts of writing in *The Book of the Duchess* links the volume of Ovid that Chaucer as narrator is reading to that of the book that the poem's reader is imagined as holding in his or her hands. Fumo calls this a "compositional consciousness"—and she explores it in relation not only to Chaucer's *Book* but also to its resonances within other texts contemporary with Chaucer, such as Langland's *Piers Plowman* and Julian of Norwich's *A Revelation of Love*. This self-consciousness about the act of writing, "when the author represents himself in the act of writing the very poem we are now reading," sets up the poem's thematics of making and remaking: Fumo traces this is in a detailed discussion of the meaning of the word "book" as any "narrative, non-lyrical written text" that expands to the poem's thematics and symbolism of black and white through Blanche and the Man in Black.

Chapters 4 and 5 focus on the book's reception, from early editors and readers as well as by more contemporary scholarship. Chapter 4 focuses on the materiality of the book and the integration of *The Book of the Duchess* in early modern discourses of biography and autobiography. This chapter does not offer new material to resolve textual questions about the flawed manuscript sources of *The Book of the Duchess* or the independent witness of Thynne's 1532 edition, which importantly supplies various missing lines from the manuscript sources. Rather, it considers how this original textual setting influenced the poem's reception, including marginal manuscript notations, the poem's concluding "envoy," and Thynne's placement of the *Book* immediately before Chaucer's *Lenvoy de Chaucer a Bukton*—which some believed was addressed to John of Gaunt—in his edition of Chaucer's *Works*, combining to shape the poem's interpretation in relationship to notions of the author's personality and involvement in historical events.

Chaucer 5 provides a detailed account of the creative responses to *The Book of the Duchess* by John Gower, John Lydgate, Charles of Orléans, and Edmund Spenser, as well as a set of anonymous poems including *The Isle of Ladies*. A poem deeply attuned to issues of textuality and reception, *The Book of the Duchess* was appropriated by authors who valued its expression of English authorial identity, and its open approach to issues of literary authority. These include John Gower's dialogues with Chaucer in *Confessio Amantis*, which reads it as a poem of love more than loss, and Lydgate's *Complaynt of a Loveres Lyfe*, which blends aspects of *The Book of the Duchess* with other Chaucerian works into a new fashioning of the dream-vision form that ends, rather than begins, with sleep. *Fortunes Stabilnes* by Charles of Orléans and the anonymous *Isle of Ladies* constitute a genuine encounter with and reworking of Chaucer's poem, while the fifteenth-century allegorical visions *The Floure and the Leafe* and *The Kingis Quair* use its central themes of dreaming, reading, and authorship for purposes that are fundamentally bookish and literary. Edmund Spenser's *Daphnaida*, a pastoral elegy composed upon the death of Lady Douglas Howard, returns the reader to the poem's commemorative purpose, as an elegy about a deceased noblewoman.

This is a book of deft literary history and sharp critical synthesis. Readers will not find in it any sustained interpretative close readings of *The Book of the Duchess* or specific passages from it, but they will benefit enormously from its lucid writing and comprehensive understanding of every aspect of this foundational text, which, as Fumo demonstrates, enshrines experimental making at the level of language, identity, and text, and offers a profoundly open-ended experience that inspires readers across time. Fumo writes beautifully and movingly about the capacity of *The Book of the Duchess* to raise questions of translation and interpretation, and communication and representation, which remain central literary preoccupations, and which prompt the wide range of responses to it to address such questions with an eye to the intimacy and vulnerability of the Chaucerian narrator. This valuable study is a "must read" and key starting-point for any reader of *The Book of the Duchess*.

DEANNE WILLIAMS
York University

KATHLEEN COYNE KELLY AND TISON PUGH, eds. *Chaucer on Screen: Absence, Presence, and Adapting the "Canterbury Tales."* Foreword by Terry Jones. Columbus: Ohio State University Press, 2016. 296 pp. $95.00 cloth; $20 e-book.

According to the *Oxford English Dictionary*, the concept of "fun" postdates the life of Geoffrey Chaucer. But he persistently uses variants of "play" and other related terms in his writing, and he famously establishes "earnest" versus "game" as a central paradigm for the understanding of the *Canterbury Tales*. Chaucer, it seems, took great joy in telling his stories, and many readers have delighted in his writing because it is humorous and indeed fun. The same cannot always be said of Chaucerian scholarship, which is sometimes so very "earnest" that it can seem dry and lifeless.

To the contrary, one of the greatest virtues of *Chaucer on Screen: Absence, Presence, and Adapting the "Canterbury Tales"* is that it is an unusually enjoyable collection to read. It is clear from the outset that this volume promises to be a little different than the norm, with a foreword written by Terry Jones, the Monty Python veteran and literary scholar, whose first words are "What fun!" A reader might lament the fact that Jones's enthusiastic foreword is only one page long, but many will agree with his view that this "immensely varied collection of essays" is both entertaining and valuable for its "illuminating" critical discourse (xi).

Chaucer on Screen is a much-needed study that offers the first comprehensive treatment of Chaucer on film. It is edited by Kathleen Coyne Kelly and Tison Pugh, with essays written by a number of well-regarded Chaucerians. As the editors explain in their introduction, the book aims to investigate "the various translations of Chaucer and his literature to film and television, pointing in particular to the disparate expectations of scholars in the academy and of consumers of visual culture" (1–2). Overall, the volume provides a thought-provoking "intervention into traditional attitudes toward Chaucer and his cinematic and televisual adaptations" (6). Yet, as is true with most any large collection of essays, certain arguments are more successful than others, and there are some gaps and issues that may leave a reader somewhat unsatisfied.

Chaucer on Screen is divided into five parts, with the first titled "Theorizing Absence." This section contains four short papers that aim to answer the long-held question of why Chaucer is so scarce on film. The contributors variously theorize the relative lack of cinematic representations of Chaucer's verse, providing suggestive answers to how and why "Chaucer's language and narrative positioning obstruct modern readings" (12) of the poet on film. Literary theorists in particular may find Part 1 to be the most intriguing section of the book, and especially the accounts by Larry Scanlon and Kathleen Forni. These critics, respectively, argue that Chaucer's writing is complexly postmodern (particularly in terms of its treatment of the "real"), a fact that makes it less accessible than the work of an author of straightforward linear narratives such as Jane Austen; meanwhile, Chaucer is shown to have a significant image problem, whereby he is viewed as both "too high and too low," not thoroughly recognizable to an American audience, and is not really considered to be "a profitable commercial property" (56). Though it is sensible for English-speaking critics to compare Chaucer with William Shakespeare, a reader might wonder whether this section really needed two separate essays that consider why Shakespeare has, comparatively speaking, been so widely present on film while Chaucer has been given scant attention. Instead, a more appropriate point of comparison for one of these chapters might have been with Dante, who has been adapted and referred to in mainstream movies more often than his fellow medieval author Chaucer.

Part 2 ("Lost and Found") explores Chaucer's remote place in the early history of Hollywood. Whereas the first section is largely speculative and theoretical, in a sign of the diversity of the volume, Part 2 presents two essays that are more firmly rooted in history and politics. Candace Barrington's essay "Lost Chaucer: Natalie Wood's 'The Deadly

Riddle' and the Golden Age of American Television" is one of the high-lights of the volume. Barrington discusses her search for a rumored tele-vision version of *The Wife of Bath's Tale*, starring the Academy Award-winning actress Natalie Wood. Barrington presents readers with an aca-demic detective story of sorts, detailing her pursuit of the film, a process that illustrated that "lost film elements" (90) can be as elusive as medie-val manuscript ephemera. Though her search for Wood's film ultimately proved to be a failure, Barrington is able to use her story to draw some interesting conclusions about ambiguous "paratexts," early American cinema, gender in Hollywood, and the challenges of medievalism. Con-sequently, Barrington's essay embodies the best features of the book as a whole, since her account is fresh, entertaining, and intellectually engaging.

The third section addresses "Presence" by exploring some of the major films inspired by the *Canterbury Tales*: Michael Powell and Emeric Press-burger's *A Canterbury Tale* (1944), Pier Paolo Pasolini's *I racconti di Can-terbury* (1972), and Brian Helgeland's *A Knight's Tale* (2001). These are perhaps the most famous movies based on Chaucer's writing, and thus they have been examined fairly extensively by critics. Essays in Part 3 by Tison Pugh, Kathryn L. Lynch, and Siân Echard illustrate why medi-evalism has increasingly been recognized as an important focus of trained medievalists, who have supported the "moral and artistic project of recu-perating the medieval past" (132) through film, a medium that can and does offer the opportunity for "lively and close reading[s] of Chaucer" (133) and his poems (to use Lynch's phrasing). These three essays, there-fore, offer some shrewd commentary on important filmic adaptations.

One movie that is probably *not* known by many readers is *The Ribald Tales of Canterbury* (1985), directed by Hypatia Lee. The reason this movie is likely unfamiliar to most Chaucerians is that it is, in fact, a pornographic film—allegedly one of the most expensive porno films ever produced. In the other essay written for Part 3, George Shuffelton offers a bold close reading of this movie, which is shown to project "a nostalgic and entirely conventional version of medieval bawdy while simultaneously rejecting the imprint of Chaucerian masculinity" via a "thorough feminine displacement of Chaucer's male authority" (149). This account illustrates that there is, it seems, something for everyone in *Chaucer on Screen*, and Shuffelton deserves credit for acknowledging that there are many types of medievalism, and for demonstrating that even taboo forms that are widely seen as too risqué for traditional academic discourse *do* have intellectual value and may offer surprising insights into the modern reception of Chaucer.

While there is much to like about the remainder of the volume, Parts 4 and 5 are where some of the most glaring problems are to be found. The fourth section comprises six essays on the BBC *Canterbury Tales* (2003). There are certainly many useful ideas to be found in this well-received series of cinematic modernizations, and the contributors' essays highlight the ways in which these adaptations deftly use Chaucerian source-material to examine crucial societal issues in the twenty-first century, such as sexuality, immigration, racism, gender inequality, and religion. Nevertheless, a reader of the entire collection might wonder why so much attention is given to this particular series of productions, in contrast to other notable cinematic versions. Also, if the BBC *Canterbury Tales* truly merits six full essays—one for each separate episode from the series—then why place length restrictions on these articles, unlike the other essays in the book? In the end, these editorial decisions mean that, on the one hand, the volume seems to value these BBC productions particularly highly but, on the other hand, the scholars were not afforded the same time and space as other contributors to articulate and support their generally helpful arguments.

The fifth and final section ("Absent Presence") features just a single essay, written by Laurie Finke and Martin Shichtman. This paper presents some very interesting commentary about the "decidedly Chaucerian" ideas found in the popular TV show *Mad Men*, especially the ways that the show, like the Wife of Bath, explores "the various publicities that can and will be attached to women" (253) in the face of social prejudices and constraints. However, as the de facto conclusion to the collection this essay seems a little out of place, as a reader may be left wanting either a companion piece, or perhaps a text that more overtly ties up the various intellectual threads of the volume. Furthermore, if *Mad Men*—a show that does *not* directly draw on Chaucer's poetic corpus—deserves a central place in the volume then why is there no specific essay on Jonathan Myerson's award-winning animated *Canterbury Tales* (1998)? And perhaps some consideration is warranted of notable references to and uses of Chaucer in other mainstream television productions (such as his comedic presence in specific episodes of the popular American sitcoms *Frasier* and *The Big Bang Theory*, for example)?

Despite some highs and lows, in general *Chaucer on Screen* is a timely and intellectually rewarding collection. It will be especially welcome to Chaucerians and medieval literature experts, who have often wondered why more of the poet's popular representations have not been given the serious academic treatment they deserve. Readers of the collection will be richly rewarded, because it provides many useful insights and, just as importantly, it is good fun to read.

GEOFFREY W. GUST
Stockton University

KATHRYN KERBY-FULTON, JOHN J. THOMPSON, AND SARAH BAECHLE, eds. *New Directions in Medieval Manuscript Studies and Reading Practices: Essays in Honor of Derek Pearsall.* Notre Dame: University of Notre Dame Press, 2014. Pp. xxii, 551. $66.00.

This volume of twenty-four essays is the latest and also grandest example of commemorative essay collections, deservedly dedicated to Derek Pearsall. The collection builds upon Pearsall's own work establishing the York Manuscripts Conference in the early 1980s. This conference and its successor at Harvard gave birth to some of the most acclaimed contemporary scholarship on medieval manuscripts and literature: including volumes such as *Manuscripts and Texts: Editorial Problems in Later Middle English Literature* (D. S. Brewer, 1987) and *New Directions in Later Medieval Manuscript Studies* (York Medieval Press, 2000)—both edited by Pearsall—and several collections of essays dedicated to Pearsall, such as *Medieval Literature and Historical Inquiry* (D. S. Brewer, 2000) and *Middle English Poetry: Texts and Traditions* (York Medieval Press, 2001).

The way this book of *New Directions* is different from the earlier festschrifts and collections, however, is how deeply the feted honoree's presence is felt throughout the volume. Rather than just offering an appreciative and celebratory introduction and a dignified photo facing the title page, the volume's editors help to map out its contents for readers with prefaces to thematic section groupings that all illustrate Pearsall's legacy helping to link medieval literary studies and book history.

As a tip-of-the-hat to Pearsall's role in establishing this standard of textuality-awareness, Part 1 of the book is titled "Celebrating Pearsallian

Reading Practices," in which Tony Spearing leads off with an article that builds upon Pearsall's work on *Troilus and Criseyde*. Spearing does so by examining Chaucer's major contribution to Middle English narrative verse, i.e., overt narrative markers of the author's participation in a tale's retelling, through the lens of narrative theorists such as Gérard Genette and Gary Saul Morson. In this, Spearing further fleshes out his concept of "autography," illustrating how it can be understood as a reaction against earlier forms of retelling existing stories. In her "Derek Pearsall, Secret Shakespearean" Martha Driver offers a metacritical piece that combs back through Pearsall's *curriculum vitae*.

Drawing on metacritism in another vein, Part 2 of the volume is as much a memorial to Pearsall's esteemed colleague at York, Elizabeth Salter, as it is a celebration of Pearsall himself. Essays from Jocelyn Wogan-Browne on affective reading in two meditations on Christ's Passion, Susan Powell on *Wynnere and Wastoure*'s connection to the Wingfield family of mid-fourteenth-century Suffolk, Katie Ann-Marie Bugyis on strategies used by the Red-Ink Annotator of *The Book of Margery Kempe*, and Sarah McNamer on the place of origin and Franciscan affiliation of the author of the Italian *Meditations on the Life of Christ* all pay homage to the enduring work Salter produced to ground Middle English literature in its international, textual, and historical contexts.

To demonstrate further the influence of Pearsall's effort to invigorate the field of literary studies with manuscript studies, Part 3 of the collection is positioned as a celebration of the thirty-year anniversary of the 1981 York Manuscripts conference. Carol Meale, for example, shows how her career-spanning interest in the book trade in London is built on the work she developed for that conference on early sixteenth-century bookseller and collector John Colyns. In her new essay, she reads Colyns's network of influence on cultural history even more deeply in an exploration of an important group of printers and book-dealers with whom Colyns gathered at Norwich in 1526. Other contributions in this section include A. S. G. Edwards's study on the cost and trade in Lydgate manuscripts in the twentieth century, A. I. Doyle's study on what can be learned about readers from marginalia in a single dispersed book collection, and Julia Boffey's study of the contexts surrounding a single witness of the *Brut* available in Huntington Library, MS HM 136.

In Parts 4 and 5 of this collection, Siân Echard and Phillipa Hardman introduce sets of essays by relatively new scholars who benefit from the "new philological" trends fostered by Pearsall, Salter, and the York and

Harvard Conferences of the 1980s and 1990s. Hilary Fox and Theresa O'Byrne, for example, write about English literary manuscripts circulating or created in Dublin. Fox uncovers links between *Piers Plowman* and James Yonge's "Governance of Princes," and O'Byrne finds paleographic evidence to link Longleat, MS 29 with Bodleian Library, e. Museo MS 232 via the scribe Nicholas Bellewe, who was closely associated with Yonge. O'Byrne productively illustrates the way resources that are being made available online are aiding the field (in this case the *Late Medieval English Scribes* website, http://www.medievalscribes.com, and the Calendar of Irish Chancery Letters [CIRCLE], http://chancery.tcd.ie). Hannah Zdansky and Karrie Fuller, too, breathe new life into old paleographic puzzles. Zdansky examines the Cotton Nero A.x scribe's possible attempts to stylize his hand to resemble older Anglo-Norman and Welsh manuscripts prized in his own time for their calligraphic beauty. Fuller then offers an analysis of the evolving and sometimes combative emotions expressed by the two scribal annotators of MS Digby 145's conflated A-and-C-text of *Piers Plowman*.

Completing these sections, Nicole Eddy explores evidence of school-aged readers composing doodles, couplets, and draft epistles to family members alongside copies of Middle English chronicles and romances such as the *Brut* and *Awyntyrs off Arthure* in Lambeth Palace, MS 491. And then, in a departure from the methodologies of other writers in the volume, Maura Giles-Watson offers a historicist argument without reference to manuscripts that bridges the late medieval and early modern periods. Giles-Watson examines the link between the rise of humanist rhetorical education in England and the systematic exclusion of women from performing drama in the Tudor era.

The section of the book most directly concerned with the reading practices in medieval England that Derek Pearsall has spent most of his career researching is Part 6, titled "Chaucerian and Post-Chaucerian Reading Practices." In this section, Elizabeth Scala digs into Pearsall's variorum edition of *The Nun's Priest's Tale* (University of Oklahoma Press, 1984) to offer a definitive new reading of Chaucer's "excessive display of quotation and allusion" (p. 361) in the tale. Sarah Baechle then provides much needed attention to the corpus of marginal glosses surviving in over thirty manuscripts of the *Canterbury Tales*—particularly those accompanying *The Wife of Bath's Prologue*. Baechle characterizes these glosses in terms of how they indicate a pattern of reading practices promulgated among Chaucer's fifteenth-century audiences in which glosses were treated as essential paratextual components of the *Tales*. Stephen Partridge, too, provides an important set of new, provisional observations about Harvard University, Houghton Library, MS Eng 530, extending the excellent work by Margaret Connolly and Linne Mooney on one of the most important fifteenth-century readers of Chaucerian texts—John Shirley.

To cap off the volume, in Part 7, Nicolette Zeeman, Jill Mann, Melinda Nielson, and Kathryn Kerby-Fulton offer new work on Langland that explores the editorial philosophies Derek Pearsall developed throughout his career, which have turned into his own "Langlandian Legacy." Mann considers afresh the manuscript evidence for the C-reviser's introduction of errors into the verse of *Piers Plowman*, and Nielson considers Langland's possible self-emendation in the context of similar revision techniques that might be found in Usk and Higdon. Kerby-Fulton explores the implications of the Oxford provenance and multiple scribes of the hypothesized Z-text to illustrate the different scribal reading practices and contemplative religious conventions in each scribe's background. Drawing these essays together are important critiques of Kane and Donaldson's edition of *Piers Plowman* informed by Pearsallian textual scholarship.

Two other pieces in the volume that are especially remarkable are Oliver Pickering's reevaluation of the *South English Legendary* poet and Peter Brown's reappraisal of a short text known as the *Canterbury Balade*. Both of these contributors pair detailed textual and historicist readings of these texts with new critical editions of them. The editions themselves will be valuable tools for scholars to use in their work and teaching for years to come, even if they do not prove definitive.

As a whole, this volume should be regarded as a landmark collection in our field. The way that the section prefaces and articles frequently refer to other content in other parts of the book reveals the commendable degree of collaboration and revision among authors and editors, in which the ideas framed originally as conference essays were developed into longer and even more significant pieces of scholarship.

This is also a beautifully produced book—and for its price could actually be acquired by many scholarly readers to own privately. To illustrate textual evidence in the essays there are vivid color images of manuscripts throughout the volume that are delightful and vibrant surprises as you turn its pages. The quality of each image reproduction, however, is fuzzier than one would like—being produced on the same paper stock as the rest of the book. It makes me wish Notre Dame Press had sprung for glossy plates even if in black and white, in order to preserve better this monument to a field of textual scholarship that relies more and more on viewing primary sources on screens rather than on pages.

The essays, however, are all models for research in this era of medieval studies that has been ushered in by the work, support, and advocacy of Derek Pearsall, his closest colleagues, and students. The volume shows that the most significant and interesting new work in late medieval literary studies not only dabbles in, but depends on, detailed attention to textual details, manuscript features, and the surviving evidence for literate cultural practices. As such it should be considered a valuable addition to research collections of any size and should be recommended to any reader looking to understand the state of the art in our field, and how it came to be.

ELON LANG
University of Texas at Austin

REBECCA KRUG. *Margery Kempe and the Lonely Reader.* Ithaca, N.Y.: Cornell University Press, 2017. Pp. xii, 241. $65.00.

Rebecca Krug begins *Margery Kempe and the Lonely Reader* by asking "Why did Margery Kempe write her *Book?*" (vii). In answering this question, Krug focuses on the *Book*'s language to argue that Kempe, an avid reader, turned to writing because the books that she read failed to provide her with adequate strategies for wrestling with negative emotions. Krug suggests that Kempe's reading and writing processes were both consolatory and collaborative, enabling her to connect with others who shared her emotional experiences and providing solutions for grappling productively with despair, shame, fear, and loneliness. While grounding her analysis in precise historical details from Kempe's biography, Krug approaches the *Book* first and foremost as a literary text, probing its linguistic structure to suggest that it draws on numerous genres—including proverbs, devotional manuals, morality plays, cycle drama, religious lyrics, prose tales, and saints' lives—to offer succor to its author as well as its readers.

Krug opens and closes her book with quotations from Adrienne

Rich's landmark feminist essay "When We Dead Awaken: Writing as Re-Vision," which traces how women readers, after experiencing the loneliness of failing to find themselves reflected in the books that they read, are moved to write books of their own. The books produced by this interplay between self and text—including *The Book of Margery Kempe*, Krug argues—create community through "the experience of realizing that what seemed like an individual, isolating experience is in fact shared with other people" (2). Krug claims that Kempe, by turning to life-writing and constructing her *Book*'s "I" as shared by author and reader, "invites her *Book*'s readers, including herself and her scribes, to participate in . . . revisionary reflection and self-construction" (7).

Krug structures her book as a series of chapters, each probing a prominent form of emotional engagement in the *Book*: comfort, despair, shame, fear, and loneliness. Chapter 1 on "Comfort," a word appearing nearly 150 times in the *Book*, argues that Kempe, after seeking and failing to find comfort in the devotional texts she read, eventually came to write her own book as a source of consolation for herself and her readers. Krug's subsequent four chapters probe ways for treating, as opposed to curing, commonly experienced negative emotions. She begins Chapter 2, "Despair," with Kempe's experience of suicidal despair in her *Book*'s opening episode, as she argues that Kempe imagines reading and writing as forms of conversation that enable her to grapple against despair. Writing the *Book*, suggests Krug, allows Kempe to engage in a conversational process of retelling, revision, and self-making that provided comfort to both writer and readers who experience despair. In "Shame" (Chapter 3), Krug analyzes Kempe's experiences of lived shame tied to sexuality and gendered embodiment, claiming that Kempe uses wordplay, rhymes, proverbial phrases, bits of lyric, and scriptural tags to depict language as having the power to combat that of negative thinking and invites potential readers to join her in experimenting with linguistic "strategies to resist feelings of worthlessness" (97). The fourth chapter, on "Fear," explores Kempe's recurring episodes of vivid, visceral fear and argues that religious drama—including *The Castle of Perseverance, Mankind*, and the N-Town *Woman Caught in Adultery*—enabled Kempe to understand fear as embodied, intensely verbal, and collective, as experienced by both the audience and the characters on stage. Krug suggests that, by failing to overcome fear over the course of the *Book*, Kempe proposes new ways of thinking about fear that allow her to understand herself as perseverant and resilient through her survival of each fearful episode. "Loneliness," the fifth and final chapter, details how Kempe grapples with ongoing loneliness and repeated loss of fellowship, as she is abandoned by travel companions and rejected by her fellow English people when she goes overseas. Krug contends that "ultimately, the *Book* itself is represented as Kempe's solution to the problem of loneliness" by "creating a community of like-minded readers" (174). Arguing that Kempe's writing was a process of self-discovery and self-revision, Krug suggests that Kempe offers her *Book* to readers as a tool with which they can likewise find themselves as connected to part of a collective with shared emotional experiences, as no longer lonely.

Margery Kempe and the Lonely Reader will appeal to scholars interested in medieval devotional culture, women writers, subjectivity, feminist autobiography, and affect studies. It takes Krug's previous work on women readers and writers (*Reading Families: Women's Literate Practice in Late Medieval England*) in new directions through its immersive engagement with one woman's literate practice. Coming after books about the *Book* such as Karma Lochrie's *Margery Kempe and the Translations of the Flesh*, Lynn Staley's *Margery Kempe's Dissenting Fictions*, Liz Herbert McAvoy's *Authority and the Female Body in the Writings of Julian of Norwich and Margery Kempe*, and Naoë Kukita Yoshikawa's *Margery Kempe's Meditations*, Krug's adds new dimension to the Kempe corpus with its sustained emphasis on literary and linguistic form. It situates itself within recent criticism on the *Book* by David Lavinsky, Jesse Njus, Julie Orlemanski, and Jessica Rosenfeld while also drawing upon Barbara Rosenwein and William Reddy's scholarship on the history of emotions.

At the same time that she provides a learned and detailed account of Kempe's literate practice, Krug reflects upon her own experience of writing *Margery Kempe and the Lonely Reader*, as she eschews the traditional book conclusion to write an afterword in which she details her ongoing engagement with Kempe's *Book* over the course of many years and traces the paths she took while writing her book. In her choice to narrate her reading and writing processes as she strove to understand Kempe's, Krug invites the readers of *Margery Kempe and the Lonely Reader* to participate in its author's self-reflection and retelling of her experiences.

As I read Krug's book, I was struck by how profoundly her exploration of the *Book*'s provision of comfort through its language resonated with my own experience. When I first encountered *The Book of Margery Kempe*, I was a very lonely reader. It was spring break of my final semester of college, and I was visiting my family, who had moved from Cleveland to San Diego the month before. I'd just broken up with my college boyfriend after many months of phone calls fraught with such long silences that I often wondered if there was anyone on the other line. I had always turned to books because they made me feel less alone, but I had not experienced that sense of textual connection in a long time. Feeling adrift and numb, I brought the *Book* with me on the week-long trip, since I needed to read it for my medieval literature class.

On that long plane ride westward, I began to read Kempe's *Book*. Lynn Staley calls it "an electrifying text," and I felt that electric connection more acutely than anything I had felt in a long, long time. The *Book*, its unruly protagonist, and its vivid language—Kempe's townspeople wishing her "in the se in a bottumles boyt," her friend claiming he would rather "ben hewyn as smal as flesch to the pott" than sleep with her, Christ telling her that she will "ben etyn and knawyn of the pepul of the world as any raton knawyth the stokfysch," her tale of the bear ostentatiously "devoydy[ng]" pear blossoms from his "tayl ende"— were hilarious, colorful, compelling, bizarre, and unlike anything I had ever encountered. As I read, I felt something click into place surely and audibly, like a seatbelt. I reveled in the unexpected kinship I felt with Kempe and in the consolation I derived from the words in her *Book*.

I entered graduate school several months later as an early modernist, but I could not get Kempe's *Book* out of my head. I adopted a cat and named her Margery Kempe. I sought out medieval seminars so that I could learn more about the *Book*. At the end of my first year, I decided to become a medievalist instead. When I told one of my professors, she looked concerned. "This isn't about Margery, is it?" she said.

Of course it was. As *Margery Kempe and the Lonely Reader* shows, Kempe facilitates connections between herself and her readers through the words in her *Book*, creating communities based in shared lived experiences of despair; shame; fear; loneliness; and, at the last, collective comfort. Through her sustained, meticulous engagement with Kempe's language, Krug makes a well researched and compelling argument for how Kempe's words, still crackling with electricity across space and time, have the capacity to help both writer and reader to feel less alone.

CARISSA M. HARRIS
Temple University

KATHY LAVEZZO. *The Accommodated Jew: English Antisemitism from Bede to Milton*. Ithaca, N.Y.: Cornell University Press, 2016. Pp. xv, 392. $65.00.

Kathy Lavezzo's fresh reading of English medieval literary, geographic, and architectural texts, *The Accommodated Jew* (no relation to Laurie Shannon's also excellent *The Accommodated Animal*), examines not the itinerant Jew but the stably housed one, proposing a "poetics of accommodation" (4) in which Jewish buildings figure as both embodied sites of anti-Christian activity and metonymic signs of Jewish spiritual "stoniness" and material hoarding. In Lavezzo's readings of medieval English anti-Semitic texts, these buildings also undermine anti-Jewish tropes by revealing identifications and permeable borders between Jews and Christians. The title refers also to the temporal mutability of the sign "Jew," for Lavezzo urges "a revision of the usual scholarly stress on supersession when analyzing antisemitism" (22), arguing instead that "antisemitic writers such as Chaucer and Marlowe invert and reverse this temporal dynamic, construing the Jew as not only a sign of a renounced carnal past, but also a changed harbinger of a material future" (23). Lavezzo's periodization allows her a similar temporal reversal; while standard chronicles of late medieval English anti-Semitism necessarily end in Jewish absence, the canny choice to trace English literature from Bede to Milton (and beyond, to Dickens) permits the book to culminate in Jewish presence.

The book goes from strength to strength. Lavezzo's prefatory remarks take us to the best-known Jewish house in English literature: Shylock's, both heavily fortified and easily breached from inside and out. Here, she provides a new argument about a well-studied text, useful for those of us who regularly teach it, and elegantly introduces a strategy for potentially subversive readings of these anti-Jewish tropes. Likewise, her analysis of the sepulchral imagery of Jewish enclosure in Bede's *On the Temple* and Cynewulf's *Elene* is both a very welcome addition to the small but growing body of work on Jews in Old English literature and an instantly essential reading of both texts. In both the Jewish temple of Bede's exegesis and the pit where Elene tortures Judas, Lavezzo reveals what she calls "privileged Jewish materialism" (30), the Christian belief that the chosen people have special wisdom about, and access to, precious objects such as the temple and the cross. The persistence of Christian desire for this fantasized Jewish privilege undermines supersessionary temporal logic.

Lavezzo chronicles a shift in views of Jewish accommodation after the Conquest, from "sepulchral" to murderous, as the key anti-Semitic trope of the "stony-hearted Jew"—embodied in Jewish buildings and enclosures—is overshadowed by anti-Semitic Marian and child-martyr tales, and in particular by the blood libel. She cannily maps her arguments onto the geography/spatial organization of medieval English towns and cities, demonstrating (for instance), that "the dark Jewish underbelly of Norwich" (74) imagined by Thomas of Monmouth in his account of the child martyr William of Norwich (the first written blood libel, as Lavezzo notes [68]), so key to the argument for Jewish expulsion, bears little relationship to the geographical centrality and conspicuousness of twelfth-century Jewish life in Norwich. Instead, this place recalls in some ways the cloister, site of Thomas's own life and work, which was also later subjected to lay Christian violence. Lavezzo finds, in fact, that the life of William stages a paradoxical form of identification between Norwich's monks and Jews in their vulnerability to the depredations of "the Christian mob" (91). This way of thinking through anti-Jewish and anticlerical violence together, as asymmetric twins— while acknowledging clerical responsibility for anti-Jewish violence— will no doubt prove useful to future scholars of the thirteenth century and beyond.

Compellingly, Lavezzo draws out the "urban currents" (108) of fourteenth-century England: capital and waste. Once again attending to spatial and material histories, she demonstrates that by sinking Jewish capital into Christian houses of worship, churchmen undermined the distinction between Jewish filth/finance and Christian purity suggested by literature such as *The Prioress's Tale*. Indeed, in mapping the events of that tale, Lavezzo deftly demonstrates that the martyred child carries Jewish excrement to a financially compromised church—could this, she asks, be an anxious commentary on the sources of ecclesiastical funding? Similarly, Lavezzo maps the Croxton *Play of the Sacrament* across Bury St. Edmunds, where it was likely performed. By juxtaposing the play's matter with the city's geography, Lavezzo argues that "its staging of Jews desecrating the host would have participated in an anti-Semitic rezoning—a morphing of contemporary space into a virtual Calvary— that was happening everywhere in the city" (144). Lavezzo also reads city and text together to "destabilize" this form of "rezoning," speculating that the play might have been staged in the Great Market, where clerics profited from lay Christian trade, near a grand house called Moyse's Hall, which evoked a commercial rather than "deicidal" (158) Judaism. In this argument, the urbane Jonathas has much in common with the audience and the clergy, and the play "doesn't so much overcome as reproduce the contradictions" of Christian Bury (170). Although it may seem overly optimistic to assert that, as a building with a vaguely Jewish name and legend, Moyse's Hall stands for "an ongoing Jewish presence in England" (171), it feels fitting in the context of a host miracle to think of the "real presence" of Jews, called forth here not only in supersessionary performance but also in a well-kept building.

The last portion of the book brings the arguments of the early chapters to bear on Marlowe and Milton, demonstrating that Jewish buildings continue to provide sites of identification and hostility for Protestant English writers. Lavezzo revisits *The Jew of Malta* for its identification of Barabas's increasing mastery of space with the desires of a Christian mercantile audience, and she centers accommodation in the seventeenth-century debates over readmitting Jews to England, arguing for *Samson Agonistes* as a neglected anti-admission text that nonetheless fails to reject the Jewish materialism it abominates. In these chapters, the explanatory promise of the book's arguments comes to fulfillment: ambivalent desire and identification mark the gazes of secular post-Reformation writers as well as pre-Conquest monks toward Jewish spaces. Yet the hopefulness of the book's aims seems temporarily to run dry here: the temporal multiplicity that Lavezzo offers elsewhere as a convincing subversion of anti-Semitic tropes reveals itself, in Milton's work, as a depressingly sustainable inconsistency: the coeval "mercantile Jew" (156) and the superseded "deicidal Jew" (144) are admittedly mutually contradictory images, but xenophobic causes have traditionally been, and remain, curiously remorseless in purveying alternative pleas.

Nearly all of the primary texts boast identifiable authors, a circumstance that allows arguments about authorial ambivalence (and particularly about subtextual identification with the Jews) recourse to biographical evidence. This is both a strength and, in some ways, a weakness. Where this information is geographical (Chaucer's route to work mapped against Jewish sites in London), it is especially interesting.

In other cases, it approaches the usual pitfalls of discerning authorial intentionality. For instance, as evidence that Cynewulf's *Elene* undermines Christian materialism, Lavezzo notes Cynewulf's "antimaterialist bent": he is a monk, and author of the world-rejecting sacred poem *Christ II* (61). Yet the biographical argument could be reversed; Christian materialism provides some of the loveliest images in *Christ II* (moon and sun are "halge gimmas" [sacred jewels (692b)]), and the poem's risen God is lavishly adorned. Perhaps, in light of Cynewulf's authorship of the more worldly *Elene*, we might see a materialist inclination shaping the apparently antimaterialist *Christ II*. Lavezzo is an exceedingly careful scholar and has no doubt considered this point; it would be worthwhile, then, for the book to include rather than allude to her antimaterialist reading of the overall Cynewulf corpus.

This study is a timely and powerful intervention at the intersection of English literature and Jewish studies. For scholars and students of medieval England, it compels rereadings of canonical texts, both those that are often taught and those that would be taught more if not for their anti-Semitic content. It will certainly become essential for the graduate training of English medievalists. For its Jewish studies audience, it is a deft study of English anti-Semitic literature. Although Lavezzo proposes a "uniquely English" form of anti-Jewishness notable for its "precocity and persistence" (5), a claim she bolsters with considerable historical evidence, she also takes aim at what critics call the lachrymose vision of Jewish history, which sees consistency in anti-Judaism and inevitability in persecution; instead, she explores the contingency and changing, often contradictory, idioms of such sentiments. This is a very current book, speaking to concerns both within and outside medieval studies, although it does not mention—nor does it need to—events of the twenty-first century. The only marks of our dangerous moment are the numerous explicit reminders of the offensiveness of anti-Jewish stereotypes and the moral wrongness of anti-Semitism: are these necessary? Perhaps they are.

MO PARELES
University of British Columbia

KARMA LOCHRIE. *Nowhere in the Middle Ages*. Philadelphia: University of Pennsylvania Press, 2016. Pp. 270. $65.00.

This book considers "utopia" and utopian thought as "word, literary genre, and concept" (2), not as a product of sixteenth-century geopolitical consciousness, but rather as a rich and nuanced presence that animates medieval writing across several genres. Citing the creation myth of the island of Utopia, related by Raphael Hythloday in Thomas More's *Utopia* (1516), Lochrie writes "Utopus-like, scholars of More's *Utopia* likewise sever his narrative utopia from his historical past, too, creating of it a conceptual and generic enclave alongside that other coeval birth, 'nascent modernity'" (6). Eschewing textual genealogies that look back reflexively (indeed, tautologically) to More's supposedly inaugural *Utopia*, Lochrie draws upon the work of theorists such as Ernst Bloch and Fredric Jameson to expand the definition of utopianism beyond historical periods or literary genres to include texts that voice utopian desires, perspectives, or "intimations" (6). These medieval "utopian experiments" (7) include Macrobius's commentary on *The Dream of Scipio*, the French and English versions of Cokaygne, *Mandeville's Travels*, and *Piers Plowman*. The utopian trajectories she traces in medieval texts—whether attitudinal, affective, or philosophical—generate their own literary histories of creation and consumption that exist alongside the more familiar utopianism of More's text and that may be placed in dialogue with it. In conceptualizing the utopian drives and imaginative projects of world-making these texts mobilize, Lochrie leaves aside apocalyptic "other worlds" of religious, visionary writing that defer or displace utopian hopes to an eschatological future.

"Utopianism, it turns out, does not always lead to Utopia," Lochrie observes (48). Each chapter gestures outward toward different literary traditions, and charts textual encounters across history and form. The utopian texts she reads do not establish a genealogy of premodern utopian thought that leads inevitably to More's *Utopia*; rather, they "develop their own utopian idioms and geographies, some of which find resonances in More's work, some of which do not" (7). Chapter 1, "Nowhere Earth: Macrobius's *Commentary on the Dream of Scipio* and Kepler's *Somnium*," explores the "cosmic utopianism" (17) of Macrobius's fourth-century commentary on Cicero's *Dream of Scipio* and Johannes Kepler's seventeenth-century *Somnium, sive astronomia lunae* ("Dream, or Lunar Astronomy"), which imagines space travel to the moon. In *The*

Dream of Scipio, Scipio's celestial vista of the earth leads to a sense of estrangement from the earth itself and a reassessment of the place of the Roman Empire within it. The dreamer's privileged perspective produces in him shame and wonder, an affective state that serves as "the beginning of utopian possibility" (29). As a speculative fiction, Macrobius's commentary offers a vision of geographical insularity that differs markedly from that of More's *Utopia*. Kepler's *Somnium* draws upon *The Dream of Scipio*'s visionary and allegorical modes to imagine earth from a lunar perspective to develop an argument about theoretical science. Together, Lochrie argues, "these two dreams offer exercises in world making, or rather, 'world re-making,' that mobilizes fabulous fictions and scientific knowledge in order to render the globe itself and our relationship to it both new and strange" (19).

Chapter 2, "Somewhere in the Middle Ages: *The Land of Cokaygne*, Then and Now," focuses on the potent tradition of Cokaygne, an imaginary island that, "like that of More's Utopia, exists somewhere and nowhere in the geographical and ontological uncanny" (52). Lochrie draws on scholars such as Ruth Levitas, Karl Mannheim, Ernst Bloch, and Fredric Jameson to theorize the role of wish-fulfillment within utopian texts while emphasizing how the Cokaygne tradition, despite its spectacular fantasies of plenty, eschews escapism in favor of more knowing (and plural) cultural critiques. Lochrie argues that despite Cokaygne's early and pervasive associations with gastronomic abundance, the "defining principle of Cokaygne is the elimination of need and unmitigated access to pleasure" rather than the "fantasy of consumption" (55). The French *Cocagne* offers culinary and sumptuary pleasures devoid of a logic of merit and severed from a moral economy of delayed gratification and reward. Goods flow in superabundance only to be abandoned, barely used: in *Cocagne* the "restricted largess of aristocratic abundance" (62) is imaginatively transformed into an alternative world characterized by a stunning excess (and thus devaluation) of material goods. In contrast, the Middle English *Land of Cokaygne* (c. 1330), preserved in British Library, MS Harley 913, redirects Cokaygne's utopian energies into a monastic satire against worldliness and materialism in which "Official culture *becomes* carnival culture" (67).

In the sixteenth century, Cocaygne becomes an icon of gross indulgence, as in Pieter Bruegel the Elder's painting *The Land of Cockaigne* (1567). As Cokaygne is transformed into a warning against gluttony and sloth, its utopian emphasis on "the elimination of labor . . . and class hierarchies" is replaced by a shrill moralism that "renders workers abject once again with respect to their responsibility to the dominant culture" (79). Moving forward in time, Lochrie considers François Rabelais's Abbey of Thélème in *Gargantua and Pantagruel* (1562–64) within the Cokaygne tradition and charts the particular attitudes toward labor resistance in the songs "Diddy Wah Diddy" in African-American folklore and "Big Rock Candy Mountain" in hobo culture. The fantastical landscapes these lyrics depict, however, offer enticements that bait the unsuspecting into slavery ("Diddy Wah Diddy") or sexual predation ("Big Rock Candy Mountain"). The chapter ends with a haunting image of Vincent Desiderio's painting *Cockaigne, 1993–2003*: an abandoned dinner table with stained table cloth and the sparse remains of a meal, in the midst of a rising sea of open art books that flood the surrounding area. Art and education themselves become objects of consumption that overwhelm and surfeit both viewer and artist. There is literally no space left in the pictorial frame for *more* art, as if tradition pushes out generative possibility, leaving only pastiche and bricolage.

Chapter 3, "Provincializing Medieval Europe: Mandeville's Cosmopolitan Utopianism," argues that *Mandeville's Travels* "dismantle[s]" (11) traditional geographical hierarchies of center and peripheries (familiar from some *mappae mundi*) to challenge received notions of Christian exceptionalism and ultimately to render medieval Europe "provincial" (as in the writing of Dipesh Chakrabarty). Lochrie identifies the decentering of Rome and Europe as a shared feature of *The Dream of Scipio* and *Mandeville's Travels*, and suggests how this perspectival shift serves as a corrective to imperialist sentiments in both texts. Mandeville's narrative and spatial digressions also strategically decenter Jerusalem within the text's cosmopolitan, utopian world geography to highlight the political, scientific, and cultural achievements of non-European and non-Christian cultures. A utopian redefinition of "cultural optics" (116) ensues from such moments of cross-cultural contact: at the court of the Great Khan, Mandeville witnesses how Christians' limited perspective renders them "cyclopsian" to non-European observers. The reversal of the Christian traveler's gaze exposes his own cultural deficiencies, although the inherent limits of his vision still inform his negative attitudes toward Jewish communities (125). This chapter ends with a reading of Richard Brome's comedy *The Antipodes* (1636), a play whose protagonist, Peregrine Joyless, is seized with a melancholy borne of an obsession with travel stories. This coda not only points toward the continued interest in *Mandeville's Travels* in the early modern period, but also suggests the alternative possibility of an (imagined) encounter with cultural diversity, one characterized by stubborn provincialism rather than cosmopolitanism (129).

Chapter 4, " 'Something Is Missing': Utopian Failure, *Piers Plowman* and *The Dream of John Ball*," reads Langland's poem in light of the utopian theories of Bloch and Jameson to argue for the poet's engagement with the affective possibilities of negative utopianism in *Piers Plowman*. Focusing on Will's education and the collective and socially constituted figure of Conscience, Lochrie shows how the apparent failures of figures such as Conscience open new utopian possibilities for the social community Langland envisions. Even the seemingly disconsolate posture of Conscience toward the end of *Piers Plowman* contains the potential for an imaginative alternative to the present, and such potential reframes the poem as a whole in "anticipatory and inaugural" terms (135). The chapter ends with a brief discussion of William Morris's *Dream of John Ball*, which, Lochrie argues, "grounds its utopian vision in failure" (12) in a manner reminiscent of *Piers Plowman* by locating "utopian hope in utopia's failure" (13).

The fifth and final chapter, "Reading Forward: More's *Utopia* Unmoored," reads More's work in light of medieval utopian traditions to argue for "the coexistence of More's utopianism with earlier utopianisms" (183). Such methods of forward reading, Lochrie writes, not only "expand the historical optic for reading Utopia," but also free *Utopia* from the "insularity of its conception" (183) and expand our own sense of the breadth of utopian possibilities. In a series of compelling readings, Lochrie considers Cokaygne in tandem with *Utopia* to elucidate the relationship between "melancholia and utopian desire" (13) and explores the geographical isolation and provinciality of the island Utopia in More's work against the cosmopolitan visions espoused by Macrobius, Mandeville, and Langland. The third section discusses the "radical pastoralism" (13) displayed by More's *Utopia* together with Langland's social vision and the fifteenth- and sixteenth-century plowman-complaint tradition.

Nowhere in the Middle Ages is a rigorous and demanding book, one whose literary history charts a journey reminiscent of Mandeville's: a strategically decentered itinerary that purposefully disrupts teleological linearity, a deliberately "discordant assemblage" (105). Perspectivism and visionary optics emerge as major throughlines in the book alongside the affective qualities of utopian idioms (wonder, shame, melancholy, hope), whether in the cosmographic heights of Scipio's dream or Kepler's lunar inhabitants, the allegorical dreams in *Piers Plowman* or *The Dream of John Ball*, or the traveler's gaze in Mandeville's travels. As a critical term, "utopia" operates across textual boundaries in ways both fascinating and frustrating. Utopian aspirations may at times be evasive and elusive, requiring critical labor to identify, let alone parse. But its seeming resistance to formal definition allows for the range of diverse texts that *Nowhere in the Middle Ages* brings into productive dialogue, and, indeed, for the infinite variability of alternative possibilities that a prescriptive model would forestall. The book's critical provocation to locate utopian thought in medieval texts, to think *with* texts across historical periods, and to reimagine the methodologies of literary history, is compelling and timely.

SARA TORRES
University of Virginia

PEGGY MCCRACKEN. *In the Skin of a Beast: Sovereignty and Animality in Medieval France*. Chicago: University of Chicago Press, 2017. Pp. 240. $45.00.

Peggy McCracken's newest book is about how "literary texts use human–animal encounters to explore the legitimacy of authority and dominion over others" (1). Over the course of *In the Skin of a Beast*, McCracken convincingly argues that medieval literature stages encounters between humans and animals to think about power dynamics among people. Yet, while animals provide a forum for thinking about relations of sovereignty among humans, this book is nonetheless careful not to overlook the specificity of the animal; indeed, it is particularly concerned with animal bodies. Furthermore, because she is concerned both with the reciprocity of encounters and with the process of asserting authority, which is never straightforward or even complete, McCracken shows a unique and valuable concern for recovering how animals have responded to humans' attempts to exercise power over them.

Thoroughly versed in poststructuralist theory, *In the Skin of a Beast* thus explores how medieval literary texts look through, at, with, and "against" animals; and while critics have been looking at animals for some while, this book's invaluable insight is that animals will also help us think through the intricacy of medieval representations of sovereignty. As McCracken acknowledges, the term "sovereignty" does risk anachronism: "We know that the notion of a 'sovereign nation-state' does not apply to the territorial governments of the Middle Ages" (4). Yet, similarly to how much may be gained from embracing the figurative functions that animals serve in medieval literature, so too is there much to be gained from bringing this concept tinged with modernity into dialogue with the medieval period, in order to think about "contractual rule and the consent to be governed" as well as the "[l]ayers of obligation and authority" that "define medieval political structures" (6) in all their complexity.

McCracken's corpus comprises a dazzling array of texts: vernacular Bibles and biblical commentaries, short didactic pieces, fables, *lais*, romances, and chansons de geste; this book also emphasizes manuscript illuminations. Its central exhibits date from the twelfth to the fifteenth century. Its geographical and linguistic scope is similarly ambitious, embracing Old and Middle French material, as well as texts originally written in Latin, Old Norse, and Middle High German. Each chapter brings together several works, and the argument advances almost more like a lyric than a narrative. Going from one chapter to the next is not simply a matter of going from "a" to "b"; rather, each new analysis returns, spiral-like, to fundamental problems addressed previously, further scrutinizing and deepening insight into them. The effect is kaleidoscopic, with increasingly intricate elements and connections brought into the mix.

The first chapter is about the flaying of animal skins, which, McCracken argues, functions as a complex "technology of human sovereignty" (12). This chapter moves from vernacular renderings of Genesis to the fifteenth-century *Conte du papegau*, which is, in turn, read alongside earlier *romans antiques*. As she proceeds through these sources, McCracken shows how flaying skins is both about survival and about relations of dominion; indeed, these skins, which were worn, exposed, written on, and so forth, are both the "material" and the "symbolic support for claims to sovereign power" (29). According to McCracken, in the Middle Ages, as in Foucault's concept of biopolitics, human sovereignty was "always already grounded on the capacity to regulate life"

(30). This chapter concludes by turning to the little-known twelfth-century *Romans des romans* in order to imagine how animals might respond to the ethics of parading their corpses.

Animal responses are, though, perhaps more at stake in the following chapter, which focuses on human–animal encounters that are cast in more affective terms. This chapter traces the (rather surprising) trope of wolves that are domesticated in a variety of saints' lives, in Marie de France's *Fables*, and in her *lai* "Bisclavret." McCracken imagines submission both as the animal behavior par excellence and as definitional of the human "social contract"; and when something, human or animal, chooses to submit, consenting to the "affective relationship" of being ruled, it stands to gain and to lose a lot.

The first chapters thus outline two quite different sorts of relationships, which frame both human–animal encounters and any relations where sovereignty is at stake more generally. The following three chapters focus on the intricate modalities through which animality and sovereignty are negotiated and renegotiated. The third chapter introduces us to a series of benevolent beasts, namely Yvain's lion and the werewolf in the thirteenth-century *Guillaume de Palerne*. This werewolf protects and provides for two exiles who, in fact, travel incognito inside bear skins. In both texts, what makes the animal "animal" (and thus the human "human") is in constant flux, as are the questions of how the human should relate to and figure the animal. In a move inspired by Derrida, McCracken concentrates on "the shared being of the sovereign and the beast"; for "if sovereign status is defined in terms of protection or the ability to protect, then the difference between the [benevolent] beast and the sovereign is not as clear" as we might think (95).

While this chapter reflects on beastliness and sovereignty in relation to exile and protection, the next is concerned with how knowledge, recognition, mirroring, desire, and—perhaps above all—gender fit into the equation. It examines snake-women, first considering the recurrent trope whereby Eve was seduced by a snake with the head of a maiden. McCracken shows how Eve recognizes herself in the snake's head, and seeks the recognition of her self-sovereignty and of her sovereignty over others (two sides of the same coin). Interactions with snake-women in *Le roman de Mélusine* and *Le bel Inconnu* are, though, about male desire for recognition, and for the recognition of his sovereignty. In subtle and complex ways, the male protagonists of these chivalric fictions mirror, and choose to reflect, the snake-women, associating both agency and the possession of knowledge with this encounter. It is thus via intricate engagements with animality, McCracken shows, that we witness how men stake claim to sovereignty and how women are distanced from power.

The final chapter is about wild men. It focuses on two late epics, *La naissance du chevalier au cygne* and *Tristan de Nanteuil*, which trouble the binary opposition of civilization and savage forest: "Becoming-human, it turns out, involves enduring kinship with animals" (131). In remarkable readings of the almost zany *Tristan de Nanteuil*, McCracken shows how gender, which is related to "reproductive logic" (154), comes about belatedly, functioning as a sort of Derridean supplement to the cross-species "becoming" of different protagonists. Because gender and reproduction arrive belatedly in this epic, there is a considerable space for, and considerable interest in, "an alternative model of social organization, troubling the security of dynasties grounded in part on the violent subjugation of animals to the needs, both material and symbolic, of humans" (156). McCracken thus reads texts nominally about the legitimacy and propagation of dynasties as calling into question man's sovereignty over animals and even modes of sovereignty that found themselves on the binary opposition of civilized man and wild beast.

In the Skin of a Beast thus brings together texts never considered in tandem. It also introduces us to a good number of "strange, hybrid, and fantastic figures": "fish knights, werewolves, contracting wolves, snake women, swan children, and bestial sovereigns" (161). Like these strange creatures and like its innovative corpus, this book's argument is unusual, complex, and provocative. Tracing a thoroughly original itinerary, it takes us from the relationship of violence to sovereignty to the intimacy of human–animal encounters. From the nexus of animality, sovereignty, exile, and protection, we journey to the relations among animality, sovereignty, gender, recognition, mirroring, choice, and knowledge, before finally exploring how gender and reproduction supplement a messy conflation of animal and human identities in the domain of the forest. The book does not "trace an evolution" but instead "insist[s] on the repetition of motifs or characterizations that put animals and humans into contact around questions of mastery, dominion, and sovereignty" (8). Indeed, the objects of study and the argument seem to converge on a deep engagement with *becoming*, in the sense that Deleuze and Guattari use the term. "Becoming," writes McCracken, "is not a transformation, not something one becomes, but a process that has no defined endpoint.

. . . Becoming destabilizes, it crosses boundaries; it works by alliance, rather than filiation" (131).

In a preface to her discussion of Marie de France's *Fables* in Chapter 2, McCracken stresses differences between the Old French *fabler* (or *fabloier*) and the Latin *vocare*:

Vocare articulates an act of sovereign decision, differentiating the animals from each other and from the human who names them; Adam calls nonhuman animals into subjection. By contrast, *fabler* insists on fictive speech. It describes telling and recounting rather than naming and calling, and defines a kind of storytelling: here the animals that speak and act in order to illustrate moral lessons for humans may also question species hierarchies and reveal the workings of power. (55)

Elements of this description seem also to apply to this remarkable book. It powerfully makes the case for the crucial but almost necessarily elusive contribution of "fictive speech," broadly conceived, to medieval and modern thinking about both animality and sovereignty. And rather than announcing an argument to which the reader is told to subscribe, this book *illustrates* its "lessons" in discursive and imaginative ways. The reader will not be called "into subjection" as such; rather, s/he will get a thoroughly new, captivating, and engaging glimpse at "the workings of power," with which to do as s/he pleases.

CHARLIE SAMUELSON
King's College London

LEE MANION. *Narrating the Crusades: Loss and Recovery in Medieval and Early Modern English Literature*. Cambridge Studies in Medieval Literature 90. Cambridge: Cambridge University Press, 2014. Pp. ix, 306; $98.00.

In his 1395 *Epistre au Roi Richart*, Philippe de Mézières urges the English and the French to cooperate in order to recover the Holy Land and spread the teachings of Christianity in the East. In making his appeal, Philippe turns to figures made famous by romance, telling Richard II and Charles VI "one of you [will] be the noble Roland and the other the very perfect Oliver . . . one of you may imitate the very valiant . . . Charlemagne and the other that very bold . . . King Arthur, when you fight against the enemies of the Faith" (116). In Philippe's letter, the discourses of chivalric fiction bleed into the political and religious concerns of the contemporary world.

Throughout *Narrating the Crusades*, Lee Manion traces similar interactions between romance narratives and the historical contexts in which they were read and purposed to ideological ends. Manion uncovers the topical resonances of a group of texts that he labels "crusading romances," a genre whose contours coalesce over the course of his book. Certainly, the problem of genre is not an unusual concern for a scholar of medieval romance, but Manion's focus on a subcategory of romance, rather than on the genre as a whole, opens up new associations among texts not often read in conjunction with one another. Of obvious interest to historians and literary scholars, medievalists and early modernists, Manion's book demonstrates the value of using literary texts, and especially romance, in the study of the crusades, and of viewing the crusades as a fruitful context for cultural production.

While scholars have previously recognized that military-focused romances such as *The Siege of Jerusalem* are relevant to crusading history, Manion extends the definition of the "crusading romance" to include texts that exhibit one or more of the features that he argues are central to "crusading discourse"—including less-than-obvious documents such as Philippe's *Epistre*. The defining tropes of crusading discourse include: imagery of the cross, military campaigns against non-Christians, and pilgrimages undertaken in conjunction with combat. These features need not all appear in a given text for it to be considered a "crusading romance," a subgenre that Manion argues is unified by a rhetorical emphasis on "loss and recovery"—both territorial and salvational. In the crusading romances, Manion claims, the conflict of the narrative focuses on "reconquest," a trope encompassing both "the recovery of legitimate possessions for Christendom as well as the individual's 'recovery' of a state free from sin" (9). Thus, *Sir Isumbras*, with its story of one knight's penitential pilgrimage, and *The Sowdone of Babylone*, with its Christian military campaigns, can be understood as part of the same tradition.

Narrating the Crusades proceeds chronologically, tracing the development of the "crusading romance" alongside the equally active evolution of crusading from the early fourteenth century through the post-Reformation period. Although much of his study focuses on romances heretofore not understood within a crusading context, Manion begins with *Richard Coeur de Lion*, a military-focused account of Richard I's participation in the Third Crusade. Manion's intervention lies in his reading of *Richard* as an "anti-nationalist" text. While the trend in *Richard* scholarship—evident in the work of Thorlac Turville-Petre, Geraldine Heng, and others—has been to see the romance as an early attempt to craft an English national identity, Manion highlights *Richard*'s interest in cross-cultural alliances. Additionally, his reading of *Richard* is distinguished from recent analyses that have foregrounded the more fantastic elements of the narrative, such as Richard's cannibalism or his demonic mother's inability to receive the Eucharist. Instead, Manion traces a lexicon of "associational forms" in the poem—words such as "frend" or "felawrade"—which, he argues, serve to highlight the "diverse, non-nationalistic" army privileged in the romance (21, 41). Throughout, Manion questions a teleological perspective that seeks familiar national concerns in premodern texts, while highlighting the intercultural context of England's crusading endeavors (65).

In Chapter 2, Manion turns to a romance not usually associated with crusading. *Sir Isumbras*—often deemed "secular hagiography" or "homiletic romance"—tells the story of a single knight's penitential journey, ending with his dominion over, and forced conversion of, eastern lands. Manion demonstrates that historical individuals often engaged in solo crusading, and by emphasizing the ties between crusading rhetoric and penance, Manion is able to read *Isumbras* as a text that resonates with this lesser-known crusading practice. If patterns of "loss and recovery" are central to the genre of the crusading romance, then *Isumbras* explores this pattern at multiple levels: the loss and recovery of the protagonist's property and family in the Holy Land, and the loss of Isumbras's spiritual compass and its recovery through his penitential journey (78). Manion claims, moreover, that *Isumbras* engages in a specific critique of western knights' failure to control the East after the fall of Acre (76, 93). We might wonder how much of the audience for *Isumbras*—or any romance deemed "topical"—would be attuned to the specific historical contexts traced in this chapter, but, as Manion reminds us, the audience for romance was broad, and it is certainly possible that some *Isumbras* readers picked up on the topical implications of the text.

Similarly, Chapter 3 investigates the topicality of two romances not often read in conjunction, *Octavian* and *The Sowdone of Babylone*. Like

Isumbras, these romances are "topical" in the sense that they can be considered tools "for evaluating or challenging social and political relations" (108). However, the contexts to which later romances like *Octavian* and *The Sowdone* respond are not those of *Richard* and *Isumbras*. Instead, these later texts react to divisions within Christianity in the late fourteenth and early fifteenth centuries, as well as to a geographical shift in crusading enterprises to locales such as Iberia.

In his final chapter, Manion joins scholars such as Helen Cooper and Andrew King in crossing traditionally defined period boundaries, reading into the early modern period for evidence of romance's transformations and continuities. For Manion's crusading context, this means tracing the continuation of "crusading narrative patterns and thought" in a period of "dramatic decline in actual English crusading activity" (146). He finds that, despite the continued printing of crusading romances such as *Richard*, *Isumbras*, and *Octavian* well into the sixteenth century, the chief resonance of the crusading romance in the early modern period was its influence on other forms and genres, evidenced in works such as James I's *Lepanto*, Edmund Spenser's *The Faerie Queene*, Christopher Marlowe's *Tamburlaine the Great*, and William Shakespeare's *Othello*. For these post-Reformation writers, the Catholic associations of the "crusading romance" constituted a challenge. However, Manion argues that early modern writers still found value in the "loss and recovery" narrative pattern of the crusading romance, using the form to "prolong and transform the medieval tradition" (157).

Studies like *Narrating the Crusades*—centered on combining the close reading of often understudied romances with historical documents that are perhaps obscure to literary scholars—show the potential insights to be gained from taking the medieval romance seriously, from seeing it not as a genre purely reliant on escapist fantasy, but as one that actively shapes and is shaped by contemporary dialogues and conflicts. Manion's study is exceptionally thorough, and his ability to connect cogent and broadly applicable literary analysis with specific and surprising historical contexts is admirable. On occasion, it is not clear how narratives of "loss and recovery" differ from the more wide-ranging "exile and return" structure that one finds so often in romance narratives. How is Havelok's recovery of his rightful crown distinct from a knight's recovery of the Holy Land in a crusading romance? And at times one might wonder why Manion selects his central literary texts when other romance examples—such as *Guy of Warwick*, or *Sir Gowther*, which Manion gestures toward but does not explore more deeply—might serve his purposes equally well. This latter question, however, just demonstrates the wider applicability of Manion's argument and encourages future scholars to explore these texts through the lens that he develops in *Narrating the Crusades*.

Overall, *Narrating the Crusades* demonstrates the topical potential of the romance, a genre whose utility is often seen to lie in its entertainment value. Furthermore, the book makes clear the need for more scholarship that crosses both disciplinary and temporal boundaries, furnishing a standard to which future studies of romance, and medieval literary texts more broadly, can aspire.

MIMI ENSLEY
University of Notre Dame

INGRID NELSON. *Lyric Tactics: Poetry, Genre, and Practice in Later Medieval England*. The Middle Ages Series, ed. Ruth Mazo Karras. Philadelphia: University of Pennsylvania Press, 2017. Pp. 224. $59.95.

In *Lyric Tactics*, Ingrid Nelson sets out to define the lyric genre as much by "what it does (its cultural work) as by what it is (its formal features)" (6). Medieval lyric—and especially insular lyric—is famously undertheorized and understudied, in part because of its divergence from post-Romantic notions of lyric form. Here Nelson proposes a new approach to lyric studies wherein form is subordinated to practice. This adjustment of emphasis, she contends, would provide a historical account of lyric in which medieval lyric is "paradigmatic rather than marginal" (6). Central to Nelson's analysis throughout are the terms tactics and strategy. The distinction from which the book takes its title is borrowed from Michel de Certeau's *The Practice of Everyday Life*. Tactics and strategy describe modes of relation to and uses of institutional forms. As Nelson explains, where strategists follow authorized and prescribed uses of these forms, tacticians navigate institutional forms in an ad hoc and improvisatory way that often results in unauthorized hybridization of forms. *Lyric Tactics* seeks to prove, then, that the lyric genre is defined by its singularly tactical relationship to institutional forms.

367

Each of the four chapters begins with a single lyric contained within a larger textual framework—a miscellany, a commonplace book, a long-form poem, and two collections of exempla. But to say that the book consists of four case studies is to undersell it. Nelson's initial reading introduces the chosen lyric, which then serves as a guide to the cultural and textual environments that medieval lyrics so nimbly navigated. Beginning with the example of "When the Nightingale Sings," the first chapter argues that the English and French lyrics of MS Harley 2253, such as "Cyl qe vodra oyr mes chauns," "De clerico et puella," and "Annot and John," actively employed the "inherently tactical" medieval concept of literary voice to distribute authority across text, performance, and audience (35). Responding to Leo Spitzer and others' characterization of the medieval lyric "I" as an "everyman" for which any "I" may be substituted, Nelson instead describes the medieval lyric voice as ethopoetic, a descriptor borrowed from medieval rhetoric. The ethopoetic voice, she explains, "is an utterance specific to both a speaker *and* his or her local and contingent circumstances" (43). In Nelson's view, then, medieval lyric voice expresses not a universal "everyman," but rather a contingent but portable "anyman," a "circumstantially qualified utterance that can nonetheless shift readily among speakers" (59). The chapter concludes by turning to the non-lyrical content of the manuscript, showing how ethopoetic vocal tactics are also central to the devotional prose of MS Harley 2253.

The second chapter turns from secular lyric to the religious lyrics of Additional MS 46919, the commonplace book of the Oxford Franciscan William Herebert (d. c. 1330). Beginning with a reading of the little-known Anglo-French lyric "Amours m'ount si enchanté," Nelson shows how friars who attempted to conscript popular lyrics for their pedagogical and pastoral strategies "had to reconcile the tactics of the lyric genre with their strategic aims for its usage" (60). More specifically, the friars' strategic aim both to instruct and to delight lay audiences with moral didactic lyric required maintaining fidelity to orthodox doctrinal meaning on the one hand, and harnessing the affective power of improvisatory musical performance on the other. The chapter situates Herebert's lyric practices within the context of post-Lateran debates about liturgical performance, emphasizing how these debates especially scrutinized the populism of fraternal preaching and the moral ambiguity of song. Through a combination of formal analysis of Herebert's lyrics and hymn translations, and an account of the cultural history of preaching and song as told by texts such as John Grimstone's 1372 preaching handbook and John of Garland's *Parisiana poetria*, Nelson shows how Herebert combined lyric formal techniques such as rhyme and equivocation with Scholastic forms such as rubrication and academic prologues. Thus, by putting the affective impact of lyric into a tactical relationship with authoritative theological meaning, Herebert proposed, through formal means, "a kind of solution to the potential conflict between fraternal song's popular appeal and its doctrinal mandate" (70).

The third chapter considers the case of Chaucer's *Troilus and Criseyde* and argues that the inset lyrics of the long-form poem illustrate Chaucer's essentially tactical lyric practices. Nelson acknowledges Chaucer's debts to the more codified continental—especially French and Italian—lyric traditions, but takes the position that Chaucer's tactical translations and adaptations of his sources connect him to an insular lyric tradition that especially "prizes the contingent, the improvisatory, and the recombinative" (90). Moreover, this formal affinity with improvisatory insular lyric practices, as Nelson has it, aligns Chaucer's poem with what she calls the political mode of "negotiation," which she contrasts with the "largely Petrarchan lyric practices that support and reify political absolutism" (91). Negotiation, a term that Nelson uses to refer to communal governance and composition, is not identical with tactics, Nelson explains, but rather a "mode made possible by lyric tactics" (94). The opening example, in this case, is Antigone's song. Through a combination of source study—an efficient account of the inset lyric's distant relationship to its continental analogues, including Machaut's *Paradis d'Amours* and *Le livre dou voir dit*—and formal analysis of Antigone's song's use of proverbs, Nelson shows how the song thematizes and enacts the mode of negotiation by means of insular lyric tactics. From here she turns to the *cantici Troili* and shows how these songs, while they adapt and translate Petrarchan poetic forms, also rely on and gesture toward insular lyric topoi. These lyric tactics, Nelson contends, resist the closure of Petrarchan absolutism.

The fourth and final chapter turns from politics to ethics. The texts under consideration in this case are Robert Mannyng's *Handlyng Synne* and Chaucer's *Legend of Good Women*. Here Nelson argues that Mannyng's and Chaucer's collections of exempla employ lyric tactics to "suggest an ethical practice that is more contingent, plural, and flexible," as opposed to the closure and absoluteness that exemplary forms might otherwise suggest (119). The first section takes the example of the

"Dancers of Colbek" episode in *Handlyng Synne*. Nelson begins with an account of casuistic ethical reasoning and its discontents to show how casuist thinking is interested in particulars, but also "tends to totalize those particularities in authorized cases" (121). Mannyng's translation of the *Manuel de pechiez*, by contrast, leans on the tactile metaphor of repeated "handlyng," and thus encourages a recursive and tactical use of the book's cases rather than a strategic and totalizing reading. Readers of Mannyng's translation find a formal aid for this recursive and indeterminate reading in the carol that is embedded in "The Dancers of Colbek," as the "carol verse is inassimilable" to any of the moral conclusions the rest of the episode suggests (129). In the next two sections, Nelson turns to Chaucer's *Legend of Good Women* and argues that the *Legend* integrates exemplary and lyric forms, and thus puts forth a "lyrical ethics" of "suspension and openness" rather than totalizing conclusions (129).

Lyric Tactics offers compelling accounts of what lyrics *do* and rich descriptions of what they *are*. A question that feels underexplored, however, is how and to what extent other neighboring genres *don't do* what lyric does. The main contenders, romance and drama, are briefly mentioned in the introduction, which promises later elaboration that the book never quite delivers. This leaves the reader wondering whether Nelson's carefully assembled theoretical framework best describes lyric, or, instead, a variety of performed genres. Further comparison with these other genres might have clarified this uncertainty, but perhaps this is too much to ask of a book that already does so much in its impressively dense pages.

This innovative and thought-provoking book will be required reading for scholars whose work is concerned with Chaucer, Middle English poetic theory, New Formalism, performance studies, or manuscript studies. Those who are interested in the long history of English lyric will also have to grapple with Nelson's challenge to reevaluate the genre in terms of its practices.

HELEN CUSHMAN
Harvard University

Sarah Elliott Novacich. *Shaping the Archive in Late Medieval England: History, Poetry, and Performance.* Cambridge: Cambridge University Press, 2017. Pp. xii, 214. $75.00.

For medievalists, the archive can be a site of fascination and frustration in equal measure, the closest we can come to a point of unmediated contact with the past as an object of study. As Sarah Elliott Novacich's important new book shows, however, the "archival desire" both to access and control the past is as much a medieval preoccupation as a modern one, and is not limited to the handling of books and artifacts. Other scholars have done much to explore the formation and dissolution of specific collections, as well as the broader ramifications of medieval documentary and book cultures, but Novacich's concern is with the idea of the archive and the many forms of desire it represents rather than with material archives themselves. Her study focuses primarily on the diverse medieval responses to three stories of world-defining collections from the Christian tradition: the Garden of Eden, which encloses a model of perfection and excludes everything else; Noah's ark, which carries a small portion of the present into the future while consigning the rest to oblivion; and the extrabiblical narrative of the Harrowing of Hell, in which the recently crucified Christ descends into the vast storehouse of hell, curating a smaller collection of souls to be saved. For medieval thinkers, Novacich argues, these episodes "represent the desire to amass collections that fully account for the world" (2); her epilogue uses the example of the "golden records" aboard the *Voyager* spacecraft to show how this desire still resonates for us.

Although the book is fairly short, it incorporates (in true archival fashion) a broad range of medieval and modern texts, performances, genres, and critical theories. While Novacich offers nuanced and insightful readings of many texts and contexts, her discussions of any single work rarely last more than a few pages: her goal is less to offer in-depth and comprehensive reevaluations of specific texts and authors than to trace the threads of common themes and concerns that link different texts and periods together. This approach is undoubtedly fruitful, and the lines of her argument are richly evocative, but readers may sometimes wonder what salient differences are being elided in these broadly defined collections. The book discusses each of its three core narratives in two parts: one focused on drama, generally mystery plays from the English vernacular cycles; and one focused on other genres, which variously include lyric and narrative poetry, chronicles, romances, and theological or devotional texts. Novacich uses these complementary discussions to reveal shared preoccupations across genres, but her discussions of medieval performance traditions are especially satisfying in their blend of textual analysis, details of historical staging practice, and modern performance theory.

The book's introduction lays both historical and theoretical groundwork for Novavich's project: it briefly acknowledges medieval authors who saw themselves contributing to or reflecting upon other kinds of archival projects, such as bureaucratic record-keeping, and it introduces the modern and medieval underpinnings of the archive theory upon which the book is based, beginning with Isidore of Seville's unpacking of the etymological resonances among archive, ark, and arcana. She considers the risks of treating "the archive" solely in conceptual terms, as Derrida and Foucault do, as well as the risk of fetishizing the material object in book history: the tension between "dustless" and "dusty" archives. Throughout the rest of the book, the theoretical approach predominates, but she also considers one pragmatic archival project with direct relevance to her work, the Records of Early English Drama, which clearly informs her careful and vivid discussions of space and movement in the mystery plays.

Novacich begins, appropriately, with the Garden of Eden, the original "garden of exemplars" (25), which is the subject of the book's first chapter, "Model Worlds." In her reading, however, the relationship between the enclosed garden and the postlapsarian world is a study in the ambiguous differentiation between originals and records or copies. She explores representations of Eden and theories of the garden-as-archive in such diverse texts as Mandeville's *Travels*, the mystery plays about Adam and Eve, and the *Roman de la rose*, showing how they play on the relationship between the walled-off garden and the world outside it, or the originary garden and the world that follows from it. In the mystery plays, for example, she considers how the boundaries between garden and world would likely have been staged in practice: the need for visibility would likely prevent fully enclosing the "garden," while the postlapsarian earth might have been "played by" the ground upon which the spectators themselves stood. The final section of the first chapter uses the notion of Edenic perfection, which would make both signification and spoken language unnecessary, to explore the tension between archive and narrative, both of which respond to the dispersed and divided character of the fallen world.

Chapters 2 and 3 turn to Noah, whose ark/archive determines both present survival and future remembrance. In the second chapter, "Ark and Archive," Novacich explores the theme of memory as expounded by Hugh of Saint Victor, who develops a mnemonic practice around the "ark of the heart" based on visualization of Noah's ark. Other nautical tales from chronicle and romance (such as *Brut*, *Émaré*, and Chaucer's *Man of Law's Tale*) make the protagonist's body an ark of memory, faith, or genealogy to be carried forward into a new world. Chapter 3, "*Uxor Noe* and the Drowned," offers a moving study of Noah's insubordinate wife in the mystery plays. Novacich argues that the wife's reluctance to enter the ark can be read as resistance to Noah's unilateral and patriarchal control of the archive of future history: she must accept "a certain loss of narrative authority in exchange for the preservation of life" (96). Her unruly "gossips" become part of a drowned history that shadows the official narrative, echoing apocryphal traditions of written records left by other antediluvian authors that might offer alternatives to Noah's control of the story.

The book's last two chapters cover the Harrowing of Hell. Chapter 4, "Infernal Archive," finds common themes in the apocryphal Gospel of Nicodemus, which describes the Harrowing, and other tales of infernal descent, such as the Middle English *Sir Orfeo*, the legend of Saint Patrick's Purgatory, and Dante's *Inferno*. In these tales, hell is a leaky archive that fails to separate past and present consistently, and in some cases its dead inhabitants, with their unruly desire to keep narrating their own stories, threaten to spill out into the present. The story of the Harrowing, then, is about controlling, framing, and managing these voices and the traditions they represent (not least the Jewishness of the Old Testament prophets and patriarchs). The final chapter, "The Harrowing of Hell: Closure and Rehearsal," turns again to the mystery plays and the literal hell mouths that might designate the gateway on stage. In calling forth the dead prophets, Christ both resurrects and imposes order upon history: the Harrowing becomes "a struggle between past and present, (partially) disguised as the former's confirmation of the latter" (141). The prophets move across the stage toward heaven, where they are effectively silenced, as unchanging eternity obviates further narrative. Novacich casts this as a form of spectral return, and shows that it speaks to the very nature of performance as reiterative: revenants from history are literally re-membered as they take on corporeal form onstage, resurrected and redeemed in the onstage space between past and future.

True to its theme, *Shaping the Archive in Late Medieval England* offers a wide-ranging collection that both opens a door to the past and problematizes our relationship with it. Its method is more exploratory and expansive than rigorously argumentative: it is a pleasure to follow Novacich's searching analysis and eloquent prose as she moves through medieval texts of almost every genre and on to Borges and NASA, but the reader carries away a set of unfolding interpretive tools and perspectives rather than a rigidly polemical position. Scholars of archive theory and performance theory will be particularly intrigued by the way Novacich brings these two bodies of thought into dialogue with each other, revealing their shared concerns with temporality, materiality, and replication. More generally, any medievalist interested in how biblical traditions were "good to think with" in broader ways (which is, perhaps, any medievalist), as well as those concerned with the intersections of modern theory and medieval cultures, will also find this both a thought-provoking study and a useful model for uncovering resonances between past and present without forcing the past to appear to us in our own image.

AMANDA WALLING
University of Hartford

STEELE NOWLIN. *Chaucer, Gower, and the Affect of Invention*. Interventions: New Studies in Medieval Culture. Columbus: Ohio State University Press, 2016. Pp. 234. $99.95.

Steele Nowlin's discussion of invention through a reconceptualization of affect is a groundbreaking study that marks a shift in our understanding of and approach to two of the most important authors in Middle English: Geoffrey Chaucer and John Gower. Nowlin examines how Chaucer and Gower "present invention as an affective force, a process characterized by emergence and potentiality" (1). Nowlin's affect is not one of emotion. It is "an intensity . . . typically described in a critical vocabulary of movement, emergence, and becoming" (1). He also broadens the definition of invention to one "that includes the dynamism and sense of potential that characterize inventional activity" (2). He clearly illustrates this relationship between affect and invention with an analysis of two cases of "paralyzed dreaming narrators": in Chaucer's *The Parliament of Fowls* and Gower's *Vox clamantis* (2). In both cases, the narrators' emotions manifest themselves in actions that lead to the creation of poetry: what Nowlin calls "the affect of invention" (12). In the remainder of the introduction, Nowlin provides an excellent overview of the scholarship on both invention and affect in medieval studies. His discussion of affect theory (13–17) explains his own contribution to this discourse within medieval studies as well as how he brings this contribution to bear on the idea of invention (17–18). In so doing, Nowlin deftly addresses a number of primary and secondary texts on invention in medieval studies (18–28). He concludes the introduction by coming back to Chaucer and Gower, again reiterating that "examining the ways in which aesthetic productions emerge through processes of invention . . . creates ways in which poetry can intervene in the discursive constructions of reality that exist outside of poetic worlds" (28). Whether or not intentional, Nowlin's chapters each follow this emergent process, which he argues is vital to the works of Chaucer and Gower, with each chapter stemming from the affect of the prior.

In Chapter 1, Nowlin explores the conceit of invention as movement in Chaucer's *House of Fame*. Nowlin emphasizes the abundance of movement in the proem to Book I, noting that it is "the primary conceptual framework" within the poem that sets the stage for its "examination of invention as movement" (40). He directs our attention to how the proem presents "dreams as affective forces" (40) and adds that the movement produced from these forces essentially displaces feeling. He marks the poem's emphasis on "*engynes* and *gynnynges*" as thought before likening "*tydynges*" as depicted in Book III's House of Rumor to images in the imagination (42–43). Referring to Chaucer's "motional quality of imagination" (43), Nowlin then demonstrates that *tydynges* are actually "inventional *gynnynges*" (50). The meticulousness with which Nowlin presents this argument, marrying the theoretical so well with the textual apparatus that Chaucer employs, is admirable. The analysis he provides of Book III to demonstrate invention as "a process of moving and becoming" is delightful (55), particularly his discussion of the eagle's speech (56–58), which adds an impressive and ultimately more productive interpretation of this moment in the poem to the existing readings.

Towards the end of the chapter, Nowlin discusses the poem's treatment of Dido as a potential inventor, which results in Geffrey appropriating her invention as his own, participating in the "misogynistic trope of masculinist invention" (68).

Chapter 2 emerges from this unresolved question of gender and invention left at the end of Chapter 1. *"The Legend of Good Women,"* contends Nowlin, ". . . actively work[s] to trigger in readers a sudden awareness of the pervasiveness of cultural constructions of gender and power" (69). He calls *Legend* "Chaucer's fullest narrative treatise on the affect of invention" and asserts it is an effort "to destabilize the antifeminist literary and cultural traditions its narratives would seem to represent" (73). Nowlin points out the impossibility for any poem to represent the affect of invention directly in a discussion of the prologue's borrowing from Boccaccio's *Filostrato*, asserting instead that the poem gestures toward this process through "displacement and movement" (77). In an attentive analysis of the legends of Cleopatra and Thisbe, Nowlin demonstrates how "Allas" becomes a "morpheme" that signals "emergent processes that . . . have already transformed into anguish and narrative entrenchment" (84). He then concludes with a discussion of *The Legend of Lucrece*, where he asserts the tale challenges the construction of gender by refusing to be subsumed into a fixed, established narrative, essentially breaking the legend as a whole from the cultural tradition(s) of misogyny it represents. Nowlin's conclusion about the poetics of the legend is especially exciting for the possibilities it opens "to the pervasive and intangible forces that construct cultural experience" (91).

Nowlin transitions into a discussion of John Gower's *Confessio Amantis* in Chapter 3. He argues that Gower's poem demonstrates the affect of invention "leak[ing] into the physical realities of narratives' fictive worlds—and even into what the poem posits to be the 'real' world outside of its own fictive frame" (93). Movement is again key in Nowlin's argument—what Gower refers to as "weie" (99)—but it is rupture that results in movement and the liquid metaphor of Envy that drive his argument here. Nowlin meticulously examines Gower's use of the word "venym" in the tale of Constantine and Sylvester, positing it as a destructive historical force from which Gower aims to rehabilitate the chronicle form. In "Three Questions," Nowlin claims we see the *"fyndyng* of new historical realities" (120), which then transitions into Chapter 4's argument about Gower's vexed relationship with the chronicle form as

it pertains to affect and invention. It is at once both "a culturally authoritative source for exemplary material" and "itself capable of resonating
with the movements of affect and invention" (123). Nowlin convincingly argues that Gower's extended use of chronicle beginning in Book
IV "suggests the emergence of a new kind of chronicle, one that encodes
the affective energies of inventional movement as an aspect of its form"
(123). He adds that the "work of invention counteracts the corrupting
effects of chronicle narratives" and that these chronicles "reinforce the
larger regenerative project of the *Confessio*" (130–31). Nowlin concludes
that Book IV of *Confessio* presents chronicles with "productive consequences" before transitioning into how Book V seems to undo such
work, as Gower critiques such use of affect as invention (143–45). The
transformational emergence comes in the way he corrects these religious
chronicles of "misbelieve"—laughter (148). He suggests that Gower
does not abandon the chronicle in this way; rather, he acknowledges
the potential limitations while maintaining the possibilities for "poetic
structure to impinge upon the structure of reality" (150).

Having discussed Gower's satire of his own use of chronicles for
invention, Nowlin returns to Chaucer's satire of such processes in Fragment VII of the *Canterbury Tales*. He situates Chaucer's work in this
section of the *Tales* as a critique of both his own and Gower's literary
experiments with the affect of invention, pointing out the exchange of
ideas between both poets. Nowlin's argument to this end using *The
Prioress's Tale* is some of the most useful analysis I have ever read. The
process of *fyndyng* lies with the reader here, writes Nowlin, and in this
way the tale "is profoundly characterized by the intersection of affect
and invention" (167). In *The Monk's Tale*, Nowlin shows us how the
issues with the monk's "chronicles" are that they treat invention as "an
end rather than a beginning" (174). Finally, in *The Nun's Priest's Tale*, he
suggests the tale's "elaborately prescriptive framework" seems to trouble
the affect of invention before he demonstrates how such a framework
participates in the satire of the tale. *The Nun's Priest's Tale*, then, "works
in concert with the other tales of Fragment VII . . . to demonstrate how
self-conscious satire is an essential part of conceptualizing affective and
inventional movements" (190). Like Gower's, Chaucer's satire does not
deny affect as invention; rather, it is a necessary part of such a process.

It is fitting that Nowlin ends his book with a conclusion that speculates on the effects of the affect of invention for Shakespeare. Nowlin's
purposes are threefold: to demonstrate early modern texts reflecting

" 'Chaucerian' and 'Gowerian' attitudes toward affect and invention";
"to propose that Shakespeare develops a kind of 'affective intertextuality' "; and, finally, to suggest a potential way in which the English
early modern poets engaged their late medieval predecessors (194). As
we continue to query the lines of periodization in our field, Nowlin's
speculations and conclusions here are a necessary addition. They, too, fit
nicely with his argument for the affect of invention: if Shakespeare pays
homage in such works as "The Phoenix and the Turtle" and *Pericles*, it's
clear he, too, experiences the poetic movement and emergence that
Nowlin shows us in Chaucer and Gower. Finally, as Nowlin alludes to
at times throughout his book, another type of such affect of invention
is critical, and I can think of no higher praise than writing that his book
stimulates its own affect of (critical) invention, opening up inroads into
discourses surrounding these and other Middle English poets.

JEFFERY G. STOYANOFF
Spring Hill College

KELLIE ROBERTSON. *Nature Speaks: Medieval Literature and Aristotelian
Philosophy*. The Middle Ages Series, ed. Ruth Mazo Karras. Philadelphia: University of Pennsylvania Press, 2017. Pp. x, 446, 10
illus. $69.95.

A. O. Lovejoy once wrote that the task of the historian of ideas is to
"trace connectedly" the "working of a given conception, of an explicit
or tacit presupposition, of a type of mental habit, or of a specific thesis
or argument" across a range of discourses and historical periods—all in
the attempt to "put gates through the fences" that separate these discourses and periods from each other.[7] In *Nature Speaks*, Kellie Robertson
has given medievalists an ambitious and often dazzling work of premodern intellectual history cast in precisely this mold. Over the course of
eight chapters, Robertson broadly outlines different models of nature in
both contemporary theory and medieval literature and philosophy by

[7] Arthur O. Lovejoy, *The Great Chain of Being* (Cambridge, Mass.: Harvard University
Press, 1936), 15–16.

tracking the fortunes of a single idea. This is the Aristotelian concept of *inclinatio*, or "inclination," which sought to explain how and why each natural creature was inclined, both temporally and physically, toward a certain end. As Robertson observes, *inclinatio* was a hot topic in both philosophy and poetry during the Middle Ages, because its power to explain certain human behaviors (such as sexual desire) often ran at cross purposes to certain orthodoxies in medieval Christianity (such as the freedom of the human will). By telling the story of *inclinatio* from the thirteenth to the sixteenth century, Robertson casts valuable light on the way that medieval culture thought about humanity's place in nature. In the process, she also makes a persuasive case for why scholars of medieval literature ought to pay better attention to natural philosophy, which both poets and philosophers inevitably drew upon whenever they sought, as she puts it, "to transform the world into words" (1).

Nature Speaks begins with three chapters that lay out its theoretical stakes and introduce two broad claims that recur through the book. The first claim is that there were two primary models for nature during the Middle Ages: "a 'transcendent' one, associated with Neoplatonic and Augustinian writers who saw nature as inscrutable and to varying degrees detached from the human world, and an 'immanent' one, associated with Aristotelian and Thomist writers who believed that the regular teleological processes observable in nature could not only reveal aspects of the divine plan but also teach us something about ourselves" (3). The second is that this dichotomy makes itself particularly felt in debates over the influence of *inclinatio* upon the will during the thirteenth and fourteenth centuries—something that Robertson demonstrates with a deft reading of the role that "kyndely enclyning" plays in Chaucer's *House of Fame*. Chapters 1 ("Figuring *Physis*") and 2 ("Aristotle's Nature") prosecute both of these claims in greater depth, by considering how nature was conceptualized, figured, and debated by both Augustinians and Aristotelians during the twelfth, thirteenth, and fourteenth centuries. Chapter 1 focuses mostly on four common figurations of Nature and her activity (ladder, book, artisan, or ax) in a wide range of texts including Gautier de Metz's *L'image du monde*, the *Prick of Conscience*, and Bartholomeus Anglicus's *De proprietatibus rerum*. Chapter 2 assesses the significance of a key event: Bishop Etienne Tempier's 1277 condemnation, at the University of Paris, of more than 219 propositions that pertained to Aristotelian natural philosophy. Robertson argues that, while the 1277 condemnation was broadly concerned with epistemology in general and "the limits of natural reason" (93), it also interrogated the particular legacy of Aristotle himself—a legacy that was often debated, as she observes, in accounts of whether or not the philosopher died a Christian death. By reading various accounts of Aristotle's end, such as the spurious *De pomo*, or select passages in Ranulph Higden's *Polychronicon*, Robertson makes it clear that the epistemological value of Aristotle's thought was hardly a settled matter during the fourteenth century.

With this theoretical groundwork laid, Robertson next turns her attention to literary representations of Nature in the work of four late medieval poets: Jean de Meun, Guillaume de Deguileville, Geoffrey Chaucer, and John Lydgate. In his *Pèlerinage de la vie humaine*, Deguileville (Chapter 4) offers a hostile response to "rationalist modes of interpreting nature" (179) by subordinating the figure of Nature to the figure of Grace Dieu. For Deguileville, God (via the proxy of Grace Dieu) wields absolute power over Nature—a position that, as Robertson notes, echoes that of the fourteenth-century "voluntarists," who held, against the "intellectualists" (or "compatibilists"), that, like the divine will, the human will was unconstrained by nature. For Lydgate (Chapter 6), "kyndely reson," or natural reason, cannot be relied upon for the grasping of metaphysical truths, since it is necessarily tied up with physical nature. For this reason, in his *Pilgrimage of the Life of Man* (itself a translation of Deguileville) and *Reason and Sensuality*, Lydgate exhorts his reader to take up exegesis rather than natural philosophy to understand the workings of nature, a conservative stance that Robertson relates to Wycliffite skepticism toward natural philosophy during Lydgate's time.

If Lydgate and Deguileville represent the "transcendent" (and orthodox) view of nature in Robertson's account, Jean de Meun (Chapter 3) and Geoffrey Chaucer (Chapter 5) are decidedly more "immanent" (and heterodox) in their opinions. In the *Roman de la rose*, de Meun explores the question of *inclinatio* by way an open-ended debate among La Vieille, Nature, and Genius, each of whom offers a different take on the matter. Where Nature largely echoes the voluntarist view on the will and *inclinatio*, La Vieille and Genius instead advocate for a version of the intellectualist position, wherein humans are entirely (in the view of La Vieille) or sometimes (in the view of Genius) driven to action purely by the motions of their flesh. Chaucer takes up these same issues in his

Parliament of Fowls and *Physician's Tale*, both of which interrogate, but do not resolve, the relation between natural *inclinatio* and human free will. Robertson argues that the *Parliament* ultimately suggests that the two respond to each other dialectically—that, in other words, natural inclination often gives rise to or shapes willful action, and vice versa. Chaucer revisits this issue in *The Physician's Tale*, where, according to Robertson, Virginius represents a man bereft of any natural *inclinatio*—a fact that explains why he is capable of the unnatural murder of his own daughter. Nevertheless, both the Physician and Virginius justify their willed actions by speaking in the voice of Nature—by claiming, that is, that their unnatural wills are in fact the result of natural inclination— and for this reason, the tale offers the reader a chilling picture of what happens "when humans are given a free pass from their animal inclinations" (277).

Robertson concludes her book by turning to what she calls "Lady Nature's last allegorical stand" (325) in Edmund Spenser's *Mutabilitie Cantos*. In the *Cantos*, which largely consist of an allegorical debate between the figure of Nature and the figure of Mutability, Nature asserts her control over the processes of natural change, which Mutability seeks to appropriate—but she does so only then to relinquish her powers to God and vanish from the scene. Nature's disappearance emblematizes, for Robertson, the early modern shift away from the figural representation of nature and toward its mathematical representation, a shift heralded by Galileo Galilei's famous claim that Nature's book is in fact "written in the language of mathematics."[8] Pivoting back to contemporary theory, she then argues that, just as the rejection of personification in early modern science had the unintended effect of "separat[ing] off the human from the non-human" (340), so too does the resistance to anthropomorphism in ecocriticism do the same. Then as now, the more we refuse to speak with nature, the less we are likely to see ourselves as part of it.

The great strength of *Nature Speaks* lies in its willingness to think big. When Robertson observes resonances between contemporary debates over "surface reading" and medieval modes of reading nature (see 73–74), or when she notes that, both in early modern science and in the work of Timothy Morton and Jane Bennett, resistance to the figuration

---

[8] Galileo Galilei, "The Assayer," in *Discoveries and Opinions of Galileo*, trans. Stillman Drake (New York: Doubleday, 1957), 239.

of nature bears an iconoclastic flavor (see 83–90; cf. 339–48), the power of her book's scope is on full display.[9] But at times, the breadth of this scope does risk eliding certain Scholastic (forgive the pun) distinctions. It is daring and original to argue, for instance, that the human soul "is properly an object of metaphysics but also of physics," since the movements of the soul in fact represent a type of "mobile being" (14)—but is it correct? Likewise, it seems right in spirit to assert that Aquinas saw a certain "continuity between the physical and metaphysical worlds" (63) because he felt that they were ordered according to analogous principles—but this formulation is somewhat misleading in its rhetorical equation of analogy with identity. In these and other cases, Robertson's tendency to paint with broad strokes makes good enough sense if we recall that she positions herself as an interlocutor of Lovejoy, Blumenberg, and other historians of intellectual *grands récits* (see 51–52). Like these scholars, Robertson is looking not to abide by the epistemological rules of any one historically constituted discourse, but to track a single "unit-idea" as it assumes various guises across many different discourses and time periods.[10] Still, it did seem to this reviewer that, at times, the care for distinctions that Robertson shows in her sensitive literary readings (especially in the Chaucer chapter) would not have diminished either these unit-ideas or her pursuit of the same.

In sum, Robertson has written a remarkable and original book. It will be required reading for any Middle English scholar pursuing work on the intersection of poetry with medieval literary theory, natural philosophy, metaphysics, ecocriticism, and the new materialisms. Medievalists who focus broadly on the history of philosophy will also want to read *Nature Speaks*, along with any and all who are curious to see how the history of ideas can help us to put more gates through more fences in our era of academic specialization.

TAYLOR COWDERY
University of North Carolina at Chapel Hill

---

[9] For the "mesh," see Timothy Morton, *The Ecological Thought* (Cambridge, Mass.: Harvard University Press, 2010), 28–38. For "vibrant matter," see Jane Bennett, *Vibrant Matter: A Political Ecology of Things* (Durham, N.C.: Duke University Press, 2009).

[10] Lovejoy, *Great Chain of Being*, 4.

NICOLE NOLAN SIDHU. *Indecent Exposure: Gender, Politics, and Obscene Comedy in Middle English Literature*. Philadelphia: University of Pennsylvania Press, 2016. Pp. 320. $69.95.

Indecent Exposure offers a field-changing and astute discussion of literary engagements with obscenity in Middle English literature. Although Nicole Sidhu's monograph focuses on fourteenth- and fifteenth-century obscene comedy in Middle English, it also provides a contextualization of this discourse in other European vernaculars and in a variety of literary and visual contexts, such as manuscript illuminations and devotional texts, sermons in particular.

Sidhu's sustained usage of "obscene comedy" as a serviceable way of categorizing the breadth of texts with which she engages is one of the most original and helpful contributions to the study of medieval comic literature. Still "in a nascent stage" (2), this category of texts is characterized by an overt preoccupation with sexuality, obscenity, domesticity, and their intersection with political governance and the fluid social structures of late medieval Britain. Sidhu's conceptual scope is deliberately capacious, as she aims to frame obscene comedy through a lens that encompasses and moves beyond traditional approaches: lexicon, genre, and the visual arts have traditionally been deployed individually as frameworks through which to read medieval comedy and obscenity. Instead, *Indecent Exposure* is deliberately multidiscursive and interdisciplinary, as it harnesses the combined efficacy of these discrete approaches in order to offer a comprehensive and nuanced analysis of this expansive literary mode. *Indecent Exposure*'s overarching theoretical scaffolding is provided by Michel Foucault's concept of "discursive formation," a persuasive hermeneutics to describe "a recognizably distinct system of thinking and speaking about women, men, and domestic power relations that would have been immediately recognizable to medieval audiences" (4). Sidhu also puts her study in constant dialogue with past and current feminist scholarship in order to unpack the misogyny that underpins many of the texts she analyzes, although she does not in turn adopt gender theory as an overt methodological framework as she constructs her argument.

Pushing forward the argument traditionally made in the different scholarly disciplines that this study brings together, Sidhu acknowledges that the obscene is a discourse controlled by the elites, but also makes a case for its "semiotic instability" (27) capable of being at once "socially normative" and "countercultural" (27).

This study is divided in two parts: Part 1 discusses Langland and Chaucer as pioneers of obscene discourse in Middle English, while Part 2 concentrates on their legacy in the fifteenth century and considers texts such as *The Book of Margery Kempe* whose comedic moments have rarely been scrutinized by scholars. This is also the case in Chapter 1, which is dedicated to William Langland's *Piers Plowman*. Sidhu posits that obscene comedy is profoundly imbricated with a critique of authority and that it provides the author with "a language and a paradigm for political analysis that is unavailable in other medieval discourse" (37). Sidhu reads Langland very much against the grain: not only does she claim his role as pioneer in the use of obscenity, therefore displacing Chaucer as the Father of Middle English comedy, but she also casts him as a writer much more invested in political thought than traditional accounts of his works as largely theological have allowed for. In the spirit of her multidiscursive approach, Sidhu contextualizes Langland's oblique uses of obscenity, or his "garbling techniques" (40), by discussing manuscript margins as spaces of sanctioned experimentation and innovation; yet, much like in *Piers Plowman*, the disruptive force of the obscene is contained in the margins and, therefore, articulates a sharp critique rather than a complete disavowal of the secular and religious hierarchies it interrogates.

As Chapter 2, which centers on Chaucer's uses of the poetics of the obscene, begins, we are already aware of his indebtedness to Langland in the process of "[u]ndoing the origins of the fabliau" (75), which Chaucer adopts but whose tropes he scrambles from within. By situating *The Miller's Tale* and *The Reeve's Tale* in the wider context of Fragment I, Sidhu exposes Chaucer's rewriting of the fabliau as a discourse capable of mounting an overt and radical critique of authority beyond its traditional limitations as temporary disruption that is however ultimately contained. As, in his tale, the Knight suppresses the predatory aggression that informs Theseus's sexual and political violence, the fabliaux that follow in Fragment I expose the ferocious repression couched in chivalric discourse. It is the persuasive recasting of *The Reeve's Tale* as a rape narrative that makes this chapter a particularly astute contribution to the scholarly debate, as Sidhu argues that in the text "we see Chaucer explicitly portraying a world where masculine contest is stripped of noble pretensions and revealed as a raw struggle for power" (92). Misogyny and violence against women become a metonymy for Chaucer's critique of aristocratic culture, which, despite the Church's policy to promote companionate marriage, placed control over women's bodies firmly in the hands of their families, as the Statute of Rapes (1382) testifies.

The second part of this study begins with a chapter dedicated to John Lydgate's mummings and poems. While many critics have previously engaged with the misogynistic quality of his works, Sidhu pushes the debate further by arguing that in a comedic context antifeminist sentiments are used to counteract anxieties generated by the dominance of powerful women in early fifteenth-century Lancastrian England (from Christine de Pizan to Joan of Navarre). To modes of female empowerment Lydgate juxtaposes an imagined "all-male political community unified across class" (115). The figure of the hen-pecked husband who is victim of a shrewish wife recuperates a trope of the traditional fabliau in order to generate sympathy and solidarity among men of all social strata. Female unruliness, therefore, ceases to be a purely domestic concern, and it is invested with public and political valence. It is, in fact, aimed at creating a desirable subject position: that of the submissive and obedient husband, a cipher of the ideal compliant citizen subjugated to the royal authority. Lollardy and the social fluidity created by the Black Death called for a return to order and a cohesive homosocial community.

Obscene comedy does not appear to be the obvious generic lens through which to read *The Book of Margery Kempe*. Nonetheless, by demonstrating that Margery played the comedic role of the unruly wife deliberately, Sidhu casts obscenity as a strategy of critique of the dominance of secular authority in fifteenth-century England. Margery's comic energy and defiance of sexual norms testify to the distinction between the relative tolerance of medieval Christianity toward her (mis)-behavior compared to society's virulent disapproval. *The Book*, therefore, reverses the traditional pattern of praising male dominance and ridiculing female rebellion: "it is the men who distrust Margery and attempt to control her who appear comically ineffective and stupid" (161). Much like in *Piers Plowman*, obscene comedy is here used as an oblique way of interrogating a resurgence of violent repression especially of Lollard activities at the time of writing; in other words, obscenity becomes "a blind behind which the author can issue potentially dangerous critiques of the powerful, in particular secular authorities" (173).

In line with its multidisciplinary ethos, the book ends with a chapter on biblical drama, which Sidhu reads as a dynamic discourse whose use of obscene comedy is aimed, once again, at critiquing "the violence and the injustice of medieval elites" (191). However, these pageants differ substantially from the conventions of medieval obscenity as they problematize the villainization and violent punishment of the unruly woman. By providing a largely unprecedented reading of these narratives in the context of late medieval practices of companionate marriage in northern Europe, *Indecent Exposure* argues for a rethinking of the uses of marital and political violence "as an effective method of securing social stability" (198). Specifically, in the context of its middle-rank affiliations, the collaboration between husband and wife created anxieties about the agency of women in artisanal classes as opposed to the more marked misogyny of the mercantile and aristocratic elites. Obscene comedy is harnessed to create a safe space in which to interrogate the repressive practices of the secular and ecclesiastical dominant social ranks.

In the introduction to *Indecent Exposure* Sidhu declares that her aim is to provide a sustained study of "the precise status of the obscene in medieval culture [which] has not been subject to close scholarly investigation" (15). I would argue that this monograph does more than that, as it casts new critical light on a number of much debated sections of her chosen texts. Although, in line with the interdisciplinarity of the project, more references to visual culture and manuscript culture would have been a welcome and useful contextualization of the material discussed, this study brings into generative dialogue a variety of incarnations of obscene comedy that expose anxieties about female agency, political governance, and the fluidity of late medieval social structures. I find the conclusion particularly poignant, as Sidhu's reflections on modern pornography make medieval obscene comedy relevant to current issues of sexuality and politics: violence against women, across time and space, always has a political valence, as it addresses metonymically the oppression of all marginalized subject positions.

ROBERTA MAGNANI
Swansea University

DAVID WALLACE. *Geoffrey Chaucer: A New Introduction*. Oxford: Oxford University Press, 2017. Pp. xiv, 172. $19.95.

David Wallace's *Geoffrey Chaucer: A New Introduction* lives up to its name in inviting its readers to look anew at Chaucer, seeing in him not the founding father of English letters but "the poet of an unfinished Englishness" (142). Wallace shows how Chaucer's Middle English absorbs influences ranging from scientific treatises to "urban noise" (44) to become a capacious and flexible poetic medium. The experimental quality of Chaucer's language is, Wallace proposes, a reason why his works are enjoying a far-reaching appeal now, in a world where English has become dominant. Wallace's dual focus on language and global reception makes his book a thought-provoking read that not only introduces its audience to Chaucer's writings but also demonstrates their present-day significance and vitality.

The introductory chapter, "Beginnings," covers both theoretical and contextual ground. It opens with a discussion of audience and persona, concepts Wallace presents as integral to Chaucer's art and to current criticism of it. The chapter then shifts, via Terry Eagleton's description of Chaucer as a "class traitor" (10), to an overview of the poet's life and times. The thesis here is that Chaucer was "first and foremost a European" (12), a claim that Wallace, of all Chaucerians, is ideally suited to expound and defend. He first makes a compelling and admirably condensed case for Chaucer's continental focus, and then vindicates the cosmopolitanism of the Middle Ages more broadly. The chapter ends with a section on war as the dark underside of the interconnected medieval world.

Insightful references to Chaucer's writings are sprinkled throughout the introductory chapter, but more developed readings begin in the second, "Schoolrooms, Science, Female Intuition." This is one of two thematic chapters that bracket a more or less chronological tour of Chaucer's writings in the book's middle three chapters. This structure is complex but effective, as it allows Wallace to trace both Chaucer's recurrent engagement with certain topics and his trajectory of development as a poet.

The second chapter examines Chaucer's interest in ways of knowing. After a brief overview of Scholasticism and exegesis, Wallace describes Chaucer's scientific expertise and his readiness to make fun of it; *The*

House of Fame, for instance, is "perched somewhere between science and farce" (33). The chapter then pivots to the relationship between women and Latinate intellectual culture, introducing the Wife of Bath as "a tissue of . . . anti-feminist texts" (36) and then, in the space of a few pages, examining gendered presentations of knowledge in *The Nun's Priest's Tale*, *The Second Nun's Tale*, *The Merchant's Tale*, *Troilus and Criseyde*, and *The House of Fame*, with references to *As You Like It* and *Sir Gawain and the Green Knight* along the way. This section is typical of the book as a whole in the expert way in which it charts a path through Chaucer's writings while referencing other medieval poems and later works of English literature. The chapter concludes with the claim that, for Chaucer, "women are different" (42) in a specifically epistemological sense. Readers who are familiar with Chaucer criticism will appreciate this chapter's illuminating perspective on his treatment of gender.

The third chapter, "A Life in Poetry," begins the chronological section of the book. Living in a world where " 'English poetry' was a contradiction in terms," Chaucer "aspires to" this label in his early works (43). The chapter examines how this aspiration leads Chaucer to learn from French models and then Italian ones, though Wallace cautions that French and Italian do not represent fully distinct creative phases. The core of the chapter discusses Machaut alongside *The Book of the Duchess* and Dante alongside *The House of Fame*. The conclusion focuses on *The Parliament of Fowls* as a case study in Chaucer's response to Italian metrics, which Wallace describes as a "liberatory" influence that may have led Chaucer to invent rhyme royal (57).

Rhyme royal provides a transition to the next chapter, "Poetry at Last: *Troilus and Criseyde*," which takes *Troilus* as a culmination of Chaucer's journey toward what he considered "poetry." Wallace shows how Italian and French influences are synthesized in this work, proposing the shorthand "Italy for poetry, France for music" (65). Even as he presents *Troilus* as a crowning achievement, Wallace also conveys a sense of its messiness: he analyzes the complex narratorial persona and proposes that this poem reveals, especially in its later books, "a poet at war with his own material" (67).

The fifth chapter, "Organizing, Disorganizing: *The Canterbury Tales*," begins with Boccaccio's *Decameron* as a foil for the *Tales*: while the former is polished and uniform, the latter displays a "formal promiscuity" and a rough, "workshop" quality (72). The experimental nature of the *Tales* comes across strongly in this chapter. Wallace places particular emphasis on the "revolutionary moment" (76) in which the Miller interrupts the Host to hijack the tale-telling game, a moment that exposes the fragility of this community of pilgrims and their narrative project. A section on genre advocates keeping "genre as an open question" when reading the *Tales* (81), and the chapter ends, by way of the Wife of Bath, the Pardoner, and Derek Zoolander, by linking genre to gender.

Chaucer's "ABC to the Virgin" is the starting-point for the sixth chapter, "Something to Believe In," which uses this often neglected work to evoke the complex reception history of Chaucer's religion. The decision to devote one of two thematic chapters to religion is provocative, and welcome: Wallace recognizes that Chaucer studies is ready for a new approach to this subject and begins to provide one, a move that makes this book something of a critical intervention as well as an introduction. Noting that "[t]he variety of belief explored in Chaucer's writing is . . . extraordinary" (89), Wallace discusses paganism, Judaism, Christianity, and Islam, in that order, presenting medieval Christianity as one form of belief among the many that fascinate Chaucer. The chapter's final two sections turn from religion to a broader understanding of spirituality. "Our Planet, Our Home" analyzes Chaucer's interest in the natural world and argues that he "anticipates . . . modern eco-criticism" (114), and "Thresholds" tracks Chaucer's use of "liminal markers" (115), reading the ending of the *Tales* as a liminal moment.

These six chapters constitute Wallace's discussion of Chaucer per se, before the final chapter turns to his global reception and reinvention. What the first six chapters offer is very much a conceptual introduction to all of Chaucer's writings, as distinct from a handbook designed to guide readers through individual poems. As such, the book is best read whole, and with the main text at 142 small pages, that is not difficult. Indeed, Wallace's writing makes it a pleasure: his style is accessible and engaging without becoming oversimplified, and it has room for occasional fun asides (e.g., "Italian has too many vowels for great war poetry" [20]). Reading the book feels like having a freely flowing conversation with someone who knows all about Chaucer and wears his knowledge lightly. Some novice readers may, however, expect a more structured, expository approach in a book labeled "Introduction," and those who have not read all or most of Chaucer's writings may struggle to follow the wide-ranging analysis at times. Students seeking information about a specific work will find that the chapter titles and subtitles do not always make it obvious where to turn, though they can rely on the index at the end. It is accompanied by a helpful timeline of Chaucer's life and a robust list of further reading that includes websites and audio-visual materials as well as primary and secondary print sources.

The book's most significant contribution to the crowded field of Chaucer introductions, and to Chaucer studies more broadly, lies in its seventh chapter, "Performance and New Chaucers." This is the chapter in which Wallace most fully develops his point about the refreshingly unformed quality of Chaucer's English—a version of the language that "shows the way to more flexible, inchoate, and spontaneous forms of expression" (123). Wallace first examines the dramatic qualities of Chaucer's writing and advocates a performative reading of his works, especially in the classroom. Teachers of Chaucer will also find useful material in the chapter's final two sections, which survey the living tradition of creative responses to Chaucer around the globe. Wallace's decision to end the book on this note is in keeping with his argument throughout: if Chaucer himself was constantly experimenting and pushing at the limits of what English can do, that same experimental energy now animates the Chaucer tradition. This book paints a compelling portrait of Chaucer as an innovator, and of his writings as (to paraphrase *The Parliament of Fowls*) old fields from which new corn is always springing.

MEGAN E. MURTON
The Catholic University of America

Books Received

Biddick, Kathleen. *Make and Let Die: Untimely Sovereignties*. New York: Punctum Books, 2016. Pp. 258. $21.00.

Biggs, Frederick M. *Chaucer's "Decameron" and the Origin of the "Canterbury Tales."* Woodbridge: D. S. Brewer, 2017. Pp. 292. $99.00.

Cornelius, Ian. *Reconstructing Alliterative Verse: The Pursuit of Medieval Meter*. Cambridge: Cambridge University Press, 2017. Pp. x, 219. $99.99.

Dearnley, Elizabeth. *Translators and Their Prologues in Medieval England*. Woodbridge: D. S. Brewer, 2016. Pp. xiii, 300. $99.00.

Edwards, Robert R. *Invention and Authorship in Medieval England*. Ohio State University Press, 2017. Pp. 280. $105.95 cloth; $19.95 e-book.

Enders, Jody. *"Holy Deadlock" and Further Ribaldries*. Philadelphia: University of Pennsylvania Press, 2017. Pp. 552. $65.00.

Garrison, Jennifer. *Challenging Communion: The Eucharist in Middle English Literature*. Ohio State University Press, 2017. Pp. 244. $105.95 cloth; $19.95 e-book.

Hanna, Ralph. *The Penn Commentary on "Piers Plowman,"* Vol. 2. University of Pennsylvania Press, 2017. Pp. 416. $89.95.

Hardman, Phillipa, and Marianne Ailes. *The Legend of Charlemagne in Medieval England: The Matter of France in Middle English and Anglo-Norman Literature*. Woodbridge: D. S. Brewer, 2017. Pp. 489. $99.00.

Kelly, Henry Ansgar. *The Middle English Bible: A Reassessment*. Philadelphia: University of Pennsylvania Press, 2016. Pp. xiv, 349. $69.95.

Machan, Tim William, ed. *Imagining Medieval English: Language Structures and Theories, 500-1500.* Cambridge: Cambridge University Press, 2016. Pp. xiii, 320. $99.99.

Nakley, Susan. *Living in the Future: Sovereignty and Internationalism in the "Canterbury Tales."* Ann Arbor: University of Michigan Press, 2017. Pp. 282. $75.00.

Tonry, Kathleen. *Agency and Intention in English Print, 1476-1526.* Turnhout: Brepols, 2016. Pp. xv, 241. €75.00.

Wadiak, Walter. *Savage Economy: The Returns of Middle English Romance.* Notre Dame: University of Notre Dame Press, 2017. Pp. xiv, 195. $45.00.

An Annotated Chaucer Bibliography, 2015

Compiled and edited by Stephanie Amsel

Regular contributors:

Mark Allen, *University of Texas at San Antonio*
Michelle Allen, *Grand Rapids Community College* (Michigan)
Stephanie Amsel, *Southern Methodist University* (Texas)
Brother Anthony (Sonjae An), *Sogang University* (South Korea)
Tim Arner, *Grinnell College* (Iowa)
Rebecca Beal, *University of Scranton* (Pennsylvania)
Debra Best, *California State University at Dominguez Hills*
Thomas H. Blake, *Austin College, Texas*
Matthew Brumit, *University of Mary* (North Dakota)
Margaret Connolly, *University of St. Andrews* (Scotland)
John Michael Crafton, *West Georgia College*
Stefania D'Agata D'Ottavi, *Università per Stranieri di Siena* (Italy)
Geoffrey B. Elliott, *Oklahoma State University*
Thomas J. Farrell, *Stetson University* (Florida)
Jon-Mark Grussenmeyer, *Rowan University* (New Jersey)
James B. Harr III, *North Carolina State University*
Douglas W. Hayes, *Lakehead University*
Ana Sáez Hidalgo, *Universidad de Valladolid* (Spain)
Andrew James Johnston, *Freie Universität Berlin* (Germany)
Yoshinobu Kudo, *Keio University* (Japan)
Wim Lindeboom, *Independent Scholar* (Netherlands)
Warren S. Moore III, *Newberry College* (South Carolina)
Daniel M. Murtaugh, *Florida Atlantic University*
Thomas J. Napierkowski, *University of Colorado at Colorado Springs*
Ashley R. Ott, *St. Louis University*
Teresa P. Reed, *Jacksonville State University* (Alabama)
Christopher Roman, *Kent State University at Tuscarawas* (Ohio)
Martha Rust, *New York University*

Thomas R. Schneider, *California Baptist University*
David Sprunger, *Concordia College* (Minnesota)
Jeffery G. Stoyanoff, *Duquesne University* (Pennsylvania)
Anne Thornton, *Abbot Public Library* (Marblehead, Massachusetts)
Winthrop Wetherbee, *Cornell University* (New York)
Elaine Whitaker, *Georgia College & State University*
Susan Yager, *Iowa State University*
Martine Yvernault, *Université de Limoges* (France)

Ad hoc contributions were made by Anna Czarnowus of the University of Silesia in Katowice, Poland, and Candace Barrington of Central Connecticut State University.

The bibliographer acknowledges with gratitude the invaluable contribution and support from Mark Allen, Professor Emeritus, University of Texas at San Antonio.

This bibliography continues the bibliographies published since 1975 in previous volumes of *Studies in the Age of Chaucer*. Bibliographic information up to 1975 can be found in Eleanor P. Hammond, *Chaucer: A Bibliographic Manual* (1908; reprint, New York: Peter Smith, 1933); D. D. Griffith, *Bibliography of Chaucer, 1908–1953* (Seattle: University of Washington Press, 1955); William R. Crawford, *Bibliography of Chaucer, 1954–63* (Seattle: University of Washington Press, 1967); and Lorrayne Y. Baird, *Bibliography of Chaucer, 1964–1973* (Boston, Mass.: G. K. Hall, 1977). See also Lorrayne Y. Baird-Lange and Hildegard Schnuttgen, *Bibliography of Chaucer, 1974–1985* (Hamden, Conn.: Shoe String Press, 1988); Bege K. Bowers and Mark Allen, eds., *Annotated Chaucer Bibliography, 1986–1996* (Notre Dame: University of Notre Dame Press, 2002); and Mark Allen and Stephanie Amsel, eds., *Annotated Chaucer Bibliography, 1997–2010* (Manchester: Manchester University Press, 2015).

Additions and corrections to this bibliography should be sent to Stephanie Amsel, Department of English, Southern Methodist University, GO2AC Clements Hall, PO Box 750283, Dallas, Texas 75275-0283. An electronic version of this bibliography (1975–2014) is available via the New Chaucer Society Web page at http://artsci.wustl.edu/~chaucer/, or directly at http://uchaucer.utsa.edu. Authors are urged to send annotations for articles, reviews, and books that have been or might be overlooked to Stephanie Amsel, samsel@smu.edu.

Classifications

Abbreviations of Chaucer's Works

ABC	*An ABC*
Adam	*Adam Scriveyn*
Anel	*Anelida and Arcite*
Astr	*A Treatise on the Astrolabe*
Bal Compl	*A Balade of Complaint*
BD	*The Book of the Duchess*
Bo	*Boece*
Buk	*The Envoy to Bukton*
CkT, CkP	*The Cook's Tale, The Cook's Prologue*
ClT, ClP, Cl–MerL	*The Clerk's Tale, The Clerk's Prologue, Clerk–Merchant Link*
Compl d'Am	*Complaynt d'Amours*
CT	*The Canterbury Tales*
CYT, CYP	*The Canon's Yeoman's Tale, The Canon's Yeoman's Prologue*
Equat	*The Equatorie of the Planetis*
For	*Fortune*
Form Age	*The Former Age*
FranT, FranP	*The Franklin's Tale, The Franklin's Prologue*
FrT, FrP, Fr–SumL	*The Friar's Tale, The Friar's Prologue, Friar–Summoner Link*
Gent	*Gentilesse*
GP	*The General Prologue*
HF	*The House of Fame*
KnT, Kn–MilL	*The Knight's Tale, Knight–Miller Link*
Lady	*A Complaint to His Lady*
LGW, LGWP	*The Legend of Good Women, The Legend of Good Women Prologue*
ManT, ManP	*The Manciple's Tale, The Manciple's Prologue*
Mars	*The Complaint of Mars*
Mel, Mel–MkL	*The Tale of Melibee, Melibee–Monk Link*
MercB	*Merciles Beaute*

MerT, MerE–SqH	The Merchant's Tale, Merchant Endlink–Squire Headlink
MilT, MilP, Mil–RvL	The Miller's Tale, The Miller's Prologue, Miller–Reeve Link
MkT, MkP, Mk–NPL	The Monk's Tale, The Monk's Prologue, Monk–Nun's Priest Link
MLT, MLH, MLP, MLE	The Man of Law's Tale, Man of Law Headlink, The Man of Law's Prologue, Man of Law Endlink
NPT, NPP, NPE	The Nun's Priest's Tale, The Nun's Priest's Prologue, Nun's Priest Endlink
PardT, PardP	The Pardoner's Tale, The Pardoner's Prologue
ParsT, ParsP	The Parson's Tale, The Parson's Prologue
PF	The Parliament of Fowls
PhyT, Phy–PardL	The Physician's Tale, Physician–Pardoner Link
Pity	The Complaint unto Pity
Prov	Proverbs
PrT, PrP, Pr–ThL	The Prioress's Tale, The Prioress's Prologue, Prioress–Thopas Link
Purse	The Complaint of Chaucer to His Purse
Ret	Chaucer's Retraction {Retractation}
Rom	The Romaunt of the Rose
Ros	To Rosemounde
RvT, RvP, Rv–CkL	The Reeve's Tale, The Reeve's Prologue, Reeve–Cook Link
Scog	The Envoy to Scogan
ShT, Sh–PrL	The Shipman's Tale, Shipman–Prioress Link
SNT, SNP, SN–CYL	The Second Nun's Tale, The Second Nun's Prologue, Second Nun–Canon's Yeoman Link
SqT, SqH, Sq–FranL	The Squire's Tale, Squire Headlink, Squire–Franklin Link
Sted	Lak of Stedfastnesse
SumT, SumP	The Summoner's Tale, The Summoner's Prologue
TC	Troilus and Criseyde

Th, Th–MelL	*The Tale of Sir Thopas, Sir Thopas–Melibee Link*
Truth	*Truth*
Ven	*The Complaint of Venus*
WBT, WBP, WB–FrL	*The Wife of Bath's Tale, The Wife of Bath's Prologue, Wife of Bath–Friar Link*
Wom Nob	*Womanly Noblesse*
Wom Unc	*Against Women Unconstant*

Periodical Abbreviations

Anglia	*Anglia: Zeitschrift für Englische Philologie*
Anglistik	*Anglistik: Mitteilungen des Verbandes deutscher Anglisten*
ANQ	*ANQ: A Quarterly Journal of Short Articles, Notes, and Reviews*
Archiv	*Archiv für das Studium der neueren Sprachen und Literaturen*
Arthuriana	*Arthuriana*
Atlantis	*Atlantis: Revista de la Asociacion Española de Estudios Anglo-Norteamericanos*
AUMLA	*AUMLA: Journal of the Australasian Universities Language and Literature Association*
BAM	*Bulletin des Anglicistes Médiévistes*
BJRL	*Bulletin of the John Rylands University Library of Manchester*
C&L	*Christianity and Literature*
CarmP	*Carmina Philosophiae: Journal of the International Boethius Society*
CE	*College English*
ChauR	*Chaucer Review*
CL	*Comparative Literature* (Eugene, Ore.)
Clio	*CLIO: A Journal of Literature, History, and the Philosophy of History*
CLS	*Comparative Literature Studies*
CML	*Classical and Modern Literature: A Quarterly* (Columbia, Mo.)
CollL	*College Literature*
Comitatus	*Comitatus: A Journal of Medieval and Renaissance Studies*
CRCL	*Canadian Review of Comparative Literature/Revue Canadienne de Littérature Comparée*
DAI	*Dissertation Abstracts International*
DR	*Dalhousie Review*
EA	*Etudes Anglaises: Grande-Bretagne, Etats-Unis*
EHR	*English Historical Review*

EIC	*Essays in Criticism: A Quarterly Journal of Literary Criticism*
EJ	*English Journal*
ELH	*ELH: English Literary History*
ELN	*English Language Notes*
ELR	*English Literary Renaissance*
EMS	*English Manuscript Studies, 1100–1700*
EMSt	*Essays in Medieval Studies*
English	*English: The Journal of the English Association*
Envoi	*Envoi: A Review Journal of Medieval Literature*
ES	*English Studies*
Exemplaria	*Exemplaria: A Journal of Theory in Medieval and Renaissance Studies*
Expl	*Explicator*
FCS	*Fifteenth-Century Studies*
Florilegium	*Florilegium: Carleton University Papers on Late Antiquity and the Middle Ages*
Genre	*Genre: Forms of Discourse and Culture*
H-Albion	*H-Albion: The H-Net Discussion Network for British and Irish History, H-Net Reviews in the Humanities and Social Sciences* http://www.h-net.org/reviews/home.php
HLQ	*Huntington Library Quarterly: Studies in English and American History and Literature* (San Marino, Calif.)
Hortulus	*Hortulus: The Online Graduate Journal of Medieval Studies* http://www.hortulus.net/
IJES	*International Journal of English Studies*
JAIS	*Journal of Anglo-Italian Studies*
JBSt	*Journal of British Studies*
JEBS	*Journal of the Early Book Society*
JEGP	*Journal of English and Germanic Philology*
JELL	*Journal of English Language and Literature* (Korea)
JEngL	*Journal of English Linguistics*
JGN	*John Gower Newsletter*
JMEMSt	*Journal of Medieval and Early Modern Studies*
JML	*Journal of Modern Literature*
JNT	*Journal of Narrative Theory*
L&LC	*Literary and Linguistic Computing: Journal of the Association for Literary and Linguistic Computing*

L&P	*Literature and Psychology*
L&T	*Literature and Theology: An International Journal of Religion, Theory, and Culture*
Lang&Lit	*Language and Literature: Journal of the Poetics and Linguistics Association*
Lang&S	*Language and Style: An International Journal*
LeedsSE	*Leeds Studies in English*
Library	*The Library: The Transactions of the Bibliographical Society*
LitComp	*Literature Compass* http://www.literaturecompass.com/
MA	*Le Moyen Age: Revue d'Histoire et de Philologie* (Brussels, Belgium)
MÆ	*Medium Ævum*
M&H	*Medievalia et Humanistica: Studies in Medieval and Renaissance Culture*
Manuscripta	*Manuscripta: A Journal for Manuscript Research*
Marginalia	*Marginalia: The Journal of the Medieval Reading Group at the University of Cambridge* http://www.marginalia.co.uk/journal/
Mediaevalia	*Mediaevalia: An Interdisciplinary Journal of Medieval Studies Worldwide*
MedievalF	*Medieval Forum* http://www.sfsu.edu/~medieval/index.html
MedPers	*Medieval Perspectives*
MES	*Medieval and Early Modern English Studies*
MFF	*Medieval Feminist Forum*
MLN	*Modern Language Notes*
MLR	*Modern Language Review*
MLQ	*Modern Language Quarterly: A Journal of Literary History*
MP	*Modern Philology: A Journal Devoted to Research in Medieval and Modern Literature*
N&Q	*Notes and Queries*
Neophil	*Neophilologus* (Dordrecht, Netherlands)
NLH	*New Literary History: A Journal of Theory and Interpretation*
NM	*Neuphilologische Mitteilungen: Bulletin of the Modern Language Society*
NML	*New Medieval Literatures*

NMS	*Nottingham Medieval Studies*
NYRB	*The New York Times Review of Books*
Parergon	*Parergon: Bulletin of the Australian and New Zealand Association for Medieval and Early Modern Studies*
PBA	*Proceedings of the British Academy*
PBSA	*Papers of the Bibliographical Society of America*
PLL	*Papers on Language and Literature: A Journal for Scholars and Critics of Language and Literature*
PMAM	*Publications of the Medieval Association of the Midwest*
PMLA	*Publications of the Modern Language Association of America*
PoeticaT	*Poetica: An International Journal of Linguistic Literary Studies*
postmedieval	*postmedieval: A Journal of Medieval Cultural Studies*
PQ	*Philological Quarterly*
Quidditas	*Quidditas: Journal of the Rocky Mountain Medieval and Renaissance Association*
RCEI	*Revista Canaria de Estudios Ingleses*
RenQ	*Renaissance Quarterly*
RES	*Review of English Studies*
RMSt	*Reading Medieval Studies*
SAC	*Studies in the Age of Chaucer*
SAP	*Studia Anglica Posnaniensia: An International Review of English*
SAQ	*South Atlantic Quarterly*
SB	*Studies in Bibliography: Papers of the Bibliographical Society of the University of Virginia*
SCJ	*The Sixteenth-Century Journal: Journal of Early Modern Studies* (Kirksville, Mo.)
SEL	*SEL: Studies in English Literature, 1500–1900*
SELIM	*SELIM: Journal of the Spanish Society for Medieval English Language and Literature*
ShakS	*Shakespeare Studies*
SIcon	*Studies in Iconography*
SiM	*Studies in Medievalism*
SIMELL	*Studies in Medieval English Language and Literature*
SMART	*Studies in Medieval and Renaissance Teaching*
SN	*Studia Neophilologica: A Journal of Germanic and Romance Languages and Literatures*

SoAR	*South Atlantic Review*
SP	*Studies in Philology*
Speculum	*Speculum: A Journal of Medieval Studies*
SSt	*Spenser Studies: A Renaissance Poetry Annual*
TCBS	*Transactions of the Cambridge Bibliographical Society*
Text	*Text: Transactions of the Society for Textual Scholarship*
TextC	*Textual Cultures: Texts, Contexts, Interpretation*
TLS	*Times Literary Supplement* (London, England)
TMR	*The Medieval Review* https://scholarworks.iu.edu/dspace/handle/2022/3631
Tr&Lit	*Translation and Literature*
TSLL	*Texas Studies in Literature and Language*
UTQ	*University of Toronto Quarterly: A Canadian Journal of the Humanities*
Viator	*Viator: Medieval and Renaissance Studies*
YES	*Yearbook of English Studies*
YLS	*The Yearbook of Langland Studies*
YWES	*Year's Work in English Studies*

Bibliographical Citations and Annotations

Bibliographies, Reports, and Reference

1. Amsel, Stephanie, and Mark Allen. "An Annotated Chaucer Bibliography, 2013." *SAC* 37 (2015): 347–400. Continuation of *SAC* annual annotated bibliography (since 1975); based on contributions from an international bibliographic team, independent research, and *MLA Bibliography* listings. 172 items, plus listing of reviews for 28 books. Includes an author index.

2. Barrington, Candace, and Jonathan Hsy. *Global Chaucers*. https://globalchaucers.wordpress.com/ (2012; accessed October 14, 2016). A crowd-sourced online reference work described as an "Online archive and community for post-1945, non-Anglophone Chauceriana." Includes listings of translations, adaptations, and recordings of Chaucer's works (especially *CT*), along with various "appropriations" by modern authors. Arranges translations by countries of origin and provides, when available, e-links to materials accessible on the Internet. Also lists various resources and includes an archive of online discussions related to the project, which was announced initially at the 2012 Congress of the New Chaucer Society.

3. Byrne, Joseph P. *Encyclopedia of the Black Death*. Santa Barbara, Calif.: ABC-CLIO, 2012. xxii, 429 pp.; illus. Includes a summary (pp. 70–71) of Chaucer's life and his literary representations of the plague ("the word appears nine times").

4. Raymo, Robert R., and Judith Glazer-Raymo, compilers; Shari Perkins and Jared Camins-Esakov, eds. *The Chaucer Collection of Robert R. Raymo*. New York: Ascensius Press, 2015. 156 pp. Catalogues the Chaucer collection of Raymo and Glazer-Raymo, which includes editions of the complete works of Chaucer, critical and literary histories, recordings of readings, and collections of Chaucer ephemera.

Recordings and Film

5. D'Arcens, Louise. "The Thunder after the Lightning: Language and Pasolini's Medievalist Poetics." *postmedieval* 6, no. 2 (2015): 191–99. Examines Pasolini's inclusion of Italian and English dialects in *I racconti*

di Canterbury / The Canterbury Tales. Reveals how Pasolini's use of dialects reflects his own theories about the importance of "language as an instrument of . . . hegemonic culture."

6. Martínez Romero, Carmen. "La lectura pasoliniana de *Cuentos de Canterbury.*" In Francisco José Salvador Ventura, ed. *Cine y religiones: Expresiones fílmicas de creencias humanas* (Paris: Université Paris-Sud, 2013), pp. 155–72. Analyzes Pasolini's version of *CT* in the context of Eco's and Pasolini's debate about semiology and the relation of reality and art. Thus, the Italian filmmaker creates a filmic narrative reflecting Chaucer's historicity of frontier, in the topics, the characters, and the notions of seriousness and of laughter.

See also no. 144.

Chaucer's Life

7. Butterfield, Ardis. "Diary." *London Review of Books*, 27 August 2015, pp. 42–43. Contemplates the writing of a literary biography of Chaucer, considering the use of archival material, the "arcades" of Walter Benjamin, and psychoanalysis. Comments on the *GP* description of the Shipman.

8. Mote, Sarah. "The Visual Arts in the Period of Geoffrey Chaucer." In Yuichiro Azuma, Kotaro Kawasaki, and Koichi Kano, eds. *Chaucer and English and American Literature: Essays Commemorating the Retirement of Professor Masatoshi Kawasaki* (SAC 39 [2017], no. 94), pp. 60–74. Provides brief descriptions of the fourteenth-century history and the life of Chaucer, and introduces late fourteenth-century visual arts, including illuminated manuscripts, stained glasses, and altarpieces with notable examples. Characterizes the fourteenth century as a period that saw a remarkable development of both vernacular literature and visual arts.

9. Strohm, Paul. *The Poet's Tale: Chaucer and the Year that Made the "Canterbury Tales."* London: Profile Books, 2014. xi, 285 pp. British reprint of *SAC* 38 (2016), no. 2.

See also nos. 3, 55, 135.

Facsimiles, Editions, and Translations

10. Ashe, Laura, ed. *Early Fiction in England: From Geoffrey of Monmouth to Chaucer.* London: Penguin, 2015. xxxiii, 423 pp. Anthology of

early English fiction including excerpts from Wace, Marie de France, Chaucer, and others.

11. Barrington, Candace, and Jonathan Hsy. "Global Chaucers." In Gail Ashton, ed. *Medieval Afterlives in Contemporary Culture* (*SAC* 39 [2017], no. 93), pp. 147–56. Provides a survey of translations and appropriations of *CT*. Examines four translations of *CT*—Afrikaans, Turkish, Brazilian Portuguese, and Mandarin Chinese—and argues how these global Chaucers enhance understanding of *CT*. Also examines works, including Luk Bey's comic book adaptation of *MilT*, that blur the line between translation and appropriation.

12. Bruinsma, Klaas, trans. *Kenterboarger teltsjes: Algemiene foarsang* (*The General Prologue*). http://www.ffu-frl.eu/PDF/Bruinsma.Chaucer .Algemiene.Foarsang.Gen.Prologue.pdf. 2013. Frisian verse translation of *GP*, with notes.

13. _____, trans. *Kenterboarger teltsjes: It teltsje fan de Mûnder* (*The Miller's Tale*). http://www.ffu-frl.eu/PDF/Bruinsma.Chaucer.Teltsjefan demoolner.STHiemstra.pdf. 2012. Frisian verse translation of *MilT*, with notes. A WorldCat record indicates that this was first published in *Trotwaer: Literair tydskrift* 3–4 (1983): 195–213; item not seen.

14. _____, trans. *Kenterboarger teltsjes: Oanrin ta it teltsje fan de Priorinne* (*The Prioress' Prologue*) and *It teltsje fan de Priorinne* (*The Prioress's Tale*). http://www.ffu-frl.eu/PDF/Bruinsma.Chaucer.It.Teltsje.fan.de .priorinne.STHiemstra.pdf. 2013. Frisian verse translation of *PrPT*. A WorldCat record indicates that this was first published in *De strikel: Moanneblêd foar Fryslân* (1970); item not seen.

15. Ensley, Mimi. "Reading Chaucer in the Tower: The Person behind the Pen in an Early-Modern Copy of Chaucer's *Works*." *JEBS* 18 (2015): 136–57. Establishes that John Harington owned a copy of William Thynne's 1542 edition of Chaucer's complete works and may have annotated it when he was imprisoned in the Tower of London. Comments on Harington's annotations and speculates on communal reading practices and Chaucer's connections to Boethius.

16. Guthrie, Steve. "On Editing *Troilus and Criseyde* Now." *TextC* 9, no. 2 (2015): 1–18. Advertises an interactive online edition of *TC*, designed to facilitate language instruction for students of Chaucer's Middle English.

17. Johnston, Hope. "Readers' Memorials in Early Editions of Chaucer." *SB* 59 (2015): 45–70. Links books as physical objects with customized Chaucer editions. Reviews how owners of early Chaucer editions

customized their copies by adding "memorial inscriptions, title-page embellishments, and portraits inserted as frontispieces." As a result of this individualization, book owners "sought to provide an overall characterization of the books and their author."

18. O'Donoghue, Bernard. *Reading Chaucer's Poems: A Guided Selection*. London: Faber & Faber, 2015. xxii, 225 pp. Presents a brief biography of Chaucer and an overview of Chaucerian criticism before discussing challenges in compiling a Chaucer edition for modern readers. Includes direct commentary on *TC* and *CT*.

19. Spencer, H. L. "F. J. Furnivall's Six of the Best: *The Six-Text Canterbury Tales* and the Chaucer Society." *RES* 66, no. 276 (2015): 601–23. Details Furnivall's founding of the Chaucer Society in 1868, and argues that his greatest contribution was his parallel text edition of *CT*, a publication that has far-reaching consequences for the later editing of Chaucer. Brief references to *Astr*, *Bo*, *WBT*, *ClT*, *KnT*, *HF*, *NPT*, and *PardPT*.

20. Wieseltier, Meir, trans. *Sipure Kanterberi* (*Canterbury Tales*). Tel Aviv: Ahuzat Bayit, 2013. 490 pp. A WorldCat record indicates that this is a Hebrew translation of Peter Ackroyd's 2009 translation of *CT*; item not seen.

See also nos. 2, 23, 29, 54, 67, 83, 123, 140, 189, 202.

Manuscripts and Textual Studies

21. Baechle, Sarah. "Chaucer, the Continent, and the Characteristics of Commentary." In Kathryn Kerby-Fulton, John T. Thompson, and Baechle, eds. *New Directions in Medieval Manuscript Studies and Reading Practices: Essays in Honor of Derek Pearsall* (*SAC* 39 [2017], no. 28), pp. 384–405. Discusses how editorial glosses and marginalia in extant manuscripts of *CT* were received and interpreted by medieval readers in the fifteenth century. Includes examination of Latin source glosses of *WBPT*.

22. Baechle, Sarah E. "Latin Glossing, Medieval Literary Theory, and the Cross-Channel Readers of Chaucer." *DAI* A77.04 (2015): n.p. Considers marginal glossing in *TC* and *CT* as examples of actual reader experience of those texts, with an eye toward recognizing different interpretations and hermeneutic approaches from relatively contemporary readers.

23. Farrell, Thomas J. "Eclecticism and Its Discontents." *TextC* 9, no. 2 (2015): 27–45. Cautions editors against eclectic emendation, assessing George Kane's method and observing how its rigor is undercut by subjectivity, particularly notions of authorial "genius." Uses *WBP*, 838 (the Summoner jeering at the Friar) as a case study to show that this indisputably Chaucerian line is always emended by eclectic editors, despite scribal consistency.

24. Harrington, Marjorie. "'That swevene hath Daniel unloke': Interpreting Dreams with Chaucer and the Harley Scribe." *ChauR* 50, nos. 3–4 (2015): 315–67. Examines Chaucer's use of dream visions and the *Somniale* tradition as contrasted with that of the Harley scribe. While Chaucer is suspicious, the Harley scribe uses the tradition as a source of knowledge. Includes an edition and translation of London, British Library, MS Royal 12.C.xii *Somniale Danielis*.

25. Horobin, Simon. "Thomas Hoccleve: Chaucer's First Editor?" *ChauR* 50, nos. 3–4 (2015): 228–50. Revisits the question of who edited the Hengwrt and Ellesmere manuscripts because the supervisory editorial hand of Hoccleve is found in both.

26. Ikegami, Masa. "The Past Forms of *SEE* in the *Canterbury Tales*: Hengwrt and Ellesmere Manuscripts and a Critical Edition." In Yuichiro Azuma, Kotaro Kawasaki, and Koichi Kano, eds. *Chaucer and English and American Literature: Essays Commemorating the Retirement of Professor Masatoshi Kawasaki* (*SAC* 39 [2017], no. 94), pp. 402–16. Compares uses of the different past forms of *see* in the Hengwrt and Ellesmere manuscripts to identify Chaucer's original forms as distinguished from the scribes' later alternations. In Japanese.

27. Jahner, Jennifer. "Reading for the End: Prescriptive Writing and the Practice of Genre." *Exemplaria* 27 (2015): 18–34. Studies a late medieval manuscript, San Marino, Huntington Library, HM 144 (c. 1500), which is a compilation of works chosen for their devotional and/ or ethical content. Uses *Mel* to show how the scribe—by omitting portions of a text and interpolating Latin proverbs and maxims in a larger script, which the Middle English then comments on—directs readers from narrative to ethical emphasis, and preserves a simpler version of the narrative framework.

28. Kerby-Fulton, Kathryn, John T. Thompson, and Sarah Baechle, eds. *New Directions in Medieval Manuscript Studies and Reading Practices: Essays in Honor of Derek Pearsall*. Notre Dame: University of Notre Dame

Press, 2014. xxii, 551 pp.; illus. Collection of interdisciplinary manuscript studies and critical essays presented at the "New Directions in Medieval Manuscript Studies and Reading Practices in Honour of the 80th Birthday of Derek Pearsall" conference on October 21–22, 2011. Includes index of manuscripts and incunabula. For essays pertaining to Chaucer, see nos. 21, 188, 231.

29. Koster, Josephine. "Masters and Commanders: Considering the Concept of the Edited Text." *TextC* 9, no. 2 (2015): 19–26. Questions the concept of a "standard edition" in the postmodern world of textual editing and uses the controversy about Adam Pinkhurst (Was he Chaucer's scribe cited in *Adam?*) as evidence that "medievalists really seek editorial closure," despite insufficient, open-ended, or ambiguous data.

30. Myojo, Kiyoko, and Noboru Notomi, eds. *What Is a Text? An Introduction to Textual Scholarship.* Tokyo: Keio University Press, 2015. xiv, 258 pp. Includes a chapter on the issues of the text of *CT.* See no. 129. In Japanese.

31. Tokunaga, Satoko. "Wynkyn de Worde's Lost Manuscript of the *Canterbury Tales*: With New Light on HRC MS 46." *ChauR* 50, nos. 1–2 (2015): 30–54. Presents textual analysis about *CT* manuscript descent, specifically, that "a copying of *W [the MS used by De Worde for his 1498 edition of *CT*]" is likely to have "led to the production of Gg [CUL, MS Gg.IV.27] and Ph[1] [University of Texas, Harry Ransom Center, MS 46], or a manuscript behind them."

32. Warner, Lawrence. "Scribes Misattributed: Hoccleve and Pinkhurst." *SAC* 37 (2015): 55–100. Critiques the methods and conclusions of various analyses of late medieval English vernacular scribes, challenging the arguments that British Library, MS Royal 17 D.XVIII is Thomas Hoccleve's holograph; that Adam Pinkhurst was "Scribe B" of Cambridge, Trinity College, MS R.3.2 (John Gower's *Confessio Amantis*); that Adam Pinkhurst was the scribe of the Hengwrt and Ellesmere *CT* manuscripts; and giving various corollary discussions. Finds "no evidence" that Pinkhurst knew Chaucer, even though he did embellish a manuscript of *Bo*, and calls for renewed attention to all pertinent and available evidence in scribal analysis.

See also nos. 51, 63, 67, 82, 85, 150, 156, 182, 189, 197, 202, 214, 217.

Sources, Analogues, and Literary Relations

33. Cornelius, Ian. "Gower and the Peasants' Revolt." *Representations* 131, no. 1 (2015): 22–51. Discusses Gower's *Visio Anglie* as a departure from his usual compositional style and from his other treatments of the Revolt. Argues that specific depictions carry out a mimetic reenactment of the Revolt, rejecting the notion that Chaucer's "moral Gower" (*TC*, V.1856) was wholly concerned with pedantry, and asserting that *Visio Anglie* fully realizes themes present in Gower's earlier work.

34. Ginsberg, Warren. *Tellers, Tales, and Translation in Chaucer's "Canterbury Tales."* Oxford: Oxford University Press, 2015. viii, 250 pp. With special consideration of Ovid, Dante, and Boccaccio as models (not sources), explores the relationship between Chaucer's predecessors and *CT* while conducting in-depth investigation into Chaucer's reworking of the original texts both through the pilgrims' tales as translations and the pilgrims themselves as translators. Examines individual characters' narrative roles in *FranT*, *WBT*, *ClT*, *MerT*, *PardT*, and *MilT*, and focuses on Chaucer's use of interruption of speech and repetition as narrative conventions.

35. Hanna, Ralph III, and Traugott Lawler, eds., using materials collected by Karl Young and Robert A. Pratt. *Jankyn's Book of Wikked Wyves.* Vol. 2: *Seven Commentaries on Walter Map's "Dissuasio Valerii" by John Ridewell, Nicholas Trivet, Eneas of Siena, and Four Anonymous Authors.* The Chaucer Library. Athens, Ga. and London: University of Georgia Press, 2014. xiv, 605 pp.; 1 b&w illus. Critical edition of seven commentaries (one excerpted) on Walter Map's Latin antifeminist treatise, with analyses of contents and impact, manuscript information, variants and emendations, extensive notes, and facing-page translations. The introduction (pp. 1–14) describes the volume, citing Chaucer's uses of Map and the commentaries, especially in *WBP*, and on the "objections to Map's satire on women" included in three of the commentaries. The notes (pp. 495–576) include recurrent comments on Chaucerian echoes in these sources, specifically *WBP*, *PF*, *FranT*, and *MerT*.

36. Haught, Leah. "In Pursuit of *Trewth*: Ambiguity and Meaning in *Amis and Amiloun*." *JEGP* 114, no. 2 (2015): 240–60. The Middle English romance *Amis and Amiloun* explores the complex concept of *trewth* in the fourteenth century. Contends that the binding oath made by childhood friends is reminiscent of the agreement of the *GP* pilgrims,

as well as pledges made in *FranT*, *ClT*, and *WBT*, but differs from the pledge binding Palamon and Arcite in *KnT*.

37. McGuire, Brigit C. "Flesh Made Word: Women's Speech in Medieval English Virgin Martyr Legends." *DAI* A76.08 (2015): n.p. As part of an examination of the image of the virgin body as "a dwelling place for God's Word," looks at Aelfric, Kempe, and *SNT*.

38. Méndez, Jerónimo. "The Bad Behaviour of Friars and Women in Medieval Catalan *Fabliaux* and Chaucer's *Canterbury Tales*." *Skepsi* 3, no. 1 (2010): 52–63. Identifies "new Romance analogues" for details in *GP*, *MilT*, *WBPT*, *PardT*, *ShT*, and *ParsT* in three fifteenth-century Catalan narratives: *Disputa de l'ase* (*The Argument of the Ass*) by Anselm Turmeda, the *Llibre de fra Bernat* (*Book of Friar Bernard*) by Francesc de la Via, and the anonymous *Col-loqui de dames* (*Symposium of Women*).

39. Rossiter, William T. "Chaucer Joins the *Schiera*: The House of Fame, Italy, and the Determination of Posterity." In Isabel Davis and Catherine Nall, eds. *Chaucer and Fame: Reputation and Reception* (*SAC* 39 [2017], no. 99), pp. 21–42. Explores how Chaucer used Petrarch, Petrarch used Dante, and Dante used Virgil: a sequence of influence that underpins Chaucer's "conception of renown" and encouraged him to lay claim to belonging to the *schiera* (band) of famous poets. Discusses references and allusions to famous poets in *HF*, the end of *TC*, and *ClP*; comments on Lydgate's, Hoccleve's, and Deschamps's praise of Chaucer; and reassesses the relative dates of composition for *HF*, *TC*, *ClPT*, and Deschamps's balade.

40. Wilson, Anna Patricia. "Immature Pleasures: Affective Reading in Margery Kempe, Petrarch, Chaucer, and Modern Fan Communities." *DAI* A77.07 (2015): n.p. Considers how the three titular authors equate excessive emotional response and similar qualities to texts with immaturity. Reads *ClPT* as Chaucer's reaction to Petrarch on the vernacular.

41. Yeager, Stephen M. *From Lawman to Plowman: Anglo-Saxon Legal Tradition and the School of Langland*. Toronto Anglo-Saxon Series. Toronto: University of Toronto Press, 2014. vii, 268 pp. Examines alliterative English writing by focusing on Anglo-Saxon legal-homiletic discourse within vernacular English poetry. Brief mention of *FranT*, *ParsT*, *MLT*, and *Mel*.

See also nos. 15, 47, 54, 78, 81, 99, 113, 117, 133, 139–40, 146, 148, 152, 155, 158–59, 161, 168, 171, 176, 182, 184, 190, 193, 195, 199, 200–201, 204–6, 210–11, 215–16, 221, 223, 225, 233.

Chaucer's Influence and Later Allusion

42. Agbabi, Patience. *Telling Tales*. Edinburgh: Canongate, 2015. viii, 124 pp. Presents a contemporary poetic adaptation of *CT*.

43. Alexander, Gavin. "The Sources of the Verse Examples in Gascoigne's *Certayne Notes of Instruction*." *N&Q* 260 (2015): 52–53. In this "first printed work of English vernacular literary criticism" (dated 1575), Gascoigne references *ParsT* (43) in arguing "For it is not inough to roll in pleasant woordes, nor yet to thunder in *Rym, Ram, Ruff*, by letter (quoth my master *Chaucer*)."

44. Bergvall, Caroline. *Meddle English: New and Selected Texts*. Callicoon, N.Y.: Nightboat, 2011. 167 pp. Includes a section entitled "Shorter Chaucer Tales" (pp. 21–51) with five pieces inspired by *CT*: "The Host Tale," "The Summer Tale (Deus Hic, 1)," "The Franker Tale (Deus Hic, 2)," "The Not Tale (Funeral)," and "Fried Tale (London Zoo)." The introduction to the volume, "Middling English" (pp. 5–19), comments on Chaucer's language as inspiration.

45. Brown, Sarah Annes. "Shakespeare and Thomas Underdowne's *Theseus and Ariadne*." *RES* 66, no. 275 (2015): 465–79. Argues that Underdowne's *Theseus and Ariadne* (1566) draws on a number of earlier versions of the myth, including Ovid's *Heroides* and Chaucer's *LGW*.

46. Candeloro, Antonio. "*Así empieza lo malo* de Javier Marías: Rumor y fama, entre William Shakespeare y Geoffrey Chaucer." *1616: Anuario de la Sociedad Española de Literatura General y Comparada* 5 (2015): 163–87. Analyzes Chaucer and Shakespeare in Javier Marías's novel, *Así empieza lo malo*. Chaucer's concepts of "fame" and "rumor," as described in *HF*, are central to Marías's depiction of contemporary men and their incapacity to face rumor and establish the truth.

47. Cooper, Helen. "Chaucer at the Edge: Middle English and the Rhetorical Tradition." *Marginalia* 19 (2015): 4–15. Plenary lecture positions Chaucer as important to sixteenth-century writers for his incorporation of the Latin rhetorical tradition—particularly the concepts of *decorum* and Augustine's three levels of style—into English, even as he does so with colorful parody and vernacular panache.

48. Croll, Angus. *If Hemingway Wrote JavaScript (1)*. San Francisco: No Starch Press, 2015. 196 pp. A collection of playful JavaScript programs, imitating or responding to well-known literary authors—Hemingway, Shakespeare, Austin, Woolf, Borges, etc.—and including brief descriptions of each writer's style. The section on Chaucer (pp.

104–11) presents a sample that echoes *GP*. Illustrated by Miran Lipo-vača.

49. De Ridder, Antonio Joaquim. "Storytelling as Preaching in Mar-guerite de Navarre's *Heptameron*." *DAI* A76.07 (2015): n.p. Examines Marguerite in the context of other historical writers of "framed short fiction," including Chaucer, and suggests commonalities with *CT*, and *ClT*, in particular.

50. Dinkler, Michal Beth. "Stories, Secular and Sacred: What's at Stake." *Religion and Literature* 47, no. 1 (2015): 221–35. Within the framework of examining Chaucer and Dostoevsky, discusses critical approaches to literary examples in relationship to teaching the Bible as literature.

51. Downes, Stephanie. "After Deschamps: Chaucer's French Fame." In Isabel Davis and Catherine Nall, eds. *Chaucer and Fame: Reputation and Reception* (*SAC* 39 [2017], no. 99), pp. 127–42. Discusses Eustace Deschamps's balade in praise of Chaucer, the Duxworth manuscript of Chaucer that belonged to Jean Angoulême, and two sixteenth-century French references to Chaucer that evince French awareness of Chaucer as a poet: an anecdote about Chaucer and his wife and a discussion of *Rom* that asserts that Jean de Meun was himself an Englishman.

52. ————. "Chaucer in Nineteenth-Century France." *ChauR* 49, no. 3 (2015): 352–70. Discusses the reception of Chaucer's poetry by nineteenth-century French critics who focused on *CT*, read Chaucer as a "European" rather than an English writer, discussed the accessibility of his language, and examined Chaucer's national literary and cultural affinities.

53. Espie, Jeff. "Wordsworth's Chaucer: Mediation and Transforma-tion in English Literary History." *PQ* 94, no. 4 (2015): 337–65. Exam-ines Chaucer's influence on Wordsworth's poetry, especially in *Lyrical Ballads* and *Ecclesiastical Sonnets*. Establishes that Wordsworth is a "Chaucerian translator," because of his engagement with Chaucerian lit-erary tradition.

54. Fumo, Jamie C. "Ancient Chaucer: Temporalities of Fame." In Isabel Davis and Catherine Nall, eds. *Chaucer and Fame: Reputation and Reception* (*SAC* 39 [2017], no. 99), pp. 201–20. Explores the "reciprocal status of antiquity and celebrity" in the reception of Chaucer, his "con-struction (and self-construction) as a vernacular authority," and the rela-tions of fame and temporality in his works, especially *MLP*. Recurrent

concerns with time, time-passing, and old age inflect his characterizations and his Ovidian poetics. Includes comments on early modern canon formation, Byron's views of Chaucer, and a 2011 on-demand reprint of *HF* by Nabu Press.

55. Galloway, Andrew. "Fame's Penitent: Deconstructive Chaucer among the Lancastrians." In Isabel Davis and Catherine Nall, eds. *Chaucer and Fame: Reputation and Reception* (*SAC* 39 [2017], no. 99), pp. 103–26. Argues that fifteenth-century verbal and visual depictions of Chaucer as an "aged penitent" (in Gascoigne, Hoccleve, Gower, Scogan, and the Bedford Hours) reflect the Derridean (and Augustinian) gaps that are evident in *Ret* and elsewhere in Chaucer's poetry. Chaucer's persistent attention to "textual mediation" evokes "the illusion of presence," or an "absent presence" whereas his followers employ echoes of him and his poetry to evoke a politically charged "secular penance" that has parallels with Lancastrian reforms.

56. Gómez, Francesc J. "El frau de l'alquimista en l'infern dantesc de Joan Pasqual i en la tradició medieval." *Magníficat: Cultura i literatura medievals* 2 (2015): 159–96. Taking as a starting-point the study of a chapter from the *Tractat de les penes particulars d'infern* by Joan Pasqual (c. 1436), traces the dissemination (and the *stemma narrationum*) of two narrative motifs: the fake alchemist and the king (Thompson, K.111.4), and the account-book of mistakes or fools (Thompson, J.1371), and places *CYT* within this tradition.

57. Hamilton, David. "Chaucer's Moose." *ChauR* 49, no. 3 (2015): 378–86. Contends that the opening of Elizabeth Bishop's "The Moose" contains several Chaucerian echoes, especially those found in *GP*.

58. Hanna, Ralph. "The 'Absent' Pardon-Tearing of *Piers Plowman* C." *RES* 66, no. 275 (2015): 449–64. Offers that when Langland revised B into C, the literary landscape was very different (from Edwardian to Ricardian poetry). Chaucerian dream vision, especially *PF* with its "emphasis upon the poetic figure who seeks to understand the world through his books and to craft this search as imaginative fiction," may be responsible for the new explicitness and clarity of *Piers Plowman* C.

59. Holsinger, Bruce. *The Invention of Fire*. New York: HarperCollins, 2015. 420 pp. Historical novel set in London, Kent, Calais, and during a pilgrimage to Durham, 1386; the second in a series that features John Gower as first-person narrator investigating criminal and political events, in this case a mass murder that involves parliamentary machinations, Nicholas Brembre's mayoralty, and the development of handguns.

Includes a range of characters both historical and fictional, with Chaucer in his role as "shire justice in Kent" and as Gower's shrewd friend and literary competitor.

60. Jacobs, Kathryn, and d'Andra White. "Ben Jonson on Shakespeare's Chaucer." *ChauR* 50, nos. 1–2 (2015): 198–215. Examines Spenserian and Shakespearean medievalism, seen by Ben Jonson as an irritating return to Chaucerian English.

61. Jones, Mike Rodman. "Chaucer the Puritan." In Isabel Davis and Catherine Nall, eds. *Chaucer and Fame: Reputation and Reception* (*SAC* 39 [2017], no. 99), pp. 165–84. Exemplifies the variety of sixteenth- and seventeenth-century versions of Chaucer, which reflects the "fragmentation, diversity, and complexity" of the English Reformation itself. Discusses Chaucer as an authority figure in the writings of polemical authors Job Throckmorton, John Clare, Matthew Sutcliffe, Richard Bancroft, and Samuel Harsnett, gauging their relative discernment in understanding Chaucer's works. Most surprising, perhaps, is Harsnett's use of *MilT*.

62. Kendrick, Laura. "Deschamps' Ballade Praising Chaucer and Its Impact." *Cahiers de recherches médiévales et humanistes/Journal of Medieval and Humanistic Studies* 29, no. 1 (2015): 215–33. Examines how Deschamps's balade 285 is a surprisingly generous recognition and glorification of Chaucer as a pioneering translator from Latin and French into English, and as an "illuminator" or enlightener of his native England. Reveals how this praise pleased Chaucer's followers, who reinforced the critical tradition of Chaucer as the first embellisher of the English language.

63. Lerer, Seth. " 'The Tongue': Chaucer, Lydgate, Chaucer's d'Orléans, and the Making of a Late Medieval Lyric." *ChauR* 49, no. 4 (2015): 474–98. The stanzas known as "The Tongue" in the Findern manuscript use source material from Lydgate's *Fall of Princes* and Chaucer's *TC* to create a coherent poem that is consistent with the manuscript's broader themes and is indebted to the literary legacy of Charles d'Orléans.

64. Munro, Lucy. *Archaic Style in English Literature, 1590–1674*. New York: Cambridge University Press, 2013. xii, 308 pp.; 4 b&w illus. Explores the use of "archaic linguistic and poetic style" in poetry and drama, 1590–1674, analyzing how combinations of anachronism and nostalgia help to influence the idea of English "nationhood." Includes

418

recurrent comments on lexical "Chaucerisms" and "Chaucer's authority," and Chapter 4, "Chaucer, Gower, and the Anxiety of Obsolescence" (pp. 69–104), explores how four early modern works express or resist concern about obsolescence through use of Chaucer and Gower, considering Book IV of Spenser's *The Faerie Queene*, the anonymous play *The Return from Parnassus*, Shakespeare and Wilkins's *Pericles*, and William Cartwright's *The Ordinary*.

65. Owens, Richard. "Caroline Bergvall Her 'Shorter Chaucer Tales.'" *postmedieval* 6, no. 2 (2015): 146–53. Examines Caroline's Bergvall's five Chaucer poems in *Meddle English* (*SAC* 39 [2017], no. 44), including discussion of their relations with Chaucer's originals. Focuses especially on Bergvall's "Fried Tale."

66. Payne, Deborah C. "Theatrical Spectatorship in Pepys's Diary." *RES* 66, no. 273 (2015): 87–105. Reveals how Pepys's performance of theatrical spectatorship allowed him to select, adjust, and even reject the pleasures of the playhouse in order to create successive, idealized versions of himself.

67. Prendergast, Thomas A. "Revenant Chaucer: Early Modern Celebrity." In Isabel Davis and Catherine Nall, eds. *Chaucer and Fame: Reputation and Reception* (*SAC* 39 [2017], no. 99), pp. 185–99. Looks at the "transition of the invented textual presence of Chaucer in the late Middle Ages to the invented personal presence of the poet in the early modern period." Comments on several spurious links between tales in the Lansdowne 851 manuscript of *CT*, by exploring various editions and uses of Chaucer's works in early modern England (especially Shakespeare and Fletcher's *Two Noble Kinsmen*), and discussing the use of Chaucer's "celebrity" in *Chaucer's Incensed Ghost* (1617), Richard Brathwait's anti-tobacco tract.

68. Rogers, Cynthia A. "'Make Thereof a Game': The Interplay of Texts in the Findern Manuscript and Its Late Medieval Textual Community." *DAI* A76.11 (2015): n.p. Explores a Middle English scrapbook from the fifteenth and early sixteenth centuries that includes some Chaucerian love literature, and considers the book's role in a performance of gentility, particularly on the part of its women readers.

69. Tambling, Jeremy. "Dickens and Chaucer." *English* 64, no. 244 (2015): 42–64. Analyzes the influence of Chaucer on several Romantic thinkers and their subsequent influence on Dickens, as well as Dickens's own reference and allusions to *CT*. Focuses on how *Our Mutual Friend* reflects medievalism in such aspects as the pilgrimage with its vast array

of characters, the device of framed narrative, and the characterization of Canterbury as the past. Allusions to Chaucer, especially in *GP* and *PardT*, are also abundant in *Our Mutual Friend*.

70. Warren, Michelle R. "'The last syllable of modernity': Chaucer in the Caribbean." *postmedieval* 6, no. 1 (2015): 79–93. Reviews references to how Chaucer is represented and appropriated in anglophone Caribbean literature and critical essays. Includes example of "fictional allusion" to *CT* in Jean Rhys's "Again the Antilles."

71. Warren, Nancy Bradley. "'Flying from the Depravities of Europe, to the American Strand': Chaucer and the Chaucer Tradition in Early America." *ELH* 82, no. 2 (2015): 589–613. Focuses on how Chaucer influenced the writings of Cotton Mather, Anne Bradstreet, and Nathaniel Ward in seventeenth- and early eighteenth-century New England.

72. Warren, Rosanna. "Stepping Out and Stepping Over: The Figure of Hyperbation." *Yale Review* 103, no. 1 (2015): 54–61. Discusses the convention of inverting or rearranging word order for poetic effect. Highlights the writing of William Dunbar, who acknowledged Chaucer to be included among the "masters who by making were remade."

See also nos. 2, 11, 39, 80, 83, 134, 179, 182, 185–86, 191, 202, 219, 230.

Style and Versification

73. Bowers, John M. "Speaking Images: Iconographic Criticism and Chaucerian Ekphrasis." In Andrew James Johnston, Ethan Knapp, and Margitta Rouse, eds. *The Art of Vision: Ekphrasis in Medieval Literature and Culture* (*SAC* 39 [2017], no. 109), pp. 55–76. Explores Chaucer's uses of ekphrasis as "expressions of an increasingly anxious desire to allow literary images to speak for themselves" in *KnT*, *BD*, and *HF*.

74. Bradbury, Nancy Mason. "The Proverb as Imbedded Microgenre in Chaucer and *The Dialogue of Solomon and Marcolf*." *Exemplaria* 27 (2015): 55–72. Uses examples from *CT*, *TC*, and the anonymous Middle English *Dialogue of Solomon and Marcolf*, read in a context created by Bakhtin's theory of "speech genres," to demonstrate the power of proverbs to transform the situations in which they are embedded. These proverbs "indicate courses of action, encapsulate worldviews, console and reconcile their recipients to the ways of this world, and mediate for

fictional characters and for readers the overwhelming variety of lived experience."

75. Crosson, Chad Gregory. "The *Canterbury Tales* and Chaucer's Corrective Form." *DAI* A77.03 (2015): n.p. Suggests that Chaucer deployed the tradition of grammatical "correction" as a metaphor for moral reform, finding examples in *CT*, *TC*, and *Adam*.

76. Knapp, Ethan. "Faces in the Crowd: Faciality and Ekphrasis in Late Medieval England." In Andrew James Johnston, Knapp, and Margitta Rouse, eds. *The Art of Vision: Ekphrasis in Medieval Literature and Culture* (*SAC* 39 [2017], no. 109), pp. 209–23. Explores the "function of faciality" in medieval poetry of Chaucer, Gower, and Hoccleve. Examines Chaucer's portraits of faces in *GP*, *MLT*, and *TC*.

77. Nishide, Kimiyuki. "The Phraseology of the 'A and B' Structure at the End of a Line in Chaucer's Verse." *Tsuru Studies in English Linguistics and Literature* 42 (2014): 1–13. Focuses on Chaucer's verse lines ending as "A and B" to find out frequent combinations of the words in A and B. In Japanese.

78. Novacich, Sarah Elliott. "On Footprints and Poetic Feet." *PQ* 94, no. 3 (2015): 201–23. Focuses on the idea of "poetic feet" of versification in poetry, and examines how travel narratives are linked to poetic language. Compares *CT*, including *ParsT*, *MkT*, *KnT*, *Tho*, *Mel*, and *TC* to Dante's *Inferno* and Mandeville's travel narratives.

See also nos. 34, 48, 72, 80, 90, 142, 159, 162, 200, 204, 234.

Language and Word Studies

79. Barrington, Candace. "Teaching Chaucer in Middle English: A Fundamental Approach." *SMART* 22 (2015): 21–32. Describes writing assignments, for an upper-division Chaucer course, that help students read *CT* in Middle English. Demonstrates how breaking the assignments into smaller steps promotes a greater understanding of fluency and discovery of unfamiliar language and ideas.

80. Bellis, Joanna. "'Fresch anamalit termes': The Contradictory Celebrity of Chaucer's Aureation." In Isabel Davis and Catherine Nall, eds. *Chaucer and Fame: Reputation and Reception* (*SAC* 39 [2017], no. 99), pp. 143–63. Describes a change in Chaucer's "linguistic fame" from fifteenth-century praise of his rhetoric and aureate diction to sixteenth-century admiration of his plain speaking: a shift that reflects the early

modern "Inkhorn Controversy" and efforts to separate "Englishness" from French. Chaucer was regarded as the "Father of English" by representatives of both groups.

81. Bourgne, Florence. "Chaucer, poète multilingue, mais jusqu'où?" *Cahiers de recherches médiévales et humanistes* 29 (2015): 199–214. Examines Chaucer's literary exchanges with contemporary French writers, including his interest in "Flaundres, in Artoys, and Pycardie." Offers how Chaucer's translation of *Rom* confirms his fascination with the duchy's growing empire, where Picard was the lingua franca.

82. Farrell, Thomas J. "The Meanings of Middle English *Wight*." *ChauR* 50, nos. 1–2 (2015): 178–97. Argues that in *CT*, *wight* could indeed mean a supernatural being and refer to Jesus Christ as Creator, which questions a long-standing editorial emendation by E. Talbot Donaldson in *WBP*, 117.

83. Hadbawnik, David. "Language Strange: Speech and Poetic Authority in Chaucer, Lydgate, Dunbar, and Spenser." *DAI* A76.11 (2015): n.p. Considers the diction of Chaucer, his successors, and *CT* editor Thomas Tyrwhitt as part of a larger argument for the interrelationship of late medieval and early modern poetic language.

84. Murchison, Krista A. "The Meaning of Middle English *Gent and Smal*." *ChauR* 49, no. 3 (2015): 371–75. Argues that the word pair "gent and smal," used in the description of Alisoun in *MilT*, meant "well-built," with connotations of noble looks and behavior.

85. Nakao, Yoshiyuki, Akiyuki Jimura, and Noriyuki Kawano. "Choice and Psychology of Negation in Chaucer's Language: Syntactic, Lexical, Semantic Negative Choice with Evidence from the Hengwrt and Ellesmere MSS and the Two Editions of the *Canterbury Tales*." *Hiroshima Studies in English Language and Literature* 59 (2015): 1–34. Compares frequencies of different negative forms as well as syntactic, lexical, and semantic negative patterns in the Hengwrt and Ellesmere manuscripts and two critical editions by Blake and Benson, respectively. Tabulates the result as statistical data and discusses the tendency and factor in the choice of negative forms or patterns.

86. Ohno, Hideshi. "The Absolute Infinitive in Chaucer: With Special Reference to Parenthetical Use of *Seien*, *Speken*, and *Tellen*." *Bulletin of Kurashiki University of Science and the Arts* 20 (2015): 131–46. Provides an overview of Chaucer's use of the absolute infinitive, and introduces its various types. Focuses especially on the uses of *seien*, *speken*, and *tellen*

in parenthetical construction and discusses their function based on statistical data.

87. Schendl, Herbert. "Code-Switching in Early English Literature." *Lang&Lit* 24, no. 3 (2015): 233–48. Discusses the main functions of code-switching in the poetry and drama of medieval England. Emphasizes how the friar in *SumT* uses the French phrase "je vous dy" to increase his authority and learnedness.

88. Simonin, Olivier. "Engagements de Gauvain et courtoisie dans *Sir Gawain and the Green Knight.*" *BAM* 87 (2015): 123–44. Explores the notion of commitment in *Sir Gawain and the Green Knight* and briefly mentions *MilT* in relation to the several meanings of the term *hend(e)*.

89. Stadnik, Katarzyna. *Chaucer's Choices through the Looking-Glass of Medieval Imagery.* Lódź Studies in Language 38. Frankfurt am Main: Peter Lang Edition, 2015. 224 pp. Uses cognitive linguistics and theories of imagery as a transmitter of culture to read the use of the Middle English word *moten* in *TC* and *KnT*.

90. Štrmelj, Lidija. "Mediaeval and Modern Metaphorical Concepts of Emotions." *ELOPE: English Language Overseas Perspectives and Enquiries* 14, no. 2 (2014): 37–47. Assesses examples from *GP*, *KnT*, *MilPT*, *WBPT*, and *SNPT*, deducing that medieval metaphors of emotion are similar to modern ones, although they depend more closely upon social categories, with negative metaphors typical of middle-class speakers, and positive ones associated with the clergy and higher classes. Examines locutions of emotion that pertain to love, jealousy, fear, anger, etc.

91. Wang, Denise Ming-yueh. "Chaucer's English and Multilingualism." *MES* 22, no. 2 (2014): 1–27. Discusses Chaucer's English inheritance from a Taiwanese-Chinese point of view. Reviews multilingualism in Chinese and medieval English cultures, and examines Chaucer's cross-cultural and multilingual literary experience in fourteenth-century England. Also addresses the question of how Chaucer's English is perceived by non-native English speakers.

See also nos. 26, 36, 44, 46, 64, 77, 110–11, 148, 150, 153–54, 187, 198, 218, 226, 232.

Background and General Criticism

92. Allen, Mark. "Memorial: John Hurt Fisher (October 26, 1919–February 17, 2015)." *ChauR* 50, nos. 3–4 (2015): 224–27. Discusses

the work and life of John Fisher and his important contribution to Chaucer studies.

93. Ashton, Gail, ed. *Medieval Afterlives in Contemporary Culture*. London: Bloomsbury, 2015. viii, 360 pp.; illus. Collection of essays covers a comprehensive range of medieval-related media, including literature, film, TV, comic-book adaptations, electronic media, performances, and commercial merchandise and tourism. For essay pertaining to Chaucer, see no. 11.

94. Azuma, Yuichiro, Kotaro Kawasaki, and Koichi Kano, eds. *Chaucer and English and American Literature: Essays Commemorating the Retirement of Professor Masatoshi Kawasaki*. Tokyo: Kinseido, 2015. iv, 420 pp. Includes seven articles related to Chaucer. See nos. 8, 26, 166, 190, 222, 226, 228. In Japanese.

95. Barrington, Candace, and Jonathan Hsy. "Global Chaucers: Reflections on Collaboration and Digital Futures." *Accessus: A Journal of Premodern Literature and New Media* 2, no. 2 (2015): n.p. Reflects on the *Global Chaucers* project, which creates a forum for world-wide non-anglophone reworkings of Chaucerian material (*SAC* 39 [2017], no. 2). Presents challenges and goals for future projects in response to scholars' diverse interests and expanding discoveries.

96. Beaumont, Matthew. *Nightwalking: A Nocturnal History of London Chaucer to Dickens*. London: Verso, 2015. vii, 469 pp. Creates a literary history of the "night side of literature" in London from the Middle Ages to the mid-nineteenth century. Considers Chaucer's "nightwalkers" in *MilT, CkT, WBT*, and *LGW*.

97. Brewer, Charlotte. "'That Reliance on the Ordinary': Jane Austen and the *Oxford English Dictionary*." *RES* 66, no. 276 (2015): 744–65. Argues that while Austen's quotations in the revised *OED* have increased in number overall, those of female authors are still extraordinarily low when compared to the canonical literary male authors: Shakespeare (c. 33,000), Walter Scott (c. 15,000), Milton (c. 12,000), and Chaucer (c. 11,000).

98. Caballero-Torralbo, Juan de Dios, and Javier Martín-Párraga, eds. *New Medievalisms*. Cambridge: Cambridge Scholars Publishing, 2015. ix, 324 pp. Collection of essays provides various approaches to the study and teaching of the Middle Ages. For essay pertaining to Chaucer, see no. 203.

99. Davis, Isabel, and Catherine Nall, eds. *Chaucer and Fame: Reputation and Reception*. Chaucer Studies 43. Cambridge: D. S. Brewer, 2015.

x, 249 pp.; 7 b&w illus. Eleven essays and an introduction (by Davis) deal with Chaucer's concern with poetic fame and/or with his poetic reputation among his contemporaries, down to the twenty-first century. The introduction (pp. 1–19) describes the essays and comments on poetic fame in *HF* and *LGW* as the topic relates to Chaucer's omissions and elisions, his uses of names and his (non-)naming of sources, and his relations with several works that influenced him, especially Boccaccio's *De mulieribus claris*. For individual essays, see nos. 39, 51, 54–55, 61, 67, 80, 202, 206, 216, 233. Includes a bibliography and index.

100. Donoghue, Daniel. "Larry Dean Benson: A Tribute." *ChauR* 50, nos. 3–4 (2015): 220–23. Provides commemorative essay on the life and accomplishments of Larry Benson.

101. Dor, Juliette. "Geoffrey Chaucer av. 1346 –v. 1400." In Bruno Méniel, ed. *Ecrivains juristes etjuristes écrivains, du Moyen Age au siècle des Lumières*. Esprits des lois, Esprit des lettres 8 (Paris: Classiques Garnier, 2015), pp. 522–26. Reviews issues of justice in *Sted* and explores how Chaucer's irony reveals his bias against medieval judicial practices in *ABC*. Also, questions the relationship among Church/Rome/nation, political vs. religious law(s), and ascending vs. descending authority in the language of *MLT*.

102. Fein, Susanna, and David Raybin. "On beyond Fifty." *ChauR* 50, nos. 3–4 (2015): 217–19. This introductory essay comments on the first fifty years of *Chaucer Review*, and looks ahead to future projects.

103. Friedrich, Jennie Rebecca. "Travail Narratives: Damage and Displacement in Medieval Travel Literature." *DAI* A77.01 (2015): n.p. Considers Chaucer as part of a larger discussion of medieval ideas of the physical damage that accrued from travel, both in the sense of a literal pilgrimage and in tropes including the "wandering heart."

104. Gabrovsky, Alexander N. *Chaucer the Alchemist: Physics, Mutability, and the Medieval Imagination*. The New Middle Ages. New York: Palgrave Macmillan, 2015. xviii, 291 pp. Views Chaucer's fascination with contemporary theories of change, both in readily visible physical form and also less visible self-reform. The book is divided into three sections: Physics, Alchemy, and Logic. The Physics section discusses *HF* as a thought experiment "where the possibilities of physical phenomena are pushed to extremes." The Alchemy section examines alchemical allegory in *FranT* with special attention to Dorigen as a "catalyst for wisdom," and allegorical imagery throughout *TC*, culminating in Troilus's

"mercurial transformation." The volume concludes with mutability in logic, particularly counterfactual "if . . . then" statements in *PF*.

105. George, Michael W. "Adversarial Relationships between Humans and Weather in Medieval English Literature." *EMSt* 30 (2014): 67–81. After examining weather patterns during the Middle Ages, suggests that the late fourteenth century experienced lower than normal temperatures and increased precipitation that would have affected harvests. Since inclement weather plays a role in *BD*, *TC*, and *MilT*, speculates that the trope of the idealized spring setting, particularly in *GP*, acts as a type of escapism, or perhaps is Chaucer's response to a year of unusually good weather.

106. Hanawalt, Barbara A. "Toward the Common Good: Punishing Fraud among the Victualers of Medieval London." In Fiona Somerset and Nicholas Watson, eds. *Truth and Tales: Cultural Mobility and Medieval Media* (*SAC* 39 [2017], no. 121), pp. 168–86. Discusses Chaucer's use of humor in describing the "thieving millers" in *GP* and *RvT*. Looks at class and social issues among food providers, including cooks, bakers, and taverners, and civic governing entities responsible for overseeing production of high-quality food. Includes brief analysis of Chaucer's Cook in *GP*.

107. James, Jonathan. "Love and Apocalypse in Chaucer's Dream Visions." *DAI* A77.05 (2015): n.p. Examines Chaucer's efforts, in *BD*, *HF*, *LGW*, and *PF*, to meld two strands of dream poetry: the philosophical and amorous subspecies of the form.

108. Johnston, Alexandra F. "Pleyes of Myracles." *English* 64, no. 244 (2015): 5–26. Takes Lawrence M. Clopper's 1990 article "*Miracula* and *The Tretise of Miraclis Pleyinge*" as a starting-point to reexamine and redefine medieval drama, asserting that *CT* presents perspective on how the drama was perceived in the fourteenth century. References *WBP* and *MilT*.

109. Johnston, Andrew James, Ethan Knapp, and Margitta Rouse, eds. *The Art of Vision: Ekphrasis in Medieval Literature and Culture.* Columbus: Ohio State University Press, 2015. vii, 307 pp. Collection of essays on ekphrastic discourse from the eleventh to the seventeenth century in texts written in Middle English, but also Medieval Latin, Old French, Middle Scots, Middle High German, and Early Modern English. For essays pertaining to Chaucer, see nos. 73, 76, 162, 234.

110. Kikuchi, Kiyoaki. *Studies in Medieval English Language and Literature I: Aspects of Middle English.* Yokohama: Shumpusha, 2015. 283 pp.

Part 1 includes several chapters on Middle English themes related to Chaucer. Chapter 1 appreciates the sound of the beginning of *GP* as associated with spring. Chapter 2 includes a brief discussion of the relationship between individualism and the use of dialect in *RvT*. Chapter 3 discusses the meaning of Chaucer's choice of English for his poetic composition. In Japanese.

111. Leahy, Michael. " 'To speke of phisik': Medical Discourse in Late Medieval English Culture." *DAI* C74.10 (2015): n.p. Considers the addition of medical terminology to the lexicons of medieval laypeople, with particular regard to its use in metaphor. Authors under consideration include Chaucer, Henryson, Rolle, and Kempe.

112. Marenbon, John. *Pagans and Philosophers: The Problem of Paganism from Augustine to Leibniz.* Princeton: Princeton University Press, 2015. x, 354 pp. Examines the influence of paganism on Christian writers from the fifth century to the eighteenth century. Includes chapter on Chaucer: "Langland and Chaucer: The Continuity of the Problem of Paganism" (pp. 214–34).

113. Marshall, Camille. "Figuring the Dangers of the 'Greet Forneys': Chaucer and Gower's Timely (Mis)reporting of the Peasant Voice." *Comitatus* 46 (2015): 75–98. Reads the Miller (whose mouth is compared to "a greet forneys" in *GP*) in the context of representations of rebel peasants in the chronicles of Thomas Walsingham, Henry Knighton, Jean Froissart, and the Anonimalle chronicler, as well as in Gower's *Vox clamantis* (Book I). The trope of fire links the peasants' literarily censored speech to the Miller's furnace-like mouth, but the Miller's subversive words are represented within the aristocratically acceptable genre of the fabliau, reinforcing how Chaucer acknowledges sociopolitical danger, but renders it comic.

114. Meyer-Lee, Robert J. "Toward a Theory and Practice of Literary Valuing." *NLH* 46, no. 2 (2015): 335–55. In an analysis of the question of literary value, argues for a pragmatic approach to understanding the value of literature, especially at present when that value is on the decline. References *GP* as general example of medieval literary valuing.

115. Milliken, Roberta. *Ambiguous Locks: An Iconology of Hair in Medieval Art and Literature.* Jefferson, N.C.: McFarland, 2012. x, 290 pp.; b&w illus. Surveys depictions of "good" and "bad" women in medieval art and literature, concentrating on how their hair characterizes them and directs viewers' attention. Includes a brief discussion of

the implications of Emelye's yellow/golden hair in *KnT* (1049–50) for the ways that it confirms her beauty.

116. Niebrzydowski, Sue. Editorial. *English* 64, no. 244 (2015): 1–4. A general introduction to the *Chaucer Reconsidered* special issue of the journal that focuses on the many genres in which Chaucer worked, as well as his primary topics.

117. Phillips-Jones, Robin. "Authority, Identity, and 'the Idea of the Vernacular' in *The Owl and the Nightingale*." *Marginalia* 18 (2015): 14–23. Destabilizes the notion of a progression of "identifiable movements" in English vernacular writing culminating in Chaucer in the fourteenth century, arguing that *The Owl and the Nightingale* (c. 1200) should be taught as an early foundational vernacular text. The poem employs "outrageous satire" through the vernacular to critique and reconfigure the form of Latin debate poetry.

118. Schiff, Randy P. "Medieval Modes of Community." *Exemplaria* 27 (2015): 352–61. Summarizes the discussions of Chaucer in Lynn Staley's *The Island Garden* (*SAC* 37 [2015], no. 23), Jamie K. Taylor's *Fictions of Evidence* (*SAC* 38 [2016], no. 135), and Jonathan Hsy's *Trading Tongues* (*SAC* 37 [2015], no. 50).

119. Schmidt, A. V. C. *Passion and Precision: Collected Essays on English Poetry from Geoffrey Chaucer to Geoffrey Hill*. Newcastle upon Tyne: Cambridge Scholars Publishing, 2015. x, 460 pp. Collection of published and previously unpublished studies of Chaucer and other writers, including the *Pearl*-poet, Hopkins, Yeats, Eliot, Jones, and Auden. Part 1, "Medieval: Chaucer and the *Gawain*-Poet," includes essays on *Bo, Form Age, KnT*, and *TC*.

120. Somerset, Fiona. *Feeling like Saints: Lollard Writings after Wyclif*. Ithaca, N.Y.: Cornell University Press, 2014. vii, 324 pp. Comprehensive study of over 500 manuscripts containing Lollard writings from 1375 to 1530. Analyzes textual culture associated with Lollardy movement. Brief references to *MLT, PardT, PhyT*, and *TC*.

121. Somerset, Fiona, and Nicholas Watson, eds. *Truth and Tales: Cultural Mobility and Medieval Media*. Columbus: Ohio State University Press, 2015. ix, 294 pp. Includes essays dedicated to Richard Green Firth that explore a variety of medieval topics. Examines issues related to oral and written cultural networks, book and social history, vernacular studies, and media studies. For essays pertaining to Chaucer, see nos. 106, 205, 209.

122. Thomas, Alfred. *Reading Women in Late Medieval Europe: Anne of*

Bohemia and Chaucer's Female Audience. The New Middle Ages. New York: Palgrave Macmillan, 2015. xv, 251 pp. Explores the influence of Anne of Bohemia, wife and consort of King Richard II, on Chaucer and his contemporaries. Proposes that Anne of Bohemia was a "possible female patron and reader" of Chaucer's texts. Focuses on *PrT*, *SNT*, *KnT*, *WBT*, and *LGW*.

123. Toner, Anne. *Ellipsis in English Literature: Signs of Omission.* Cambridge: Cambridge University Press, 2015. x, 255 pp. Studies various kinds of narrative suspension and ellipsis in English literature, and includes comments on a reference to *SqT* in the expository essay that accompanies the Gothic tale "Sir Bertram, a Fragment" (1773). Connects the essay with Thomas Tyrwhitt's edition of *CT* (1775) where asterisks "first appear" at the end of *SqT*, and surmises that the editorial history of the tale would have differed if there had been "an explicit mark of interruption in the medieval orthographic repertoire."

124. Yoshikawa, Naoë Kukita, ed. *Medicine, Religion and Gender in Medieval Culture.* Woodbridge: Boydell and Brewer, 2015. xi, 293 pp. Investigates religious and medical medieval discourses in the Middle Ages. For essay on Chaucer, see no. 183.

See also no. 197.

The Canterbury Tales—General

125. Archer, Jayne Elizabeth, Richard Marggraf Turley, and Howard Thomas. " 'Soper at oure aller cost': The Politics of Food Supply in the *Canterbury Tales.*" *ChauR* 50, nos. 1–2 (2015): 1–29. Proposes connections between the *CT*—especially Chaucer's Plowman, the apocryphal *Plowman's Tale*, and *RvT*—and ideas about food supply. Provides an overarching argument that anxieties about farming and the politics of how food was distributed in late fourteenth-century England tie together many of the tales and pilgrims' words.

126. Duprey, Annalese. " 'Lo, pitee renneth soone in gentil herte': Pity as Moral and Sexual Persuasion in Chaucer." *EMSt* 30 (2014): 55–66. Surveys how pity functions as a lover's emotional ploy that establishes a power relationship in *CT*. Focuses on *MerT* and *FranT* and explores to what extent May and Dorigen create agency for themselves by participating in the exchange of suffering for pity and love.

127. Ji-yeon, Choi. "Re-reading Chaucer's Women: Focusing on

Fabliau and Clothing." *MES* 23, no. 2 (2015): 145–59. Focuses on fabliau and the clothing of Chaucer's women in *MilT*, *WBT*, and *RvT*, and claims that "women's desire and independent will are materialized by means of [the] Wife of Bath's clothing."

128. King, Pamela M. *Medieval Literature 1300–1500*. Edinburgh: Edinburgh University Press, 2011. xiv, 242 pp. Provides close readings of canonical medieval texts, including *Piers Plowman*, Malory's *Morte Darthur*, and *CT*. Emphasizes *KnT*, *GP*, *MilT*, *PrT*, *SumT*, *PardT*, and *FrT*.

129. Matsuda, Takami. "Vernacular Literature of Medieval Europe: Chaucer's *Canterbury Tales*." In Kiyoko Myojo and Noburu Notomi, eds. *What Is a Text? An Introduction to Textual Scholarship* (*SAC* 39 [2017], no. 30), pp. 81–104. Refers to Paul Zumthor's notion of *mouvance*, and argues that *CT* should be understood not as a single text but as a group of different, co-existent texts. In Japanese.

130. Scala, Elizabeth. *Desire in the "Canterbury Tales."* Interventions: New Studies in Medieval Culture. Columbus: Ohio State University Press, 2015. x, 225 pp. Presents Lacanian analysis of desire in *CT* that focuses on the "circulation of the signifier" and the generative power of misrecognition/misreading. Clarifies the meaning and function of fundamental concepts (subject, signifier, Other, aggressivity, Symbolic order, etc.) and identifies in *GP* the functions of desire ("longen" [line 12]) and contestation. Examines paired tales that epitomize aspects of desire and its manifestations in language and narrative, and ways that it "pervades and constitutes the discourse" of *CT*. Considers *KnT* and *RvT* (mediated by *MilT*), *WBT* and *ClT*, and *PhyT* and *SNT*. Refers to *MLT*, *FranT*, and *ShT*.

131. Workman, Jameson S. *Chaucer and the Death of the Political Animal*. The New Middle Ages. New York: Palgrave Macmillan, 2015. xvii, 274 pp. Studies "the architecture of Chaucerian metapoetics" in *CT* and reads several tales as Neoplatonist texts. Criticism of *MilT*, *ManT*, and *NPT* is framed by a consideration of the corrupted natural philosophy of the old man in *PardT*. Nicholas's impalement in *MilT* signals the failure of his naturalistic, materialistic philosophy. *ManT* presents art's metaphysical descent down the Neoplatonic "chain of love" via a naturalistic, domesticated revision of Ovidian sources that depicts linguistic dissolution. *NPT*, "the definitive nursery rhyme of medieval Platonism," achieves a return to the Golden Age by illustrating both the "conflict between Human Art (Chauntecleer's world) and Human History (the

widow's world)" and between Pertelote's naturalism and Chauntecleer's literary Neoplatonism, only to achieve resolution in Chauntecleer's escape into prelapsarian silence in a tree.

132. Wu, Hsiang-mei. "Chaucer and Prejudices: A Critical Study of 'The Canterbury Tales.'" *DAI* C74.10 (2015): n.p. Examines treatment of several *CT* narrators and characters and sees examples of "othering" and hostile prejudice toward those characters. Proceeds from there to possible continuations of those prejudices in contemporary readings.

133. Zuraikat, Malek. "The Anti-Crusade Voice of Chaucer's 'Canterbury Tales.'" *DAI* A76.07 (2015): n.p. Argues that along with Langland and Gower, Chaucer's writings, especially *CT*, may be read as an indirect critique of crusading.

See also nos. 18, 20, 22, 34, 38, 42, 49, 74–75, 79, 128, 168, 190, 192, 221.

CT—The General Prologue

See nos. 12, 36, 48, 57, 69, 76, 90, 105, 110, 114, 125, 128, 130, 145, 163.

CT—The Knight and His Tale

134. Britton, Dennis Austin. "From the *Knight's Tale* to *The Two Noble Kinsmen*: Rethinking Race, Class, and Whiteness in Romance." *postmedieval* 6, no. 1 (2015): 64–78. Establishes how Shakespeare and Fletcher used "images of Africanness to link race and class" in *The Two Noble Kinsmen*, and claims this differs from Chaucer's concern with the "racial alterity" and "whiteness" of the Amazonian women in *KnT*.

135. Byeong-yong, Son. "The Political Nature of Romance: Focusing on Knight's Tale." *MES* 22, no. 2 (2014): 61–81. Looks at the political and social context of Chaucer's life, and claims that in *KnT* Chaucer appropriated and transformed the conventions of romance to reflect his own political views about medieval kingship.

136. Chapman, Juliana. "Melodye and Noyse: An Aesthetic of *Musica* in *The Knight's Tale* and *The Miller's Tale*." *SP* 112, no. 4 (2015): 633–55. Contends that Chaucer employs music as a literary aesthetic, which creates a "structure of narrative mirroring," in *KnT* and *MilT*.

137. Johnston, Andrew James. "Chaucer's Postcolonial Renaissance." *BJRL* 91, no. 2 (2015): 5–20. Analyzes how *KnT* and *SqT* engage with the Orientalist discourses buttressing contemporary humanist Italian discussions of visual art, especially in terms of the subjects of classicism and of optics.

138. Magnani, Roberta. "Policing the Queer: Narratives of Dissent and Containment in Chaucer's *The Knight's Tale*." *MFF* 50 (2014): 90–126. Discusses Emily's subjectivity and "empowered devotional femininity" in *KnT*. Contends that Chaucer's "queer hermeneutics" adjusts "traditional concepts of masculinity and femininity" within *KnT*.

139. Schrock, Chad D. *Consolation in Medieval Narrative: Augustinian Authority and Open Form.* New York: Palgrave Macmillan, 2015. xv, 240 pp. Explores how Abelard, Chaucer, and Langland used consolatory narratives in their writings. Chapter 5 (pp. 107–27) explores Augustinian and Boethian concerns in *KnT*.

See also nos. 19, 36, 73, 78, 89–90, 115, 119, 122, 128, 130, 199.

CT—The Miller and His Tale

140. Beidler, Peter G. *The Lives of the Miller's Tale: The Roots, Composition and Retellings of Chaucer's Bawdy Story.* Jefferson, N.C.: McFarland, 2015. viii, 275 pp.; 32 b&w illus. Describes how Chaucer adapted his source, *Heile of Beersele*, increasing the "theatricality" of plot and details in making *MilT*, concentrating on the architectural setting (house and window), dramatic details, and additional "scenes." Surveys and summarizes various later translations and adaptations of *MilT* for adults and children: prose, verse, drama, musical, novels, graphic novels, film, and television. Includes the texts of recent (2014) adaptations by Peter N. Miller (excerpt) and Gareth Machin (complete), both previously unpublished but available from the authors.

141. Slefinger, John. "The Two Alisouns: The Miller's Use of Costume and His Seduction of the Wife of Bath." *EMSt* 30 (2014): 155–64. Explores how the Miller might be interacting with the Wife of Bath when he presents Alisoun, whose description "represents an attempt to control and win the Wife of Bath's sexual attention while undercutting any agency or interiority she may have."

142. Smilie, Ethan. "*Goddes Pryvetee* and a *Wyf: Curiositas* and the Triadic Sins in the Miller's and Reeve's Tales." *C&L* 65, no. 1 (2015):

4–26. Explains that the medieval notion of *curiositas* (illicit pursuit of knowledge) entails concupiscence of the eyes, concupiscence of the flesh, and worldly pride, showing that these vices are a theme that links *MilT* and *RvT*, particularly evident in a series of puns ("pryvetee," "queynte," etc.). By offering a variety of characters that are guilty of *curiositas*, Chaucer deflates the intellectual pretentiousness of the vice.

See also nos. 11, 13, 34, 61, 84, 88, 90, 96, 105–6, 108, 127–28, 130–31.

CT—The Reeve and His Tale

143. Blackwell, Alice. "'Right in his cherles termes wol I speke': Chaucer's Self-Defeating Reeve and His Self-Destructing Tale." *MedPers* 76 (2015): 163–80. Although the Reeve claims a moral high ground by telling a story that deals out justice to its dishonest miller, this revenge does not accord with the moral virtue of justice nor with the amoral fabliau genre, undermining the Reeve's sanctimony and raising unanswered questions about the degree of consent given by the women who become instruments of the clerks' revenge.

See also nos. 106, 110, 125, 127, 130, 142.

CT—The Cook and His Tale

See nos. 96, 106.

CT—The Man of Law and His Tale

144. Czarnowus, Anna. "Ethnically Different Mothers-in-Law in Chaucer's *Man of Law's Tale* and Its 2003 BBC Adaptation." In Rafal Boryslawski, Czarnowus, and Lukasz Neubauer, eds. *Marvels of Reading: Essays in Honour of Professor Andrzej Wicher* (Katowice: Wydawnictwo Uniwersytetu Ślaskiego, 2015), pp. 103–13. Assesses representation of the mothers-in-law in *MLT* and their equivalent in the BBC adaptation, where the mother-in-law is of Iranian origin, but looks on Custance from a highly racist perspective.

145. Johnson, Eleanor. "English Law and the Man of Law's 'Prose' Tale." *JEGP* 114, no 4 (2015): 504–25. Argues that the Man of Law

depicts himself as a traditionalist in law. Through his presentation in *GP*, his conversation with the Host, and his tale, the Man of Law separates himself from negative views of lawyers in the wake of the 1381 Rising. In claiming that he will give a tale in prose, he refers to the veracity of his story rather than its form.

146. O'Connell, Brendan. " 'Struglyng wel and myghtily': Resisting Rape in the *Man of Law's Tale.*" *MÆ* 84, no. 1 (2015): 16–39. Unlike Constance in Trevet and Gower, Custance in *MLT* does not speak with her would-be rapist; further, she immediately struggles with him and receives divine aid in overcoming him. Asserts that Chaucer's treatment of this scene demonstrates knowledge of the law concerning self-defense and justifiable homicide.

147. Richmond, Andrew M. " 'The broken schippus he ther fonde': Shipwrecks and the Human Costs of Investment Capital in Middle English Romance." *Neophil* 99, no. 2 (2015): 315–33. Discusses *MLT* within analysis of shipwrecks and depictions of seashores in Middle English romances.

See also nos. 41, 54, 76, 101, 120, 130, 188.

CT—The Wife of Bath and Her Tale

148. Burrow, J. A. "Nature in *King Hart.*" *RES* 66, no. 276 (2015): 624–33. Considers how Nature brings forces to bear that "incline" Hart to feel and behave the way he does in *King Hart*. Argues that Chaucer's Wife of Bath uses the same technical term when she says "I folwed ay myn inclinacioun / By vertu of my constellacioun" in *WBP*.

149. Delony, Mikee C. "Weaving the Sermon: The Wife of Bath's Preaching Body in the *Canterbury Tales.*" In Priscilla Pope-Levison and John R. Levison, eds. *Sex, Gender, and Christianity* (Eugene, OR: Cascade Books, 2012), pp. 33–57. Examines connections between women's weaving and preaching by focusing on Alisoun. Uses the metaphor of weaving to establish how Alisoun "wove textiles and words as a mode of female expression and critique of the patriarchal church's interpretation of sacred knowledge."

150. Edwards, A. S. G. "The Wife of Bath's Sixth Man (*Canterbury Tales*, III 21)." *ChauR* 49, no. 3 (2015): 376–77. Argues that *WBP*, 21 should be emended from *fifthe* to *sixte*.

151. Morrison, Stephen. "Editing Middle English Texts: Spin-offs for

the Oxford English Dictionary." *BAM* 86 (2015): 37–52. Analyzes the Wife of Bath's "deceptive nature of fine outward show," in terms of her dress and clothing, as opposed to her inner purity in *WBT*.

152. Nakley, Susan. " 'Rowned she a pistel': National Institutions and Identities According to Chaucer's Wife of Bath." *JEGP* 114, no. 1 (2015): 61–87. Establishes how *WBT*'s treatment of sovereignty and of civic and domestic institutions "redefine[s] English nobility as a national form of identity" that crosses class and gender boundaries. Further argues that Chaucer's anachronistic use of Dante in the old woman's sermon creates a sense of nobility based not on heritage but on "shared ethical standards of virtuous living" and "civic responsibility."

153. Parsons, Ben. "Beaten for a Book: Domestic and Pedagogic Violence in *The Wife of Bath's Prologue*." *SAC* 37 (2015): 163–94. Identifies relations between domestic and pedagogical violence in *WBP*, establishing that its vocabulary is "redolent of the classroom" and arguing that Jankyn's treatment of Alison grants her agency, albeit unintentionally. Describes the motivations and restrictions of wife-beating and student-beating in medieval discourse and assesses how in the final altercation in *WBP* the contradictions between two sets of prescribed limits on violence reveal awareness of the need for disciplinary restraint.

154. Stadolnik, Joseph. "The Stuff of Metaphor: *Fyr* and *tow* in the Prologue to the *Wife of Bath's Tale*." *ES* 96, no. 1 (2015): 15–21. Argues that the Wife's *fyr* and *tow* not only warn against sexual temptation but are also a contemporary "reference to the fatal accident at the *bal des ardents* at the French royal court in 1393, which very nearly took the life of Charles VI."

155. Takana, Hidekuni. "Bāsu no nyōbō no monogatari no fusawashi-sa-kō" ("The Fitness of *The Wife of Bath's Tale*"). *Bulletin of Seikei University* 46 (2011): 13–22. Compares *WBT* with its Middle English analogues and comments on the relations between *WBPT* and *ShT*. http://repository.seikei.ac.jp/dspace/bitstream/10928/86/1/bungaku-46_13-22.pdf (accessed January 12, 2016). In Japanese.

See also nos. 19, 21, 23, 34–36, 82, 90, 96, 108, 122, 127, 130, 141, 158, 173, 188, 194.

CT—The Friar and His Tale

See nos. 23, 128.

CT—The Summoner and His Tale

156. Whearty, Bridget. "The Leper on the Road to Canterbury: The Summoner, Digital Manuscripts, and Possible Futures." *Mediaevalia* 36/37 (2015/2016): 223–61. Examines the Summoner in *GP* in connection with representations of leprosy and discusses the limitations of the digital manuscripts used to research findings.

See also nos. 23, 87, 128.

CT—The Clerk and His Tale

157. Hui-jeong, Seon. "The Clerk's Ironic Storytelling in The Clerk's Tale." *MES* 22, no. 2 (2014): 31–59. Examines the irony and paradoxes of *ClT*, claiming that through the tale, the Clerk "challenges an audience as Griselda's impassive patience challenges Walter." Views the Clerk as a "complicated figure of utter submissiveness and essential silence like Griselda."

158. Ida, Hideho. "A Literary Comparison between Chaucer's 'The Clerk's Tale' and Its Latin and French Originals." *Doshisha Global and Regional Studies Review* 4 (2015): 45–65. Points out lines of *ClT* not included in either of the Latin and French sources and considers the meanings of these additions by Chaucer. Argues that Walter is characterised as stricter in *ClT* and discusses the narrator Clerk's position in relation to the Wife of Bath. In Japanese, with English abstract.

159. Normandin, Shawn. "From Error to Anacoluthon: The Moral of the 'Clerk's Tale.'" *N&Q* 260 (2015): 218–19. In rendering Petrarch's explanation for why God tests humans in the form of a disjointed sentence (*ClT*, 1153–61), Chaucer points out its irrationality. Argues how this ploy resonates with the Clerk's expression of qualms about Petrarch at the beginning of his tale.

160. Rodríguez Mesa, Francisco José. "Entre exégesis y adición: El papel del Prólogo al 'Cuento del erudito' en la adaptación de Chaucer del de insigni obedientia et fide uxoris." In Elisa Borsari, ed. *En lengua vulgar castellana traduzido: Ensayos sobre la actividad traductora durante la Edad Media* (San Millán de la Cogolla: Cilengua, 2015), pp. 121–33. Evaluates Chaucer's strategies of adapting his Italian sources in *ClT*. He uses three paratexts to adjust the original story to the specific narratological and structural microcosm of *CT*: *ClP*, the conclusion explaining

what Petrarch meant in Griselda's story, and the sarcastic epilogue questioning the validity of the Italian's purpose for an English context.

See also nos. 19, 34, 36, 39–40, 49, 130.

CT—The Merchant and His Tale

161. Al-Garrallah, Aiman Sanad. "The Cunning Wife/Fruit Tree Syndrome: Chaucer's *The Merchant's Tale* and Seven Arabic Stories." *Neohelicon* 42 (2015): 671–86. Suggests Arabic texts not as sources for *MerT*, but as fellow exemplars of certain similar "universal" archetypes (tree, garden, billet-doux, key). Juxtaposes Arabic tales (some from *The Arabian Nights)* with *MerT*, and organizes stories by tree type (pear, sycamore, palm). Reads the shared archetypes through a Jungian lens, comparing them to the shadow, anima, animus, and persona. Refers to *hortus conclusus* and *locus amoenus* as integral to these archetypal manifestations of a "collective unconsciousness" or "ur-myth."

162. Schuerer, Hans Jürgen. "The Soul of Ekphrasis: Chaucer's 'Merchant's Tale' and the Marriage of the Senses." In Andrew James Johnston, Ethan Knapp, and Margitta Rouse, eds. *The Art of Vision: Ekphrasis in Medieval Literature and Culture (SAC* 39 [2017], no. 109), pp. 224–42. Argues that ekphrasis in *MerT* is an "engagement with the union of language and the inner senses." In particular, examines "ekphrastic moments . . . between physical expression and the psyche" in Chaucer's treatment of marriage in *MerT*.

163. Zedolik, John. "'The gardyn is enclosed al aboute': The Inversion of Exclusivity in the *Merchant's Tale*." *SP* 112, no. 3 (2015): 490–503. Treats control as a thematic device in *MerT* and in *CT* at large. January seeks to control May through literal enclosure, but is himself figuratively controlled by May and Damian, becoming a keeper kept. Conversely, the pilgrim narrator of *CT* relinquishes the closed form of the *GP* descriptions and gives control over to the other pilgrims, maintaining partial control by becoming a participant himself.

See also nos. 34–35, 126.

CT—The Squire and His Tale

164. Karnes, Michelle. "Wonder, Marvels, and Metaphor in the *Squire's Tale*." *ELH* 82, no. 2 (2015): 461–90. Argues that *SqT* is an

exception among medieval romances because it investigates things that are not what they seem. The first section of the tale scrutinizes the mechanics of marvels and wonder; the second explores the mechanics of stories, especially figurative language. Draws heavily on appeals to medieval philosophical theories and finds that the tale links literature to marvels, claiming that such an association was crucial to the development of literary theory in England.

165. Kikuchi, Akio. "'Ancestral voices prophesying war': The Representation of the Mongol Empire in Chaucer's *Squire's Tale*." *Tohoku Romantic Studies* 2 (2015): 1–14. Considers why the tale of the Mongol Empire is allocated to the young Squire. Points out the Squire's idealistic representation of the royal family of the Empire and discusses Chaucer's possible attitude toward *SqT*, taking fourteenth-century political affairs into account. In Japanese.

166. Matsuda, Takami. "The Interruption of the *Squire's Tale*: The Disillusionment of Wonder in the *Canterbury Tales*." In Yuichiro Azuma, Kotaro Kawasaki, and Koichi Kano, eds. *Chaucer and English and American Literature: Essays Commemorating the Retirement of Professor Masatoshi Kawasaki* (*SAC* 39 [2017], no. 94), pp. 44–59. Argues that the medieval notion of wonder helps to explain the Franklin's interruption of *SqT*. The Squire presents the marvels in his tale as explainable in scientific terms, in accord with the philosophical notion of wonder. The Franklin similarly intends to reframe romance marvels in scientific terms and does not want the Squire to forestall him. In Japanese.

See also nos. 123, 137.

CT—The Franklin and His Tale

167. Douglas, Blaise. "Bonds in a Selection of Middle English Breton Lays." In Claire Vial, ed. *"A noble tale / Among us shall awake": Approches croisées des "Middle English Breton Lays" et du "Franklin's Tale"* (*SAC* 39 [2017], no. 174), pp. 17–25. Explores the notion of commitment in connection with the contradictory and untenable verbal pledges in *FranT*.

168. Gaston, Kara. "The Poetics of Time Management from the *Metamorphoses* to *Il filocolo* and *The Franklin's Tale*." *SAC* 37 (2015): 227–56. Examines the management of time in the "Aeson episode" of Ovid's *Metamorphoses* (Book VII), the Tale of Menedon in Boccaccio's *Filocolo*,

and *FranT*, focusing on Medea's *carmen*, Tebano's magic, Dorigen's complaint, and their parallels with poetic composition. Dorigen's complaint conveys a sense of "productive contingency" and resists order or completion, suggesting that what remains unsaid can be powerfully evocative (as in *LGW*) and that the "establishment of interpretive perspective . . . [is] an event that takes place in time" (as in *CT*).

169. Greene, Darragh. "Moral Obligations, Virtue Ethics, and *Gentil* Character in Chaucer's *Franklin's Tale*." *ChauR* 50, nos. 1–2 (2015): 88–107. Argues that the Franklin presents a formula for happiness: living a life of *gentilesse* as opposed to the principle of adhering to a law-based system of morality.

170. Hardyment, Christina. *Pleasures of the Table: A Literary Anthology*. London: The British Library, 2015. 240 pp., illus. Focuses on literary food writing and includes brief discussion of the Franklin's hospitality in *FranT*.

171. Kowalik, Barbara. "Czytanie cudów w *Panu Gawenie i Zielonym Rycerzu i Opowieści Franklina*" ("Reading Marvels in *Sir Gawain and the Green Knight* and *The Franklin's Tale*"). In Rafal Boryslawski, Anna Czarnowus, and Lukasz Neubauer, eds. *Marvels of Reading: Essays in Honour of Professor Andrzej Wicher* (Katowice: Wydawnictwo Uniwersytetu Śląskiego, 2015), pp. 159–74. Discusses the idea of the marvelous in the *Gawain*-poet's Arthurian romance and in *FranT*. Argues that the marvels in *FranT* are indispensable to the genre, producing the effect described by Tolkien as *eucatastrophe*.

172. Morrison, Stephen. "Serious Play and Playful Seriousness in *The Franklin's Tale*." In Claire Vial, ed. *"A noble tale / Among us shall awake": Approches croisées des "Middle English Breton Lays" et du "Franklin's Tale"* (*SAC* 39 [2017], no. 174), pp. 27–34. Focuses on how playfulness breaks the limits of existential constraint in *FranT*.

173. Ruszkiewicz, D. "'Fair is foul and foul is fair': Appearance vs. Reality in *The Franklin's Tale* and *The Wife of Bath's Tale*." In Claire Vial, ed. *"A noble tale / Among us shall awake": Approches croisées des "Middle English Breton Lays" et du "Franklin's Tale"* (*SAC* 39 [2017], no. 174), pp. 35–44. Studies shifting perspectives on love, marriage, and honor in *FranT* and *WBT*.

174. Vial, Claire, ed. *"A noble tale / Among us shall awake": Approches croisées des "Middle English Breton Lays" et du "Franklin's Tale."* Paris: Presses Universitaires de Paris Ouest, 2015. 105 pp. Volume focuses on

literary heritage of Breton lay narratives, with emphasis on *FranT*. For three essays pertaining to Chaucer, see nos. 167, 172, 173.

See also nos. 34–36, 41, 104, 126, 166.

CT—The Physician and His Tale

175. Jae-cheol, Kim. "The Sovereignty and Bare Life in Chaucer's 'Physician's Tale.'" *MES* 23, no. 2 (2015): 25–47. Investigates the logic of "sovereignty" in *PhyT*, and how sovereignty is transferred from God, to nature, then to Virginia, and back to the people who "subvert the entire political order" toward the end of the tale. Sovereignty is directly associated with extreme violence in *PhyT*.

See also nos. 120, 130, 183.

CT—The Pardoner and His Tale

176. Armijo Canto, Carmen Elena. "De Odo a *Canterbury* y el *Libro de los gatos*." *Anuario de letras: Lingüística y filología* 46 (2008): 33–52. Explores thematic parallels between Odo of Cheriton's *Sermones* and *Fabulae* and *PardT*. Though not intended to prove any direct influence of the former on the latter, shows how some topics that were widespread in ecclesiastical texts were adopted in literary texts for entertainment purposes.

177. Lavinsky, David. "Turned to Fables: Efficacy, Form, and Literary Making in the *Pardoner's Tale*." *ChauR* 50, nos. 3–4 (2015): 442–64. Argues for the effectiveness of the Pardoner's speech in light of his use of fables and exempla rather than *officium*. *PardT* affirms the power of literature over that of the Pardoner's own duplicitous nature.

178. Minnis, Alastair. "Fragmentations of Medieval Religion: Thomas More, Chaucer, and the Volcano Lover." The Presidential Address. The New Chaucer Society. Nineteenth International Congress, July 16–20, 2014. University of Iceland, Reykjavík. *SAC* 37 (2015): 3–27. Traces evidence of anatomical votive offerings, particularly genital renderings, in Roman practice, Reformation commentary, and modern accounts, presenting them as background to reading the Host's commentary on the Pardoner's cullions (*PardT*, 951–55). The Pardoner's genitalia are "imagined as a fecundating relic," with satiric implications.

179. Simpson, James. "Not Yet: Chaucer and Anagogy." The Biennial Chaucer Lecture. The New Chaucer Society. Nineteenth International Congress, July 16–20, 2014. University of Iceland, Reykjavík. *SAC* 37 (2015): 31–54. Explores aspects of anagogical reading practices and their relations with social prediction and prophecy. Reformation readers perceived predestinarian and prophetic themes in spurious Chaucerian texts, although Chaucer himself seems to distrust prophecy and certainty about the future. However, *PardT* is prophetic "in a variety of ways," reflecting Chaucer's fears of civic disruption that he anticipated when contemplating the breakdown of the sacramental system of penance. Also comments on anagogy in Julian of Norwich, *Piers Plowman*, and *Pearl*.

See also nos. 19, 34, 69, 120, 128.

CT—The Shipman and His Tale

180. Coley, David K. "Money and the Plow, or the *Shipman's Tale* of Tithing." *ChauR* 49, no. 4 (2015): 449–73. Argues that *ShT* comments on fourteenth-century controversies regarding tithing and examines the connections drawn between international finance and agrarian production.

181. Epstein, Robert. "The Lack of Interest in the *Shipman's Tale*: Chaucer and the Social Theory of the Gift." *MP* 113, no. 1 (2015): 17–48. The exchanges of goods and services in *ShT* are often read following Bourdieu's theory that self-interest motivates all human actions. Claims that this analysis does not take into account other motivating factors clearly present in the tale, such as conjugal affection and the pleasures of generosity and friendship.

See also nos. 7, 130, 155.

CT—The Prioress and Her Tale

182. Blurton, Heather, and Hannah Johnson. "Reading the *Prioress's Tale* in the Fifteenth Century: Lydgate, Hoccleve, and Marian Devotion." *ChauR* 50, nos. 1–2 (2015): 134–58. Examines manuscript circulation of *PrT* showing Chaucer's reception as a Marian poet. This tale

was not only used in devotional texts but was responded to in this register by Lydgate and Hoccleve.

183. Magnani, Roberta. "Chaucer's Physicians: Raising Questions of Authority." In Naoë Kukita Yoshikawa, ed. *Medicine, Religion and Gender in Medieval Culture* (*SAC* 39 [2017], no. 124), pp. 45–64. Explores interconnection among medicine, religion, and gender, as well as Chaucer's engagement with Marian doctrine, in *PrPT* and *PhyT*.

184. Park, Hwanhee. " 'To ben holden digne of reverence': The Tale-Telling Tactics of Chaucer's Prioress." *Comitatus* 46 (2015): 99–116. Invokes the medieval ideal (exemplified by *Ancrene Wisse*) of establishing self-identity and authority by memorizing and performing texts. The Prioress does this by "over-identifying" with the clergeon. Briefly considering the anti-Semitism of the tale, argues that it may be read in the context of hagiographical tradition, where all "pagans" are usually denounced.

See also nos. 14, 122, 128.

CT—The Tale of Sir Thopas

185. Carlson, David R. "Skelton, Garnesche, and Henry VIII: Revels and Erudition at Court." *RES* 66, no. 274 (2015): 240–57. Discusses how Skelton persistently mocks Henry's awarding knighthood to Garnesche by likening him to the silliest knights of romance. Claims that this portrayal of knighthood is influenced by Chaucer's mockery of knights in *Th*.

See also no. 78.

CT—The Tale of Melibee

186. Barrington, Candace, and Jonathan Hsy. "Remediated Verse: Chaucer's *Tale of Melibee* and Patience Agbabi's 'Unfinished Business.' " *postmedieval* 6, no. 2 (2015): 136–45. Focuses on the "mirroring structure" of Agbabi's "Unfinished Business" in *Telling Tales* (*SAC* 39 [2017], no. 42) and *Mel*. Also reflects on the inherent "problematizing of translation" that accompanies transforming *Mel* into contemporary poetry.

See also nos. 27, 41, 78.

442

CT—The Monk and His Tale

See nos. 78, 188.

CT—The Nun's Priest and His Tale

187. Parsons, Ben. "*Collie* and Chaucer's 'Colle.'" *N&Q* 260 (2015): 525–29. Although the phrase "Colle oure dogge" (*NPT*, 3383–86) has been cited as support for the notion that "collie" derives from a medieval pet name, a review of attestations of *colle* provides no evidence that dogs given that name tended to be members of the sheep-herding breed.

188. Scala, Elizabeth. "Quoting Chaucer: Textual Authority, the Nun's Priest, and the Making of the *Canterbury Tales*." In Kathryn Kerby-Fulton, John T. Thompson, and Sarah Baechle, eds. *New Directions in Medieval Manuscript Studies and Reading Practices: Essays in Honor of Derek Pearsall* (*SAC* 39 [2017], no. 28), pp. 363–83. Examines Derek Pearsall's Variorum Edition of *NPT* and suggests that the Nun's Priest's "self-conscious literary performance transforms" the tales of *CT*, which are enhanced by Chaucer's quotations, allusions, and references to his own works. In particular, Chaucer's act of "self-quotation" is highlighted in *NPT*. Also discusses *MLT*, *WBPT*, and *MkT*.

189. _____. "Seeing Red: The Ellesmere Iconography of Chaucer's Nun's Priest." *Word & Image* 26, no. 4 (2010): 381–92. Shows that the Nun's Priest is often illustrated in manuscripts and books, even though he is not described in the *GP*, arguing that the illustrations are informed by the Host's comments on the Priest and by the description of the protagonist of *NPT*, the "red-topped rooster," Chauntecleer. Surveys illustrations in extant manuscripts of *CT*, and examines portraits of the Nun's Priest in visual history. Includes 10 color illus.

See also nos. 19, 131.

CT—The Second Nun and Her Tale

190. Ikegami, Keiko. "The Second Nun's Tale: From a Viewpoint of Saints' Legends." In Yuichiro Azuma, Kotaro Kawasaki, and Koichi Kano, eds. *Chaucer and English and American Literature: Essays Commemorating the Retirement of Professor Masatoshi Kawasaki* (SAC 39 [2017], no. 94), pp. 30–43. Discusses *SNT* from several perspectives related to

saints' legends, including the representation of the saint in *SNT*, the etymology of Cecilia, the sources of *SNT*, the Second Nun as a narrator, *SNT*'s position in *CT*, and Chaucer's attitude toward religion. In Japanese.

See also nos. 37, 90, 122, 130, 223.

CT—The Canon's Yeoman and His Tale

191. Ziolkowski, Theodore. *The Alchemist in Literature: From Dante to the Present*. New York: Oxford University Press, 2015. xiii, 237 pp. Surveys the figure of the alchemist and the uses of alchemical imagery in western literature, focusing on how satire and trivialization of the subject gave way to more esoteric uses, especially as the practice of alchemy gave way to chemistry. Includes a summary (pp. 28–32) of *CYT* as an early example of satire with touches of esoteric knowledge, and suggests in passing how John Lyly's *Galathea* (1592) is "indebted extensively" to Chaucer's tale.

See also no. 56.

CT—The Manciple and His Tale

See no. 131.

CT—The Parson and His Tale

See nos. 41, 43, 66, 78.

CT—Chaucer's Retraction

192. Riley, Deirdre. "Retraction and Recollection: Chaucer's Apocalyptic Self-Examination." *Mediaevalia* 36/37 (2015/2016): 263–90. Reads *Ret* as the culmination of Chaucer's growing self-knowledge that unifies *CT*.

See also no. 55.

Anelida and Arcite

193. Miller, T. S. "Chaucer's Sources and Chaucer's Lies: *Anelida and Arcite* and the Poetics of Fabrication." *JEGP* 114, no. 3 (2015): 373–400. In A*nel*, a poem about the faithless lover Arcite, the poet narrator is also false both in specific details and in reference to his putative sources. Argues that Chaucer emphasizes "the deception inherent in his poetic process" in a poem that claims to preserve memory but "fabricates" its own claims to authenticity and truthfulness.

A Treatise on the Astrolabe

See no. 19.

Boece

194. Eckert, Ken. "Chaucer's *Boece* and Rhetorical Process in the Wife of Bath's Bedside Question." *Rhetorica: A Journal of the History of Rhetoric* 33, no. 4 (2015) 377–92. Reveals similarities in the rhetorical strategies of the *wyf* in *WBT* and Lady Philosophy in *Bo*.

195. Wuest, Charles. "Chaucer's Variations on a Boethian Theme." *DAI* A76.10 (2015): n.p. Considers Chaucer's repeated engagement with a passage from the *Consolation* in *Bo*, several shorter works, *PF*, and *TC*, leading to an argument that Chaucer ultimately suggests that some limits of translation are insurmountable.

See also nos. 19, 32, 119, 225.

The Book of the Duchess

196. Dunai, Amber Rose. "Dreams and Visions in Medieval Literature." *DAI* A77.03 (2015): n.p. Considers *BD* in a larger survey of dream visions, with particular attention to "connections [to] the conventions of medieval mystical texts."

197. Fumo, Jamie Claire. *Making Chaucer's "Book of the Duchess": Textuality and Reception*. New Century Chaucer Series. Cardiff: University of Wales Press, 2015. 244 pp. Studies the history of interpretation of *BD*, surveying scholarly commentary, material transmission, and late medieval/early modern creative reception. Emphasizes the (re)making of *BD*

over time, by means of the interrelated textual processes of writing, reading, and reception modeled within the poem itself. As a work that, paradoxically, has been both marginalized and freighted with canonical import, *BD* impacts our understanding of Chaucerian authorship, English and French vernacularity, and the late medieval culture of book production in ways that demand fuller reckoning.

198. Hardaway, Reid. "A Fallen Language and the Consolation of Art in the *Book of the Duchess*." *ChauR* 50, nos. 1–2 (2015): 159–77. Links *BD* with Freudian method, arguing that the poem "foreshadows" psychoanalysis through its depiction of how certain uses of language can heal trauma from painful memories.

199. McNamara, Rebecca F. "Wearing Your Heart on Your Face: Reading Lovesickness and the Suicidal Impulse in Chaucer." *Literature and Medicine* 33, no. 2 (2015): 258–78. In *BD*, Chaucer reinvents the *dits amoreux* tropes of Froissart (in *Le paradis d'Amours*) and Machaut (in *Le jugement dou roy de Behaingne*), applying Galen's humoral medicine to depictions of the lovelorn knight. Likewise, in *KnT*, the banished Arcite's plight foregrounds humoral imbalance and melancholy, and his death is described in Galenic detail. Establishes how both texts invite the audience to a closer and more empathic reading of suicidal characters than is usually available within the "artifice" of *fin'amors* poetry.

200. Stanbury, Sarah. "The Place of the Bedchamber in Chaucer's *Book of the Duchess*." *SAC* 37 (2015): 133–61. Contextualizes the bedchamber of *BD*, exploring its adaptations of French source material, the otherness of France, the social and psychological implications of beds and textiles, and the imagery of black and white. Emphatically English in its wordplays and domestic situation, *BD* locates the process of poetic composition "on English ground."

201. Winders, Susan Melissa. "Reading Medieval Courtesy." *DAI* A76.11 (2015): n.p. While attempting to locate courtesy literature in a larger literary milieu, examines Machaut and *BD* on the way to an examination of Langland.

See also nos. 73, 105, 107.

The Equatorie of the Planetis

The House of Fame

202. Boffey, Julia, and A. S. G. Edwards. "The Early Reception of Chaucer's *The House of Fame*." In Isabel Davis and Catherine Nall, eds.

Chaucer and Fame: Reputation and Reception (*SAC* 39 [2017], no. 99), pp. 87–102. Surveys knowledge of and responses to *HF* from the earliest manuscripts and printed editions to Alexander Pope's adaptation, *The Temple of Fame* (1710), with commentary on early uncertainty about the title and author of *HF*, and on the "ways in which Chaucer's poem embedded itself into various kinds of literary consciousness."

203. Caballero-Torralbo, Juan de Dios. "Literary Overtones, Self-Fashioning and Poetics in Chaucer's *The House of Fame*." In Juan de Dios Caballero-Torralbo and Javier Martín-Párraga, eds. *New Medievalisms* (*SAC* 39 [2017], no. 98), pp. 149–76. Surveys themes and plots in *HF*, comments on its sources, and discusses its "narrator-character."

204. Davis, Rebecca. "Fugitive Poetics in Chaucer's *House of Fame*." *SAC* 37 (2015): 101–32. Argues that motion in *HF* is "not the antithesis to form but its condition of possibility." Water imagery links Boethian "enclynyng," the littoral "field of sand" that signals transition between Books I and II, and the eel-trap shape of the House of Rumor; Geffrey is a "second Aeneas" who is making literary tradition. Various puns (e.g., sand/sound, tides/tidings) and the "anaphoric circles" of repeated "O"s in lines 1961–76 engage formal and thematic concerns so that *HF* shares some formal features with *Pearl* and anticipates the restless poetics of *CT*. Includes 5 b&w figures.

205. Hahn, Thomas. "Don't Cry for Me, Augustinius: Dido and the Dangers of Empathy." In Fiona Somerset and Nicholas Watson, eds. *Truth and Tales: Cultural Mobility and Medieval Media* (*SAC* 39 [2017], no. 121), pp. 41–59. Provides a "newly broadened context for Chaucer's obsession with Dido," and looks at Chaucer's narrators in *HF* and *LGW*.

206. Havely, Nick. " 'I wolde . . . han hadde a fame': Dante, Fame, and Infamy in Chaucer's *House of Fame*." In Isabel Davis and Catherine Nall, eds. *Chaucer and Fame: Reputation and Reception* (*SAC* 39 [2017], no. 99), pp. 43–56. Describes how in Book III of *HF* Chaucer engages with Dante's *Commedia*, especially Canto XI of the *Purgatorio*; focuses particularly on speaking silences, tacit allusions, and concerns with infamy.

207. Orlemanski, Julie. "Scales of Reading." *Exemplaria* 26 (2014): 215–33. Reads *HF* as an example of how a literary work constructs "discursive scale," making us self-conscious about how we read and interpret, when we read closely, and when we distance ourselves and see the text in relation to genres and systems, history, literary tradition. The

poem's "vertiginous changes of scale" confront us with the "epistemological and ethical consequences" of the level at which we read.

208. Rezunyk, Jessica. "Science and Nature in the Medieval Ecological Imagination." *DAI* A77.06 (2015): n.p. Uses *HF*, among other texts, to demonstrate a versatile permeability between "science and the humanities" in the medieval period, in contrast to current more isolated approaches to these disciplines.

209. Van Dussen, Michael. "Tourists and *Tabulae* in Late-Medieval England." In Fiona Somerset and Nicholas Watson, eds. *Truth and Tales: Cultural Mobility and Medieval Media* (*SAC* 39 [2017], no. 121), pp. 238–56. Discusses significance of tables and "narrative *tabulae*" in late medieval England. Addresses the tabular text in *HF*.

See also nos. 19, 39, 46, 54, 73, 99, 104, 107, 210, 216.

The Legend of Good Women

210. Kanai, Noriko. " 'Sely Dido': A Study of Dido in the Legend of Dido." *Baiko Studies in Language and Culture* (Society for the Study of International Languages and Cultures of Baiko Gakuin University) 6 (2015): 72–80. Focuses on the legend of Dido in *LGW* and compares its representation of Dido in Virgil's *Aeneid*, Ovid's *Heroides*, and *HF*. Argues that Dido in *LGW* desires Aeneas more actively than in other versions and that *LGW* presents her positively as conforming to nature as opposed to social norms. In Japanese, with English abstract.

211. Schuurman, Anne. "Pity and Poetics in Chaucer's *Legend of Good Women*." *PMLA* 130, no. 5 (2015): 1302–17. Discusses "the narrator's rhetoric of pity," alluding to Augustine, Aristotle, Cicero, and others, while arguing that both pity and poetry involve "a kind of authentic inauthenticity" that is unstable, paradoxical, and contingent in *LGW*.

See also nos. 45, 96, 99, 107, 122, 168, 205.

The Parliament of Fowls

212. Obenauf, Richard. "Censorship and Intolerance in Medieval England." *DAI* A77.01 (2015): n.p. As part of a consideration of censorship, subjects several works, including *PF*, to a hypothetical "model of intolerance" based on Abelard, Ockham, and John of Salisbury.

213. Powrie, Sarah. "Knowing and Willing in Chaucer's *Parliament of Fowls.*" *ChauR* 50, nos. 3–4 (2015): 368–92. Contends that *PF* challenges the medieval idea of judgment, based in reason, by also taking into account affective forces.

See also nos. 35, 58, 104, 107, 195.

The Romaunt of the Rose

214. Robinson, Olivia. "Re-contextualising the *Romaunt of the Rose*: Glasgow, University Library MS Hunter 409 and the *Roman de la Rose.*" *English* 64, no. 244, (2015): 27–41. Argues that *Rom* should be recontexualized, viewing the work not as a Chaucerian fragment, which perpetuates a fragmentary approach to the work, but as part of a tradition of translation. Analysis of decorated initials and borders in Hunter 409 rearticulates the work and reveals its conformity with "wider *Rose*-transmission patterns."

See also no. 51.

Troilus and Criseyde

215. Besserman, Lawrence. "Biblical *Figura* in Chaucer's *Troilus and Criseyde*, ll. 1380–86: 'As don thise rokkes or thise milnestones.'" *ChauR* 49, no. 3 (2015): 344–51. Notes that the visual imagery of falling rocks and millstones Pandarus uses to convince Troilus of his future success is associated with death and destruction in the Bible, which actually undermines Pandarus's argument in *TC*.

216. Blamires, Alcuin. "'I nolde sette at al that noys a grote': Repudiating Infamy in *Troilus and Criseyde* and *The House of Fame.*" In Isabel Davis and Catherine Nall, eds. *Chaucer and Fame: Reputation and Reception* (*SAC* 39 [2017], no. 99), pp. 75–86. Surveys classical and medieval skeptical views of the significance of fame and contrasts the attitudes toward reputation expressed by Criseida in Boccaccio's *Filostrato* and Criseyde in *TC*, focusing on the heroines' views about infamy before leaving Troy. Chaucer's character briefly rejects the opinions of others and, like the narrator of *HF*, "glimps[es] something interesting about personal sufficiency," without ultimately disregarding reputation.

217. Carlin, Martha. "Thomas Spencer, Southwark Scrivener (d.

1428): Owner of a Copy of Chaucer's *Troilus* in 1394?" *ChauR* 49, no. 4 (2015): 387–401. Thomas Spencer, a scrivener, purportedly owned a copy of *TC* in 1394. Presents the historical record regarding Spencer's life, since if this claim is true, it represents the only recorded instance of one of Chaucer's works circulating during his lifetime.

218. Clark, Laura. "Stretching the *Sooth*: Use, Overuse, and the Consolation of *Sooth* in Chaucer's *Troilus and Criseyde*." *Neophil* 99, no. 3 (2015): 493–504. Examines how the three main characters in *TC* use *sooth* to define their characterizations. Claims that Chaucer's use of *sooth* also "produces tension" in *TC*.

219. Dunai, Amber. "'Ane doolie sessoun' and 'ane cairfull dyte': Cresseid and the Narrator in Henryson's *Testament of Cresseid*." *ChauR* 50, nos. 3–4 (2015): 420–41. Examines the parallels between Cresseid and the narrator showing Cresseid's eventual transformation while the narrator fails to understand the moral point. Includes comments on Chaucer's narrator in *TC*.

220. Garrison, Jennifer. "Chaucer's *Troilus and Criseyde* and the Danger of Masculine Interiority." *ChauR* 49, no. 3 (2015): 320–43. Contends that masculine obsession with interiority, especially that marked by courtly love, enables "powerful men to ignore the destructive public consequences of their political" actions. Yet, *TC* reveals "that such separation between the public and private is illusory."

221. Honda, Takahiro. "An Aspect of Chaucer's 'Death' in *Troilus and Criseyde*." *Research Reports* (Fukushima National College of Technology) 55 (2014): 125–30. Compares *TC* with Boccaccio's *Il filostrato* and points out there are two kinds of death for Troilus in *TC*, as well as salvations in the Chaucer and Boccaccio texts. Traces the continuity of the theme of death from *TC* to *CT*. In Japanese, with English abstract.

222. Kawasaki, Masatoshi. "Chaucer's *Troilus and Criseyde* and the Poetics of Space." In Yuichiro Azuma, Kotaro Kawasaki, and Koichi Kano, eds. *Chaucer and English and American Literature: Essays Commemorating the Retirement of Professor Masatoshi Kawasaki* (SAC 39 [2017], no. 94), pp. 121–41. Discusses the various ways in which the treatment of space in *TC* functions in relation to the characterizations, the development of the plot, and the changing role of the narrator. In Japanese.

223. Kirkpatrick, Robin. "The Pace of Praise: Might Theology Walk Together with Literature?" *Religion & Literature* 47, no. 3 (2015): 1–24. Focusing on *TC*, argues that Chaucer relied heavily on previous works, primarily Dante's *Divina commedia*, for theological and linguistic

direction. Contends that Chaucer, like Dante, does not merely regurgitate biblical narratives, but expands on them, and states that Chaucer's works display a sincere devotion to the Virgin, the Crucifixion, and the Resurrection, identified "as characteristically Dantean." Also discusses *ABC* and briefly mentions *SNT*.

224. Megna, Paul. "Emotional Ethics in Middle English Literature." *DAI* A77.02 (2015): n.p. Considers the connection between ethics and emotional response in several Middle English texts, including *TC*.

225. Murton, Megan. "Praying with Boethius in *Troilus and Criseyde*." *ChauR* 49, no. 3 (2015): 294–319. Argues that Chaucer's interpretation of Boethius, as shown in two key passages in *TC*, his translation of *Bo*, and a significant *Bo* manuscript, "enables him to present Troilus as a genuinely Boethian hero who channels philosophical insight into religious devotion."

226. Nakao, Yoshiyuki. "'Assege' in Chaucer's *Troilus and Criseyde*: Investigating the Cognitive Process of Siege." In Yuichiro Azuma, Kotaro Kawasaki, and Koichi Kano, eds. *Chaucer and English and American Literature: Essays Commemorating the Retirement of Professor Masatoshi Kawasaki* (*SAC* 39 [2017], no. 94), pp. 358–79. Examines the implications of "siege" in *TC* from cognitive viewpoints. Argues that the siege of Troy as a prototype of "siege" is repeated in metaphorically diversified forms such as Pandarus's enclosure of Troilus and Criseyde, and that this "siege" is structured in terms of different speech agents, cognitive processes, and combinations of different spaces. In Japanese.

227. ———. *The Structure of Chaucer's Ambiguity*. Studies in English Medieval Language and Literature 6. Frankfurt am Main: Peter Lang Edition, 2013. xiii, 309 pp. Based on an earlier Japanese book, *The Structure of Chaucer's Ambiguity* (*SAC* 28 [2006], no. 54), this republished English version analyzes the "parole aspect of language" within an expanded study of ambiguity in *TC*. Proposes an original theoretical framework, "double prism structure," which brings together elements of cognitive linguistics, semantics, and pragmatics.

228. Oka, Saburo. "Reading Chaucer's *Troilus* from an Anthropological Point of View." In Yuichiro Azuma, Kotaro Kawasaki, and Koichi Kano, eds. *Chaucer and English and American Literature: Essays Commemorating the Retirement of Professor Masatoshi Kawasaki* (*SAC* 39 [2017], no. 94), pp. 3–19. Begins with attempts to position Chaucer, *TC*, and the reading subject (the author himself), and reads the Prologue and Epilogue of *TC* in literary, historical, and anthropological terms. In Japanese.

229. Raby, Michael B. "Attention and Distraction in Middle English Literature." *DAI* A77.03 (2015): n.p. Considers medieval understandings of the relationship between attention and distraction or diversion, using several texts, ranging from Augustine to Walter Hilton, Julian of Norwich, and *TC*.

230. Round, Nicholas G. "Máximo Manso: Love's Fool." *Hispanic Research Journal* 11, no. 1 (2010): 82–93. Argues that Pérez Galdós's *El amigo Manso* (1882) echoes *TC* in its concern with philosophical consolation, the theme of kinds of knowledge, and the narrator protagonist's mocking of his mourners in the afterlife. Like Troilus, Manso is an idealistic lover whose beloved does not match his ideal.

231. Spearing, A. C. "Narrative and Freedom in *Troilus and Criseyde*." In Kathryn Kerby-Fulton, John T. Thompson, and Sarah Baechle, eds. *New Directions in Medieval Manuscript Studies and Reading Practices: Essays in Honor of Derek Pearsall* (*SAC* 39 [2017], no. 28), pp. 7–33. Discusses how *TC* is a "renarration" of earlier medieval narratives and reveals how Chaucer uses the "autographic 'I'" in Book II of *TC*. Focuses on "aspects of narrative freedom" used by Chaucer throughout *TC*.

232. Stampone, Christopher. "Choreographing *Fin'amor*: Dance and the Game of Love in Geoffrey Chaucer's *Troilus and Criseyde*." *ChauR* 50, nos. 3–4 (2015): 393–419. Examines the use of *daunce* in the poem in order to explore the way dancing is linked to rhetoric in the interactions between the main characters.

233. Strakhov, Elizaveta. "'And kis the steppes where as thow seest pace': Reconstructing the Spectral Canon in Statius and Chaucer." In Isabel Davis and Catherine Nall, eds. *Chaucer and Fame: Reputation and Reception* (*SAC* 39 [2017], no. 99), pp. 57–74. Reviews the presence of Statius's *Thebaid* in *TC*, exploring in detail the juxtaposition of Statian and Ovidian material in Cassandra's explanations of Troilus's dream of the boar, explaining Chaucer's elision of Boccaccio from his poem as Chaucer's imitation of Statius's "poetics of disavowal," and commenting on Chaucer's complex use of the list-of-poets topos in *TC*, V.1782.

See also nos. 18, 22, 39, 63, 74–76, 78, 89, 104–5, 119–20, 195.

Lyrics and Short Poems

An ABC

See nos. 101, 223.

Adam Scriveyn

See nos. 29, 75.

Former Age

234. Stanbury, Sarah. "Multilingual Lists and Chaucer's *The Former Age*." In Andrew James Johnston, Ethan Knapp, and Margitta Rouse, eds. *The Art of Vision: Ekphrasis in Medieval Literature and Culture* (*SAC* 39 [2017], no. 109), pp. 36–54. Examines relationship of ekphrasis and inventory lists in *Form Age*. Reflects on "relationship between material things and the categories that classify them in multilingual England."

See also no. 119.

Lak of Stedfastnesse

See no. 101.

Proverbs

235. Stanley, E. G. "Proverbe of Chaucer." *N&Q* 260 (2015): 358–60. Given his "frequent equivocalness" on matters of high seriousness, there is good reason to believe that *Prov*, a "riddling poem" (*NIMEV* 3914) is Chaucer's work, philologists' objections on the basis of its inaccurate *compace/embrace* rhyme notwithstanding.

Chaucerian Apocrypha

236. Burrow, John. "*The Tale of Beryn*: An Appreciation." *ChauR* 49, no. 4 (2015): 499–511. One scribe included the *Tale of Beryn* in his copy of *CT*. The Prologue presents Chaucer's pilgrims after they arrive at Canterbury, and the tale is appropriate to its teller, a merchant. Argues that the *Beryn* author was "an intelligent and attentive reader of Chaucer."

237. Eckert, Kenneth. " 'He clothed him and fedde him evell': Narrative and Thematic 'Vulnerability' in *Gamelyn*." *Medieval and Early Modern English Studies* 22, no. 2 (2014): 131–46. Connects the *Tale of*

Gamelyn to Chaucer with respect to concerns of class, legal, and cultural issues, and focuses on the theme of vulnerability as an important conceit of the poem.

See also nos. 67, 125, 179.

Book Reviews

238. Allen, Mark, and John H. Fisher, eds. *A Variorum Edition of the Works of Geoffrey Chaucer Volume II. The Canterbury Tales: The Wife of Bath's Prologue and Tale*, Parts 5a and 5b (*SAC* 36 [2014], no. 12). Rev. Alan Baragona, *Speculum* 90, no. 1 (2015): 224–26.

239. Arner, Lynn. *Chaucer, Gower, and the Vernacular Rising: Poetry and the Problem of the Populace after 1381* (*SAC* 37 [2015], no. 155). Rev. Hisashi Sugito, *SIMELL* 30 (2015): 127–36.

240. Barr, Helen. *Transporting Chaucer* (*SAC* 38 [2016], no. 70). Rev. Elizabeth Scala, *RES* 66, no. 275 (2015): 569–70.

241. Beidler, Peter G. *Chaucer's Canterbury Comedies: Origins and Originality* (SAC 35 [2013], no. 46). Rev. Hideshi Ohno, *SIMELL* 30 (2015): 107–19. In Japanese.

242. Brewer, Derek. *The World of Chaucer.* Trans. Hisato Ebi and Bunichi Asakura (Tokyo: Yasaka Shobo, 2010). Rev. Yuko Tagaya, *SIMELL* 30 (2015): 121–26. In Japanese.

243. Burrow, John A. *English Poets in the Late Middle Ages: Chaucer, Langland and Others* (*SAC* 36 [2014], no. 84). Rev. Elizabeth Robertson, *MLR* 110, no. 3 (2015): 808–10.

244. Carney, Clíodhna, and Frances McCormack. *Chaucer's Poetry: Words, Authority and Ethics* (*SAC* 37 [2015], no. 61). Rev. Susan Yager, *JEGP* 114, no. 4 (2015): 589–92.

245. Collette, Carolyn P. *Rethinking Chaucer's "Legend of Good Women"* (*SAC* 38 [2016], no. 209). Rev. Kara Doyle, *JEGP* 114, no. 4 (2015): 592–94.

246. Denery, Dallas D. II, Kantik Ghosh, and Nicolette Zeeman, eds. *Uncertain Knowledge: Scepticism, Relativism, and Doubt in the Middle Ages* (SAC 38 [2016], no. 77). Rev. Jordon Kirk, *SAC* 37 (2015): 285–87.

247. Fisher, Matthew. *Scribal Authorship and the Writing of History in Medieval England* (*SAC* 38 [2016], no. 16). Rev. Michael Johnston, *SAC* 37 (2015): 293–96.

248. Forni, Jane. *Chaucer's Afterlife: Adaptations in Recent Popular Culture* (*SAC* 37 [2015], no. 38). Rev. Sebastian J. Langdell, *N&Q* 260 (2015): 319–20.

249. Grady, Frank, and Andrew Galloway, eds. *Answerable Style: The Idea of the Literary in Medieval England* (*SAC* 38 [2016], no. 82). Rev. E. Gordon Watley, *MP* 112, no. 4 (2015): E292–E294.

250. Hodges, Laura F. *Chaucer and Array: Patterns of Costume and Fabric Rhetoric in the "Canterbury Tales," "Troilus and Criseyde" and Other Works* (*SAC* 38 [2016], no. 105). Rev. Nicole D. Smith, *RES* 66, no. 275 (2015): 567–68.

251. Johnson, Eleanor. *Practicing Literary Theory in the Middle Ages: Ethics and the Mixed Form in Chaucer, Gower, Usk, and Hoccleve* (*SAC* 37 [2015], no. 70). Rev. Ryan McDermott, *SAC* 37 (2015): 296–300; Jessica Rosenfeld, *MP* 113, no. 2 (2015): E73–E75; Winthrop Wetherbee, *JEGP* 114, no. 4 (2015): 154–56.

252. Kerby-Fulton, Kathryn, John T. Thompson, and Sarah Baechle, eds. *New Directions in Medieval Manuscript Studies and Reading Practices: Essays in Honor of Derek Pearsall* (*SAC* 39 [2017], no. 28). Rev. Kevin Gustafson, *JEBS* 18 (2015): 279–81.

253. King, Pamela M. *Medieval Literature 1300–1500* (*SAC* 39 [2017], no. 128). Rev. Stephanie Fox, *English* 64, no. 244 (2015): 71–72.

254. Klitgård, Ebbe. *Chaucer in Denmark: A Study of the Translation and Reception History 1782–2012* (*SAC* 38 [2016], no. 8). Rev. Kari Anne Rand, *ES* 96, no. 4 (2015): 475–76.

255. Lenz, Tanya S. *Dreams, Medicine, and Literary Practice: Exploring the Western Literary Tradition through Chaucer* (*SAC* 38 [2016], no. 88). Rev. Lola Sharon Davidson, *Parergon* 32 (2015): 252–53.

256. Malo, Robyn. *Relics and Writing in Late Medieval England* (*SAC* 37 [2015], no. 130). Rev. Elizabeth Allen, *MP* 112, no. 4 (2015): E288–E291.

257. Mann, Jill. *Life in Words: Essays on Chaucer, the Gawain-Poet, and Malory* (*SAC* 38 [2016], no. 89). Rev. Laura K. Bedwell, *Christianity and Literature* 65 (2015): 108–10; Andrew Galloway, *RenQ* 68, no. 3 (2015): 1126–28; T. Miller, *Sixteenth Century Journal* 46 (2015): 816.

258. Minnis, Alastair. *The Cambridge Introduction to Chaucer* (*SAC* 38 [2016], no. 90). Rev. Corey Sparks, *SAC* 37 (2015): 305–7.

259. Mooney, Linne R., and Estelle Stubbs. *Scribes and the City: London Guildhall Clerks and the Dissemination of Middle English Literature,*

1375–1425 (*SAC* 37 [2015], no. 12). Rev. Ceridwen Lloyd-Morgan, *English* 64, no. 244 (2015): 72–74.

260. Murrin, Michael. *Trade and Romance* (*SAC* 38 [2016], no. 135). Rev. Maia Farrar, *Comitatus* 46 (2015): 268–70.

261. Nakao, Yoshiyuki. *The Structure of Chaucer's Ambiguity* (*SAC* 39 [2017], no. 85). Rev. Kikuchi Kiyoaki, *SEL* 56 (2015): 219–23.

262. Pugh, Tison. *Chaucer's (Anti-)Eroticisms and the Queer Middle Ages* (*SAC* 38 [2016], no. 93). Rev. Wan-Chuan Kao, *SAC* 37 (2015): 307–11.

263. Raymo, Robert R., and Judith Glazer-Raymo, compilers. Shari Perkins and Jared Camins-Esakov, eds. *The Chaucer Collection of Robert R. Raymo* (*SAC* 39 [2017], no. 4). Rev. Derek A. Pearsall, *JEBS* 18 (2015): 302–4.

264. Rigby, Stephen, and Alastair J. Minnis, eds. *Historians on Chaucer: The "General Prologue" to the "Canterbury Tales"* (*SAC* 38 [2016], no. 118). Rev. A. S. G. Edwards, *Literature and History* 24, no. 2 (2015): 89–91.

265. Rosenfeld, Jessica. *Ethics and Enjoyment in Late Medieval Poetry: Love after Aristotle* (*SAC* 35 [2013], no. 33). Rev. Monica Brzezinshi Potkay, *MP* 112, no. 3 (2015): E217–E219.

266. Somerset, Fiona. *Feeling like Saints: Lollard Writings after Wyclif* (*SAC* 39 [2017], no. 120). Rev. Emily Steiner, *MP* 113 (2015): E4–E7.

267. Somerset, Fiona, and Nicholas Watson, eds. *Truth and Tales: Cultural Mobility and Medieval Media* (*SAC* 39 [2017], no. 121). Rev. Joel Fredell, *SAC* 15 (2015): 321–25.

268. Strohm, Paul. *Chaucer's Tale: 1386 and the Road to Canterbury* (*SAC* 38 [2016], no. 2). Also titled *The Poet's Tale: Chaucer and the Year that Made the "Canterbury Tales"* (*SAC* 39 [2017], no. 9). Rev. Orlando Bird, *Financial Times*, January 24, 2015, p. 10; Peter Brown, *History Today* 65, no. 7 (2015): 61; Sam Leith, *Spectator* 327, no. 9725 (2015): 32; Sebastian Sobecki, *SAC* 37 (2015): 325–28.

269. Van Dijk, Conrad. *John Gower and the Limits of the Law* (*SAC* 38 [2016], no. 96). Rev. Jonathan M. Newman, *SAC* 37 (2015): 328–31.

270. Wakelin, Daniel. *Scribal Correction and Literary Craft: English Manuscripts 1375–1510* (*SAC* 38 [2016], no. 26). Rev. Rory G. Critten, *SAC* 37 (2015): 333–35; Susan Powell, *JEBS* 18 (2015): 314–19.

271. Yeager, Stephen M. *From Lawman to Plowman: Anglo-Saxon Legal Tradition and the School of Langland* (*SAC* 39 [2017], no. 41). Rev. Eric Weiskott, *SAC* 37 (2015): 338–41.

Author Index–Bibliography

The New Chaucer Society
Twentieth International Congress
July 10–15, 2016
Queen Mary University of London, Mile End

SUNDAY, JULY 10

9:30–5:15: Teachers' Workshop (Arts 2, Rms. 316, 317, 320)

9:30–10:00: Morning Coffee

10:00–11:30: Round Table (Susanna Fein, David Raybin, John Fyler, Candace Barrington, Isabel Davis, David Wallace, Kara McShane, Leah Haught)

11:30–12:45: Business Meeting

12:45–1:45: Lunch

2:00–3:30: Relevance/Difference—Both? (Sally Frostic, Mary Kay Waterman, Mark Randolph, Cristin VanderPlas, Timothy Cox, Jaclyn Silvestri)

3:30–3:45: Coffee

3:45–5:15: Reading Medieval Today (Ruth Lexton, Karen Patton-McShane, Lori Ayotte, Lisa Warman)

10:00–4:00: Graduate Student Workshop (by application only) (Bancroft, David Sizer)

10:00–10:45: London Scribes and Scripts (Simon Horobin)

10:45–11:00: Coffee

11:00–11:45: Correcting (Daniel Wakelin)

11:45–12:30: Illumination and Reading Practices (Jessica Brantley)

12:30–1:30: Lunch

1:30–2:15: Paper and Materials (Orietta Da Rold)

2:15–3:00: Binding (Alexandra Gillespie)

3:00–3:15: Tea

3:15–4:00: Print (Alexandra da Costa)

10:00–5:00: Trustees' Meeting (Arts 2, Rm. 217)

1:00–5:00: Early Registration (Arts 2 Lobby)

12:45: Lunch for Trustees and Teachers (Arts 2, Rm. 317)

5:30: Wine Hour for Trustees and Teachers (Arts 2 Lobby)

7:30: Evening Gathering for Graduate Students at Bancroft Arms, 410 Mile End Road

MONDAY, JULY 11

8:30–4:30: Registration (Arts 2 Lobby)

9:30–10:30: Business Meeting (Arts 2 Lecture Theatre)

10:30–11:00: Coffee Break

11:00–12:30: Welcome and Plenary Session (People's Palace Theatre)
Moderator: Paul Strohm (Emeritus, Columbia University)

"Did Shakespeare Live in Chaucer's London?"
Discussants: Helen Barr (Lady Margaret Hall, Oxford), Farah Karim-Cooper (Shakespeare's Globe), Bruce Holsinger (University of Virginia), Gordon McMullan (King's College London)

12:30–2:00: Lunch

2:00–3:30: Sessions: Group 1

Session 1A, Round Table: Queer Manuscripts: The Textuality of Error (1) (Bancroft 1.13)
(Thread: Error)
Organizers: Roberta Magnani (Swansea University) and Diane Watt (University of Surrey)
Chair: Diane Watt

- "Temporal Orifices in the Huntington MS HM 114 *Troilus*," Sara Petrosillo, University of California, Davis
- "The Queer and Broken Text: The Rhetoric of Fragmentation in Fifteenth-Century Manuscript Compilations of *The Canterbury Tales*," Samantha Katz Seal, University of New Hampshire
- "Marginalia as Cop: Policing Queer Temporality in Harley 2382," Miriamne Ara Krummel, University of Dayton
- "Queer Margins and the Hermeneutics of Manuscript (Non-) Conformity," Catherine S. Cox, University of Pittsburgh-Johnstown
- "Cecilia among the Saints: William Cotson, the Queerness of Print and the Autumn of the Middle Ages," Zachary E. Stone, University of Virginia

Session 1B, Round Table: Chaucer and the Digital Age (Bancroft 1.13a)
(Thread: Medieval Media)
Organizer and Chair: Kara Crawford (The Bishop's School)

- "Tools for 'best sentence and moost solaas': Using Digital Tools to Introduce Chaucer," Lee Read, Wilde Lake High School
- "Teaching Writing through Chaucer: A Lesson on Plagiarism and Source Integration," Jennifer Alberghini, CUNY Graduate Center
- "The Variant Archive: Mining Manly and Rickert," Andrew Kraebel, Trinity University
- "Geoffrey Chaucer, Game Designer?" Betsy McCormick, Mount San Antonio College

Session 1C, Seminar: Popularizing Pedagogy in the Late Middle Ages (Skeel Lecture Theatre)
(Thread: *Scientiae*)
Organizers: Susan Phillips (Northwestern University) and Claire Waters (University of California, Davis)
Chair: Claire Waters

- "Personification as Pedagogy," Katharine Breen, Northwestern University
- "Schooling Synonymy," Irina Dumitrescu, University of Bonn
- "'A suffisant Astrolabie': Pedagogy and the Poetics of Know-How," Lisa H. Cooper, University of Wisconsin-Madison
- "Vernacular Confession as Pedagogical Innovation? Confessional Formulas and the Manuscript Anthology," Robyn Malo, Purdue University
- "Robert Grosseteste and the Castle of Love: 'English Theology' through the Ages," Ryan McDermott, University of Pittsburgh
- "'A Christian Mannes Bileeve,' Women Readers, and Vernacular Theology," Nicole D. Smith, University of North Texas

Pre-circulated materials for this seminar can be found at http://newchaucersociety .org/hub/entry/1c-popularizing-pedagogy-in-the-late-middle-ages.

Session 1D, Paper Panel: The East of England (Bancroft 1.15) (Thread: Chaucerian Networks)
Organizer and Chair: Stephen Partridge (University of British Columbia)
- "'Through all this region': Ritual Murder Cults in Late Medieval East Anglia," Heather Blurton, University of California, Santa Barbara
- "*Doubilness*, Prudence, and Sovereign Personhood in John Lydgate's *Troy Book*," Andreea Boboc, University of the Pacific
- "The Illuminators of the East of England: Localising Decorated Copies of Middle English Literature," Holly James-Maddocks, Saint Louis University

Session 1E, Paper Panel: Performing Gendered Sacred Spaces (Bancroft 3.26)
(Thread: Ritual, Pageant, Spectacle)
Organizer and Chair: Emma Lipton (University of Missouri)
- "The Space of the *Hortulanus*: Liturgical Drama in Medieval Convents," Margaret Pappano, Queen's University
- "Queer Sanctity in the Digby *Mary Magdalene*," Meisha Lohmann, Binghamton University

Session 1F, Round Table: Are We Dark Enough Yet? Pale Faces 2016 (Arts 2 Lecture Theatre)

(Thread: Corporealities)
Organizer and Chair: Jeffrey J. Cohen (George Washington University)
- "#PaleFacesMatter?" Wan-Chuan Kao, Washington and Lee University
- "Beyond the Anglophone Inner Circle of Chaucer Studies," Candace Barrington, Central Connecticut State University
- "Races without Bodies: The Medieval Invention of Whiteness," Jerrell Allen, Indiana University
- "Pale like Me: Resistance, Assimilation, and 'Pale Faces' Sixteen Years On," Cord Whitaker, Wellesley College
- "The Unbearable Whiteness of Medieval Studies," Dorothy Kim, Vassar College

Session 1G, Round Table: Networks in Late-Medieval Manuscripts (PP1)
(Thread: Chaucerian Networks)
Organizer and Chair: Michael Madrinkian (University of Oxford)
- "Middle English Manuscript Networks and Non-Networks," A. S. G. Edwards, University of Kent
- "Provincial Scribal Networks," Michael Johnston, Purdue University
- "Multilingual Manuscripts on the March of Wales," Helen Fulton, University of Bristol
- "Through the Maze via the Margins: Establishing the Evidence for Manuscript Networks in the Age of Chaucer," Kenna L. Olsen, Mount Royal University
- "'Go litel bok': The Circulation of Chaucer's *Troilus and Criseyde*," Simon Horobin, Magdalen College, Oxford

Session 1H, Round Table: The Social Worlds in *Troilus and Criseyde*
(David Sizer Lecture Theatre)
Organizers: John M. Hill (US Naval Academy) and Lawrence Besserman (Hebrew University)
Chair: John M. Hill
- "'Myn owen swete herte': Love and Lies in *Troilus and Criseyde*," Natalie Hanna, University of Liverpool
- "Binding, Bliss and Boethius: Prayer in *Troilus and Criseyde*," Sheri Smith, Cardiff University
- "'These fragments have I shored against my ruins': Citation as Pathology in *Troilus*," Maud McInerney, Haverford College

- "The Business of Translating Love in *Troilus and Criseyde*," Brian Gastle, Western Carolina University

Session 1I, Paper Panel: Surveillance (1): Making Visible (PP2)
Organizer and Chair: Sylvia Tomasch (Hunter College, CUNY)
- "Everywhere & Nowhere: Surveilling the Friars," Thomas Goodmann, University of Miami
- "Neighborhood Watch," Ellen K. Rentz, Claremont McKenna College
- "Surveilling the Leper: A High Stakes Game," Sealy Gilles, Long Island University–Brooklyn

3:30–4:00: Coffee Break

4:00–5:30: Sessions: Group 2

Session 2A, Round Table: London Living: Topographies, Orientations, Hardware (Arts 2 Lecture Theatre)
(Thread: London: Books, Texts, Lives)
Organizer and Chair: Sarah Stanbury (College of the Holy Cross)
- "The Local: Middle English Proximities," Matthew Boyd Goldie, Rider University
- "Public Inns, in and around London," Martha Carlin, University of Wisconsin-Milwaukee
- "Criseyde's Paved Parlor, in Troy and Troynovant," Joyce Coleman, University of Oklahoma
- " 'Þe ȝateȝ stoken watȝ neuer ȝet': London, the New Jerusalem, and the Hardware of 'Entre,' " Laura Varnam, University College, Oxford
- "Metaphors Chaucer Lived By," Marion Turner, Jesus College, Oxford

Session 2B, Paper Panel: Problem Texts (1) (Bancroft 1.13)
(Thread: Error)
Organizer and Chair: Megan Cook (Colby College)
- " 'The book of the xxv. Ladies'? Reading Errors Productively in Chaucer's Catalogues," Gania Barlow, Oakland University
- "The Other 'Ploughman's Tale': Reading Pseudo-Chaucer in Oxford, Christ Church MS 152," Zachary Hines, University of Texas at Austin
- "The Implausible Plausibility of the Canterbury Interlude," Thomas Prendergast, College of Wooster

Session 2C, Round Table: Household Knowledges (1) (PP2)
(Thread: *Scientiae*)
Organizer and Chair: Glenn Burger (Queens College and The Graduate Center, CUNY)
- "Field Knowledge in Gentry Households," Nadine Kuipers, University of Groningen
- "Medical Miscellanies and the Dissolving of Household Hierarchies," Michael Leahy, University of Nottingham
- "Domesticating Health Knowledge with the *Régime du corps*," Jennifer Borland, Oklahoma State University
- "Chantry Culture and 'Household Knowledges,'" Isabel Davis, Birkbeck, University of London

Session 2D, Paper Panel: Chaucerian Shibboleths (1): Age of Faith (PP1)
(Thread: Uses of the Medieval)
Organizers: Ryan McDermott (University of Pittsburgh) and Michelle Karnes (Stanford University)
Chair: Ryan McDermott
- "Fides," Miri Rubin, Queen Mary University of London
- "Historicism," Ed Craun, Washington and Lee University
- "Doctrine," Megan Murton, Catholic University of America

Session 2E, Paper Panel: Texts in Plays/Plays in Texts (Bancroft 1.13a)
(Thread: Ritual, Pageant, Spectacle)
Organizer and Chair: Tamara Atkin (Queen Mary, University of London)
- "Lyric Writing in the N-Town Plays," Ann Killian, Yale University
- "*Everyman* and English Humanism," Katie Little, University of Colorado-Boulder
- "Playing by the Book: Women, Books of Hours, and Medieval Marian Drama," Sue Niebrzydowski, Bangor University

Session 2F, Paper Panel: Sweetness: The Possibilities of Pleasure (Bancroft 1.15)
(Thread: Literary Forms)
Organizers: Peggy Knapp (Carnegie-Mellon University), Richard Newhauser (Trinity University), and Jessica Rosenfeld (Washington University in St. Louis)

Chair: Peggy Knapp
- "Strange Magic," David Raybin, Eastern Illinois University
- "'For shrewednesse, hym thoughte the tale swete': Pleasure and Alienation in Chaucer's Writing," Walter Wadiak, Nanyang Technological University, Singapore
- University of California-Berkeley, "The Particularities of Pleasure: The Face of Sensation," Maura Nolan

Session 2G, Paper Panel: Chaucerian Controversialisms (Bancroft 3.26)
(Thread: Uses of the Medieval)
Organizer and Chair: Michael P. Kuczynski (Tulane University)
- "Catholic Chaucer: Confessional Controversy and the Early Modern Canon," Nancy Bradley Warren, Texas A&M University
- "'A subject seldom handled by ladies': Recusant Readings of Medieval Women," Ana Sáez-Hidalgo, Universidad de Valladolid
- "John Gower and That Old Time Religion," R. F. Yeager, University of West Florida

Session 2H, Paper Panel: Varieties of Literacy (Skeel Lecture Theatre)
Organizers: Christopher Cannon (New York University) and Emily Steiner (University of Pennsylvania)
Chair: Elizabeth Robertson (University of Glasgow)
- "Miraculous Multitasking and Misbehaving Minds: Attention and Devotional Literacy," Katherine Zieman, University of Oxford
- "Chaucerian Reception: Insights from New Philology and Historical Pragmatics," Jeremy Smith, University of Glasgow

Session 2I, Paper Panel: Middle English Literature and the Archives (1): London (David Sizer Lecture Theatre)
Organizers: Julia Boffey (Queen Mary University of London) and Ryan Perry (University of Kent)
Chair: Julia Boffey
- "*Saint Erkenwald* and the Library of Old Saint Paul's," Brendan O'Connell, Trinity College Dublin
- "Hoccleve in the Archives," Peter Brown, University of Kent, Canterbury

- "The London Archival Context for Chaucer Studies," Matthew Payne, Westminster Abbey

5:30–6:30: **Poster Session (Octagon)**
Organizers: Ruth Evans (Saint Louis University) and Laura Saetveit Miles (University of Bergen)
Launch of Poster Session. During this session, poster presenters are invited to stand alongside their posters to field questions and engage in discussion. Posters will be exhibited for the duration of the Congress.

- "Trecento Illuminated Biccherna and Gabella book covers at the Archivio di Stato, Siena, Italy," Stephanie Amsel, Southern Methodist University
- "Visualizing Interiority: Corporeal Metaphor, Cognition, and the Affective Reader," Sarah Baechle, University of Notre Dame
- "Chaucer's Chessboard: Reading Spaces and Spaces for Reading in the *Book of the Duchess*," Annika Cunningham, University of Michigan
- "Picking up the Pieces: Affect, Gender, and Medieval Studies," Lara Farina, West Virginia University
- "Reading Fish in Ashmole 61," Maia Farrar, University of Michigan
- "Screen-Shotting Fragment I," Moira Fitzgibbons, Marist College
- "Antanaclasis, Paranomasia, Barbarismus: Varieties of Chaucerian Word Play and Scribal Variance in the Hengwrt and Ellesmere MSS," R. James Goldstein, Auburn University
- "Seven Seals of the English Apocalypse," Karen Gross, Lewis & Clark College
- "A 'Haphazard' Miscellany? Some Thematic Links between Booklets 1 and 4 in London, Lambeth Palace, MS 306," Alison Harper, University of Rochester
- "Weaving for Mary: The Suggestion of Performing Patronage in Santa Maria Maggiore," Tania Kolarik, University of North Texas
- "Aurality and Visuality in the Mise-en-Page of Chaucerian Manuscripts," Ruen-chuan Ma, Columbia University
- "Differences and Distances of the *Piers Plowman*: The A-Version Manuscripts," Tomonori Matsushita, Senshu University
- "Tables of Contents in Lydgate's *Fall of Princes*," J. R. Mattison, Jesus College, Oxford/University of Toronto
- "A Litel Thyng and a Myrie Tale," Mariah Min, University of Pennsylvania

- "Chaucer's Language Embodied: Progressive Diminution in *Sir Thopas*," Yoshiyuki Nakao, Professor Emeritus, Hiroshima University
- "Syllabic Noise: Visual/Sonic Cross-Hatching in L'Envoy de Chaucer," Christine Neufeld, Eastern Michigan University
- "The Augmented Palimpsest: From Chaucer to ChaucAR," Tamara O'Callaghan, Northern Kentucky University, and Andrea Harbin, SUNY Cortland
- "'Gladly wolde he lerne and gladly teche': Multimodal Literacies and *The Canterbury Tales*," Jessica Rezunyk, Bayview Glen
- "To Err Is Scribal: Correction Practices in Two Manuscripts of Lydgate's *Siege of Thebes*," Justyna Rogos-Hebda, Adam Mickiewicz University in Poznan
- "London: The English New Jerusalem," William M. Storm, Eastern University
- "Chaucer in Scotland: Networks of Transmission," Katherine Terrell, Hamilton College
- "'Inglourious Bâtarde': Tracing the Impact of Neurological Disorders and Ageing in the Work of Scribes," Deborah Thorpe, University of York
- "Chaucer's *Boece*: Literary(?)," Krista Sue-Lo Twu, University of Minnesota-Duluth
- "Reginald Pecock and Speculative Grammar in the Vernacular," Erin Wagner, Urbana University
- "Other Kinds of Extinction: W. S. Merwin's Medieval Poetics," Erica Weaver, Harvard University

6:30–7:30: Reception, Generously Sponsored by Boydell & Brewer (Octagon)

TUESDAY, JULY 12

9:00–10:30: Sessions: Group 3

Session 3A, Paper Panel: London Bridge (Bancroft 1.13)
(Thread: London: Books, Texts, Lives)
Organizer and Chair: Catherine Sanok (University of Michigan)
- "Vagrants and Viaducts: Representing London Bridge in *The Cook's Tale*," Sarah Breckenridge Wright, Duquesne University

- "The Box Seats: Severed Heads and the Pageantry of London Bridge," Sheila Coursey, University of Michigan
- "Becket at London's Bounds: Sainthood and the Architectures of Citizenship," Jennifer Jahner, Caltech

Session 3B, Round Table: Queer Manuscripts: The Textuality of Error (2) (PP1)
(Thread: Error)
Organizers: Roberta Magnani (Swansea University) and Diane Watt (Surrey University)
Chair: Roberta Magnani

- "Trans Textuality," M. W. Bychowski, The George Washington University
- "The Queerness of Miscellanies," Kathleen E. Kennedy, Penn State-Brandywine
- "I See It, but I'm Not Quite Sure What It Is; or, The Discomfort with *Cleanness* as a Naked Text," James Staples, New York University
- " 'Oueral enker-grene': How Queer is the Green Knight in British Library MS Cotton Nero A.x.?" Amy Louise Morgan, University of Surrey
- "Traumatic Displacement in the Alliterative *Morte Arthure* and Malory," Lucy Allen, University of Cambridge

Session 3C, Seminar: Medieval Multimodalities/Digital Multimodalities (Skeel Lecture Theatre)
(Thread: Medieval Media)
Organizers: Dorothy Kim (Vassar College) and Katharine Jager (University of Houston-Downtown)
Chair: Dorothy Kim

- "Hyperreading Then and Now," Meg Worley, Colgate University
- "Beyond Sound, Image and Text: The (More) Hidden Modes of the Manuscript," Kate Maxwell, University of Tromsø
- "Medieval Re-mediations of The Apostles' Creed for Multimodal Interpretive Communities," Laura Kendrick, Université de Versailles
- "Multimodality and Wall Text Verses in Manuscript," Heather Blatt, Florida International University
- "The Multimodal and the End of Silence," Susan Yager, Iowa State University

- "Linguistic Ecology and Hybrid Mothers," Mark Amsler, University of Auckland
- "Exploring Medieval Mulitmodality through Pedagogy of Making and Remediation," Elon Lang, University of Texas at Austin, and Robin Wharton, Georgia State University

Pre-circulated materials for this seminar can be found at http://newchaucersociety.org/hub/entry/3c-seminar-medieval-multimodalities-digitalmultimodalities.

Session 3D, Round Table: The Experience of Fiction (1) (PP2) (Thread: *Scientiae*)
Organizers: Marco Nievergelt (Institut d'Etudes Avancées de Paris) and Julie Orlemanski (University of Chicago)
Chair: Marco Nievergelt

- "The Value of 'Chaf', or Chaucer's Praise of 'Folye,'" Darragh Greene, University College Dublin
- "Fiction as Ethical Exercise," Laura Ashe, Worcester College, Oxford
- "'It seems impossible, but it's necessary': The Poetics of Fiction in the *Secretum philosophorum*," Jessica Lockhart, University of Toronto
- David Lavinsky, "'Why ask why?': Romance, Counterfactuality, and the Making of Fiction," Yeshiva University, New York

Session 3E, Round Table: Narrative Conduits (Bancroft 1.13a) (Thread: Chaucerian Networks)
Organizer: Leila K. Norako (Stanford University) and Kristi J. Castleberry (Lyndon State College)
Chair: Kristi J. Castleberry

- "'Þe marches of þe cee': Navigable Waterways and the Shaping of Narrative in Kyng Alisaunder and Titus and Vespasian," Andrew M. Richmond, Ohio State University
- "Wandering 'on the Rokke (. . .) Over the see': The Ocean as Natural Boundary and Narrative Conduit in Charles of Orleans's English Dream," Amber Dove Clark, University of Texas
- "Monmouth's Thames: Unpredictable Messenger of Divine Will," Sarah Crover, University of British Columbia
- "Souls and the Sea in the Digby *Mary Magdalene*," Gina Marie Hurley, Yale University

Session 3F, Paper Panel: Corporeal Fluidity: Written in Stone (Bancroft 1.15)

(Thread: Corporealities)
Organizer: Liz Herbert McAvoy (Swansea University)
Chair: Megan Cook
- "Petrified Women and Stony Animacy in William Caxton's c. 1480 *Metamorphose*," Sophia Wilson, King's College London
- "Bodies and Buildings: The Jews of Lincoln and the Hereford Mappamundi," Kathy Lavezzo, University of Iowa
- "Toward a Theology of Maternity: Margery Kempe's Built Environment," Mary Beth Long and Kim Sexton, University of Arkansas-Fayetteville

Session 3G, Round Table: Literary Value in 2016 (Bancroft 3.26) (Thread: Literary Forms)
Organizer and Chair: Robert J. Meyer-Lee, Agnes Scott College
- "What Is the Literary Value of a Name?" Siobhain Bly Calkin, Carleton University
- "The Literary and the Humanistic in 2016," Thomas J. Farrell, Stetson University
- "Lyric Values," Ingrid Nelson, Amherst College
- "Chaucerian Ephemera and Literary Value," Amy Goodwin, Randolph-Macon College
- "Meter as a Specifically Literary Practice," Eric Weiskott, Boston College

Session 3H, Paper Panel: Surveillance (2): Hearing, Reading, Writing (David Sizer Lecture Theatre)
Organizer and Chair: Sylvia Tomasch, Hunter College (CUNY)
- "'Writen in his tables': Surveillance as Inscription and Erasure in Chaucer," Ashley Ott, Saint Louis University
- "Eyewitness to History or Spy for the English? Historical Research as Surveillance in Robert Mannyng of Brunne's *Chronicle*," Jacqueline M. Burek, University of Pennsylvania
- "'Youre names I entre heer in my rolle anon': The List and Parchment Roll as Controlled Space," Martha Rust, New York University

Session 3I, Round Table: Did Chaucer Have a Mother Tongue? In Memory of David Trotter (Arts 2 Lecture Theatre)
Organizers: Christopher Cannon (New York University) and Emily Steiner (University of Pennsylvania)

Chair: Ardis Butterfield (Yale University)
- "Was There a Mother Tongue in the Later Middle Ages?" Marjorie Curry Woods, University of Texas at Austin
- "Gram/marians and Mother Tongues," Georgiana Donavin, Westminster College, Salt Lake City
- "Father Chaucer, Mother Tongue," Colette Moore, University of Washington
- "Gower's Vernaculars: Interlanguage and Gender," Jonathan Hsy, George Washington University

Respondent: Ardis Butterfield

10:30–11:00: **Coffee Break**

11:00–12:30: **Presidential Address (People's Palace Theatre)**
Chair: Ardis Butterfield (Yale University)
- "The litel erth that here is," Susan Crane, Columbia University

12:30–2:00: **Lunch**

2:00–3:30: **Sessions: Group 4**

Session 4A, Paper Panel: London and the Senses (Bancroft 1.13)
(Thread: London: Books, Texts, Lives)
Organizer and Chair: Marion Turner, University of Oxford
- "Quiet Riot: Sound Studies and Chaucer's Ear for the City," Joseph Taylor, University of Alabama
- "Thinking by Heart: Feeling and the Chaucerian Brain," Jenny Boyar, University of Rochester
- "The Funerary Sensorium," Elizabeth Edwards, University of King's College

Session 4B, Round Table: Textual Error/Textual Correction (Bancroft 1.13a)
(Thread: Error)
Organizer and Moderator: Thomas J. Farrell, Stetson University
- "Revisiting Error: Scholarly vs. Scribal Mistakes," Misty Schieberle, University of Kansas

- "Error, Expansion, Translation: The Host's Stanza," Warren Ginsburg, University of Oregon
- "Obscenity as Error: Correcting Chaucer's Obscenities in BL, MS Additional 35286," Carissa Harris, Temple University
- "Variance, Error, Authority: The Part-Divisions of the *Knight's Tale*," Stephen Partridge, University of British Columbia

Session 4C, Paper Panel: *Curiositas* (Bancroft 1.15)
(Thread: *Scientiae*)
Organizer and Chair: Patricia Clare Ingham, Indiana University
- "Curiosity's Fall: *The Miller's Tale* and Anti-Intellectualism," Richard Newhauser, Arizona State University, Tempe
- "*Curiositas* and *Curatio* in East Anglian Drama," Helen Cushman, Harvard University
- "Of Kings and Craftsmen: The Power of Curious Works," Anke Bernau, University of Manchester

Session 4D, Paper Panel: Town and Country Networks in Chaucerian Britain (Bancroft 3.26)
(Thread: Chaucerian Networks)
Organizer and Chair: Helen Fulton, University of Bristol
- "'Is not this my friend?': Urban Social Networks and *Troilus and Criseyde*," Cathy Hume, University of Bristol
- "'By meenes and brocage': The Politics of Intercession in Chaucerian Networks," Megan Leitch, Cardiff University
- "Networks of Scribes and Patrons in Chaucerian London," Linne Mooney, University of York

Session 4E, Round Table: Material Culture and Early British Performance (Skeel Lecture Theatre)
(Thread: Ritual, Pageant, Spectacle)
Organizer and Chair: Gail McMurray Gibson, Davidson College
- "Drama in Alabaster: An Intermedial Comparison," Jessica Brantley, Yale University
- "Putting the Pageant Wagon before the Play in York," Christina M. Fitzgerald, University of Toledo
- "Houses, Halls, and Roofed Chambers: The Ark as Playhouse," Sarah Stanbury, College of the Holy Cross

- "The Semiotics of Holy Matter in Early English Drama," Jay Zysk, University of South Florida
- "Instrumental Drama," Shannon Gayk, Indiana University, Bloomington

Session 4F, Seminar: (Dis)abling the Human/Animal Body (PP2) (Thread: Corporealities)

Organizers and Chairs: Haylie Swenson (George Washington University) and Liam Lewis (University of Warwick)

- "(Very) Close Encounters: Curiosity and Pain in Marie de France's 'The Peasant and the Beetle,'" Abby Ang, Indiana University
- "Got Your Nose! Animality as Humanity in *Bisclavret*," Teresa P. Reed, Jacksonville State University
- "Animals, Gesture, and Communication despite It All," Karl Steel, Brooklyn College and the Graduate Center, City University of New York
- "Animal Prostheses and Enabling Technologies in Chaucer's *Squire's Tale*," Jessica Chace, New York University
- "The Bear and the Baby: Lumps of Flesh in the Bestiary and *The King of Tars*," Andrea Whitacre, Indiana University

Session 4G, Paper Panel: Chaucerian Shibboleths (2): Teleology (Arts 2 Lecture Theatre) (Thread: Uses of the Medieval)

Organizers: Ryan McDermott (University of Pittsburgh) and Michelle Karnes (Stanford University)
Chair: Michelle Karnes

- "Telos," Rita Copeland, University of Pennsylvania
- "Entelechy," D. Vance Smith, Princeton University
- "Eschatology," Ryan McDermott, University of Pittsburgh

Session 4H, Round Table: Digital Approaches to Middle English Editing (David Sizer LT)

Organizers: Akiyuki Jimura (Hiroshima University and Okayama University of Science) and Yoshiyuki Nakao (Hiroshima University and Fukuyama University)
Chair: Yoshiyuki Nakao

- "Encoding Wayfinding Techniques in the Hagiographies of Oxford,

Bodleian Library, Laud Misc. 108," Shay Hopkins, University of California at Santa Barbara
- "The Cotton Nero A.x. Project: Digital Approaches to the *Gawain*-Poems," Murray McGillivray, University of Calgary
- "The Manuscripts and Editions of the *Canterbury Tales*: Textual Variations and Readings," Hideshi Ohno, Kurashiki University of Science and the Arts
- "Editing *Piers Plowman: Translatio* and Transformations," Timothy Stinson, North Carolina State University
- "Lydgate in Three Dimensions: Considering Digital Representation and Context in Holy Trinity, Long Melford," Matthew Davis, North Carolina State University

Session 4I, Paper Panel: Traveler's Tales and Medieval Ethnographies: Encountering Religious Diversities (PP1)
Organizer and Chair: Christine Chism, University of California, Los Angeles
- "An Iberian Jew in London: Solomon ha-Levi/Paul of Burgos's Purim Letter," Steven F. Kruger, Queens College and The Graduate Center, CUNY
- "Ethnographic Encounters and Religious Debate in *Alexander and Dindimus*," Stephanie Pentz, Northwestern University
- "Jerusalem in the Myddel: Oppositional Geography and Prester John's Christian Empire in *The Book of John Mandeville*," Sierra Lomuto

3:30–4:00: **Coffee Break**

4:00–5:30: **Sessions: Group 5**

Session 5A, Round Table: Problem Texts (2) (Bancroft 1.13)
(Thread: Error)
Organizer and Chair: Megan Cook, Colby College
- "Chaucer's Problem Poem: The 'inexplicable,' 'rambling,' 'tedious,' 'puzzling' *House of Fame*," Dabney Bankert, James Madison University
- "Mis-taking Chaucer in 'The Complaint of the Prisoner against Fortune,'" Kathleen Burt, Middle Georgia State University
- "'So sleigh arn clerkes olde': Forgery, Plagiarism, and Bad Scholarship," Brooke Hunter, Villanova University
- "Contemplating Emptiness in Two Early Manuscripts of *The Cloud of Unknowing*," Sarah Noonan, St. Mary's College

Session 5B, Paper Panel: Charisma (Arts 2 Lecture Theatre)
(Thread: Medieval Media)
*Organizers: Irina Dumitrescu (University of Bonn) and Laura Saetveit Miles
(University of Bergen)*
Chair: Holly Crocker, University of South Carolina

- "Kingly Charisma: Royal Image-Crafting in Late Medieval England,"
  Noelle Phillips, Douglas College
- "Chaucerian Charisma; or, What C. S. Lewis Really Did," David Wallace, University of Pennsylvania
- "Gawain's Charisma," Patricia Clare Ingham, Indiana University

Session 5C, Laboratory: Reading the Arts Curriculum (Skeel Lecture Theatre)
(Thread: *Scientiae*)
Organizer: D. Vance Smith, Princeton University

This session is designed to explore some common university texts that
would have structured the intellectual *habitus* of Chaucer's university-
educated contemporaries. Participants will explore what it was like to
be an arts student in Oxford and Cambridge as well as sample some
of the texts that were regularly lectured upon in the so-called "three
philosophies" (rational, natural, and moral). After some general remarks
on the late medieval university curriculum, discussion will center around
short readings from subjects including ethics, logic, natural philosophy,
and rhetoric. Discussion leaders will include Martin Camargo (University of Illinois at Urbana–Champaign), Kellie Robertson (University of
Maryland), Jessica Rosenfeld (Washington University in St. Louis), and
D. Vance Smith (Princeton University).

*Pre-circulated materials for this session can be found at http://newchaucersociety
.org/hub/entry/5c-reading-the-arts-curriculum.*

Session 5D, Round Table: After Chaucer (PP2)
(Thread: Chaucerian Networks)
*Organizers: Aditi Nafde (Newcastle University) and Elon Lang (University of
Texas at Austin)*
Chair: Elon Lang

- "Form and Fashion in Lancastrian Poems," Jenni Nuttall, St. Edmund Hall, Oxford
- "Secularized Contemplation: Chaucer's Lyrics in the Fifteenth Century," Gabriel Haley, Concordia University
- "How Are Authors Made? Reading Chaucer and Hoccleve with the Encyclopedists," Helen Hickey, University of Melbourne
- " 'He fo in herte is vnto wommen alle': Antagonism and Ambivalence in Hoccleve's *The Series*," Madeleine L. Saraceni, Yale University
- "A Late Middle-English Literary Decorator: Chaucerian Echoes in the *Sowdone of Babylone*," Phillipa Hardman, University of Reading

Session 5E, Round Table: Teaching with Torture: Violence as Spectacle in the Classroom (Bancroft 1.13a)
(Thread: Ritual, Pageant, Spectacle)
Organizer and Chair: Nicole Nyffenegger, Bern University

- "Mean Girls: Gender and Violence in Abu Ghraib and Chaucer's *Prioress's Tale*," Sarah Nangle, University College Dublin
- "Spitting Images: Pedagogies of Purity, Spectacle, and Violence in the *Prioress's Tale*," Cara Hersh, University of Portland
- " 'This is ynogh, Grisilde myn': Personal Suffering and Public Subjugation in the *Clerk's Tale*," Dianne Berg, Tufts University
- "The Reader as Spectator in John Foxe's *Actes and Monuments*," Kathrin Scheuchzer, University of Bern
- "Cloaked in Virtue, Soaked in Blood: Romantic Narrative as Disguise in *The Knight's Tale*," John Hoarty, Saint Ignatius College Prep

Session 5F, Paper Panel: Embodied Emotions, Emotional Bodies (1): Falling and Fallen Bodies (Bancroft 1.15)
(Thread: Corporealities)
Organizer: Stephanie Downes, University of Melbourne
Chair: Barry Windeatt, Emmanuel College, Cambridge

- " 'Double Sorwe': Embodied Emotion and Gendered Bodies in *Troilus and Criseyde*," Victoria Blud, Centre for Medieval Studies, University of York
- "The Anatomy of a Swoon in Chaucer's *Book of the Duchess*," Lynn Shutters, Colorado State University
- "Arcite's Inexpressible Love: *Hereos* and Bleeding in *The Knight's Tale*," Rachel Levinson-Emley, University of California, Santa Barbara

Session 5G, Paper Panel: The Limits of the Literary (1): Spiritual Constraints and Literary Possibilities (PP1)
(Thread: Literary Forms)
Organizers and Chairs: James Simpson (Harvard University) and Eva von Contzen (University of Freiburg)
- "The Vernicle and the Archive," Catherine Sanok, University of Michigan
- " 'Thou getest fable noon ytoold for me': Journey, Genre, and Community in *The Parson's Prologue*," Jonathan Stavsky, Hebrew University of Jerusalem
- "Guillaume de Deguileville and the Limits of Didactic Allegory: Literary Authorship as Residual Subjectivity," Marco Nievergelt, Institut d'Etudes Avancées de Paris

Session 5H, Paper Panel: Middle English Literature and the Archives (2): The Continent (Bancroft 3.26)
Organizers: Julia Boffey (Queen Mary University of London) and Ryan Perry (University of Kent)
Chair: Ryan Perry
- "Public Texts in London: Evidence from Central European Manuscripts," Michael Van Dussen, McGill University
- "A Southwark Tale: New Documents on Gower, Chaucer, and *The Canterbury Tales*," Sebastian Sobecki, University of Groningen

Session 5I, Paper Panel: Conscience and Confession (David Sizer LT)
Organizer and Chair: Nicole D. Smith, University of North Texas
- " 'Shryfte wythoute repentaunce': Confession as Narrative Medicine in *The Book of the Duchess*," Pamela M. Yee, University of Rochester
- "Memory and Sapience in Dunbar's Confession Poems," Kate Ash-Irisarri, Liverpool Hope University
- "Lay but Ordained? Rational but Patient? Conscience in *Piers Plowman*," Nicolette Zeeman, University of Cambridge

5:30–7:00: Special Event: Lavinia Greenlaw (People's Palace Theatre)

One of the UK's most important poets, Lavinia Greenlaw, will be reading from her latest book of poetry, *A Double Sorrow*, which imaginatively recreates Chaucer's *Troilus and Criseyde* via a sequence of more than 200 poems, each seven lines long and working over three rhymes, loosely in the manner of rhyme royal, with stunning results. The book was short-listed for the 2014 Costa Poetry Award, and the *Guardian* writes that its words are "shadowed by the mystery that is the mark of real poetry."

7:00–8:00: **Reception, generously sponsored by the English departments of Birkbeck, University of London; King's College London; Queen Mary University of London; University College London; and the Centre for Late Antique and Medieval Studies, King's College London (Octagon)**

WEDNESDAY, JULY 13

9:00–10:30: **Sessions: Group 6**

Session 6A, Round Table: Literary Afterlives of Medieval London (Arts 2 Lecture Theatre)
(Thread: London: Books, Texts, Lives)
Organizer and Chair: Bruce Holsinger, University of Virginia
- "Charles Dickens's Medieval London," Andrew Lynch, University of Western Australia
- "Soiled Knights and Mean Streets: The London of Medieval Crime Fiction," Anne McKendry, University of Melbourne
- "The Detective's Tale," Oliver Harris, Novelist
- "*The Clerkenwell Tales* and the Aesthetic of Place," Courtney Catherine Barajas, University of Texas, Austin
- "William Morris, *News from Nowhere*, and the Built Environment," John Ganim, University of California–Riverside
- "Cromwell's London," Theresa Coletti, University of Maryland

Session 6B, Paper Panel: Scribal Error (Bancroft 1.13)
(Thread: Error)
Organizers: Andrew Kraebel (Trinity University) and Daniel Wakelin (University of Oxford)
Chair: Andrew Kraebel
- "Taking Scribal Error to Court: Variation and Authority in Statute Collections," Anya Adair, Yale University

- "*Errare* in Romance," Paul A. Broyles, University of Virginia
- "The Influence of Error: Reconsidering the Authorial Revision of *Piers Plowman*," Michael Madrinkian, University of Oxford

Session 6C, Round Table: Beyond the Imagetext (Skeel Lecture Theatre)
(Thread: Medieval Media)
Organizers: Jessica Brantley (Yale University) and Ingrid Nelson (Amherst College)
Chair: Jessica Brantley

- "Framing Problems: User Interface and the Late Medieval Illustrated Manuscript," Ashby Kinch, University of Montana
- " 'The sleighte and the compassynge': Word and Image in Manchester, John Rylands Library, MS English 1," Nicholas Perkins, St. Hugh's College, Oxford
- "Autographs, Allographs, and the Imagetext in Manuscript Culture," Sonja Drimmer, University of Massachusetts, Amherst
- "Singing the *Dirige*: Job and Imaginative Ascetic Practice," Amy Appleford, Boston University
- "Manuscript Is the New Digital," Catherine Brown, University of Michigan

Session 6D, Round Table: The Mathematical Imaginary (Bancroft 1.13a)
(Thread: *Scientiae*)
Organizer: Tekla Bude, Newnham College, Cambridge

- "Chaucer's Arabic Mathematical Divination: Geomancy in *The Knight's Tale* and *Troilus and Criseyde*," Shazia Jagot, University of Southern Denmark
- "Why Can't Chaucer Count?" Alexandra Gillespie, University of Toronto
- "Algebraic Notation, Poetic Conceit, and the Development of the Symbolic," Valerie Allen, John Jay College, CUNY
- "Calculation Anxiety: Debt in the *Canterbury Tales*," Anne Schuurman, University of Western Ontario

Session 6E, Round Table: Public Interiorities (Bancroft 1.15)
(Thread: Ritual, Pageant, Spectacle)
Organizer: Katherine Zieman, University of Oxford

Chair: Fiona Somerset, University of Connecticut

- "Inside Out: Anchoritic Performances among the Laity," Michelle M. Sauer, University of North Dakota
- "Lay Religious Exemplarity in Eleanor Hull's Psalm Commentary," Sara Fredman, Washington University in St. Louis
- "Public Interiority and Family Feeling at the Court of Edward III," Sarah McNamer, Georgetown University
- "A Script for the Mumming at Eltham: Christmas, 1400," William Askins, Community College of Philadelphia

Session 6F, Round Table: Divergent Bodies and the Making of the Middle Ages (PP2)
(Thread: Corporealities)
Organizers: Richard H. Godden (Tulane University) and Dorothy Kim (Vassar College)
Chair: Dorothy Kim

- "The Goddess of 'thre formes': Diana, Metamorphosis, Divergence and the Politics of Identity Formation," Roberta Magnani, Swansea University
- "Killing Hermengild and Converting England: Displays of Male Control in *The Man of Law's Tale*," Elizabeth Melick, Kent State University
- " 'To-bollen for wrathe': The Discourse of Disability in *Piers Plowman*," Dana Roders, Purdue University
- "Sweet Fruits and Barren Figs: Separating Christian and Jewish Zoophytes in Fifteenth-Century East Anglian Drama," Robert W. Barrett, Jr., University of Illinois at Urbana–Champaign

Session 6G, Round Table: Translating Global Chaucers (PP1)
(Thread: Uses of the Medieval)
Organizer and Chair: Candace Barrington, Central Connecticut State University

- "*Vilains mots!* Nineteenth-Century French Translations of the *Canterbury Tales*," Stephanie Downes, University of Melbourne
- "In the Margins of the Polish *Parlement of Foules*," Marcin Ciura, Independent Translator
- "Reinventing Chaucer's *Sir Thopas* from a Turkish Perspective," Züleyha Çetiner-Öktem, Ege University

- "When Global Chaucers Go Local: Reading Chaucer in Taiwan," Denise Ming-yueh Wang, National Chung Cheng University, Taiwan

Session 6H, Paper Panel: Sensing Nature (Bancroft 3.26)
Organizers: Justin L. Barker (Purdue University) and Ingrid Pierce (Purdue University)
Chair: Richard Newhauser, Arizona State University, Tempe
- "Unnatural Gardens: Natural Space and Literary Artifice in Dream Poetry," Lotte Reinbold, University of Cambridge
- "The Feelings that Follow Chaucer's Whelp," Myra Wright, Queens College, CUNY
- "Feeling English: Fatherly Love and Childish Desire in Chaucer's *Treatise on the Astrolabe*," Jamie Taylor, Bryn Mawr College

Session 6I, Paper Panel: Materiality and Materialism (David Sizer LT)
Organizers: Katherine Little (University of Colorado) and Nicholas Perkins (University of Oxford)
Chair: Isabel Davis, Birkbeck, University of London
- "'Longa est series . . . malorum': The Necklace of Harmonia from Statius to Chaucer," Daniel Davies, University of Pennsylvania
- "The Country in the City: Materialisms of 'Rural' Texts at the End of the Fifteenth Century," Kathleen Tonry, University of Connecticut

Respondent: Elizabeth Schirmer, New Mexico State University

10:30–11:00: **Coffee Break**

11:00–12:30: **Sessions: Group 7**

Session 7A, Paper Panel: Overlapping Errors (Bancroft 1.13) (Thread: Error)
Organizer: Robert S. Sturges, Arizona State University
Chair: Marilynn Desmond, SUNY Binghamton
- "London's Burning: The Queer Tongue of Chaucer's Prioress," Jane Gilbert, University College London
- "'A Land Born of Varied Seed': Exile, Error, and Englishness in

Gower's *Vox clamantis*," Leah Klement, Caltech/The Huntington Library

- "'(P)eruertyd' History and Elected Rulers: Fictions of Sovereignty in *St. Erkenwald*," Lee Manion, University of Missouri

Session 7B, Paper Panel: Media and the Medieval Manuscript (Bancroft 1.13a)
(Thread: Medieval Media)
Organizers: Linne Mooney (University of York) and Wendy Scase (University of Birmingham)
Chair: Wendy Scase

- "The Networked Corpus: Thinking beyond the Codex in Digital Manuscript Studies," Angela Bennett, University of Nevada, Reno
- "Archive or Scriptorium? Digital Scholarship and Textual Studies," Robin Wharton, Georgia State University and Elon Lang, University of Texas at Austin
- "Pan-insular Medieval Translation Networks and the Digital Hive Mind," Victoria Flood, Durham University, and Aisling Byrne, University of Reading

Session 7C, Round Table: Curiosity in Theory and Practice (PP1)
(Thread: *Scientiae*)
Organizer: Patricia Clare Ingham, Indiana University
Chair: Richard Newhauser, Arizona State University, Tempe

- "The Philosopher in the Pit: Blumenberg, Chaucer, and the History of Theoretical Curiosity," Michael Raby, McGill University
- "Langland's Curious God," Jennifer Sisk, University of Vermont
- "Magic and the Space of Curiosity in *Saint Erkenwald*," Elizabeth Allen, University of California–Irvine
- "Curiositas and the Unwilling Narrator: Chaucer Reading Langland," Alastair Bennett, Royal Holloway, University of London

Session 7D, Round Table: Bohemia (PP2)
(Thread: Chaucerian Networks)
Organizer and Chair: Michael Van Dussen, McGill University

- "Between England and Bohemia: *Insurgent Gentes* in Motion," Fiona Somerset, University of Connecticut
- "Fed Up with the Miracle: Popular Response to Wyclif's Eucharistic

Critique in England and in Bohemia," Marcela Perett, North Dakota State University

- "Reappraising 'First seith Boece': Thomas Arundel, Anne of Bohemia's Funeral, and Other Metropolitan Anecdotes," Ryan Perry, University of Kent
- "Anne of Bohemia and Female Learning at the Royal Court of Prague," Alfred Thomas, University of Illinois at Chicago

Session 7E, Paper Panel: Performing Gendered Chaucerian Spaces (Bancroft 1.15)
(Thread: Ritual, Pageant, Spectacle)
Organizer and Chair: Emma Lipton, University of Missouri
- "Performing Female Masculinity in the Margins: Glosses on *The Wife of Bath's Prologue*," Laura Saetveit Miles, University of Bergen
- "Gender and Space in *The Reeve's Tale*," Emilie Cox, Indiana University
- "'Women desire of al thynges soverayntee': Chaucer, Vernacular History, and Female Power," Anna Johnson Lyman, University of Pennsylvania

Session 7F, Paper Panel: The Limits of the Literary (2): The Literary and Non-Literary, Convergence and Divergence (Bancroft 3.26)
(Thread: Literary Forms)
Organizer: Jonathan Stavsky (Hebrew University of Jerusalem) and Tom Stillinger (University of Utah)
Chair: Tom Stillinger
- "Literature as Aberration," Kara Gaston, University of Toronto
- "Chaucer and the Poetics of Listing," Eva von Contzen, University of Freiburg
- "Letters of Our Lady: Marian Poetry and the Edges of the Literary," Claire Waters, University of California, Davis

Session 7G, Seminar: Medieval and Modern in the Classroom (David Sizer LT)
(Thread: Uses of the Medieval)
Organizer and Chair: Katharine Breen, Northwestern University
- "Chronology as Teleology: Rethinking Timelines in the Medieval and

Early Modern Survey," Stephanie Batkie, The University of Monte-
vallo
- "From *Tars* to Targaryen: Teaching Medieval and Modern Miscegena-
  tion Narratives," Thomas Blake, Austin College
- "Chaucer and Frankenstein," Kara Crawford, The Bishop's School
- "*Bailey's Cafe* as Epilogue to the *Canterbury Tales*," Suzanne Edwards,
  Lehigh University
- "English Drama—Then and Now," Sarah W. Townsend, University
  of Pennsylvania

*Pre-circulated materials for this seminar can be found at http://newchaucersociety
.org/hub/entry/7g-medieval-and-modern-in-the-classroom.*

**Session 7H, Medieval Lectio: A Schoolroom Laboratory (Arts 2
Lecture Theatre)**
*Organizers: Christopher Cannon (New York University) and Emily Steiner
(University of Pennsylvania)*
Magister: Dr. Kurt Smolak, University of Vienna
This session will investigate the procedures of basic literacy training in
the age of Chaucer by reenacting them. In the first half of the session,
"students" will be introduced to a Latin school-text (or some aspects of
it) by a teacher proceeding entirely in Latin; in the second half, the
classroom experience will be discussed by participants as well as members of the audience. A central area of interest will be the complexities
involved in teaching a new language *in* that language, but the laboratory will also offer the opportunity for participants to repeat the wholly
Chaucerian experience of a pedagogy that ignores the vernacular they
share. Volunteers interested in participating as students should write to
Chris (cc131@nyu.edu) or Emily (steinere@english.upenn.edu) prior to
the congress (no knowledge of Latin required!).

**Session 7I, Paper Panel: Fifty Years of the *Chaucer Review*: Look-
ing Back, Looking Forward (Skeel Lecture Theatre)**
*Organizers: Susanna Fein (Kent State University) and David Raybin (Eastern
Illinois University)*
Chair: Susanna Fein
- "Valuing Chaucer," Robert J. Meyer-Lee, Agnes Scott College
- "Myn auctor Lollius," Leah Schwebel, Texas State University

- "Chaucerian Retrospect," Robert Edwards, Pennsylvania State University
- "Then and Now," Helen Cooper, Magdalene College, Cambridge

12:30–2:00: **Lunch**

2:00–3:00: **Graduate Workshops—Senate House Special Collections Reading Room**

3:00–4:00: **Hands-on workshop with tour of early print collections (by application only)**

2:00–5:00: **Half-day Excursions**
During the afternoon, a range of excursions will be offered; many of these excursions are limited to a small number of participants, and registration for places, and further details, will be available as part of the online registration: *http://eshop.qmul.ac.uk/browse/extra_info.asp?compid = 1&modid = 2&deptid = 34&catid = 1&prodid = 582*

The excursions will include:
1. Coach trip to Eltham Palace (generously supported by English Heritage). A stunning medieval palace with the Courtauld family's 1930s modernist house attached, nestling in woodland in southeast London. Chaucer was Clerk of the Works at Eltham Palace; he is said to have supervised the building of the bridge over the moat there. Eltham Palace also was the setting for one of Lydgate's mummings, the favorite royal residence of Henry VI and Edward IV, and where the young Henry VIII grew up. Visitors can see the medieval tiltyard and the magnificent Great Hall, and will be taken on a tour of the medieval and modern parts of the house. **Those who have signed up for the tour should gather at The Curve at 1:45 (coach A) and 2:00 (coach B); your coach allocation is marked on your ticket.**
2. A walking tour of medieval London, led by Paul Strohm and Elliot Kendall (convened by Marion Turner and Bruce Holsinger as part of their "London: Books, Texts, and Lives" thread). Details of where to gather are included in your Eventbrite registration.
3. A walking tour of London and Southwark, led by Martha Carlin and

490

    Caroline Barron. Details of where to gather are included in your Eventbrite registration.

4. Westminster Abbey Muniments tour. Details of where to gather are included in your Eventbrite registration.

5. Visit to the library of St. Paul's Cathedral, generously supported by the Archdeacon of London, the Ven. Nick Mercer. Details of where to gather are included in your Eventbrite registration.

6. Visit to the Worshipful Company of Barbers, led by James Carley. Details of where to gather are included in your Eventbrite registration.

6:30–7:45: Theatre Performance: Poculi Ludique Societas, *The Pride of Life* (People's Palace Theatre)
PLS (Poculi Ludique Societas), an acclaimed theater company affiliated with the University of Toronto, is proud to present a fully professional production of the late fourteenth-century morality play *The Pride of Life*, co-directed by Matthew Sergi and Ara Glenn-Johanson, and made possible by generous support from the Connaught Fund's New Researcher Award. This cast of six women will playfully reframe the antifeminist themes in the text; since only the first half of the *Pride* manuscript survives, they draw on audience input to improvise the play's lost conclusion differently at every showing. The medieval music trio, Pneuma Ensemble, will provide musical accompaniment.

8:00–9:00: Two Special Events
Multilingual Chaucer: Patience Agbabi (Arts 2 Lecture Theatre)
Convener: Candace Barrington
Open event
An Evening of Medieval Music by Opus Anglicanum (Arts 2 Drama Studio)
Convener: Sarah Salih
Ticketed event
Please sign up at http://tinyurl.com/z6n7ysw.

THURSDAY, JULY 14

9:00–10:30: Sessions: Group 8

Session 8A, Round Table: Teaching Chaucerian Cruxes (Bancroft 1.13)

(Thread: Error)
Organizer and Chair: John Longo, The Colorado Springs School
- "Beyond the 'Marriage Group,'" Rosemary O'Neill, Kenyon College
- "Bequeathing Error by Design," Mark Sherman, Rhode Island School of Design
- "'A Continuous Thread of Revelation': The Value of Juxtaposition," Mary Kay Waterman, The Lovett School
- "Material Girls: Teaching *The Wife of Bath's Prologue and Tale* and *The Shipman's Tale*," Suzanne Hagedorn, College of William and Mary

Session 8B, Paper Panel: How They Thought Then (PP1)
(Thread: Medieval Media)
Organizers: Katherine Zieman (University of Oxford) and Sarah Noonan (St. Mary's College)
Chair: Sarah Noonan
- "The Medium Is the Medicine: Middle English Healing Charms," Nancy Bradbury, Smith College
- "Crosses in the Margins: Gestural Mark-Making and User Engagement in the Medieval Codex," J. D. Sargan, University of Oxford
- "In Plain Text: Reading Boring Manuscripts," Daniel Wakelin, University of Oxford

Session 8C, Round Table: Household Knowledges (2) (David Sizer LT)
(Thread: *Scientiae*)
Organizer and Chair: Glenn Burger, Queens College and The Graduate Center, CUNY
- "MS Harley 2253: What Women Read at Home," Jennifer Sapio, University of Texas
- "Cambridge University Library Ff.2.38," Raluca Radulescu, Bangor University
- "Household Books and Ethics," Rory Critten, University of Berne/University of Fribourg
- "Knowing Things," Myra Seaman, College of Charleston
- "The Worshipful Eel: Object and Network in Caxton's *Book of the Knight of the Tower*," Elliot Kendall, University of Exeter

Session 8D, Paper Panel: Mediating Italian Literature (PP2)
(Thread: Chaucerian Networks)

Organizer: Kara Gaston, University of Toronto
Chair: Leah Schwebel, Texas State University

- "Boccaccio's *Filostrato* and the *Histoire ancienne jusqu'à César* (Second Redaction): The Matter of Troy in Naples and London," Marilynn Desmond, Binghamton University, SUNY
- "'Laurence' and 'Bochas' in Lydgate's *Fall of Princes*," Taylor Cowdery, University of North Carolina, Chapel Hill
- "The *Decameron* Effect," William Robins, Victoria University/University of Toronto
- "The Problem of Friendship: Theorizing Affective Reception in Chaucer," Anna Wilson, University of Toronto

Session 8E, Conversation: A Pilgrimage to Safe(r) Spaces: Classroom Crossroads of Identity (Bancroft 1.13a)
(Thread: Corporealities)
Organizers: Ben Ambler (Arizona State University) and Carol L. Robinson (Kent State University)
Chair: Helen Young, University of Sydney
An informal discussion on building safe(r) spaces in our medieval classrooms.

Session 8F, Seminar: Chaucerian Debate and Dialogue (Bancroft 1.15)
(Thread: Literary Forms)
Organizer and Chair: Neil Cartlidge, Durham University

- "What if Chaucer Knew *Disciplina clericalis?*" Gabriel Ford, Davidson College
- "Fragments of Debate: Group Experience in the Headlinks of the *Canterbury Tales*," Jonathan Forbes, University of California, Santa Barbara
- "Chaucer's Messy Nests: Constructing Gendered Debate in the *Canterbury Tales*," Wendy Matlock, Kansas State University
- "Polyphony in the *Canterbury Tales*: Chaucer, Debate and Polemic," Jonathan Fruoco, Université Grenoble Alpes/ILCEA 4
- "'Fro this noyse unbynde': The Victory of Suspense in Poetic Debates," Megan E. Palmer, University of California, Santa Barbara

Pre-circulated materials for this seminar can be found at http://newchaucersociety .org/hub/entry/8f-chaucerian-debate-and-dialogue.

Session 8G, Paper Panel: Arts of Dying (1) (Bancroft 3.26)
Organizer and Chair: Amy Appleford, Boston University
- "Death Is Money: Buying Trouble with the Pardoner," Roger A. Ladd, University of North Carolina at Pembroke
- "The Trial as History: York's 'Last Judgment,'" Emma Lipton, University of Missouri
- "*Patience*, Plague Flight, and the Art of *Not* Dying," David K. Coley, Simon Fraser University

Session 8H, Round Table: What Do We Want out of Book Reviews (and Book Reviewers)? (Skeel Lecture Theatre)
Organizer and Chair: Kellie Robertson, University of Maryland
This session will offer an informal conversation about issues surrounding book reviewing in medieval studies. What sorts of best practices should govern the book review process? How are reviews assigned? What is the impact of the review process? What role do book reviews play as the role of the scholarly monograph itself changes? Participants will include A. S. G. Edwards (*YWES*), Patricia Clare Ingham (*TMR*), Robert J. Meyer-Lee (*JEGP*), Timothy Stinson (*Digital Philology*), and Marion Turner (*Speculum*).

Session 8I, Round Table: What if It's True? Paul Strohm's New Chaucer Biography (Arts 2 Lecture Theatre)
Organizer and Chair: Lynn Staley, Colgate University
- "Chaucer's Audience," Karma Lochrie, Indiana University
- "Extensions of the Local in *Chaucer's Tale*," R. D. Perry, University of California, Berkeley
- "What Can We Now Know about Chaucer that He Didn't Know about Himself?" David Matthews, University of Manchester
- "Chaucer in the Customs House," Ethan Knapp, Ohio State University

10:30–11:00: **Coffee Break**

11:00–12:30: **Sessions: Group 9**

Session 9A, Paper Panel: Early Modern Readers "Correcting" Medieval Texts (Bancroft 1.13)

(Thread: Error)
Organizers: Clarissa Chenovick (Fordham University) and Frederic Clark
(New York University)
Chair: Clarissa Chenovick

- "Elias Ashmole and Franciscus Junius: Two Seventeenth-Century Annotators of Chaucer," Megan Cook, Colby College
- "Obliteration as Correction: Destroying the 'Pope' in Early English Print," Vaughn Stewart, University of North Carolina, Chapel Hill
- "Sanity before 1700: Seventeenth-Century Precedent to Reassurance by Dryden-the-Catholic," Betsy Bowden, Rutgers (Emerita)

Session 9B, Paper Panel: The University II.0 (Bancroft 1.13a)
(Thread: *Scientiae*)
Organizers: Thomas Goodmann (University of Miami) and Thomas Prender-
gast (College of Wooster)
Chair: Thomas Goodmann

- "Jewish Spaces, Academic Debts, and the Building of Medieval Oxford," Jenny Adams, University of Massachusetts, Amherst
- "A Medieval Look at the Modern, Corporate University," Matt Brumit, University of Dallas
- "Punctuation and Public Speaking in Medieval Oxford: The Case of William Herebert's Accents," Marjorie Harrington, University of Notre Dame

Session 9C, Round Table: Narrative Conduits (Bancroft 1.15)
(Thread: Chaucerian Networks)
Organizer: Leila K. Norako (Stanford University) and Kristi J. Castleberry
(Lyndon State College)
Chair: Leila K. Norako

- "Taking the Waters: Rivers, Oceans, and Identity in Gower and Chaucer," Valerie B. Johnson, Georgia Institute of Technology
- "The Boatman's Song: Riverside Authorship and Literary Form in Thomas Hoccleve's *Male regle*" Sam McMillan, Pennsylvania State University
- "Moral Conduct and Cultural Conduits," Jeremy DeAngelo, Rutgers University
- "Navigating New Floodwaters in Old English Verse," Sharon Rhodes, University of Rochester

- "Fluvial Selves: Rivers and Identity in *Pearl*," Randy P. Schiff, SUNY Buffalo

Session 9D, Round Table: Emotions at Law (PP1)
(Thread: Ritual, Pageant, Spectacle)
Organizers: Andreea Boboc (University of the Pacific) and Conrad van Dijk (Concordia University of Edmonton)
Chair: Andreea Boboc

- "The Emotional Language of the Law: A Case Study of *Anelida and Arcite*," Rebecca F. McNamara, University of Western Australia
- "Giving the Slip: Divine Justice and Emotional Life," Emily Steiner, University of Pennsylvania
- "Envy and Justice," Jessica Rosenfeld, Washington University in St. Louis
- "Chaucerian Anger," Paul Megna, University of California, Santa Barbara
- " 'On kneys I knelyt and mercy culd implore': An Examination of Kneeling in Relation to Emotions Experienced at Law," Jennifer Hough, Liverpool Hope University

Session 9E, Round Table: Embodied Emotions, Emotional Bodies (2) (PP2)
(Thread: Corporealities)
Organizer: Stephanie Downes, University of Melbourne
Chair: Mary C. Flannery, University of Lausanne

- "Bodies on the Mind: Chaucer and Gower," Corinne Saunders, University of Durham
- "Fainting or Feinting? The Rhetorical Swoon," Sarah Kelen, Nebraska Wesleyan University
- " 'Biblotte it with thi teris ek a lite'; or, The Art of Faking It," Juliette Vuille, Lincoln College, Oxford
- "The Sensation of Our Own Decay: Sensing Pain in Middle English Literature," Amanda Barton, Saint Louis University
- "Chaucer's Tears: 'Outrageous Wepyng,'" Barry Windeatt, Emmanuel College, Cambridge

Session 9F, Seminar: Contemporary Medievalist Poetry (Skeel Lecture Theatre)
(Thread: Uses of the Medieval)

Organizer: Jane Chance, Rice University
Chair: Robert Stanton, Boston College
- "Themes and Techniques from Medieval Poetry," Thomas Cable, University of Texas, Austin
- "The Uncertain Middle Ages," Paul Hardwick, Leeds Trinity University
- "Embodiment and Medievalism in *V*," Sarah Kate Moore, University of Washington
- "Longing for Words: The Medievalist Poetics of Marie Howe," Mary Kate Hurley, Ohio University
- "At the Edge of the Known: A Contemporary Poetics of the *Via negativa*," John Fry, University of Texas, Austin
- "Postfeminist Vernacularity," Jane Chance, Rice University

Pre-circulated materials for this seminar can be found at http://newchaucersociety.org/hub/entry/9f-contemporary-medievalist-poetry.

Session 9G, Round Table: Chaucer's Langland (Arts 2 Lecture Theatre)
Organizers: Stephanie Batkie and Eric Weiskott
Chair: Stephanie Batkie
- "The Ploughman's Tale," Christopher Cannon, New York University
- "A Tale of Two Plowmen: The Mid-Sixteenth-Century Reception of *Piers Plowman* and *The Plowman's Tale*," Mimi Ensley, University of Notre Dame
- "Chaucer's Langland's Boethius," Frank Grady, University of Missouri–St. Louis
- "Running Wild: Beast Allegory in Chaucer and Langland," Elizaveta Strakhov, Marquette University
- "Did Chaucer Know *Piers Plowman?*" Lawrence Warner, King's College London

Session 9H, Round Table: The Social Worlds in *Troilus and Criseyde* (David Sizer LT)
Organizers: John M. Hill(US Naval Academy) and Lawrence Besserman (Hebrew University)
Chair: Lawrence Besserman
- "Elegizing Criseyde: Chaucer and Henryson's Use of *Ubi sunt*," Jill Fitzgerald, US Naval Academy

- "*Troilus and Criseyde*, Book II: Speech, Property, and Late Medieval Widowhood," Kathryn McKinley, University of Maryland–Baltimore County
- "Sliding Sovereignties: Criseyde's Politics in Word and Deed," Susan Nakley, St. Joseph's College, NY
- "Virtual and Objective Images of the Social Worlds in *Troilus and Criseyde*," Anna Narinsky, Independent Scholar

Session 9I, Paper Panel: Material Mysticism (Bancroft 3.26)
Organizer and Chair: Nicholas Watson, Harvard University
- "Wisdom, Who Is Christ: Henry Suso and the Performance of Gender in Mystical Theater," Steven Rozenski, University of Rochester
- "Materiality in Language: Form and Transcendence in Julian and the *Cloud*-author," Kerilyn Harkaway-Krieger, Indiana University
- "Chaucer's Fart and Julian's Treasure," Jim Knowles, North Carolina State University

12:30–1:30: **Lunch**

1:30–3:00: **Sessions: Group 10**

Session 10A, Round Table: *The Legend of Good Women*: Chaucer's Mistake? (1) (Bancroft 1.13)
(Thread: Error)
Organizers: Betsy McCormick (Mount San Antonio College), Leah Schwebel (Texas State University), and Lynn Shutters (Colorado State University)
Chair: Betsy McCormick
- "Ugly Feelings; or, The Affects of Failure in *The Legend of Good Women*," Glenn Burger, Queens College and The Graduate Center, CUNY
- "The Thingness of Chaucer's Broken *Legend*," Steele Nowlin, Hampden–Sydney College
- "Dialectics of Failure in *The Legend of Good Women*," Matthew Irvin, The University of the South
- "Becoming the Villain: Misogyny, Authorship, and Erroneous Ethics in *The Legend of Good Women*," April Graham, Rutgers, The State University of New Jersey
- "*The Legend of Good Women*: Chaucer's Failed Collection?" Sophia Yashih Liu, National Taiwan University

Session 10B, Paper Panel: The Audible Medieval Past (1) (PP1)
(Thread: Medieval Media)
Organizer and Chair: Joseph Taylor, University of Alabama, Huntsville
- "Voicing Identity, Community, and Diversity in The Second Shepherds' Play: Polyphony as Medieval English Dramatic Experience," Rosemarie McGerr, Indiana University, Bloomington
- " 'Vpon heʒe and down low': The Sonoric Landscape of *Sir Gawain and the Green Knight*," Jamie Friedman, Westmont College
- "Fnorteth," Jeffrey Jerome Cohen, George Washington University

Session 10C, Round Table: Encyclopedic Experiments (Bancroft 3.26)
(Thread: *Scientiae*)
Organizers: Kellie Robertson (University of Maryland) and Emily Steiner (University of Pennsylvania)
Chair: Kellie Robertson
- "Encyclopedic Vision and Compendial Form in the *De regimine* Tradition: Poets and Popular Constitutionalism," Matthew Giancarlo, University of Kentucky
- "Technologies of Time: Astronomical Clocks as Universal History," Elly Truitt, Bryn Mawr College
- "Visualizing Knowledge in the *Breviari d'amor*," Joy Partridge, The Graduate Center, CUNY
- "The Medieval Theory of Everything: Wax, Eggs, Color, and the Whole World," Suzanne Akbari, University of Toronto

Session 10D, Paper Panel: Richard Bury and His Circle (Bancroft 1.13a)
(Thread: Chaucerian Networks)
Organizer and Chair: Neil Cartlidge, Durham University
- "Manuscripts as Social Media in the Circle of Richard Bury," Thomas Hahn, University of Rochester
- "Dreams of Necessity in *The Nun's Priest's Tale*: Chaucer as a Reader of Thomas Bradwardine," Edit Anna Lukács, University of Vienna
- "Robert Holcot's Pagans: Faith, Justice, and Community in the Reign of Edward III," Jack Bell, Duke University

Session 10E, Round Table: The Sensuous Body (Bancroft 1.15)
(Thread: Corporealities)

Organizers: Richard Newhauser (Arizona State University, Tempe) and Larry Scanlon (Rutgers University)
Chair: Larry Scanlon

- "Blazon and the Green Knight," Sylvia Tomasch, Hunter College
- " 'Noght wol I knowe compaignye of man': Masculine Conceptions of Autonomous Femininity in *The Knight's Tale*," Casey Ireland, University of Virginia
- "Fair Nudity: Unexpected Erotic Effects in the Late Middle Ages," Laura Pereira, University of Santiago de Compostela
- "The Corporeal Performance of the Wife of Bath's Desiring Body," Oya Bayıltmış Öğütcü
- "The Mouth in the *Song of Songs*," Julie Orlemanski, University of Chicago

Session 10F, Seminar: Meters and Stanza-Forms: The Favorite and the Forgotten (Arts 2 Lecture Theatre)
(Thread: Literary Forms)
Organizers: Jenni Nuttall (University of Oxford) and Eric Weiskott (Boston College)
Chair: Eric Weiskott

- "Middle English Verse Phlebotomy: Medicine in Rhyme," Jessica Henderson, Centre for Medieval Studies, University of Toronto
- "Rhymes without Lines and Reading for Balance," Daniel Sawyer, University of Oxford
- "Chaucerian Rhyme-Breaking," Ruth Evans, Saint Louis University
- " 'With heigh stile he enditeth': The Uses of Rime Royale," Katharine Jager, University of Houston-Downtown
- "Chaucer's Headless Lines," Ad Putter, University of Bristol
- "Dipodic Meter in the Age of Chaucer," Nicholas Myklebust, Regis University
- "Blank Verse and the Unrhymed Line in Middle English Poetry," Amanda Holton, University of Reading

Pre-circulated materials for this seminar can be found at http://newchaucersociety .org/hub/entry/10f-meters-and-stanza-forms-the-favorite-and-theforgotten.

Session 10G, Round Table: New Histories of the English Language (Skeel Lecture Theatre)
Organizer: Seeta Chaganti, University of California, Davis

Chair: Jeremy Smith
- "Generative Form," Sarah Novacich, Rutgers University
- "Language History Is Religious History: Vernacular Textuality and Religious Reform, 1100–1500," Nicholas Watson, Harvard University
- "Smooth or Rough? Lydgate and the History of the English Language," Andrea Denny-Brown, University of California, Riverside
- "Avant-Garde Medievalism and the Aesthetics of Linguistic History," Daniel Remein, University of Massachusetts, Boston

Session 10H, Round Table: Chaucer in the College Classroom (PP2)
Organizers: Disa Gambera (University of Utah) and Peter Travis (Dartmouth College)
Chair: Disa Gambera
- "Selling Chaucer: The Draws and Dangers of TV Adaptations in the Classroom," Robert Stretter, Providence College
- "Teaching Chaucer on the Border," Elizabeth Schirmer, New Mexico State University
- "Remediating Chaucer and the Middle Ages," Sandy Feinstein, Pennsylvania State University, Berks
- "Gamifying Chaucer's *Canterbury Tales*," Daniel Kline, University of Alaska, Anchorage

Session 10I, Round Table: Anchorite Spirituality (David Sizer LT)
Organizers: Michelle M. Sauer (University of North Dakota) and Susannah Mary Chewning (Union County College)
Chair: Michelle Sauer
- "The Physicality of Absence: Katharine Hardell and St. Bartholomew's," Will Rogers, University of Louisiana at Monroe
- "The Orchard inside the Walls," Jennifer Brown, Marymount Manhattan College
- "Julian in a Nutshell; or, A Room with a View," Sheila Fisher, Trinity College
- "Conceptualizations of the Anchorhold in Two Middle English Translations of Aelred's *De institutione inclusarum*," Amanda Wetmore, University of Toronto
- "Stones of the Heart: Love, Sex, and Mineral Transformation," Liam Lewis, University of Warwick

3:00–3:15: **Break**

3:15–4:45: **Sessions: Group 11**

**Session 11A, Paper Panel: Foreign Capital: Texts, Contact, and
Culture in Late Medieval London (Arts 2 Lecture Theatre)**
(Thread: London: Books, Texts, Lives)
Organizer and Chair: Sebastian Sobecki, University of Groningen
- "The Lee and Wighton Families Read Mandeville: Manuscripts and
  Travelers in Fifteenth-Century London and Italy," Anthony Bale,
  Birkbeck, University of London
- "The Pardoner as Connoisseur: Encountering the Wine Trade as For-
  eign Capital in Chaucer and Gower," Craig Bertolet, Auburn Univer-
  sity
- "Costly Bodies: Trade and Travel in *Blanchardyn and Eglantine*," Ruth
  Lexton, Wellington College

**Session 11B, Round Table: *The Legend of Good Women*: Chaucer's
Mistake? (2) (Skeel Lecture Theatre)**
(Thread: Error)
*Organizers: Betsy McCormick (Mount San Antonio College), Leah Schwebel
(Texas State University), and Lynn Shutters (Colorado State University)*
Chair: Leah Schwebel
- "Fathers and Daughters in Chaucer's *The Legend of Good Women*,"
  Nicole Sidhu, East Carolina University
- "The Pedagogy of Failure: Teaching *The Legend of Good Women* in the
  Undergraduate Chaucer Course and Beyond," Barbara Zimbalist,
  University of Texas at El Paso
- "Chaucer's Good Women as Marvelous Failures," Tara Williams,
  Oregon State University
- "Mansplaining: Chaucer, Cupid, Lydgate, and Tanner 346," Kara
  Doyle, Union College

Respondent: Elizabeth Robertson, University of Glasgow

**Session 11C, Round Table: The Audible Medieval Past (2) (Ban-
croft 1.13)**
(Thread: Medieval Media)
Organizer and Chair: Joseph Taylor, University of Alabama, Huntsville

- "Chaucer Makes Noise," Daniel Ransom, University of Oklahoma
- "The Sound of the Inner Word and Chaucer's Words to the Host," Norm Klassen, St. Jerome's University in the University of Waterloo
- "Sound in the Works of the *Pearl*-Poet," Ingrid Pierce, Purdue University
- " 'This hole *Elementarie*': Contested Letters, Orthography, and Sound in Early English Poetry," David Hadbawnik, American University of Kuwait

Session 11D, Round Table: The Experience of Fiction (2) (Bancroft 1.13a)
(Thread: *Scientiae*)
Organizers: Marco Nievergelt (Institut d'Etudes Avancées de Paris) and Julie Orlemanski (University of Chicago)
Chair: Julie Orlemanski

- " '(T)he rokkes been aweye': Fictionality and 'apparence' in *The Franklin's Tale*," Rebecca Davis, University of California, Irvine
- "Rethinking 'the Historian's Right of Invention,' " Joanna Bellis, Merton College, Oxford
- "Old Rehearsals, New Inventions: Fictional Elements Antithetical and Integral to Medieval Sermons," Erika Harman, University of Pennsylvania
- " 'Tyme and Space': Graphing Fiction in the *Canterbury Tales*," Angela Jane Weisl, Seton Hall University
- "The (Real) Elephant in the Room: Bestiary Fictionality," Carolynn Van Dyke, Lafayette College

Session 11E, Seminar: Teaching Drama after Chaucer (PP2)
(Thread: Ritual, Pageant, Spectacle)
Organizer and Chair: Theresa Coletti, University of Maryland

- "Teaching Drama after Chaucer: Open-Scripting the Play of Noah," Christine Chism, University of California, Los Angeles
- "John Phillip's *Plaie of Pacient Grissell* and Late Medieval Drama," Holly Crocker, University of South Carolina
- "Fragments, Framing Devices, and Female Literacy: Teaching the N-Town Marian Material," Leah Haught, University of West Georgia
- "Troubling (and Troubled) Identities: Teaching the Prioress with the *Croxton Play of the Sacrament*," Kara McShane, Ursinus College

- "Incompletion and Interaction: Teaching *The Pride of Life*," Matthew Sergi, University of Toronto
- "The Wife of Bath as Spectator," Emma Maggie Solberg, Bowdoin College

Precirculated materials for this seminar can be found at http://newchaucersociety .org/hub/entry/11e-teaching-drama-after-chaucer.

Session 11F, Paper Panel: Intent and the Haphazard in Medieval Books (PP1)
(Thread: Literary Forms)
Organizers: Elizaveta Strakhov (Marquette University), Zachary Hines (University of Texas at Austin), and Boyda Johnstone (Fordham University)
Chairs: Zachary Hines and Elizaveta Strakhov
- "Imposing Order upon Chaos: The Mysterious Materiality of Later Medieval Manuscripts," Venetia Bridges, University of Leeds
- "Accidentally Medieval Books: Compiling Chaucer in the Sixteenth Century," Jason Escandell, University of Texas at Austin
- " 'Blynde entencioun' and 'sodeyn hap': The Inclusion of Chaucer's Lyrics in Fifteenth-Century Manuscript Anthologies," Julia Boffey, Queen Mary University of London

Session 11G, Round Table: Arts of Dying (2) (Bancroft 1.15)
Organizer and Chair: Amy Appleford, Boston University
- "Affective Dying and Loving in Chaucer's *Troilus and Criseyde*," Sif Rikhardsdottir, University of Iceland
- " 'Meche mournynge and myrthe was mellyd togeder': The Politics of Mourning in the Alliterative *Saint Erkenwald*," Sarah Wilson, Northwestern University
- "Ante *Ars moriendi*: Eschatological Clusters in Middle English Manuscripts," J. Justin Brent, Presbyterian College
- "The Soul in Pain: The Doctrine of Purgatory in Late Medieval English Social Practice," Colin Fewer, Purdue University Northwest

Session 11H, Round Table: Aberrant Adventures (Bancroft 3.26)
Organizer and Chair: Susan Crane, Columbia University
- "Havelok's Long Arms," Lynn Staley, Colgate University
- "(Ab)errant Heroics in *Richard Coer de Lyon*," Leila K. Norako, Stanford University

- "Civilian Casualties: Interrogating Knightly Heroism in *Beues of Hamtoun*," Jenna Stook, Mount Royal University
- "A Damsel on a Quest: Malory's Elaine of Astolat," Kristi J. Castleberry, Lyndon State College
- "Sir Bors's Choice: Representing Mental Adventures," Karla Taylor, University of Michigan

Session 11I, Round Table: Medievalisms (David Sizer LT)
Organizer and Chair: Thomas Prendergast, College of Wooster
- "Refashioning a Prophetic Author in Chaucerian Apocrypha," Kimberly Fonzo, University of Texas at San Antonio
- "Dryden's Chaucer, Cressy's Julian, and the Future of Middle English," Vicki Larsen, University of Michigan, Flint
- "Chaucer's London in Historical Novels for the Young," Velma Bourgeois Richmond, Holy Names University
- "*The Famous History* (and the renowned fictionality) *of the Knight of the Burning Pestle*," Jade Standing, University of British Columbia
- "Medieval Reanimation at the Turn of the Twentieth Century," Adin Lears, SUNY, Oswego

6:00–7:00: Plenary Session: Biennial Chaucer Lecture (The Porter Tun at the Brewery, 52 Chiswell Street, EC1)
Chair: Susan Crane, Columbia University
Introduction: David Matthews, University of Manchester
- "Chaucer's Silent Discourse," Stephanie Trigg, University of Melbourne

The Biennial Chaucer Lecture, the reception, and the Congress banquet will take place at the Brewery, a magnificent space built in 1750, in the heart of the City of London.

7:00: Reception and Congress Banquet (The Porter Tun at the Brewery)

The reception is open to all Congress delegates. Sign-up for the banquet will be available as part of online registration.

FRIDAY, JULY 15

Coach Trip to Canterbury
NCS will provide coach transport to Canterbury, allowing delegates to

visit the charming medieval city and its stunning cathedral. Coaches will leave Queen Mary in the morning and will leave delegates near the historic city center; coaches will return to London in the late afternoon/ early evening, and will aim to have delegates back in London by about 7 p.m.

We understand that some delegates may also wish to travel independently and take the (faster, but more expensive) train from London Stratford International to Canterbury. We will provide an itinerary of Canterbury's many historical sites to all congress delegates.

Index

Page numbers of illustrations are indicated in the index by *italics*.